Japanese/Korean
Linguistics
Volume 6

Japanese/Korean Linguistics

Volume 6

Edited by
Ho-min Sohn &
John Haig

Published for the
Stanford Linguistics Association by
CSLI Publications
Center for the Study of Language and Information
Stanford, California

Library of Congress Cataloging-in-Publication Data

Conference on Japanese/Korean Linguistics (1st : 1989 : University of Southern
    California)
            Japanese/Korean Linguistics/edited by Hajime Hoji
                p. cm.
            Includes bibliographical references and index.
            ISBN 1-57586-089-9
            ISBN 1-57586-088-0 (pbk.)
1. Japanese language–Congresses. 2. Korean language–Congresses.
3. Japanese language–Grammar, Comparative–Korean–Congresses.
4. Korean language–Grammar, Comparative–Japanese–Congresses. 5.
Linguistics–Congresses. I. Hoji, Hajime. II. Stanford Linguistics Association. III.
Center for Study of Language and Information (U.S.) IV. Title.
PL503.C6   1989   90-2550
495.6–dc20   CIP

∞The acid-free paper used in this book meets the minimum requirements of the
American National Standard for Information Sciences—Permanence of Paper for Printed
Library Materials, ANSI Z39.48-1984.

Contents

Part IV
Syntax   333

Part V
Semantics　　493

Part VI
Discourse　　563

Preface

With the long-term goal to foster the development of an active, cooperative academic community in Japanese and Korean linguistics at both the national and international levels, the annual Japanese/Korean Linguistics Conference has evolved into the most prestigious and competitive among all the scholarly conferences of its kind. Through the previous five conferences, many intriguing and fascinating linguistic facts and generalizations, as well as commonalities and interesting disparities existing between Korean and Japanese, have been uncovered to an enormous extent. The 6th Conference contributed greatly to further revealing various mystified phenomena greatly to further revealing various mystified phenomena in Japanese and Korean, adding significant insights to our linguistic perspective.

For the first time since its inception in 1989, the Japanese/Korean Linguistics Conference was held outside of Southern California and the University of Hawaii was honored to host the 6th Conference at its Center for Korean Studies on August 8 through 10, 1995. A host of interested faculty and students of the University of Hawaii were indeed grateful for the occasion.

The Conference was a great success. Thirty-nine insightful papers in diverse areas in Japanese and Korean were presented. From a total of 127 submitted abstracts these had been selected through an intensive process of evaluation by approximately fifty reviewers. We were blessed with two distinguished guest speakers. Samuel Martin, Professor Emeritus of Far Eastern Linguistics at Yale University, and Noriko Akatsuka, Professor of Japanese at UCLA.

The success of the Conference was due also to the hard work of the abstract reviewers, Organizing Committee members and those who served as moderators, as well as a generous grant provided by the Korea Foundation. The Organizing Committee members were University of Hawaii's Haruko Cook, John Haig, Dong Jae Lee, William O'Grady, and Ho-min Sohn, and Mainland's Noriko Akatsuka (UCLA), Young-mee Cho (Rutgers University), Patricia Clancy (UC Santa Barbara), Hajime Hoji (University of Southern California), Masayo Iida (Stanford University), Shoichi Iwasaki (UCLA), and Sung-Ock Sohn (UCLA). We are also grateful to the following graduate students for their assistance: Kayoko Fujita, Akiko Hagiwara, Jeyseon Lee, Min-Sun Song, and Naoko Yoshinaga.

This volume is composed of the revised versions of most of the papers presented at the 6th Conference. As usual, the guest speakers' papers were presented first, followed by papers in historical linguistics, phonology, syntax, semantics, and discourse, in that order.

Part I

Guest Papers

Un-Altaic Features of the Korean Verb

SAMUEL E. MARTIN
Yale University

1.0. This study compares certain features of Korean verbs with features found in the Turkic, Mongolian, and Tungusic languages and those of Japanese.[1] Menges 1975 (21, 23, 58) criticized Miller 1971 for deriving OJ "*nar-u, nas-u* 'become'"[2] from *ni* + a proto-Altaic verb stem for the reason that (as Poppe 1976:472 phrases the argument) "two verbal stems never combine or merge in the Altaic languages, which is correct". Leaving aside other details of Menges's criticism (such as Miller's ill-supported postulation of a proto-Altaic stem *$\ddot{a}l_2$-), his rejection of the direct derivation of the OJ stems *nar-* and *nas-* from *ni* is justified. Menges does not mention the derivation of the OJ copula *nar-i* perhaps because Miller was not explicit about that superficially similar stem and failed to give the background of the quoted remark from Martin 1966:226, which was in the context of an etymology comparing J **nar-* and **nas-* with K *na-* 'emerge, get born' and *nah-* 'give birth to'.[3] When Miller later (1988:416) was critical of Martin for taking seriously "the long-standing traditional explanation of the generation of the copula by contraction, ...*nari* < **...ni ari* ··· even though the formulation violates everything else we know about the history of the language" I thought he was referring to the failure of **ni ar-* to implode as **n[y]er-* in accordance with the narrow view of Japanese compressive devices elaborated in Miller 1975, and THAT is surely not "everything else we know about the history of the language".

2.0. The Japanese noun predicator called the copula (in Martin 1966 the "pseudo-copula") is a complex structure built on *ni*, as shown by evidence that is surely overwhelming, even for those who may share Miller's disdain for the indigenous scholarship that made this the "traditional explanation". The focused forms of noun predication, for example, are ··· *ni fa/mo ar-* parallel to the focused forms *ku fa/mo ar-* for adjective predication. The reduction of the unfocused *n[i] ar-* → *nar-* is parallel to the later reduction of *k[u] ar-* → *-kar-*, leading in each case to a new paradigm. The reduction was optional: *na-dǫri ni ara-mu wo* (K 3:10) 'I will be your bird', *fyitǫ ni ar[y]i se-ba* (K 30:7) 'were you a man'. Similarly parallel is the structure for predicating subjective adjectival nouns with *tǫ*, which takes the form ··· *tǫ (fa/mo) ar-* with a reduction of the unfocused *t[ǫ] ar-* → *tar-*. In each of these structures, the expected predicative form (made just like those of *nar-u* 'become' and *nas-u* 'create')[4] is ···*ar-u* but in most syntactic situations that form is replaced by the infinitive ···*ar-i*, as is true of the verb *ar-* 'exist' itself, both as a full verb and as an auxiliary following the infinitive to make the OJ perfect-resultative structure *-yi ar-[y]i* > *-ye[y]r-[y]i* by way of a crasis that will pass Miller's muster though it happens to represent "the traditional explanation". Examples: *fyina wo ofyer[y]i* (K 101:24) 'has covered the hinterland [of the south]', *sumyi katabukyer[y]i* (K 106:3) 'the corners have sagged', *ima mo nǫkǫr[y]er[y]i* (B 7:4) 'remain even now', *yǫsu-ka tǫ nar[y]er[y]i* (B 18:4) 'it has become the refuge'. The last example is interesting in that it exemplifies both the subjective copula *tǫ* '(treated) as', in an adverbialized predication of the preceding noun, and the verb *nar-* 'become', which more commonly is preceded by the objective copula *ni*, as in *faru ni si nare[y]-ba* (M 1047) 'when it gets to be spring'.

2.1. But where do the morphemes *ni*, *tǫ*, and *ku* come from? Martin 1987:801 treated *ni* and *tǫ* as "essive particles", respectively objective and subjective. The morpheme *ku* functions as a kind of nominalizer, and it was attached to the root **a-* (of the stem **a-ra-* 'be') to make a postadnominal noun *aku* 'fact' that followed a truncated form of the attributive to create a structure *-[u] aku*, as in **katar[-u] aku* → *kataraku* 'what it tells' (M 852) and **sur[u] aku* → *suraku* 'that he does' (NS 18a), and the adjective attributive **-kyi aku* → *-kyeku* 'what is ··· ' (see Martin 1975:839, 1987:805). The adjective infinitive sometimes engenders a derived noun (Martin 1975:398). It functions as a postadnominal in Aomori, where A-*i ku* 'that it is A' corresponds to A-*ku* of the mainstream dialects (Martin 1975:399 n.8). When we consider Ryūkyū forms we discover that a fourth morpheme *-sa* underlies a complex paradigm A-*s[a] a(r)-* beside A-*k[u] a(r)-*. In standard Japanese A-*sa* makes an abstract noun 'A-ness'. I suggest that in proto-Japanese *sa* was to *ku* as *tǫ* was to *ni*, subjective vs objective versions of the predicator, though the semantic difference is not easily demonstrated. It is to be noted that three of these morphemes *ni* 'be N', *tǫ* '(treated) as N', and *ku* 'be A', together with the adverb *sa* 'so'[5] that sounds like *-sa*, are the only non-verbs that attach *te[y]*, the "gerund" marker. This was normally appended to the verb infinitive and is itself the infinitive of the perfect auxiliary *te[y]-* < **ta-Ci-*, usually cited in the predicative(/attributive) form as *tu(ru)* 'finish (doing)', to be compared with the Korean bound auxiliary for the retrospective aspect $-t^e/a-$ < $-ta-$.[6] It is unclear whether with these cases of *ni* and *sa* we can include the allative particles PLACE *ni* and (dialect) PLACE *sa*, which mean the same thing as PLACE *fye* 'to PLACE' (from a quasi-free noun 'direction'). The anomalous "instrumental" marker *mo-te* 'with' is generally taken as a contraction of *mot-[y]i te[y]* 'holding' (< **mota-Ci ta-Ci*). It is also unclear whether the reciprocal *to* 'with (as the other party)' is to be identified with the subjective copula. The morphemes *to* and *ku* in some or all their manifestations may be developments from the noun *toko* 'place' (to which Korean *'theh* 'site' has been compared) and the morpheme *sa* is often taken to be a truncation of *sama* 'appearance, direction', but (as suggested in Martin 1987:805) the *-ma* may have been suffixed to an original *sa*. That *sa* I would venture to associate with the bound honorific auxiliary of Old Japanese *-···(a)-sa-* and of Korean *···(ᵘ/o)-s i-*, taken by Martin 1996a (§1.3) as an incorporated bound noun *s(o)* < **sa* 'fact' in a circumlocution 'it is [the case] that ··· '. (The use of J *sama* as an honorific postnoun and title began not much before 1400.)

Martin 1990:489 posits a proto-Japanese essive verb 'be' with these forms: *na-* root and subjunctive ("mizen-kei"), *n-i* infinitive ("ren'yō-kei"), *n-o* attributive (< eastern-dialect adnominal), *n[-u]* (central-dialect) attributive / predicative that is the source of the "nigori" nasal-voicing in N + N compounds, **n-u* predicative (replaced by the infinitive or infinitive + *ar-*). But whether the noun predicator *nar-i* is derived from a particle or an infinitive it does not violate Menges's rule that two verb stems never combine to make a compound verb in the Altaic languages, for the infinitive form of Japanese is not a raw "stem" but a stem + the ending *-(C)i* though that fact is often obscured by compressions in making the surface forms. The Altaic languages permit the linking of verbs to make what is sometimes called "compound verbs" by putting non-final members of the structure into a continuative form such as the gerund 'does and (also/then/so)', and that is the normal way that compound verbs are made in Japanese, too.

It should be kept in mind that before the 13th century the Japanese structures that consist of a noun or an adjective + *ni, ku, to* (and probably *sa*) + a verb, whether auxiliary or not, were punctuated by junctures both before and often after those markers, so that not only were the component verbs pronounced in separate phrases, but so too were these monosyllables. Today those looser constructions are tightened into single phrases, and a similar tightening is taking place for many of the structures of gerund[7] + (auxiliary) verb that have, in terms of versatility, largely replaced the structures of infinitive + verb found in the earlier language. The reduction of unfocused N | *ni* | *ar-* → N | *nar-* was a particularly early instance of that tightening of phrases. In Martin 1987 I proposed that the structure Adjective + *kyi* / *s[y]i* (also set off by juncture on both sides) was a similar compression of *ku* / *sa* + *ar-yi*, and that fits nicely with the development of the extended conjugations of the adjective in Old Japanese and in the Ryūkyūs. The *ku* and the *sa* may very well have cognates outside Japanese, but looking for the source of *kyi* and *s[y]i* in a fantasized proto-Altaic morphology is, in my opinion, misguided. The adjective stem was used rather freely as an adnominal in Old Japanese, and the languages of the Ryūkyūs continue to use the stem in that and other versatile ways, though the mainstream Japanese dialects have tightened the structure of Adjective + Noun into lexical compounds.

2.2. From what is said above, it is clear that the Japanese structures usually called "compound verbs" are in keeping with the patterns found in the Altaic languages, for they are made up of an inflected form (the infinitive, made with the suffix *-i*) of one verb stem + a following verb stem, and these were pronounced as separate phrases, punctuated by juncture, before around 1200. Even cases which superficially seem to consist of a raw verb stem with a verb appended, such as OJ *sas-agey-* 'hold up, offer' are properly treated as contractions from linked verb phrases: *sas[i]-agey-* < **sas[a-Ci] anka-Ci-*.

3.0. Korean, too, has structures that link verb phrases, by putting the first verb in a paradigmatic form marked by an ending such as that of the infinitive -ᴗ*e/a* or of the gerund -ᴗ*kwo*. But the Korean lexicon is unusual in that it also has genuine compounds of raw verb stem + verb stem. In that respect, it is quite unlike Tungusic, Mongolian, Turkic, and Japanese.

Some of these compounds occur in modern Korean but are not attested in Middle Korean: kēl-ttu- 'float under the water', **chi-salli-** 'praise highly, flatter', **sekk-pakkwu-** 'take the wrong one, mistake it', tul-mēy- 'tie (straw sandals) to one's feet', ... Some are attested from Middle Korean but do not survive today: *kulk-sis-* 'scour and wash', *ses-twuph-* = *ses[k]-twuph-* 'mix and cover', *twup-teth-* = *twup[h]-teth-* 'cover up (another's guilt)', *puzu-thi-* 'smash, shatter', ... And a good number of compound verbs are attested both in modern Korean and in Middle Korean: **mulu-nok-** < *mulu-nwok-* 'get fully ripe, mature, reach its prime', **pulu-cic-** < *pulu-cici-* vi 'shout, yell', **puth-cap-** < *put-cap-* 1463 Pep = **put[h]-cap-* vt 'seize, grasp, get, hold', po-salphi- < ᴗ*pwo-sol*ᴗ*phi-* vt 'take care of, watch over', ... In 1400+ Kwan-yek there is an example of *na-ka-* (#106) 'go out', but the *na-* can be taken as the common contraction of the infinitive ᴗ*na-*ᴗ*a* (cf #107 *tule kata* < ᴗ*tu*ᴗ*l-e* °*ka-* 'go in'); Middle Korean has many examples of both ᴗ*na*ᴗ*a* °*ka-* and ᴗ*na (-)* °*ka-*. There are no clear examples of compound verbs in 1103 Kyeylim, but a few are found in the hyangka poems as interpreted by Kim Wancin 1980: *mas-pwo-* (= *mac-pwo-*) 'meet, confront, see' (1:6, 11:9 [but the first stem in both is written with a semantogram]), *pwupuy-wul-* 'make a rubbing noise' (21:3), *pi[l]-solW-* 'say in prayer' (7:4 [semantograms with phonogram support for the elision], 20:4 [semantograms]), *swos-na-* 'spurt out' (16:4 [semantograms]), *swumki-cwu-* 'kindly hide'

(7:8 [semantograms]), *skoy-toT-* 'awake' (24:4 [semantogram]), *hel-ni-* 'go on falling apart' (1:4 [semantograms]), *hyey-naz-* 'advance the count [of the years]' (1:4 [semantograms]), *nil^{u}ol-wo-* 'reach here' (19:10 [the first stem is a semantogram perhaps with semantophonogram support]). It could be argued that the orthography was simply ignoring a paradigmatic ending (such as the infinitive - ˙*a* or the gerund - ˙*kwo*) but the phonogram supporting the semantogram in *pi[l]-solW-* is evidence to the contrary.[8] In modern Korean the compound verb may carry a somewhat different meaning from the the the structure of infinitive + verb stem. as shown by **tōl-po-** 'take care of, look after, attend to' and **tola po-** 'turn around/back, ... '.

3.1. What can we say about these un-Altaic compound verbs of Korean? In Middle Korean they appear to be readily constructable, and of the 2200+ stems listed in Martin 1997 from eight to ten percent can be identified as compounds of stem + stem, depending on the generosity of our inclusion of bound stems. But the structure of stem + BOUND stem is found in Tungusic, Mongolian, and Turkic, too; the bound stem is usually described as a formant or suffix, as in the many stems formed with the Altaic verbalizer *-la-*. And bound stems occur also in Japanese, as shown by the OJ passive, causative, and honorific formations, as well as the future *⋯(a)-ma-* and the negative *⋯(a)-na-*, to say nothing of the various derivational formants described in Martin 1987:671-2, 790-6.

A Korean verb can be attached to a simple verb stem, or to the stem of a compound verb:

(1a) $^{\circ\circ}$*pwuy-*˙˙*tuT-* = $^{\circ\circ}$*pwuy-*˙˙*tut-/tu*˙*l[u]-* < *-*tu*˙*tu-* 'meander, wander' ← $^{\circ\circ}$*pwuy-* = $^{\circ\circ}$*pwuy-/pwuy*˙*y-* 'twist' + ˙˙*tuT-* = ˙˙*tut-/tu*˙*l[u]-* < *⁺*tu*˙*tu-* 'drop, fall'

(1b) $^{\circ\circ}$*pwuy*˙˙*tut-*°*ni-* 'go on wandering/meandering' ← $^{\circ\circ}$*pwuy-*˙˙*tuT-* + °*ni-* 'go'

(2a) *ton-*˙*ni-* < *tot-*˙*ni-* < **toT-*°*ni-* 'walk about, come and go'

(2b) *ses-tonni-* = *ses[k]-tonni-* (< *-tot-ni-*) 'go around/on (keep) mingling' ← *sesk-* + *ton-*˙*ni-* (< *tot-*˙*ni-* < **toT-*°*ni-*); **wul-pu(lu)-cic-** 'bawl' ← **wū(l)-** 'cry' + **pulu-cic-** 'shout' (< **pulu-/pull-** 'shout' + **cic-** 'bark; croak')

From what is said here, we might conclude that modern Korean would have a higher ratio of compound verbs than Middle Korean, but I am not sure that is true. Comparable statistics for the modern language are not yet available. And the poetic nature of the sparse data on Old Korean may mask the true situation of the earlier time.

3.2. How were the Middle Korean compound-verb stems accentuated? The most common pattern preserves the underlying accentuation of both members of the compound, as if they were separate words. For a list of such compounds, see Appendix 1. Other patterns preserve the accent of the first member only (Appendix 2) or the second member only (Appendix 3). Apparently there are no compounds that ignore both accents and yield an all-low stem. Compound members with the unmarked low pitch are perforce treated as "preserving" that accentuation.

For the most part the patterns violate the automatic pattern of low-high that we would like to reconstruct for all proto-Korean words, and this suggests that these stems came into being at a time (or at times) after proto-Korean underwent development into historic Korean.[9] There is other evidence for that. When the basic shape of the stem was "extrasyllabic", in that it contained a coda violating the rules for the canonical shape of a syllable, it was reduced — and not only before a consonant, as in *ses-moy-* = *ses[k]-moy-* < **sesk-moy-* 'tie them all up together' and *put-cap-* = *put[h]-cap-* < *puth-cap-* 'seize, grasp, get, hold', but also before a vowel, as in *ses-elk-* = *ses[k]-elk-* < **sesk-elk-* 'bind / tie them together' and in *put-ˮan-/-aˊn[o]-* = *put[h]-ˮan-/-aˊn[o]-* < **puth-aˊno-* 'hold it in one's arms, hug'. The coda *···lk* was, apparently, pronounceable: *kulk-pis-* 'scratch and comb oneself'. But its final stop became the onset of the following syllable when that syllable started with a vowel: *mol.k-anc-* 'settle clear'. The coda *···h* of *tah-* 'come in contact; touch; arrive' elided regardless of the following onset: *ta-cwoch-* < *ta[h]-cwoch-* 'closely follow', *ta-tilG-/-tilo-* < **ta-tiloG-* < **ta[h]-tilok-* 'thrust against, butt; approach; attack, defy'.[10] Yet other stems with the coda *···h* pushed the final aspirate into the next syllable when possible: *ceh-* 'fear' + *twuˊli-* 'fear' → *cethwuˊli-* 'fear', *ceh-* 'fear' + *-p⁴o-* 'apparent' → *cephu-* 'be fearsome / fearful', *ˮtywoh-* 'be good' + *kwuc-* 'be bad' → *ˮtywokhwuc-* '(whether it) be good or bad'. The coda *···lh* also pushed the final aspirate into the next syllable when possible: *kulthalh-* < *kulh-talh-* 'boil and decoct, boil it down', *ilthulˊGi-* < *il[h]-tulˊGi-* 'suffer a fiasco, get thwarted, lose out'. From the early part of the 16th century the coda *···c* [ts] normally reduced to *···s*, as in *mac-pat-* > *mas-pat-* 'contact, hit' but in the 15th century it sometimes stayed intact: *mac-°na-* = *mas-°na-* (> *man-°na-* from the 16th century).

3.3. In certain compound verbs the first stem is one of the "irregular" type that had two shapes in Middle Korean. (We include the "regular" *···l-* stems with the irregular types because they too appeared in two shapes, as shown in Martin 1997.) Often the stem appears in a compressed shape of one syllable rather than the etymologically original shape, which was basically dissyllabic, though the dissyllabicity is sometimes masked when the minimal vowel ⁴o of the second syllable is suppressed in attaching suffixes. When the first member of a compound is one of these two-shape stems, it always appears in the compressed shape:[11]

ˮket-°na- 'walk across; cross' ← *ˮkeT-* = *ˮket-/keˊl[u]-* < **keˊtu-* 'walk' + *°na-* 'emerge'

tot-ˊni- 'walk about, come and go' < **tot-°ni-* ← *toT-* = *tot-/tol[o]-* < **toto-* 'run' + *°ni-* 'go; go on, continue'

ˮyes-°pwo- ← *ˮyez-* = *ˮyes-/yeˊz[u]-* < **yeˊsu-* 'spy on' + *°pwo-* 'look'

῁*kip-sesk-* 'mix/blend and weave' ← ῁*kiW-* = ῁*kip-/ki῀W[ᴸ⁄₀]-* <
*ki῀pᴸ⁄₀- 'sew (up), patch, mend'

˙*ko-ta˙tom-* = ˙*ko[l]-tat˙om-* < *˙*ko[˙lo]-ta˙tom-* 'tidy up, arrange, put
in good order' ← ˙*ko(l)-/˙ko῀l[o]-* < *˙*ko˙lo-* 'grind; put an edge on;
polish' + *ta˙tom-* 'trim it, prune it, smooth it; adorn'

tu-nwoh- = *tu[l]-nwoh-* 'lift and put/place it; lift it up' ← [῁]*tu(l)-/
tu῀l[u]-* < **tu῀lu-* 'hold; lift, raise, hold up' + *nwoh-* 'put'

nolp˙tu- = *nol-˙ptu-* 'pop/spring up' ← [῁]*no(l)-/no῀l[o]-* < **no῀lo-*
'fly' + ˙*ptu-* 'float; widen the gap, depart, leave'

῁*nilp˙tu-* = ῁*nil-˙ptu-* 'pop/spring up' ← ῁*ni(l)-/ni῀l[ᴸ⁄₀]-* < **ni῀lᴸ⁄₀-*
'arise' + ˙*ptu-* 'float; widen the gap, depart, leave'

῁*pil-mek-* 'beg (for one's food)' ← ῁*pi(l)-/pi῀l[ᴸ⁄₀]-* < **pi῀lᴸ⁄₀-* 'beg;
pray; borrow' + *mek-* 'eat'

῁*kem-sek-* 'turn black with rot' ← ῁*kem-/ke῀m[u]-* < **ke˙mu-* 'be black'
+ *sek-* 'rot'

῁*kel-anc-* 'seat oneself, take a seat' ← ῁*ke(l)-/ke῀l[u]-* < **ke˙lu-* 'hang
it' + *a(n)c-* = *anc-, ac-* 'sit'

῁*i-sis-* < ῁*i[l]-sis-* < **i῀lᴸ⁄₀-sis-* 'wash out, rinse' ← ῁*i(l)-/i῀l[ᴸ⁄₀]-* <
*i῀lᴸ⁄₀- 'rinse (grain)' + *sis-* 'wash'

Dissyllabic stems from **···lᴸ⁄₀l-, *···lᴸ⁄₀G-* < **···lᴸ⁄₀k-,* or **···sᴸ⁄₀G-* <
*···sᴸ⁄₀k-, however, elide the final consonant of the underlying form:

pulu-cici- 'shout, yell' = *pulu[l]-cici-* ← *pulu-/pull-* < **pulul-* (1) 'call,
summon, invite', (2) 'sing, sing out, shout; sing of'

puzu-thi- 'smash, shatter' = *puzu[G]-thi-* ← *pᴸ⁄₀zG-/pozo-* < **pᴸ⁄₀osᴸ⁄₀G-*
< **pᴸ⁄₀osᴸ⁄₀k-* 'crush, smash' + ˙*thi-* 'hit, beat'

pulu-twot- 'swell up' = *pulu[G]-twot-* ← *pulG-/pulu-* < **puluG-* <
*puluk- 'get full' + *twot-* 'sprout; rise'

wulu-ceksi- 'bawl' = *wulu[G]-ceksi-* ← *wulG-/wulu-* < **wuluG-* <
*wuluk- 'howl, roar' + *cek˙si-* 'make/let it get wet, soak it; stain;
defile'

salo-mwut- 'bury alive' = *salo[G]-mwut-* ← *salG-/salo-* < **saloG-* <
*salo-k- 'let one live' + *mwut-* 'bury'

twolo-˚(h)hye- < **twolo[G]-˚(h)hye* 'pull/turn it around' ← *twolG-/twolo-*
< **twoloG-* < **twolo-k-* 'turn it, make/let it turn' + ˚*(h)hye-* 'pull'

twulu-˚(h)hye- < **twulu[G]-˚(h)hye-* 'turn it around; turn it over' ←
twulG-/twulu- < **twuluG-* < **twulu-k-* 'encircle, surround; turn it
around, whirl it, make it revolve' + ˚*(h)hye-* 'pull'

The initial onset of the later member of a compound may lenite:

῁*hyey-Ga῀li-* < **῁hyey-ka῀li-* 'considers, ponders; figures out; counts'
← ῁*hyey-* 'reckon, count; think, consider, figure' + *ka῀li-* 'branch off,
be forked'

hey-Gwat- < **hey-Wat-* < **-pat-* 'disperse it, dissolve it' ← *hey-*
'scatter' + *pat-* 'butt'

mol-[¨]Goz- = **mol[o]-[¨]Gos-/mol[o]-Go˙z[o]-* < **molo[G]-ko˙so-* vt
'cut out' ← *molG-/molo-* < **moloG-* < **molok-* vt 'cut out' + *[¨]koz-*
= **¨kos-/ko˙zo-* < **ko˙so-* 'cut'
¨twol-˚Gwo- = *¨twol-˚Wwo-* = *¨twol-˚pwo-* vt 'look around; take care of,
look after' ← *¨two(l)-/two˙l[o]-* < **two˙lo-* vi/vt 'turn (around/back/to)'
+ *˚pwo-* vt 'look, see'

4.0. In both Korean and Japanese a verb form is made up of a STEM +
an ENDING. There are both simple stems with no internal structure and
complex stems, which consist of a stem + one or more formants. The
formants are bound auxiliaries, and the stem to which they are attached
may be either free or bound. (Bound stems — and, for that matter, bound
auxiliaries — can also be called ROOTS.) The endings are a small set of
paradigmatic markers, and these may contain further structure: certain
endings are simple, but others are complex and contain more than one
morpheme. Our modern paradigms have proliferated the endings by
compressing larger structures that originally consisted of a verb form with
a simple ending and other elements, such as particles and auxiliaries. The
stem does not occur without an ending, but in Japanese the infinitive
ending -*i* has been absorbed by certain stems, namely those that end in ···*i-*
or ···*e-*, and that leaves the stem looking as if it were free.

4.1. Many Japanese verb infinitives underlie derived nouns that were
originally made by atonicizing the infinitive form. The transitive infinitive
[Tōkyō] *hazime*[7] = [old Kyōto] *fazi*[7]*me* < **pansima-Ci-Ci*[7] from an
atonic stem means 'begins it' (cf [Tōkyō] *hazimari*[7] = [old Kyōto]
fazima[7]*ri* < **fazimari*[7] < **pansima-ra-Ci*[7] 'it begins') and the infinitive
underlies the noun *hazime* < *fazime* 'the beginning' (atonic). The intransitive infinitive [Tōkyō] *noko*[7]*ri* < [old Kyōto] [7]*nokori*[7] < **[7]no̜ko̜-ra-Ci*[7]
from a tonic stem means 'it remains' (cf *noko*[7]*s-* < **[7]no̜ko̜-sa-* 'leaves it')
and underlies the noun *nokori*[7] < [7]*nokori* 'remainder' (this form is
preaccented in Kyōto and the accent is heard as initial low pitch) from an
atonic low-register noun in old Kyōto. These two stems are derived from a
low-register root **[7]no̜ko̜* that is probably cognate with MK *nwoh-* 'put it
aside' according to Martin 1966:239, #175 (see below). Every stem has an
infinitive form, but many stems lack an infinitive-derived noun; that form
is not a part of the verb paradigm but belongs with the derivational
morphology of the nouns, and each must be specified in the lexicon.

In Japanese of the 11th century and earlier the atonic stems and roots
were marked by HIGH register and the tonic stems and roots were marked
by LOW register. High and low refer to the pitch of the initial syllable, but
one explanation of the proto-Japanese accent system hypothesizes that the
registers were originally distinguished by vowel length, and that the initial
syllable of a low-register word was long. In our example: **no:ko* →
*no:ko-ra-, **no:ko-sa-*. Cf Mg *nöö-* < pMg **nöge-* 'put away, store,

save'; Tg *nee-, neekuu-, neeke-, neekči-* 'put' < pTg **nee(ke)-*. The same etymon may be present not only in Korean *nwoh-* 'put, put aside; release, let go/escape' but also in Korean neh- (dial. yeh-) < MK *nyeh-* 'put/let in' ? < **nih-* and in Japanese *nigey-* < **ninka-Ci-* = *nogar-* < **nonka-ra-* 'escape' and *nigas-* < **ninka-sa-* = *nogas-* < **nonka-sa-* 'let escape'. The extra *n* in the proto-Japanese forms for 'escape' may be an emphatic infix or perhaps it just echoes the initial nasal. That would leave us with pKJ roots **noka-/*nika-* 'release, escape' and **noko-* 'put, put away' for further comparison with the Mongolian and Tungusic verbs. It is unclear just how Korean *nyeh-* ? < **nih-* acquired the specialized meaning 'put/let in', but cf Khalkha *nöh(ö)-* 'fill in, compensate, mend'. It is also unclear whether these etyma are connected with J **noko-* and **nuka-* 'remove' (cf Tg *luk-* 'take off/out' and Starostin 1991:75 who reconstructs pA **luk'E*), as well as **oku-* 'put, put aside; send' (= K *nwoh-*). Cf also written Mg *niyu-* = Khalkha *nuu-/nöö-* 'hide, conceal' (Kuribayashi 1968:296).

4.2. The view of the Japanese verb presented here does not allow the stem to occur without a paradigmatic ending. An alternative view would say that the infinitive IS the stem and account for the lack of the -*i* ending in certain other forms by rules truncating the stem. That view is implicit in the pedagogical treatment of Jorden and Chaplin 1962-3 where the verb infinitive is called the "stem" of the verb, and the syntactic similarity with the adjective infinitive *(-)ku*, called the "adverbial", is not addressed as such. It would be possible to defend such a view and still preserve the infinitive morpheme -*i* if that morpheme were redefined as simply "verb marker". While I do not favor this approach, let me point out that it would mean that the Japanese verb "stem" DOES occur freely, in fact much more so than its Korean counterpart. In my view of Japanese verbs the real stem is the form Japanese grammarians call the "mizen-kei". That is the form to which various "subjunctive" elements are attached, such as the three bound auxiliaries -*na-* 'negative', -*ma-* 'future/probable', and -*sa-* '(subject-exalting) honorific', as well as the focus particle *ba* < **n pa* used as hypothetical 'if': OJ *sirani* 'unknowing' (K 23:10; 45:4, 6) < **sira-n[a]-Ci* (negative infinitive), *komu* 'will come' (K 51:5, 87:4) < **ko-m[a]-u*, *twofa-sa-n[y]e* 'please ask [for news of me]' (K 86:5) < **t(w)opa-sa-na-Ci*,[12] *ina-ba* 'when (in future) I go away' (K 5:35) ? < **ina-m[a] pa*.[13]

4.3. What is a verb? Suppose we assume that every language has two large lexical categories, as well as various smaller categories. The larger of the two major categories we label "noun", the smaller "verb". Some verbs are made from nouns, and many nouns are made from verbs, but the lexicon consists preponderantly of primary nouns. It is possible to characterize the noun or the verb both syntactically and semantically. There are also words that we would like to characterize semantically as "adjectives"; their primary function is to describe nouns. In some languages these are morphologically and syntactically closer to verbs, in others to nouns.

In Korean, as far back as we can see, the adjective stem is paradigmatically identical with the verb stem both in form and in categories; the only difference is that for semantic reasons certain forms are lacking, specifically those that express commands, propositions, intentions, and processes. Some of the Korean adjectives can also function as intransitive verbs with the meaning 'become ⋯ ' rather than 'be ⋯ ', but more often that meaning is expressed by a periphrastic expression 'become so that it is ⋯' using the intransitive verb toy- < towoy- < toWoy- < *topoy- vi 'become'. In modern Japanese the adjective has a paradigm much like that of the verb as far as categories go (like Korean, lacking certain categories), but the forms are different from those of the verb, and the paradigms developed later.

4.4. The adjective stem in Korean is much like the verb stem with respect to forming compounds and the like. In Japanese the adjective stem, unlike the verb stem, can enter into compounds, and it is the form to which are attached auxiliaries such as su^7gi- 'be/do overly', as in ta^7ka- 'expensive' + su^7gi- → $taka$-su^7gi- 'be too expensive'. But the verb, as mentioned above, must be put into the infinitive form: no^7m-i + su^7gi- → $nomi$-su^7gi- 'drink too much'. A few of the Japanese adjective stems also underlie free nouns (or vice versa),[14] and some of the stems referring to subjective sensations can be used alone as an exclamation (Martin 1975: 815): *Aa ita!* 'Ouch, it hurts!'

The Japanese adjective stem was relatively free compared with the verb stem (and with the Korean adjective stem). There are no cases of the Japanese raw verb stem + verb stem (or of verb stem + noun), but several adjective-adjective compounds occur: $hoso$-na^7ga- 'long and narrow/slender' < *foso-naga-* (attested 1603), $huru$-ku^7sa- 'old and stale' < *furu-kusa-* (attested 1106). And adjective stem + noun is common. Before entering into a compound with a following noun the verb stem has to be extended with the infinitive ending, as in *iri-e* 'inlet (stream)' < *ir[y]i-ye* < *ir[a-C]i* (? < *dira-Ci*) 'enter' + *ye* (< ?*d(y)o*) 'inlet; branch'. But the adjective stem needs no extension: *waka-kusa* 'young grass' (K 5:46, 6:10). For Old Japanese it is unclear whether a given string is to be taken as an adjective-noun compound or as a looser structure of adjective | noun. For other structures that contain the adjective stem see Martin 1987:813-5.

The Korean adjective stem also makes a few compound nouns by direct attachment to a noun: **nulk-tali** 'an old animal; an old person' ← nulk- adj 'old' + tali 'leg', **mip-sang** 'a disgusting face, appearance, or act' < miw- adj 'hateful' + *SANG* 'appearance', *polk-˚cwuy* (1489 Kup-kan 6:68a) = ¨polk-˚cwuy [first accent unexplained] (1527 Cahoy 1:12a= 22b) 'bat' ← *polk*- adj 'bright; red' + ˚cwuy 'rat'.[15]

4.5. Unlike Japanese, Korean permits also compounds of verb-stem + noun → noun: *twu ˙ti-˙cwuy* (> **twuteci**) 'mole' ← *twu ˙ti-* = *tuwuy-* vt 'upset; rummage' + ˙*cwuy* 'rat'; *pipuy-hwal* (1775 Yek.e po 45b) 'the bow of a bowstring drill' ← *pi ˙puy-* 'rub' + *hwal* 'bow'; *pwus-twos* (1775 Yek.e po:42a) '(paired) winnowing mats' (> **puttwu**) ← *pwuch-* vt 'fan' + *twosk* 'mat'; ˙*pswus-¨twolh* 'whetstone' [first accent unexplained] ← *pswuch-* 'graze, glance' + ¨*twolh* 'stone'; ˙*mas-tang* vnt (> **mattang** adj-n) 'making it suitable' [first accent unexplained] < *mac-* vi 'suit, fit, match' + *TANG* 'suitability'.[16] Modern examples: ik-pancwuk 'half-cooked (= hot-water) dough', petq-(n)i 'protruding teeth', kkekciq-son 'heroic measure'.

A few Korean verb stems also occur as free adverbs: *somos* adv 'thoroughly; penetratingly' ← *somoch-* vt 'pierce', tēl 'less, little' < *¨*tel* (*can ul tel mek.u.l ye* 1747 Songkang 2:6b) ← ¨*te(l)-/te ˙l[u]-* < *te ˙lu-* vt 'lessen it', *mich* < *mis* adv 'and (extending to), and also' ← *mich-* vi 'attain, reach',[17] *tet* adv 'additionally, added on top' ← *teth-* 'grope/ fumble for; stammer; *add on*',[18] *kulu* 'wrongly, mistakenly, mis⋯ ' < *kulG-/kulu-* < *kuluG-* < *kuluk-* adj 'be wrong' (and vt 'untie, loosen'), cf the noun/adverb *kulus* 'a mistake; by mistake' ?< *kulu-s* (or *kulG-us*) or < *kuluch-* vi 'go amiss/astray'. The stem of *pi ˙lus-* 'begin it' is used as an adverb, *pi ˙lus* 'for the first time', and also as a noun in the phrase *pi ˙lus ¨ep.si* 'with no beginning' (1482 Nam 1:75a).[19]

A number of verb stems are identical with nouns, from which most seem to have been derived:[20]

kwop 'double' → *kwop-* 'get doubled'

ne ˙chwul (> **nenchwul**) 'vine, tendril' → *ne ˙chwu(l)-/ne ˙chwu ˙l[u]-* < *ne ˙chwu ˙lu-* vi 'vine out'

nwu ˙pi < ˙*NAP-QUY* 'quilt (garment)' → *nwu[˙]pi-* vt 'quilt'

˙*twoy* 'measure' (? < Chinese *dŏu* = ¨*TWUW/¨TYE* 'peck measure, dipper' + -˙*i*) → ˙*twoy-* vt 'measure it'

˙*stuy* 'belt' ?< ⋯ *s ˙TAY* (1103 Kyeylim #236 ˙*SSILQ-˙TAY* 'silk belt') → *stuy-* vt 'wear (as a belt), gird oneself with'

˙*poy* 'belly' → *poy-* vt 'get pregnant with (child), conceive'

˙*soym* 'a source, a (well)spring' (?< ˙*soy-* 'leak') → ¨*soym-* (?= ¨*soym-/ *soy ˙m[ᵘ/o]-* < *soy ˙mᵘ/o-*) vi 'spring/spurt up'

˙*sin* ?< *˙*syen* 'shoes' (1103 Kyeylim #231 ˙*SSYENG*), perhaps from Chinese *xuàn* '(put into) shoe-last (mold)' (Karlgren 1923:249) → ¨*sin-/ si ˙n[ᵘ/o]-* < *si ˙nᵘ/o-* vt 'wear it on one's feet'; compare *pwosyen* (> **pesen**) 'socks, bootees' (1103 Kyeylim #232 ˙*PPOY SSYENG*), perhaps < ˙*PWO* 'cloth' (or ˙*pwoy* ?< ˙*PWO* + -*i* 'hemp cloth') + 'shoes'. LKM 1958:109 compared *pwosyen* with Manchu *foji* 'skin covering for boots and shoes' [Norman], but that goes back to something like *fomoči* or *fomon*, related to Evenki *hemčurē* 'fur boots' (Tsintsius 2:366a).

˙*anh* 'inside' → ¨*an-/a˙n[o]-* < **a˙no-* vt 'hug, embrace'

˙*phwum* 'bosom' or (1481 Twusi 10:42b, somehow overlooked by Martin 1992:69) 'chest width' (? < ˙*ph[u]-wu-m* 'blooming, opening up') → ˙*phwum-* vt 'embrace, hug'

pwo˙moy (→ *pwonoy* [sic] > *pwonuy*) 'the inner husk (as of a chestnut)' → *pwo˙moy-* vi 'rust'

ye˙mul 'chopped hay, fodder' (Pak 1:21b) → *ye˙mu(l)-/ye˙mul[u]-* < **ye˙mulu-* vi 'get ripe, ripen, mature' [The semantic relationship is unclear.]

*mwo˙zi > *mwo[ ]i* (?1775 Han-Cheng 13:62b) > *mwongi* (1748 Tongmun 2:35, ?1775 Han-Cheng 14:39b) > ˙*mwoy* (1586 Sohak 4:12b) > ˙*mey* (1527 Cahoy 2:10a=19b) noun 'food, fodder' → *mwo˙zi-* vt 'feed'

˙*ko(˙)mol* 'drought' → ˙*ko˙mo(l)-/˙ko˙mo˙l[o]-* < *˙ko˙mo˙lo-* vi 'go without rain, be rainless, be drought-dry'

But the following noun is probably derived from the verb:

kᵉ/a˙li 'branch, fork' ? < **kᵉ/a˙li[-˙i]* der n < *kᵉ/a˙li-* vi 'branch off, be forked'

The verbs might have been formed at any time. The formation of ˙*kis* 'nest' → ¨*kiz-* < **ki˙zo-* 'roost (in a nest)' requires more delicate timing because of the accent of the noun (canonically imposed?) and the final vowel of the verb (the vestige of a suffix?).

Certain structures of noun + verb are best to be regarded as syntactic: subject + verb, or object + verb. Koreans have always freely omitted the nominative and accusative markers in many kinds of sentences, especially when the subject/object is short and is directly followed by the verb. But in some instances a change in shape or accentuation indicates a compound, and in some the syntactic valences of the noun and verb show that the noun is not to be taken as the subject or object, but plays some other role. Examples: ˙*stuy-˙cho-* vt 'gird/encircle oneself with' ← ˙*stuy* 'belt' + ˙*cho-* vt 'attach', *mal˙moy-¨zam-/-za˙mo-* = *mal˙moy-¨sam-/-sa˙mo-* vt 'arise from, be in consequence of, be due to, accord with' ← *mal˙moy* 'reason, cause; furlough' + ¨*sam-/sa˙m[o]-* < **sa˙mo-* vt 'make (it into ···)'. I treat as idioms certain of these structures often listed as compounds by Korean lexicographers, such as the following (cf LCT 1971:322):

   ˙*him nip-* vt/vi 'owe to, be indebted for' ← ˙*him* 'power' + *nip-* vt 'incur; wear'

   ˙*him ˙psu-* vi 'endeavor; exercise influence' ← ˙*him* 'power' + ˙*psu-* vt 'use, apply'

   ˙*nwun ¨mel-* vi 'go/be blind' ← ˙*nwun* 'eye' + ¨*me(l)-/me˙l[u]-* < **me˙lu-* adj 'be far'[21]

   ˙*kwuy mek-* vi 'go/be deaf' ← ˙*kwuy* 'ear' + *mek-* vt 'eat; ··· '

Structures of bound adverb + verb are also often regarded as compounds, but sometimes I prefer not to do so: ¨*pi ¨wuz-* = ¨*pi ¨wus-/wu˙z[u]-* <

*wu˚su- bnd adv + vt 'sneer at'. If that is treated as one word, the spelling requires the phoneme string to be ¨pi¨Gwu⋯ (otherwise the spelling would be ¨pi¨ywu⋯), but I think a juncture must have kept that realization from happening.

4.6. Verb stems comprise a class that is largely closed in both Japanese and Korean, and so is the class of (predicable) adjective stems. When words with the semantic characteristics of a verb or an adjective are borrowed into these languages from Chinese or English, they are treated as if nouns and are predicated by an auxiliary of one sort or another. In Korean both the verbal noun and the adjectival noun are predicated with the auxiliary **ha-** < MK °ho-/˚ho˚y- 'do/be'. Japanese verbal nouns are predicated with the auxiliary *si-* ← proto-Japanese *sǫ- 'do', but the adjectival nouns are predicated with the copula, for which the paradigmatic forms are made up of one of the essives, *ni* (objective) or *tǫ* (subjective), + the auxiliary *a(r)-* 'be'. Some of the verbal and adjectival nouns can never be separated from the predicating auxiliary, even by a focus particle. The inseparables are usually short.

4.7. While the usual practice is to modify nouns by processes of adnominalization that put the predication into an adnominal form, usually called "attributive" in Japanese and "modifier" in Korean, both languages have a number of primary adnouns (Martin 1975:742-754, 1992:146-153), and these vary in the extent to which they can be separated from the modified nouns they precede. Some occur only as adnouns, others have wider uses such as noun or adverb; most have transparent origins as other parts of speech. Japanese has very few primary adnouns. There is a gradation of freedom between adnouns and versatile prefixes, which can be described as bound adnouns, just as there is between adverbs and bound adverbs. In Japanese, juncture sometimes serves as a criterion for differentiating adnoun or adverb from prefix; cf the "pseudo adnouns" of Martin 1975:750-3.

5.0. We have seen that Korean differs from the Altaic languages in allowing compounds of one verb stem with another. It differs in that respect also from Japanese, provided we do not regard the infinitive form as the stem. But the attested Korean compound verbs were probably created after the various stages of morphological development described in Martin 1996a that led to the birth of the unusual verb conjugations and the emergence of accentual distinctions. If proto-Korean lacked compound verbs, then it was more like Altaic and Japanese. But if the feature of verb-stem compounds could develop within Korean, what kept that from happening in the other languages?[22]

5.1. There is another difference between some of the Altaic languages and Korean. The Korean verb stem rather freely forms compounds with other verb stems and to some extent with nouns, but it does not occur by itself without an ending. The only exceptions seem to be stems that are directly derived from nouns and a very small number of stems that are directly adverbialized (§4.6). In Turkic and Mongolian the verb stem freely appears with no ending and then serves as a simple imperative: Mongolian *gar* 'go away!', Chuvash *kay* 'go!', Turkish *(bana) bak* 'look (here)!'. The Tungusic verb stem is more like the Korean[23] in that it usually requires a suffix, but that is not always true.[24] There are two kinds of imperative, present and future, and in most cases these are distinctively marked for person and number (singular / plural). That is a far more elaborate scheme than the Korean imperative, which is made with the suffix -*(ᵘ/o)la*. In Middle Korean the ending could be preceded by - *kᵉ/a-*, the bound auxiliary of the effective aspect:[25]

> *kap˙ka˙la* (1447 Sek 6:22b) '[telling us to] repay' (?1468⁻ Mong 31b) ← *kaph-* 'repay'; *is˙ke˙la* [imperative] (?1517⁻ ¹No 2:72b) 'stay' ← *is(i)-* 'be, stay', ··· *ho˙ke˙la ¨mal˙la* (?1517⁻ ¹No 2:57a) 'you [two] need not ··· ' ← *˙ho-/˙ho˙y-* 'do/be'

After /y/ or /l/ the effective is lenited to - *Gᵉ/a-*:

> *¨pskeyGa˙la* (1481 Twusi 24:37a) '(in order to) penetrate it' ← *¨pskey-* vt 'pierce', vi 'get pierced', *¨nil˙Ge˙la* '(Pals,) get up!' (?1517⁻ ¹No 1:38a) ← *¨ni(l)-/ni˙l[ᵘ/o]-* 'arise', *¨salGa˙la* '[saying you] stay alive!' (1481 Samkang hyo:20a) ← *¨sa(l)-/sa˙l[o]-* < **sa˙lo-* 'live'.

A shortened shape turns up in certain passages. In Martin 1992 I treated these as elision of the velar stop, - *˙[k]ᵉ/a-*, and assumed that the effective imperative is what is found in *pi˙se˙la* (?1517⁻ Pak 1:44a) 'comb my hair!' = **pis˙[k]e˙la* ← *pis-* vt 'comb (one's hair)'. I have changed my mind and now say that the form is *pi˙se ˙la* with the plain infinitive followed by an exclamatory particle,[26] as in the modern equivalent, where -ᵉ/a la expresses the plain-style command and -(u)la is used only in indirect quotations ('told one to do it'). What changed my mind was the realization that *tu˙le ˙la* (1459 Wel 10:21a) 'listen [to my words]!' ← *tuT-* = *tut-/tul[u]-* < **tutu-* vt 'listen, hear' could not very well be a contraction **tut˙[k]e˙la* nor, given its accentuation, could *a˙la˙la* (1447 Sek 19:26a) '[you] be aware [of this]' and (23:45b) '[you people] be aware [of this]!' be a contraction of *¨al˙Ga˙la* (?1468⁻ Mong 31b) '[telling us to] recognize [the obligation]' ← *¨a(l)-/a˙l[o]-* < **a˙lo-* vt 'know, recognize, realize'. Other examples: *pa˙ta ˙la* (?1517⁻ ¹No 2:27a) 'offer [a firm price]!' ← *pat-* vt 'get; offer, give', *ipata ˙la* (1459 Wel 23:89b) 'give her solace' ← *ipat-* vt 'entertain', *¨pwoa ˙la* (1447 Sek 23:13a) 'look at it!' ← *˙pwo-* vt 'see, look'. With *tas˙ka( )˙la* (1459 Wel 23:77b) 'practice [the Way]' ← *task-* 'polish, practice', it is difficult to say which structure is present, *tas[k]-˙ka-˙la* or *task-˙a ˙la*. The modern differentiation of direct imperative (-ᵉ/a la) from indirectly quoted command must have set in later than the 15th and 16th century texts, for in them we find both forms used in quotations as well as in direct commands: *˙twue ˙la* (1459 Wel 7:8a) '[said to] put it (back) away' ← *˙twu-* 'put away', *sam˙ka˙la* '[gather and] show respect!' (1447 Sek 23:13a) ← *sam˙ka-* 'show restraint/respect'. In modern Seoul the string /kala/ represents both ka-la, an indirectly quoted command '(telling one) to go', and ka[-a] la, a plain-style direct command 'go!', sometimes said as kake la, a survival of *˙*kakᵉ/a˙la*. But in Middle Korean the optional shortening of the infinitive ˙*ka-˙a* is ˙*ka*, so the lack of an initial accent tells us that *ka˙la* (1447 Sek 6:22b '[tells him to] go' is the aspectually unmarked imperative, and the same is true of *phye˙la* (1447 Sek 23:31b) '[I told him to help] spread it' ← ˙*phye-* 'spread it', for otherwise we would expect *˙*ka˙la* and *˙*phye˙la*. It would seem that the modulated forms ¨*ka˙la* (1463 Pep 2:51a) and ¨*phye˙la* (1463 Pep 2:218a) could be taken either way, but we fail to find the modulated infinitives *¨*ka(-˙a)* and *¨*phye(-˙e)* else-where, nor do we expect them, for the modulator[27] is never used before certain endings, including the infinitive (Martin 1992:271).

I am uncertain whether the emphatic particle in the structure verb + -ᵉ/a la (and, by analogy, in modern -ke la and the -ne la of o-ne la = w-a la 'come!') is to be etymologically equated with the la of adjective + -ᵉ/a 'la < MK -˙ᵉ/a 'y˙la, contracted from i-˙la, the lenited form of the copula i-˙ta. If so, we can ask whether the simple imperative ending ⃗(ᵘ/o)˙la is the same etymon, and if so, a lenition of -˙ta, the indicative assertive. But that is highly speculative in view of two likely examples in 1103 Kyeylim: *wola* 'come' (#322 QWO-LA) and (with the effective) *acokala* 'sit' (#317 A-˙CUK-KA-LA). There are three examples in the hyangka, according to Kim Wancin's interpretation: *pella* (10:4) 'let them be arrayed!' ← ¨*pe(l)-/˙pe˙l[ul]-* (also *pe˙l[ul]-*) < *¨*pe˙lu-* vi 'spread', and (with the effective) *swos-nakela* (16:4) 'let it gush forth!' ← *swos-˙na-* and *nilukela* (15:4) 'let it reach!' ← *ni˙lu-* = *ni˙lu(l)-/ni˙lul[u]-* < *ni˙lulu-* vi 'reach'. As in these examples, the imperative was not always second-person in reference, and its shape is identical to that of the intentive/purposive ⃗(ᵘ/o)˙la, the predecessor of modern -(u)le (purposive) '[go] to do' and -(u)lye (intentive) 'intend to do'; there is an example of that, too, in the hyangka: *tas.kela* (8:4) '(come) in order to practice' (?= *task-ula*, ?= *tas[k]-ke-la*) ← *task-* 'polish; practice'. In *pwo˙la ka˙la* (?1517-¹No 1:67b) 'you go see!', the first form is the purposive, the second the imperative. An example of the effective intentive: ˙*mwo.m ol* ¨*kalmka˙la* ˙*honwon* ˙*t ila* (1481 Twusi 21:29b) 'seeks to hide himself' ← ¨*kalm-/kal˙m[o]-* 'hide it'. The variant -(u)la survives in certain structures, often with an extra l that is sometimes heard in Seoul, especially in the structure -(u)lla 'y, from a contracted quotation, and -(u)lla, the prospective adjunctive (Martin 1992:866-7).[28]

Like the intentive and purposive, the imperative was probably made on ⃗(ᵘ/o)l, the prospective modifier (= imperfect/future adnominal) ending, with a semantic development like that in English "Willya lend me a hand, please!" ← "will you?". All these structures, including the imperative,

seem to be from $-(^{l\!l}\!o)l + \cdot i + \cdot ka$ '(the question) whether it is to be/do'
$> -(^{l\!l}\!o) \cdot l\, i \cdot [k]a = -(^{l\!l}\!o) \cdot l\, i \cdot (y)a > (1) -(^{l\!l}\!o) \cdot l\, [i]\, ya$ and $> (2) -(^{l\!l}\!o) \cdot l$
$[i\, y]a$. I assume that in all cases the postmodifier $\cdots \cdot ya$ 'question' is from
$\cdots \cdot i \cdot ka$ ("is it that $\cdots$?") and is unrelated to the OJ question particle ya,
though the postmodifier $\cdot ka$ must be cognate with J ka 'the question
(whether)'. Korean nominalizations with $\cdots \cdot i$ 'the fact (that $\cdots$)' can
function as unmarked questions as well as statements (perhaps with an
ellipted copula), and that is the source of the modern interrogative ending
$-ni < -(^{l\!l}\!o) \cdot n\, i$ or $-\cdot no- \cdot n\, i$ of the plain style.

5.2. Old Japanese has an imperative form that after a consonant stem
ends in $-ye$ and after a vowel stem ends in $\cdots yo$ (= eastern dialect $\cdots ro$
after $\cdots ey$, but not $\cdots iy$ or $\cdots yi$), and these forms all survive in the modern
language. Old Japanese examples: $susumye$ (B 18:4) 'go forth!', $ne[y]\, yo$
(M 831) = $ne[y]\, ro$ (M 3499 [eastern]) 'sleep!', $tukey\, ro$ (M 4420
[eastern]) 'attach it!' but $okiy\, yo\, okiy\, yo$ (M 3873 [eastern]) 'get up! get
up!', $kyi\, yo$ (M 15) 'wear it'.[29]

The form in front of yo (or ro) might be identified as the infinitive, for
that ending ($-yi < *-i$ or $*-Ci$) is absorbed into the stem-final front vowel.
Or it might be the stem itself. The stem $myi- < *mi-$ 'see, look', to which
are attached the auxiliaries $-ma-$ (future), $-na-$ (negative), and $-sa-$ (honorific), among others, has the infinitive $myi < myi[-yi] < *mi-Ci$. In Martin
1987 I assumed that the distinctive form of the imperative of a consonant-
final OJ stem contained the infinitive (e.g. $susum-yi < *susuma-Ci$) + an
exclamatory particle a ($susumye < *susum-i\, a$) and that the vowel-stem
form before yo or ro was the infinitive. In a few examples the OJ infinitive (or stem?) occurs alone as a command: myi (M 1, 15) = $myi\, yo$
(M 27) 'look!'. But there are no examples of consonant-stem infinitives
like $susumyi$ used alone as a command. And there is one clear example of
a stem occurring alone as a command: $faya\, ko$ (M 15, M 3636, M 3717)
'come quickly!' There are no OJ examples of $*ko\, yo$ or the shorter $*ko\, i$
that led to the later form koi, nor are there examples of $*kyi\, yo$ or of the
infinitive $kyi < kyi[-yi] < *ki-i\, (< *ko-Ci)$ used alone as a command. No
attestations of an eastern version $*ko\, ro$ or $*kyi\, ro$ are found, either.
Another example that is probably a stem: $se\, yo$ (M 15) 'do it!' (the future
is $se-m\cdots$). We assume that the stem $se-$ was earlier $*so-$ (like $*ko-$ 'come'
but with the high accentual register rather than the low). The infinitive is
$si < (*)se[y] < *so-Ci$, and in modern Japanese we find $si\, ro$ as the
eastern version of $se\, yo$. The basis for reconstructing $*so$ for the stem is
the structure of negative adverb (na) + infinitive ($V-yi$) + so that
expresses prohibitions: $na\, omofyi\, so$ 'don't worry!' (M 506), $na\, yakyi\, so$
(M 3452 [eastern]) 'don't burn it', $na\, yase[y]\, so$ (M 3586 [eastern]) 'don't
let yourself waste away', and even $na\, se\, so$ (M 4487) 'don't do it!'. This
structure was heard in modern times by Miyara Tōsō (1954:170) in a
remote village of Shizuoka prefecture: $naa\, ki\, so$ 'don't come'.[30]

While OJ *kǫ* 'come!' (? < **kǫ:*) and perhaps *se* (? < **sǫ*) 'do!' make it attractive to treat the form before *yǫ* (and *rǫ*) as the unsuffixed stem rather than the infinitive, evidence in favor of the infinitive is found in the dialect of the Hachijō islands, where V-*i ro* occurs for the consonant-final stems (KggD 819b): *kaki ro* = standard *kake* 'write it!', in contrast with *kake ro* 'hang it!'. Also relevant: there are examples of OJ *na* V-*yi [sǫ]* with the *sǫ* absent: *na tǫwerafyi* (M 4385 [eastern]) 'may [the waves] not surge', *na tayе[y]* (M 3501 [eastern]) 'let [the words] not end'. In the modern language the honorific infinitive *o*-V-*i* can be used alone (and also followed by *yo* or *ne*) as a command; cf Martin 1975:965, where the usage is explained as an optional ellipsis of *nasai* < *nasare*, which is the imperative of the honorific 'do'. In western Honshū and eastern Kyūshū a lengthened infinitive is used for the vowel-ending stems: *okii* 'arise!', *ukee* 'accept it!' Sporadically in various parts of Japan the vowel-stem verbs are restructured to go with the consonant stems that end in ···*r*- and the appropriate imperative is made on that: *okire* 'get up!' and *ukere* 'accept it!. In the modern language *ro yo* and the shortened *ro i* both occur (Martin 1975:960) and there are dialect reports of *re* ? < *ro i* (960), *e* < *ye* < *yo* (919, 935), and *ya(i)* ? = *ya i* (960).

5.3. Miller 1971:18-9 says that the "Old Korean imperatives in -*ra* ··· clearly go directly ··· with the Old Japanese imperatives in -*rö*", treating the disparity in vowels as due to "the *ö/a* ablaut relationship". It is unclear whether (as his choice of symbols would seem to indicate) he is referring to the "ablaut relationship" he sees within Japanese, which is a way of describing a pattern of vowel alternation found in etymologically related forms within the language, or to that of pA *a/o* (pp. 135, 279, 284, and 289), which is said to explain forms claimed to be cognate that have different vowels in each of the languages compared.[31] But both J *rǫ* and *yǫ*, as we have seen, are emphatic particles and contribute to the making of a command only when they follow the infinitive. As emphatic particles they have other uses, too; see the articles on *rǫ* in Nkd and Jdb. There was no emphatic particle **ra* in Old Japanese and it is hard to say whether the particle *ya* is related to *yǫ* or not. Perhaps Miller thinks that pKJ (or even pA) had an etymon **r$a/_o$* which was handed down to Korean in one "gradation", to Japanese in the other − and not handed down at all, presumably, to the "other Altaic languages". But what strikes me as more interesting than any sort of external comparison is the relationship within Japanese between the dialect variants *rǫ* and *yǫ* (? < **dǫ*), in view of similar pairs such as the passive bound auxiliaries ···*(a)-re[y]*- < **-ra-Ci*- and ···*(a)-ye[y]*- < **-ya-Ci*- ? < **-da-Ci*.[32]

The *la* of the Korean exclamatory structure -*^{e}/a* 'la = -*·^{e}/a* 'y *·la* could have originated as a particle, but I take it as the lenited form of the indicative assertive ending -*ta* < -*·ta* − which, to be sure, could itself have originated as a particle. The (quotative) imperative ending -*ula* <

-$^{u}\!o$ ˙*la*, on the other hand, seems to have come from a structure based on the prospective modifier -$($$^{u}\!o)l$, as explained in §5.1. Despite the superficial appeal of the comparison, I do not think the Korean and Japanese imperative formations have a common origin.

5.4. The independent existence of *kǫ* 'come' and *sǫ* (> *se*) 'do' makes it plausible that all the Japanese stems may earlier have served as commands. If so, proto-Japanese shared this feature with Tungusic, Mongolian, and Turkic, but was different from Korean. Of all these five languages, only Korean permits the compounding of verb stems, but that feature, as we have observed, may very well have been absent from proto-Korean. There is no evidence that the earlier speakers of Korean ever used the verb stem as a command, so we must assume they did not. That single feature, then, is the only significant way that the earliest stage of the Korean verb system differed from the verb systems found in the Turkic, Mongolian, Tungusic, and Japanese language families.

Notes

1 Modern Korean forms, printed in boldface, are written in the Yale Romanization: **wu** = [u] but abbreviated to just **u** after **p ph pp m y**; elsewhere **u** = [ɨ]; **o** = [o]. But forms written before 1933 and those from Ceycwu island, printed in boldface italics, are represented in a version of the Yale system that permits differentiation from *wo* of the now lost vowel called **alay a** (= *alay o*), a low back vowel which once functioned as the unrounded counterpart of [o] and the low counterpart of [ɨ]: *u* = [ɨ] everywhere, *wu* = [u], *o* = [ɔ], *wo* = [o]. The Middle Korean voiced fricative phonemes are represented by *W* (labial), *z* (apical), and *G* (velar or laryngeal); the morphophoneme *T* represents the alternation of the phoneme *t* with *l* (and **t** with **l**). Following the 15th-century spelling conventions, a single dot (˙) marks high pitch and a double dot (¨) marks a rise from low to high; the low pitch is left unmarked, and the low dot (the period) is used only as a device to separate symbols when they might be misinterpreted as a dyad. The hollow dot (˚) marks a verb stem of the high/low type, and the double hollow dot (˚˚) marks a verb stem that is rising but just low before certain endings. Readings of Chinese characters are in italicized small capital letters; they are taken from the prescriptions of 1448 Tongkwuk, which tried to impose certain distinctions of Middle Chinese that were ignored in Korean speech. In accentual patterns the notations H and L represent high and low pitch, respectively. The symbol C represents any consonant, and V is any vowel or vocalic nucleus. While brackets and slashes are used to delimit phonetic and phonemic transcriptions, the slash is used also to show alternants ("or") and the brackets are used to delimit elided strings in certain formulations. Forms

from other languages are cited as found in the sources (with minor adjustments, such as -ng for -ŋ), or as in Martin 1996a. The designation of Korean texts follows the practice of Martin 1992:401-6, where the full titles can be found. Japanese forms are in the notations of Martin 1978. Abbreviations in citing forms:

J = Japanese

K = Korean

Ma = Manchu (written Manchu unless otherwise specified)

MCh = Middle Chinese (as codified from 600 and later)

MK = Middle Korean (as attested in Hankul texts from 1445)

Mg = Mongolian (written Mongolian or "general" Mongolian unless otherwise specified)

OCh = Old Chinese (from texts of 1000 BC and later)

OJ = Old Japanese (the central dialect of texts of around 600-800)

OTk = Old Turkic (as found in texts from 800 and later)

pA = proto-Altaic

pJ = proto-Japanese

pK = proto-Korean

pKJ = proto-Korean-Japanese

pKTg = proto-Koreo-Tungusic (from Kim Tongso 1981)

pMg = proto-Mongolian

pTg = proto-Tungusic

pTk = proto-Turkic

Tg = Tungusic (proto-Tungusic or "general" Tungusic)

Tk = Turkish or Turkic (proto-Turkic or "general" Turkic)

2 Miller's gloss should be amended to "'become, create' respectively".

3 MK *nah-* also means 'weave' but that is not a semantic extension along the lines of "give birth to" > "create, produce" > "weave". Instead, it is a homophonous verb stem, for which there is a likely cognate in Mg *nehe-* 'weave' (Buryat *neke-* < proto-Mg *neke-; cf Kuribayashi 1989:294). Tsintsius 1:618b says that Evenki *neke-* 'knit' was borrowed from the Mongolian stem. Incidentally, J *nas-* 'create' is used to mean 'give birth to' in certain dialects, such as Ibaraki. Modern K **nai** 'age' might be taken to be a derived noun from **nah-** < MK *nah-*, but it may instead represent the accretion of -i (a common noun extension in dialects) to **na** < MK ʾ*nah* 'age', to which comparisons can be made of Mg Khalkha *nas* 'age' (Dagur *nase* not *nasi) and Tk *yaš* 'age', *yašaa-* 'live (a long time, a number of years)'. Kim Tongso (1981:129, 132) gives a pTg root *nas- 'age' (noun). He fails to provide the source of the reconstruction, but it appears to be Tsintsius 2:587a: Evenki *nahun* 'age' and Solon *nasā* 'age, year of life', both of which she says are loans from Mongolian, citing written Mg *nasu(n)* and Mg *nasa(n)* and comparing OTk *yaš* 'year; life' and Yakut *sas* 'year; life; ⋯ '.

4 These I would take back to a stem (or an infinitive) + an auxiliary, but that is not directly relevant to the issues examined in this paper.

5 The first element of the form *sa-te* 'so, as it is' is identified as the adverb *sa(a)* 'like that', which is associated with the mesial deictic *so* 'that', as the *ka-* of *ka-ku* (and *ka-ku te*) is associated with the proximal deictic *ko* 'this', though other uses of *ka* (as in *ka no* = modern *ano*) are the distal deictic. The alternation of OJ /o/ with /a/ is a matter of "ablaut" (apophony) according to Miller; see §5.3.

6 The auxiliary is compared in Martin 1995 with the Korean bound auxiliary for the retrospective aspect $-t^e/a-$ < $-ta-$. The farfetched comparison by Miller 1971:285ff of the Japanese gerund with an Altaic instrumental suffix was effectively dismissed in Menges 1975:110-11 from the standpoint of the Altaic data, but the comparison is bad from the Japanese side, too. Apparently Miller was unaware that at least until the 12th century J *te* was set off from the preceding verb infinitive by a juncture marking it as a separate word, as is clearly shown by the attested accents. The traditional Japanese treatment of *te* as a kind of connective particle (setsuzoku-joshi) is not wide of the mark; see the next note. Miller seeks to find a complex inflectional system for Macro-Altaic like what is reconstructed for Indo-European, but the Japanese and Korean evidence does not support his ambitions. The later systems have gained their complexity through processes of morphological accretion and compression. Internal evidence points to simpler systems for earlier stages of these two languages, and the more convincing external morphological comparisons depict at best an inflectional system for the original Macro-Altaic language (if it existed) that must have been meager and sparse.

7 In Old Japanese the "gerund" is the infinitive + *te[y]*, itself the infinitive of the perfect auxiliary usually cited in the predicative and attributive (= adnominal) forms as *tu(ru)*. The structure was gradually tightened into a single word and often, under the influence of changes in prosody, the gerund forms were further compressed in differing ways in different areas of the country.

8 The orthography of the hyangka is complex and it has been interpreted in many ways. A Korean word was often written with a semantogram, a character representing the Chinese word for the same meaning, or with a semantophonogram, a character representing the sound that is heard in the Korean translation of the character but not representing that Korean word. Some of the semantograms are followed by a phonogram (or a semantophonogram) that supports the Korean translational reading by providing a hint of the final syllable or its coda. Both semantograms and phonograms are ordinary Chinese characters and it can be difficult to decide whether a given character is to be taken as one or the other. That is one reason that there are various interpretations of a given hyangka poem.

9 The fact that *pwo˙nay-* 'send' carries the automatic LH accentuation is evidence that it was not created as a compound of 'see' + 'send' for we would expect **˙pwo-¨nay-* < **˙pwo-* + **na-˙i-*. This strengthens the comparison (LKM 1958:106, #9) with Ma *bene-* 'send away' and *benji-* 'send here', though there are other problems with that; cf Tsintsius 1:125a, and 1:94b, calling our attention to Ma *bonggī-* 'send away'. Why are there no other Tungusic forms?

10 This supports the derivation of *tatoT-* = *tatot-/tatol[o]-* < **tatoto-* vi 'arrive' from *tah-* + *toT-* 'run' proposed in Martin 1996a.

11 A possible exception: *kilu-˙khu˙key* (1518 Sohak-cho 10:11a) '[gets] to be long/tall and big' ought to be **(¨)kil-˙khu˙key* if it is from *¨ki(l)-/ki˙l[^{u}⁄$_{o}$]-* < **ki˙l^{u}⁄$_{o}$-* adj 'be long', vi 'get big, grow (= **cala-**)' + *˙khu-* adj 'large'. But Wmk treats the first part as a hapax adverb with the same meaning as *ki˙li* 'for a long time' and that may be the best explanation: '[gets] to be great for a long time'. Perhaps the original stem **ki˙l^{u}⁄$_{o}$* survived as a direct adverbialization, but if so what happened to the accent? This differs slightly from the case of *palo* 'right away, directly' from *palG-/pa˙lo-* < **pa˙loG-* < **pa˙lok-* adj 'be right' where the derivation is < **pa˙lo[G]*, but also has somehow lost the accent. Another explanation for our exception would take the first component as *kilG-/kil^{u}⁄$_{o}$-* < **kil^{u}⁄$_{o}$G-* < **kil^{u}⁄$_{o}$-k-* vt 'raise, grow': *kilu[G]-˙khu˙key* '[gets] raised to be great' if that can be seen to be a translation of the Chinese locution, which literally means "achieves distance". Or indeed as an adverb, but one directly derived from **kil^{u}⁄$_{o}$[G]-* rather than **ki˙l^{u}⁄$_{o}$-*. A similar case is *kelu-ptwuy-* vt 'jump over' < *kelG-/kelu-* < **keluG-* < **keluk-* vt 'jump over, skip, omit' + *ptwuy-* vi 'jump'. But, unlike *kilu*, Wmk does not recognize *kelu* as an adverb.

Another adverb with a puzzling accentuation is *˙il* (1463 Pep 2:178b, 1481 Twusi 14:20b, 1482 Nam 1:21a) < *ilG-/il^{u}⁄$_{o}$-* < **il^{u}⁄$_{o}$G-* < **il^{u}⁄$_{o}$ok-* adj 'be early'. To that stem we can compare pA **ēr₁* 'early' (Street 1974:13, Poppe 1960:106 − I have removed their dot from atop the *e*), but a greater resemblance can be seen in Turkic *ilk(i:)*, *ilik* 'first, early'. Miller 1975:153 offered as a Japanese cognate the first part of *ari-ake* with the inadequate gloss 'dawn, daybreak'. The Japanese word means 'a daybreak with the moon still in the sky' and the OJ word *ari-ake[y]*, written with the semantograms STAY (*zai*) + OPEN (*kai*) or BRIGHT(EN) (*mei*), also referred to the time around the 20th day of the lunar month when such moonlit daybreaks most often occur. The traditional explanation of the word 'a dawn when it [the moon] is still there', far from being a "folk-etymology", as Miller dismisses it, is probably correct. The semantic weight is on the persistence of the moon, not the earliness of the dawn.

12 The OJ bound desiderative auxiliary *na-* is probably a semantic extension of the negative auxiliary, with which it is formally identical, and the

form *ne* 'won't you/they do it?' = 'I want you/them to do it' seems to be either (1) *ne[y]*, the raw stem used as an imperative (see §5.2) and followed by the emphatic particle *i* (= *yo*), or (2) *n[y]e* the infinitive (*n[y]i* < *na-Ci*) used as an imperative + the exclamatory particle *a*. Without the particle (···*a-na*) the auxiliary stem means 'shall I not do it?' = 'I want to do it; I will do it', an exhortative addressed to the speaker himself.

13 This reconstruction implies another use of the raw stem − here, that of the future auxiliary *ma-*, in which the structure is put into subdued focus ("if it is given that ··· ") with the particle *fa* < **pa* to express the OJ hypothetical 'if (perchance); when (in the future)'. The particle is thought to have originated as a noun meaning 'situation' or 'place', probably cognate with the Korean postmodifier **pa** < MK ˙*pa*. The Korean morpheme appears in hyangka 25:7 in a phrase taken as ˙*tye* ˙*pa* 'that [is the vow of Samantabhadra = Viśvabhadra]' by Kim Wancin 1980:210 (others have preferred the reading ˙*i* ˙*pa* 'this'), where it marks the identified (the topic) in an identificational sentence, quite like a common use of the Japanese particle *wa* < OJ *fa* < **pa*. Another OJ structure with this marker is the provisional *-(r)eba* = *-(r)e[y]-ba* 'when (in the past); whenever; if (= provided that); since, because' < **-(r)a i n pa* (< ···), consisting of the root of the auxiliary underlying the attributive ending + the post-adnominal *i* 'fact' (fossilized in Japanese, more common in Korean) + the adnominal marker *n* 'of' + *pa* 'situation'. The formation of the provisional is parallel to that of the OJ concessive *-(r)eydo (mo)* = *-(r)e[y] do (mo)* 'even if/though; but' < **-(r)a i n to (mo)* with the noun *to* 'place; situation', etymologically close to *toko* and *tokoro*, to all of which we compare Korean the 'site; status' < MK ˙*theh* , ··· *tey* 'place; situation' < MK ··· ˙*t* ⁿ*oy* / ᵉ*ay* (postadnominal + locative particle) 'at the place/fact that ··· ', with the bound noun *t* that is found directly attached to stems in MK *-t* 'the fact that ··· ' + ˙*i* nominative (source of the suspective ending *-ci* < MK -˙*ti* 'the uncertain fact that ··· '), ˙*ol* accusative, or ˙*on* subdued focus. (For the Korean forms, see Martin 1992:787b, 814b-5a, 818b, 821b. And for more on the Japanese forms, see Martin 1975:552-9, 1987:104-9.) Though in some of its uses the modern Japanese gerund *V-te* is quite similar to Korean *V-n* **tey** the structures are not etymologically connected. The Korean cognate for the Japanese gerund (< *te[y]* < **ta-Ci*, the infinitive of the perfect auxiliary), as mentioned in §2.1 above, is the bound auxiliary -˙*t*ᵉ*/a-* < -˙*ta-* that marks the retrospective aspect (Martin 1995).

14 But the few examples seem to be special cases, such as the four colors *si⁷ro* 'white', *ku⁷ro* 'black', *a⁷ka* 'xanthic (red/brown)', and *a⁷o* 'cyanic (blue/green)', on the unusual accentuation of which Vovin 1994:30 offers a new and attractive theory.

15 This example may be compromised by the comparison (LKM 1958:109 #57) with one of the two Manchu words for 'bat', *ferehe singgeri* (*singgeri* 'rat'). It takes a bit of digging to find cognates elsewhere among Tungusic

languages. Lamut (Even) has *"kevëc"* = [kewə̌č] in Tsintsius and Rishes 281b but *"kevec"* = [keweč] in Tsintsius 1:386a, quite different from Lamut *elduki* = Evenki *eldukī* in Tsintsius 2:446b, with Olchi *xele*, Orok *xelen* ('swallow'!), and Nanai *xeregdepī*, *xeregdexī*, and *xeremdeki*, all ?< pTg *pere(g)*. (Initial *p⋯ became *x⋯ in southern Tungus, but *f⋯ in Manchu and zero in northern Tungus.) The dictionaries are unclear on the Mongolian word(s); Hangin 1970 has *bagvaaxai*. One Middle Chinese word for 'bat' was *pyuk*, and Cantonese uses a compound of that + 'rat' (*fūk-syú*) to mean 'bat'. No, English "bat" is surely not *b[Vk] + [r]at*, though it is unclear how the final apical came about, for the ME ancestor was *bakke*, a word borrowed from Scandinavian, with no further history. The word "rat" goes right back to an Indo-European form with virtually the same pronunciation.

[16] A non-example: LCT 1971:224 and 1964:553a misread *"elGuy-phi"* for *el˙Guyn ˙phi* (1466 Kup 2:30b) 'blood clot'. A productive type: the bound adjectival noun *˙tos* 'seeming' could attach directly to the verb stem in Middle Korean, optionally omitting the adnominal ending (Martin 1992:822b), and relics of this usage can be found for modern tus (Martin 1992:840a).

[17] Cf Japanese *mita-* 'get full', *mita-sa-* = *mita-Ci-* 'fill' (Martin 1966:232 #90); pA *büte-* 'be completed' (Street 1974:10): Tk *büt-* 'become complete'; Mg Khalkha *büte-* (Dagur *bute-*) 'be achieved, get completed', *büten* < *bütün* 'whole, entire, full' borrowed into Evenki *hutun*. But Starostin 1991:111 compares the J stem with pTg *milte-* 'full' (Tsintsius 1:536-7 under Lamut *miltəre*) and written Mg *meltei* 'overfill' to reconstruct pA *milẗ'V-*. With *"te(l)-/te˙l[u]-* < *te˙lu-* vt 'lessen it' LKM 1958:108 compared Ma *dulga* 'not full' = [Norman] 'half filled', but that word is probably to be put with Ma *dulim-ba* 'middle, center' from pTg *dulin* (Tsintsius 1:222-3) : written Mg *duli* 'medium'.

[18] The '*add-on' meaning is found in the compound verb *twup-teth-* vt 'cover up (another's guilt)': *twup-te˙thul ˙ss i˙Gwo* (1462 [1]Nung 7:54b), *twup-tet˙ti* (1475 Nay 3:7b). Identifying *tet* as an adverb in *tet pu˙thi˙m ye n'* 'if you apply still more on top' (1489 Kup-kan 3:18b) follows the analysis of LCT 1971:411, but Wmk treats the example as a compound verb *tet-pu˙thi-*, like modern tes-puchi-. It is unclear how or whether these words relate to the adverb *te* 'more'.

[19] Cf J *hito-tu* < *fyito̧-tu* < *pito̧-tu* 'one' (Martin 1966:238 #157) and Tk *bi:r* 'one'. The variant stems *ni˙lu-* = *ni˙lu(l)-/ni˙lul[u]-* < *ni˙lu˙lu-* and *ni˙lo-* = *ni˙lo(l)-/ni˙lol[o]-* < *ni˙lo˙lo-* 'reach' occur as the adverbs *nilu* and *nilo* 'possibly, can' (with flattening of the accent), as in *e˙lwu nilu* 'can possibly' (1463 Pep 5:42a) and *"mwot nilu* (1447 Sek 13:8a) 'cannot possibly', and as defective verbal nouns in the structures *ni˙lu [˙]hi* (1481 Twusi 11:7b) and *ni˙lo ˙hi* (?= /ni˙lu˙hi/) (1586 Sohak 5:9b) 'so as to reach', also *ni˙lul ˙hi* (1482 Kum-sam 1:35a).

20 Japanese, too, has a few nouns that are identical to verb stems (Martin 1975:397-8, 1987:65). Unlike Korean, most of the derivation seems to be deverbal. Exceptionally *naf-* < **napa-* 'weave into rope' may have been derived from the noun *nafa* < **napa* 'rope', for the verb was not attested before 1010, while the noun dates back to the Man'yō-shū. Korean has possible cognates in MK *nwoh* 'string, cord' (1103 Kyeylim #308, #309 (ˊ)*NA*) and (ˊ)*pa* 'rope; [dial.] string' ?< *˙*pah* (1103 Kyeylim #308 ˙*PHAK*) — cf Martin 1992:49), but no verb. The lack of a high accent on MK *nwoh* 'string' calls for the reconstruction of **nwo˙ho* according to Whitman's formulation (see Martin 1996a), but another possibility would be that it is a contraction of a compound **nwo-˙pah* or that both 'string' and 'rope' are different truncations of an original dissyllable *nwo˙pa(h)* ?< **na˙pa*. But there are likely cognates for *˙*pah* 'rope' in Tk *ba:-* 'tie/bind it' → Turkish *bağ* 'rope, bond', *bağ-la-* 'tie it', Mg *bag-la-* 'tie up, wrap', and J *o* < *wo* < **bo* 'thong, cord, tie', which are more satisfying than the comparison with J *wa* 'loop; wheel' and *wana* 'snare' made by Miller 1982:397. Miller brings in also OJ *wanak-* 'tie (around) the neck, strangle' but that scantly attested verb may well be a variant of *unag-* 'hang around one's neck' from the noun *una* 'nape of neck; head', a possibility overlooked in Martin 1987, which (like Miller) followed the traditional association with *wana* (Jdb 821-2). Additional complications are offered by the modern dialect forms **kkunap(h)ul** and **kkunaphal** (and mysteriously **khuntaphul**) 'string', **kkun** < *˙*kinh* and **no-kkun** 'string' (also **kin-kkun** and **cīn-kkun**, perhaps from **kīn** 'long'). Martin 1966:240 (#186) attempted to extract a stem **nap-** from **kkunapul** but that seems less promising than other possibilities. The assignment by Wmk to *˙*pa* of the expected high accent is based on a single citation from ?1517- ¹No 2:36a, and an earlier occurrence on the same page does not carry the dot. J *tuna* 'rope, line' may or may not be connected with *tunag-* < **tuna-na-ka-* and *turane[y]-* < **tura-na-Ci-* 'put in a row, link', but the *-na* could be a separate morpheme attached to a truncation of *turu* < *tura* 'vine; bowstring', which may be cognate with K **cwul** < *˙*cwul* 'line, cord', pKJ **cur(u)* if we are willing to give up the hallowed comparison of the Korean word with OJ *sudi* < **sunti* 'tendon; sinew; line'; cf Martin 1966:235 (#126), 243 (#226).

In Tungusic we find several noun/verb pairs such as Nanai *xedun* 'wind' and *xedun-* '(wind) to blow', Manchu *aga* 'rain' and *aga-* 'to rain', *jalu* 'full' and *jalu-* 'get/be full', etc. (See Sunik 1962:96-104).

21 The dictionaries treat 'blind' as a different stem from 'far', and support for that may be found in the distinction made by Tungusic cognates such as Nanai *balī* 'blind' vs *bala* 'long ago', for which Kim Tongso 1981:113-5 reconstructs pTg/pKTg **balī-* 'blind' and **bala-* 'distantly past > far' but identically pK **mäl* for both etyma. Mongolian cognates are *balay* 'blind' and *balar* 'obscure, dim, distant [past]'. The only cognate possibility I

have found in Turkic is Yakut *boloor* 'get dim'. The only Japanese possibility seems to be *moya-moya* 'misty, dim' < *moya* 'haze, fog, mist', of obscure origin and unattested before 1600. The forms for 'blind' and 'far' must have derived from a single etymon (DIM/FAR), perhaps independently in each language except Korean, where the shape stayed the same for both.

22 According to Bloomfield 1933:416 "Primitive Indo-European did not use verb-stems as compound-members" and (417) English and German independently developed the usage. But what he has in mind is compound types such as noun+verb ("water-ski") or verb+noun ("killjoy", "bake-shop", "driveway", "breakfast"), not verb+verb. Recent additions to the English vocabulary include a few compounds such as "hang-glide", "freeze-dry", and "stir-fry" (a loan-translation from Chinese), but some, such as "jump-start" and "kick-start", may be formed by way of a noun interpretation of one of the stems. Lass 1994:198 says that N+V compounds like the modern English "sky-dive" and "carbon-date" are doubtful for Indo-European and uncertain for proto-Germanic. It has been suggested that the proliferation of compound verbs in Middle Korean might be due to the influence of Chinese. If that were true, we would expect them to be used to translate Chinese compounds, but typically what the MK compound verb translates is a single Chinese morpheme.

23 Ramstedt 1952:83 was wrong in assuming that modern Korean ye-po 'look here! hey!', ili o 'C'mere!', and cip ey ka 'Go home!' contain unsuffixed stems. The form ka is a contraction of the infinitive ka[-a] < MK ˙ka(-˙a); o and po are contractions of o-o and po-o with the marker for a particular style that is called "authoritative" or "semiformal" in Martin 1992.

24 Examples of the raw stem used as an imperative: Manchu *tuhe* 'fall down!' (Sunik 1962:99), *ara* 'write!' (Sunik 1962:336), *ala* 'tell it!' (Sunik 1962:144) — in Sibe followed by an emphatic particle *ale ee* (Yamamoto 1969:58 #1346), Sibe *taa* 'look!' (Yamamoto 1969:7 #173).

25 The effective aspect is a kind of aorist that sometimes refers to the past and more often to a definite future; it is the source of the modern future-presumptive *-keyss-*. The effective aspect contrasts with the processive aspect -˙*no-* < pK *-na-* and the retrospective/perfect aspect -˙t^{e}/*a-* < pK *-ta-*. Martin 1995 says that two of the bound auxiliaries are a specialized use of the verbs ˚*ka-* 'go' and ˚*na-* 'emerge', and that the third is cognate with the J perfect auxiliary *(V-i) ta-* (usually cited in the finite forms *tu/turu*). After the verb ˚*ka-* itself, the auxiliary -˙k^{e}/*a-* was usually (but not always) replaced by -˚n^{e}/*a-* < *˙*nyo-*, a form hypothesized to account for the stem variants ˚*nye-* and ˚*ni-*, cognate with the J perfect auxiliary *V-i na-* (usually cited in the finite forms *nu/nuru*) and perhaps with the J verb **ina-* 'go away'. But I may well be wrong in my reconstruction of **nyo-*, since we could account for ˚*nye-* as a breaking of the vowel in ˚*ni-*,

and that may be supported by other such cases, e.g. *˝kiT- > *˝kyeT- > modern kyēT- 'get oily', as it seems obvious from ki˙lum 'oil' (Martin 1996a n.11). The aspect markers can be followed by many of the same endings as the simple stems, but the infinitive -˙^{e}/a is not attached to -˙t^{e}/a- or -˙no- and it is absorbed by the vowel of -˙k^{e}/a- in the effective infinitive that is used in the structures -˙k^{e}/a ˙za (< *˙sa) 'only if one to does' and -˙k^{e}/a ˚ci- 'want to do'. An example of *nika cila* 'want go' in 1103 Kyeylim (#323) is written ˙NIK-KA-˙ZIP-LA.

26 There is another exclamatory expression that consists of the infinitive + the quoted form of the copula indicative assertive [i]la, lenited from [i]ta. It is mostly limited to the stems of adjectives and the quasi-adjectives iss- 'exist; have' and ēps- 'lack'. The plain-style command iss.e la 'Stay!' (also heard as iss.ke la) sounds the same as (cāymi) iss.e 'la 'it is (fun)!' But /chwuwela/ can only mean 'Gee it's cold!' In Middle Korean the abbreviated form of the copula was 'y˙la and the exclamatory adjective expressions were -˙^{e}/a 'y˙la. The meaning of the quoted copula here is somewhat like the English use of "I tellya ··· !" or "Lemme tellya ··· !" Apparently such expressions could be made with the MK verbs, too: ˝won ˙kil˙h ol ni˙ce 'y˙la (1482 Nam 1:28b) 'Why, I forget the road I came!' A poetic version of the expression is -˙e 'ylwo˙ta with the variant (emotive) copula ˙ilwo˙ta (Martin 1992:273-4), as seen in sa˙lwol ˝i˙l uy is˙kwu.m ul ni˙pe 'ylwo˙ta (1481 Twusi 22:54a) 'I get pulled by the events to be lived out'.

27 The modulator is a bound auxiliary -˙w^{u}/o- that is freely applied to stems to create new forms used in several ways (often vacuously). After certain vowels the suffix is frequently reduced to nothing, but it leaves a trace on monosyllabic stems by imposing the rising tone represented by the double dot: ˚ka-˙wo- → ˝ka- 'go', ˚nye-˙wu- → ˝nye- 'go', ˚pwo-˝wo- → ˝pwo- 'look, see', ˚twu-˙wu- → ˝twu- 'put away'. For more on the modulated forms see Martin 1992:269-73. It has been suggested (Martin 1995:8) that a cognate for the modulator is to be found in the pJ auxiliary *w^{u}/o- ?< *b^{u}/o-, the root that underlies the OJ infinitive wi[y] < *w^{u}/o-i ?< *b^{u}/o-Ci- 'be'.

28 In two 16th-century Chinese-Korean phrasebooks there are uses of -(^{u}/o)˙la to refer to actions in the past. These may be due to the influence of the sentence-final Chinese particle ··· le, which marks either a completed act or a sudden realization. For example, in reply to the question ˝ne y ˝en˙cey ˙won˙ta (?1517- Pak 1:51a) 'When did you come?' the answer is ku˙ce-kulp˙ph uy ˝wo˙la 'I came three days ago', and in reply to the question ˝ne y ˝en˙cey [WANG-KING] ˙uy ˙sye˙pte nan˙ta (?1517- ¹No 1:1a) 'When did you leave Wángjīng?' the answer is ˙na y ˙i˙tol s chwo holo s ˙nal [WANG-KING] ˙uy ˙sye˙pte ˝na˙la 'I left Wángjīng on the first of this month'. Notice also the Middle Korean usages that mean 'doing in alternation' and 'does and then; whereupon' (Martin 1992:851b).

29 Eastern forms are found in some of the regional gazetteers called fudoki and in the Azuma ("Eastern Japan") poems of the Man'yō-shū (M 3348-3569) and the "sakimori" poems (M 4293-4516) attributed to border guards sent to Kyūshū from the east.

30 Another possibility: the final element might be the emphatic particle so (= modern zo, Ryūkyū du/ru) described in Martin 1992:110. But the derivation from 'do' is more convincing, in view of such structures as na kari so-n[y]e (M 20) 'I want them not to cut [the grass]' and na nar[y]i so-n[y]e (M 14) 'we do not want [the god] to cry out', with the stem-following suffix -n[y]e (desiderative, with 2nd or 3rd person subject) of sazakyi torasa-n[y]e (K 69:5) '(I want you to) seize the wagtail!', wa ga na twofa-sa-n[y]e (K 86:5) 'ask for (my name =) news of me!', and sukey ni ko-n[y]e (K 15:9) 'come to our aid!', itself the imperative of a bound auxiliary (desiderative, more often 1st person) that appears unsuffixed in yuka-na (M 15, 2103) 'I want to go' and, followed by an exclamatory particle, kadukyi se-na wa (K 39:6) 'let's dive in!'. The infinitive is -n[y]i as in naka-n[y]i mo (M 4178) 'let it [the bushwarbler] sing' and nifofa-n[y]i (M 1694) 'may it [the wisteria] waft its odor [to me] and ⋯ '. The attributive -nu is found in ko-nu ka mo (M 3867) 'I hope it comes'. There are no attestations of the predicative, but it should have the same shape. The auxiliary is probably a semantic specialization of the negative -na- "won't I ⋯ ?!", "can't it be that ⋯ ?!". See Yoshida 1973:437-74.

31 As Menges (1975:8) says, the Altaicist use of the term "ablaut" is rather different from the way it is used with respect to Indo-European, where the word refers to systematic apophony in the inflectional systems, of the sort exemplified by English "drink, drank, drunk" and "sing, sang, sung". The Altaicists use the term to refer to semantic differentiations between pairs of morphemes by choice of vowel. Even where connotational consistencies can be found, as in the Korean "heavy" and "light" isotopes (or the English pairs "teeny" vs "tiny", "sheen" vs "shine"), these vowel variations are poor support as such for external etymologies, however much they may inform − or misinform − us with respect to the prehistory of the individual languages.

32 Also to be considered is the OJ emphatic particle so or zo (Martin 1987:110). If we assume that the pronunciation was [tso] or [ndzo] that will help explain the modern Ryūkyū reflex du (usually from du or do), which is weakened in Okinawa to ru so that it concides with the reflexes of OJ ro and ru: kani ru yaru < kani du yaru < (*)kane do yaru < *kane zo ya [? = fa] aru 'it is money', in which the first /ru/ represents the emphatic particle and the final /ru/ represents the attributive ending of the verb, for that form is obligatory when an emphatic or interrogative particle occurs earlier in the sentence. This is an example of the Okinawan preservation of a literary construction that is called "kakari-musubi": the ru < du < do < zo is the "kakari" (the enhancing particle) and the final

-*ru* is the "musubi" (the wrap-up ending). The Okinawan copula seems to be from *ya* (= *fa*) + *a(r)*-, as is indicated by the negative: *kani ya qaran* 'it is not money', corresponding to OJ *kane ni (fa) aranu* ⋯. On "kakari-musubi" see the illuminating paper by Whitman in this volume.

Bibliography

Benzing, J. 1955. Die tungusischen sprachen: versuch einer vergleichenden grammatik. Wiesbaden: Steiner.

Bloomfield, L. 1933. Language. New York: Holt.

Hangin, J.G. 1970. A concise English-Mongolian dictionary. Indiana U.

Jdb = Omodaka et al. 1967. Jidai-betsu kokugo dai-jiten: jōdai-hen. Tōkyō: Sansei-dō.

Jorden, E.H. and Chaplin, H.I. 1962-3. Beginning Japanese. Yale University Press.

Kang Sinhang. 1980. "Kyeylim ¹yusa" yenkwu. Seoul: Sengkyun-kwan University Press.

Karlgren, B. 1927. Analytic dictionary of Chinese and Sino-Japanese. Paris: Guethner.

KggD = Kokugo-gakkai. 1980. Kokugo-gaku daijiten. Tōkyō: Tōkyō-dō.

Kim Tongso. 1981. Hankwuk-e wa TUNGUS-e uy um.wun pikyo yenkwu. Taegu: Hyosung Women's University Press.

Kim Wancin [Kim, Wan-jin]. 1980. Hyangka haytok-pep yenkwu. Seoul: SNU Press.

Kuribayashi Hitoshi. 1989. "Mongoru-kei sho-gengo taishō kihon goi [Comparative basic vocabularies for Mongolian languages]". [Tōkyō University of Foreign Studies, ILCAA] Gengo bunka sesshoku ni kansuru kenkyū [Studies of linguistic and cultural contacts] 1:153-383.

Lass, R. 1944. Old English: a historical linguistic companion. Cambridge University Press.

LCT = ¹Yu Changton. 1964. ¹Yi-co-e sacen. Seoul: Yensey tay-hak.kyo.

LCT = ¹Yu Changton. 1971. Ehwi-sa yenkwu. Seoul: Senmyeng munhwa-sa.

LKM = ¹Yi Kimun [Lee, Ki-Moon]. 1958. "A comparative study of Manchu and Korean". UAJ 30:104-93.

Martin, S.E. 1966. "Lexical evidence relating Korean to Japanese". Language 42:185-251.

Martin, S.E. 1987. The Japanese language through time. New Haven: Yale University Press.

Martin, S.E. 1992. A reference grammar of Korean. Tōkyō: Tuttle.

Martin, S.E. 1995. "On the prehistory of Korean grammar: verb forms". Korean Studies 19:1-13.

Martin, S.E. 1996a. Consonant lenition in Korean and the Macro-Altaic question. Korean Studies Monograph. University of Hawaii Press.

Martin, S.E. 1996b. [This paper.]

Martin, S.E. 1997. The verb forms of Middle Korean: a dictionary and index.

Menges, K.H. 1975. Altaische studien 2: Japanisch und Altaisch. Wiesbaden: Steiner.

Miller, R.A. 1971. Japanese and the other Altaic languages. University of Chicago Press.

Miller, R.A. 1975. The footprints of the Buddha. American Oriental Society.

Miller, R.A. 1982. "Japanese evidence for some Altaic denominal verb-stem derivational suffixes". Acta Orientalia Hungarica 36:391-403.

Miller, R.A. 1988. Review of Martin 1987. Language 64:413-7.

Miyara Tōsō. 1954. Fūdo to kotoba. Tōkyō: Iwasaki-shoten.

Mun Senkyu. 1972. Cosen-kwan yek.e yenkwu. Seoul: Kyengin munhwa-sa.

Nkd = Nihon kokugo dai-jiten. 20 vols. 1972-6. Tōkyō: Shōgak[u]-kan.

Norman, J. 1967. A Manchu-English dictionary. Taipei.

Poppe, N. 1976. Review of Menges 1975. Journal of Japanese Studies 2:470-4.

Poppe, N. 1960. Vergleichende grammatik der altaischen sprachen: 1. Vergleichenden lautlehre. Wiesbaden: Harrassowitz.

Ramstedt, G.J. 1952. Einführung in die altaische sprachwissenschaft 2: formenlehre. Mémoires de la Société Finno-ougrienne 104:2 [sic].

Starostin, S.A. 1991. Altayskaya problema i proiskhozhdenie yaponskogo yazyka. Moskva.

Street, J.C. 1974. On the lexicon of proto-Altaic: a partial index to reconstructions. Madison, Wisconsin.

Sunik, O.P. 1962. Glagol v tunguso-man^{y}chzhurskikh yazykax. Moskva.

Tsintsius, V.I. 1975-7. Sravnitel^{y}nyy slovar^y Tunguso-Man^{y}chzhurskikh yazykov. 2 vols. Leningrad: Nauka.

Wmk = Hankul Hak.hoy. 1992. Wuli mal khun sacen, vol 4. Seoul: Emun-kak.

Yamamoto Kengo. 1969. Manshū-go kōgo kiso-goi shū. Tōkyō: Tōkyō Gaikoku-go Daigaku.

Yoshida Kanehiko. 1973. Jōdai-go jodō-shi no shi-teki kenkyū. Tōkyō: Meiji-shoin.

Texts

B = 753 Bussoku-seki no uta
K = 712 Koji-ki
M = 622-733 Man'yō-shū
NS = 720 Nihon-Shoki
hyangka: cited from Kim Wancin 1980

1103 Kyeylim = Kyeylim ¹yusa (Jílín lèishì): from Kang Sinhang 1980
1400⁺ Kwan-yek = Cosen-kwan yek.e (Cháoxiān-guǎn yìyǔ): cited from Mun Senkyu 1972
1447 Sek = Sekpo sangcel
1459 Wel = Wel.in sekpo
1462 ¹Nung = ¹Nungen kyeng enhay
1463 Pep = Pep-hwa = Myopep ¹yenhwa-kyeng enhay
1466 Kup = Kwukup-pang enhay
?1468⁻ Mong = Mongsan hwapep pep.e ¹yaklok enhay
1475 Nay = Nayhwun
1481 Samkang = Samkang hayngsil-to
1481 Twusi = Twusi enhay [cho-kan]
1482 Nam = [Yengka-taysa cungto-ka] Nammyeng-chen [sensa] kyeysong enhay
1489 Kup-kan = Kwukup kan.i-pang
?1517⁻ ¹No = [Pen.yek] ¹Nokeltay
1518 Sohak-cho = [Pen.yek] Sohak
1527 Cahoy = Hwunmong cahoy
1586 Sohak = Sohak enhay
?1775 Han-Cheng = Han-Cheng munkam

Appendix 1

The compound verb preserves the accentuation of both components. In the absence of attestations requiring a different assignment, we assume this accentuation as the default.

L-L ← L + L

hey-ic- vt 'turn back (the wind)' ← *hey-* vt + *ic-* vi

kulk-pis- vt 'scratch and comb oneself' ← *kulk-* vt + *pis-* vt

kulk-sis- vt 'scour and wash' ← *kulk-* vt + *sis-* vt

kulthalh- = *kulh-talh-* vt 'boil and decoct, boil it down; worry' ← *kulh-* vt + *talh-* vi

mol.k-anc- vi 'settle clear' ← *molk-* adj + *a(n)c-* vi

moyGelk- < *moy-elk-* vt 'tie them together' ← *moy-* vt + *elk-* vt

moy-cwoc- vi '(mouth) get tightly shut' ← *moy-* vt + **cwoc-* vi

put-cap- < **puth-cap-* vt 'seize, grasp, get, hold' ← *puth-* vt + *cap-* vt

put-cwoch- < **puth-cwoch-* vt 'adhere to and follow, follow implicitly, revere (as leader)' ← *puth-* vt + *cwoch-* vt

pwos-task- = *pwos[k]-task-* vt 'roast/toast (beans or sesame)' ← *pwosk-* vt + *task-* vt

cwos-puth- vt = *put-cwoch-*

ses-elk- = *ses[k]-elk-* vt 'bind/tie together' ← *sesk-* (vi/)vt + *elk-* vt *ses-moy-* = *ses[k]-moy-* vt 'tie them all up together' ← *sesk-* (vi-/)vt + *moy-* vt

ses-moyc- = *ses[k]-moyc-* vt 'tie them all up together' ← *sesk-* (vi-/)vt + *moyc-* vt

ses-mwot- = *ses[k]-mwot-* vi 'mingle/mix together' ← *sesk-* (vi-/)vt + *mwot-* vt

ses-pak- = *ses[k]-pak-* vt 'impress/inlay as a mixture' ← *sesk-* (vi-/)vt + *pak-* vt

ses-twuph- = *ses[k]-twuph-* vt 'mix and cover' ← *sesk-* (vi-/)vt + *twuph-* vt

swos-kulh- vi 'boil up' ← *swos-* vi + *kulh-* vi

ta-cwoch- = *ta[h]-cwoch-* vt 'closely follow' ← *tah-* vi + *cwoch-* vt

ta-wat- < **ta[h]-Wat-* < **-pat-* vt 'bump; bump into' ← *tah-* vi + *pat-* vt

tas-pwosk- = *tas[k]-pwosk-* vt 'polish well, scrub hard' ← *task-* vt + *pwosk-* vt

twup-teth- = *twup[h]-teth-* vt 'cover up (another's guilt)' ← *twuph-* vt + *teth-* vt

tik-mek- vt 'peck and eat, peck at' ← *tik-* vt + *mek-* vt

hywok-tyek- adj 'be fine, small, tiny' ← *hywok-* adj + *tyek-* adj (= ˝*cyek-*)

pwos-talh- < **pwos[k]-talh-* vt 'roast down, reduce by roasting' < **pwosk-talh[i]-* ← *pwosk-* vt + *tal˙hi-* (= *talh-˙i-*)

mas-pat- < **mac-pat-* ?vt 'contact, hit' ← *mac-* vi + *pat-* vt

L-L/LL ← L + L/LL

hey-toT- = *hey-tot-/-tol[o]-* < **hey-toto-* vi 'scatter and run' ← *hey-* vt + *toT-* = *tot-/tol[o]-* < **toto-* vi

mac-toT- > *mas-toT-* = *mas-tot-/-tol[o]-* < **mac-toto-* vi 'run into, encounter, meet up with' ← *mac-* vt + *toT-* = *tot-/tol[o]-* < **toto-* vi

mwot-toT- = *mwot-tot-/-tol[o]-* < **mwot-toto-* vi 'run together (into a group)' ← *mwot-* vt + *toT-* = *tot-/tol[o]-* < **toto-* vi

put-toT- = *put[h]-tot-/-tol[o]-* < **puth-toto-*) vi 'adhere, cling' ← *puth-* vt + *toT-* = *tot-/tol[o]-* < **toto-* vi

L-LL ← L + LL

ses-alpho- = *ses[k]-alpho-* adj 'be a mixed pain/ailment' ← *sesk-* + *alpho-* < *alh-po-* adj

ses-tilG-/til⁴o- < **ses[k]-til⁴oG-* < **sesk-til⁴ok-* (or **-tit⁴ok-*?) vt 'mix, mingle' ← *sesk-* vt + *tilG-/til⁴o-* < **til⁴oG-* < **til⁴ok-* (or **tit⁴ok-*?) vt

ta-tilG-/-tilo- < **ta-tiloG-* < **ta[h]-tilok-* (or **-titok-*?) vt 'thrust against, butt; approach; attack, defy' ← *tah-* + *tilG-/til⁴o-* < **til⁴oG-* < **til⁴ok-* (or **tit⁴ok-*?) vt

hey-tilG-/-tilu- < **-tiluG-* < **-tiluk-* vt 'suddenly scatter' ← *hey-* vt + *tilG-/til⁴o-* < **til⁴oG-* < **til⁴ok-* (or **tit⁴ok-*?) vt

hey-mulG-/-mulu- < *-*muluG-* < *-*muluk-* vi 'get destroyed' ← *hey-*
vt + *mulG-/mulu-* < **muluG-* < **muluk-* vt

mak-colG-/-colo- < *-*coloG-* < *-*colok-* vt 'cut off (so as to block)' ←
mak- vt + *colG-/colo-* < **coloG-* < **colok-* vt

kwut-polo-/-poll- < *-*polol-* adj 'be firm and stiff' ← *kwut-* adj +
polo-/poll- < **polol-* adj

L-LL ← L + L-R/LH

nwop-nos.kaW- adj 'be high and low' ← *nwoph-* adj + *nos-"kaW-* =
nos-"kap-/nos-ka˙W[o]- < *noc-ka˙po-* adj

L-LL ← L + LH

moyGelkhi- < *moy-elkhi-* vi 'get tied together' ← *moy-* L + *el˙khi-* (<
elk-˙hi-)

ses-hulli- = *ses[k]-hulli-* vt 'mix/mingle tears' ← *sesk-* L + *hul˙li-* (<
**hulul-˙i-*) vt

ses-tonni- = *ses[k]-tonni-* (< *-tot-ni-*) vi 'go around/on (keep) mingling'
← *sesk-* L + *ton-˙ni-* (< *tot-˙ni-* < **toT-˙ni-*) vi

L-R ← L + R/LH

ses-"pay- = *ses[k]-"pay-* vi ' [the world and the Way] perish from getting
mixed up' ← *sesk-* vt + *"pay-* = *"pay-/pay˙y-* vt 'destroy,
exterminate; capsize'

kulk-"cwuy- (= -*"cwuy-/-cwuy˙y-*) vt 'grasp, clutch, clench' ← *kulk-* vt
+ *"cwuy-* = *"cwuy-/cwuy˙y-* < *cwu˙i-* (?< *cwu-˙i-*) vt

kwut-"sey- adj 'be firm and strong' ← *kwut-* adj + *"sey-* < *se˙i-* adj

L-R ← L + R/LH

cap-"cwuy- (= -*"cwuy-/-cwuy˙y-*) vt 'grab and grasp, rake it in/up' ←
cap- vt + *"cwuy-* = *"cwuy-/cwuy˙y-* < *cwu˙i-* (?< *cwu-˙i-*) vt

mas-"kolm-/kol˙m[o]- = *mac-"kolm-* < **mac-kol˙mo-* vt 'answer,
respond' ← *mac-* vi + *"kolm-/kol˙m[o]-* < **kol˙mo-* bnd v (? =
"kolW- vt)

mas-"ni(l)-/-ni˙l[⁴/o]- = *mac-"ni(l)-/-ni˙l[⁴/o]-* < **mac-ni˙l⁴/o-* vt 'meet'
← *mac-* vi + *"ni(l)-/ni˙l[⁴/o]-* < **ni˙l⁴/o-*

ses-"ni(l)- = *ses[k]-"ni(l)-/-ni˙l[⁴/o]-* < **sesk-ni˙l⁴/o-* vi 'arise mingled
(with)' ← *sesk-* vt + *"ni(l)-/ni˙l[⁴/o]-* < **ni˙l⁴/o-* vi 'arise'

ses-"tuT- = *ses[k]-"tuT-* (< *"tut-/tu˙l[u]-* < **tu˙tu-*) vi 'fall pell-mell'
← *sesk-* vt + *"tut-/tu˙l[u]-* < **tu˙tu-* vi

kes-"tuT- = *kes[k]-"tuT-* (< *"tut-/tu˙l[u]-* < **tu˙tu-*) vi 'break off (and
fall)' ← *kesk-* L + *"tuT-* = *"tut-/tu˙l[u]-* < **tu˙tu-* vi

cwuk-"sa(l)- vi 'live and/or die' ← *cwuk-* vi + *"sa(l)-/sa˙l[o]-* <
**sa˙lo-* vi 'live'

ep-"tuT- = *ep-"tut-/-tu˙l[u]-* < **eph-tu˙tu-* vi 'fall down (on one's
face)' ← *eph-* vt + *"tut-/tu˙l[u]-* < **tu˙tu-* vi

ptwuy-"nwo(l)-/-nwo˙l[o]- < **ptwuy-nwo˙lo-* vi 'jump about, romp,
frolic' ← *ptwuy-* vi + *"nwo(l)-/nwo˙l[o]-* < **nwo˙lo-* vi

L(L)-R (< LH) ← L(L) + R (< LH)

  mul-"he(l)-/-he˙l[u]- < **mul[u]-"he(l)-/-he˙l[u]-* < **mulu[G]-he˙lu-*
  vt 'destroy' ← *mulG-/mulu-* < **muluG-* < **muluk-* vt + *"he(l)-/*
  he˙l[u]- < **he˙lu-* vt

LL-R/LH ← LL-R/LH

  mulu-"keT- = *mulu-"ket-/-ko˙l[o]-* < **mulu[l]-ko˙to-* vi 'step back' ←
  mulu-/mull- < **mulul-* vi + *"keT-* = *"ket-/ke˙l[u]-* < **ke˙tu-* vi
  mulu-˙ko(l)-/-˙ko˙l[o]- < **mulu[G]-˙ko˙lo-* vt 'grind it fine/soft' ←
  mulG-/mulu- < **muluG-* < **muluk-* adj/vi + *˙ko(l)-/˙ko˙l[o]-* <
  *˙ko˙lo- vt

L-LH ← L + LH

  cwos-tu˙tuy- vt 'follow (the model of)' ← *cwoch-* vt + *tu˙tuy-* vt
  hey-cwo˙chi- vi 'get followed around' ← *hey-* vt + *cwo˙chi-* vt
  kwup-hil˙hwu- vt 'bend (body), stoop' ← *kwup-* vi/adj + *hil˙hwu-* vt

L-LH(H) ← L + LH(H)

  ses-pe˙mu˙l- ← *ses-pe˙mu(l)-* = *ses[k]-pe˙mu(l)-/-pe˙mu˙l[u]-* ← *sesk-*
  vt + *pe˙mu(l)-/pe˙mu˙l[u]-* < **pe˙mu˙lu-* vi

L-H ← L + H

  he-˙thi- = *hey-˙thi-* vt 'scatter, strew' ← *hey-* vt + *˙thi-* vt
  pskay-˙thi- vt 'break it' ← *pskay-* vt + *˙thi-* vt

L-H ← L(L) + H

  tot-˙ni- (> *ton-˙ni-*) < **toT-˙ni-* vi 'walk about, come and go' ← *toT-*
  = *tot-/tol[o]-* < **toto-* vi + *˙ni-* vi

L-H/L ← L + H/L

  pskay-˙(h)hye- vt 'break it' ← *pskay-* vt + *˙(h)hye-* vt
  mas-˙pwo- < *mac-˙pwo-* vt 'confront' ← *mac-* vi + *˙pwo-* vt
  swos-˙na- vt 'spurt out' ← *swos-* vt + *˙na-* vi

L-H/L ← L(L) + H/L

  tut-˙pwo- vt 'listen and look, hear and see' ← *tuT-* = *tut-/tul[u]-* <
  *tutu- vt + *˙pwo-* vt

LL-H/L

  hulu-˙ni- vi 'flow along/away' ← *hulu-/hull-* < **hulul-* vi + *˙ni-* vi
  tuwuy-˙(h)hye- vt 'overturn it, upset' ← *tuwuy-* vt + *˙(h)hye-* vt

LL-H ← LL + H

  tuwuy-˙thi- vt 'turn it/them over' ← *tuwuy-* vt + *˙thi-* vt

L-L(L) ← L + L(L)

  mac-toT- > *mas-toT-* = *mas-tot-/-tol[o]-* < **mac-toto-* vi 'run into,
  encounter, meet up with' ← *mac-* vi + *toT-* = *tot-/tol[o]-* < **toto-* vi

LL-L(L) ← LL + L(L)

  kolo-tilG-/-til^{u}o- < **-til^{u}oG-* < **-til^{u}ok-* vt 'cut across, intersect' ←
  kolo- adj + *tilG-/til^{u}o-* < **til^{u}oG-* < **til^{u}ok-* (or **til^{u}ok-?*) vt

LL-L ← LL + L

  mulu-nik- < **mulu[G]-nik-* vi 'get soft and ripe (or well-cooked)' ←
  mulG-/mulu- < **muluG-* < **muluk-* adj/vi + *nik-* vi

mulu-nwok- < **mulu[G]-nwok-* vi 'get fully ripe, mature, reach its prime' ← *mulG-/mulu-* < **muluG-* < **muluk-* adj/vi + *nwok-* vi

mulu-sip- < **mulu[G]-sip-* vt 'chew it soft, chew well' ← *mulG-/mulu-* < **muluG-* < **muluk-* adj/vi + *sip-* vt

mulu-tih- < **mulu[G]-tih-* vt 'pound it soft' ← *mulG-/mulu-* < **muluG-* < **muluk-* adj/vi + *tih-* vt

tuwuy-ic- vi 'get overturned/upset' ← *tuwuy-* vt 'overturn it, upset' + *ic-* vi 'wane; get chipped'

LL-R/LH ← LL + R/LH

mulu-ˮtuT- = *mulu-ˮtut-/-tu˙l[o]-* < **mulu[G]-tu˙tu-* vi 'collapse' ← *mulG-/mulu-* < **muluG-* < **muluk-* adj/vi + *ˮtuT-* = *ˮtut-/tu˙l[u]-* < **tu˙tu-* vi

L-HL ← L + HL

ses-˙nuli- = *ses[k]-˙nuli-* vt 'mix them down' ← *sesk-* vt + *˙nuli-* vt

LH-L ← LH + L

ke˙twu-cap- vt 'concentrate on, stick close to; closely supervise; hold up (the ends of a skirt)' ← *ke˙twu-* (< *ket-˙wu-*) vt

te˙wuy-cap- vt 'grab hold of' ← *te[˙]wuy-* vt + *cap-* vt

mwo˙two-cap- vt 'gather and grasp' ← *mwo˙two-* (< *mwot-˙wo-*) vt + *cap-* vt

ˮmul˙li-cwoch- vt 'pursue in retreat' ← *mul˙li-* (< **mul[u]l-˙i-*) vt + *cwoch-* vt

mul˙li-Gwat- < *mul˙li-Wat-* < **-pat-* 'spurn; repel' ← *mul˙li-* (< **mul[u]l-˙i-*) vt + *pat-* vt

mi˙li-Gwat- < **mi˙li-Wat-* < **-pat-* vt 'push hard' ← **mi˙li-* (< **mi˙l[ᵘo]-˙i-*) + *pat-* vt

no˙li-Gwat- < **no˙li-Wat-* < **-pat-* vt 'lower it' ← *no˙li-* vi + *pat-* vt

LH-L ← LH + R (< LH)

pol˙ki-kay- vt 'clear it up, make it get clear' ← *pol˙ki-* vt + *ˮkay-* (< *ka˙i-*) vi

LH-R ← LH(H) + R/LH

ke˙two-ˮpwu(l)-/-pwu˙l[u]- < **-pwu˙lu-* vt 'blow together (into a heap)' [= *ketwu-pwu(l)-* not attested till 1747] ← *ke˙two-* (< *ket-˙wo-*) = *ke˙twu-* vt + *ˮpwu(l)-/pwu˙l[u]-* < **pwu˙lu-* vt

nelu-ˮtuT- = *nelu-ˮtut-/nelu-tu˙l[u]-* < **nelu-tu˙tu-* vi 'get widely scattered'

te˙pu-ˮsa(l)- = *te˙pu[l]-ˮsal-/-sa˙l[o]-* < **te˙pu[l]-sa˙lo-* vi 'live together' ← *te˙pu(l)-/te˙pu˙l[u]-* < **te˙pu˙lu-* vt + *ˮsa(l)-/sa˙l[o]-* < **sa˙lo-* vi

ken˙ti-ˮcwuy- (= *-ˮcwuy-/-cwuy˙y-*) vt 'swindle, obtain by swindling' ← *ken˙ti-* vt + *ˮcwuy-* = *ˮcwuy-/cwuy˙y-* < *cwu˙i-* (? < *cwu-˙i-*) vt

ke˙twu-ˮcwuy- (= *-ˮcwuy-/-cwuy˙y-*) vi 'get tightened, drawn up, shriveled' ← *ke˙twu-* (< *ket-˙wu-*) vt + *ˮcwuy-* = *ˮcwuy-/cwuy˙y-* < *cwu˙i-* (? < *cwu-˙i-*) vt

el˙Gi-"nwol- vi 'engage in fornication, play around' ← *el˙Gi-* (< *e˙l[u]-*
˙Gi-) vt + *"nwo(l)-/nwo˙l[o]-* < **nwo˙lo-* vi

R-L ← R (< LH) + L

"kam-polk- adj 'be dark red' ← *"kam-/ka˙m[o]-* < **ka˙mo-* adj + *polk-*
adj

"kem-pulk- adj 'be dark red' ← *"kem-/ke˙m[u]-* < **ke˙mu-* adj + *pulk-*
adj

R-R/LH ← R (< LH) + R/LH

"tep-"ta(l)-/ta˙l[o]- < **-ta˙lo-* vt [sic] 'heat it' ← *"teW-* = *"tep-/*
te˙W[u]- < **te˙pu-* adj + *"ta(l)-/ta˙l[o]-* < **ta˙lo-* vi [sic]

"ti-"nay- vt 'let it pass (move past); experience, undergo' ← ← *"ti-* =
"tiy- < *ti-˙i-* = *ti-˙[G]i-* vt + *"nay-* vt < **na-˙i-*

"nay-"swuy- (= -*"swuy-/swuy˙y-*) vt 'exhale (a breath)' ← *"nay-* vt <
*na-˙i- + *"nay-* vt + *"swuy-* = *"swuy-/swuy˙y-* vt < **swu-˙i-*

"ey-"two(l)-/-two˙l[o]- < **"ey-two˙to-* vt 'hover hesitantly around (a
person)' ← *"ey-* vi + *"two(l)-/two˙l[o]-* < **two˙lo-* vi/vt

R-LL ← R (< LH) + LL

"nem-toT- = *"nem-tot/-tol[o]-* < **ne˙mu-toto-* 'run beyond/over' ←
"nem-/ne˙m[u]- < **ne˙mu-* vt + *toT-* = *tot-/tol[o]-* < **toto-* vi

R-LH ← R (< LH) + LH

"polp-tu˙tuy- vt 'step on and trample' ← *"polW-* = *"polp-/pol˙W[o]-* <
*pol˙po- vt + *tu˙tuy-* vt

"kam-pho˙lo- < **ka˙mo-pho˙lo-* adj 'be dark blue, blue-black' ←
"kam-/ka˙m[o]- < **ka˙mo-* adj + *pho˙lo-* adj

"kem-phu˙lul- vi 'turn (get to be) dark blue' ← *"kem-/ke˙m[u]-* <
*ke˙mu- adj + *phu˙lul-* vi(< *"LH)

R-H/L ← R + H/L

"cwuy-˚cwu- vt 'grasp and give' ← *˚˚cwuy-* = *"cwuy-/cwuy˙y-* < *cwu˙i-*
(? < *cwu-˙i-*) vt + *˚cwu-* vt

"ti-˚na- vt 'pass, move past' ← *"ti-* = *"tiy-* < *ti-˙i-* = *ti-˙[G]i-* vt + *˚na-*
vi

"nem-˚na- vi 'get exciting, get to be fun' ← *"nem-/ne˙m[u]-* <
*ne˙mu- vt + *˚na-* vi 'emerge

R-H < R + H

*"nay-˙thi-*₁ vt 'throw away, discard; drive away, expel'

*"nay-˙thi-*₂ < **"nay-thi˙i-* vi 'get discarded (thrown away); get expelled'

R-H/L ← R + H/L

"et-˚ni- vt 'go on (keep) getting' ← *"et-* vt + *˚ni-* vi

LL-LH ← LL + LH

twulu-hil˙hwu- = *twulu[G]-hil˙hwu-* vt 'whirl it around' ← *twulG-/*
twulu- < **twuluG-* < **twulu-k-* vt + *hil˙hwu-* vt

tuwuy-hil˙hwu- vt 'overturn it, upset' ← *tuwuy-* vt + *hil˙hwu-* vt

LH-H/L ← LH + H/L

ka˙two-"hye- vt 'keep under control, oversee' ← *ka˙two-* vt + *˚hye-* vt *kel˙Gwuy-°hye-* vt 'attract, draw (in)' ← *kel˙Gwuy-* (< **ke˙l[u]-˙Gwu-i-*) vt + *°hye-* vt

wum˙chi-˙hye- vt 'pull it in, withdraw' ← *wum˙chi-* vt + *°hye-* vt

LH-H ← LH + H

ku˙chi-˙thi- vt 'make/let one put an end to it' ← *ku˙chi-* vt + *˙thi-* vt

LH-LH ← LH-LH

ka˙two-hil˙hwu- vt '(make efforts to) keep under control, oversee, look after' ← *ka˙two-* vt + *hil˙hwu-* vt

pi˙li-nwu˙li- adj 'be putrid' < *pi˙li-* adj + *nwu˙li-* adj

LH-LH ← LH + LH/R

ku˙chi-nwu˙lu-/-¨nwull- < **kuchi-nwu˙lul-* vt 'restrain, suppress, inhibit, hold back, control' (cf *kus-nwu˙lu-/-¨nwull-*) ← *ku˙chi-* vt + *nwu˙lu-/¨nwull-* < **nwu˙lul-* vt

wu˙ki-nwu˙lu-/-¨nwull- < **wu˙ki-nwu˙lul-* vt 'press down' ← *wu˙ki-* vt + *nwu˙lu-/¨nwull-* < **nwu˙lul-* vt

H-R ← H + R/LH

°spwop-¨tuT- (= *¨tut-/tu˙l[u]-* < **tu˙tu-*) vi 'come unplugged and fall out' ← *°spwop-* vt + *¨tuT-* = *¨tut-/tu˙l[u]-* < **tu˙tu-* vi

°ptut-¨tuT- (< *¨tut-/tu˙l[u]-* < **tu˙tu-*) vi 'fall, drop' ← *°ptut-* vi + *¨tuT-* = *¨tut-/tu˙l[u]-* < **tu˙tu-* vi

H-L(L) ← H + L(L)

°thi-toT- = *°thi-tot-/-tol[o]-* < **°thi-toto-* vt 'push up' ← *°thi-* vt + *toT-* = *tot-/tol[o]-* < **toto-* vi

°skoy-toT- = *°skoy-tot-/°skoy-tol[o]-* < **°skoy-toto-*) vi 'wake up, come awake' ← *°skoy-* vi 'awake' + *toT-* = *tot-/tol[o]-* < **toto-* vi

H-L ← H + L

°thi-pat- vt 'butt/hit/push against' ← *°thi-* vt + *pat-* vt

H-LH

°ptut-tul˙Gi- vt 'drop it, make/let it fall' ← *°ptut-* vi + *tul˙Gi-* vt (< **tu˙l[u]-˙Gi-* < **tu˙tu-Gi-*)

H-LH ← H/L-LH

°pwo-sol˙phi- vt 'take care of, watch over' ← *°pwo-* vt 'see, look' + *sol˙phi-* vt 'investigate'

HH-H/L ← HH + H/L

˙tu˙li-°(h)hye- vt 'pull/draw it in' ← *˙tu˙li-* vt + *°(h)hye-* vt

HH-L(L) ← HH + L(L)

˙tu˙li-toT- < *-tot-/tol[o]-* < **-toto-* vi 'run in, run toward here' ← *˙tu˙li-* vt + *toT-* = *tot-/tol[o]-* < **toto-* vi

HL-R (< LH) ← HH + R/LH

˙tuli-¨pu(l)-/-pu˙l[u]- < **-pu˙lu-* vt 'blow it in' ← *˙tu˙li-* vt + *¨pwu(l)-/pwu˙l[u]-* < **pwu˙lu-* vt

HL-R/LH ← HH + R/LH

˙tuli-¨swuy- vt 'inhale (a breath), breathe in' ← *˙tu˙li-* vt + *°°swuy-* = *¨swuy-/swuy˙y-* vt

H-RL ← H/L + RL
 twu- ¨*kyesi-* vi 'be/stay put away' ← *twu-* + ¨*kyesi-* vi
H-H/L ← H/L + H/L
 wo-˚*ka-* vi 'come and go' ← *wo-* vi + ˚*ka-* vi
H-HL ← H-HL
 thi-˚*swo-* vt 'shoot hard at' ← *thi-* vt + ˚*(s)swo-* vt
H-H ← H + H
 thi-˚*ptu-* vt 'raise/lift (one's eyes)' ← *thi-* vt + ˚*ptu-* vt
 thi-˚*thi-* vt 'raise, lift, toss up' ← *thi-* vt + ˚*ptu-* vt
H-R/LH ← HH + R/LH
 thi-¨˚*swuy-* (= -¨*swuy-/-swuy*˚*y···*) vt 'breathe hard'

Appendix 2

The compound verb preserves the accent of the first component only.
L-L ← L + [R] (< LH)
 cap-tu(l)-/-tul[u]- < **cap-tulu-* vt 'catch, seize, detain' ← *cap-* vt
 'catch, take, hold' *[*¨*]tu(l)-/tu*˚*l[u]-* < **tu*˚*lu-* vt
 put-tu(l)-/-tul[u]- < **puth-tulu-* vt 'grab, seize, take hold of' ← *puth-*
 + *[*¨*]tu(l)-/tu*˚*l[u]-* < **tu*˚*lu-* vt
L-L(L) ← L + R/LH
 ses-kyeT- = *ses[k]-kyeT-* vt 'intertwine, cross (one's fingers)' ← *sesk-*
 (vi/)vt + ¨*kyeT-* = ¨*kyet-/kye*˚*l[u]-* < **kye*˚*tu-* vt
L-L ← [R] (<LR) + L
 tu-nwoh- = *tu[l]-nwoh-* vt 'lift it and put/place it; lift it up' ← *[*¨*]tu(l)-/*
 tu˚*l[u]-* < **tu*˚*lu-* vt + *nwoh-* vt
LH-L ← LH + R (< LH)
 pol˚*ki-kay-* vt 'clear it up, make it get clear' ← *pol*˚*ki-* vt + ¨*kay-* (<
 ka˚*i-*) vi
LH-L ← LH + H/L
 ke˚*twu-hye-* vt 'pull them together' ← *ke*˚*twu-* vt + ˚*hye-* vt
LH-L ← LH + [R]/LH
 ke˚*twu-tu(l)-/ke*˚*twu-tul[u]-* < **ke*˚*twu-tulu-* vt 'take/tuck/gather up' ←
 ke˚*twu-* vt + *[*¨*]tu(l)-/tu*˚*l[u]-* < **tu*˚*lu-* vt
H-L < H + H/L
 ˚*pcoy-hye-* vt 'wildly cut open' ← ˚*pcoy-* vt 'cut open, lance' + ˚*(h)hye-*
 vt 'pull, drag'
H-LL ← H + R/LH
 ˚*psu-ze(l)-/*˚*psu-zel[u]-* < **psu[l]-selu-* vt 'sweep up, clean it up' ←
 ˚*psu-* vt + ¨*se(l)-/se*˚*l[u]-* < **se*˚*lu-* vt

Appendix 3

The compound verb ignores the accent of the first component.

L-L ← R/LH + L

mi-cwoch- < *mi[l]-cwoch-* < vt 'follow, pursue' ← ¨*mi(l)-/mi˙l[⁴⁄₀]-* < **mi˙l⁴⁄₀-* vt + *cwoch-* vt

no-swos- < *no[l]-swos-* vi 'soar in flight' ← [¨]*no(l)-/no˙l[o]-* < **no˙lo-* + *swos-* vi

nol-pwuch- vt 'incite, stir up' (> *nol-Gwuch-*) ← [¨]*no(l)-/no˙l[o]-* < **no˙lo-* vi + *pwuch-* vt

sey-Gwet- < **se˙i-pat-* adj 'be forceful, powerful, strong' ← °°*sey-* < *se˙i-* adj + *pat-* vt

pey-Gwat- < **pey-Wat-* < **-pat-* vt 'repulse' ← ¨*pey-* < *pe˙[h]i-* vt + *pat-* vt

L-L(L) ← R/LH + LL

cwuy-mulG-/-mulu- < **cwuy-muluG-* < **cwu(i)-muluk-* vt 'finger it, fumble with, massage; coax' ← ¨*cwuy-* = ¨*cwuy-/cwuy˙y-* < *cwu˙i-* (?< *cwu-˙i-*) vt + *mulG-/mulu-* < **muluG-* < **muluk-* vt

L-R < R + R

pskey-¨tulW- < ¨*pskey-¨tulW-* = ¨*pskey-¨tulp-/-tul˙W[o]-* (< **˙tulpu-*) vt 'penetrate'

LL-R/LH ← LH + R/LH

kulhuy-¨tuT- = *kulhuy-¨tut-/-tu˙l[u]-* < **-tu˙tu-* vi 'come untied/ unfastened/undone, get loose' ← *kul˙huy-* vt + ¨*tuT-* = ¨*tut-/tu˙l[u]-* < **tu˙tu-* vi

ke˙twu-tu(l)-/ke˙twu-tul[u]- < **ke˙twu-tulu-* vt 'take/tuck/gather up' ← *ke˙twu-* vt + [¨]*tu(l)-/tu˙l[u]-* < **tu˙lu-* vt

LL-L ← LH-L

twoyGwo-wat- < **-Wat-* < **-pat-* vt 'intensify/augment and heighten it' ← *twoy˙Gwo-* vt 'make it thick/severe/hard' + *pat-* vt

Towards a Theory of Desirability in Conditional Reasoning

NORIKO AKATSUKA
University of California, Los Angeles

1. Introduction

I have been working on conditionals for over fifteen years[1]. At the abstract level, I could say that I chose conditionals because I was interested in the following questions:

1. What is linguistic pragmatics?
2. Is semantics separable from pragmatics?
3. Why and how is language a reflection of the human mind?

---

[1] My special thanks go to Pat Clancy, Shoichi Iwasaki, and Susan Strauss for their valuable suggestions and criticisms at various developmental stages of this paper.

In addition to the 6th J/K Conference at the University of Hawaii, earlier versions of this paper were presented at the following Japanese institutions: International Christian University, Tokyo; Kobe University; Nagoya University; Tohoku University; and Tsukuba University.

This study was partially supported by a UCLA Academic Senate Research Grant and a Sasakawa Faculty Research Grant from the Center for Japanese Studies at UCLA.

Though conditionals themselves represent an extremely fascinating research topic, I chose to study them not for their own sake, but instead as a key to finding answers to these fundamental issues in general linguistics.

Everyone will agree that the notion of truth has played a central role in the long tradition of the study of semantics, in particular, in the inquiry of conditional reasoning. First and foremost, the "if-then" construction has been regarded as a linguistic device for valid reasoning and logical argumentation. Consequently, the natural language conditional has been typically compared to the mathematical conditional, " $p \supset q$ ", where the relevant notions are truth-values, i.e., True and False. Until quite recently, much research on conditionals in linguistics as well as in such related fields as psychology and language acquisition has been conducted under the strong influence of that rationalistic tradition (cf. Traugott, ter Meuleln, Reily & Ferguson 1986, Haiman 1978). As for counterfactual conditionals, their study has been virtually the monopoly of logicians and philosophers (cf. Jackson 1991), and the major concern of these disciplines has been the logical problem of truth conditions, i.e., to specify under what conditions a particular instance of counterfactual reasoning is 'true' or 'valid'.

Through years of research, however, I have become more and more convinced that the speaker's evaluative stance, i.e., DESIRABLE/UNDESIRABLE plays a crucial role in understanding many instances of conditional reasoning in everyday life. Take, for example, the familiar adult speech to young children such as, "if you touch it, you'll get burned." In a recent cross-linguistic study (Clancy, Akatsuka, Strauss; forthcoming), we examined how Japanese, Korean, and American parents use conditionals when talking to very young children of less than three years of age. Based on a total of 84 hours of spontaneous discourse data, we discovered that what we called "predictive" conditionals such as the above was one of the three most common semantic types of conditionals in all three languages. According to our analysis, "predictive" conditionals express the speaker's prediction, "UNDESIRABLE-leads-to-UNDESIRABLE" and the speaker's stance, "THAT'S UNDESIRABLE, SO I DON'T WANT IT TO HAPPEN." Since the types of functions served by "predictive" conditionals, e.g., warnings, threats, and prohibitions, exemplify the earliest type of discourse to which we humans are exposed in the process of socialization and language acquisition, it is reasonable to assume that the natural logic of UNDESIRABLE-leads-to-UNDESIRABLE in conditional reasoning is universally acquired by children of any language and any cultural background at a very early age.

The major goal of the present study is to share with the reader for the first time a full picture of my theory of desirability in conditional reasoning. I have had the great fortune of having access to the data collected in Japanese, Korean, and English by Iwasaki, Kawanishi, and Strauss, respectively, just following the 1994 Northridge earthquake near Los Angeles. In this study, I hope to show how and to what degree a qualitative analysis of cross-linguistic data can shed light on the understanding of the inherent relationship between the speaker and counterfactuality in everyday life.

The paper will consist of two major divisions, Section 2 and Section 3. Section 2 is a discussion on what originally motivated my interest on conditionals in general. It will provide a brief overview of the literature and philosophy on conditionals which impacted my thinking at the time. I would like the reader to understand how and why I have become an advocate of the "desirability hypothesis" in conditional reasoning, and what exactly this hypothesis is. Section 3 is an examination of counterfactual reasoning in everyday life. It will be divided into two smaller sections, 3.1 and 3.2. In 3.1, I will introduce Fauconnier's (1985) theory of mental spaces as a more current view on counterfactual conditional reasoning and will systematically demonstrate why and how it fails to account for usages of counterfactuals in everyday situations. In 3.2, I will examine instances of counterfactual conditionals excerpted from the aforementioned 1994 LA earthquake data and will contrast these with Fauconnier's made-up examples. A working hypothesis will then be presented to answer questions such as "When and why do we typically use counterfactuals?" or "What are we doing when we invoke counterfactuals into daily conversation?"

2. Background
2.1 The first encounter

I first became interested in conditionals in about 1975, when I was starting out as an Assistant Professor at the Department of Linguistics at the University of Chicago and at the same time audited a course in mathematical linguistics. Many linguists at that time were using symbolic logic to formally represent linguistic semantics--by "formally" I mean in the sense of clearly and concisely. In that class, I learned that the analysis of conditionals was traditionally regarded as being within the territory of mathematical logicians and philosophers rather than that of linguists. I also learned that many brilliant people had been trying to come up with some analysis of the logical meaning of conditionals for a long time, and yet there was (and even still now is) very little agreement about the underlying semantics of conditionals.

As a result of that experience, I started to think that in Japanese, two- and three- year olds can understand and use conditional forms such as *Mama, itcha iya* 'Mommy, don't go' (literally 'if you go, I'll hate it') and puzzled over the following question: Since young children understand and use these types of utterances right away, how could conditionals be as complicated as they were made out to be? I gradually started to think that perhaps the first premise of many scholars is wrong--the premise that people try to represent the meaning of natural language conditionals using mathematical logic. In the domain of mathematics, there is no 'speaker', no 'listener', and no evolution of time. The notion of true and false in mathematical logic does not need the existence of people. If 2 + 2 is 4, 2 + 2 will always equal 4 even after every human being disappears from earth. It is an impersonal, eternal truth. I began to think then that perhaps conditionals belong to an entirely different domain--the domain where what counts is the speaker, the listener, and the progression of time.

Of course, initially this was only my gut feeling and for a long time I didn't know how to go about substantiating this new premise. I then realized that the examples in logic textbooks are all in English, and that I should look at my own language. For example, in modern Japanese, the antecedent clause in *konya shujin ga kaette ki-tara tazunemashoo* 'If/When my husband comes back tonight, I'll ask him' can express either 'if' or 'when'. In order to accurately determine whether the meaning is a conditional or a temporal one, one must consider what the speaker is thinking about with respect to her husband coming home, that is, whether it involves a certainty or an uncertainty. If it is just a regular business day, he would be expected to come back at the end of the day. But if he is out of town on business and the wife does not know whether he will be coming tonight or tomorrow, the reading would be 'if'. I also learned at that time that the Korean conditional marker *-myen* behaves in exactly the same way as *-tara*, particularly with respect to the possible alternation in meaning between 'if' and 'when'.

2.2 Benveniste (1971)

Around the same time that I began to get seriously interested in conditionals, I first read Benveniste's (1971:223) famous article, "Subjectivity in Language", which starts with the question, "If LANGUAGE is, as they say, the instrument of communication, to what does it owe this property?" I was quite moved when he questioned the fact that people have equated language to a 'communicative tool', and then asked the question that if language is simply a 'tool' how do we explain where all of these properties come from? If language is a tool or an instrument, you could throw it away and replace it with a new one. However, there is no way to separate language from human beings. In Benveniste's words, "Language is in the nature of man, and he did not fabricate it" (pp. 223-224). He also said that the real nature of language only shows up in discourse--"Many notions in linguistics, perhaps even in psychology, will appear in a different light if one reestablishes them within the framework of discourse" (p. 230).

Most importantly, Beneveniste characterized the speaker as being the 'subject' of consciousness. This type of perspective on the relationship between language and the speaker made me begin to understand how modern Japanese and Korean conditionals work, for example. That is, one basically needs to look into the consciousness of the speaker to see whether the utterance is a conditional or a temporal. One must know whether the speaker considers the issue at hand as being within the realm of certainty or uncertainty at the very moment of utterance.

2.3. The initial puzzle

Even though the natural language conditional has typically been compared with the mathematical conditional, there are actually very few scholars who subscribe to the view that the natural language "if" behaves exactly like "⊃". One well-known exception is, of course, Grice (1975). Recall that Grice's famous maxims of conversation and his concept of conversational implicatures were originally conceived to defend his theoretical position that the natural language connectives such as "if", "and", and "not" are semantically equal to their counterparts in classical logic. Around the time that I seriously started to look at the natural language conditional, Grice's ideas became available through publication (1975) for the first time and quickly gained popularity among linguists. As a result, there were a good number of "orthodox" Griceans--certainly more than there are now.

The following is one of the puzzles that I faced at the early stages of my work on conditionals (e.g., 1983). Refer to the classical truth table represented in Table 1. If the value of both p and q are (T), then the evaluation of the whole conditional statement is also (T) as is evident in the first line. Similarly, if the value of both p and q are (F), the evaluation of the whole is (T), as is evident in the last line:

Table 1: Classical Truth Table

p	q	p ⊃ q
True	True	True
True	False	False
False	True	True
False	False	True

Focusing on the last line, one will note that a particular type of puzzle emerges--a puzzle which involves a contrast of two types of conditionals. For the first type, imagine a situation where an American mother is crying at her daughter's funeral, saying: "If I hadn't given her the car keys, this accident wouldn't have happened." If we adopt the truth table analysis, the antecedent, 'if I hadn't given her the car keys' is F(alse), since the mother had given her daughter the keys, and the consequent clause, 'this accident wouldn't have happened' is also F, since it actually did happen; thus the whole utterance is evaluated as T. This corresponds to the fourth line of the classical truth table (i.e., F F = T). Now compare this sentence with the following conditional: "If this sandwich was made this morning, you're

Shirley Temple," excerpted from the movie "Gaslight". At the time that this movie was made, Shirley Temple was one of the most popular child stars in America One crucial contextual element here is that this conditional is uttered by an angry male customer to a middle-aged, unattractive woman working behind the counter of a diner. What the speaker is saying is that 'this sandwich can't possibly have been made this morning'--it was dry and tasted bad, and he was unhappy about it. The truth-value of the first clause is F, and of course the interlocutor is not Shirley Temple, so that is F also. With the value of both p and q being F, the value of the whole conditional statement is evaluated as T (i.e., F F = T).

Now let's compare the first conditional with this one. Both conditionals are of the type F F = T, but the first one truly expresses the speaker's heartfelt sorrow and regret, while the second one expresses the speaker's cynical and nasty attitude towards his interlocutor, implying something like "I don't believe such nonsense, you old hag". The mental attitudes of the two speakers in each conditional are totally different. Given this, what does the logical analysis of F F = T say about the inherent difference of emotion associated with the two conditionals? Absolutely nothing. Furthermore, the truth-value approach fails to tell us anything about why the first conditional can begin a conversation, while the second one cannot. The "if" clause of the second type of conditional must always be a repetition of what the previous speaker has just asserted; it cannot originate in the speaker's own mind.

The formula F F = T clearly does not tell us anything at all about these differences. This is precisely what inspired me to choose conditionals as my focus of study. There seemed to be an entire domain of interaction and emotion that simply could not be accounted for, or even noticed, by the traditional philosophical approach--and this domain is the domain of desirability.

3. The Desirability Hypothesis

In recent years, I have been suggesting that natural language conditionals are an important device for encoding the speaker's evaluative stance of desirability (e.g. Akatsuka, forthcoming; Clancy, Akatsuka, Strauss, ibid; Akatsuka & Sohn 1994, Mays 1994). Table 2 below juxtaposes my desirability table with the traditional truth table:

Table 2: Akatsuka Desirability Table
vs. Classical Truth Table

DESIRABLE TABLE (Akatsuka)			TRUTH TABLE (classical logic)		
p	q	if p then q	p	q	p ⊃ q
Desirable	Desirable	Desirable	True	True	True
———	———	———	True	False	False
———	———	———	False	True	True
Undesirable	Undesirable	Undesirable	False	False	True

I first arrived at the desirability table hypothesis when I realized that a statement such as the following can function as either a "promise" or "threat": "If you eat my cookies, I'll whip you" (Akatsuka 1991). For most of us who consider being whipped as undesirable, a natural interpretation of this statement would be a threat. However, it also could be a genuine promise if the speaker knows that the listener enjoys being whipped. Thus, in the first reading, the speaker wants the addressee to eat the cookies, while in the second, s/he does not. Clearly, based on this type of reasoning, speakers are using a contingency relationship between the antecedent and the consequent of natural language conditionals to express their desirability stance, as follows:

DESIRABLE leads to DESIRABLE
or
UNDESIRABLE leads to UNDESIRABLE

I believe that the natural logic working in our everyday reasoning is extremely simple, and that in many uses of conditionals, the logic is actually "Desirable leads to Desirable" and "Undesirable leads to Undesirable". The first type of conditional expresses the speaker's attitude "THAT'S DESIRABLE, SO I WANT IT TO HAPPEN." Conversely, "Undesirable leads to Undesirable" conditionals express the speaker's attitude "THAT'S UNDESIRABLE, SO I DON'T WANT IT TO HAPPEN."

The most dramatic, empirical support for the desirability table hypothesis has come from my recent joint research with Pat Clancy, of UCSB, and Susan Strauss, of UCLA, involving the types of conditionals used by parents to their children (Clancy, Akatsuka, & Strauss; ibid). In this study we investigated how Japanese, Korean, and American parents use conditionals when talking to very young children and analyzed the types of conditionals the parents use. Examples of the type of questions we asked ourselves are: What kind of input using conditionals are Japanese, Korean, and American children of one-, two-, and three- years of age exposed to? Could it really be the case that the conditional sentences children are hearing do, in fact, relate to issues of true vs. false, or is it more an issue of DESIRABLE (i.e., desirable-leads-to-desirable) or UNDESIRABLE (i.e., undesirable-leads-to undesirable)? Since the children in all three language samples were very young, these conversations were particularly rich in such speech acts as commands, prohibitions, and granting permission.

In order to analyze desirability in the datasets of the three languages in an objective fashion, we first identified the frequently recurring types of events, actions, and states that can be reliably judged as desirable or undesirable on independent grounds. These objective criteria were refined and collapsed into six categories: safety, health, social acceptability, success, emotional well-being, and positive evaluation. On the basis of these criteria, we coded the content of every conditional clause in our data as "desirable", "undesirable," or "neutral." Table 3 shows that the majority of conditionals in our data in all three languages (59% in Japanese, 71% in Korean, and 58% in English) follow the logic of Desirable-leads-to--Desirable or Undesirable-leads-to-Undesirable.

Only 4% of the conditionals in Korean and English, and 11% in Japanese reverse the expected relationship between desirable events/desirable outcomes and undesirable events/undesirable outcomes; and of these anomalous conditionals, 43% are not actually counterexamples to this natural logic, since they are concessives. Concessive conditionals, by definition, exhibit a counter-to-expectation relationship between antecedent and consequent, as in the following examples:

(1) Japanese: (Child wants to sit on mother's lap to eat)

   M: *dakko shinaku-temo   taberu desho*
       'even if I don't hold you, you can eat, can't you?'

(2) Korean: (Child turns on TV and tells everyone to look; her mother tells her that the program she's interested in isn't on)

   M: *pwa to maynnal kuke eps-canha*
       'even if we look, that's never on.'

In concessive conditionals, undesirable antecedents (not sitting on mother's lap) leads to desirable consequences (being able to eat) while desirable antecedents (watching TV) lead to undesirable consequents (not seeing the desired program). Since it is the inherent nature of concessives to reverse the usual desirability relations found in conditionals, they can be seen as the exception that proves the rule.

Table 3. Desirability Analysis of All Conditional Sentences (Clancy, Akatsuka, Strauss; forthcoming)

Antecedent	Consequent	Japanese (N=149)	Korean (N=131)	English (N=129)
desirable	desirable	.25	.18	.29
undesirable	undesirable	.34	.53	.29
desirable	undesirable	.01	.02	.008
undesirable	desirable	.10	.02	.03
neutral		.30	.25	.38

3. Counterfactuals and desirability

Recall the counterfactual conditional expressing the mother's grief that we discussed in Section 2.3. We can now understand that the antecedent clause, 'If I hadn't given her the car keys' is not a matter of true vs. false, but rather giving her the car keys is either a 'desirable' action or an 'undesirable' action. Giving her the car keys turned out to be an undesirable thing; the desirable situation would have been not giving them to her. The counterfactual conditional, "If I hadn't given her the car keys, this accident wouldn't have happened' uttered by a lamenting mother in any language expresses the logic of "desirable-leads-to-desirable" and the speaker's attitude, "That's desirable, so I want it to happen". Why, then, does it express the mother's deep sorrow and regret? It is because she KNOWS that what she wants is absolutely unattainable[2].

In 1985, I claimed that conditionals are identifiable not by their syntactic forms, but by the speaker's attitude at any given point within the epistemic scale in Table 4. Here it is shown that the speaker's evaluation of the realizability of p ranges in value from zero (i.e., counterfactuals) to one (i.e., realis).

Table 4: The epistemic scale (Akatsuka 1985)

REALIS		IRREALIS	
know (exist x)	get to know (exist x)	not know (exist x)	know not (exist x)
	newly-learned information		counter-factual

---

[2]   The reader is referred to my discussion of the epistemic scale and counterfactuality in Akatsuka (1985).

3.1. Critique of Fauconnier's (1985) account of counterfactuality

In the recent cognitive semantics movement, Fauconnier (1985) has attempted to provide an account of counterfactuality in the framework of his theory of mental spaces. I will demonstrate that Fauconnier's vision of counterfactuality is inadequate in shedding light on everyday counterfactual reasoning, essentially because this perspective remains under the strong influence of the tradition of logic.

First, consider example (3), appearing in the original as (F52). Fauconnier presents this example as an everyday occurrence of a counterfactual context.

(3) [originally appearing as (F52)]

A1: If Napoleon had been Alexander's son, he would have won the battle of Waterloo.
B1: But he would have died long before that.
A2 : Well, suppose he lived a very long life, without ever aging, or that Alexander was resurrected in Corsica in the eighteenth century...

Now, let me ask the readers to re-read this made-up conversation very carefully and see whether they can come up with any clear idea of what speaker A is saying by uttering (A1). Is the speaker saying that Napoleon was not as great a military leader as Alexander? If this is the case, why doesn't he say so more directly, i.e., "If Napoleon had been Alexander" rather than Alexander's son? And what about speaker B's reaction to (A1)? Is (B1) a joke? And if it is a joke, why is speaker A proposing such 'absurd' conditions as an immunity to aging and the possibility of resurrection for a mortal man in (A2)? It would appear here that A is trying to make (A1) an instance of 'valid' reasoning. Does this mean, then, that by uttering (A1) speaker A is more interested in the imaginary father-son relationship between Alexander and Napoleon than in Napoleon's military prowess itself? I must say that I am totally puzzled and unable to deduce the speakers' intentions in any of the lines in the above excerpt.

One could probably claim that it is primarily due to the lack of prior discourse context that we find it difficult to comprehend the speakers' intentions in (3). However, I would strongly disagree with that line of thinking. Instead, I would plainly argue that contrary to Fauconnier's claim, (3) cannot possibly be a reflection of ordinary usages of counterfactuals. I doubt that any conversation even remotely resembling this one would ever occur in spontaneous discourse; and regarding the ability to deduce the speaker's intention in using counterfactual conditionals in spontaneous discourse, I will argue that the user's intention is, on the contrary, normally quite obvious, not just to the interlocutor, but to the general audience as well. This point will be demonstrated in detail in the examination of authentic discourse data such as our 1994 LA earthquake data.

Crucially, just like logicians and philosophers' analyses of counterfactuals, Fauconnier's theory is not at all interested in the question "when a speaker uses a counterfactual conditional, what is s/he really doing?" This point becomes much clearer when we examine Fauconnier's concept of 'space-builders'. According to Fauconnier, various linguistic elements such as "if" and "wish" as well as "not" and "prevent" are considered to be "space-builders". As such, they are supposed to be capable of setting up a counterfactual mental space which functions in such a way that "some relation (sic)", which does not hold in the parent space (i.e. the speaker's belief world), may be satisfied in the counterfactual space. In this light, consider the utterances listed in (4), which appear in the original as (F3-F6) (emphasis original).

(4) [appearing in the original as F3, F4, F5, and F6]

(F3)
If Lucky had won, I would be rich. I would have moved to Tahiti.
(F4)
I *wish* Lucky had won. I would be rich.
(F5)
Fortunately, the fire did *not* cross the highway. My house would have been destroyed.
(F6)
Luckily, the fire was *prevented* from crossing the highway. My house would have been destroyed.

Note that the speakers of (F3)-(F4) sound unhappy because what they wanted to happen did not happen. In contrast, the speakers of (F5) - (F6) sound extremely happy. They are virtually saying, "Boy! Am I fortunate/lucky! My house wasn't destroyed!" However, in Fauconnier's theory of spaces, the speaker's mental attitude is virtually of no relevance whatsoever. Fauconnier simply states that in all four of the above utterances, "the first sentence can be understood to set up a counterfactual space (incompatible with the origin), and the second one expresses some relation satisfied in that counterfactual space (pp. 109-110)."

Fauconnier totally ignores the significance of the attitudinal adverbs "fortunately" and "luckily" in the first sentences in (F5) and (F6) and claims that counterfactuality in the second sentence is *lexically imposed* by the words "not" and "prevent" because these words are strong space-builders, much stronger than "if" and "wish" in (F3) and (F4) respectively. Fauconnier does, however, recognize the fact that "if" and "wish" do not always function as successful space-builders, as illustrated in (5), originally appearing as (F10):

(5) [originally appeared as (F10)]

I wish you would help me tomorrow.
(Compatible with your actually helping)

In sharp contrast, however, when we examine the 1994 LA earthquake data in the next section, it will become crystal-clear that it is not the lexical power of negatives such as "not" and "prevent" that has 'imposed' the counterfactuality in (F5) and (F6); rather, as will be demonstrated, it is the speaker who has intentionally invoked counterfactuals into the discourse for specific purposes, e.g., complaining or rejoicing. To illustrate this point in preview, notice that the omission of the attitudinal adverbs from Fauconnier's examples result in an unnatural occurrence of counterfactuals in the second sentence, as illustrated in (6) below:

(6)
a) [from (F5)] ??The fire did not cross the highway. My house would have been destroyed
b) [from (F6)] ?? The fire was prevented from crossing the highway. My house would have been destroyed.

While it is clear that the notion of desirability plays absolutely no role in Fauconnier's theoretical framework, we have seen that Fauconnier's own examples unwittingly serve as testimony to the critical importance of the consideration of the speaker's attitude to an adequate theory of counterfactual reasoning in everyday life.

3.2 A Case Study from the 1994 Los Angeles Earthquake Data

3.2.1 Background

On the morning of Monday, January 17, 1994, an unusually strong earthquake hit the Los Angeles area at approximately 4:30 a.m. It was a holiday, not a regular working day. When the earthquake hit, most people were at home, still fast asleep. Thanks to this, the casualties were miraculously small.

About five weeks after the earthquake, audio-and video-taped narratives about the earthquake experiences were collected from UCLA students who are native speakers of Japanese, Korean, and American English. These data were collected by Iwasaki (Japanese), Kawanishi (Korean) and Strauss (English). The students were total strangers until they met for the first time at the data collection site. The students were paired up and were asked to talk to each other for approximately 20-25 minutes about their personal experiences during the earthquake. The student pairs were left alone in the room which was equipped with a video camera and supplemental audio recording device. For the purpose of this study, I will restrict the analysis to one particular excerpt from the Japanese conversational data.

3.2.2 Co-construction of counterfactuals in Japanese data

In the following, I will focus on one Japanese excerpt which followed a 15 minute exchange of the two speakers' respective experiences about things such as where they were at the time of earthquake, how frightening it was, and what kind of damage they suffered (relatively small). This excerpt is shown in (7):

The structure of (7) is clearly divided into 3 parts: (a) the opening, (b) co-construction of counterfactuals 'if not p, not q' by the two speakers, where p and q stand for REALITY (e.g., p = "the earthquake occurred at 4:30 a.m." and q = "casualties were very small"), and (c) the closing. Note that the speakers are saying essentially the same thing in the opening and closing. In the opening, speaker H says "*Asa de yokatta* (We were lucky it was in the morning)" and in the closing, speaker A repeats exactly the same thing, "*Asa de yokatta*".

(7)

(a) Opening	H:	demo nee *asa de yokatta* desu yo ne?
		gozen yoji han de?
	A:	atashi mo omotta-n desu yo.
(b)	H:	moshi nee
"if not p,		kore ga nee imagoro
not q"	A:	= kore ga nee, yuugata no:
	H:	ima toka ne
	A:	rasshuji no goji toka ne ha ha ha ha
	H:	soo soo soo
		yuugata no rasshuji no goji toka:
	A:	ha haha haha ha
	H:	ano toshokan nanka de mada gakusei nanka
		ir < iru jikan dattara:
	A:	iru san yoji toka:
	H:	moo atama kara saa hon ga ochitekite:
	A:	aa zaa sugokatta desu nee.
	H:	haiuei furiiuei nanka mo zenbu nee
	A:	zenbu
	H:	sundanshichattara moo
	A:	kanbotsushichatte:
	H:	shisha nanka . juubai gurai n natta deshoo nee?

(c) Closing A: nn atashi mo omotta-n su. *asa de yokattn* -n
                 daroo na tte
             H: nnn
             A: minna neteru toki datta kara
             H: honto hukoo chuu no saiwai desu yo:
             A: nn
             H: =nn nn

[English version of (7)]

(a) Opening H: but, see, we were lucky it happened in the morning,
                    at four thirty, right?
             A: I thought about that, too.

(b)
"if not p,   H: If it had happened around now (in the late
not q"   afternoon)
             A: (it) had happened in the evening
             H: now or something
             A: at rush hour, like five o'clock   ha   ha
             H: right, right, right. rush hour-- 5:00 in the evening
             A: ha haha haha ha
             H: well like at the library, if it was the time the students
                    were still there
             A: like three or four o'clock or
             H: well, on their heads, the books would fall, and
             A: Oh, like "crash" -- it would've been terrible.
             H: the highway, freeway, all of them.
             A: All of them
             H: If they had been cut then
             A: they would have collapsed and
             H: The death toll would've been 10 times more, right?

(c) Closing A: So, I thought too that we were lucky it happened
                 in the morning.
             H: Yeah.
             A: everybody was sleeping at that time, so
             H: Right, it was the only blessing within this disaster.
             A: Yeah.
             H: =Yeah, yeah.

What is so remarkable about these Japanese data is that its abstract
structure is quite similar to that of Fauconnier's examples in (4),
(particularly (F5) and (F6)), even though Fauconnier's examples are

monologic and (7) is a dialogue. One important difference is that in the latter there is no occurrence whatsoever of the words "not" or "prevent". In this light, I would like to propose here that contrary to Fauconnier's claim, what 'imposes' a long stretch of co-construction of counterfactuals by the two speakers is the initial exchange of "*Asa de yokatta desu yo ne*? (Weren't we lucky it happened in the morning!)" and "*atashi mo omotta n desu yo* (I thought about it, too!)". This is precisely the role of the sentence initial English attitudinal adverbs, "fortunately" and "luckily" in (F5) and (F6).

What are the two speakers doing by co-constructing "if not p, then not q" here? Notice that all of the co-constructed counterfactuals reflect the logic of Undesirable-leads-to-Undesirable. In sharp contrast to Fauconnier's 'absurd' conditions, all co-constructed "if not p" components here represent a variety of situations which could have actually happened and could have resulted in much greater casualties. The two speakers have shared an unusually undesirable experience, but they could come out of it relatively unharmed, and they are congratulating themselves by conveying the message "it could've been much worse." Recently, Strauss & Kawanishi (1996) have used the 1994 LA earthquake data for their pioneering study on assessment strategies in Japanese, Korean and American English. One of their findings is that Japanese speakers often participate in co-construction activities to establish common ground, contrary to the claim made by others, e.g., Ono & Yoshida (1996) that speakers of Japanese do not 'finish each other's sentences'. In fact, example (7) used here is excerpted from one of Strauss & Kawanishi's examples illustrating collaborative finishes in Japanese. What deserves our special attention is that counterfactuals are used here to establish emotional solidarity between the two speakers.

Throughout the 1994 LA earthquake data, Undesirable-leads-to-Undesirable counterfactuals typically appear regardless of which language the speakers use. Based on this, I hypothesize that the following is a proto-typical usage of counterfactual conditionals in everyday life. Ultimately, this hypothesis will have to be examined in the light of cognitive psychology.

> Hypothesis: When we humans undergo some unusual experiences, we tend to reappraise/appreciate REALITY in terms of desirability in comparison/contrast with hypothetical situations which actually could have happened.

This unusual experience does not have to be something undesirable. It can be an extremely pleasant one, such as the successful completion of a difficult task. As such, it is easy to find counterfactuals expressing the author's gratitude in the acknowledgments sections of many different types of writings[3]. Example (8) is a clear example taken from a popular paperback on the Vietnam War:

(8)
Dear America could not have been completed without their dedication, insights, and commitment to the intrinsic value of these writings. (Edelman, ed. Dear America: Letters Home From Vietnam. 1985)

This type of counterfactual also expresses the logic of Undesirable-leads -to-Undesirable. The conditional as a whole hypothetically expresses the worst situation that the speaker can think of, namely, the non-existence of the very object which is the source of the present happiness. For this reason, the counterfactual can express a strong sense of gratitude by conveying the message that "you and you alone are responsible for bringing about the happy PRESENT moment."

4.   Conclusion

I have tried to demonstrate how discourse-based research on conditionals has culminated in the construction of a theory of desirability in conditional reasoning. By doing so, I hope that I have also shown that fundamentally our study addresses itself to general questions in linguistic theory:

1. What is linguistic pragmatics?
2. Is semantics separate from pragmatics?
3. Why and how is language a reflection of the human mind?

The research results overwhelmingly indicate that the most typical counterfactual conditionals occurring in everyday life are direct reflections of the deeply felt emotions of ordinary people. This is a concept that appears to be totally ignored by the rationalistic tradition of counterfactuals. I conclude by suggesting that an adequate theory of cognitive semantics will have to incorporate in some way a theory of desirability as delineated in the present study.

---

3   "Gratitude counterfactuals" also appear often in the acknowledgement sections of MA theses and Ph.D. dissertaions.

References

Akatsuka, N. (1983) Conditionals. *Papers in Japanese Linguistics,* 9, 1-33.

Akatsuka, N. (1985). Conditionals and epistemic scale. Language 61 (3), 625-639.

Akatsuka, N. (1991) Dracula Conditionals and Discourse in *Interdisciplinary Approaches to Language: Essays in Honor of S.Y. Kuroda,* edited by C. Georgopoulos and R. Ishihara. Kluwer Academic Publishers. Dordrecht/Boston/London. pp. 25-37.

Akatsuka, N. (forthcoming). Negative conditionality, Subjectification, and Conditional Reasoning. In R. Dirven & A. Anthansiadou (Eds), *On Conditionals Again..* John Benjamins.

Akatsuka, N. & S-O. Sohn. (1994) Negative conditionality: The case of Japanese -tewa and Korean -taka. In Akatsuka (Ed.) *Japanese/Korean Linguistics 4,* pp. 203-220. CSLI/Stanford.

Benveniste, E. (1971). *Problems in General Linguistics.* U of Miami Press. Coral Gables.

Clancy, P., Akatsuka, N., & Strauss, S. (forthcoming) Deontic modality and conditionality in adult-child discourse: A cross-linguistic study. In A. Kamio (Ed), *Approaches in Functional Linguistics.* John Benjamins.

Fauconnier, G. (1985) *Mental Spaces.* The MIT Press.

Grice, H.P. (1975). Logic and conversation. In P. Cole and J.L. Morgan (Eds.), *Speech acts, Syntax and semantics 3,* New York:Academic Press.

Haiman, J. (1978). Conditionals are topics. *Language* 54..3:564-89.

Jackson, F. (Ed). (1991). *Conditionals.* Oxford readings in philosophy. New York:Oxford University Press.

Mayes, P. (1994). Conditionals and the Logic of Desirability: An Interview with Noriko Akatsuka. In Strauss & Kreuter (Eds.), *Issues in Applied Linguistics ,* Vol. 5, No. 2. pp. 449-461.

Ono, T. & Yoshida, E . (1996). A Study of Co-Construction: We Don't Finish Each Other's Sentences. In Akatsuka, Iwasaki & Strauss (Eds.) *Japanese/Korean Linguistics 5.* CSLI/Stanford pp.115-130.

Strauss, S. & Kawanishi, Y. (1996). Assessment Strategies in Japanese, Korean, and American English. In Akatsuka, Iwasaki & Strauss (Eds.) *Japanese/Korean Linguistics 5.* CSLI/Stanford. pp. 149-166.

Traugott et al. (1986). *On Conditionals.* Cambridge:Cambridge University Press.

TEXTS

Edelman, B. (1985) *Dear America: Letters Home from Vietnam..* Pocket Books.

1994 Northridge Earthquake data. (1994) Iwasaki, Kawanishi, and Strauss.

Part II

Historical Linguistics

On the Origins of Japanese Sentence Particles *ka* and *zo*

CHARLES J. QUINN, JR.
Ohio State University

Introduction

When words come to be applied in relating other linguistic structures, such as phrases, words, and morphemes, to one another, they are said to grammaticalize (or grammaticize).[1] In the process, a word comes to relate, in regular ways, to a greater variety of other meanings, and its original meaning typically becomes more abstract. This can be seen, for example, in the case of French *pas* 'step', which, in addition to its use as a common noun, came to be used as an optional, intensifying component in negating clauses, added to the negative marker *ne*, so that *ne ... pas* 'not a step' served to strengthen the negation of verbs of movement, and eventually, of any verb.[2] A word that at one time was used in contexts limited to those that involved 'steps' in the sense of walking, progressing, and so on, then, provided first a way of strengthening a plain negative, and in time simply the normal way to negate a clause. Today, in spoken French, people routinely use *pas* as the sole marker of clause negation, to the exclusion of *ne*, so that in effect the negative strengthener has outsurvived the original negative morpheme itself.

---

[1] I would like to thank Bob Ramsey, Leon Serafim, Sasha Vovin and John Whitman for comments on earlier versions of this paper. I am grateful to Samuel E. Martin for the same, but also for his example in giving internal evidence the hardest look possible.

[2] See Hock 1986: 194, Schwegler 1988. Both are cited in a discussion of the same in Hopper and Traugott 1993: 58.

Another phenomenon often observed as a word grammaticalizes is the lingering of constraints that applied to the word before it gained its added, more abstract function. These can usually be seen to follow from some aspect of the meaning of the source word. For example, as Hopper and Traugott (1993:3) point out, the English 'be going to' future, "as an original aspectual, ... can occur in constructions where a future formed with *will* cannot:

a. If interest rates are going to climb, we'll have to change our plans.

b. *If interests will climb, we'll have to change our plans."[3]

Hopper and Traugott refer to this effect as the "persistence of meaning" (1993:3), and attribute the incompatibility of 'will' here to its nonaspectual, original meaning of intention. There are several features in the behavior of Old Japanese (OJ) sentence particles *ka* and *so/zo* that smack of the persistence of earlier meanings, apparent quirks that might not seem so arbitrary if we could but construct a story that leads to where we find them at the time of the earliest texts. This paper attempts such an archaeology of their travels.

In OJ texts, which date from the Nara period[4] (710-784), particles *ka* and *so/zo* (later *zo*) function both in sentence-final position and medially, after focused words or phrases, and the latter use (i.e. the kakari-musubi construction) appears to have been based on the former.[5] The hypothesis proposed here is that sentence-final *ka* and *so/zo* began, respectively, as demonstrative pronouns *ka* 'that over there/already known' and *so* 'that there facing me/now evident/just mentioned' were added to a sentence as an afterthought kind of clarification of that sentence's topic, in (1) seeking or (2) establishing the identification of the referent of that *ka* or *so*. In other words, *Ima ka* 'Is it now?' would have evolved from *Ima? -- ka* 'now? -- that one (known to us)'. Similarly, *Ta so* 'who is it?' would have evolved from *Ta? -- so* 'who? -- that (there facing me/now evident/just mentioned)'. While *Ima ka* is a yes/no question, it differs from other such questions (e.g. *Ima ku?* 'Are they coming now?'[6]) in that it seeks to IDENTIFY some assumed referent with the category expressed as *ima* 'now'. It is this function of seeking an identification that a question like *Ima ka* 'Is it now?'

---

[3] From Hopper and Traugott 1993:3.

[4] These include the poetic anthology *Manyooshuu* (completed ca. 759), sung verses recorded in the *Kojiki* 'Records of Ancient Matters' (712) and *Nihongi* 'Chronicles of Japan' (a.k.a. *Nihon shoki*, 720), *senmyoo* 'imperial edicts' (collected in the *Shoku Nihongi* 'Records of Japan, continued', collection for which commenced in 797), and the Shinto prayers called *norito*.

[5] See Ôno et al., eds., 1974, for Ôno's summary of his original arguments of this view.

[6] This question type contrasts with the Referential Predicate (explained below) *Ima kuru* 'Is it that they're coming now?', in which we typically find a different inflected form and a final *ka*, which can be interpreted as 'it', the referent presupposed in the asking of such a question.

shares with a content interrogative like *Ta so* 'Who is it?'. Both seek the identification of a referent, the existence of which is presupposed in the act of asking such a question. The difference is that while one proposes a particular identification (*ima* 'now'), the other goes no further than to propose a category within which an identification is to be made (*ta* 'who' for people, *izure* 'which one' for countable items of any kind, *izuko* 'where' for a location, etc.). A fact that is very relevant to this discussion is that questions that seek an identification presuppose a referent. The referent presupposed in the asking is routinely expressed in English with the pronoun 'it' ('Is it now?', 'Who is it?').[7] It is this referent for which an identification is sought. Since, as the two examples from Old Japanese suggest, such questions were routinely accompanied by a particle *ka* or *so/zo*, one wonders if these might have somehow indexed that presupposed referent.

OJ documents show the use of homophonous forms *ka* and *so* as demonstrative pronouns and as components in lexicalized and quasilexicalized forms like *kare*, *sore*, *ka no*, and *so no*, where their contribution can be understood as equivalent to what they meant when standing alone. Both *ka* and *so* were used in senses spatial, personal, and epistemic, much as their present descendents *a-* and *so-* are. Might it not have been the case that the *ka* and *so/zo* that we find at the end of identification-seeking questions in Old Japanese were originally these demonstrative pronouns, used to refer to the assumed referent -- time, person, place, etc. -- for which an identification was sought? The nature of these questions, along with the fact that *ka* and *so/zo* were not used in non-identifying yes/no questions, suggest these OJ sentence particles (*syuuzyosi* 'final particles') may well have been the grammaticalized descendants of the pronouns *ka* and *so*. In particular, it would have been their use in referring deictically to information as known, referrable, or otherwise accessible that suited them to serve in such a role: *ka* in the sense of 'that one (already) evident/known' and *so* as 'that one right there/now evident/just mentioned'.

We also find *ka* and *so/zo* attested in Old Japanese in statements and exclamations, and here, too, they make sense as grammaticalized descendants of the same demonstrative pronouns, added after a sentence to drive home the identity of the referent, which can be understood as a *ka* 'that one already known' or a *so* 'that one just evident/mentioned'. These meanings can be seen to survive, somewhat attenuated but nevertheless discernable, in the more grammaticalized uses of *ka* and *so/zo* that are attested in Old Japanese and later. It therefore seems possible and, as I will argue here, quite reasonable, to understand the OJ sentence particles *ka* and *so/zo* as having originated as demonstrative indexes of the referent presupposed in the asking of an identification question (the 'it' of 'Who is it?' or an 'Is it X? kind of question') or the assertion of a statement of

---

[7] Of course, if the copula 'be' is used, English grammar also requires an overt 'it', which is not the case in questions like 'Now?'

identity (the 'it' of 'It's --'). Each particle, *ka* and *so/zo*, is found[8] in both questions and in statements in Old Japanese and Early Middle Japanese, [9] but when analyzed from the etymological perspective propsed here, this breadth of distribution can also be seen to make good sense.

The hypothesis for OJ *ka*

Let us summarize the hypothesis for OJ sentence particle *ka* first. We may begin with demonstrative pronoun *ka*. One of the attested uses of OJ and EMJ pronoun *ka* and its relatives *kare* 'that one over there/already known', *ka no X* 'that X over there/already known' among others, is in reference to readily accessible information, whether it is ostensively evident (perceptually present) to the speaker and addressee, or not. Like its present-day functional equivalent *a- (are, atira, asoko, ano,* etc.*),* 'that over there/the familiar one', demonstrative *ka* was used to refer to things evident in a shared spatiovisual field but detached from both speaker and addressee. This reference to things mutually accessible in the same spatiovisual field, at equal remove, seems a likely bridge to referring to things mutually accessible in some nonimmediate spatial domain, such as over a great distance, or over time. It is not surprising to find that *ka* (again like *a-* today) was used in reference to information assumed to be accessible, whether it was presently perceived, or not. OJ and EMJ *ka*, whether used as a free morpheme (*ka ha,* etc.) or bound morpheme (*kare, kanata*), referred to information a speaker assumed a hearer to have access to just as he had access to it; when this information was not ostensively evident, the assumption was that it was accessible in memory. *Ka* was also used in reference to things the speaker himself had access to in memory but not in his present situation or discourse. For want of a better term, this kind of reference to information assumed to be 'there' when it was not ostensively 'here' can be called EPISTEMIC DEIXIS -- 'pointing to' some information as known. In this use, the reference of *ka* has been established outside the present discourse moment -- prior to it in time, or removed from it in space, and is thus available as a memory, familiar and already known, if not yet (re)identified with a common noun, noun phrase, epithet, nominalized clause, or whatever. This is the meaning of demonstrative *ka* that could have played a central role in the uses that are attested for OJ particle *ka*.

Under the hypothesis described, *ka* questions would have been proposals for identifying a known, presupposed entity originally expressed by pronoun *ka* 'the one already known', with the entity (e.g. *ima* 'now') or category (e.g. *ta(re)* 'who') expressed by the nominal predicate preceding this *ka*. Questions posed with *ka*, then, can be understood as having had their origins in an unresolved juxtaposition of one referent (e.g. *ima* 'now') or category name (e.g. *izure* 'which one') with another, epistemically more certain entity (*ka* 'that known one', 'it'), as, again, in *Ima? — ka* 'now? -- that one' > 'Is it now?'. Answering *Ima? — ka* would thus have meant confirming or disconfirming the identification or equation of *ima* with the

---

[8] This is true today even of *zo* as well of *ka*, albeit only in fossilized phrases like *itu zo ya* 'When was it?', *nani to zo* 'somehow', etc.

[9] The language attested in documents from the Heian period (784-1188).

referent of pronoun *ka* . Similarly, to ask *Izure ka* 'which one?' would have been to ask 'which one' (*izure*) is to be identifed with 'the one' already known (*ka*), and this is precisely what *Izure? -- ka* 'which one? -- that one' would have meant. Furthermore, the same epistemic deixis we attribute to OJ *ka* may be observed in the two inflected forms it cooccurred with, the rentai or izen. This will be taken up below, in the description of Referential Predicates. In this way, given the epistemic deixis practiced with demonstrative *ka* 'that, the familiar one', 'it', the question arises: could not the OJ particle *ka* have been this very pronoun *ka*, reanalyzed and grammaticalized?

The scenario outlined thus far is not, in itself, difficult to imagine. For one thing, it provides a reason for the long-remarked fact that in Old and Early Middle Japanese, the *zyosi* 'particle' *ka* is attested only after nominals (nouns or nominalized clauses), and not after the unmarked predicative (the *syuusi* 'end stop') form. For another, since all OJ and EMJ *ka* questions were requests for identification -- whether "yes/no" questions (*Ima ka*) or information ('wh-') questions (*Izure ka*) -- it is not difficult to think of the *ka* itself as originally referring to the known entity that such requests for identification necessarily presuppose. *Ka* the particle would have had its start referring to the same kind of 'it' the existence of which is assumed in questions like 'Is it now?' and 'Which one is it?' -- each of which entails a something to ask about.

At the same time, it must be admitted that this is not a commonly held view of the history of demonstrative *ka*, least of all in Japan. It has been pointed out, for example, that in the extant OJ texts, demonstrative pronoun *ka* occurs hardly at all as a stand-alone pronoun (e.g. with focus-restricting *ha*, as in *ka ha*), but mostly in lexical and quasilexical forms like *kare* 'that one we know' and *ka no* (e.g. *ka no X* 'that X we both/all know') (cf. Hashimoto 1983). This fact, together with an increase in the number of attested uses of freestanding *ka* in the Heian period (794-1192), has led Hashimoto and others to the conclusion, which has gone largely unchallenged, that *ka* was new in Old Japanese, became more established in Early Middle Japanese, and then died out.

These distributional facts must be interpreted with some care. Since the bulk of Nara period Japanese texts take the form of short, lyric verse, not exposition or narrative, the scant attestation of pronoun *ka* (or the roughly synonymous *kare*, for that matter) in these documents may have been more a consequence of the conventions of lyric verse than a fact of language use in general. We might ask, rather, why a deictic pronoun like *ka* should be used with any frequency at all in verse, in the absence of a particular, personally known addressee -- whether in its sense of 'that one over there (visible to both of us)' or in its sense of 'the one we already know'. If it is used at all in short OJ lyric verse, a defining quality of which is response to a present moment, we might rather expect it to be used in introspective reference to the poet's thoughts.[10]

The next oldest group of Japanese texts, which survive from the Heian period (Early Middle Japanese), includes a variety of narratives, as well as lyric verse, and it has been noted by Hashimoto and others that by this time demonstrative pronoun *ka* was more widely used. It is still, however, more often attested embedded in lexicalized and quasilexical forms, as it was in the Nara texts. Etymologically, *kare* may have got its start as a strengthened form of *ka*, but by the Heian period, it is clearly the default pronoun for referents of a 'that one over there/that we already know' sort. I would add that while this becomes clear in the Heian period, it was probably so in the Nara period, too. The richer variety of the Heian texts, in particular the great body of narratives that was produced, means that the Heian data differ from the Nara data in both variety and sheer volume. Is it any surprise that some words should be more in evidence? Where the Nara texts provide the philologist with a single, narrow casement window, looking out on just a few genres of language use (verse and song, mainly lyric, imperial edicts, prayers), the Heian texts provide, so to speak, four walls of large windows, along with infrared binoculars, hidden microphones, and more. It seems crucial to think first in terms of the genres in which we find these forms used, before attempting conclusions about the language in general.[11]

If sentence particle *ka* did in fact evolve from pronoun *ka*, an evolutionary story like the one just outlined has a familiar plot line, as such stories go: the progressive grammaticalization of demonstrative *ka* would have gone hand-in-hand with the strengthening and eventual replacement of pronoun *ka* with *kare* by the time of Old Japanese. It seems unwarranted to conclude that since there are fewer tokens of independent pronoun *ka* in the Nara period texts and more in the Heian period texts, that pronoun *ka* was but new and on the rise in Old Japanese, and became established only later, in Early Middle Japanese. For one thing, this conclusion ignores the Old Japanese attestation of *ka* in words like pronoun *kare* and quasi-words like prenominal specifier *ka no* [noun] 'that familiar [noun]'. The more likely scenario, it seems, would have demonstrative pronoun *ka* old and in decline in Old Japanese -- stranded on islands of certain very common phrases and words, and -- the hypothesis of this paper -- as the sentence-final clitic that indexed a desire to have some known 'that' or 'it' identified. That there are

---

[10] Cursory examination of the evidence suggests that this may have been the case, but I will not pursue this question further here.

[11] Hashimoto 1983 also proposes that distal/already known demonstrative *ka* was a later, secondary development of proximal *ko/ka* 'this here/ that I'm now thinking of'. It is difficult to follow his argument that the sense of epistemic familiarity of *ko/ka* 'this' was basic for historical *ka*, and its spatial 'that over there' use derived from this (if I understand correctly). However, since it is the epistemic deixis of *ka* that my hypothetical etymology depends most on, *ka*'s possible origins in the epistemic use of proximal *ko* are not necessarily relevant. What is more, even in Hashimoto's history of *ka*, epistemic deixis is there all along.

more instances of pronoun *ka* in EMJ texts than in the OJ texts (but not more than *kare*) was most likely the consequence of the explosive increase in the number and variety of genres written in Japanese in the Heian period. Prounoun *ka* would still have been on its way out as the default distal demonstrative pronoun; it was still underused in comparison to the synonymous *kare*.

The hypothesis for OJ *so/zo*

Now, what of OJ particle *so/zo*? By a similar reanalysis, it seems likely that the epistemic use of mesial demonstrative pronoun *so* to refer to a referent as 'that one evident right there/now/just mentioned' evolved into the more abstract function of identifying a discourse referent as 'the one' or 'that'. The probable origins of sentence particle *so/zo* in demonstrative pronoun *so* was first suggested by Fujitani Nariakira, in his grammatical treatise *Ayuishoo* (1773 [1960]), and this etymology is generally accepted today. The specifics of how this might have come about, however, does not seem to have been addressed by either Fujitani or anyone else, perhaps because the referring function of *so/zo* is thought to be self-evident. In particular, it does not seem to have been noted that *so* could have been used after a sentence to confirm its topic, as a kind of afterthought . This would explain its final position as a consequence of what has long been a very common move in Japanese, attested since the earliest texts.

Since sentence particle *so* is used in both statements and information ('wh-') questions, the more naturally an etymology fits both uses, the more preferable it should be. In statements, following up with pronoun *so* would have meant that the information *so* followed was to be taken as a point in need of being driven home. In *Umasi kuni so* 'It's a fine land' (MYS 1.2[12]), for example, *so* yields an act of positive identification, whereby a referent just established in that discourse (*Yamato no kuni* 'the Land of Yamato') is identified as *umasi kuni* 'a fine land'. Under the etymology herewith proposed, the *so* of *Umasi kuni so* would have got its start in this role as demonstrative pronoun *so* added as an afterthought intended to clarify or drive home the referent of the predicate *umasi kuni*: *Umasi kuni -- so* 'a fine land, that one (just mentioned, under discussion)!'

So is attested not only in statements of positive identification in Old Japanese (and Early Middle Japanese, as *zo*), but also in questions posed with content interrogative words like *ta(re)* 'who', *izure* 'which one', *nado* 'why', and so on. This use with content interrogatives is illustrated in the *ta(re) so* 'who is it?' (< *ta(re), so* 'who? -- that (one just noted/evident)') example cited above. In fact, sentence particle *so* is not attested in Old Japanese or Early Middle Japanese in the asking of questions except in combination with a content interrogative word or phrase. Consequently, the interrogative use of *so* can be understood simply as the grammaticalized consequence of adding demonstrative pronoun *so* to emphasize that there was a referent in need of identification in terms of what was just mentioned, viz. the "wh-" phrase. Since the use of an interrogative word like *izure* entails a

---

[12] *Manyooshuu* Book 1, poem number 2.

referent, the use of a pronoun here would be redundant and, thus, emphatic. Indeed, interrogative words like *izure* in Old Japanese and Early Middle Japanese did not require a following *ka* or *so/zo*, even if they were commonly accompanied by them. The effect of adding the redundant reference of a pronoun *ka* or *so* to a content interrogative word, then, would have emphatically marked that word as at issue, problematic, and in need of being dealt with. If this is what *so/zo* meant when used after interrogative words, it differs very little from what pronoun *so* would have contributed to statements of positive identification, as just described. Thus, the interrogative side of combinations like *ta(re) so* 'who is it?' would have come not from the final *so*, but from the *ta(re)*, *nani* 'what', etc. *So* would have been involved here by virtue of emphasizing, by adding its overt reference, as an afterthought, to the referent already implicit in the question word; its point would have been simply that there was a *so* 'that one recently evident/just mentioned' that needed to be dealt with, specifically, identified. In this way, the use of pronoun *so* with interrogative phrases that sought identification would have been based on the same referential function that underwrote its use in making positive identifications.

Finally, to repeat a point made in passing above, it is noteworthy that from OJ through Early Middle Japanese, particles *so* and *zo*, like *ka*, follow only lexical nouns and nominalized clauses, and not clauses inflected in the *syuusi* 'end stop' form. It would thus appear that they were all involved in the predication, specifically identification, of nominals.[13] It is not too much to say that they functioned as a kind of copula. If we are going to categorize these words as they are usually categorized, that is, as *syuuzyosi* 'final [sentence] particles', we must admit that they were of a species different from vocative *yo* or ejaculative *ya*, both of which followed either nominals or *syuusi*-inflected clauses. By the hypothesis proposed here, the quasi-copular function of *so*, *zo*, and *ka* would have come about through the use of demonstrative pronouns *ka* and *so* to clarify the referent of the preceding nominal as 'that one already known' and 'that one just mentioned', respectively. However, they would have become full fledged sentence particles only when they came to follow non-nominals as well as nominals.

These etymologies for *ka* and *so/zo* and the process whereby each would have come to be reanalyzed as a sentence particle, might also render some additional facts coherent which otherwise remain a bit anomalous. There is, for example, the ordering of component particles in exclamations (*Waga sato ka mo* 'That's my home village!' ?< *ka mo* 'that one, even') and ironic questions (*ahi-mi-te noti ha ahazi mono ka mo* 'after coming together, not meet [again]?' (MYS 2087) ?< *ka mo* 'that mutually remembered one [i.e. meeting], even'). This construal would give us a reason for the violation of the canonical ordering [[[case particle] focus/quantifying particle] sentence particle] that a string like *ka mo* (and later, perhaps, *ka ha*) seems to exhibit. If an exclamatory or ironic [[sentence] + [[*ka*] *mo*]] is viewed as the relic of an afterthought pronoun *ka*

---

[13] The term nominal covers lexical nouns, deverbal nouns, noun phrases, and nominalized clauses.

'that known, familiar one' added to a sentence in surprise or incredulity (hence the reading of *mo* as 'even'), the appearance of a focus/quantifier particle (*mo*) governing a sentence particle (*ka*) can be understood as the grammaticalized descendant of an earlier noun phrase (*ka*) expanded in scope (i.e. beyond expectations) with *mo*.

Unfortunately, while this interpretation of *ka mo* supports nicely the etymology proposed here for particle *ka*, it seems more likely that the *mo* in *ka mo* had scope not over a pronoun *ka*, but over the entire sentence, including what was probably an already grammaticalized sentence particle *ka*: [[[sentence] *ka*] *mo*]. The *mo* and *ha* that we find at the end of sentences already concluded with particle *ya*, *ka*, or *zo* (listed in most dictionaries of earlier Japanese as *yamo*, *yaha*, *kamo*, *kaha*, and *zomo*) can be understood as the same inclusive focus/quantifying *mo* and restricted focus/quantifying *ha*, but the ironic and exclamatory meanings associated with these paired particle compounds can be more consistently explained if we see the focus/quantifying particle (*mo* or *ha*) as governing the entire [[sentence] + sentence particle] complex, and used by the speaker or writer to present that entire complex to the ongoing discourse in a restricted (resigned, belittling) way with *ha* or an expanded (inclusive, remarkable, surprised) way with *mo* (Quinn 1987, and forthcoming). *Ahazi mono ka mo* 'What, not meet?' (as above), then, would have had the ironic ring it had because the *ka* of *Ahazi mono ka* problematized the equation of 'it' (our situation) with 'a fixed fact that we won't meet', and *mo* quantified this identification as beyond the bounds of what the speaker expected – 'additional' in the sense of unforeseen or surprising. The sentence so quantified then becomes a kind of topic (*X mo*) for an unspoken comment, unspoken because it is a foregone conclusion: *Ahazi mono ka mo* ... The effect would have been pragmatically motivated (one typically wants to see one's beloved again), and something like 'The identification "it is a fixed fact that we won't meet" is too much [to entertain].' The same kind of 'dangling topic *qua* foregone conclusion/ comment' construal seems a viable etymology for *yamo*, *yaha*, *kaha*, and *zomo*, as well. It does not seem that *ka mo* should have worked any differently.

Even if combinations like *kamo*, *kaha* (unattested till the Heian period), and *zomo* do not have their origins in an afterthought [[demonstrative pronoun] + *mo*], this does not mean that the afterthought demonstrative pronoun etymology proposed above for particles *ka* and *so*/*zo* is cast in doubt. All it means is that the grammaticalization of pronouns *ka* and *so* to sentence particles would have been underway before people began framing entire [[sentence] + particle] complexes with focus/quantifying particles like *mo* and *ha*.

The story sketched so far for *ka* and *so*/*zo* becomes a bit more convincing when it is fleshed out with more detail. Let us therefore take a closer look at each of the characters in the tale, across a range of attested uses. The examples cited have been selected almost entirely from Old Japanese, since it is at this stage in the history of the language that the functional carryover from the homophonous pronouns *so* and *ka* to sentence particles *so*/*zo* and *ka* would presumably have been strongest.

OJ Sentence particle *ka*

The OJ particle *ka* is generally understood in Japanese scholarship as a marker of *gimon* 'doubt', that is, a speaker-internal matter, with no necessary involvement of an addressee. When used at the end of a sentence, *ka* has scope over that sentence. There is informal consensus that it also means basically the same thing -- doubt -- when it is used to mark a nonfinal phrase in the construction known as kakari-musubi 'government-closure'. In this latter use, however, the doubt is focused on the constituent immediately governed by *ka*. It is the former of these uses, the sentence-final one, that will be considered in this section; the nonfinal use will be taken up subsequently. In either case, juxtaposing a word or phrase with pronoun *ka* would have been a way to problematize its relation to the assumed referent that *ka* would have pointed to. Indeed, problematizing an identification seems an apt gloss on what the *gimon* 'doubt' interpretation of particle *ka* gets at.

OJ *ka* is the ancestor of present-day *ka*, and like its descendant, most typically marks the sentence that precedes it as a question, whether self-directed or addressed to someone else. This is generally true, but *ka* has changed considerably since the eighth century, as has *so/zo*, the other sentence particle examined here. In reviewing the facts about *ka*, we can begin by observing that *ka* occurred regularly after nouns in Old Japanese, as in examples (1) through (3).

(1) Kaminaduki sigure no   tune   ka   MYS 19.4259
    Tenth month drizzle GEN custom DI[14]
    'The Tenth Month: is it a constant of rain?'

(2) ... kehu ka asu   ka to ...   MYS 15.3587
        today DI tomorrow DI Q
    ' ... [waiting quietly, thinking] "Is it today? Is it tomorrow?"'

(3) ... Watatumi ha kususiki   mono ka   MYS 3.388
        Sea Deity RF be inscrutable[RT] one   DI
    'The Sea, is he an inscrutable one!'

As the third of these examples suggests, despite the general association of *ka* with the marking of interrogative mood in OJ, in many of its contexts of use the particle's effect shaded off into something more akin to exclamation, by way of indexing some surprise or disbelief at the point made by the clause. The English translation reminds us that this is not an unusual discourse function for the morphology or syntax of interrogatives to take on, then or now, East or West.

Somewhat more remarkable is the fact, already alluded to, that OJ *ka*, whether in questions or exclamations, was used only after nouns and

---

[14] Abbreviations and symbols are listed in the Appendix that follows the list of references.

noun phrases, as above, or nominalized clauses, as in the following examples.[15]

(4) ... kokobaku mo mi   no   sayakeki   ka   MYS 17.3991
     this much IF view GEN refreshing^{RT} DI
     'Such a refreshing a sight it is (is what it is).'

(5) Sizukeku mo kisi   ni   ha nami   ha yose-keru ka   MYS 7.1237
     softly   IF shore LOC RF waves RF lap-EEF^{RT} DI
     'It's true, I see, that the waves lap on the shore so softly.'

The main clauses of (4) and (5) are inflected in the RENTAI 'adnominal' (a name that refers to another use of the same form, that of modifying nouns). In (4) and (5), however, the noun head is missing, and the rentai inflection serves to nominalize that clause and mark it as referring to the information it contains, rather than presenting or establishing it anew. Even when used in the predication of exclamations[16] or warnings, rentai-inflected information is typically more established, given, assumed, or otherwise authoritative than some other, less established information, which it is used to ground.[17] In both (4) and (5) inclusive focus particle *mo* indicates that the manner expression it governs (*kokobaku* and *Sizukeku*, respectively) includes more than one would have expected, and *mo* is for this reason a common component in exclamatory clauses that end in *ka*.

Finally, we may ask how necessary a component a familiar referent, the kind of epistemically referrable referent that pronoun *ka* pointed to, might be in the examples just provided. For example, in (1), repeated below for convenience's sake, the speaker assumes that the there is something 'constant' (*tune*) with which the Tenth Month can be identified; the question is, is it 'a constant of drizzle'?

(1) Kaminaduki sigure no   tune   ka   MYS 19.4259
     Tenth month drizzle GEN custom DI
     'The Tenth Month: is it the rain that is its constant?'

In (2) as well, the question assumes that there is a day -- someday soon -- to be identified as the one when the beloved returns.

---

[15] When the identity of an inflected form is central to the point under discussion, that form is marked with an abbreviation superscripted after the English gloss equivalent: mizen 'not yet so', renyoo 'predicator-linked', syuusi 'end stop', rentai 'noun-linked', and izen 'already so'. A functional reanalysis (Quinn 1987, forthcoming) of the the early Japanese inflectional paradigm posits (a) an unmarked, nonreferential group consisting of infinitives (renyoo, mizen) and finite (syuusi) forms; and (b) a marked, referential pair consisting of infinitive (izen) and finite (rentai) forms.

[16] Thanks to Shoichi Iwasaki (p.c.) for the reminder that rentai-inflected clauses and exclamation are by no means incompatible.

[17] Quinn 1987, chapter 8.

(2) ... kehu ka asu   ka to ...   MYS 15.3587
      today DI tomorrow DI Q
    ' ... [waiting undefiled, thinking] "Is it today? Is it tomorrow?"'

In both of these examples, then, we have questions that assume a referent to
be identified, the kind of referent that pronoun *ka*, in its epistemic sense of
'familiar, known one', referred to. The point with *ka* is not just that it
'follows nouns and nominalized clauses', as the dictionaries and handbooks
tell us, but more basically that it is used in questions that present those
nouns and nominalized clauses as identical with some presupposed referent.

    The same is true of the examples that cross into the exclamatory,
(4) and (5), where an identification or characterization is not only predicated
(the syuusi inflection would be sufficient for that), but predicated as referrable
information, in an 'It's [clause], [is how it is]' kind of locution. At the very
least, a main clause governed by *ka* put the identity of some referent at issue,
whether in the form of a genuine question or in the form of exclamation,
incredulity, surprise, and so on. In the absence of an interrogative word, the
mere presence of *ka* alone is no guarantee that a *ka*-concluded sentence is
actually a question that requests an answer.

    If particle *ka* had its start in indexing an assumed referent, this same
function may perhaps be glimpsed in the constraint that required, through
Old Japanese and Early Middle Japanese alike, that any predicator (*yoogen* or
inflecting word) governed by particle *ka* take the form of a referring
expression, that is, be nominalized. The inflected forms involved were the
rentai 'adnominal' and izen 'already so'. When used as a nominalized
clause, as in examples (4) and (5), repeated below, a rentai clause functioned
in discourse as a kind of EPISTEMIC DEIXIS, in that it indexed a speaker's or
writer's assumption that the information therein expressed was referrable, in
other words somehow established, assumable, or known.

(4) ... kokobaku mo mi   no   sayakeki   ka   MYS 17.3991
      this much IF view GEN refreshing^{RT} DI
    'Such a refreshing a sight it is (is what it is).'

(5) Sizukeku mo kisi ni   ha nami ha yose-keru ka   MYS 7.1237
      softly   IF shore LOC RF waves RF lap-EEF^{RT} DI
    'It's true, I see, that the waves lap on the shore so softly.'

A rentai-nominalized main clause like these would have been used with its
own illocutionary force, with or without the *ka*, but in either case, such a
main clause can be understood as prompting a repredication of the clause's
ideational content (IC) in an identifying 'It's (that) IC' way, instead of
simply introducing that IC to the discourse anew. (This latter function was
handled by the SYUUSI 'endstop' form.) An afterthought *ka* would have
emphasized this repredication, adding its own reminding reference of '-- that
situation'.

Such rentai-nominalized main clauses are functionally analogous to clauses nominalized with *no* today,[18] and will be termed REFERENTIAL PREDICATES, or RPs for short (Quinn 1987, 1996, forthcoming). Examples (4) and (5) show RPs at work indexing the factuality of what the speaker has recognized as 'how things are'. As these examples suggest, the factuality of rentai nominalization is CONTINGENT: it depends on the speaker's act of referring, based on the speaker's construal of 'how things are' at that point in the discourse, for the purposes of what s/he has to say. In this speaker-contingent, evidential sense, the RP created with rentai-nominalization can be said to be discourse-delimited, or FINITE.[19]

We can understand the role of the final *ka* in these examples of finite RPs as follows: the rentai inflection marks the predicator and what it governs as something the speaker regards as referrable information (i.e. marks the predicator as a finite RP), and this is repredicated with *ka*. Insofar as *ka* functioned in the predication of nouns (examples (1), (2), (3)) and nominals (examples (4) and (5)), and was neither a dedicated interrogative particle nor the only way to ask a question, it seems more accurate to say that it functioned in a way that was somewhat copular. More on this below. First, it is necessary to have a look at the other inflected form that kept regular company with sentence-final *ka*. Clauses predicated with this inflection can be understood as a second, nonfinite variety of RP.

The NONFINITE RP takes the form of an IZEN ('already so'[20])-inflected clause, and indexes the speaker's construal of that state of affairs as a fact that did not depend on his or her own experience so much as on recognition of what was what in the world. A predicator inflected in the izen form functioned in Old Japanese as a REFERENTIAL INFINITIVE, a partner to the the finite rentai. Like the head-internal rentai-inflected clause, the izen nominalized the clause and marked it as information somehow more established than other information in the immediate discourse context.[21] It differed from the rentai in that it referred to a clause's content not as contingently or subjectively so, but rather as absolutely and objectively so.

(6) ... ihebito no   ihahi-mata-ne   ka   MYS 15.3688
       family GEN keep pure-wait-NEG[IZ] DI
    'Is it the failure of those at home to wait in ritual purity?'

This line ventures an identification of the cause of the speaker's husband's not having returned home from a mission abroad. As the infinitive partner of

---

[18] The EXTENDED PREDICATE in Jorden's analysis of present-day Japanese (Jorden with Noda 1987 (Part 1):178).

[19] This construal of the term "finite" is purely for the purposes of labeling a distinction regularly marked by OJ inflection.

[20] There was nothing aspectual about this inflected form, despite its name. See Quinn 1987, chapter 9, for an interpretation based on a study of its various functions.

[21] Not only in other independent clauses, but also in hypotactic linking to a superordinate clause, effected by consequential -*ba*, antithetical -*do*, or simply zero (interpreted either way).

the finite rentai, the izen infinitive can be understood as indexing an absolute, objective kind of givenness, in contrast to the rentai's more contingent, situation-particular referentiality -- a contrast somewhat like that obtaining today between clauses nominalized with *mono* 'thing' (*Muzukasii mon(o) desu yo.* 'It's a difficult thing/business/matter [any time, any place].') on the one hand, and *no*, on the other (e.g., *Muzukasii n(o) desu yo.* 'It [the situation under discussion] is difficult [is how it is].') In (6), the speaker is wondering if it is such a hard fact, beyond her personal ken and control, that might have led to her husband's failure to return home.

In (4) and (5), then, particle *ka* is used in the predication of contingent (finite, rentai-inflected) RPs, and in (6) it is used in the predication of an absolute (nonfinite, izen-inflected) RP. It is a fact of OJ that if a clause concluded with an inflecting form (verb, adjective, verb- or adjective-derived suffix), *ka* was not used unless that clause was inflected in the rentai or izen form, that is, unless it was a nominalized clause -- more specifically, a RP -- contingent (rentai-inflected) or absolute (izen-inflected). As examples (1)-(3) show, *ka* was also used to conclude clauses that ended with a noun or noun phrase. On the face of it, *ka* seems to have had a role in the predication of nominals, whether lexical NPs or nominalized RP clauses.

Was *ka* basically interrogative, and its presence in exclamatory or confirmative sentences derivative of the interrogative function? Or was the interrogative function more an association that emerged in symbiotic relation with other, more clearly interrogative elements in the same clause, such as the *i-*[22] ('wh-') words? Can all of *ka*'s attested functions in OJ -- from interrogative to exclamatory/confirmative -- be derived from a common basic meaning interacting differentially with respectively different contexts? I believe they can. For the moment, let us draw a tentative, minimalist conclusion based on the evidence examined thus far: sentence particle *ka* was an overt way to make an identification (as in examples (3), (4), and (5)) or to seek an identification (as in examples (1), (2), and (6)). An 'identifying' construal of *ka* thus covers the exclamatory/confirmative uses and the interrogative uses as well. While we have no record of the intonation contours with which *ka* was used, we can assume that intonational differences could have provided disambiguation when needed. For the most part, however, pragmatic cues seem to have been clear enough without such suprasegmental help, as our ability to tell the difference today suggests.

The Quasi-copular Identification of *ka*

The use of *ka* in content interrogatives involves the same identifying function. As example (7) reminds us, presupposition is a necessary component of content interrogative sentences.

(7) ... aha-mu to ihu ha   tare naru   ka   MYS 12.2916
      meet-OPT Q say RF who COP^{RT} DI
      'Who is it that says "Let's meet"?'

---

[22] Many interrogative words (*izure, izuko, iku-*, etc.) in early Japanese begin with an *i-*; hence this abbreviation.

There is no asking 'Who is it who says so?' without presupposing that someone does say so; no asking 'Who saw it?' without assuming that someone saw it; no asking 'What did you have to eat?' without assuming that 'you ate something'; and so on. If the interrogative RP (RT-inflected clause *tare naru* here) can be understood as seeking an identification (identification being the function of inflecting copula *nari*, too), the *ka* can be read as emphasizing this requested identification, as a final predicator. The 'double predication' is realized by the use of the inflecting copula *nari* in the RP and noninflecting, quasicopular *ka* as the overt predicator of the RP.

In short, an interpretation of *ka* that relates it to a presupposed element makes logical sense. When we seek to identify something, we necessarily presuppose that there is such a something that we can refer to, whether in asserting an identity for it or asking if a proposed identity fits it. Whether we assert 'It's tomorrow', for example, or ask 'Is it tomorrow?', both messages assume an 'it' for which 'tomorrow' is posed as a possible identity. Since an assumed referent ('it') is a factor in all the attested uses of *ka* in Old Japanese, from content interrogatives to exclamations, we can reasonably conjecture that *ka* might have referred to that assumed referent, the 'it' assumed when making or seeking identifications. The existence in OJ of a homophous demonstrative pronoun, *ka* 'that one over there/already familiar', which seems to have been in the process of being displaced by the morphologically complex *kare* ('id.'), suggests that this could have indeed been the case.

When pronoun *ka* came, by this route, to be used to identify nominals, to say, in effect, 'It's N' of them, it took on a more grammatical role. As *ka* gave up ground to *kare* in the role of distal/familiar demonstrative reference, it remained embedded in words like *kanata* 'that direction/far away' and *kare* itself; it seems likely too that the specifier *ka no* 'that over there/one we know' too had achieved lexical status. But as OJ and then EMJ particle *ka*, it was living a very active second life, playing the variety of related roles that we have examined.

OJ and EMJ *ka* is clearly not a simple interrogative marker. Its use is restricted to referring expressions (nominals), and to questions that involved presupposition, that is, requests for identification of an assumed referent. Furthermore, content (*i-*) questions were quite askable without *ka*, and presuppositionless yes/no questions did not use *ka*, but rather *ya*, which is taken up just below. This leaves us with a very copula-like *ka*, even if its use was severely constrained by the fact that it did not inflect. Pronouns can take on copular functions, it has been shown, if there is some reason for them to be used in syntactic locations where they serve a copular function, such as identification. Li and Thompson (1977) review scholarship on this phenomenon from a variety of languages (Mandarin, Hebrew, Palenstinian Arabic, Wappo), and for their main study, that of Mandarin, argue convincingly that a demonstrative pronoun (*shì* 'this') used resumptively became reanalyzed as the copula *shì* that is in use today. Using *shì* 'this' to emphasize an already mentioned referent, as in *Zhī́ ér shì zhǐ, shì bù rèn yě* 'to use him knowing [that he'd rebel], this was unkind.', positioned the word where it could be understood to assert the noun that followed it, that is, mean not only 'this', but 'this is'. If this happened with a demonstrative pronoun in a SVO language, it is not that different in kind from the reanalysis proposed here for *ka* and *so/zo* in SOV Japanese. In the case of Japanese, however, copular roles are a stop along a route that runs on into particlehood. But this is getting ahead of our story.

Ka was not the only sentence particle used in interrogative sentences in Old Japanese. Another particle, *ya*, was also used routinely in the posing of questions, and used more broadly than *ka*. Unlike *ka*, sentence-final *ya* was not subject to the constraint that the inflected clause (verbal, adjectival, copular, inflecting suffix) it governed be an RP. *Ya* was used on both RPs and on unmarked, presupposition-free finite clauses. Since understanding what *ya* was should help in understanding what *ka* was not, a brief review of *ya*'s uses is in order.

Entirely (inter)personal: Sentence particle *ya*

Ka was not used to conclude sentences the main predicator of which was inflected in the unmarked finite (syuusi 'endstop') form, although such sentences were also used in posing questions. But syuusi-inflected interrogative clauses were limited to straightforward yes/no questions ('IC?'), and these were not Referential Predicates (i.e., not of the form 'Is it that [IC]?'). The sentence particle used in syuusi-inflected questions was *ya*.

(8) ... imo ni   tuge-tu   ya   MYS 18.4138
      love LOC convey-PF^{SS} RS
      'Have you told my love/my wife?'

The particle *ya* functioned in Old Japanese in several ways, all of which can be said to have had something vocative, or addressee-oriented, about them. We find *ya* manifested not only in questions but also in apostrophe and interjection (*hayasikotoba*) in verse and song -- facts that suggest that *ya* may have been related to the uniquely vocative *yo*. At the least, it seems safe to say that *ya* served to call attention (typically that of one's addressee) to the whole or a part of one's message. When applied over an entire sentence, this attention was routinely sought in the process of posing a yes-no question, as in (8) above.[23] In terms of Halliday's three metafunctions of language (cf. Halliday 1985), *ya*'s use in calling an addressee's attention to something, typically for the purpose of resolution, means that it functioned INTERPERSONALLY, without any direct motivation of a TEXTUAL or IDEATIONAL sort.[24] While *ya* and *ka* are generally thought of as the two interrogative particles of earlier Japanese, the identifying, quasi-copular

---

[23] Ironic (*hango* 'opposite language') interpretations can be understood as the consequence of uttering what was formally a question in the face of an already obvious answer.

[24] Halliday's TEXTUAL metafunction refers to the linguistic differentiation of different kinds of information, as in new/old, referential/nonreferential, definite/indefinite, etc. IDEATIONAL signification is, roughly speaking, propositional: the who, what, and how of linguistically expressed states, events, and acts.

function manifested by *ka* is nowhere evident in *ya*'s uses, and *ya* was not used in the posing of *i-* ('wh-') questions at all. While sentence-final *ka* followed only RT- or IZ-inflected RPs, sentence-final *ya* followed any inflected form, presupposing (RT, IZ) or not (RY, SS). In other words, a presupposition-free question could only be concluded with *ya*, not *ka*.

As this brief survey of the uses of OJ *ka* and *ya* suggests, if *ka* was an interrogative marker, it was hardly the functional equivalent of a simple question mark. It was used, as we have seen, with presupposition-based yes/no questions (i.e., 'Is it that [IC]?' RPs), but not in presupposition-free (syuusi-inflected) yes/no questions (simple 'IC?' questions). Again, the syuusi-inflected questions would be capped with *ya*, not *ka*. In its sentence-final use, then, *ka* participated in the predication of sentences that referred to some assumed or known information as they sought or marvelled at an identification. Not surprisingly, it was *ka*, and not *ya*, that was used with content interrogatives, whether as a whole sentence (as in (7) above), or as part of a construction that seems to have begun as an identification-seeking 'it' cleft, a use to which we now turn.

The kakari-musubi construction and OJ *ka*

Ka's use in a clause-internal, focus-raising role probably began as an 'it' cleft, in which *ka*, used in a quasi-copular way to designate a constituent the identity of which is at issue.[25] This produces the kakari-musubi construction, illustrated in (9), (10), and (11). Example (9) is a question asked in reference to 'the moon that ought to shine', mentioned (... *teru beki tuki wo*) in the line preceding the one quoted here:

(9) ... sirotahe   no kumo ka kakuseru   MYS 7.1079
     white-hemmed GEN cloud DI be hidden^{RT}
     'Is it a white cloud that has has hidden it?'

The construction is named for its two components, a focused phrase (the KAKARI 'one in charge') and a specially inflected predicator that concluded the sentence (the MUSUBI 'binding, closure'). As the meaning of kakari suggests, the construction has long been viewed as an agreement phenomenon, whereby the presence of a certain particle on the kakari (*ka*, *so/zo*, *ya*, *namu*, *koso*) triggers a special, non-syuusi inflection on the sentence's final predicator (a rentai or izen form). The present discussion is limited to the role of *ka* in this construction. In kakari-musubi, *ka* was the most common, if not exclusive, means of marking focus on content interrogative words and phrases. (*So/zo* also participated in content questions, but less often and in a more restricted way, a point taken up with *so/zo*, below.)

(10) ... itu   ka koe-na-mu   MYS 1.83
     when DI cross-PF-OPT^{RT}
     'When is it we'll cross it?'

---

[25] The functional resemblance to it-clefts of kakari-musubi sentences in which the kakari is focused with *ka* and so/zo is noted and discussed in Quinn 1987.

(11) ... nani ka sayareru   MYS 5.870
    what DI is interfering[RT]
'What is it that is in the way?'

    As mentioned, in the *kokugogaku* 'national [i.e. Japanese]
linguistics' tradition, *ka* is understood as a marker of 'doubt' (*gimon*). By
this, scholars seem to mean an inability or unwillingness on the part of the
speaker or writer to affirm or assert something. 'Doubt', on this construal,
has to do with the speaker's assessment of a proposition itself and/or
relations within it (Is it the case, i.e. true, as a whole? What happened?
Who did what?, etc.), and less to do with addressing this doubt to some
addressee. If *kokugogaku* scholars were to put this in terms of Halliday's
metafunctions, they might say that *ka* is involved in making textual
distinctions about a message's I(deational) C(ontent), whether as a whole
('Is it that [IC]?') or in part ('Is it X that [IC]?'), in addition to its
interpersonal significance. In this way, *kokugogaku* has made a place for
questions speakers pose to themselves or utter in exclamatory surprise, and
in the bargain distinguished *ka* from *ya*. Unlike *ka*, *ya* is concerned less
with IC than with reaching out to an addressee; in *kokugogaku*, its meaning
is characterized as *toi* 'asking', as in chapter 4 of Sakakura 1993.

    As the above examples suggest, however, we can go further and say
what it is that is doubted: the identity of a referent, whether that referent is
(a) the situation under discussion (the 'it' for which an identity is sought in
terms of a proposed IC, as in 'Is it now?' or 'Is it (that) you're coming?')
or (b) a person, thing, time, place, and so on (the 'it' for which an identity
is sought in 'When is it that you're coming?'). *Ka* can thus be understood
as an index of DOUBTED IDENTITY, whether it is used at the end of a
sentence, of an entire proposition, or used of a single phrase, in the kakari-
musubi construction.

    What is it about *ka* that led it to function in these ways? As
suggested in the initial sketch of *ka*'s etymology, in each of the examples
presented above, it is possible to read *ka* as pronoun *ka* 'that/the one
known/it', in an afterthought or right-dislocated position. This is because
all OJ uses of sentence or focus particle *ka* involve presupposing a referent,
just the kind of referent that was routinely expressed with the homophonous
pronoun *ka*, and because afterthought right-dislocation is very much in
evidence in Old Japanese, where it basically served to clarify the reference
assumed for the preceding clause, as a kind of redundant and therefore
emphatic reminder of that clause's topic. This meant that such postposed or
right-dislocated information would have scope over the entire clause --
which is of course a feature of sentence particles in general. At all events,
this interpretation of *ka* can be schematized roughly as the kind of utterance
formalized as (12a), below. From (12a) evolved (12b), which set the stage
for (13a) and, subsequently, kakari-musubi (13b). The formulae in (12)
show how nominal predication with *ka* may have arisen; those under (13)
show how, by a self-similar process, the kakari-musubi construction
probably emerged and continued to evolve.

(12a) nominal (= noun, RP clause, etc.) -- *ka* 'that, it'.

                                     (afterthought demonstrative *ka*)

(12b) nominal *ka*   'Is it [nominal]?'   (quasi-copular *ka*)
                           'It's [nominal]!'

(13a) nominal *ka* -- RP   'Is it [nominal]? -- RP'
          (Quasi-copular *ka* predicates kakari of kakari-musubi;
                    RP clause added as afterthought.)

(13b) nominal *ka*, RP   'Is it [nominal] that [RP]?'
          (*Ka* still identifies; RP a constituent of same sentence.)

(13c) [nominal *ka* + RT-inflected predicator]$_{RP}$
           'Is it that [emphasized nominal + predicate]?'
          (*ka* = focus, not predication; entire sentence now RP)

The difference with kakari-musubi (as it first emerged, represented in (13a)) is that the *ka*-predicated nominal sentence is now itself followed by an afterthought in the form of an RP (hence the rentai inflection of *ka*-focused kakari-musubi). In terms of example (11) *Nani ka sayureru* 'What is it that's in the way?', this meaning would have resulted from a grammaticalization of **Nani ka -- sayareru* 'What is it? -- that one in the way.' As the afterthought structure of (13a) further grammaticalized, that is, as the afterthought came to be perceived as part of the sentence, we get the kind of *ka*-focused kakari-musubi generally attested in Old and Early Middle Japanese (13b). However, there are also sentences with *ka*-focused kakari phrases where, as with *ya*- and *namu*- focused ones, the RP includes the whole sentence, and not just the musubi. This is the 'Is it that [emphasized nominal + predicate]?' of (13c).[26] The demise of the kakari-musubi construction came when the rentai-inflected clause lost its referential 'that --' sense, and became the default form for presuppositionless sentences.

To back up, however, the focus that *ka* initially created on the constituent it marked (as in (13a and b) in a kakari-musubi construction was very similar to, and much the product of, the identification-seeking role it played at the end of a nominal sentence (12b). Focusing on an element internal to the clause, or the marking with *ka* of an element internal to the clause, can be understood as a development that emerged after this sentence-final use had grammaticalized to the point where *ka* had taken on some kind of predicative significance, described above as quasi-copular. The kakari-marking in the kakari-musubi construction would have begun as a quasi-copular predication with *ka*, and the rentai-inflected predicate that follows it in the same sentence (the musubi) would have been there as an afterthought, to clarify what was presupposed in the preceding predication with *ka*. In other words, the same move -- an afterthought confirmation of the topical scope of the main predication -- not only put *ka* at the end of a nominal

---

[26] Quinn 1987, 1994, and 1996 discuss this difference between *ka* and *so/zo* on the one hand and *ya* and *namu* on the other. The whole sentence RP reading of *ka*- and *so/zo*-focused kakari musubi sentences is treated in Quinn, forthcoming.

sentence (12a), and got it involved in the business of predicating nominals (12b), but also put the rentai-inflected clause (an RP) there too (13a), in the case of the kakari-musubi construction (13b).

Ôno Susumu's (e.g. Ôno et al., eds. 1974) account of the origins of kakari-musubi includes an insight that fits in the evolutionary scenario summarized in (12) and (13) above. He proposed that the rentai-inflected predicator was, properly understood, the topic of the kakari phrase in the kakari-musubi construction, and that the kakari particles had all been sentence particles before they became kakari particles. At an earlier stage of the language, he suggested, the kakari phrase (nominal + kakari particle) had been the predicator (*yoogen*) of the sentence, and the ordering of the constituents the unmarked topic + comment, theme + rheme sort. Thus, at an earlier stage of the language, there would have been no way to express the meaning of sentences like (9) and (11) other than by means of sentences like (14a) and (14b):

(14a) *Kakuseru (ha) sirotahe no kumo ka.
'The thing that hid it, is it a white cloud?'

(14b) *Sayareru (ha) nani ka
'The matter in the way, what is it?'

Then, according to Ôno, an 'inversion transformation' (*tooti-hoo*) flipped these constitutents into the order of the historical examples (9, 10, 11), and the kakari-musubi construction was born. Ôno leaves it at that: this inversion was a process in pre-OJ sentence syntax whereby one dominant sentence type produced another. Nothing in the process, as he describes it, is motivated by anything like an afterthought (which has the advantage of being something real speakers routinely did), and there is no mention of presupposition, for example. But he was certainly right about the predicative origins of the kakari particles and the predicative nature they imparted to the phrases they governed, as well as in seeing the rentai-inflected predicator as somehow scope- or topic-setting.

However, what Ôno explains as a diachronic change of one sentence type into another by 'inversion' can also be interpreted as the emergence of an alternative sentence type that was used to different purposes. By this analysis, kakari-musubi would have arisen not in an across-the-board transformation of one sentence type into another, but rather through the grammaticization, or routinized reinterpretation, of an afterthought (the RP) as an internal constituent of a clause. In terms of (13a-c) above, this would mean that the RT-inflected predicator would have started out as a right-dislocated 'afterthought' attempt to clarify the topical scope of the preceding predicator (governed by quasi-copular *ka*), and then over time, have been reanalyzed by speakers as a constituent in a single sentence (13b), on the way to becoming the main predicator of that single sentence (13c). In terms of what (sentence particles *ka* or *so/zo*) evolved into what (emphatic phrase particles *ka* and *so/zo*), Ôno's account is a different way of saying what is described as the reapplication of (12b) in (13a).

OJ Sentence particle *so/zo*

We turn now to *so/zo*, which displays both a distributional and functional similarity to *ka*. In Old Japanese, this particle is found with both a voiced and unvoiced intial consonant. In Early Middle Japanese, the voiced *zo* has won out, and this is the sentence particle that survives today, used to assert and index a variety of affective stances having to do with certainty, from encouragement (*Ii zo!* 'Awriiight!', 'Way to go!'), to threats (*Yurusanai zo.* 'I won't stand for it.'), to milder warnings (*Sa, iku zo!* 'OK, here we go!'), among others.

In Old Japanese, we find *so/zo* used, like *ka*, in the predication of nominals. Whereas *ka* figured in putting the identity of some assumed or presupposed referent at issue, *so/zo* served primarily to establish or assert an identification, as in (15) through (18) below. The EI label refers to *so/zo*'s primary function of establishing identity.

(15) Umasi kuni so Akidusima Yamato no   kuni ha.   MYS 1.2
      is fine land EI p.n.   p.n.   GEN land RF
      'It's a fine land -- Akizushima, the Land of Yamato.'

(16) Natuyase   ni   yosi   to ihu mono so.
      summer weight loss LOC is good Q say thing EI

      munagi tori   mese.   MYS 16.3853
      eel   catch eat
      'It's something said to be good for summer weight loss: catch and eat eels.'

(17) Sikisima no   Yamato no   kuni ha kotodama no
      [epithet] GEN p.n.   GEN land RF word-spirit GEN

      tasukuru kuni so.   MYS 13.3254
      help   land EI
      'The land of Yamato is a land that the word-spirit helps.'

(18) ... yo   no   naka ha kazu   naki   mono so. MYS 17.3973
      world GEN midst RF number is lacking thing EI
      '... the world is nothing worth counting.'

If we examine the contexts in which the above examples were used, it is not difficult to read the *so* as referring to some referent just mentioned in the discourse, or about to be mentioned, which is a meaning that demonstrative *so* 'that one right there/now evident/just mentioned' could have contributed. In (15), it is *Yamato no kuni* 'the Land of Yamato' that is being identified by means of *so*, and this name was just mentioned (prior to what is quoted in (15)) in the same poem. Thus, *Umasi kuni so* can be read as *Umasi kuni, so* 'A fine land, that' with little change in meaning. In a similar way, *kotodama no tasukuru kuni so* in (17) can be read as ... *tasukuru kuni, so* 'a land that the word-spirit helps, that', if we read *so* here as referring to the ... *Yamato no kuni* that was just mentioned. Example (18) allows the same possibility, in that the *so* that predicates *kazu naki mono* can be read as reterring to the just mentioned *yo no naka*, as an afterthought topic: *kazu naki mono, so* 'a worthless thing, that'.

While its basic function was to establish an identification, *so/zo* was also used, like *ka*, in the predication of interrogative words and phrases, that is, in the seeking of an identification. This function is illustrated in the following examples.

(19) Hototogisu nani no   kokoro zo.   MYS 17.3912
     cuckoo   what GEN heart EI
     'Cuckoo, what are your intentions?'

(20) Izuku yori ki-tari-si   mono zo.   MYS 5.802
     where from come-PRF-EF thing EI
     'What manner of being are they, coming from we know not where?'

(21) Waga seko wo   itu zo ima ka to matu nahe ni   MYS 8.1535
     my   man ACC when EI now DI Q wait time LOC

     omo ya ha mie-mu aki no kaze huku.
     face RS RF become visible-SUP autumn GEN wind blow
     'As I wait for my man, [thinking] "When is it? Is it now?",
     will his face appear? The fall winds blow.'

(22) Ta   so, kare.   MYS 8.1535
     when EI that one (over there)
     'Who is it, that person over there?'

(23) Rei   nara-zu   ihu ha tare zo.   MS 7
     precedent COP-NEG say RF who EI
     'The one who speaks out so differently there, who is it?'

(24) Are,   ta   so ya.   MS 104
     that one over there who EI RS
     'That person over there, who is it?'

However, it is only when used after interrogative words and phrases, as in (19) through (24), that *so/zo* is used in the posing of a question. Here again, we may imagine *so* or *zo* as pronoun *so* 'that right there/just evident/ mentioned', and see how such an interpretation fits the context. It works well enough in example (19), where the speaker is addressing the cuckoo and asking about its behavior (singing), which s/he has observed and is, indeed, responding to: *nani no kokoro, so* 'what do you mean by it, that?' The final *so* of (20) could easily refer to the *kodomo* 'children' just mentioned in the same poem; these 'children' are indeed the topic of this question, so a reading like *izuku yori kitarisi mono, so* works fine as 'What ... are they, ..., those [little] ones?' In (21), the longed for appearance of the speaker's husband's face, mentioned in the next line, could well be the referent of a pronoun *so*, if we read *ima so* as *ima, so* as 'now, that [event]?' If we read *ta, so* into the *ta so* of (22), pronoun *so* would refer to the same referent as pronoun *kare*, postposed here as an afterthought topic. Or, it could be understood as referring to that referent less directly, through the word *kare*. This would make it an instance of of demonstrative *so*'s role in referring to information established in the discourse (in contrast to *ka* and *kare*).[27] Reference to something just mentioned might explain the use of a pronoun *so* in (24), to refer to the topic *are*. Example (23) is straightforward; pronoun *so* could refer to the just mentioned topic *rei nara-zu ihu* 'the one who speaks out so differently'. Or it might have been addressed to the very person who so spoke out; this would give us *so* in the mesial sense of 'the one in front of me', or 'you'. In either case, the referent is outside the speaker's present location, but nearby -- whether ostensively or in the discourse.

At this point, we may take note of a certain complementarity in the functions participated in by *ka* on the one hand, and *so/zo* on the other. Each OJ particle had its main function, which we have characterized as problematizing, and thus seeking, an identification for *ka*, and making an identification for *so/zo*. *Ka*, however, also played a central role in the predication of exclamatory identifications (especially when focus/quantifying particle *mo* was also involved), just as *so/zo* participated in the seeking of identifications, provided an interrogative word was involved. Why should this be? We might say that because *ka* was a marker of doubt, a question particle, it lent itself to expressing disbelief and surprise, and thus exclamatory identification, under the right conditions. This is probably true in some sense, but why was *ka* and not *ya* put to work in this way? We might take a similar tack for the use of *so/zo* in information questions, and note that in its role as positive identifier, it serves to emphasize the interrogative word. That it does this is true enough, but why not just use *ka*?

The answer would seem to lie a little further back in history, before either word became a sentence or focus (kakari) particle. Demonstrative pronoun *ka* would have fit the role of seeking identifications better than *so* because of its potential for referring to familiar, previously established referents -- the kind of referent that an identification-seeking question routinely presupposed. Demonstrative *so* would not have been as well suited to this function, since it referred to information just recently evident (nearby at the moment of speaking, or just mentioned in the ongoing discourse). But this very function of pointing out referents that are only now evident, yet outside the speaker, would have made demonstrative *so* well suited to making new identifications. Demonstrative *ka* would have been less well suited to this role, since it referred instead to already established knowledge. If *ka* were to be used in making new identifications, it might be

---

[27] But *ta(re)* shows such an affinity for *so/zo*, as opposed to *ka*, in Old Japanese and Early Middle Japanese, that combinations like *ta so* and *tare zo* may well have been collocational or, in the case of *ta so*, lexical. This would of course mean that the use of *so* was no longer a choice situated in the act of speaking, but something that simply came as part of asking 'who?' Pronoun *so* could have become associated with *ta(re)* by refferring to either 'you', or to a person just referred to in the discourse.

expected to do so with a referent that had been known all along, but not recognized or appreciated for what it was until just now -- a fair characterization of some, if not all, of the referents for which we find *ka* used to make exclamatory identifications (cf. examples (3), (4), (5) above).

Perhaps it does not need mentioning, but the same sort of afterthought scope or referent checks with demonstrative pronouns, which we hypothesize may have put pronouns *ka* and *so/zo* after content interrogatives, remain common in today's spoken language. Consider, for example, the following.

(25) Nan da, are.
what COP that one (we know/over there)
'What is [it]?--that.' 'What's THAT?'

(26) Nani, sore.
what that one (just mentioned/right there)
'What [is it]? -- that you just said.' or 'What do you mean by that?'

(27) Dare, sore.
who that one (just mentioned/right there)
'Who [is it]?--that one.' or 'Who's THAT [you're talking about]?'

Given the presupposing nature of content interrogatives, and the use of demonstrative *ka* to refer to assumable, already known referents, pronoun *ka* (and today, *are*) would seem far better suited to such work than *so*. Indeed, in terms of pure numbers, the use of *ka* in OJ and EMJ content interrogatives clearly outstrips that of *so*. But what if the content question were about something just mentioned, or just evident in the speech situation? If the question was about the identity of such a referent, this might have been a role for demonstrative *so*, since it was in the business of this kind of reference. Examples (19) through (24) seem to suggest such a contextual motivation for the use of *so/zo* with content interrogatives.

One final point to make concerning OJ and EMJ sentence-final *so/zo* is that, again like *ka*, this identifying, quasi-copular particle, true to this function, followed only referring words, that is, nouns and nominalized clauses. If *so/zo* predicated an inflecting word (verb, adjective, copula, inflecting suffix), that word occurred in its nominalizing rentai inflection, in a finite Referential Predicate, as described for *ka* earlier.

(28) Aga koromo sureru   ni   ha ara-zu ... hagi   no   sureru   so.
my robes   rubbed^{RT} LOC RF be-NEG bush clover GEN rubbed^{RT} EI
'It's not that my robes are relief dyed; it's that the bush clover rubbed against them [when I went to Takamatsu].'   MYS 10.2101

This poem shows us how an RP might be predicated with either the inflecting copula *nari* (here clefted into its *ni* and *ari* components, to support the contrastive use of restricted focus/quantifying particle *ha*) or the noninflecting quasi-copula *so/zo*. The referent under identification with these RPs is the stain on the speaker's robes. The speaker is at pains to identify how is it that they got that way. The first RP tells us 'It's not that they've been relief dyed (whatever else may have happened)', and the second RP identifies what is actually the case: 'It's that they've been rubbed against by the bush clover.'

(29) ... uti-ide-haberi-nuru zo.   TM
     come out-(-)-PF^{RT} EI
     'It's that I'm going to come out [with it].'

Example (29) is from *Taketori monogatari* 'Tale of the Bamboo Cutter' (Early Middle Japanese), specifically a scene in which the heroine, Kaguyahime, explains to her earthly stepparents why she is so distraught. This statement is made just before she reveals to them a truth she has long felt she could not: that that she must return to the moon. In the sentence immediately preceding (29), she has identified her behavior up to this point (*ima made sugosi-haberi-turu nari* 'It's that I've let it [revealing the truth, that she must return to the moon] pass until now'); note the use of an RP, predicated with inflecting copula *nari*. She then relents (*sa nomi ya ha* 'that, I just [couldn't do]'), and speaks the line quoted in (29). This RP, with the help of *zo*, identifies her present situation, which explains to her parents why they are finally about to hear what she the goes on to confess.

     Both (28) and (29) show *zo* in its quasi-copular role of identifying a referent evident in the immediate context (the stain on the robes in (28), the imminent confession in (29)) with an RP.

OJ *so/zo* in kakari-musubi

     Like *ka*, *so/zo* was also used medially after focused phrases, in the kakari-musubi construction. A *so/zo* on the kakari phrase serves to identify it with the the description given in the following rentai-inflected musubi. Thus, while *ka*'s basic function, at the end of sentences and in kakari-musubi, was to seek an identification, *so/zo*'s was to establish one. In both cases, the kakari phrase was to be identified with the description given in the rentai-inflected musubi, which, as we have seen, most likely originated in an afterthought topic.

     While interrogative words occur regularly in the kakari of Old Japanese kakari-musubi examples, even in OJ, *so/zo* is little attested with them in this context, and in Early Middle Japanese, it tends to occur mainly with *ta(re)*.

(30) Tare zo oho-mahe ni   mawosu.   Kojiki (ge, Yuuryaku)
     who EI (+)-front   LOC say (-)^{RT}
     'Who is it who speaks before [the Throne]?'

(31) Tare so kono ya   no   to osoboru.   MYS 14.3460
     who EI this   house GEN door push^{RT}
     'Who is it who pushes on the door of this house?'

(32) ... momizi   wo   ba tori-te so sinohu.   MYS 1.16
     red leaves ACC RF take-PF EI appreciate^{RT}
     'It's [after] having picked them that I enjoy them.'

The identifying function of *so/zo* in this construction would have simply been the quasi-copular nominal-predicating use described above for examples (15) through (26). (This use would have been the grammaticalized product of demonstrative pronoun *so* used as an afterthought confirmation of the referent of the preceding predicate.) The stages whereby pronoun *so/zo* became quasi-copular *so/zo*, and the quasi-copular, the kakari particle, would have been the same as described for *ka* in (12) and (13). The particle *so/zo* would have reached particle status when it lost its predicating punch, and simply emphasized one constituent of a single RP (a development analogous to (13c) above). This seems to have been underway from early on, in sentences like (33).

(33) ... a ga   noreru   uma   so tumaduku ihe   kohu   rasi   mo.
        I GEN be riding horse EI trips   home long for seems IF
        '[It's that] the horse I'm on stumbles. They must miss us at home!'
                                                                    MYS 3.365

A superstition apparently held that if a traveler's horse tripped on the road, people you left back home were thinking of you. There is clearly an emphasis on *uma* 'horse' here, but it may not have been so strong as a translation like 'It's the horse I'm on, he stumbles' or 'It's my horse that stumbles' would suggest. Since the speaker's conclusion (*kohu rasi mo*) is based on the fact of the horse's having stumbled, and not on it having been the horse (as opposed to the speaker) that stumbled, the best interpretation for the kakari-musubi of (33) would seem to be one that takes the NP focused with *so* as internal to a single RP, the main predicator of which is *tumaduku*. What the speaker is saying is something along the lines of 'What's happened is --. That means --!'

To sum up, *so/zo*'s primary use was to establish rather than problematize an identification. Its secondary function, which emerged only in the company of content interrogatives, was to put an identification at issue. In this way, *so* complements *ka* precisely, since *ka*'s primary function was to put an identification at issue, to problematize it. It was only in the absence of 'wh-' words that *ka* became involved in the establishment of identifications, and then less with commitment than in surprised recognition. This complementary sharing of functional load parallels in a striking way the difference between the different kinds of epistemic deixis expressed with demonstratives *ka* and *so*: the already known, preexisting familiarity indexed by *ka*, and the familiarity created by either presence in the here-and-now ('that right there, by you'), or by recent mention in the current discourse (discourse deixis, anaphora), of *so*.

Conclusion

There are, then, several "funny" things about Old Japanese (and Early Middle Japanese, for that matter) sentence (*syuu zyosi*) and focus (kakari *zyosi*) particles *ka* and *so/zo*, that suggest a persistence of some earlier meanings. These quirks can be taken as preliminary evidence that particles *ka* and *so/zo* originated in demonstrative pronouns *ka* and *so*, respectively. First, there is the homophony of the particles with the pronouns -- hardly conclusive in itself, but a hint of the kind that Roman Jakobson, for one, would insist on looking into. There is the ubiquitous use in Japanese, then and now, of an afterthought utterance of a completed predication's scope, or topic. This was done with pronouns or other referring expressions in Old Japanese, as it is done today, after content interrogative predicates (cf. (25) through (27) above) as well as other kinds.

Another odd thing about particles *ka* and *so/zo* is that they only governed referring expressions, that is, nominals. But this makes perfect sense if we understand them as quasi-copular predicators, whose job it was to problematize (*ka*) or make (*so/zo*) an identification -- a function that can be shown to follow naturally from demonstrative pronouns *ka* and *so*. It seems clear that *ka* and *so/zo* would have done just this, if uttered after the kinds of clauses that we find them used after in the extant texts. These quasi-copular functions (problematizing and making an identification, respectively) can also be seen to fit a functional, dynamic account of the parts played by *ka* and *so/zo* in the kakari-musubi construction.

There is also the possibility, examined briefly here, that when operating outside their basic uses (problematizing an identification for *ka*; making one, for *so/zo*), each tends to show an affinity for contexts where the associated demonstrative pronoun's particular kind of reference would make sense. When *ka* participates in a positive identification, for example, it is often an identification of a long-standing, previously known referent in what is for the speaker new terms, and surprised recognition. When *so/zo* is used in problematizing an identification with an *i-* ('wh-') word, this often happens in contexts in which the scope of that interrogative word is something that is ostensively present, or has just been mentioned.

What, finally, of evidence for the identity of *ka* or *so/zo* from related languages? While in the case of *so/zo* there is no apparent Korean cognate, for *ka* there is the interrogative particle attested in middle Korean as *ka/kwo*. The course of development hypothesized in this paper has been kept internal to Japanese, in the interests of seeing how convincing the internal case might be and what avenues of investigation it might suggest for the origins of possible long-lost relatives. It may be that Korean interrogative *ka/kwo* and Japanese *ka* were one and the same morpheme in an earlier Koreo-Japonic, or even Tungusic, ancestor. Or, it may be that they were parallel but historically distinct developments internal to Korean and Japanese, respectively.[28] It would help to know what kinds of etymologies have been proposed for *ka/kwo* . It does not seem that *ka/kwo* was a simple interrogative marker, although my knowledge of the matter is at present too limited to hazard even a guess as to how its use was constrained.

Be that as it may, if a convincing case for a single Koreo-Japonic *ka/kwo* is to be made, it would seem that it will be made with a study that not only notes the obvious phonological and rough functional (i.e.

---

[28] There are numerous instances in the natural world where morphologically (anatomically) similiar organisms have evolved independently, just as organisms with a common ancestor may go on to develop similar features, each independently of the other.

interrogative) similarities, but also explores the question of discourse-pragmatic similarities, as they are attested or not, in the extant Old Japanese, Early Middle Japanese, and Middle Korean texts, to begin with. Insofar as the story proposed here for the reanalysis and grammaticization of Japanese *ka* is a plausible one, it provides a testable hypothesis for the origins of either an earlier Koreo-Japonic (-Tungusic?) *ka/kwo* or of parallel but historically unrelated developments of *ka/kwo* in Korean and *ka* in Japanese. But these are questions for another day.

References

Fujitani Nariakira. 1776 (1960). *Ayuishoo*, in Nakada Norio and Takeoka Masao, eds., 1960. *Ayuishoo shinchuu 'Ayuishoo* newly annotated'. Tokyo: Kazama Shobo.

Halliday, M.A.K. 1985. *An Introduction to Functional Grammar*. London: Edward Arnold.

Hashimoto Shiroo. 1983 (S 57). "*Shijigo no shiteki tenkai*," pp. 217-40 in Kawabata Yoshiaki et al., eds., *Kooza Nihongo-gaku 2: Bunpoo-shi*. Tokyo: Meiji shoin.

Hock, Hans H. 1986. *Principles of Historical Linguistics*. Berlin: Mouton de Gruyter.

Hopper, Paul J. and Elizabeth Closs Traugott. 1993. *Grammaticalization*. New York: Cambridge University Press.

Jodaigo jiten henshu iinkai, eds. 1967. *Jidai betsu kokugo daijiten, joodai-hen*. Tokyo: Sanseido.

Jorden, Eleanor Harz with Mari Noda. 1987. *Japanese: the Spoken Language Part 1*. New Haven: Yale University Press.

Katagiri Yoichi, Fukui Teisuke, Takahashi Masaji, and Shimizu Yoshiko, eds. 1972. *Taketori monogatari, Ise monogatari, Yamato monogatari, Heichuu monogatari*. Nihon koten bungaku zenshuu. Tokyo: Shogakukan.

Kojima Noriyuki, Kinoshita Masatoshi, Satake Akihiro, eds. 1971-75. *Manyooshuu* vols. 1-4. Nihon koten bungaku zenshuu. Tokyo: Shogakukan.

Li, Charles. 1977. *Mechanisms of Syntactic Change*. Austin: University of Texas Press.

Li, Charles, and Sandra A. Thompson. 1977. "A Mechanism for the Development of Copula Morphemes," pp. 419-444 in Charles Li, ed. 1977. *Mechanisms of Syntactic Change*. Austin: University of Texas Press.

Nakada Norio and Takeoka Masao, eds., 1960. *Ayuishoo shinchuu 'Ayuishoo* newly annotated'. Tokyo: Kazama Shobo.

Nakada Norio, Wada Toshimasa, and Kitahara Yasuo, eds. 1983. *Kogo daijiten*. Tokyo: Shogakukan.

Ogiwara Asao and Konosu Hayao, eds. 1973. *Kojiki, Joodai kayoo*. Nihon koten bungaku zenshuu. Tokyo: Shogakukan.

Ôno Susumu, Maeda Kingoro, and Satake Akihiro, eds. 1974. *Iwanami kogo jiten*. Tokyo: Iwanami shoten.

Ôno Susumu. 1993. *Kakari* musubi *no kenkyuu*. Tokyo: Iwanami shoten.

Quinn, Charles J. 1987. *A Functional Grammar of Predication in Classical Japanese*. University of Michigan Ph.D. dissertation. Ann Arbor: University Microfilms International.

Quinn, Charles J. 1994. *Kodai Nihongo* 'kakari-musubi' *kinoo ron* ('A Functional Study of the kakari-musubi construction in Early Japanese'). *Nihon Bunka Kenkyu Hokoku* 30: 1-49.

Quinn, Charles J. 1996. "Point of View in the Clause: A Rhetorical Look at *Kakari-Musubi*," in robert Borgen, Thomas Hare, and Sharalyn Orbaugh, eds. 1996. *The Distant Isle: Essays and Translations in Honor of Robert H. Brower*. Ann Arbor: University of Michigan Center for Japanese Studies.

Quinn, Charles J. Forthcoming. *A Reader's Grammar of Classical Japanese* (tentative title). Ann Arbor: University of Michigan Center for Japanese Studies.

Sakakura Atsuyoshi. 1993. *Nihongo hyoogen no nagare* ('The stream of expression in Japanese'). Iwanami seminaa bukkusu 45. Tokyo: Iwanami Shoten.

Schwegler, Armin. 1988. "Word-order changes in predicate negation strategies in Romance languages," *Diachronica* 5: 21-58.

Appendix of abbreviations and symbols

ACC accusative (*wo*)
COP copula (*nari*)
DI doubted identity (*ka*)
EI established identity (*so/zo*)
EF established fact (*-ki*)
EEF externally established fact (*-keri*)
GEN genitive
IC ideational content
IF inclusive focus/quantification (*mo*)
IZ izen
LOC locative (*ni*)
MS *Makura no sooshi*
MYS *Manyooshuu*
NEG negation
OPT optative (*-mu*) ☐

PF perfective (*-tu, -nu*)
PRF perfect (*-ri, -tari*)
Q quotative (*to*)
RF restricted focus/
     quantification (*ha*
RP referential predicate
RS response soliciting (*ya*)
RT rentai
TM *Taketori monogatari*
(+) honorific
(-) humble

The *Kakari* Particle *Namu* in Heian Discourse

J. PAUL WARNICK

Brigham Young University / Ohio State University

0. Introduction[1]

The *kakarimusubi* construction seems to occupy a prominent position in discussions of Classical Japanese,[2] in part because of its frequent occurrence in classical texts and in part, perhaps, because it is has no formal counterpart in modern Japanese. *Kakarimusubi* is usually described as a 'phenomenon' (*gensyoo*) of Classical Japanese (e.g. see Shibatani 1990, Iwabuchi 1977, Oono 1974, Nihongo Kyooiku Ziten 1982, Nihon Kokugo Daiziten 1973, Nihon Bunpoo Daiziten 1971), and because it has been viewed traditionally as a syntactic phenomenon, discussion often seems to begin and end with a description of its syntactic properties, with little discussion of any discourse or pragmatic functions associated with it. Oono (1993) points out that most research regarding *namu*, for example, has examined only the genres in which it was used and how often it appeared. As recently as a dozen years ago, it was noted that little had been done in investigating the substance of the relationship between the particles and their corresponding predicates in

---

[1] I am greatly indebted to Charles Quinn for helpful comments regarding this paper and also for many enlightening discussions on this and other related topics.

[2] Defined here primarily as the language used during the Heian period.

91

kakarimusubi (Hoojoo 1983).   Since that time, a few notable works have appeared (e.g. Quinn 1987, 1994, Oono 1993, Takeuchi 1986), although there is still much room for fruitful research examining the nature of *kakarimusubi* in discourse contexts.   While its syntactic nature is also important and interesting, one wonders what discourse functions were associated with *kakarimusubi* that led to its use in some places while not in others and what factors led to the use of a given *kakari* particle rather than another.

In this paper I will focus on the *kakari* particle *namu*[3] and attempt to identify the discourse functions associated with its use. I will first review how this particle has been treated in discussions of *kakarimusubi* and then discuss the nature of its use in a selection from *Genji Monogatari*. I hope to show that an examination of the discourse contexts of its use demonstrate that there is more to *namu* than its syntactic properties.

1.   *Kakarimusubi*

The term *kakarimusubi* refers to a construction in which the occurrence of a *kakari* particle in a sentence influences or affects the inflection of the predicate. With particles *zo, namu, ya, ka*, and *koso*, the main clause predicate does not appear in the usual *syuusi* inflection (the conclusive or non-past indicative form). With the first four, rather, the accompanying predicate, the *musubi*, appears in the *rentai* inflection (the attributive or adnominal form). In the case of *koso*, the main clause predicate appears in the *izen* inflection[4] (the realis conditional or provisional form).   I will focus on the *rentai* inflection here, inasmuch as it provides the *musubi* for *namu*.

Kakarimusubi is thus referred to as an agreement relation (e.g. see Oono 1974, Nihon Kokugo Daiziten 1973).   Shibatani (1990) calls the *kakari* particle a 'relation opener', with the *musubi*, the agreeing inflected predicate, providing the 'tying' or 'conclusion'.

2.   *Namu*

The particle *namu* is generally grouped with *zo* as an emphatic particle, said to give emphasis to the element it follows (Oono 1993, Shibatani 1990, McCullough 1988, Iwabuchi 1977, Iwai 1976, Ikeda 1975, etc.). *Namu* is characterized as being somewhat softer, or less forceful than *zo*. In addition,

---

[3]The sequence *namu* has multiple interpretations in Classical Japanese; in using the term I am referring to the *kakari* particle only (discussed below).

[4]In the Nara period, adjectival predicates associated with *koso* appeared in the *rentai* inflection as well.

Iwai (1976) indicates that *namu* is used to call attention to the element it marks. Oono (1974) says that it indicates a softened, polite conclusion or decision.

Its distribution in classical texts shows that it appeared frequently in representations of spoken language in telling tales, in conversations, letters, and so forth, as well as cases where the narrator speaks to the reader (*soosizi*) (Takeuchi 1986). Evidently its use was relatively rare in more ritualized language forms such as *waka* poetry (Quinn 1987, Kokubo 1985, Oono 1993). This would indicate that in addition to its function of emphasizing, it also indexed a certain interpersonal stance on the part of the speaker in relation to the hearer, a stance which seemingly was not generally appropriate for more formalized genres. Takeuchi (1986) points out that *namu* tended to be used when the speaker was showing awareness of and concern for the hearer. She points out that its emphatic nature consists of its highlighting in order to heighten the interest and concern of the hearer regarding what is being said, suggesting a desire to have the hearer accept what is being said sympathetically.

The origin of *namu* as a *kakari* particle is not entirely clear, although it seems to have come from *namo*, an attested form used in the Nara period (Oono 1993, Takeuchi 1986, Hoojoo 1983, Hashimoto 1969, Sansom 1928). According to Quinn (personal communication), perhaps an earlier ancestor is *naru mo*, also an attested form, with *naru* being the *rentai* form of the copula *nari*. If this is the case, and if the *mo* is the inclusive focus particle, which seems likely, this gives credence to the idea that the use of *namu* indexes an interpersonal stance, since *mo* also relies on shared knowledge in that it presupposes familiarity with the set in which the marked element is to be included.

The examples below, taken from *Genji Monogatari*, do seem to indicate that there is more involved with the use of *namu* than mere emphasis.[5]

(1)   ... namida wo   sahe <u>nan</u> otosi-   haberi-<u>si</u>.   (p.142)
         tear   ACC IFP KP let fall be   FACT

---

[5]Note that all Japanese references are from Nihon Koten Bungaku Zensyuu (Shogakukan, 1970); the English references are taken from the Seidensticker (1976) translation. The occurrences of *namu* are underlined, as are the *rentai* inflections in the predicates (the *musubi*). Note that *namu* is also rendered *nan*. The transcription reflects the orthographic representation in the text. A list of abbreviations used in the glosses appears in Appendix A. While the glosses are not detailed completely, they are sufficient for my purposes here. A complete list of the occurrences of *namu* discussed here is shown in Appendix B, in the order of appearance in the text.

'... and I would join them in their sniffling ... ' (p.25)

(2)   ... sasuga ni   wa ga   misute- te- N   noti wo
        indeed COP I   GEN discard ASP SUP after ACC
      sahe _nan_, omohiyari   usiromi- tari- _si_. (p.151-2)
      IFP KP be considerate care for ASP FACT
      'She was seeing to my needs even now that I had apparently
      discarded her.' (p.30)

(3)   ... onoko simo _nan_, sisainaki   mono ha   haberu-me_ru_ to ...
        man EMP KP meaningless thing RFP be   SUP QUOT
      (p.162)
      'A stupid, senseless affair, a man tells himself, ... ' (p.35)

Note that in the first two examples *namu* immediately follows the particle *sahe*, which is a particle of inclusive focus. *Sahe* serves to indicate that the element it marks is to be included with other elements of the same sort (McCullough 1988, Ikeda 1975). In (3), *namu* follows *simo*, a combination of particles which is said to emphasize the preceding element (Ikeda 1975). Obviously, in none of these cases is one of the particles dependent on the other for its interpretation as a particle of emphasis or focus. It would seem then, that if *namu* can immediately follow a separate, independent particle of emphasis or focus, as seen here, with both particles (*sahe* and *namu*, or *simo* and *namu*) having scope over the same portion of the sentence (*namu* obviously having scope over the preceding particle as well), we must conclude there is more to *namu* than its function in providing emphasis. I will return to this point again shortly.

3.   Functions of *Kakarimusubi*

In reference to *kakarimusubi*, Yamaguchi (1987) points out that if *kakari* particles related only to the element they follow, they would not be expected to have an effect on the form of the predication at the end of the sentence. They would be no different from any other particle, since all particles serve to relate the preceding element to something else.

Yamaguchi suggests, rather, that the *kakari* particles seem to have scope over much more. He discusses Nitta's idea that a sentence has two levels, one which represents the expression situation (*iiarawasi zitai*) and one the expression attitude (*iiarawasi taido*). Nitta suggests further that this expression attitude has a judgment modality (*handan no muudo*) and a transmission or communication modality (*dentatu no muudo*). The former consists of various aspects of the judgment about the expression situation, while the latter consists of various aspects of the communication as related to the hearer. If Nitta is correct in suggesting that *kakarimusubi* is the province of the latter, the communication modality, it is not merely a syntactic phenomenon; there is something about *kakarimusubi* which relates to the relationship between the speaker, the information, and the hearer.

Yamaguchi goes on to say that the idea of a sentence having an objective aspect (Nitta's expression situation) and a subjective aspect (Nitta's expression attitude) is widely accepted. This distinction corresponds to Halliday's (1985) representation of meaning as having ideational, textual, and interpersonal components. The ideational meaning refers to the context of what is represented (Nitta's expression situation), the textual to the context of how the information is staged, and the interpersonal to the context of an interactive exchange (Nitta's expression attitude) (see Quinn 1987, 1993). If *kakarimusubi* is, in fact, part of the transmission or communication modality related to the expression attitude, we should be able to see how consideration of the hearer is involved in the use of *namu*. This I will attempt to do below.

It is interesting to note that McCullough (1988) and Oono (1974) claim that *kakarimusubi* affects the inflection of the predicate without changing the meaning of the sentence. The meaning to which they refer can only be understood as the ideational meaning or the expression situation.

Quinn (1994) provides a careful attempt at establishing a coherent theory regarding the functions of *kakarimusubi*. He claims that *namu* serves to raise for the hearer the focus of the element it marks, with the accompanying *musubi* serving to confirm the proposition which includes that focus. This suggests there is a textual component (in Halliday's terms) to *namu* in that it affects the way the utterance is staged. As a point of reference, Quinn states that *zo* identifies the element it marks, with the accompanying *musubi* indicating the presupposition underlying the identification. Both *namu* and *zo* serve to highlight, but the purpose of that highlight differs.

Elsewhere, Quinn (1987) discusses the relationship between the use of *namu* and that of the modern *ne(e)*, suggesting a common function between them. He states that as with *ne(e)*, *namu* serves to suggest to the hearer that the portion of the message it marks is presented by the speaker as a place to 'touch base', a solicitous gesture on the part of the speaker indicating s/he is addressing the hearer sympathetically. This indicates an interpersonal stance, and agrees with Nitta's contention that there is a 'communication' modality associated with *kakarimusubi*. These arguments suggest that while there is no ideational component to *namu*, there is a textual and an interpersonal component involved.

4. The *Rentai* inflection and the indexing of information

As noted above, the predicate associated with *namu* appears in the *rentai* inflection. Quinn (1994) summarizes the various uses of the *rentai* inflection in Japanese, including those in *kakarimusubi*, and notes a common function: all the nonadnominal uses of the *rentai* inflection serve to nominalize a clause and in each case, the nominalization seems to index a certain level of commitment to the factuality of the information in the given clause. In main clauses, the nominalization serves as a referential predicate, 'grounding' that predicate and offering it as established information. It also often serves, more specifically, to provide explanation linking the predicate with the discourse context. It has been argued that the modern *no da* construction is the functional counterpart of this use of the *rentai* inflection (see Iwasaki 1993, Horie 1993, Yamaguchi 1987, Quinn 1987).

In terms of *kakarimusubi* appearing with the *rentai* inflection then, the *kakari* clause is the focus against the backdrop of the grounded *musubi*, with the *musubi* also providing links to the surrounding discourse (see Quinn 1987, 1993). The idea of established information or commitment to the factuality of information is discussed in the work of both Prince (1978) and Kamio (1994) as well.

Prince discusses how discourse context affects the use of wh-clefts and it-clefts in English. Based on an examination of the contexts of use for each, she concludes that each has a specialized function in English discourse. Example (4) is from Prince (1978:883).

(4) a. What John lost was his keys.
     b. It was his keys that John lost.

Prince points out that these two sentences have the same ideational meaning, to use Halliday's term, or the same expression situation, to use Nitta's term, namely, that John lost his keys. What differs is the indexing of the speaker's stance with regard to the information. Prince claims that wh-clefts mark the information in the wh-clause as assumed or assumable as given, which she defines as 'in the hearer's consciousness'. It-clefts, on the other hand, mark information in the that-clause as being a known fact (although not necessarily known to the hearer), with no assumption about the hearer's thinking. Each construction then suggests a different stance regarding how the information is related to the parties involved.

In related work, Kamio (1994) has developed the idea of territory of information. His theory suggests that the selection of a given syntactic structure is affected by the relationship of the information to the 'territory' of the speaker and that of the hearer. He provides the following examples (1994:70).

(5) a. Watasi, atama ga itai.
         I   head NM ache

'I have a headache.'

b.   ??Watasi, atama ga itai- tte.
       I   head NM ache HM
       Lit. 'I hear I have a headache.'

In (5a), the information is about the speaker's own experience. It would be considered part of the speaker's 'territory' but it would not be assumed to be part of the hearer's territory. Hence, a 'direct' syntactic form is used to express that information. Since the speaker's own headache is information in the speaker's territory, Kamio states that (5b), which indicates that the information is hearsay, is 'quite odd'. This is due to the conflict between the function of *tte* in indicating hearsay and the fact that information regarding the headache is expected to be knowledge available to the speaker through direct, personal experience.

These ideas (from Prince and Kamio) are relevant to *kakarimusubi* as well, in that this construction seems to be used when the speaker is assuming a particular stance in relation to the hearer and to the information at hand. In terms of Quinn's analysis, for example, *zo* is used when the speaker assumes that the information it marks is in his/her own territory, while not within that of the hearer. That is, the speaker is providing an identification s/he assumes is new to the addressee.

On the other hand, *namu* would be used when the speaker assumes that there is some overlap between his/her own territory and that of the hearer. By using *namu*, the speaker is indexing an interpersonal stance, indicating that the information *namu* marks is assumed to be understood or understandable (shared or shareable) by the hearer. In the next section, I will discuss a few of the examples I have examined which show that the focus provided by *namu* is clearly different from the identification focus associated with *zo* and *ka* (providing and seeking, respectively), as well as the questioning function of *ya*.

5.   Data and discussion

As noted above, *namu* is more likely to appear in texts which lend themselves to the use of elements with an interpersonal stance rather than in more ritualized genres. Since conversations do lend themselves to the expression of interpersonal stance, I selected the 'rainy night discussion' (*amayo no sinasadame*) of the 'Broom Tree' (*Hahakigi*) chapter of *Genji Monogatari* to examine the functions of *namu* in the context of discourse. This discussion plays a prominent role in the tale, inasmuch as it seems to be the catalyst that starts Genji on his search for love (Washimi 1981).

In the discussion, Genji and Too no Chuujoo, close friends since childhood, spend a rainy night relating their opinions of and experiences with women of different social station. They are joined by two young courtiers, Hidari no Muma no Kami and Too Shikibu no Joo. These two are urged by Genji and his friend to share their own stories and experiences. The intimate nature of the conversation and the relationship between the four men make this an ideal setting for examining interpersonal stance in discourse. This section of the tale provides an extended representation of their conversation, and we may conclude, at the very least, that the language represented is not atypical of actual Heian speech.

Bruner (1990) points out that stories are particularly 'viable instruments' for social negotiation. Relationships are negotiated and renegotiated through the telling of stories. Hence, the interpersonal and textual aspects of this discussion may be considered at least as important as its ideational one.

There were thirty-eight cases of *namu* in this portion of the tale. One case appeared in a section from the narrator (*soosizi*) and was therefore excluded from this study; I examined only those cases where *namu* was used in the conversation among the four men. As seen in Table 1, of the resulting thirty-seven cases, Genji used *namu* once, and Too no Chuujoo (Chujo hereafter) five times. Hidari no Muma no Kami (Muma no Kami) was responsible for twenty-three occurrences, and Too Shikibu no Joo (Shikibu) for eight. The latter two figures include cases when the speaker was quoting someone else in the process of relating a story. Table 1 also gives a rough estimate of how much each man contributed to the conversation as a whole. While not a strict correlation, the relative frequency of the use of *namu* corresponds with the overall contribution of each man to the conversation, showing that the ratio of the use of *namu* in the passage was fairly evenly distributed among the four men.

TABLE 1
Relative Use of *Namu* and General
Contribution to the Conversation

Participant	No. Uses of *Namu*	% of Total Uses of Namu	% of Conversation
Genji	1	2.7	3.5
Chujo	5	13.5	21.1
Muma no Kami	23	62.2	66.1
Shikibu	8	21.6	9.3
Totals	37	100.0	100.0

The first occurrence of *namu* in this passage appears in the initial part of the discussion. Chujo has asked to see Genji's love letters. As he is looking through some of them, Genji suggests that Chujo himself probably has quite a collection and expresses interest in seeing his friend's letters.

(6)   sate <u>nan</u>, kono zusi mo kokoroyoku hiraku be<u>ki</u> to ...   (p.132)
        then KP this   file IFP gladly   open EXP QUOT
        'When I have seen it I shall be happy to throw my files open to you.'
                (p.21)   (Genji)

Genji is confirming that he would readily open his files once Chujo has afforded the same opportunity: 'Then, you see, it's a situation where you can expect me to be happy to open my files.'

The next occurrence appears when Chujo laments to Genji that there are few flawless women.

(7)   ... yauyau   <u>namu</u> mi- tamahe- si<u>ru</u>.   (p.132)
            gradually KP   see (humble) know
        'This is a sad fact which I have learned over the years.'   (p.21)
        (Chujo)

The *namu* here is highlighting the fact that he came to this realization over time. Again, the interpersonal meaning is consistent with this use: 'What happened was, gradually, you see, I came to see ... '

The third case to be discussed (repeated from (1) above) occurs when Muma no Kami is talking about when he was a boy and would listen to the women read the old romance tales and how he would find the stories moving, just as the women did.

(8)   ... namida wo   sahe <u>nan</u> otosi- haberi-<u>si</u>.   (p.142)
            tear   ACC IFP KP let fall be   FACT
        '... and I would join them in their sniffling ... '   (p.25)   (Muma no
        Kami)

As noted above, the *namu* immediately follows the focus particle *sahe*. The *namu* is not needed to emphasize the tears per se; focus is brought to *namida wo* through the use of *sahe*. Rather, the *namu* seems to be commending the tears to the audience in a solicitous 'This is what I think you can appreciate -- I would even let fall the tears, you see.'

It is interesting to note the ordering or 'layering' of particles here. Not only is there a particle (*namu*) following *sahe*, it is preceded by a particle (*wo*) as well. The *wo* is a case particle, *sahe* is a focus particle, and the *namu* has an interpersonal function. This same kind of ordering can be seen in modern Japanese as well (e.g. *Nara kara wa ne ... , Nihon ni mo sa ... *). Quinn (personal communication) points out that with multiple particles, the relative ordering remains constant: the case particle appears first, followed by a particle of focus, which in turn is followed by a 'sentence particle', or in other words, a particle that modulates the preceding information interpersonally. The outermost type is always of an interpersonally significant nature, which further supports the idea that there is something interpersonal about *namu*.

The next example appears when Muma no Kami is discussing talent in calligraphy and painting and comparing the work of a master with that of one without great skill.

(9)   ... naho   ziti   ni   nan yori-   keru. (p.146)
        all the more essence LOC KP approach FACT
        '... the real thing is the real thing.' (p.27) (Muma no Kami)

Again, the *namu* serves as a textual highlight as well as functioning interpersonally. It signals that the speaker assumes the hearer will agree that what the work of a master is approaches the essence of a thing.

Example (10) appears when Muma no Kami is relating what he told a woman whom he found to be overly jealous. He told her that if she could lose her jealousy,

(10)   ... ito   ahare   to   nan omohu beki. (p.149)
        very feeling QUOT KP feel   EXP
        '... my affection is certain to grow.' (p.29) (Muma no Kami quoting his comment to the woman)

The *namu* in this case again can be understood to function similar to the *ne(e)* of modern Japanese: `(If you could lose your jealousy, then) you could expect me to feel affection, you see.' Note that *ne(e)* also appears within a sentence, as well as in sentence-final position, and serves to draw the hearer's attention by highlighting and indicating concern that the hearer is attending to the conversation and has understood what has been said to that point. As with *namu*, *ne(e)* also may appear following a variety of syntactic elements, including particles, nouns, and the verbal gerund.

Example (11) (from (2) above) occurs when Muma no Kami goes to see a woman he had not visited for some time. She was gone that particular day but he arrived and found his clothes laid out just as he liked them.

(11)　　... sasuga ni　wa ga　　misute- te-　N　noti wo　sahe <u>nan</u>,
　　　　　indeed COP I　GEN discard ASP SUP after ACC IFP KP
　　　　omohiyari　　usiromi- tari- <u>si</u>.　(p.151-2)
　　　　be considerate care for ASP FACT
　　　　'She was seeing to my needs even now that I had apparently
　　　　discarded her.'　(p.30)　(Muma no Kami)

As noted above, the *namu* here appears immediately following the focus
particle *sahe*. With both appearing together, there seems to be more than just
emphasis going on in the case of *namu*. It seems that the use of *namu* suggests
to the listeners that this is the part to which the speaker would like to draw
their attention and in addition suggest a shared understanding of the
significance of what he is saying.
　　　　In the next example, Muma no Kami is relating a incident when a
friend joined him one night as he traveled to his father's residence. The friend
indicated that

(12)　　kŏyohi hito　　matu-　ramu yado <u>nan</u>, ayasiku　kokoro
　　　　tonight person waiting　SUP　house KP　strangely heart
　　　　kurusi<u>ki</u>　to　　te ...　(p.154)
　　　　tormented QUOT CCB
　　　　'He was much concerned, he said, about a house where he was sure
　　　　someone would be waiting.'　(p.31)　　　　　(Muma no Kami quoting
　　　　the friend)

Again we note that the *namu* is providing focus (or highlight) on the lodging
where the woman would be waiting. It also serves to touch base with the
listener and present this information with an expectation of understanding.
The friend would certainly know that　Muma no Kami himself was
experienced in visiting women and would understand.
　　　　The last example we will examine is that which appeared in (3)
above. Shikibu is relating his affair with a woman socially much superior to
him. He suggests the futility of such a relationship.

(13)　　... onoko simo <u>nan</u>, sisainaki　　mono ha　haberu-me<u>ru</u>
　　　　man　EMP KP　meaningless thing RFP be　　SUP
　　　　to ...　(p.162)
　　　　QUOT
　　　　'A stupid, senseless affair, a man tells himself, ... '　　(p.35)
　　　　(Shikibu)

More literally, he is saying 'It seems there are senseless things men do too, you know.' With the *namu* following *simo*, which itself provides emphasis, we are again led to ask why the *namu* appears if its only function were to emphasize. As noted above, since it appears outside the focus particle *simo*, it must be somehow relevant to interpersonal concerns. It serves to highlight the marked element as the part of the sentence the speaker would like to use to 'touch base' with the listener. It proposes confirmation related to the information expressed and also confirmation suggested by the speaker that the listener is attending to the details of the story as the speaker intends. Particles like *sahe* and *simo* function as quantifier-like focus particles, while the nature of the focus with *namu* has more to do with modality and with the predicate.

In these various examples, we can see that *namu* certainly serves to focus or highlight the element it marks. However, to limit it to this function is to overlook its use in many discourse contexts. As we have seen, its use appears to be consistent with the confirmatory function of the modern *ne(e)*.

While not necessarily arguing that *ne(e)* has derived from *namu*, it is interesting that we seem to see the same functions in the same kinds of environments. Of course, it is impossible to 'prove' that *namu* had to have some interpersonal function. Being removed in time, we cannot see, for example, the reaction of the listeners when *namu* was used (nods, etc.). However, given the nature of its use, as seen in these examples, the best reading of *namu* seems to be as an index of interpersonal stance. It use does seem to carry interpersonal connotations.

Finally, in reference to the syntactic nature of the use of *namu* in this passage, it is interesting to note the kinds of syntactic elements followed by *namu*.

TABLE 2
Syntactic Elements Marked by *Namu*

Type	Count
Particles	14
Verbs/Zyodoosi	10
Nouns	7
Adjectives	4
Adverbs	2
Total	37

Table 3 shows the kinds of elements appearing as the final part of the predicates providing the *musubi* for *namu* in this passage. They are shown here in their *syuusi* inflections.

TABLE 3
Musubi Elements Appearing with *Namu*

Type	Count
ki	10
besi	8
keri	5
'bare' verb	5
'bare' adjective	2
meri	2
(no overt *musubi*)	2
raru	1
mazi	1
zu	1
Total	37

Future research will focus on the syntactic environments in which *namu* appears, based on the information in Tables 2 and 3, in a closer examination of the textual functions associated with *namu*.   It is interesting to note here, however, that *ki*, a subjective index of evidentiality occurs twice as often as its objective counterpart *keri*, which is not unexpected considering personal experiences are being related in this passage.   A majority of the predicate types appearing with *namu* in this passage are ones that index evidentiality or personal involvement, which is consistent with the nature of a discussion where intimate stories are told, subjective evaluations are made, and the speaker touches base with his listeners.

Table 4 indicates the relative frequency of *namu* in comparison with the other *kakari* particles appearing in the passage with an overt *musubi* element (the lack of one can sometimes lead to alternate interpretations).

TABLE 4
Relative Use of *Kakarimusubi* Constructions

Particle	Count
namu	37
zo	10
ka	10
ya	7
koso	16
Total	80

Namu was by far the most common *kakari* particle found in this selection, appearing in about 58% (37 of 64) of the cases with *rentai* inflection and about 46% (37 of 80) of the *kakarimusubi* cases overall. Again, this is not unexpected, given the nature of the conversation and the interpersonal nature of *namu*. Other *kakari* particles have more of an ideational aspect and have to do with the identification of discourse referents or questioning, as noted above. Due to the confirmative function of *namu*, providing a means whereby the speaker 'touches base' with the hearer, in a discussion among four acquaintances wherein they relate to each other similar intimate experiences, a speaking style which frequently uses such a device is not surprising.

6. Conclusion

In this paper I have reviewed briefly how *kakarimusubi* in general and *namu* in particular have been viewed traditionally and also more recently in more careful attempts to determine their associated discourse functions. I have examined occurrences of *namu* in a selection from *Genji Monogatari* that represents extended oral narrative and commentary. In looking at these examples in the context of their occurrence in discourse, it seems Quinn's (1994) analysis does explain the use of these constructions with greater accuracy and clarity than perhaps traditional analyses. Textually, *namu* highlights (against the ground of the *musubi*), but interpersonally, it does this by suggesting confirmation, assumed agreement, and shared knowledge.

There is much more work to be done in examining other representations of conversation, from *Genji Monogatari* as well as from other texts. Other kinds of examples need to be examined as well, such as cases where the narrator is addressing the reader (*soosizi*). There is more work to be done in examining the textual functions of *namu* by examining its use in relation to the surrounding predicates in the given context (the 'topography' of the discourse).

This kind of data provide the basis for a better analysis of the discourse functions of *namu*. A richer understanding of the functions of this and other *kakarimusubi* constructions contributes to a better accounting of *kakarimusubi* and thereby to a deeper understanding of classical texts and the culture which produced them.

APPENDIX A
Abbreviations Used in Glosses

ACC	Accusative particle	INST	Instrumental particle
ASP	Aspectual	KP	Kakari particle
CCB	Coordinate clause boundary	LOC	Locative particle

COND	Conditional	NEG	Negative
COP	Copula	NEG-EXP	Neg. Expectation
EMPH	Emphatic particle	NM	Nominative (Kamio)
EXP	Expectation	PL	Plural
FACT	Evidential	QUOT	Quote particle
GEN	Genitive	RFP	Restricted focus prt.
HM	Hearsay marker (from Kamio)	SUP	Suppositional
IFP	Inclusive focus particle		

APPENDIX B[6]
Examples of *Namu* in the 'Rainy Night Discussion'

1.   sate   <u>nan</u>, kono zusi mo kokoroyoku hiraku be<u>ki</u> to ...   (p.132)
       then KP   this   file   IFP gladly   open EXP QUOT
       'When I have seen it I shall be happy to throw my files open to you.'
       (p.21)   (Genji)

2.   ... yauyau   <u>namu</u> mi- tamahe- si<u>ru</u>.   (p.132)
       gradually KP   see (humble) know
       'This is a sad fact which I have learned over the years.'   (p.21)
       (Chujo)

3.   ... mi otorise-   nu   yau   ha   naku <u>nan</u> aru be<u>ki</u>
       compare unfavorably NEG situation RFP not   KP   be EXP
       to ...   (p.133)
       QUOT
       'The fact is not up to the advance notices.'   (p.22)   (Chujo)

4.   ... naka   no   sina ni   <u>nan</u>, hito   no   kokorogokoro
       middle GEN rank LOC KP   person GEN hearts
       onogazisi no   tatetaru omomuki mo mie- te,   wakaru
       several   GEN form   inclination IFP appear ASP be separated
       beki koto   katagata   ohokaru be<u>ki</u>.   (p.134)
       EXP thing various places many   EXP
       'When you come to the middle ranks, each woman has her own little
       inclinations and there are thousands of ways to separate one from
       another.'   (p.22)   (Chujo)

5.   ... omohu yori tagaheru koto <u>nan</u>, ayasiku   kokoro tomaru
       think   than different thing KP strangely heart   remain
       waza   na<u>ru</u>.   (p.136)

---

[6]As noted above (footnote 5), all Japanese references are from Nihon Koten Bungaku Zensyuu (Shogakukan, 1970); the English references are taken from the Seidensticker (1976) translation.

situation be
'The first surprise is hard to forget.'   (p.23)   (Muma no Kami)

6.   ... ohokaru naka   ni   mo e   <u>nan</u> omohisadamu-mazikari-
       many   within LOC IFP NEG KP select   NEG-EXP
    ke<u>ru</u>. (p.137)
    FACT
    'A man sees women, all manner of them, who seem to be beyond
    reproach, but when it comes to picking the wife who must be
    everything, matters are not simple.'   (p.24)   (Muma no Kami)

7.   ... taraha- de   asikaru   beki daizi-   domo <u>namu</u>
       sufficient NEG unpleasant FACT importance PL   KP
    katagata ohoka<u>ru</u>.   (p.138)
    various many
    '... the qualifications are altogether too many.'   (p.24)
    (Muma no Kami)

8.   ... namida wo   sahe <u>nan</u> otosi- haberi-<u>si</u>. (p.142)
       tear   ACC IFP KP let fall be   FACT
    '... and I would join them in their sniffling ... '   (p.25)
    (Muma no Kami)

9.   ... nan   naku siizuru   koto <u>nan</u>, naho   makoto no
       defect not   produce thing KP all the more real   GEN
    mono-no-zyauzu ha   sama koto ni   miewakare-
    master   RFP form thing LOC be distinguished
    habe<u>ru</u>. (p.145)
    be
    '... the perfection of the form announces that it is from the hand of a
    master.'   (p.26-7)   (Muma no Kami)

10.   ... sono kokorosirahi okite nado   wo   <u>nan</u>, zyauzu ha
      that care   place and so forth ACC KP   master RFP
    ito   ikihoi koto ni,   waromono ha   oyoba-nu
    very power thing LOC inferior   RFP reach NEG
    tokoro ohoka-me<u>ru</u>. (p.146)
    area   many SUP
    'It is here that the master has his own power. There are details a
    lesser painter cannot imitate.'   (p.27)   (Muma no Kami)

11.   ... naho   ziti   ni   <u>nan</u> yori-   ke<u>ru</u>. (p.146)
      all the more essence LOC KP approach FACT
    '... the real thing is the real thing.'   (p.27)   (Muma no Kami)

12.   ... zinen   ni   kokoro wosameraruru yau   ni   <u>nan</u>
      natural COP   heart calm   situation LOC KP
    haberi- <u>si</u>. (p.147)
    be   FACT

'In the course of time I began to mend my ways.' (p.27) (Muma no Kami)

13. ... tada   kono nikuki   kata hitotu <u>nan</u> kokoro wosame-zu
   merely   this   irritating   fault   one   KP   heart   calm   NEG
   haberi- <u>si</u>. (p.148)
   be   FACT
   '... save the one thing I found so trying.' (p.28) (Muma no Kami)

14. ... ito   ahare to   <u>nan</u> omohu be<u>ki</u>.   (p.149)
   very   feeling QUOT KP feel   EXP
   '... my affection is certain to grow.'   (p.29)   (Muma no Kami
   quoting his comment to the woman)

15. ito   kurusiku <u>nan</u> aru bekereba ...   (p.149)
   very   trying   KP be EXP
   'It will be much harder to pass the months and years in the barely
   discernible hope that you will settle down and mend your fickle
   ways.' (p.29) (Muma no Kami quoting the woman)

16. ... katamini somuki- nu   beki kizami ni   <u>namu</u> a<u>ru</u> to ...
   mutually part   ASP EXP time   COP KP   be QUOT
   (p.149)
   'Maybe you are right. Maybe this is the time to part.'   (p.29)
   (Muma no Kami quoting the woman)

17. ... sasuga ni   wa ga   misute- te-   N   noti wo   sahe <u>nan</u>,
   indeed COP   I   GEN discard ASP SUP   after ACC IFP KP
   omohiyari   usiromi- tari- <u>si</u>. (p.151-2)
   be considerate   care for   ASP FACT
   'She was seeing to my needs even now that I had apparently
   discarded her.' (p.30) (Muma no Kami)

18. arisinagara ha   e   <u>nan</u> misugusu-mazi-   <u>ki</u>. (p.152)
   as till now RFP NEG KP overlook   NEG-EXP FACT
   'Yet she went on saying that she could not forgive the behavior I had
   been guilty of in the past.'   (p.30)   (Muma no Kami quoting the
   woman)

19. aratame- te   nodoka ni   omohinara- ba   <u>nan</u>
   change   ASP settle   COP   consider so   COND KP
   ahimiru   be<u>ki</u> ...   (p.152)
   have relationship with   EXP
   'If I would settle down, she would be very happy to keep company
   with me.' (p.30) (Muma no Kami quoting the woman)

20. ... ito   itaku   omohinageki-te   hakanakunari-haberi-
   very   painful grieve   ASP die   be
   ni- sika- ba,   tahaburenikuku <u>namu</u>
   ASP FACT   because   regrettable   KP

oboe-   haberi-<u>si</u>. (p.152)

feel   be   FACT

'She was sad I gathered, and then without warning she died. And the game I had been playing came to seem rather inappropriate.' (p.30) (Muma no Kami)

21.   ... sabakari nite   ari- nu   beku <u>nan</u> omohi-tamahe-ideraru<u>ru</u>.

so   INST be ASP EXP KP recall (humble)

(p.152)

'I continue to regret what I had done.' (p.30) (Muma no Kami)

22.   ... sono kata mo gusi-   te,   urusaku <u>nan</u> haberi-<u>si</u>

that field IFP possess ASP superior KP be   FACT

to   te ... (p.152)

QUOT CCB

'... and in sewing she could have held her own with Princess Tanabata.' (p.30) (Muma no Kami)

23.   koyohi hito   matu- ramu yado <u>nan</u>, ayasiku   kokoro

tonight person wait SUP house KP   strangely heart

kurusi<u>ki</u>   to   te ... (p.154)

tormented QUOT CCB

'He was much concerned, he said, about a house where he was sure someone would be waiting.'   (p.31)   (Muma no Kami quoting the friend)

24.   ... mabayuki   kokoti <u>nan</u> si- haberi-<u>si</u>. (p.155)

disagreeable feeling KP feel be   FACT

'... I was very annoyed.' (p.31) (Muma no Kami)

25.   ima yori noti ha,   masite   sa   nomi <u>nan</u> omou-

now from after RFP   much more that way only   KP feel

tamaheraru be<u>ki</u>. (p.156)

(humble) EXP

'I have no doubt that the wariness will grow as the years go by.' (p.32)   (Muma no Kami)

26.   ... nasakenaku utatearu   koto wo <u>nan</u>, saru   tayori

heartless   unpleasant thing ACC KP suitable connection

ari-te,   kasumeihase- tari- ke<u>ru</u>, ... (p.158)

be ASP say indirectly ASP FACT

'Then ... my wife found a roundabout way to be objectionable.' (p.33) (Chujo)

27.   kore <u>nan</u>, e   tamotu-maziku   tanomosigenaki kata nari-

this KP NEG keep   NEG-EXP unpromising   sort be

ke<u>ru</u>. (p.160)

FACT

'She was, I fear, not the sort of woman one finds it possible to keep for very long.' (p.34) (Chujo)

28. ... kasikoki onna   no   tamesi   wo   <u>nan</u> mi-   tamahe-
    wise   woman GEN example ACC   KP   know (humble)
    <u>si</u>. (p.161)
    FACT

'... I knew a remarkably wise woman.' (p.35) (Shikibu)

29. ... subete kuti   akasu beku   <u>nan</u> habera-zari- <u>si</u>. (p.161)
    all   mouth open FACT KP   be   NEG FACT

'In a word, I was awed into silence.' (p.35) (Shikibu)

30. ... wa ga   hutatu no   miti utahu wo   kike to   <u>nan,</u>
    I GEN two   GEN way sing ACC listen QUOT KP
    kikoegoti-haberi-sika-   do, ...   (p.161)
    tell   be   FACT however

'... he made reference, among other things, to a Chinese poem about the merits of an impoverished wife.' (p.35) (Shikibu)

31. ... sono mono o   si   to   si-   te   <u>nan,</u>
    that person ACC teacher QUOT consider ASP KP
    wazuka naru ...   (p.162)
    few   be

'... and under her tutelage I managaed to turn out a few things in passable Chinese myself.' (p.35) (Shikibu)

32. ... hazukasiku <u>nan</u> mie-   haberi-<u>si</u>. (p.162)
    be daunted KP   appear bc   FACT

'... a man ... is somewhat daunted at the thought ... '   (p.35) (Shikibu)

33. ... onoko simo   <u>nan,</u> sisainaki   mono ha haberu-me<u>ru</u>
    man EMPH KP   meaningless thing RFP be   SUP
    to ...   (p.162)
    QUOT

'A stupid, senseless affair, a man tells himself, ... '   (p.35) (Shikibu)

34. ... kokoroyamasiki monogosi nite   <u>nan</u> ahi- te- habe<u>ru</u>.
    irritating   screen   INST KP   meet ASP be
    (p.163)

'She insisted on talking to me through a very obtrusive screen.' (p.35) (Shikibu)

35. ... ito   kusaki ni   yori   <u>nan,</u> e   taimen tamahara-<u>nu</u>.
    very foul   LOC depend KP   NEG meet   receive NEG
    (p.163)

'When I have disencumbered myself of this aroma, we can meet once more.' (p.36)   (Shikibu quoting the woman)

36. ... yosibami   nasakedata-zara- mu nan, meyasukaru be<u>ki</u>.
       put on airs   act elegant NEG SUP KP   becoming EXP
       (p.166)
       '... it is safer not to make a great show of taste and elegance; ... '
       (p.37)   (Muma no Kami)
37. ... hitotu hutatu no   husi ha   sugusu   beku <u>nan</u>
       one   two   GEN point RFP leave as is EXP KP
       a- bekari-ke<u>ru</u>   to ...   (p.166)
       be EXP   FACT QUOT
       '... she should keep back a little of what she is prepared to say.'
       (p.38)   (Muma no Kami)

References

Abe, Akio, Ken Akiyama, and Gen'e Imai, eds. 1970. Genji monogatari.
       Nihon Koten Bungaku Zensyuu, Vol. 1. Tokyo: Shogakukan.
Bruner, Jerome. 1990. Acts of meaning. Cambridge, Massachusetts:
       Harvard University Press.
Halliday, M.A.K. 1985. An introduction to functional grammar. London:
       Edward Arnold.
Hashimoto, Shinkichi. 1969. Zyosi/zyodoosi no kenkyuu. Tokyo:
       Iwanami.
Hoojoo, Tadao. 1983. Kokugo bunpoo ronsoo. Tokyo: Meiji Shoin.
Horie, Kaoru. 1993. From zero to overt nominalizer NO: a syntactic
       change in Japanese. Japanese/Korean linguistics 3, ed. by Choi
       Soonja, 305-321. Stanford: CSLI.
Ikeda, Tadashi. 1975. Classical Japanese grammar. Tokyo: Toho Gakkai.
Iwabuchi, E. 1977. Bungo bunpoo. Tokyo: Shuei Shuppan.
Iwai, Yoshio. 1976. Genji monogatari gohookoo. Tokyo: Kasama Shoin.
Iwasaki, Shoichi. 1993. Functional transfer in the history of Japanese
       language. Japanese/Korean linguistics 2, ed. by Patricia M. Clancy,
       20-32. Stanford: CSLI.
Kamio, Akio. 1994. The theory of territory of information: the case of
       Japanese. Journal of Pragmatics 21.67-100.
Kokubo, Takaaki. 1985. Ookagami no gohoo. Tokyo: Meiji Shoin.
Matsumura, Akira, ed. 1971. Nihon bunpoo daiziten. Tokyo: Meiji
       Shoin.
McCullough, Helen Craig. 1988. Bungo manual. Ithaca, New York:
       Cornell University East Asia Program.
Nihon Daiziten Kankookai. 1973. Nihon kokugo daiziten. Tokyo:
       Shogakukan.

Ogawa, Yoshio, ed. 1982. Nihongo kyooiku ziten. Tokyo: Taishukan.

Oono, Susumu. 1974. Kihon zyodoosi kaisetu. Iwanami kogo ziten. Tokyo: Iwanami.

_____. 1993. Kakarimusubi no kenkyuu. Tokyo: Iwanami.

Prince, Ellen F. 1978. A comparison of wh-clefts and it-clefts in discourse. Language 54.883-906.

Quinn, Charles J. 1987. A functional grammar of predication in classical Japanese. Doctoral dissertation, University of Michigan.

_____. 1993. Clause as text: the staging of information in classical Japanese and kakari-musubi. Ms., The Ohio State University.

_____. 1994. Kodai nihongo 'kakarimusubi' kinooron. Nihon Bunka Kenkyuuzyo Kenkyuu Hookoku 30.144-192.

Sansom, George. 1928. An historical grammar of Japanese. Oxford: Clarendon Press.

Seidensticker, Edward G., tr. 1976. The tale of Genji. New York: Alfred A. Knopf.

Shibatani, Masayoshi. 1990. The languages of Japan. Cambridge, England: Cambridge University Press.

Takeuchi, Michiko. 1986. Heian zidai wabun no kenkyuu. Tokyo: Meiji Shoin.

Washimi, Toshihisa. 1981. Amayo no sinasadame hyoosyaku Tokyo: Kasama Shoin.

Yamaguchi, Yoshinori. 1987. Kaku katuyookei no kinoo. Kokubunpoo Kooza 2, ed. by Akiho Yamaguchi, 1-36. Tokyo: Meiji Shoin.

The Origin of Register in Japanese and the Altaic Theory

ALEXANDER VOVIN
University of Hawaii at Manoa

THE ORIGIN OF REGISTER IN JAPANESE AND THE ALTAIC THEORY

Alexander Vovin
University of Hawai'i at Mânoa

To the memory of Murayama Shichirô
村山七郎先生の御霊に捧ぐ

0. Introduction

This article has two major goals: it proposes a new hypothesis regarding the origins of accent register in Japanese, deriving it from the loss of contrast between initial voiceless and voiced obstruents in Proto-Japanese as compared to Proto-Altaic. Its second purpose is to demonstrate that there is, therefore, another set of untrivial phonetic correspondences between Japanese and reconstructed Altaic, which, as I hope, will further contribute to the elimination of the still partially existing skepticism regarding the Altaic origins of Japanese. Since the reconstruction of Proto-Japanese accent in some respects remains controversial, I will start from a detailed discussion of this controversy.

1. Traditional reconstruction of Proto-Japanese accent system

All mainland Japanese dialects may be divided into three groups according to their accent systems: Eastern, Western, and Kyûshû. It is quite customary to use Tôkyô dialect as a representative of the Eastern group, Kyôto dialect as a representative of the Western, and Kagoshima dialect as a representative of Kyûshû. The next chart shows the typical accentual behavior of bimoraic nouns with and without a following particle:[1]

gloss	Tôkyô	Kyôto	Kagoshima	class/reconstr.
'nose'	hana LH	hana HH	hana HL	2.1/HH-H
	hana-ga LH-H	hana-ga HH-H	hana-ga LH-L	
'person'	hito LH	hito HL	hito HL	2.2a/HH-L
	hito-ga LH-H	hito-ga HL-L	hito-ga LH-L	
'stone'	isi LH	isi HL	isi HL	2.2b/HL-L
	isi-ga LH-L	isi-ga HL-L	isi-ga LH-L	
'foot'	asi LH	asi HL	asi LH	2.3/LL-L
	asi-ga LH-L	asi-ga HL-L	asi-ga LL-H	
'chopsticks'	hasi HL	hasi LH	hasi LH	2.4/LH-H
	hasi-ga HL-L	hasi-ga LL-H	hasi-ga LL-H	
'monkey'	saru HL	saru LF	saru LH	2.5/LH-L
	saru-ga HL-L	saru-ga LH-L	saru-ga LL-H	

Two basic characteristics are important in establishing an accent class in the traditional system: register and locus of an accent. Register is determined by the pitch of the initial mora in a word. Thus, classes 2.1 and 2.2 belong to high register, and classes 2.3, 2.4, and 2.5 to low register. The locus of an accent is on the high-pitched mora followed by a low-pitched one: the lack of such a combination makes a word unaccented. Thus, in Proto-Japanese classes 2.1, 2.3, and 2.4 are unaccented, and classes 2.2 and 2.5 are accented. In Kyôto-type dialects both register and locus are important, in Tôkyô-type only locus is relevant, and in Kagoshima-type only register.

According to the traditional point of view, the Kyôto-type system of accent is more archaic than the Tôkyô-type system and, thus, is closer to the Proto-Japanese (PJ)[2] system. The latter is considered to be a deviation

---

[1] The accentual reconstruction presented here follows Martin 1987.

[2] In this article, the following abbreviations are used: AZ (Azeri), BUR (Buriat), CHUV (Chuvash), J (Modern Japanese), K (Modern Korean), KALM (Kalmyk), KAZ (Kazakh), KHAL (Khalkha Mongolian), MA (Manchu), MJ (Middle Japanese), MK (Middle Korean), MM (Middle Mongolian), OJ (Old Japanese), OK (Old Korean), OT (Old Turkic), PA (Proto-Altaic), PAI (Proto-Ainu), PJ (Proto-Japanese), PK (Proto-Korean), PM (Proto-Mongolic), PMT (Proto-Manchu-Tungus), PT (Proto-Turkic), RM (*Ruiju myôgishô*), SAR-U (Saryg-Uighur), SOL (Solon), TUR (Turkish), TURK (Turkmen), TUV (Tuvinian), WM (Written Mongolian), YAK (Yakut).

from the Kyôto system (Kindaichi 1971: 934).

2. Ramsey's reconstruction of the Proto-Japanese accent system

However, this point of view was challenged by Tokugawa Munemasa (Tokugawa 1972) and S. Robert Ramsey (Ramsey 1979; 1980). Both scholars point out the fact that dialects with Kyôto-like accent systems are surrounded by dialects with a Tôkyô-like accent system. Such geographical distribution certainly makes it difficult to claim that the archaic area is in the middle, while the areas exhibiting innovation are on the borders. Tokugawa especially casts doubt on the archaic nature of the 2.5 accent class, preserved exclusively in Kyôto-type dialects (Tokugawa 1972:314). The key point in Ramsey's reconstruction is an assumption that only pitch change was important in the proto-system, and that there were no pitch distinctions *per se*: in other words, Ramsey eliminates register and preserves only locus (Ramsey 1979:174). Ramsey further suggests that Kyôto-type dialects moved the locus of accent one mora to the left compared to the more archaic Tôkyô-type dialects (Ramsey 1980:64-65). Another important point in Ramsey's hypothesis is his interpretation of accent marks in the Late Heian dictionary *'Ruiju Myôgishô'* (1081 A.D.). Ramsey suggests that in the *'Ruiju Myôgishô'* PINGSHENG (even tone) renders high pitch and SHANGSHENG (rising tone) renders low pitch (Ramsey 1979:165), (Ramsey 1980:65-67), while in the traditional interpretation *pingsheng* is considered to reflect low pitch and *shangsheng* high pitch (Martin 1987:84,118). Thus, the difference between the traditional interpretation and Ramsey's interpretation of the *'Ruiju Myôgishô'* accent classes for bimoraic words is the following (Ramsey 1980:66):

accent class	traditional	Ramsey
2.1	HH-H	LL-L
2.2	HL-H	LH-L
2.3	LL-H	HH-L
2.4	LH-H	HL-L
2.5	LH-H[3]	HL-L

Ramsey's conclusion is that register in Japanese is not important, and the primary distinction is locus, which is preserved in modern-day Tôkyô speech (Ramsey 1979:174).

However, there are several counterarguments against Ramsey's proposals: philological evidence, evidence from Korean loanwords in Japanese and Japanese loanwords in Ainu, structural evidence from dialects, and

---

[3] The evidence for the existence of the 2.5 class in RM is very meager, and, therefore, it is safer to consider that the RM language lacked a distinction between 2.4 and 2.5. This does not mean, however, that 2.5 in Modern Kyôto is necessarily an innovation.

comparative evidence from Altaic.

3.1 Philological evidence for the equations EVEN=LOW and RISING=HIGH

Ramsey argues that there is no way of knowing what labels 'even tone' and 'rising tone' meant in Middle Chinese (1979:161). However, he does not refer to an important article by Mei Tsu-lin, who demonstrated beyond any reasonable doubt that 'even tone' was long, low and level and 'rising tone' was high, level and short (Mei 1970). Mei has also clearly demonstrated that rising tone originated from a final glottal stop (1970: 88-97). Therefore, there is hardly any room for speculation that 'rising tone' might be low: from the numerous examples in many diverse languages of the world such as Tibeto-Burman, Austroasiatic, Paleosiberian etc. we know that glottal stop is normally associated with a high pitch. Moreover, logically it is strange if a high pitch is denoted by a dot in the lower left corner, but a low pitch by a dot in the upper left corner, of a character.[4] In any case, there is no direct evidence that would support Ramsey's point of view.

Ramsey further argues that we cannot know the values of 'even' and 'rising' for Japanese, since 'we could not be sure which of the many Chinese dialects of the time the Japanese were attempting to imitate' (1979: 161). We certainly do not know that, but all the positive evidence we have in the Japanese tradition: the description of the Middle Chinese tones in the 'Hobogirin' (Mei 1970: 94), the description of the Middle Chinese tones in the 'Shittan zô' (880 AD) by the monk Annen (Mei 1970: 91-93, 98-100), and musical notation in the shômyô (Rai 1951) give support for the interpretation of 'even' as LOW and 'rising' as HIGH in Japanese, too.

3.2 Evidence from early Korean loanwords in Old Japanese

One would expect that early Korean loanwords in Old Japanese will either preserve original Korean pitches or will be pretty close to them. It would be absolutely inconceivable if the pitches flip-flopped. However, that is the case if Ramsey's reconstruction is accepted. Frederick Kortlandt (who accepted Ramsey's point of view) in a recent publication writes: 'we can only speculate about the origin of the tonal differences between MK pwuthye and J hotoke HHH 'Buddha', MK tyel H and J tera LH 'temple', MK koïr LL and J koori HHH 'district', MK nat H and J nata LL 'hatchet'' (Kortlandt 1993:64). No need to speculate, however, if one assumes that the traditional reconstruction is right as far as register is concerned:

---

[4] Cf. from the point of view of typology, that Late Middle Korean low pitch is also described as a pingsheng (Yi Swungnyeng 1961/1985, 66), and it is also attested in modern Hamkyeng dialects (Ramsey 1978, 84). Why should the Japanese use the reverse notation?

gloss	RM (traditional)	RM (Ramsey)	Middle Korean
'Buddha'	fotoke LLL	fotoke HHH	pwuthye LL
'temple'	tera HL	tera LH	tyel H
'district'	kofori LLL	kofori HHH	koWol LL
'hatchet'	nata HH	nata LL	nat H
'bowl'	fati LL	fati HH	pali LL

Middle Korean pitches turn out to be identical with pitches in early Korean loanwords in Japanese in the traditional reconstruction.

3.3. Evidence from early Japanese loanwords in Proto-Ainu

I present external evidence for pitch contours exhibited by archaic Japanese loanwords in Proto-Ainu (PAI). There are many Japanese loanwords in modern Ainu dialects, and quite a few of them turn out to be recent, e.g., Obihiro *huton* 'futon' < J *huton* 'futon', Yakumo, Obihiro *hon* 'book' < J *hon* 'book' etc. Nevertheless, there are also several very old loanwords. Since Proto-Ainu is probably younger than Proto Japanese by at least three hundred years (Vovin 1993b:155), I do not claim that these loanwords were borrowed from Proto-Japanese, but they go back at least to the end of the first millenium A.D. All Japanese dialects adjacent to Ainu are dialects with Tôkyô-type accent systems. Thus, if the ancestors of the speakers of these dialects used Tôkyô-type accents, it is natural to expect that speakers of Proto-Ainu would borrow loanwords with Tôkyô-type accents. In fact, however, as I will show below, the oldest Japanese loanwords in Proto-Ainu exhibit accentuation almost identical to the traditional interpretation of the *'Ruiju Myôgishô'* accents and Proto-Japanese accent system reconstructed in Martin 1987, which suggests that the accent system of Tôkyô-type dialects deviated from the Kyôto-type system. Anyway, it is difficult to suppose that the Ainu borrowed the accentuation of its oldest Japanese loanwords from the mid-15th century Kyôto dialect, when, according to Ramsey, Kyôto dialect underwent an accent shift from Tôkyô-type to their modern type (Ramsey 1980:75). Even more unrealistic would be a suggestion that Proto-Ainu borrowed from some Kyôto-type dialect in northern Japan which then disappeared without a trace. Thus, the speakers of dialects in northern Japan probably used an Old-Kyôto-type system of accent (in the traditional interpretation) at the end of the first millenium A.D.

Hattori Shirô suggested that Proto-Ainu did not have pitch accent, because high pitch in the Saru dialect of Hokkaidô corresponds to a long vowel in Raichiska dialect of Sakhalin (Hattori 1967). However, high pitch in Hokkaidô dialects does not always correspond to a long vowel in Sakhalin dialects and a long vowel in Sakhalin dialects may also correspond to low pitch in Hokkaidô dialects. Moreover, there are two distinct systems of accent among Hokkaidô dialects, one represented by the southernmost Yakumo dialect, and the other by all other dialects. In addition, there is evidence that one of the Kuril Ainu dialects, recorded by Stepan Krasheninnikov, exhibited both pitch accent and vowel length (Vovin 1993b:66). Detailed argumentation for the reconstruction of pitch distinctions as well as vowel length in Proto-Ainu is presented in Vovin (1993b: 65-68).

There are some limitations to the reconstruction of the Proto-Ainu accent systemd due to the following circumstances:

1) None of the modern Ainu dialects preserved the Proto-Ainu accent system, though Yakumo has the most archaic type.

2) Every Ainu word in isolation is accented, that is, there is at least one high-pitched syllable. Thus, without a following suffix it is impossible to tell an oxytonic class LH from an atonic class LL, since in isolation both look like oxytonic LH[5]. Numerous published Ainu folklore texts do not show accentuation; thus the most important source on Ainu accentuation is Hattori's dictionary of Ainu dialects (Hattori 1964), which normally shows only a possessive form of nouns besides a form in isolation. However, only a few Ainu nouns have a possessive form.

3) A closed syllable almost always has a high pitch. Thus, if a loanword from Japanese acquires an Ainu prefix ending in a consonant, the whole complex will have low prototonic contour HL[L], and there is no way to reconstruct the basic pitch contour of this loanword.

4) The Proto-Ainu high prototonic class HH[H] is not preserved as such in any of the modern dialects, and is reconstructed on the basis of correspondence of oxytonic class LH in Soya to low prototonic class HL in Yakumo, Saru and Nayoro dialects. Thus, if Soya data are lacking, it is impossible to tell this class from low prototonic HL.

Nevertheless, there are several old loanwords from Japanese where I am confident of the reconstruction of Proto-Ainu accent. I provide these words in the chart below:

gloss	Proto-Japanese[6]	Tôkyô	Kyôto	Proto-Ainu
'metal'	*kana-Ci HH (2.1)	kane LH	kane HH	*kaani HHH
'paper'	*kanpi HL[7] (2.2a)	kami LH	kami HL	*ka[n]pi HL
'cup'	*tuki HL (2.2b)	tuki LH	tuki HL	*tuuki HLL
'bone'	*pone LL (2.3)	hone LH	hone HL	*pOnE LL
'skin'	*kapa LL (2.3)	kawa LH	kawa HH[8]	*kApL
'board'	*ita LH (2.4)	ita HL	ita LH	*ita LH

---

[5] Ainu accent is different from Japanese, since it is a rise of pitch, not a fall, that marks the locus.

[6] Cited according to Martin 1987.

[7] PJ 2.2a HL-L < *HH-L

[8] Irregular accent in Kyôto.

'hammer'	*tutu-Ci LH (2.4)[9]	tuti LH[10]	tuti LH	*tuuti LLH
'saw'	*no̱ko̱ LF (2.5)	noko HL	noko LF	*noko LH
'bag'	*pukurwo LLL (3.4)	hukuro LHH	hukuro HLL	*pukuru LLH
'ladle'	*pisaku LHH (3.6)	hisyaku LHH	hisyaku LLH[11]	*pisaku LLH
'medicine'	*kusuri LHF (3.7a)	kusuri LHH	kusuri LHF	*kusuri LHL

As can be seen from this chart, Proto-Ainu displays a system of accent quite different from the Tôkyô-type dialects of Eastern Japan but very close to the Proto-Japanese accent system. There is no difference between accent classes 2.4 and 2.5, but this may be accounted for by the fact that PAI *ita LH 'board' and PAI *noko LH 'saw' do not have possessive forms with following suffixes. Nevertheless, both classes have initial low pitch as in Kyôto, not high as in Tôkyô. Moreover, PAI *kusuri LHL 'medicine' almost exactly reflects PJ *kusuri LHL-L < *LHH-L (3.7a), and its accent is different from PAI *pisaku LLH 'ladle' < *PJ *pisaku LHH-H (3.6). Thus, I believe that Proto-Ainu presents separate evidence for the existence of accent classes 2.5 and 3.7, different from 2.4 and 3.6 in PJ, and that these classes in Kyôto-type dialects are an archaism inherited from PJ, not an innovation (see also 3.4 below).

In the same way, accent class 2.3 is represented in Proto-Ainu as LL-H (PA *ponE=hE LL-H), but not as HH-L, the latter being Ramsey's interpretation for this class in 'Ruiju Myôgishô' (Ramsey 1980:66). Accent class 2.1 is obviously high without a fall, and not vice versa, and class 2.2 starts with high pitch, not low.

There is also an example where Proto-Ainu accent helps to reconstruct the appropriate accent class for Proto-Japanese in cases where irregular accent correspondences between dialects do not provide a decisive answer. Martin proposes either 2.1 or 2.4 for PJ *pora 'cave' (Martin 1987:414). PAI *pO[O]ra H[L]L ?< *H[H]L 'cave' obviously serves to reject 2.4 and suggests 2.1 or perhaps even 2.2.

Therefore, both Old Korean loanwords in Japanese and Japanese loanwords in Ainu present the same favorable evidence for the traditional reconstruction of Proto-Japanese pitches and for the traditional interpretation of pitches in 'Ruiju Myôgishô.'

3.4. Comparative evidence for the archaic nature of class 2.5

Another significant piece of the evidence against Tokugawa-Ramsey theory of the innovative nature of Kyôto-type accent comes from evidence for the archaic nature of accent class 2.5, which exists exclusively in Kyôto-type dialects. Among the five accent classes reconstructed for Japanese bimoraic

---

[9] Martin suggests here development 2.4 ?< 3.5 (Martin 1987: 557).

[10] Irregular accent in Tôkyô.

[11] Irregular accent in Kyôto.

words, accent class 2.5, which has falling pitch (F) on the second mora, is the smallest. Its small size and the peculiar character of its distribution has led both scholars to suggest that it is secondary (Tokugawa 1972; Ramsey 1979, 1980). However, Evgenii Polivanov proposed in 1924 that accent class 2.5 resulted from a loss of a pre-PJ final *-*m*, and he provided comparisons of Kyoto Japanese *turu* LF 'crane' (< PJ **turu* 2.5) and *asa* LF 'morning' (< PJ **asa* 2.5) with K *twulwumi* 'crane' (MK *twolwomi/twulwumi* HLL< PK **twulwum-i* HL-L) and K *achim* 'morning' (MK *achom* LH < PK **acV$_{[-front]}$m* LH) 'morning' (Polivanov 1968/1924:152). Whitman further added to this list also comparisons of OJ *pyiyu* 'pigweed' (PJ **pidu* 2.5) with MK *pìlúm/pilom* 'id.' (< PK **pidVm* LH) and OJ *paru* 'spring' (PJ **paru* 2.5) with MK *pwóm* 'id.' (Whitman 1985:202). The last example represents certain problems in the regularity of phonetic correspondences, so it is better excluded for the time being. The list can, however, be continued with the following parallels from Korean and other Altaic languages, as I have already noted elsewhere: PJ **saru* 'monkey' also belongs to accent class 2.5, and tentative pre-PJ reconstruction **sarum* is perfectly paralleled by WM *sarma-ɣcin* 'monkey' (Vovin 1994:250). Also, stems of Japanese quality verbs designating color when used as nouns belong to accent class 2.5 in spite of the fact that they belong to different accent registers when used as quality verbs: *siro-* B 'is white', and *siro* 2.5 'white [color]', *aka-* A 'is red', and *aka* 2.5 'red [color]', *awo-* B 'is green/blue', and *awo* 2.5 'green/blue [color]', *kuro-* A 'is black', and *kuro* 2.5 'black [color]'. Our pre-PJ reconstruction would suggest a nominalizer *-*m*, which is reminiscent of the same nominalizer *-m* in Turkic and Korean (Vovin 1994:250).

3.5. Evidence from dialects for register in Proto-Japanese

As I already mentioned above, one of the strongest of Ramsey's arguments is that Kyôto-type dialects are surrounded by Tôkyô-type dialects. Moreover, Ramsey mentions the fact that there is a pocket with a Tôkyo-type accent in southern Nara prefecture, which he believes to be the remains of an earlier type (Ramsey 1979:172). However, this argument works nicely only as long as we do not take into consideration that there are other dialects besides those which exhibit either Tôkyô-type or Kyôto-type systems. Ramsey's theory is built largely on the comparison of Tôkyô dialect with Kyôto dialect and it does not account for the fact that Kagoshima-type Kyûshû dialects and all Ryukyuan dialects exhibit a system which provides evidence for register but not for locus in Proto-Japanese, though he is well aware of the fact: 'This correspondence between Kagoshima-type dialects and Old Kyoto is straightforward, but it is difficult to understand in terms of the proto-system if we suppose that only pitch changes and not the pitches themselves were distinctive' (Ramsey 1979:174). However, if we compare the following data from the Ryukyuan dialect of Shuri (Okinawa island) and Kagoshima with reconstructed values for PJ:

gloss	Shuri	Kagoshima	class	reconstruction
'nose'	hana HL	hana HL	2.1	HH-H
'person'	hwitu HL	hito HL	2.2a	HH-L
'stone'	ʔisi HL	isi HL	2.2b	HL-L
'foot'	ʔasi LL	asi LH	2.3	LL-L
'chopsticks'	haasi LLL	hasi LH	2.4	LH-H
'monkey'	saru LL	saru LH	2.5	LH-L

we will realize that there is no evidence supporting the claim that 'only pitch changes were distinctive in the proto-system': neither Kagoshima nor Shuri show any traces of pitch changes. Moreover, given the following family tree for Japanese dialects:

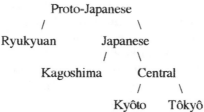

one can clearly see that while pitch changes are attested on the most shallow level — exclusively in Central dialects — the evidence for relevance of pitches themselves is supported by the two higher levels.[12] Therefore, there is strong dialectal evidence for the view that pitches themselves were distinctive in Proto-Japanese, while there is no similar evidence for the pitch changes; on the contrary it is possible to conclude that pitch change may in fact be an innovation, typical of Central dialects. The same can be said about the crucial point Ramsey makes about the merger of the classes 2.2 and 2.3: bizarre as it is, it never occurred other than in the Central dialects, and, therefore, may have little or no impact on reconstruction of the proto-system.

---

[12]Maner Thorpe in his dissertation (1983: 236) designed a new tree for Japanese languages/dialects, where he groups together in one group the Kyûshû dialects, Ryûkyûan, and Azuma Old Japanese as opposed to central Japanese. The major evidence he cites is based on morphology, which is not convincing from my point of view, and meanwhile common phonetic innovations he proposes between these three groups can at best be called very imaginative, as they are nothing but an artifact of his analysis of both the Proto-Japanese and Proto-Ryukyuan vowel systems. At the same time, lexical evidence and other more important phonetic features unite both Kyûshû and Azuma Old Japanese with Central Japanese and oppose them to Ryukyuan.

Finally, only nouns present evidence for locus, while both verbs and adjectives can be divided into two register classes, according to the pitch of the initial syllable: A (high) and B (low), neither of them showing any trace of a locus (Martin 1987: 191-218). If locus is to be the major feature of Japanese accent, as claimed by Ramsey, it is unclear why it has been preserved only by nouns.

3.6. Comparative Altaic evidence for the register in PJ

If one accepts the point of view presented above, namely that there is enough evidence for maintaining the traditional reconstruction of the Proto-Japanese accent system, where register is the most important distinction, then the next natural question would be regarding the origin of the register distinction. It is obvious that a prosodic feature like register cannot be inherent in language just as tones are not the inherent language feature. Therefore, it should come from somewhere. Two substantial attempts to explain the origin of initial Japanese pitches are known to me: Martin 1987 and Starostin 1990, 1991:83-85, and forthcoming.

Martin proposed that in first syllable all high-register words had short vowels and all low-register words had long (1987: 249-53). There is, however, some evidence that there was a vowel length in Proto-Japanese independent of lower register (Hattori 1978-79; Vovin 1993b).

Starostin came with a cardinally different proposal. First he suggested, revising Murayama's 1962 proposal concerning the accentual correspondences between Japanese and Korean, that the correspondences between the genetically related Japanese and Korean words, and not those which represent Korean loanwords in Japanese, are actually the opposite to what was proposed by Murayama: thus, he claimed that a Japanese high pitch corresponds to a Korean low pitch, and vice versa (1990: 44-47; 1991:83-85). Later he expanded his original claim, including also vowel length attested in Proto-Manchu-Tungus and Proto-Turkic. Starostin proposes to reconstruct four accentual types or tones for Proto-Altaic (forthcoming):

	PT	PMT	PK	PJ
Type 1	*VV	*V	*L	*H
Type 2	*V	*VV	*H	*L
Type 3	*V	*V	*L	*H
Type 4	*V	*V	*H	*L

However, the number of exceptions, when correspondences are straightforward, is very considerable, and many of them include such obvious cognates as PJ *mí 'water', PMT *muu 'id.', and PK *múl 'id.' Therefore, I believe that Starostin's theory does not really have a solid basis.

On the contrary, it seems that Japanese registers may have originated from a loss of certain consonant distinctions of Proto-Altaic. This hypothesis seems especially likely since there are only two series of initial bilabial and dental stops and one series of velar in Proto-Japanese as compared to three series in Proto-Altaic. The correspondences among these three series and their reflexes in Japanese are as follows:

Proto-Altaic	Proto-Japanese
*p'-	*p-
*p-	*p-/*b-
*b-	*b-/*p-
*t'-	*t-
*t-	*t-/*d-
*d-	*d-/*t-
*c'-	*t-
*c-	*t-/*d-
*j-	*d-/*t-
*k'-	*k-
*k-	*k-
*g	*k-

What especially attracts attention here is that reflexes of Proto-Altaic voiceless unaspirated and voiced stops in Proto-Japanese are pretty chaotic: both can be reflected sometimes as PJ *C[-voice] or C[+voice], but it seems that there is no specific pattern. Starostin suggests that there was a secondary devoicing of pre-PJ *b- and *d- (Starostin 1991:70-71), but it still remains unclear why this devoicing occured in some cases but not in the others.

Since it seems impossible to establish regular and unambiguous reflexes of PA initial voiceless unaspirated and voiced stops in PJ stops, I believe that it becomes possible to look for these reflexes in prosodic features. From this point of view the very existence of registers in Japanese is suggestive: we know from numerous examples from other languages that loss of a voiceless/voiced distinction is likely to lead to a development of tonal distinctions. Particularly, the loss of the [+voice] feature of an initial consonant will lead to the acquisition of a low pitch, and contrastively, syllables beginning with a [-voice] consonant will acquire high pitch. Therefore, I propose the following tentative rule: PJ high register corresponds to PA initial voiceless stop (aspirated or unaspirated), PJ low register corresponds to PA initial voiced stop. Let us try to verify this hypothesis by investigating the evidence, first from nouns, and then from verbs.

Taking into consideration the following system of reflexes of PA initial stops in daughter languages:

PA	PJ	PMT	PK	PM	PT
*p'-	*p	*p	*p-	*h-	*Ø-
*p-	*p-	*p-	*p-	*h-	*b-
*b-	*b-	*b-	*p-	*b-	*b-

PA	PJ	PMT	PK	PM	PT
*t'-	*t-	*t-	*t-	*t-	*t-
*t-	*t-/*d-	*d-	*t-	*d-	*d-
*d	*d-/*t-	*d-	*t-	*d-	*y-
*c'-	*t-	*c-	*c-	*c-	*c-
*c	*t-	*j-	*c-	*d-	*d-
*j	*d-/*t-	*j-	*c-	*j-	*y-
*k'-	*k-	*x-	*k-/*h-	*k-	*k-
*k-	*k-	*k-	*k-	*k-	*g-/_V[front][13]
*g	*k-	*g	*k-	*g-	*g-/_V[front][13]

one can see that certain Altaic languages are crucial for determining the exact nature of an initial stop in Proto-Altaic, and that lack of data from these languages may lead to lack of evidence for the voiceless or voiced nature of a particular initial consonant in Proto-Altaic. For example, if a Japanese word has a parallel only in Korean, it is not included in the following list, because Korean merged all three series of initial PA stops into one, with the sole exception of occasional reflexes of PA *k'- as *h-, and therefore Korean data are almost useless for our purposes. Thus Korean parallels are provided only if there are parallels in other Altaic languages which can shed any light on the problem of interrelation between voiced/voiceless consonants in Altaic and registers in Japanese. Similarly, only reflexes in Proto-Manchu-Tungus differentiate all three series of Proto-Altaic initial velars, and only reflexes in Proto-Turkic differentiate all three series of PA initial dentals. If in the first case the Proto-Manchu-Tungus reflexes are lacking, we need combined evidence from both Proto-Turkic and Proto-Mongolian to establish the identity of a Proto-Altaic initial velar. In the case of absence of Proto-Turkic evidence for Proto-Altaic initial dentals, even the combined evidence from all other languages will not help us to find out whether we are dealing with a Proto-Altaic voiced or voiceless unaspirated consonant. Needless to say, only comparisons that can support or contradict the above rule are included below.

4. New hypothesis regarding the origins of register in Proto-Japanese

I propose the following hypothesis regarding the origins of register in Proto-Japanese:

Proto-Japanese LOW register < PA initial VOICED (*b, *d, *j, *g);

Proto-Japanese HIGH register < PA initial VOICELESS (*p', *p, *t', *t, *c', *c, *k', *k).

Below I present comparative evidence in favor of this hypothesis.

[13] PT preserves an opposition between voiced and voiceless velars only before front vowels (Starostin 1991: 8).

NOUNS

Proto-Japanese	Proto-Altaic

1.1 H-H

*káN 1.1 'fragrance' (OJ *ka*)
cf. *kag-* A 'to smell' < *kán-k-

PA *k'aŋo- 'nose' > PMT *xoŋo- 'nose',
PK *koh H;'nose'; PM *kaŋ-bar 'nose';
PT *kaŋ/ñ 'nose'.

*ká-Cí 'hair' (OJ *key*)

PA *k'ïl$_1$ 'id' > PMT *xil-ŋa 'hair'; PK
*kal-h 'head hair'; PM *kilga-sun 'horse
hair'; PT *kïl$_1$ 'hair'.

*kwó 'child' (OJ *kwo*)

PA *kuŋa 'id' > PMT *kuŋa- 'id', ?PM
*kümün 'person'

*kǫ́- 'this' (OJ *ko-*)

PA *k'V- 'id' > PT *ku 'id.', MK *kù*
'that'

*tí 'blood' (OJ *ti*)

PA *t['Ji 'id' > PM *ti-sun

1.2 H-L

*dáCi or *díCa 'branch'
(OJ *ye*)

PA *tal$_1$V 'id.' > MK *cwùlkí* LH 'stem'
(of a plant), PT *dal 'branch'.

*kú[-]Cì 'fang' (OJ *kiy*)

PA *k'ü- 'tooth, fang' > PMT *xü-kte
'tooth'

*pí 'sun', 'day' (OJ *pi*)

PA *p['Jies- '[sun]light' > PMT
*po:s[V]- *'light' , MK *pyèth* 'sunlight'

exception

*dá 'arrow' (OJ *ya*)

PA *da 'arrow', 'bow' > PT *ya:ñ 'bow',
'arrow'

1.3a L-L

*bàn 'I', 'we' (OJ *wa-*)

PA *bän 'I', *ba/*bu 'we'

*bì 'well' < *bu-Ci (OJ *wi*)

PA *bul$_1$- 'spring' > PT *bul$_1$-ak, ?WM
bulaɣ 'id'

*pì 'ice' (OJ *pi*)

PA *bu- 'id' > PMT *bu-kse, PT *bur$_2$,
PK* èlV̂- 'to freeze' (>MK :el-)

*dwò 'night' (OJ *ywo*)

PA *dolV- 'id'> PMT *dolbo, ?PT *yal$_1$
'rest' (Sevortian 1989:85).

*dù 'hot water' (OJ *yu*)

PA *dul$_1$V 'hot', 'warm' > PT *jïl$_1$ï-, PM
*dula-, ?PMT *du:l- 'warm'

*kwò ?<*kuCa 'flour'
(OJ *kwo*)

PA *gul$_1$V- 'id.' > PM *gulir 'id.' (> WM
ɣulir), MK kòlò(kolG-) 'id.'

exceptions:

*kò-Cì 'tree' (OJ *kiy, kǫ-*)

PA *k'iñee '[cherry]-tree' > PMT *xiñee
'cherry-tree'

*tà 'rice-field' (OJ *ta*)

PA *t'al$_1$a 'field', 'steppe' > PM *tala,
PT *tal$_1$a, MK *tùlúh*

1.3b L-H

*dà 'house' (OJ *ya*)　　　　　　　PA *ju: 'id' > PMT *ju:, OT *yurt*

exceptions:

*pàn 'tooth' (OJ *pa*)　　　　　　PA *pal₁V 'molar', 'hammer' > PMT *palV 'molar', 'hammer', PM *halu-qa 'hammer'

pò-Cí 'fire' (OJ *piy, po-*)　　　　PA *p'ër₁ 'id' > OT ört 'fire', 'flames'; MK pul 'fire'

2.1 HH-H

*páná 'nose' (OJ *pana*)　　　　PA *p['lu:ñV 'smell' > PMT *pu:ñ- 'smell', 'to smell' (Tsintsius 1975-77.2: 349); PM *hüni-r 'id.' (MM hünir, KH üner, DAG hunu:-).

*páná-Ci 'feather' (OJ *pane*)　PA *p['luña- 'hair', 'down' > PMT *puñe 'down' > MA *fuñexen*; PM *hü-sün < *hün-sün 'hair', 'down'

*pátí 'bee' (OJ *pati*)　　　　　PA *p'ar₁ï 'id.' > OT arï, MK *:pel* 'id.' < PK *pèlV´

*pínsá 'knee' (OJ *piza*)　　　　PA *p'eñ- > PMT *peñŋe 'id.'

*pósí 'star' (OJ *posi*)　　　　　PA *p'iol₂V 'id.' > PM *ho(l)-dun, PT *yïL-dïr₂, MK *:pyel*

*kọsí 'waist' (OJ *kọsi*)　　　　PA *k'el₁V 'id.' > PT *kel₁ 'waistband', MK *hèlí* 'waist'

*kúmá 'nook', 'inside (OJ *kuma*)　PA *k'uŋV 'navel', 'cavity' > PMT *xuŋu 'navel' (Tsintsius1975-77.2: 280), PK *kwùmu-k 'cavity', PM *küyi'navel'.

*twórá 'tiger' (OJ *twora*)　　PA *t'u:l₁ku 'carnivore' > SOL tu:lge 'wolf' (Tsintsius 1975-77.2: 210), PT *tül₁ki/*til₁kü 'fox' (OT *tilkü*, TUR *tilki*, TURK *tilki*, CHUV *tilë*, KAZ *tülkü*) (Räsänen 1969: 480).

*tọrí 'bird' (OJ *tọri*)　　　　PA *t'or₁ï 'kind of a bird' > PMT *tura:kii 'crow', 'daw', 'rook'(Tsintsius 1975-77.2: 218); PK *tolk 'chicken'; PM *tura-Gu-n 'raven' (MM *turaGun*, WM *toro:*, KH *turliax*, BUR *turla:G*, KALM *turla:G*); PT *torïga 'small bird', 'lark' (OT *torïga*).

*túmá-Ci 'claw', 'nail' (OJ *tumey*)　PA *t'ubV 'id.' > MK *thwop* 'claw', 'nail'; PM *tuGur 'hoof'; PT *tubñak 'hoof'

*dó-tú 'four' (OJ *yọ-tu*)　　　PA *tö- 'id.' > PMT *di-, PM *dö-, PT *dö- 'id.'

Evidence is not conclusive:

*dá-tú 'eight' (OJ *ya-tu*)   PA *c/jab > PMT *jab 'id.'

*(d)íbó 'fish' (OJ *iwo*)   PA *c/jibV- > PM *jiɣa-sun 'id.'

2.2a HH-L

*kákí 'fence' (OJ *kakyi*)   PA *k[ʻ]al$_1$kV 'fence', 'shield' > PM *kalka 'shield', 'fence', 'screen' > WM *qalqa* 'shield', 'fence', 'screen'; KH *xalx* 'shield', 'fence', 'screen'; BUR *xalxa* 'shield', 'fence', 'screen'; PT *kalka-[n/ng] 'shield'.

*k[ói]-tá 'north' (OJ *kiyta*)   PM *koi-tu 'north', 'back'.

*pó[n]twó 'interval', 'time'   MA *fonde* 'time'
(OJ *potwo/podwo*)

*tóbó 'ten' (OJ *towo*)   PA *cuba- > PMT *cuwa- 'id.'

*túrá 'vine' (OJ *tura*)   PA *dVl$_1$V- 'vine' , 'hawthorn' > PMT

*jali-kta 'hawthorn',   'willow'; PM *dolu-gana 'hawthorn'

2.2b HL-L

*pórò 'hood' (MJ *foro*)   PA *pʻo:r$_2$V 'top' > PMT *poro-n 'top of the head' (Tsintsius 1975-77.2: 334), PM *horai 'top [of the head]' (MM *horai*, KII *oroi*), PT *u.$_1$/*ʻö:r$_2$ 'on top', 'upper part' (OT *üzä/özä*, TURK *üzär* , YAK *üüsä/üösä*).

*(d)ísò- 'stone' (OJ *isi*)   PA *tiəl$_2$o 'id.' > PMT *jolo, PK *twòlV̆, PM *cila-ɣun, PT *daal$_2$ 'id.'

*túkà 'mound' (OJ *tuka*)   PA *tukʻa- > PMT *tuka 'earth', 'ground'

2.3 LL-L

*dàmà 'mountain' (OJ *yama*)   PA *daba- 'mountain pass', 'to cross the mountain' > PMT *daba- 'id.', PM *daba- 'id.'

*pàrà 'belly' (OJ *para*)   PA *bäl$_1$a 'id.' > PK *poli > MK póy 'id.' ; PT *be:l$_1$ 'waist'.

*(d)ìrò 'face', 'color' (OJ *iro*)   PA *dür$_2$u 'id.', 'pattern', 'form' > PMT *duru-n 'form', 'outlook', 'pattern', 'design'; PM *düri 'form', 'outlook'; PT *yü:r$_2$ 'face'.

*kùtù 'shoes' (OJ *kutu*)   PM *gutu-l 'id.'

*tòsì 'year' (OJ *tosi*)   PA *dïl$_2$V 'year' > MK *twòls 'anniversary', PM *jil 'year', PT *yal$_2$ 'year (of age)'

*tùkù- 'moon' (OJ *tukiy*)   PA *dVl$_1$kV- 'moon' > PT *yal$_1$- (> OT *yal-ciq* (Nadeliaev 1969: 228); PK *tVlh

> OK *tolh-, MK *tól* 'moon'.

*bàtà 'intestines' (OJ *wata*) PT *bod 'body' > OT *bod*, TUR *boy*, SAR-U *poz*, AZ *boy*, TURKM *boy*, CHUV *pü* 'body', 'height', TUV *bot* 'self'

exceptions:

*pànkì 'foot' (OJ *pagi*) PA *pal₁kV 'foot', 'leg' > PMT *palga-n 'foot', 'leg'; PK *pal H 'foot'; PT *balak 'ankle'.

*pòtǒ 'vagina' (OJ *potǫ*) PA *p['Jutu 'id.' > PK *pwoti, PM *hutu-γun

*tàkwò 'octopus' (OJ *takwo*) PMT *taku-ra 'octopus', 'shell' (Tsintsius 1975-77.2: 154)

*kàpà 'skin', 'bark' (OJ *kapa*) PA *k'a:p'a 'id.' > PK *kàph- 'id.', PM *kaγu-da-sun 'bark', PT *ka:puk 'bark', 'shell'.

*pàrà 'field' (OJ *para*) PA *p'al₁a 'id.' > Ewen *ha:linr ə* 'meadow', PK *pel(h) 'field' (MK *phéli*, K *pel/phel*), PT *ala-ŋ 'ground', 'plain' (> OT *ala ǥ* TUR *alan*, TURKM *ala ǥ* YAK *ala:-s*).

*tàkà-Ci 'peak' (OJ *takey*) PT *da:g 'mountain'

*tòkì 'time' (OJ *tǫkyi*) *c'ak['JV 'id.' > PK *cek, PM *caγ, PT *ca:k 'id.'

*tùtì 'earth' (OJ *tuti*) *t'owVr₂ > PMT *tu:rV 'earth' (Tsintsius 1975-77.2: 217-18); PM *toγur- 'earth'; PT *to:r₂ 'dust', 'earth'.

2.4 LH-H

*kàtá 'shoulder' (OJ *kata*) *gar₁a 'arm', 'branch' > PM *gar 'hand', 'arm', PMT *gara 'branch', PT *kar₁ï 'arm'.

*kàrí 'wild goose' (OJ *kari*) *ga:ru 'goose', 'swan' > PMT *ga:ru 'swan', 'eagle-owl', MK *kùlyèkí* 'wild goose', PT *kar₂ 'id.'

*kàsú 'dregs' (MJ *kasu*) MA *gasan* 'carrion'.

*pàntá 'skin' (OJ *pada*) PMT *balda 'sheepskin'

*kàkí-Ca 'cock', 'fowl' (OJ *kakye*) PMT *ga:ki 'crow'

*kàCí 'paddle' (OJ *kai*) PMT *gawu 'pole for pushing the boat', *ga- 'to push boat with a pole' (Tsintsius 1975-77.1: 134)

2.5 LH-L
exception

*pìrû 'leech (OJ *piru*) *p['Jiru 'a kind of worm' > PMT *piru

'worm', 'bug'; MK pèlGéy LH 'worm'
or pyèlwók LH 'flea'

3.1 HHH-H
*kárántá 'body' (J karada)

*k['] ar₁ï 'body', 'belly' > PK *kari 'body'?,
'belly'? > MK kali-spye (kali-spye kali
hon tay 'ribs [are] a place on kali ' Yu
1964: 19), K kalpi 'ribs'; PT *karïn 'belly'.

3.5b LLH-H < *LLH-L
exception
*kòkòró 'heart', 'soul'
(OJ kokoro)

*kökö-r₂ 'breast' > PMT *xuku-n/
*kuku-n (Tsintsius 1975-77.2:254-255);
MK kwokoyyang 'kernel'; PM *kökün
'breast'; PT *gökür₂ 'breast'

3.7b LHL-L
*pìtó-tù 'one' (OJ pito-tu)

*pir₁V- > MK pìlú-sé 'for the first
time', K pilose; PT *bir₁ 'one'

exception
*koonpo 'spider' (OJ kumo)

*keemV 'spider' > PMT *kææm[p]i
'water spider'; PK *kemu- > MK
kèmúy 'spider'.

4.10 LHLL
*kàsásà(n)kì 'magpie'
(OJ kasasagi)

PMT *gasa 'a kind of a bird' (Tsintsius
1975-77.1: 143)

VERBS
Proto-Japanese
A:
PJ *tár- 'suffice' (OJ tar-)

Proto-Altaic

PA *col₁[V]- 'be full', 'suffice'
> PMT *jalu-, PT *dol- 'be full',
MK cólà- 'suffice'

PJ *kík- 'hear' (OJ kyik-)

PA *k'ul₁- 'ear' > PM *kul-ku
'middle ear'/'earwax', PT *kul₁-
kak, MK kwúy 'ear'

PJ *kórós- 'kill' (MJ koros-)

PA *k['] oro- 'id.' > PM
*koro[-]g

PJ *kádwóp- 'go [back and forth]'
(OJ kaywop-)

PA *kedV 'go' > PT *ge:t- 'go',
PM *ködel- 'move',
MK :ket/l- < PK *kedV- 'walk'

PJ *kúp- 'eat' (OJ kup-)

PA *keb- 'chew' > PM *kebi-
(MM kebi-, KALM kew-), PT
*käb- (VEWT 244)

PJ *kóron-p- 'roll','tumble'

PA *kul₁V- > PT *kul₁- 'id.'

(MJ *korob-*)

PJ *kánk- 'smell' (OJ *kag-*)

(VEWT 298a), K *kwulu-* 'roll'

PA *k'aŋo 'nose' > PMT *xoŋo-PK *koh H; PM *kaŋ-bar, PT *kaŋ/ñ

exceptions:

PJ *bí- 'be' (OJ *wi-*)

PA *bi- > PMT *bi-, PM *bü- 'be'

PJ *dák- 'burn' (OJ *yak-*)

PA *dak- > PMT *deg-je-, PT *yak-, MK *thó-* < *tVkV-

B:

PJ *pì-da-Ci- 'get cold' (OJ *pyiye-*)

PA *bege- 'id.' > PMT *begi:- 'get cold' (Tsintsius 1975-77.1: 119), PM *bege-re 'shiver' (MM begere-, KH beere-).

PJ *kò̱- 'come' > (OJ *ko̱-*)

PA *gel$_1$- 'id.' > PT *gel$_1$-

PJ *kìr- 'cut' (OJ *kir-*)

PA *gir$_1$- 'id.' > PMT *gir- (Tsintsius 1975-77.1:153)

PJ *kò̱nò̱m- 'like', 'be fond of' (OJ *ko̱no̱m-*)

PA *gunV > PMT *gu:n- 'think'/'say'; PM *guni- 'be sad'/'miss'

exceptions:

PJ *tàt- 'stand' (OJ *tat-*)

PJ *tò̱r- 'take' (OJ *to̱r-*)

PA *cur$_1$- > PT *dur$_1$- 'id.'

PA *t'ïr- 'take', 'hold' > PMT *turV- 'hold', 'support' (Tsintsius 1977: 220), MK *tül-* 'take'

ADJECTIVES
Proto-Japanese
A:

Proto-Altaic

PJ *kátá- 'hard' (OJ *kata-*)

PA *kata- 'hard' > PMT *kata-, PM *kata-ɣun, PT *kat-, MK *kwùt-*

PJ *kúrá- 'dark' (OJ *kura-*)

PA *k[']ar$_1$a 'black' > PM *kara, PT *kar$_1$a

PJ *káná-si- 'sad', 'beloved', (OJ *kanasi-*)

PA *k[']ana- > PT *kan- 'be satisfied' (OT *qani* 'satisfaction', 'joy' (Nadeliaev 1969: 417-8))

PJ *tápútwo- 'sacred', 'exalted' (OJ *taputwo-*)

PA *tap'V- > PM *tabi- 'sacrifice', 'offering', 'venerate', 'respect' (WM *tabi-g* (Lessing 1960: 761)

PJ *túrá- 'hard to bear', 'bitter'
(OJ tura-)

PA *t[']ur₁a- > PT *t/dur₁ï 'unpleasant', 'hateful' (OT turï (Nadeliaev 1969: 587))

B:

PJ *pùtwò- 'fat'/'thick' (OJ putwo-)

PA *bVdV- > PM *büdü-gün 'thick', PT *bädü-k 'big', MK pùlù- 'is full', 'is bulgy'

PJ *bàkà- 'young' (OJ waka-)

PA *baka- > PM *baga 'young', 'small'

PJ *dò̱-'good' (OJ yo̱-)

PA *diogV 'good' > PT *yag-, MK tyoh-

PJ *tìká- 'close' (OJ tika-)

PA *dIka 'close' > PMT *daga 'close' ?PM *daɣa- 'follow', PT *yak-ïn, ?K taumn 'next' ?< *tah-um

PJ *dùta-ka- 'rich' (OJ yutaka)

PA *juja- 'rich'/'fat' > PM *juja-ɣan 'fat'/'thick'

exceptions:

PJ *tàkà- 'high'/'mountain' (OJ takey)

PA *taka-> PT *daag 'mountain'

The number of exceptions in the high register is really insignificant, and therefore I come to the conclusion that Proto-Altaic initial voiceless consonants are reflected in Proto-Japanese as high register. There are more exceptions among low-pitched words, and I suggest that low pitch in Proto-Japanese may have a complex origin. While some of the low-pitched words possibly go back (as I demonstrated above) to the Altaic words with initial voiced consonants, low pitch in exceptions may reflect vowel length, according to Martin 1987.

A reasonable question may arise: how to explain register distinctions in words beginning with vowels or sonorants? A possible speculative answer to this question is that Proto-Japanese typologically was very similar to modern Shuri dialect of Ryukyuan, which distinguishes smooth vocalic onset versus an initial glottal stop for vowel-initial words and preglottalized versus plain nasals for sonorant-initial words. This contrast in modern Shuri is of a secondary nature and has nothing to do with register in Proto-Japanese. Nevertheless, a similar contrast might have existed in Proto-Japanese and it might have given reflexes with high and low registers in words beginning with vowels or sonorants. It is also possible that instead of an initial glottal stop there was a different laryngeal:

HIGH REGISTER	LOW REGISTER
*ʔV- or *HV-	*V-
*ʔn- or *Hn-	*n-

It is not clear so far what Altaic correspondences this tentative system may have, but I prefer to put it forward as a working hypothesis needing further investigation.

References

Hattori, Shirô. 1964. Ainu go hôgen jiten. Tôkyô: Iwanami.

------------------. 1967. Ainu go on'in kôzô to akusento. Onsei no kenkyû 13. 207-223.

------------------. 1978-79. Nihon sogo ni tsuite. 1-22. Gengo.

Hirayama, Teruo. 1989/1960. Zenkoku akusento jiten. Tôkyô: Tôkyôdô.

Kindaichi, Haruhiko. 1971. On'in henka kara akusento henka e. Kindaichi hakushi beiju kinen ronshû. Tôkyô: Sanseidô, 929-956.

Kortlandt, Frederick. 1993. The Origin of the Japanese and Korean Accent Systems. Acta Linguistica Hafniensia 26.57-65.

Lessing, Ferdinand D. 1960. Mongolian-English Dictionary. Berkeley and Los-Angeles: University of California Press.

Martin, Samuel E. 1987. The Japanese Language Through Time. New Haven and London: Yale University Press.

Mei, Tsu-lin. 1970. Tones and Prosody in Middle Chinese and the Origin of the Rising Tone. Harvard Journal of Asiatic Studies 30. 86-110.

Murayama, Shichirô. 1962. Nihongo no tungûsugo teki yôso. Minzokugaku kenkyû 26/3.

Nadeliaev, V.M., ed. 1969. Drevnetiurkskii slovar'. Leningrad: Nauka.

Polivanov, Evgenii D. 1968/1924. K voprosu o rodstvennykh otnosheniiakh koreiskogo i altaiskikh iazykov. Stat'i po obshchemu iazykoznaniiu. Moskva: Nauka, 156-164.

Ohno, Susumu. 1990/1974. Kogo jiten. Tôkyô: Iwanami.

Rai, Tsutomu. 1951. Kan'on no shômô to sono seichô. Gengo kenkyû 17-18: 1-46.

Ramsey, S. Robert. 1978. Accent and Morphology in Korean Dialects. Kwukehak chongse, 9. Seoul: Thap Chwulphansa.

------------------. 1979. The Old Kyôto dialect and the Historical Development of Japanese Accent. Harvard Journal of Asiatic Studies, v. 39/1.157-175.

------------------. 1980. Nihongo no akusento no rekishi teki henka. Gengo 9/2.64-76.

Ramstedt, Gustav J. 1949. Studies in Korean Etymology. Mémoires de la Société Finno-Ougrienne 95. Helsinki: Suomalais-Ugrilainen Seura.

Räsänen, Martti. 1969. Versuch eines Etymologisches Wörterbuchs der Türksprachen. (VEWT) Lexica Societatis Fenno-Ugricae XVII/1.

Helsinki: Suomalais-Ugrilainen Seura.

Starostin, Sergei A. 1990. O iapono-koreiskikh aktsentnykh sootvetstviiakh. Tezisy dokladov konferentsii 'Sravnitel'no-istoricheskoe iazykoznanie na sovremennom etape'. 44-47. Moscow: Institut slavianovedeniia i balkanistiki.

------------------. 1991. Altaiskaia problema i proiskhozhdenie iaponskogo iazyka. Moscow: Nauka.

------------------. forthcoming. On vowel length and prosody in Altaic languages. Festschrift für Vitalij Shevoroshkin zum seiner 60. Geburstag. ed. by Alexis Manaster Ramer.

Thorpe, Maner L. 1983. Ryûkyûan language history. Doctoral dissertation, University of Southern California.

Tokugawa, Munemasa. 1972. Towards a family tree for accent in Japanese dialects. Papers in Japanese Linguistics 1:2 (translated by James D. McCawley). 301-320.

Tsintsius, Vera I. et al. 1975-77. Sravnitel'nyi slovar' tunguso man'zhurskix iazykov, vol. I-II,
Nauka, St. Petersburg (Leningrad).

Vovin, Alexander. 1993a. Long Vowels in Proto-Japanese. Journal of East Asian Linguistics 2.125-134.

------------------. 1993b. A Reconstruction of Proto-Ainu. Leiden: E.J.Brill.

------------------. 1994. Genetic Affiliation of Japanese and Methodology of Linguistic Comparison. Journal de la Société Finno-Ougrienne 85.241-256.

Whitman, John B. 1985. The Phonological Basis For the Comparison of Japanese and Korean. Doctoral dissertation, Harvard University.

Yi, Swungnyeng 1961/1985. Cwungsey kwuke munpep. Seoul: Uylyu munhwasa.

Yu, Changton. 1987/1964. Yico e sacen. Seoul: Yensey tayhakkyo chwulphanpu.

Word-Initial Low Register in Proto-Japanese[1]

MORIYO SHIMABUKURO
University of Hawaii at Manoa

This paper provides evidence that Proto-Japanese (PJ) had vowel length in the initial syllable and word-initial low REGISTER associated with an initial-syllable long vowel, and also reconstructs PJ phonemic vowel length and the phonetic SUPRASEGMENTAL feature of low initial register on the basis of the Ryukyuan initial long vowel, which I consider to be a remnant of the original long vowel.

Martin (1987: 262) suggests that the correlation between initial-syllable vowel length and initial low pitch may have existed in Japanese. He points out that Ryukyuan disyllabic nouns contain an initial long vowel belonging to historical accent classes 2.3 (LL) and 2.4 (LH) and that their initial low pitch in Japanese is a reflex of original initial-syllable vowel length.

I have examined Okinawan disyllabic and trisyllabic nouns containing an initial long vowel and have found that in general they are initially low pitched. Examples[2] are as follows (Throughout this paper B mean low initial pitch and C is low tonic (2.4 and 2.5)[3]):

---

[1] I woud like to express my gratitude to Professor Leon A. Serafim for his helpful comments and advice in the writing of this paper.
[2] As far as examples used in this paper are concerned, the sources are:
Shuri: *Okinawa go jiten* (1963).
Nakijin: Nakasone (1983).
Onna: Hirayama and et al. (1966) and Nakamoto and Shinozaki (1988). Other Okinawan dialects: Hirayama and et al. (1966), Hirayama (1967) and Uemura

Shuri	Nakijin	Onna	Oo	
kaamii B	kaamii B		kaamii B	'tortoise'
uuN B	uunuu B		uuN B	'axe'
naaka B	nahaa C	naaka B		'relation'

A few exceptions are also found, but they may be accounted for as compounds, borrowed words, or words with secondary vowel length (see Serafim, 1994). The following Shuri examples are taken from *Okinawa go jiten* (A means high initial pitch).

kuuri A 'ice' : This is a borrowed word. The Ryukyu is located in the area of semi-tropical. No natural 'ice' is found. The word for 'ice' in Japanese is *koori* 3.1 (HHH).

kiimusi A 'cater-pillar' : This word is composed of the words *kii* A 'hair' and *musi* A 'bug'.

kaara A 'river' : The initial-syllable vowel length is due to a /w/ deletion between the vowels in the syllable; *kawara* > *kaara*.

Vovin (1993) reconstructs some Proto-Okinawan (PO) and PJ long vowels based on a hypothesis that some dialects preserve PO vowel length in word-initial syllables. Vovin does not take the word-initial low register into account. In my version of PJ, since I suggest that there was a correlation between initial vowel length and initial low pitch, I reconstruct a PJ suprasegmental feature different from Martin's and Vovin's (some of my PJ forms happen to be the same as Vovin's. See below). I suggest the following ten PJ forms.

1. PJ *kaanp$^{u}/_{o}$-Ci 3.4, 3.5, 3.6 or 3.7[4] 'mold'. Martin (1987: 431) and Vovin (1993: 127) suggest PJ *kanp$^{u}/_{o}$-Ci 2.1 and PJ *kaanp$^{u}/_{o}$-Ci 3.1 for the word meaning 'mold' respectively. Notice that my PJ

(1959).

Sakishima (southern Ryukyu dialects): Hirayama and et al. (1966), Hirayama (1967) and Uemura (1959).

[3] More specifically, the accent type C means HL for two mora, HLL for three mora, LLHL for four mora and LLLHL/LLHHL for five mora words.

[4] I propose that PJ *kaanp$^{u}/_{o}$-ci has word-initial low pitch, but I am not certain to which historical accent class it belongs at present because of lack of data.

reconstructed form differs from both Martin's and Vovin's in pitch pattern. Other than that mine and Vovin's are the same. Concerning the PO word for 'mold', Vovin (1993: 127) reconstructs PO *kaabui A based on Shuri *kaabui* B and Nakijin *haabui* C[5]. However, taking both Serafim's PJ etymology for 'mold' (Serafim, 1993) and Shuri and Nakijin forms into account, I rather reconstruct PO $*kaab^{o(o)}/_{uu}ri$ C. The Old Japanese (OJ) form for 'mold' is *kabiy* (Martin, 1987: 431). Furthermore, the Middle Korean (MK) word *kwomphuy* RL[6] means 'become moldy' and the Early Modern Korean word for 'mold' is *kwom*. Regarding Modern Korean dialects, the cognates are *kwoomphangi* in Seoul (Martin 1987: 162), *koompheyi* in Kyengnam and *komsaku* in Kyengpuk[7]. Moreover, as far as Modern Japanese accent is concerned, the words meaning 'mold' are *kabi* LH in Tokyo, *kabi* HH in Kyoto and *kabi* HL in Kagoshima dialects (Hirayama, 1960: 138).

    2. PJ *kuunpo* 3.7 'spider'. The PJ words for 'spider' that Martin (1987: 463) and Vovin (1993: 128) have proposed are *?*kunpo* (<? **konpo*) 2.5 and *kuumpo* 3.7 respectively. the difference between them lies in the vowel length of the first syllable and in the syllable-final nasal in the same syllable. Hattori (1979: 108-109) reconstructs PJ *koobu* 'spider' on the basis of Kyushu dialects *kobu, koobu, kubu* and the Ryukyuan words meaning 'spider'. Vovin (1993: 128) proposes PO *kuubu/*koobu* C on the basis of Shuri *kuubaa* B, Oo *koobu* B, Nakijin *hubu* C (HL) and Onna *kuubaa* B. I suggest PO *koobu* C 'spider'. Kabira[8] *goolu* and Taketomi *koo?tara*[9] also retain the initial-syllable vowel length. The Modern Japanese accents of the word 'spider' are Tokyo *kumo* HL, Kyoto *kumo* LH and Kagoshima *kumo* LH (Hirayama, 1960: 204). I might add that Thorpe (1983: 333) reconstructs Proto-Ryukyuan (PR) *kobu* 'spider'.

    3. PJ *saaru* 3.7 'monkey'. Martin's (1987: 518) PJ for 'monkey' is *saru* 2.5, and Vovin's (1993: 129) is *saaru* 3.7. I reconstruct PO *saaru* C 'monkey' since Shuri *saaruu* B, Nakijin *saaruu* C[10], Oo *saaru* B, Onna *saaru* B and Kume *saaru* B are initially low pitched. Vovin (1993: 129) suggests PO *saaru* C 'monkey'. In addition, other Ryukyuan examples for 'monkey' are Tokashiki *saaruu* B and Kumejima *saaruu* B. In Modern Tokyo dialect the suprasegmental feature of the word *saru* is HL, in Kyoto LH and in Kyushu dialects such as Kagoshima and Miyakonojo, LH (Hirayama, 1960: 41).

---

[5] In Vovin (1993:127), the accent class is given as A, but in fact it is C (LLHL) (see Nakasone, 1983).
[6] RL means rising low pitch.
[7] Korean examples are taken from Vovin (1993: 127).
[8] Kabira, Ishigaki.
[9] The symbol ? stands for a voiceless glottal stop in this paper.
[10] *Saaruu* is LLHL: word-initial low register and accent on the third mora. See also footnote 3.

4. PJ *kaanka-Ci 3.7 'shadow'. Martin (1987: 432) suggests PJ *kanka-Ci 2.5. Vovin (1993: 127) reconstructs PJ *kaanka-Ci 3.7. The reason that Vovin reconstructs the initial-syllable long vowel is due to the evidence of PO *kaagai which is based on Okinawan dialects such as Shuri, Oo, Nakijin and Onna. Based on the following cognates--Shuri kaagaa B, Oo kaagi B, Nakijin kaagaa C[11], Onna k'aagi B, Kume kaagi B, Haneji haaga B, Ishikawa kaagi B, Yomitan kaagi B, Naha kaagi B, Kochinda kaagi B, and Nakazato kaagi B, --I reconstruct PO *kaagai C. This reconstruction completely agrees with Vovin's (PO *kaagai B). The OJ cognate is kagey (Martin, 1987: 432). In addition, the cognate kaagi B is also found in Daitoo, Tokashiki, and Kumejima. As for accent patterns of the cognate words in Modern Japanese dialects, they are kage HL in Tokyo, kage LH in Kochi, Kagoshima and Miyakonojo, and kage LF[12] in Kyoto.

5. PJ *paatwo 3.4 'pigeon'. This is based on Okinawan Shuri, Nakijin, and Oo cognates and also on the hypothesis of word-initial low register, but happens to be exactly the same as Vovin's. Martin (1987: 402) suggests PJ *patwo 2.3. Vovin (1993: 126) reconstruct PJ *paatwo 3.4. He reconstructs a long vowel for the word for 'pigeon' based on Shuri, Oo and Nakijin. These dialects are considered to retain an archaic vowel length in the first syllable. Shuri hootu B, Oo hootu B and Nakijin pootuu B are examples. Vovin (1993: 126) suggests PO *paatu B for 'pigeon'. I rather suggest PO *pootu B. The OJ cognate is fatwo (Martin, 1987: 402). In addition, other Ryukyuan dialects having word-initial low pitch but having lost vowel length are: Ishigaki patu LL, Ohama patu LL, Taketomi patu LH, Kuroshima patu LH, Hateruma paton LH, Iriomote patuna LLH, and Yonaguni hatu LH. In Modern Tokyo, Kyoto and Kagoshima dialects, the word hato is pronounced HL, LF, and LH respectively.

6. PJ *oonp[(a)-C]i 3.5 'belt, girdle'. Vovin (1993: 129) suggests PJ *oon[p-C]i 3.5. Martin (1987: 503) reconstructs PJ *onp[a-C]i 2.4. Regarding PO, I reconstruct *?uubi B based on Shuri ?uubi B, Onna ?uubi B, and Oo ?uubi B. Vovin (1993: 129) reconstructs PO *?uubi B as well. Hirayama (1960: 39) describes the accent patterns of the word obi in Modern Japanese as follows: Tokyo obi HL, Kyoto obi LH, Kagoshima and Miyakonojo obi LH, and Toyama obi LL.

7. PJ *uusu 3.5 'mortar'. In Okinawan dialects, words for 'mortar' are ?uusi B in Shuri, ?usi C in Nakijin, ?uusu B in Onna, and ?uusi B in Kume. The first three forms of the Okinawan dialects taken into account, Vovin (1993: 129) produces PO *?uusu C 'mortar'. My PO is *?uusu C. Martin (1987: 564) suggests PJ *usu 2.4 'mortar'. Vovin (1993: 129) reconstructs PJ *uusu 3.5 on the basis of both the cognates in the Okinawan dialects and Proto-Ainu (PA) *niisu A (HLL) 'mortar'. He believes that PA *niisu results from the combination of PA *nii 'tree' and

---

[11] In Vovin (1993: 127), Nakijin kaagaa is classified as accent type A, but it is LLHL; That is, accent type C (see Nakasone, 1983 and see also footnote 3).
[12] LF indicates low falling pitch.

PA *uusu* 2.4 'mortar'.   In addition, other Ryukyuan dialects such as Daitoo, Aguni, and Kumejima also retain an original long vowel and word-initial low register: *?uusi* B (Hirayama, et al.,1966). The accent patterns of the word *usu* 'mortar' in Tokyo, Kyoto, Kagoshima, and Toyama are HL, LH, LH, and LL respectively (Hirayama, 1960: 39).

8. PJ *wooka(C)i* 3.7 'bucket'. Martin's (1987: 505) PJ form is *bo-kaCi* (> *wo-key* > *woke* 2.5).   I reconstruct PO *wuuki* C 'bucket': Shuri *wuuki* B, Nakijin *huki* C, Onna *wuuki* B, Kume *wuuki* B, Haneji *wuki* B, Ishikawa *wuuki* B, Yomitan *wuuki* B, Naha *wuuki* B, Kochinda *wuuki* B, and Nakazato *?uuki* B.   Other Okinawan dialects retaining the initial-syllable vowel length are Hentona *uuki*, and Nago *wuukii* (their accent classes are not certain).   Furthermore, in Ryukyuan Taketomi the word form for 'bucket' is *buuki* (the pitch pattern of the word is not available in the literature). In addition, Thorpe (1983: 269) reconstructs PR *woke*. According to Hirayama (1960: 41), in Modern dialects the accent patterns are: Tokyo *oke* HL, Kagoshima *oke* LH, and Kyoto *oke* LF.

9. PJ *iiki* 3.5 'breath'. Martin's (1987: 422) reconstruction for 'breath' is PJ *iki* 2.4 (? < *ika-Ci). The OJ form is *ikyi* (Martin, 1987: 422). My PO *?iici* C 'breath' is based on Shuri *?iici* B, Nakijin *?ici* C, Onna *?ici* B, and Oo *?ici* B, Ishikawa *?iici B*, Yomitan *?iici* B, Naha *?iici* B and Nakazato *?iici* B. Thorpe (1983: 268) reconstructs PR *iki* 'breath'. In Modern Japanese dialects, the words for 'breath' are as follows: *iki* HL in Tokyo, *iki* LH in Kyoto and Kagoshima, and *iki* LL in Toyama (Hirayama, 1960: 39).

10. PJ *mooko* 3.7 'bridegroom, son-in-low, companion'. The OJ form is *mwokwo* (Martin, 1987: 487).   In Okinawan dialects, the words meaning 'bridegroom' are *muuku* B in Shuri, Naha, Onna, Ishikawa, Hanji, Yomitan, Kochinda, Nakazato and Hentona, *muuhu* B in Oku and Haneji, *muku* B in Oo, and *muhu* C in Nakijin. Furthermore, in Ryukyuan as a whole there are more dialects having the initial-syllable vowel length and low register. Their cognates are *muuku* B in Tokashiki and Kumejima and *muuhu* B in Izena. I suggest PO *muuku* C 'bridegroom'. In addition, Thorpe (1983: 332) reconstructs PR *moko*. Regarding Japanese-mailand dialects, the suprasegmental features of the word *muko* are HL in Tokyo, LF in Kyoto and LH in Kagoshima.

Whitman's /-r-/ deletion rule (Whitman 1985: 21-23 and 1991) deletes /-r-/ when a preceding vowel is short. However, there are a number of initially low-pitched nouns with the syllable structure *(C)Vr-* in Japanese. If Whitman's hypothesis is correct, it is possible that those nouns originally had a long vowel before the /-r-/ and that somehow the long vowel has gotten shortened but kept the word-initial low register. Therefore, the word *doro* (LL) 'mud', for example, was *dooro* (LLL) in PJ. The following are Japanese nouns belonging to the historical accent class 2.3, taken from Martin (1987) and compared with Okinawan cognates.

	Japanese	Shuri	Nakijin	PJ
'color'	iro	ʔiru B	ʔiruu B	*iiro
'black'	kuro	kuruu B	kuruu B	*kuuro
'paste'	nori	nui B	nu'i B	*noori
'mud'	doro	duru B	duruu B	*dooro/*ntooro[13]

A problem of this analysis is that cognates of this type in Ryukyuan do not contain the expected initial long vowel. However, I suggest that this analysis is more general. Further research needs to be done regarding the lack of vowel length where expected in the given subset of Okinawan examples.

Conclusion

In this paper I have suggested ten PJ forms and ten PO forms based on the Ryukyuan initial-syllable long vowel which may have been associated with low register. The following have been suggested in this paper.

	PJ		PO	
1. 'mud'	*kaanp^u/$_o$-Ci	3.4, 3.5,	*kaab$^{o(o)}$/$_{uu}$ri	C
2. 'spider'	*kuunpo	3.7	*koobu	C
3. 'monkey'	*saaru	3.7	*saaru	C
4. 'shadow'	*kaanka-Ci	3.7	*kaagai	C
5. 'pigeon'	*paatwo	3.4	*pootu	B
6. 'girdle'	*oonp(a)-Ci	3.5	*ʔuubi	B
7. 'mortar'	*uusu	3.5	*ʔuusu	C
8. 'bucket'	*wooka(C)i	3.7	*wuuki	C
9. 'breath'	*iiki	3.5	*ʔiici	C
10.'bridegroom'	*mooko	3.7	*muuku	C

These proto-forms are in general different from the ones which have been reconstructed in the literature, such as those in Martin and in Vovin, in accent class and initial vowel length. I believe that word-initial low register existed in relation to the word-initial long vowel, and the evidence from the Ryukyuan dialects supports the PJ and PO forms.

As for the nouns belonging to historical accent class 2.3, as mentioned above, there is not much evidence to support their PJ forms with an initial long vowel. Regarding this problem, further research needs to be done.

---

[13] In Ohama, Ishigaki the word for 'mud' is *duuru*. This is the only evidence to support the form PJ *dooro*. Martin (1987: 391) reconstructs PJ *ntoro* 2.3 'mud'. In MK, the word meaning 'dirty, muddy' is *teerep-* RL (Whitman, 1991: 527).

References

Hattori, Shiro. (1979) Nihon sogo ni tsuite [About Proto-Japanese], *22 Gengo*.

Hirayama Teruo, Oshima Ichiro, and Nakamoto Masachie. (1966) *Ryuukyuu hoogen no soogooteki kenkyuu* [A comprehensive study of Ryukyuan]. Tokyo:Meiji Shoin.

Hirayama Teruo. (1967) *Ryuukyuu Sakishima hoogen no soogooteki kenkyuu* [A comprehensive study of southern Ryukyuan dialects]. Tokyo:Meiji Shoin.

Hirayama Teruo. (1989) *Zenkoku akusento jiten* [A dictionary of pitch accents in all dialects]. Tokyo:Tookyoodoo Shuppan.

Martin, Samuel E. (1987) *The Japanese language through time*. New Haven and London: Yale University Press.

Nakamoto Masachie and Shinozaki Koichi. (1988) Okinawa hontoo Shuri to Onna no akusento [Accent in Shuri and Onna of Okinawa island], *Ryuukyuu no hoogen 13*:1-61. Hoosei Daigaku Okinawa Bunka Kenkyuujo.

Nakasone, Seizen. (1983) *Okinawa Nakijin hoogen jiten* [A Dictionary of the Nakijin dialect]. Tokyo.

Okinawa go jiten [A dictionary of the Okinawan language]. (1963) Tokyo: Okurasho Insatsukyoku.

Serafim, Leon A. (1993) *The Importance of Vovin's Proto-Japanese etymology for 'mold'*, ms.

Serafim, Leon A. (1994) *Vowel length in Japanese and Ryukyuan*, ms.

Thorpe, Maner. (1983) *Rkyukyuan language history*, PhD. dissertation, USC.

Uemura Yukio. (1959) Ryuukyuu hoogen ni okeru 1-2 onsetsu meishi no akusento no gaikan [General view of accent in Ryukyuan mono- and disyllable Nouns], *Kokuritsu Kokugo Kenkyujo ronshuu 1:Kotoba no Kenkyuu:121-140*. Tokyo.

Vovin, Alexander. (1993) Long vowels in Proto-Japanese, *Journal of East Asian linguistics 2:125-134*.

Whitman, John B. (1985) *The phonological basis for the comparison of Japanese and Korean*, Ph.D dissertation, Harvard.

Whitman, John B. (1991) *A rule of medial *-r- loss in Pre-Old Japanese*, ms.

Another Source of M ~ B Variation in Japanese

BLAINE ERICKSON
University of Hawaii at Manoa

1. Introduction

In Japanese, *m* and *b* vary with one another, both synchronically and diachronically. There are at least three sources for this variation: one superstratal, one adstratal, and one substratal. The discussion will start with Old Japanese, the language of Heijōkyō (present-day Nara) in the eighth century CE and the earliest well-attested form of Japanese. (The *Wèizhì*, a Chinese historical account dated 57 CE, has the earliest attested Japanese, but the first sizable and reliable corpus dates from the 700s.) The sources of m ~ b variation from that time will be examined before moving on to other related phenomena in later periods.

2. Superstratal Evidence

The superstratal evidence is based on loans, namely the two main strata of borrowings from Chinese. Although the extensive body of work on the reconstruction of Middle Chinese can be incorporated

I would like to thank Leon A. Serafim for his many helpful suggestions and comments, and also for his unflagging support. My thanks also to Gerald B. Mathias, from whom I have received numerous insights, many of which are central to this paper. I also would like to thank Robert N. Huey, for his help in tracking particularly elusive references. Finally, I wish to thank Samuel E. Martin for his encouragement. Any errors or deficiencies herein are my responsibility alone, of course.

into this section, the majority of the data are from Japanese itself.

2.1 Go'on and Kan'on

GO'ON are the ON'YOMI (Chinese readings) of characters as interpreted by the Japanese at the time of the first great wave of Chinese influence, which began during the late fifth century CE and continued into the sixth century. KAN'ON are the on'yomi from the next wave of Chinese borrowings, from the late seventh through the eighth centuries CE (Okimori 1989: 46; Shibatani 1990: 120–21). As is evident from the dates, Go'on were borrowed during the pre-Old Japanese period, and Kan'on during the height of the Old Japanese period.

2.1.1 Go'on

The character for Go in Go'on, 呉, is the same one used for the Wú area of south China. (Wú is the modern Mandarin; EARLY MIDDLE CHINESE [EMC] is reconstructed as *ŋɔ [Pulleyblank 1991: 325].) For this reason, the Go'on are often said to represent the Chinese of that area, and this variety of Chinese is dated to about the sixth century (Pulleyblank 1991: 2–3; Shibatani 1990: 120). However, Gerald B. Mathias (personal communication) has observed that the Go'on are remarkably similar to Sino-Korean readings, and suggests that the Go'on might better be regarded as the Japanese interpretation of the Korean pronunciation of Chinese characters, rather than being based directly on Early Middle Chinese. Whitman (1985: 14) also supports this view. This hypothesis has two factors in its favor: geography and history. As for geography, Korea is simply closer to Japan than south China. Interactions between Japan and the continent, whatever their nature, would have been easier through the Korean peninsula than with South China if for no other reason than proximity. As for history, it is known from the *Kojiki* (*Record of Ancient Matters*, 712 CE) and the *Nihon Shoki* (*Chronicles of Japan*, 720 CE) that Koreans taught the Japanese how to write (Seeley 1991: 4–9; Shibatani 1990: 126). Additionally, it is clear that there were interactions and perhaps even close ties between Japan and Korea, including large-scale migration from Korea, from the Yayoi period (300 BCE–250 CE) through the Kofun period (250–552) (Barnes 1986; Hanihara 1991a: 246–47 et passim; Nelson 1974: 1017; Sahara 1992; Sansom 1958; Turner 1991: 98 et passim). For these reasons, Mathias' hypothesis will be accepted herein.

More evidence against the hypothesis that Go'on are from the Wú region can be adduced from Pulleyblank 1984. Pulleyblank noted that Wú may have been used pejoratively, to contrast pronunciation that differed from that of the Táng capital of Cháng'ān (Pulleyblank 1984: 74). This negative label may have been applied to the existing strata of Chinese borrowings in Japan (now known as Go'on), to distinguish that older style of pronunciation from the newer and 'proper' Kan'on (see § 2.1.2).

2.1.2 Kan'on

Kan'on, the readings from the late seventh and early eighth centuries, are regarded as representing the 'correct' Chinese pronunciation of the time. The Kan of Kan'on, 漢, is the same character read Hàn in Mandarin, which is both the name of the Hàn dynasty (206 BCE–220 CE) and the ethnonym the (northern) Chinese use for themselves. That Kan'on represent a more 'Chinese' pronunciation is also supported by historical evidence, for monks and scholars from Japan made trips to Táng China, and brought their learning back to Japan with them (Sansom 1958; Shibatani 1990: 121). There were also trips made by Chinese monks to Japan, but their numbers seem to have been far fewer than those of the Japanese going to China. As Whitman noted, Kan'on pronunciations were based on contact with (LATE) MIDDLE CHINESE (LMC) speech (Whitman 1985: 9–10, 14 et passim); historical data support this view (i.e., the presumed date for Late Middle Chinese and the date of Kan'on borrowings coincide).

2.1.3 Differences between Go'on and Kan'on

A number of differences between Go'on and Kan'on can be shown. Although the following statements will be made as general rules, there are exceptions to these (as there are to all) generalizations.

First, Go'on and Kan'on often differ in their vowels. Open-syllable Go'on tend to have one (short) vowel, whereas open-syllable Kan'on tend to have two vowels (often one long [i.e. two-mora] vowel in modern Japanese). Go'on vowels are usually identical to their values when the same characters are used as MAN'YŌGANA (characters used as a syllabary) in the *Kojiki* and the *Man'yōshū* (*Collection of a Myriad Leaves*, ca. 759) (Mathias: personal communication). A typical example would be 賣, 'to sell', which has the following values: Go'on *me*, Kan'on *bai*, and man'yōgana *mê* (the carat represents the A-type vowel [i.e. KŌRUI], the details of which are not relevant herein). As noted above, Go'on vowels are also similar to Korean values for the same characters.

Next, although both Go'on and Kan'on have voiced, voiceless, and nasal initial consonants, voiced Go'on initials (usually) correspond to voiceless Kan'on initials, while nasal Go'on initials (usually) correspond to voiced Kan'on initials. An example of the latter is illustrated above with 賣 'to sell'; an example of the former would be 夏 'summer', Go'on *ge*, Kan'on *ka*. As noted by Pulleyblank, by the time of Late Middle Chinese, upon which Kan'on are based, the Chinese voiced initials had become 'partly devoiced' with breathy aspiration (i.e. breathy voice) (1984: 67–68), thus explaining the voiced Go'on to voiceless Kan'on correspondence (for a dissenting view, see Ramsey & Unger 1972: 279–283).

Why, then, do Go'on nasal initials correspond to Kan'on voiced initials? The answer lies partly in changes between Early Middle Chinese and Late Middle Chinese. The Early Middle Chinese nasals had become prenasalized stops in the Táng standard dialect: Late Middle Chinese. This 'is evident from the transcription practice of the period as well as from Kan'on and from Tibetan transcriptions of Chinese' (Pulleyblank 1984: 68). Pulleyblank also wrote that this innovation did not spread far beyond the Táng capital and did not affect the post-Táng development of the standard language. For simplicity's sake, they are represented as plain nasals in Pulleyblank's reconstruction of Late Middle Chinese (Pulleyblank 1984, 1991).

Does this really explain why Go'on nasal initials correspond to Kan'on voiced initials? It does if one assumes that Old Japanese (i.e. contemporaneous to Kan'on) voiced initials were prenasalized. There is the danger of circular reasoning here, except that the Tibetan evidence also favors the hypothesis that EMC nasals became LMC prenasalized stops. The hypothesis (widespread in historical Japanese circles; see Unger 1977: 8) that the OJ phonemes /b/, /d/, /g/, and /z/ were phonetically prenasalized will be accepted herein. There is dissent over whether the obstruent component was voiced or not; this question will be discussed in § 4.1.

2.2 The Ramsey and Unger Account

The change between Go'on-period nasals and Kan'on-period voiced obstruents, based on Ramsey & Unger 1972, was covered in Unger 1977: 33–35; this is recounted here.

In brief, there was one (relevant) change in Chinese between the time of Go'on and Kan'on borrowings: nasal initials became prenasalized stops, except for those syllables which ended with a velar nasal, which remained unchanged. There were two changes in Japanese between the time of Go'on and Kan'on borrowings. One was that voiced initials either deleted or became homorganic glides (specifically, *b > w, *d > y, *g > Ø, *z > Ø); the other was that voiced initials of the Go'on stratum of vocabulary, and only the Go'on stratum, became prenasalized obstruents.

If the changes of the Ramsey and Unger explanation have been correctly presented, they represent a violation of the NEOGRAMMARIAN HYPOTHESIS: Sound Change Knows of No Exception. As the Neogrammarian Hypothesis remains an invaluable tool in historical linguistics, any interpretation that disposes of it is to be questioned at the very least, and discarded if it cannot be supported by an explanatory conditioning factor or subsequent (and regular) sound change. In this light, the hypothesis put forward in Ramsey & Unger 1972 must be thoroughly re-examined, and perhaps, ultimately, replaced.

Ramsey and Unger have the facts of Go'on and Kan'on in their favor, but they do not appear to have Japanese comparative evidence on their side. Although the Ryūkyūan evidence favors a *b > w change in mainland Japanese, Whitman (1985: 18–19) argued against a *d > y change in Japanese, based on Ryūkyūan data. If one agrees with Whitman, then it becomes a critical weakness in the Ramsey and Unger account, and one must discard their hypothesis.

Regardless of what the exact changes were, the fact remains that there are countless nasal-voiced stop doublets in Japanese, such as Go'on *mai*: Kan'on *bei* for 米 'rice' (EMC mɛj', LMC mjiaj´ [Pulleyblank 1991: 213]), and Go'on *nai*: Kan'on *dai* for 内 'inside' (EMC nwəj^h, LMC nuaj` [Pulleyblank 1991: 223]). Without the Ramsey and Unger theory, another explanation for the correlation of Go'on nasal initials to Kan'on voiced initials must be sought. Although a replacement for that theory is beyond the scope of this paper, it would seem likely that between the time of Go'on and Kan'on borrowings, Japanese voiced stops became prenasalized, and thus accorded exactly with LMC prenasalized initials derived from EMC nasal initials.

3. Adstratal Evidence

Native Japanese doublets form the most important and most puzzling part of the m ~ b variation problem. As will be seen, there are two distinct layers involving this type of evidence; they will be examined by date, for the different dates correspond to different types of evidence and phenomena.

3.1 Old Japanese Evidence

There are numerous examples of labial consonants varying with each other. Old Japanese examples of this phenomenon were presented in Serafim 1978: 15–18. Rather than attempt to account for these (and other) doublets by some as-yet unknown paradigmatic or derivational relationship, Serafim hypothesized that there were '[t]wo dialect groups [which] contributed words to the lexicon of Central Japanese of the Nara and Heian periods' (Serafim 1978: 5). Identification of which words belong to which dialect has yet to be undertaken, but if such a task were possible, it would represent an important step forward in Japanese historical linguistics.

For m ~ b variation specifically, Serafim presented eight sets, with a total of 27 lexical forms exemplifying the sets. These are presented below in Table 1 (reproduced, with minor simplifications in glosses, from Serafim 1978: 18). Note that Serafim used *nb* for the phoneme identified as /b/ herein.

Set	Corr.	Word	Gloss
1	nb	*kunbo*	'geographical depression'
	m	*kuma*	'corner'
2	nb	*ama-tönb-*	'fly through the sky'
		ama-tönb-u-ya	'flying through the sky' M
		tönb-	'fly'
		tönba-s-	'cause to fly'
	m	*ama-ndam-u*	'sky flying' M
3	nb	*pinboroki*	'sacred tree'
	m	*pîmorökî*	id.
4	nb	*sinba-r-*	'tie up (using force)'
	m	*sima-r-*	'tie up'
		sime-	'tie'
5	nb	*kunbar-*	'distribute'
	m	*kumar-*	id.
		mi-kumar-i	'place that distributes water'
6	nb	*sunbë-*	'unite (under one's rule)'
	m	*sumê (-ra)-*	'royal'
7	nb	*yu-nbar-i*	'urine'
	m	*mar-*	'excrete'
8	nb	*omo-nbuku-*	'head towards'
		omo-nbukë-	'cause to face towards'
		kata-nbuk-	'lean'
		kata-nbukë-	'cause to lean'
	m	*omo-muk-*	same as omo-nbuku-
		omo-mukë-	same as omo-nbukë-
		muk-	'face towards'
		mukë-	'cause to face towards'

TABLE 1. M ~ B VARIATION FROM SERAFIM 1978

Key

circumflex (ˆ) over a vowel indicates that the vowel
    is A-type, i.e. kōrui
dieresis (¨) over a vowel indicates that the vowel is
    B-type, i.e. OTSURUI
M indicates that the word is a MAKURAKOTOBA
    (stereotyped epithet)
Corr. stands for correspondence

These and other examples present strong evidence in favor of Serafim's hypothesis of dialect mixture. As is expected in the case of admixture, borrowed words do not necessarily replace existing words; rather, they augment the lexicon, often with a slightly difference nuance, or with a different but similar semantic range (Serafim 1978: 6). An example of this in English is *shirt*, which is a direct inheritance from proto-Germanic, coexisting with *skirt*, a borrowing from Old Norse, a closely related Germanic language (Hock 1991: 410 et passim; Robinson 1992). There are numerous other borrowings from Old Norse, representing the same phenomenon. Serafim proposed that a similar set of borrowings in Old Japanese is the best explanation for the doublets found in the Old Japanese corpus.

As late as the beginning of the Old Japanese period, there may have been a significant number of immigrants from the Korean peninsula. This further supports Serafim's hypothesis, for it is thought that the people who were migrating from the mainland spoke a now-extinct language that was closely related to Japanese (Serafim: personal communication). However, no large-scale migration is attested (or hypothesized in Serafim 1978 or herein) for the Heian period. In this situation, borrowing will be dialectal, and possibly unintentional on the part of the borrowers (Thomason & Kaufman 1988: 44–45).

3.2 Post-Old Japanese Evidence

Serafim 1978 dealt with those examples of alternation which are from the Old Japanese period. There are, however, other examples of m ~ b alternation where one or both members of the pair is from a period later than Old Japanese. The pairs to be examined herein (and absent from Serafim 1978) are presented in Table 2.

Word 1	Gloss	Word 2	Gloss
amu	'bathe'	*abu*	id.
Kamata	'oven field'	*kabayaki*	'oven-broil'
katamuku	'to lean'	*katabuku*	id.
kemuri	'smoke'	*keburi*	id.
samisii	'be sad'	*sabisii*	id.
samurafu	'to serve'	*saburafu*	id.
san (<samu)	'three'	*Saburau*	Saburō (name, '3rd son')
tōkimi	'corn'	*tōkibi*	id.
tomosii	'poor'	*tobosii*	id.
umu	'give birth'	*ubuya*	'birthing hut'

TABLE 2. EXAMPLES OF M ~ B VARIATION

Checking the date of the first attestation of the members of each doublet is the first step. Once dates are known, particular doublet sets can be included (or excluded) as exemplars for the hypothesis to be presented herein. See Table 3. Texts of first attestation are taken from Ōno et al. 1990; dates are from Shinmura 1991 and *Nihon Koten Bungaku Daijiten* 1984.

In order to better study this, it is necessary to gather as many examples as possible, and to date the first attestation of each word. I leave this more in-depth analysis to the future; for now, the words listed above will serve as a starting point.

Word	Text	Date
amu	K	905
abu	MS	1000
kama- (ta)	W	Heian period (794–1185)
kaba- (yaki)	—	
hatamuku	H	1240
katabuku	MS	1000
kemuri	KS	1656
keburi	K	905
samisii	—	
sabisii	G	1000
samurafu	O	Muromachi period (1392–1568)
saburafu	K	905
samu (> san)	MY	759
Sabu-rau	G	1000
(tō-) kimi	MY	759
(tō-) kibi	—	
tomosii	MY	759
tobosii	T	18th century
umu	K	712
ubu- (ya)	N	720

TABLE 3. M ~ B WORDS WITH TEXTS AND DATES OF EARLIEST ATTESTATION

Key
— Unattested in Ōno et al.

G	*Genji Monogatari*	MY	*Man'yōshū*
H	*Heike Monogatari*	N	*Nihon Shoki*
K	*Kokinshū*	O	*Otogizōshi*
KS	*Kusōshishō*	T	*Tensō Zenbonkushū*
MS	*Makura no Sōshi*	W	*Wamyō Ruijushō*

Of the examples above, several must be discarded due to no attestation of one member of a pair. These are *kama-/kaba-*;

samisii/sabisii; and *tōkimi/tōkibi*. Next, since both *umu* and *ubu* are from the Nara period, they are more likely to be examples of dialect borrowing (as discussed in Serafim 1978) and are therefore not relevant to this discussion. Finally, there is a third member of the *saburafu/samurafu* set, namely *samorafu*, which is dated to the Nara period (Ōno et al. 1990: 589). This earlier member of the triplet will be ignored herein, because its vowel alternation and date suggest that it is best considered under Serafim's dialect borrowing hypothesis.

This leaves six pairs for consideration. This is an unfortunately small number, and it is to be hoped that conclusions drawn from these examples can be supported by further evidence, to be gathered at a later date.

4. Selected Issues in Old Japanese Phonology

Before moving on to the central thesis of this paper, it is necessary to enter into discussions of selected issues in Old Japanese phonology, in particular, the OJ antecedents to modern /b/, /d/, /g/; and /z/; and the fricativization of *p.

4.1 Phonetic Status of Voiced Obstruent Phonemes

It is widely assumed that the phonemes realized as voiced obstruents in Modern Japanese, namely /b/, /d/, /g/, and /z/, were nasal-obstruent clusters in Old Japanese (the development of affricates is irrelevant herein). Many suggest that the obstruent components were voiceless at first, and later assimilated to the voicing of the prenasalization to become voiced. The reasons for proposing that the obstruent component was voiceless are tied to the hypothesis (advanced in Martin 1987 and elsewhere; rejected in Whitman 1985) that the pre-OJ voiced obstruents either lenited to glides or deleted entirely (see § 2.2). It is argued that if the obstruent portion of the nasal-obstruent clusters were voiceless, then they would not have lenited or deleted.

The changes that affected the nasal-obstruent clusters are as follows: $*^mp > *^mb > b$; $*^nt > *^nd > d$; $*^\eta k > *^\eta g > g$, and $*^ns > *^nz > z$. These changes are conflated in Rules 1 and 2.

$$[+\text{cons}] > [+\text{voi}]/[+\text{nas}]\_$$

RULE 1. ASSIMILATORY VOICING

$$[+\text{nas}] > \emptyset/\_[+\text{cons}]$$

RULE 2. DELETION OF PRENASALIZATION

The phonetic status of these phonemes, phonemicized as /b/, /d/, /g/, and /z/ herein, is relevant to the proposed changes of § 5.

4.2 Fricativization of /p/

The Old Japanese phoneme *p has given rise to the modern phonemes /h/, /f/, and, of course, /p/; it is also the source of some instances of /w/ and Ø (see Vance 1987: 9–47 for a discussion of the phonemicization of Modern Japanese). Although the series of changes and conditions for those changes are fairly complex, it is possible to give a simplified account which will suffice for the purposes of this discussion. In short, *p > [ɸ] except next to obstruents (even this is a controversial and overly simplistic statement, but the environments in which *p remained [p] have no bearing on this discussion). Later, in some environments, [ɸ] further lenited to [w] (probably with a voiced bilabial fricative as an intermediary stage, i.e. ɸ > β > w); [w] (including [w] < *w) then deleted everywhere except before /a/. [ɸ] changed to [ç] before /i/ and /y/, and to [h] before /e o a/; it remained unchanged before /u/. (Under the influence of English, [ɸ] now occurs before all vowels. It has therefore changed from an allophone of /h/ to a separate phoneme /f/. See Vance 1987: 21.)

The issue of when *p changed to [ɸ] has been debated by many, but in the absence of firm evidence, many people gave in to either agnosticism, as exemplified by Unger, who wrote 'it does not matter whether fricative articulation began to replace stop articulation as early as Old Japanese' (Unger 1977: 19); or to the a priori assumptions of the traditional Japanese account, which holds that the change had already occurred by the Nara period. This latter position is solidly rejected by Pulleyblank, who noted that if *p had already changed to [ɸ] by the Nara period, one would expect the man'yōgana of the *Nihon Shoki* to have employed initial LMC *f- for presumed OJ [ɸ]. No such examples can be found; instead, LMC *p- was employed to represent OJ *p (Pulleyblank 1984: 156). On this basis, the change *p > ɸ can not have occurred any earlier than the late eighth century. The change must have happened by the time of the Portuguese arrival in Japan, for Portuguese records from the 16th century indicate [ɸ] as the value before /u/ (Okimori 1989; Vance 1987: 19–21). The question remains as to when the change occurred; an implication of this paper's thesis narrows the date of the change to sometime in the early Heian period.

5. Hypothesized Sound Change and Substratal Evidence

The remaining members of the m ~ b alternation set, presented in Tables 2 and 3 in § 3.2, suggest that there was a sound change of m > b in some dialect(s) of Japanese, and that this change occurred at some point in the late 10th century. However, from the data and hypothesis presented below, it will be shown that the original sound change was b > m; that this change occurred in a less-prestigious dialect; and that the opposite change, m > b, was a hypercorrection, or was otherwise socially motivated.

5.1 Hypothesized Processes and Intermediary Stages

At some point either contemporaneous to or shortly after the change *p > [ɸ], it is hypothesized that, in some dialects, the voiced counterpart of *p, *ᵐp or *ᵐb, became ᵐɸ or ᵐβ. It is highly unlikely that voicelessness of the fricative could have been maintained with nasalization, and it is therefore hypothesized that the phonetic realization of this segment would have been as a (pre)nasalized voiced bilabial fricative, without oral closure, i.e. [β]. It is further supposed that this nasalized bilabial fricative merged with /m/. The support for this latter supposition is based in part on this hypothesized segment's phonetic similarity to [ɱ], a voiced nasal labiodental fricative, and what Pullum and Ladusaw wrote about this segment: that it is never found as phonologically distinct from /m/ (Pullum & Ladusaw 1986: 96). Even if this segment were somehow maintained as distinct from /m/ for those speakers for whom the change occurred, it would not have been perceived as distinct for those speakers who did not have this change. If this is so, then the nasal fricative proposed herein would have merged, or would have been perceived as merged, with /m/, and this then becomes the process by which /b/ changed to /m/.

Another possibility is that *ᵐb lost its oral component directly, without an intermediate nasal fricative stage; that is, that it simply changed to [m]. Given the long history of Japanese to weaken labial consonants, this is a reasonable supposition. However, this is merely an account of the facts without an explanation; an explanation is to be preferred, and that is what is offered herein.

It is possible that the proposed change did not affect all instances of original /b/; that is, that the sound change did not go to completion (the theory of Lexical Diffusion must be appealed to here; see Hock 1991: 649–52 et passim). However, it happened in enough environments, for enough speakers, to lead to the adaptation of the changed form of certain words in the lexicon of the capital, as evidenced by the examples cited in § 3.2 and Table 2 above.

The data presented in Table 2 are equally split between the change m > b and b > m, and therefore do not suggest one change over the other. It is proposed herein that the earlier change was b > m, and that this change was phonetically motivated. The opposite change, m > b, was either motivated by some sort of rule reversal (my thanks to John Whitman for pointing this out to me; an example of this would be r-insertion in some varieties of British English [Wells 1982: 222–27]), or by social factors. The explanation put forth herein is that those who did not distinguish between /m/ and /b/, or those whose pronunciation of /b/ was such that other speakers could not hear it as distinct from /m/, were of a socially less-prestigious group than those for whom /b/ and /m/ were both phonetically and phonologically distinct. There is, of course, no way to prove this directly, unless one can find something from the Heian period corpus of literature that would suggest this.

The closest I have come to finding such evidence is in passages from both *Genji Monogatari* (*The Tale of Genji*) and *Makura no Sōshi* (*The Pillow Book of Sei Shōnagon*). In the former, there is mention of the vulgarity of a certain governor's speech (Murasaki 1963: vol. 5 p. 132, 1976: 937); in the latter, the commoners were said to have too many syllables in their speech (Sei 1967: 16, 1991: 25). There are other mentions of commoners' speech in these works; however, since there are any number of ways in which accents can differ, there is no way to know exactly how the commoners' speech differed from that of the writers.

5.2 Date of Change

Since the proposed change assumes that the fricativization of *p occurred before (or at the same time as) the *^{m}b > [m] change, and the data presented in Table 3 show that the post-Old Japanese m ~ b variation happened between the beginning and the end of the 10th century, it is further proposed that both this change and the change it was dependent upon, *p > [Φ], occurred sometime during the tenth century. Further post-Old Japanese examples of m ~ b variation should support this conclusion.

That there is a relatively large distance between the first attestation of this change and some later attestations (for other words) should not be overly surprising. After all, not all words which underwent this change would necessarily have been employed in all texts. There is also the question of the spread of the change: perhaps earlier writers did not have certain examples of this change in their lexicons that later writers did have. Finally, there is the issue of the accuracy of texts. It is well-known that errors will be introduced when texts are copied, and that some of these errors are 'corrections' made by later writers.

5.3 Supporting Evidence

In order to support the changes proposed herein, in addition to data from Japanese itself, data from other languages need to be included. In the absence of actual data, the kind of data that would support the central hypothesis will be listed.

First, examples of voiced stops changing to homorganic nasals should be presented. This change has occurred in certain of the Salish languages (Erickson 1993); as many other examples as can be found should be examined to see whether they might support or refute the central hypothesis of this paper.

Second, discussions of hypercorrection should also be examined. For this, the work of Labov should be reviewed, as well as the relevant sections of Thomason & Kaufman 1988, and Hock 1991.

Finally, I hope that parallel phenomena within Japanese itself will support the hypotheses proposed herein; such a discussion, however, is beyond the scope of this paper.

6. Conclusion

This is a preliminary explanation of how certain examples of m ~ b variation in Japanese came about. In order to determine which words can be accounted for with this hypothesis, as many examples of m ~ b variation as possible need to be found and dated. Those from the Nara period would be best accounted for by Serafim's doublet hypothesis; those later than the eighth century could support the sociolinguistic hypothesis proposed in this paper. Furthermore, relevant examples of similar changes from other languages would strengthen the hypothesis put forward herein. Finally, I hope that feedback from others will help me to shed light on this issue.

Appendices
Appendix I:
List of Chinese and Japanese Terms, Given in Characters

Cháng'ān 長安

Genji Monogatari 源氏物語

Go'on 呉音

Heijōkyō 平城京

Heike Monogatari 平家物語

Kan'on 漢音

Kofun 古墳

Kojiki 古事記

Kokinshū 古今和歌集

kōrui 甲類

Kusōshishō 句双紙抄

Makura no Sōshi 枕草子

makurakotoba 枕詞

man'yōgana 万葉仮名

Man'yōshū 万葉集

Nara 奈良

Nihon Shoki 日本書記

Otogizōshi 御伽草子

otsurui 乙類

Táng 唐

Tensō Zenbonkushū 天草全本句集

Wamyō Ruijushō 倭名類聚鈔

Wèizhì 魏志

Yayoi 弥生

Appendix II:
Romanization

Japanese romanization in the text is Hepburn; in linguistic examples, it is Kunreisiki, except for the addition of *f*, which represents the post-Nara period-premodern value of the modern Kunreisiki *h*.

Mandarin is romanized in Hànyŭ Pīnyīn.

References

Barnes, Gina L. 1986. Jiehao, Tonghao: Peer Relations in East Asia. In John F. Cherry, ed. Peer Polity Interaction and Socio-Political Change. Cambridge: Cambridge University Press.

Erickson, Blaine. 1993. Reconstruction of Proto-Coast Salish. ms.

Hanihara, Kazurō. 1991a. Dual Structure Model for the Formation of the Japanese Population. In Hanihara, ed., 1991b: 244–251.

————, ed. 1991b. Japanese as a Member of the Asian and Pacific Populations (アジア太平洋地域の中の日本人). International Research Center for Japanese Studies, International Research Symposium No. 4, 1990. Kyoto: Kokusai Nihon Bunka Kenkyū Sentā.

Hock, Hans Henrich. 1991. Principles of Historical Linguistics. Berlin: Mouton de Gruyter.

Martin, Samuel E. 1987. The Japanese Language Through Time. New Haven: Yale University Press.

Murasaki, Shikibu (紫式部) (Yamagishi Tokuhei (山岸徳平), ed.) 1963. Genji Monogatari (The Tale of Genji). Nihon Kogo Bungaku Taikei 18. Tokyo: Iwanami. 4th printing, 1965.

————. (Edward Seidensticker, trans.). 1976. The Tale of Genji. New York: Alfred A. Knopf.

Nelson, Andrew Nathaniel. 1974. The Modern Reader's Japanese-English Character Dictionary. Tokyo: Charles E. Tuttle. 2nd revised edition, 16th printing, 1984.

Nihon Koten Bungaku Daijiten Editorial Committee (日本古典文学第辞典編集委員会). 1984. Nihon Koten Bungaku Daijiten (日本古典文学第辞典). Tokyo: Iwanami.

Okimori, Takuya (沖森卓也). 1989. Nihongoshi (日本語史, History of the Japanese Language). Tokyo: Ōfūsha. 5th printing, 1992.

Ōno, Susumu, Akihiro Satake, & Kingorō Maeda, eds (大野晋, 佐竹昭広, 前田金五郎). 1990. Kogo Jiten (古語辞典, Dictionary of Classical Japanese), revised edition. Tokyo: Iwanami. 5th printing, 1994.

Pulleyblank, Edwin G. 1984. Middle Chinese: A Study in Historical Phonology. Vancouver: UBC Press.

————. 1991. Lexicon of Reconstructed Pronunciation in Early Middle Chinese, Late Middle Chinese, and Early Mandarin. Vancouver: UBC Press.

Pullum, Geoffrey K. & William A. Ladusaw. 1986. Phonetic Symbol Guide. Chicago: University of Chicago Press.

Ramsey, S. Robert & James Marshall Unger. 1972. Evidence of a Consonant Shift in 7th Century Japanese. Papers in Japanese Linguistics 1:2: 278–95.

Robinson, Orrin W. 1992. Old English and its Closest Relatives: A Survey of the Earliest Germanic Languages. Stanford: Stanford University Press.

Sahara, Makoto. 1992. Rice Cultivation and the Japanese. Acta Asiatica 63: 40–63.

Sansom, George. 1958. A History of Japan to 1334. Stanford: Stanford University Press.

Seeley, Christopher. 1991. A History of Writing in Japan. Leiden: E. J. Brill.

Sei, Shōnagon (清少納言) (Kikan Ikeda (池田亀鑑), ed.) 1967. Zenkō Makura no Sōshi (全講枕草子, The Complete Pillow Book of Sei Shōnagon). Tokyo: Shibundō (至文堂). 2nd printing, 1968.

——————. (Ivan Morris, trans.) 1991. The Pillow Book of Sei Shōnagon. New York: Columbia University Press.

Serafim, Leon A. 1978. Doublets in Japanese Native Vocabulary: A Contribution to the Consonant Phonology of Prehistoric Japanese. ms.

Shibatani, Masayoshi. 1990. The Languages of Japan. Cambridge: Cambridge University Press.

Shinmura, Izuru (新村出), ed. 1991. Kōjien (広辞苑). Tokyo: Iwanami. 4th edition.

Thomason, Sarah Grey & Terrence Kaufman. 1988. Language Contact, Creolization, and Genetic Linguistics. Berkeley: University of California Press.

Turner, Christy G., II. 1991. Sundadonty and Sinodonty in Japan: The Dental Basis for a Dual Origin Hypothesis for the Peopling of the Japanese Islands. In Hanihara, ed., 1991b: 96–112.

Unger, James Marshall. 1977. Studies in Early Japanese Morphophonemics. Bloomington: Indiana University Linguistics Club. 1977 publication of 1975 dissertation.

Vance, Timothy J. 1987. An Introduction to Japanese Phonology. Albany: State University of New York Press.

Wells, J.C. 1982. Accents of English 1: An Introduction. Cambridge: Cambridge University Press. 3rd reprint, 1992.

Whitman, John Bradford. 1985. The Phonological Basis for the Comparison of Japanese and Korean. Harvard University dissertation.

Kakarimusubi from a Comparative Perspective

JOHN WHITMAN
Cornell University

1. *Kakarimusubi* (KM: representative references are Ôno, 1993 and Quinn, to appear) refers to a syntactic pattern in premodern Japanese where the scope of of a constituent marked with a particular type of particle (*kakari zyosi*) is demarcated by ADNOMINAL (*rentaikei*) or REALIS-CONDITIONAL (*izenkei*) marking on an associated predicate (*musubi*). After providing a brief structural characterization of the pattern, this paper places it in a broader typological context, and returning to premodern Japanese, proposes a structural analysis. The final section of the paper discusses the apparent areal isolation of the KM pattern in northeast Asia.

2. Structural characterization

In the KM pattern of premodern Japanese, four particles appear with adnominal marking on the associated predicate: [-wh] interrogative *-ya* (1), [±wh] ([+wh] after the 8th century) interrogative *-ka* (2), -interrogative focus *-namu* (< *-namo*) (3), and ±interrogative focus *-zo* (<*-so*) (4). Throughout this paper, the particle and relevant marking on the associated predicate are indicated in boldface. Examples follow:

(1) Ofotomo no Dainagon φa [tatu   no kubi no tama **ya**]   (*TM*)
    Otomo GEN Councillor TOP   dragon GEN head GEN gem Q
    tor-i-te   oφas-i-tar-**u**
    take-RY-PERF.RY   come.HON-RY-PERF-RT
    'Did Otomo no Dainagon get the gems on the dragon's head?'

(2) kakaru   miti φa   [ikade **ka**] imas-**uru**   to   (*IM* 9)
    this.kind road TOP   how   Q   go(HON)-RT COMP
    if-u   wo   mi-re-ba   mi-si   φito   nari-ker-i
    say-RT ACC   see-IZ-COND see-PAST.RT person   be-RY-PAST-SS
    'When (he_i) heard (someone) say, "How is it that you are on this road?" it was a person that (he_i) had encountered before.'

161

(3) titi   φa   naφobito   ni-t-e   (*IM* 10)
    father TOP ordinary.person be-PERF-RY
    [φaφa **namu**]   φuziφara   nar-i-ker-**u**
    mother-EMPH   Fujiwara   be-RY-PAST-RT
    'Father was an ordinary person; it is Mother who was a Fujiwara.'

(4) [kano φati wo sute-te,   mata iφ-i-ke-ru   yori **zo**] (*TM*)
    that bowl ACC discard-PERF.RT again say-RY-PST-RT from FOC
    omo na-ki   koto wo ba 'φadi   wo   sut-u'   to φa iφ-i-ker-**u**
    face lack-RT fact ACC TOP shame ACC discard-SS C TOP say-RY-PST-RT
    'It is from (his) speaking again after having discarded that bowl
    that brazen-faced behavior came to be called "discarding shame".'

A fifth ±interrogative focus particle -*koso* appears with realis-conditional
(*izenkei*) marking on the associated predicate:

(6) [tir-e-ba **koso**] itodo   sakura φa   medeta-**kere**   (*IM* 82)
    fall-IZ-COND   the more cherry TOP wonderful-IZ
    uki.yo-ni   [nani **ka**]   φisasi-kar-u   bek-i
    sad.world-in   what Q   long-V-RT   MOD-RT
    'It is because they fall that cherry blossoms are so fine;
    in this woeful world what should be longlasting?'

The semantic differentiation of the particles in the KM pattern and its
historical development are central topics of Japanese historical syntax; I
will not dwell on them here. Instead I would like to sketch in (7) a very
rough structural characterization of the pattern for the purpose of
typological comparison:

(7) a. The KM particle designates the scope-bearing constituent (the K-
        marked element) in a SCOPED (focus, interrogative) construction.
    b. The K-marked element is contained in a clause whose predicate
        (the M-marked predicate) takes a nominalizing ending.
    c. The M-marked predicate indicates the scope of the K-marked
        element.
    d. There are locality restrictions on the relationship between the K-
        marked element and the M-marked predicate.

The point of (7a) is clearest in examples like (2) and (5), where the K-
marker is a [+wh] interrogative particle. Hence much of the following
exemplificatory discussion about (7c) and (d) centers on wh-question
markers of this type.

The KM pattern in wh-questions is independently interesting for the perspective it gives on the syntactic marking of wh-questions in general. The basic components of wh-questions are usually identified as a wh- or Q-marker and a wh-phrase; this treatment has been standard in the generative tradition since Baker (1970). The former element in this treament conflates two roles: it marks the scope of the question, and also the type (function or mood) of the clause (in the sense of Cheng 1991). The KM wh-question pattern shows that these two functions must be distinguished: scope is marked by adnominal M-marking on the predicate, while the type of the clause (interrogative) is marked by K-marking with -*ka* on the wh-phrase in situ. Thus we know by the position of adnominal marking that the scope of the question in (2) is over the clause headed by *imasuru*; (2) could never be interpreted as a matrix question. It is easy to imagine a treatment that associates abstract [+wh] marking with adnominal M-marking: but such a treatment would overlook the fact that adnominal marking is not necessarily associated with an interrogative function in the KM pattern.

The type of scope most plausibly associated with the other four KM particles in premodern Japanese is focus (of course in classical Praguean terms the scope of a wh-phrase is a subtype of focus). [-Wh] -*ya* marks the focus of yes/no questions. -*Zo* survives in modern Japanese as a sentence final emphatic particle and is often rendered in translations from the premodern language by means of a pseudocleft with sentence-final -*zo* on the K-marked constituent in predicate position. -*Namu* does not survive in modern Japanese, but this particle is typically translated by literary scholars using one of the variety of devices for marking focus in modern Japanese, such as exhaustive listing -*ga* for the subject of the second clause in (3) in the *Nihon koten bungaku zensyû* modern Japanese translation (Katagiri et al 1972: 143):

(8) Titi   wa nami   no mibun no   hito de,
    father TOP ordinary GEN rank GEN person be
    haha **ga** Huziwara no   de   datta.
    mother NOM Fujiwara   GEN issue was
    'Father was a person of ordinary rank; <u>Mother</u> was a Fujiwara.'

The import of (7b) is obvious for the four premodern Japanese KM particles that appear with adnominal M-marking. -*Koso* alone requires, after the 8th century, realis conditional marking of the sort normally found on subordinate 'although' or 'because' clauses. As far as I know this pattern is typologically unique to Japanese, but it is consistent with (7b). Realis conditional marking is 'nominal' in a synchronic sense because it marks verbal adjuncts; diachronically many attempts have been made to derive this verbal form from the adnominal ending (see for example Unger 1977). It is relevant to the discussion in §4 that this form is also presuppositional (i.e. realis).

It is difficult to exemplify (7c) and (d) with data from premodern Japanese alone, since definitive statements about scope marking and locality restrictions require access to intuitions about ungrammatical sentences and impossible meanings. I therefore introduce these aspects of the structural definition of KM in the following section.

3.0 KM in a living language

Gair (1983) identifies a pattern in Sinhala (Indo-Aryan: Sri Lanka) that has the properties of (7); this pattern (especially its [+wh] interrogative subtype) has been studied intensively in recent dissertations by Kishimoto (1991) and Sumangala (1993). We can see (7a-b) exemplified in (9-11) below:

(9) Siri [mokak də]   keruwe   (Gair & Sumangala 1991: 1)
    Siri what   Q   did-E
    'What did Siri do?'

(10) Siri [waduwædə də] keruwe   (G&S 1991: 5)
     Siri woodworking Q   did-E
     'Was it woodworking that Siri did?'

(11) Siri [waduwædə tamayi]   keruwe   (G&S 1991: 2)
     Siri woodworking EMPH   did-E
     'It was indeed woodworking that Siri did.'

In (9), a wh-question, the wh-phrase *mokak də* 'what-Q' is K-marked by the interrogative particle -*də*. The scope of the question is indicated by M-marking with -*e*, a type of nominalizing verbal suffix. In (10), -*də* marks the focus of a yes/no question. In (11), non-interrogative focus is marked by the particle -*tamayi*. In the absence of a K-marker the verb in (11) takes a non-nominalizing conclusive ending:

(12) Siri waduwædə   keruwa   (G&S 1991: 2)
     Siri woodworking   did-A
     'Siri did woodworking.'

Interrogative -də also marks questions without a preverbal K-marked element, as do the Japanese interrogative K-markers. In this case in Sinhala the predicate appears in a conclusive, not a nominal form, like premodern Japanese -ya but unlike -ka :

(13) oya   pot-ak   gatta də   (Kishimoto 1992: 7)
     you   book-QINDEF   bought Q
     'Did you buy a book?'

As (14a-b) show, premodern Japanese -ya followed the conclusive (shûshikei) form of the associated predicate, while -ka followed the adnominal (rentaikei) form:

(14) a. ware   wo   ba   sir-a-zu   ya   (IM 62)
        me   ACC TOP   know-MZ -not.SS Q
        'Don't you know me?'

     b. waraɸabe-to   ɸaradati-tamaɸ-er-u   ka   (GM 5)
        children-with squabble-HON-PERF-RT Q
        'Have you been fighting with the children?"

3.1   Long-distance readings

Gair (1983) demonstrates that (7c) holds for the KM pattern in Sinhala. In embedded contexts, M-marking on the predicate disambiguates the scope of wh-questions:

(15) [Siri [mokak də] keruwe kiyəla]   amma   kalpənaa-keruwa
     Siri what Q did-E   COMP   mother thought-A
     'Mother thought (about) what Siri did.'   (G&S 1991: 1)

(16) [Siri [mokak də] keruwa kiyəla]   amma   kalpənaa-keruwe
     Siri what Q did-A   COMP   mother thought-E
     'What did Mother think that Siri did?'   (G&S 1991: 1)

In (15), M-marking on the embedded predicate indicates an embedded question, while in (16) M-marking on the main clause predicate indicates a matrix question.

Japanese grammarians have tended to assert that KM in premodern Japanese is essentially clause-bounded: that is, M-marking occurs on the predicate of the clause immediately containing the K-marked constituent. If this were actually the case, M-marking could not function as a type of scope marking, and

KM would be simply a mechanical (and very unusual) kind of concord. In fact in their interpretation of KM sentences, literature specialists have not treated it so. Consider for example the following exchange between Take no Okina and Kaguyahime from *Taketori monogatari*. Take no Okina asks Kaguyahime to clarify her (very stringent) requirements for an acceptable suitor:

(17) T: somosomo [[[ika   yau nar-u kokorozasi ar-a-m-u]   φito] ni **ka**
in first place what kind be-RT love have-MZ-SUP-RT person DAT Q
aφa-m-u]   to   obos-**u** ...
wed-SUP-SS   COMP think-RT/SS
'In the first place [what kind of love]$_i$ do you think that you would
want to marry a person that has t$_i$?' ...

K: [[[nani bakari no   φuka-ki]] wo **ka** mi-m-u]   to iφ-a-m-**u**
what degree GEN deep-RT ACC Q see.MZ-SUP-SS C say-MZ-SUP-RT/SS
'[How deep (a love)]$_i$ shall I say that I would like to see t$_i$?'

Despite the fact that the wh-expressions are separated from the matrix predicate by two clause boundaries (and one NP boundary), these are clearly matrix questions. Unfortunately in (17) M-marking is morphologically obscured in the written language. This is because the suppositional ending -*mu* (occuring four times) and the matrix predicate *obos-u* 'think' (honorific) both have segmentally[1] identical adnominal and conclusive forms. Thus this example lacks the morphological perspicuity of the Sinhala contrast in (15-16). However the long-distance (matrix) interpretation of the wh-questions in (17) is not in question: the example shows at a minimum that the KM question strategy did not restrict premodern Japanese to a clause-bounded interpretation of wh-questions!

[1] The accentuation of adnominal verb forms was distinct, at least for 'high' register verbs (Type-A in Martin 1987). Martin (191-8) analyzes the adnominal ending as atonicizing for both accentual classes of verbs, but notes (350-1) that in Kamakura materials Type-B adnominal forms have a tonic pattern identical to the conclusive. *Obosu* 'think' most likely belongs to this class. Martin (351) also observes that suppositional -*mu* appears to atonicize the preceding verb stem in both adnominal and conclusive contexts. Nevertheless, the atonicizing analysis of the adnominal ending raises the distinct possibility that M-marking was originally suprasegmentally unambiguous.

Morphologically unambiguous examples of long-distance KM in premodern Japanese tend to be difficult to find because of the segmental homphony of the adnominal and conclusive forms of most bridge verbs (*iφ-u* 'say', *omoφ-u* 'think') and the suppositional ending, which is common in questions. Matsuo (1936: 94-5) uses the paucity of such examples to dispute the view that KM across the boundary of a complement clause might have represented correct usage. However one of Matsuo's own morphologically unambiguous examples, from *Yamato monogatori* , gives us a clear (if poetically complex) case of a long-distance KM question:

(18) [tamakusige   φuta tose a φ-a-nu   kimi ga mi wo   (*YM* 4)
    comb-box   2   year meet-MZ-not -RT you GEN body ACC
    akenagara ya φa   ar-a-m-u]   to   omoφ-i-si
    red-still   Q TOP be-MZ-SUP-SS COMP think-RY-PAST(RT)
    'Did I think of your person, which I have not seen for two years, still in the red (vestments of the fifth rank)?'

This example is a poem contained in a letter read by the protagonist of the story, who is waiting for news of an expected promotion to fourth rank in the new year. The poem in the letter, from an acquaintance in the capital, is his first indication that the promotion will not be forthcoming.[2] The force of the yes/no question (which is rhetorical) depends upon it having matrix scope; were the question embedded, the protagonist would still not know whether he had been promoted or not. M-marking on the matrix predicate in this instance is deliberate: its purpose is to mark matrix scope.

3.2 Locality restrictions

Gair (1983) further shows that the KM pattern in Sinhala is subject to a locality condition which appears to basically equivalent to subjacency (see Kishimoto 1991):

(19) *oyaa [[kau də liyəpu] potə] kieuwe?   (Kishimoto 1991: 13)
    you   who Q wrote   book] read-E
    'Who did you read the book that t wrote?'

---

[2]*Tamakusige* is a *makura kotoba* ('pillow-word') for *ake-* in its punned meaning of 'open' (here, 'open the new year'), and also for *φuta* in its punned meaning of 'lid' (of a box). The poem builds from a triple entendre based on *ake* 'red' (the designated robe color of the protagonist's current status, fifth rank), *ake-* 'open', and the comb-box trope.

(20) oyaa [[kauru liyəpu] potə də]   kieuwe?   (Kishimoto 1991: 12)
      you   who   wrote book Q]   read-E
      'Who did you read the book that t wrote?'

In (19) K-marking is directly on the wh-element, which is separated from the M-marked predicate by a complex NP boundary. The result is ungrammatical. In (20) K-marking is on the entire island (complex NP) constituent, which is therefore subjacent to the M-marked predicate; the result is ungrammatical.

    These facts correspond exactly to the judgements of Japanese grammarians about the premodern KM pattern. For example Yamada Yoshio (1952) shows that K-marking inside syntactic islands does not trigger M-marking on the matrix predicate, for adjunct clauses (1952: 570-1, 574-5) and complex NPs (1952: 583-4). The point here is that in an example like (17), for instance, K-marking with [+wh] -ka cannot appear inside the complex NP containing the wh-expression:

(21) [[ika (*ka) yau (*ka) nar-u kokorozasi (*ka) ar-a-m-u]
      what (Q) kind (Q) be-RT love   (Q)   be-MZ-SUPP-RT
      φito]   ni   ka   aφa-m-u]   to   obos-u
      person DAT Q   marry-SUPP-SS   COMP think-RT

K-marking must instead appear on the entire island constituent, in this case the complex NP headed by "person". This is identical to the Sinhala pattern in (19-20).

4. KM as a cleft in situ pattern

    Gair (1983) takes property (7d) as a diagnostic for movement, as do Kishimoto and Sumangala.[3] Gair points out that corresponding to the pattern in (9, 11) in Sinhala are examples where the focused element is overtly displaced to the end of the clause:

[3]These researchers differ as to the level of representation where movement occurs (and where therefore the relevant locality restriction applies). Kishimoto takes the view that Sinhala wh movement is abstract. Sumangala argues that movement is syntactic but involves a null wh-element, following Watanabe's (1992) analysis of Japanese. Gair, Kishimoto, and Sumangala all assume that the relevant locality restriction is Subjacency. Yanagida (1995) takes a different view, arguing that locality retrictions in the KM pattern as well as other wh-in-situ patterns constrain movement of the K-marker to the position where the wh item takes its scope.

(22) Siri keruwe   [mokak də]
    Siri did-E   what Q
    'What did Siri do?'

(23) Siri keruwe   [waduwædə **tamayi**]
    Siri did-E   woodworking EMPH
    'It was indeed woodworking that Siri did.'

Gair proposes that (22-23) are derived by a type of focus movement, and that the original examples (9-11) are derived by the abstract (i.e. LF) counterpart of this movement. Both types of movement are constrained by subjacency, accounting for the contrast between (19) and (20). KM in the unmoved pattern thus emerges as a type of in-situ focus construction.

This analysis is reminiscent of Ôno Susumu's (1955, 1993) diachronic account of the premodern Japanese K-markers which appear with adnominal M-marking. On this account the K-markers originate as sentence-final particles. The KM pattern itself originates from the pseudocleft pattern present at all historical stages of Japanese. Right dislocation or 'inversion' of the topic with the presupposition in the pseudocleft pattern of (24) results in the order of (25). Omission of topic marking on the presupposition and dropping of the copula as in the premodern version of the 'inversion' pattern (26), leads to reanalysis as KM. Inverted pseudocleft sentences like (?6) are thus hypothesized as the diachronic source for the actual KM pattern in sentences like (3).[4]

(24) **Pseudocleft version of (8)**
    [Huziwara no de   datta no] wa h a h a da (yo)
    Fujiwara GEN issue was COMP TOP mother be EMPH
    'The one who was a Fuziwara was mother.'

(25) **Pseudocleft version of (8) with focus inverted/right dislocated**
    haha   da (yo), [Huziwara no   de   datta no] wa
    mother   be EMPH Fujiwara GEN issue was COMP TOP
    'It was mother, the one who was a Fujiwara.'

---

[4]Note that if Ôno's account is correct, we should expect to find 'long distance' KM examples like (17-18), since a long-distance construal is surely an option in the pseudocleft pattern.

(26) **Premodern version of (25), (copula and topic marking optional)**

φaφa	(nar-i) **namu**[5]	[φuziφara	nar-i-ker-u]	(φa)
mother (be-SS) EMPH?		Fujiwara	be-RY-PAST-RT	(TOP)

The (synchronic) inversion analysis actually works better for Sinhala, since this language lacks overt topic or nominative marking, and has a null copula in the present tense. As a diachronic account of Japanese KM, the inversion analysis has been subject to criticism (thus recently Kinsui 1994). As a synchronic analysis of Sinhala the analysis faces the difficulty pointed out by Sumangala (1993): extracting the focused element from within the topic/presupposition and inserting it in the position of a predicate nominal is a lowering operation, as shown schematically for such a derivation of the Japanese example (24):

(27) [PRESUPPOSITION ... t_i ....]   FOCUS$_i$ (COPULA)

[$_S$ [t_i Huziwara no de   datta no]   wa   [$_{VP}$ hahai   (da)]]

    Fujiwara   GEN issue was COMP TOP   mother   be

Nevertheless there are compelling aspects to the intuition that a cleft structure is involved in the KM pattern. The same intuition is behind the tendency of literary scholars to translate KM sentences with cleft-like equivalents, in particular with the device of the extended predicate. The cleft-like aspects of the KM pattern center on the fact that the presupposition is nominalized, and the focused element extruded from the presupposition in terms of its scope.

The weakness of the inversion analysis is that it takes as its point of departure the pseudocleft structure in (24, 27). This is not surprising, since pseudoclefts are the only overt cleft structure in Sinhala and Japanese. These languages lack an overt equivalent of the English *it*-cleft structure in (28b):

		PRESUPPOSITION		FOCUS	
(28)	a.	[Who was a Fujiwara]	is	[mother].	(Pseudocleft)

		FOCUS	PRESUPPOSITION	
	b.	It is [mother]	[that was a Fuziwara].	(*It*-cleft)

---

[5]A difficulty for Ôno's hypothesis is the fact that *namu<namo* does not occur as a sentence-final emphatic particle; the homophonous sentence particle *namu< namo* follows the irrealis (*mizenkei*) form of inflecting stems and expresses volition or exhortation.

This syntactic gap is likely related to the absence of VP-internal extraposition structures in verb-final languages such as Sinhala or Japanese. However the very existence of this syntactic gap suggests the possibility that we might look for an abstract equivalent, much as generative syntaticians have associated an abstract equivalent of wh-movement with in-situ wh-questions in languages (such as Japanese and Sinhala) where wh-phrases are not moved in the syntax. The possibility that comes to mind is that KM is the pattern of an *it*-cleft in situ.

At first glance it is not entirely clear what the structure of an in-situ equivalent of (28b) should be. The focus predicate nominal in *it*-clefts is a subcategorized complement of the copula on many analyses (Jesperson 1927, Chomsky 1977). If we take seriously the idea that the copula is a pleonastic element, however, the requirement that the copula (and its complement, the focus element) are obligatory components of the construction disappears. It is plausible to hypothesize that an overt focus element external to the presupposition is required only when the 'operator' internal to the presupposition is silent, as in Chomsky's analysis of English *it*-clefts (29):

	FOCUS	PRESUPPOSITION
(29)	It is [mother]$_i$	[OP$_i$ that t$_i$ was a Fuziwara].

When the 'operator' internal to the presupposition is overt, it requires no antecedent (speaking informally), rendering the structure on the left-hand side of (29) superfluous. On the view that I have proposed, the KM clause in (3) has the surface syntactic structure in (30a). At an abstract level of representation it takes on the structure in (30b), which is also the structure of (29) once pleonastic material is omitted:

(30) a. [φaφa **namu**   φuziφara   nar-i-ker-u]
          mother-EMPH   Fujiwara   be-RY-PAST-RT

    b. [[φaφa **namu**]$_i$ [t$_i$ φuziφara   nar-i-ker-u]]
          mother-EMPH   Fujiwara   be-RY-PAST-RT

I think there are several pieces of evidence for the analysis of KM as an in-situ cleft pattern. Nitta Yoshio (1984) observes that KM in premodern Japanese does not occur in imperative and exclamatory contexts, and points out that this shows a close relationship between K-marking and the modal force of the clause. The first of these facts can be accounted for by the morphological fact that imperative marking is incompatible with the types of M-marking attested in premodern Japanese (although why this is so needs to be explained). The reason for the second fact is less obvious. We are used, for example, to finding close connections between the syntax of exclamations and the syntax of questions; thus we might expect to find an exclamatory subtype of the KM pattern.

Inspection of English *it*-clefts, however, reveals that they are excluded from the subject/aux inversion+negation exclamatory pattern: the exclamatory pattern which shares the basic syntax of yes/no questions. Consider the distribution of English *it*-clefts over modal clause types in (31):

(31)   **Modal clause-type restrictions on clefts**
    a. Always be punctual.   (imperative)
    b. Aren't you punctual!   (exclamatory)
    c. It is you who is always punctual. (declarative)
    d. Isn't it you who is punctual?   (interrogative)
    e. *Be it you who is always punctual. (imperative)
    f. *Isn't it you who is punctual!   (exclamatory)

Copular sentences in general allow both imperative (a) and syntactically marked (inversion+negation) exclamatory patterns (b). *It*-cleft equivalents of (a-b) are possible with declaratives (c) and interrogatives (d). But both imperative (e) and exclamatory (f) patterns are disallowed with the corresponding clefts.

A second piece of support for the *it*-cleft in situ analysis is typological. If the cleft analysis of KM is correct, Sinhala and premodern Japanese fall into the class of languages where wh-questions take a cleft pattern (Givon 1979). A crucial fact about languages of this type is that the cleft pattern in questions appears always to be of the *it*-cleft, not the pseudocleft type. Above I pointed out that overt syntactic analogues of the *it*-cleft pattern seem to be absent in verb-final languages. If this correlation is correct, the only possible realization of the it-cleft pattern in verb-final languages is as a cleft in situ; this would then be the expected pattern in questions formed from clefts.

5.   KM from an areal standpoint

It is fairly clear that KM in Japanese is not an innovation of the central dialects attested in premodern literary texts, since it is attested in Ryûkyûan (Kokuritsu Kokugo Kenkyûjo 1963).[6] The following Shuri data is from Ohnishi (1995), based on Kokuritsu Kokugo Kenkyûjo 1963:

---

[6]The consensus among scholars in Japan seems to be that the Ryûkyûan dialects which attest KM appear only to show adnominal M-marking, not the realis conditional (*izenkei*) pattern associated with *-koso* (6) (Ohnishi 1995). This

(32) a. sjumuçi   'jun-uN
          book   read-CONC
          'read a book'
      b. sjumuçi   'jun-uru   Qcu
          book   read-ADNOM   person
          'a person reading a book'
      c. 'waa ga   'jun-uN
          I   NOM   read-CONC
          'I read'
      c. 'waa ga   du   'jun-uru
          I   NOM FOC 7   read-ADNOM
          'I read'

From an areal standpoint, however, KM as fully defined in (7) appears
to have no other complete exponent in northeast Asia. In the remainder of
this paper I would like to briefly explore the distribution of patterns
similar to (7) in the areal vicinity of Japanese.

Alexander Vovin has pointed out to me the possible existence of a
pattern similar to KM in certain Tungusic languages. The data in (33-37)
from Ewen (Lamut) clearly show the pattern of K-marking (7a):

(33) asal-gu   olra-w beci-i?   (Benzing 1955: 121)
      women-Q   fish-ACC   3PL
      'Do the women catch fish?'

(34) uliki-w-gu   bu-ri-s,   hulica-m-gu?   (Benzing 1955: 111)
      squirrel-ACC-Q give-PAST-2S fox-ACC-Q
      'Did you give a squirrel or a fox?'

---

would be consistent with the likelihood that the *koso+ izenkei* KM pattern is
a relatively recent innovation in the small number of 8th century examples
where it occurs (I am grateful to Alexander Vovin for bringing this likelihood
to my attention). However Leon Serafim (p.c.) reports that the *koso+izenkei*
pattern is attested in some Ryûkyûan (Okinawan) dialects. Resolution of this
issue is important for determining the antiquity of the *koso+izenkei* pattern.

7The Shuri focus particle *-du* may be cognate with the premodern
Japanese K-marker *zo* (?< *so*), although its initial /d/ is not the
regular Shuri correspondence for either initial in the premodern
Japanese form (Kokuritsu Kokugo Kenkyûjo 1963: 178)

(35) aman-si   timina   hør-jin-gu, ətə-n-gu?   (Robbek 1989: 148)
father-2S tomorrow   go-fut-Q   not-FUT-Q
'Is your father going tomorrow or not?'

(36) hu-kkə   on   ulm-is?   (Benzing 1955: 112)
you-FOC   why   squirrel.hunt-2PL
'(But) why do <u>youse</u> hunt squirrels?'

(37) hi-kkə   ərə-w   əmu-rə-s   (Robbek 1989: 147)
you-FOC   this-ACC   bring-PRES-2S
'(But) you bring this.'

-Gu/-ku marks the focus element in yes/no questions (Benzing 1955: 111) internally to the clause (33, 34); it also marks the clause type in clause-final position (34, 35). These functions correspond to those of premodern Japanese *-ya* and instantiate (7a). *-Kka/-kkə*is analyzed as marking contrastive focus (36,37).

What is less clear from the Ewen data is the existence of parallels to (7c-d). Historically verbal forms marked for subject agreement have a nominal source ('participial' in Benzing's terminology), but this is true irrespective of the presence of K-marking. As (33-37) show, K-marking appears with a wide range of tense and aspect endings.

Korean presents a pattern that is almost the obverse of what we see in Ewen. Korean lacks clear counterparts of K-marking (7a). On the other hand, Korean evinces (7b-c), if we allow wh-expressions to stand in for the role of K-marked elements. A tradition going back to Ramstedt (1939) identifies the prefinal endings *-n-* and *-l(q)-* in Korean interrogatives as adnominal (Martin 1954, Kim Wancin 1957, Lee Ki-moon 1961/72; see Suh 1990 for a review of these and subsequent studies of Korean interrogative pattterns). The adnominal suffixes also provide the basis for sentence patterns that are not fixed in an interrogative function, but adnominal marking is obligatory in questions with verbal predicates. As Lee (1961/72: 144-5) points out, this is part of the fundamentally 'nominal' character of interrogatives in Late Middle Korean (LMK) in particular.

What Lee is referring to is the fact that the sentence final interrogative particles *-(k)a* (-wh), *-(k)wo* (+wh) and *-ta* (±wh) attach only to nominal or adnominal forms. The first two particles attach directly to predicate nominals (38, 39), the abstract nominalizer or 'formal noun' *i* '(fact) that' (40) or to the adnominal forms of verbal predicates (41). The particle *-ta* (used in direct questions of intent with a second person subject: An 1965) attaches only to adnominal forms of verbals (42):

(38) i   stol i   neh-uy   cyeng   **ka**   (*Wel.in sekpo* 8: 94).
this girl-NOM your-GEN servant Q
'Is this girl your servant?'

(39) Pwuthye-y   nwu   **kwo**   (*Wel.in sekpo* 17: 34).
Buddha-NOM   who   Q
'Who is the Buddha?'

(40) mozom-kwa   nwun-kwa-y   i cey
heart-and   eye-and-NOM   this time
etuy   is-no-n-y   **wo**   (*Nungem kyeng enhay* I 46)
where be-PROC-ADNOM -fact Q
'Where is the mind and eye now?'

(41) CINSIL an-i-n **ka**   hoy-a ne-y UYSIM ho-kwo (*Wel.in sekpo* 10: 38)
truth not-be-ADNOM Q do-INF you-NOM doubt do-ing
'Wondering if it is not the truth you doubt and...'

(42) ne-y SIN ho-no-n **ta**   ani ho-no-n **ta**   (*Sekpo sangcel* 9: 26)
you-NOM do-PROC-ADNOM Q not do-PROC-ADNOM Q
'Do you believe or not?'

The fact that the interrogative particles attach only to nominal or adnominal forms is suggestive of two possibilities about the earlier grammar of the language. First, the status of *-(k)a* and *-(k)wo* as postnominal particles suggests they may have originally had a wider distribution inside the sentence as well as in sentence-final position. There is no obvious source for *-(k)a*, although it seems likely that its origin is related to the source for the modern postvocalic nominative particle. In the case of *-(k)wo* a potential related form is the adverb *kwos* 'just, precisely' (?< *kwo+(u)s* adverbial suffix).

Second, there is some reason to believe that the adnominal ending + question particle forms in (41-2) represent the earlier pattern in the language. Forms involving adnominal ending + *i* '(fact) that' + question particle are periphrastic, based on the Late Midddle Korean extended predicate pattern formed around *i*.[8] Furthermore, An (1965) shows that the

[8]Co-option of the nominal head of an extended predicate pattern as a question marker is reminiscent of contemporary Japanese questions in *no*, the 'formal noun' head of the modern Japanese extended predicate pattern. *No* in this pattern is clearly on its way to

pattern of adnominal ending +(k)a/(k)wo (41) was restricted to embedded questions (sometimes used in ellipted matrix contexts). This pattern becomes (re-)established in matrix questions after the 16th century, perhaps in compensation for the loss of the adnominal + *ta* pattern (42). The general tendency for embedded clauses to preserve the syntax of an earlier stage of the language suggests that the pattern may originally have been the general one, restricted during the LMK period due to the popularity of the extended predicate pattern. If this is so, Korean may have regularly marked questions with adnominal forms of predicates in conformity with (7c).

The use of adnominal forms of predicates in clause-final position is restricted in LMK: patterns where this is possible require that the adnominal form be followed by a (normally postnominal) particle (such as the concessive ending *-kenul* < *-ke-* effective + *-n* adnominal + *ul* accusative: Martin 1992: 606). Loss by adnominal forms of the ability to appear as a bare clause-final endings would have eliminated the possibility for a complete counterpart of the KM pattern in (7), but I have suggested here that the components for an earlier synthesis of such a pattern are still present in the language of the 15th century.

Abbreviations (premodern Japanese)
RY = ren'yôkei = CONT(INUATIVE) IZ = izenkei = COND(ITIONAL)
RT = rentaikei = ADNOM(INAL)   SS = shûshikei = CONC(LUSIVE)

Premodern Japanese texts cited
TM = *Taketori mongatari* (859) YM = *Yamato monogatari* (c. 950)
IM= *Ise monogatari* (900)   GM = *Genji monogatari* (1002)

References
An Pyenghuy. 1965. Hwuki cwungsey kwuk.e uy uymun-pep ey tayhaye. Hakswulci (Kenkwuk University). Reprinted in An (1992), 136-67.
_____ 1992. Kwuk.e-sa yenkwu. Seoul: Mwunhak kwa ciseng-sa.
Baker, C. L. 1970. Notes on the description of English questions: the role of an abstract question morpheme. Foundations of Language 6. 197-219.
Benzing, Johannes. 1955. Lamutische grammatik. Wiesbaden: Franz Steiner Verlag.

---

reanalysis as a question marker, much like modern Korean *-ni* (< *-n* adnominal + *i* '(fact) that').

Cheng, Lisa. 1991. On the typology of wh-questions. Doctoral dissertation, MT.

Chomsky, Noam. 1977. On wh-movement. A festscrift for Morris Halle, ed. by P. W. Culicover, T. Wasow, and P. Kiparsky. New York: Holt, Rinehart & Winston.

Gair, James. 1983. Non-configurationality, movement, and Sinhala focus. Presented at the Linguistics Association of Great Britain, Newcastle, September 1983.

Gair, James & Lewala Sumangala. 1991. What to focus in Sinhala. Proceedings of ESCOL 1991.

Givon, Talmy. 1979. On understanding grammar. New York: Academic Press.

Jesperson, Otto. 1927. A modern English grammar III. London: Allen & Unwin.

Katagiri Yôichi, Fukui Teisuke, Takahashi Shôji & Shimizu Yoshiko. 1972. Nihon koten bungaku zensyû 8. Tokyo: Shogakukan.

Kim Wancin. 1957. -N, -l tongmyengsa uy thongsa-cek kinung kwa paltal ey tay haye. Kwuk.e yenkwu 2.

Kinsui Satoshi. 1994. (Heisei 4 nen · 5 nen ni okeru Kokugogakkai no tenbô) Bunpô (shiteki kenkyû). Kokugogaku 177: 9-19.

Kishimoto Hideki. 1991. On the nature of quantificational expressions and their logical form. Doctoral dissertation, Kobe University.

Kokuritsu Kokugo Kenkyûjo. 1963. Okinawago jiten. Tokyo: Ôkura-shô.

Lee Ki-moon. 1961. Kwuk.e-sa kaysel. Seoul: Mincwung sekwan. (Second edition 1972).

Martin, Samuel. 1954. Korean morphophonemics. Baltimore: Linguistic Society of America.

_____ 1987. The Japanese language through time. New Haven: Yale University Press.

_____ 1992. A reference grammar of Korean. Rutland: Tuttle.

Matsuo Sutejirô. 1936. Kokugohô ronkô. Tokyo: Bungaku-sha.

Ohnishi Takuichirô. 1995. Hôgen ni okeru syûshikei to rentaikei, mata kakarimusubi ni tuite no oboegaki. Presented at the Kokuritsu Kokugo Kenkyûjo, June 1995.

Ôno, Susumu. 1955-6. Nihon koten bunpô 1-10. Kokubungaku kaishaku to kanshô .

_____ 1993. Kakarimusubi no kenkyû. Tokyo: Iwanami shoten.

Nitta Yoshio. 1984. Kakarimusubi ni tuite. Kenkyû shiryô nihon bunpô 5, joshi-hen (1), ed. by K. Suzuki. Tokyo: Meiji shoin.

Quinn, Charles. To appear. Functional perspectives on predication in Japanese. Ann Arbor: Michigan Monographs in Japanese Studies.

Ramstedt, John. G. 1939. A Korean grammar. Helsinki: Mémoires de la société finno-ougrienne 82.

Robbek, V.A. 1989. Iazyk Evenov Berezovki. Leningrad: Nauka.

Suh Chung-mok. 1990. Uymun-pep. Kwuk.e yenkwu eti kkaci oassna, ed. by Sewul tayhakkyo tayhakwen Kwuk.e Yenkwu-hoy , 291-310. Seoul: Tonga chwulphan-sa.

Sumangala, Lewala. 1993. Long distance dependencies in Sinhala: the syntax of focus and wh Questions. Doctoral dissertation, Cornell University.

Unger, James. 1977. Studies in early Japanese morphophonemics. Bloomington: Indiana University Linguistics Club.

Watanabe Akira. 1992. Subjacency and s-structure movement of WH-in-situ. Journal of East Asian Linguistics 1: 255-292.

YamadaYoshio. 1952. Heian-chô bunpô-shi. Tokyo: Hôbunkan.

Yanagida Yûko. 1995. Focus projection and wh-head movement. Doctoral dissertation, Cornell University.

Pre-Sino-Korean and Pre-Sino-Japanese: Reexamining an Old Problem from a Modern Perspective

MARC H. MIYAKE
University of Hawaii at Manoa

0. Defining Pre-Sinoxenic

The Chinese language[1] has unquestionably exerted enormous influence upon its neighbors. In Vietnamese, Korean, and Japanese, this influence has been especially great at the lexical level. Each of these languages has a stratum of loanwords from MIDDLE CHINESE, the language of the Tang Dynasty.[2] These strata—SINO-VIETNAMESE (SV), SINO-KOREAN (SK), and

---

[1]For ease of exposition, I will treat 'the Chinese language' throughout this paper as a single entity even though it may have split into heterogenous 'dialects' if not 'languages' as early as Han times. Korean, Japanese, and Vietnamese were probably not influenced by exactly the same variety of 'Chinese'.

[2]Actually, each of these strata (Sino-Vietnamese, Sino-Korean, and Sino-Japanese) is composed of several strata (GO-ON, KAN-ON, etc.), some with

SINO-JAPANESE (SJ)—are collectively known as SINOXENIC (SX).[3] Sinoxenic loanwords are directly associated with Chinese characters, display generally regular sound correspondences with Middle Chinese, and are unquestionably loans from Chinese.

However, not all Chinese loanwords in Vietnamese, Korean, and Japanese are Sinoxenic. Each of these languages has Chinese loanwords which are considered to be 'native' and are not usually, if ever, associated with Chinese characters.[4] These non-Sinoxenic words were generally borrowed at periods predating the Tang Dynasty.[5] I call these earlier strata of loanwords PRE-SINOXENIC (PSX). The sub-varieties of Pre-Sinoxenic are PRE-SINO-VIETNAMESE (PSV), PRE-SINO-KOREAN (PSK), and PRE-SINO-JAPANESE (PSJ).

1. Previous studies of Pre-Sinoxenic

Most studies of Chinese loanwords in Vietnamese, Korean, and Japanese have focused on Sinoxenic as opposed to Pre-Sinoxenic. No large-scale works devoted to Pre-Sinoxenic as a whole or of any of its sub-varieties exist, except for Kamei's monograph on Pre-Sino-Japanese (1954) and Ray's dissertation on Pre-Sino-Vietnamese (1979). A chapter in Kim (1971) is perhaps the longest treatment of Pre-Sino-Korean to date. This is unfortunate because Pre-Sinoxenic may reveal much about the nature and intensity of Sinitic influence

---

relics predating Middle Chinese. For this paper, I will generally ignore these subdivisions and treat each variety of Sinoxenic as a unified 'stratum' in contrast to the strata of non-Sinoxenic Chinese loan words.

[3]This term was coined by Martin (1953: 4).

[4]Other than as KUNYOMI in Japanese and as 'native' glosses for Chinese characters in Vietnamese and Korean.

[5]There are a large number of exceptions to this rule of dating in Korean. Many words were borrowed from Middle Chinese or Old Mandarin, lost their association with characters, and became 'nativized'. I will examine only a few of the 'decharacterized' Middle Chinese loans in this paper, since (1) I believe that most of them are uncontroversial and obvious borrowings and (2) my main interest in this paper lies in pre-Middle Chinese borrowings—Pre-Sinoxenic in the strict sense. For an examination of the 'decharacterized' Middle Chinese and Old Mandarin borrowings in Korean that are not covered in this paper, see Martin (1992: 96-98). A future version of this paper will expand its scope to include all of these 'decharacterized' borrowings in Korean, regardless of their source (Old Chinese, Middle Chinese, or Old Mandarin). Perhaps a cover term for these borrowings may be 'NATIVIZED SINO-KOREAN', which avoids specifying the date of borrowing.

in East Asia prior to the Tang Dynasty.

The few extant studies on Pre-Sinoxenic such as Karlgren (1926), Kamei (1954), Ray (1979), and Kim (1971) have all viewed the subject from Karlgrenian perspectives.[6] Bernhard Karlgren's views on Chinese language history remain influental even today. However, much counterevidence against them has surfaced in recent decades. Many post-Karlgrenian reconstructions of Chinese have appeared, but perhaps the most radical among them are those of Baxter (1992) for OLD CHINESE and Pulleyblank (1984, 1991) for Middle Chinese.

Innovations in reconstruction are not limited to Chinese. Previous work on Pre-Sino-Korean and Pre-Sino-Japanese predated the important recent advances made by Ramsey and Unger (1972), Whitman (1991), Ramsey (1993), and others.

Our picture of Chinese, Korean, and Japanese language history has changed radically since even 1971, when Kim's chapter on Pre-Sino-Korean was published. Many of the words in these paper were proposed to be Pre-Sino-Korean and Pre-Sino-Japanese when the predominant reconstructions of Old and Middle Chinese were Karlgrenian and when many sound changes in Korean and Japanese were yet unknown.[7] Will these etymologies still appear valid once they are reexamined from a modern perspective?

2. Goals, methodology, and assumptions of the present study

This paper attempts to evalute the validity of approximately 70 proposed Chinese etymologies for Korean and Japanese words. My focus will be primarily, though exclusively, on phonological similarity between the Korean and Japanese words and their presumed Chinese sources. Non-phonological factors such as semantics will be mentioned though not emphasized. Kamei (1954) attempted to refute most of Karlgren's (1926) Pre-Sino-Japanese etymologies on largely semantic and cultural grounds. I do not wish to duplicate his work here; rather, I wish to concentrate on how modern views on historical phonology affect the validity of Pre-Sino-Korean and Pre-Sino-Japanese etymologies. These etymologies will be classified according to their probability into five categories ranging from most likely to least likely.

---

[6]Although Ray and Kim are not Karlgrenian purists—Ray uses Mineya's (1972) Karlgren-like reconstruction of Middle Chinese and Kim revises Karlgren's Old Chinese reconstructions to a limited extent—their work predates the radical post-Karlgrenian innovations in Chinese reconstruction found in Pulleyblank (1984, 1991), Baxter (1992), and elsewhere.

[7]These include Whitman's (1991) rules of *-r- and *-m- loss in Japonic and Ramsey's (1993) origin of aspirated stops from earlier *hV*-stop sequences in Korean.

59 of the proposed Pre-Sino-Korean and Pre-Sino-Japanese etymologies given here are respectively from Kim (1971) and Karlgren (1926). The others are from a variety of sources:

'arrive' bamboo (MK) 'that 1': suggested by Ho-min Sohn (at University of Hawai'i at Mānoa roundtable, 'Issues in the genetic relation of Korean and Japanese'; 1994)

'bowl' 'Buddha' (OJ), 'temple' (OJ, MC/OC 2nd etymology): from Martin (1991: 278).

'fish': suggested by Barbara E. Riley (personal communication, 1995)

'flay' (MK), 'rice1' (OJ), 'spirit' (Koguryo), 'that 2' (MK, OJ) and 'vessel' (MK): from Whitman (1990: 518-20, 522).

'hare 'summer' (MJ, OJ), 'spade' MK 2nd cognate: from Ono et al. (1990).

'house' (NK), 'rice 3': suggested by Leon A. Serafim (personal communications,1994, 1995)

'rat': suggested by Hashimoto (1978: 103-04)

'spade': suggested by Whitman (1990: 534, 543)

The remaining etymologies were suggested by me.

I have excluded most of the Korean borrowings from Middle Chinese and all of the Korean borrowings from OLD MANDARIN from this paper. For the reasoning behind this, see note 5.

The proposed Pre-Sino-Korean words are cited in Yale MIDDLE KOREAN (MK) romanization following Martin (1992), even if the words are NEW KOREAN (NK). Thus NK *o* is written here as *wo*, as in Middle Korean. Pitch accent is not indicated. This paper will focus largely on validating etymologies based on segmental phonological criteria. If a suspected Pre-Sinoxenic word and a Chinese word survive the 'first round' of tests of segmental similarity, then it is worthy for a 'second round' of tests of supersegmental (pitch accent and tone) similarity. Because (1) many Pre-Sinoxenic etymologies can be eliminated on segmental grounds alone and (2) Old Chinese, the supposed source of most Pre-Sinoxenic words, probably had no phonemic tones, this paper consists only of the 'first round' of segmental tests. I will incorporate the 'second round' of supersegmental tests into a future version of this paper.

The proposed Pre-Sino-Japanese words are cited in my own romanization. The initial of ha-gyō is spelled *p*. KŌOTSU distinctions are marked by 1 or 2 following the vowel. Although this notation does not hint at any particular phonetic interpretation of the distinction, I will assume that *i1* and *e1* are more palatal than *i2* and *e2* and that *o1* is more rounded than *o2,* which may be phonetically schwa. Pitch accent is not indicated for the reasons given above.

Both the EARLY MIDDLE CHINESE (EMC) and Old Chinese (OC) reconstructions are my own. The former is a revision of Pulleyblank (1984, 1991). The latter is a highly tentative revision of Baxter (1992) which is still in progress. Early Middle Chinese is the language of the Sui Dynasty *Qieyun* rhyme dictionary of 601 (Pulleyblank 1991: 1). This language may possibily be an artificial standard, with more rhyme categories than in any variety of Chinese at the time.[8] Unlike Baxter's (1992) Old Chinese, which is intended to represent the language of the *Shijing,* 'Old Chinese' here is largely an internal reconstruction of Early Middle Chinese incorporating additional elements from XIESHENG evidence. It is an abstraction intended to represent earlier distinctions and is not intended to represent Chinese at a specific date and place. Explanations of my Early Middle Chinese and Old Chinese orthographies will be given when needed below.

This paper presumes that Korean and Japanese evolved from PROTO-KOREO-JAPONIC (PKJ), according to the scheme established in Whitman (1991).[9] However, this assumption will not affect many of my judgments on the etymologies examined here. If it is correct, then some of the Pre-Sino Korean and Pre-Sino-Japanese words may have been Chinese loans into Proto-Koreo-Japonic as opposed to its daughter languages, Korean and Japanese. Even if the Proto-Koreo-Japonic hypothesis is incorrect, some of the Pre-Sino-Japanese words may have been borrowed, if not inherited, from Korean peninsular intermediaries such as Koguryo.

I have excluded Pre-Sino-Vietnamese from this study because Vietnamese borrowing from Chinese was probably not involved in a situation parallelling between Korean peninsular and Japonic languages. Presumably Pre-Sino-Vietnamese words were directly borrowed from some variety of Chinese, without intermediaries.[10]

---

[8]Many of the possibly artificial rhyme distinctions involve the presence or absence of vowel length in my reconstruction of Early Middle Chinese.

[9]Leon A. Serafim coined the term 'Proto-Koreo-Japonic.' Whitman (1990) uses the term 'Proto-Japanese-Korean.'

[10]This assumption underlies Pre-Sino-Vietnamese studies. Chinese loans in Mu'ò'ng (the closest relative to Vietnamese; the equivalent of 'Ryūkyūan' to Vietnamese) and Tai languages are assumed to have been borrowed through Vietnamese intermediaries due to Vietnamese cultural and political dominance. However, the possibility remains that some Pre-Sino-Vietnamese words were borrowed through Tai or other intermediaries.

This study is concerned not only with whether a given word was a loan from Chinese or not, but also with whether such loans were transmitted directly to Korean or Japanese or not. The transmission possibilities for Chinese loanwords are outlined below:

Possible routes of Chinese loan transmission in Northeast Asia; groupings after Yi (1971).

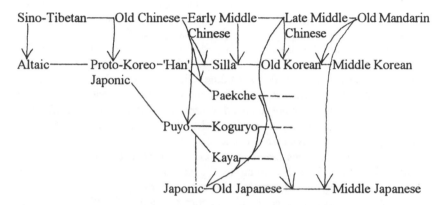

I will attempt to answer the following questions for each proposed Pre-Sino-Korean and Pre-Sino-Japanese word in this paper: Was the word genetically inherited at the Proto-Koreo-Japonic level and not borrowed from Chinese at all? Could Chinese or Sino-Tibetan instead have borrowed the word from Proto-Koreo-Japonic or Altaic rather than the other way around? Was the word borrowed from Chinese, and if so, borrowed by whom, with or without intermediaries? Answering these questions will add not only to our knowledge of Chinese-Koreo-Japonic contacts but also to that of contact within the Koreo-Japonic sphere.

3. Classification of data

I have sorted the 70 proposed Chinese etymologies for Korean and Japanese words into five grades according to their probability.

'Passing' grades, 'A' through 'C', are given to Korean and Japanese words which are probably cognate with the Chinese words.

Grade 'A': The phonological fit between the Korean and/or Japanese word and the proposed Chinese source is good. The word is definitely a loan from Chinese.

Grade 'B': The phonological fit between the Korean and/or Japanese word and the proposed Chinese source is imperfect. However, I still suspect the word to be a loan from Chinese. In some cases, non-phonological factors favor Chinese etymologies.

Grade 'C': The phonological fit between the Korean and/or Japanese word and the proposed Chinese source is imperfect. Although this word is probably cognate with its Chinese counterpart, it may not be a loan from Chinese. Korean and/or Japanese may have inherited the word while Chinese borrowed it from a non-Chinese language.

'Failing' grades, 'D' and 'F', are given to Korean and Japanese words which are probably not cognate with the Chinese words.

Grade 'D': The phonological fit between the Korean and/or Japanese word and the proposed Chinese source is imperfect. Morphological and semantic factors conspire to render Chinese etymologies improbable. I doubt that the word is a loan from Chinese. It may just be a look-alike, though the slim possibility of 'passing' as a cognate remains. Further examination may elevate a few Grade D words to Grade B (and vice versa).

Grade 'F': The antithesis of Grade A. The phonological fit between the Korean and/or Japanese word and the proposed Chinese source is poor. The word is definitely not a Chinese loan.

The grades I am most sure about are A, C, and F. I am less sure about some of the words in the grades in-between, B and D. Although this classifcation is somewhat tentative, I will organize my analysis of the data below according to the five grades. Each subsection will list the words in a certain grade arranged primarily by subclass (k, j, kj, pkj, etc.) and secondarily by alphabetical order of glosses. These lists will be followed by comments on the classes of words. Limitations of time and space prevent me from in-depth analyses of all individual etymologies.

The codes following the grades (A-F) indicate the possible direction of loans:

a = Borrowed by Chinese or Sino-Tibetan from Altaic? Hence native to Proto-Koreo-Japonic?

k = Attested only in Korean? Borrowed by Korean peninsular language from Chinese after Proto-Koreo-Japonic split? Or borrowed or inherited at Proto-Koreo-Japonic level?

j = Attested only in Japonic? Borrowed by Japanese either from Korean peninsular language (leaving no cognate in Middle Korean) or directly from Chinese after Proto-Koreo-Japonic split? Or borrowed or inherited at Proto-Koreo-Japonic level?

kj = Attested in both Korean, Japonic? Borrowed by Japanese from Korean peninsular language after Proto-Koreo-Japonic split?

k,j = Attested in both Korean, Japonic? Borrowed separately by Korean peninsular language and Japanese from Chinese after Proto-Koreo-Japonic split.

pkj = Attested in both Korean, Japonic? Borrowed or inherited at Proto-Koreo-Japonic level.

x = Borrowed by Chinese or Sino-Tibetan from unknown source.

4. Analysis of data

4.1 Analysis of grade A etymologies

Grade A etymologies:

錢 'money': OJ *zeni*, EMC **dzian*, OC **dzyan*; grade Aj

行蹟 'achievement': MK *hoyngtyek*, EMC **xraangh tsiak*, OC **graangs tsyak*, grade Ak

水 'liquor': MK *swuvul*, EMC **sywiiq*, OC **hlwiq*; grade Ak

俗 'vulgar': MK *sywok*, EMC **zuok*, OC **zwok*; grade Ak

屐子 'wooden sandal': MK *kyekci*, EMC **giak ts++q*, OC **gyak ts+q*, grade Ak

鉢 'bowl': MK *pali*, OJ *pati*, EMC **pat*, OC **pat*; grade Akj

個 'counter': (NK *kay*), (SJ Kan-on *ka*, SJ Tō-on *ko*), EMC **kaah*, OC **kaays*; grade Ak,j

Only one grade A word is exclusive to Japanese: 'money'. The phonological match is perfect, since EMC **dzian* was phonetically [dzien] with medial *-e-*, as indicated by Go-on *zen*. Furthermore, 'money' was not an concept indigenous to Japan and hence is a word conducive to importation. *zeni* has at least three possible origins: (1) It may be a nativization of the Go-on pronunciation. (2) It may have come through a Korean peninsular intermediary via trade with one of more of the peninuslar states. (3) It may have borrowed directly from Chinese by Japonic envoys sent to China or from Chinese visitors to Japan. Note that Korean does not have a cognate for this word (New Korean has *twon*), though perhaps one or more of the lost peninsular languages (Koguryo etc.) may have had one.

Most of the grade A words are exclusive to Korean. 'Achievement', 'liquor', and 'vulgar' are probably all loans from LATE MIDDLE CHINESE (LMC)[11] rather than Early Middle Chinese:

'achievement': MK *hoyng tyek*, LMC *$*hxraanyh\ tsiec$*, SK *hayng cek*

'liquor': MK *swu(vul)*, LMC *$*sxüyq$*, SK *swu*

'vulgar': MK *sywok*, LMC *$*sxüok$*, SK *swok*

Note the similarity of the Middle Korean, Late Middle Chinese, and modern Sino-Korean forms.[12] Because these words were borrowed during the period of Sino-Korean borrowing, they are actually Nativized Sino-Korean (see note 5) as opposed to Pre-Sino-Korean. Since these words do not tell us anything about pre-Tang contact between China and Korea, I will not discuss them further. For further examples of Nativized Sino-Korean, see Martin (1992: 96-98).

The grade A word 'wooden sandal' is probably a loan from Early Middle Chinese or Old Chinese, not Late Middle Chinese. Although the first half of the word, MK *kyek*, could be from LMC *$*giac$*, EMC *$*giak$*, or OC *$*gyak$*, the second half of the word, MK *ci*, matches better with EMC *$*ts++q$* or OC *$*ts+$* than with LMC *$*tszq$*.[13] It may or may not be Pre-Sinoxenic due to its indeterminate dating.

---

[11]Late Middle Chinese is the language of Chang'an, the Tang capital, in the seventh and eighth centuries (Pulleyblank 1991: 2-3). It is the basis for Kan on and most of Sino-Korean and Sino-Vietnamese. All Late Middle Chinese reconstructions are my revisions of Pulleyblank (1991).

My Chinese orthography is phonemic rather than phonetic.

Tonal spelling conventions in Early Middle Chinese and Late Middle Chinese: Syllable final -*q* and -*h* represent SHANGSHENG and QUSHENG respectively. They are not intended to represent final glottal stop or -*h*, although creakiness and breathiness may have been secondary features of tones in Early Middle Chinese and Late Middle Chinese. PINGSHENG and RUSHENG are unmarked.

Segmental spelling conventions in Early Middle Chinese and Late Middle Chinese: Syllable-initial *q* represents glottal stop. *x* represents a voiced *h* in Early Middle Chinese and represents low register in Late Middle Chinese. Hence LMC *hx represents voiceless h followed by a vocalic nucleus with low register tone. *ny* represents palatal *n*. Doubling of vowels indicates vowel length.

q represents a glottal stop in all positions in Old Chinese.

[12]I use modern Sino-Korean readings because those in the *Tongkwuk cengum* and other sources of the Middle Korean period are too artificial.

[13]Late Middle Chinese *z* represents a syllabic *z*, found in Mandarin *si, zi, ci*.

The grade A word 'bowl' was probably first borrowed by a Korean peninsular language from OC *pat. Then it was probably borrowed by Japanese as *pati from speakers of that Korean peninsular language, possibly via Buddhism, since the word ultimately derives from Sanskrit *pātra* (Martin 1991: 278). Note that both the Middle Korean and Old Japanese forms share a final -i, which may have been (1) a suffix in the unknown peninsular language or (2) a vowel added by the peninsular language, whose syllable structure may have required open syllables like Old Japanese. This word may be proof of the transmission of Buddhism through Korean peninsular intermediaries. See the discussions of other Buddhist vocabulary in section 4.2.

Although the grade A word '(generic) counter' is treated as the Sino-Korean reading of [個], I list it here because it is a loan from Old Chinese, not Late Middle Chinese, the source of most of Sino-Korean. It retains the Old Chinese syllable-final glide -y which is lost in Early Middle Chinese.[14] Compare NK *kay* with PSV *cái* [ka:j] 'generic counter', also derived from OC *kaays. These words are of course cognate with the Sino-Japanese Go-on and Kan-on *ka* and the Tō-on *ko*. Many Vietnamese, Korean, and Japanese counters are of Chinese origin. The Old Chinese origins of NK *kay* and PSV *cái* imply that counters were imported into Korean peninsular languages and Vietnamese at an early date. The lack of an Old Chinese-derived generic counter in Japanese may mean that either (1) the older Old Chinese-derived form *kai or *ke2 < *kai, probably an import from a Korean peninsular language, was replaced by the later forms *ka* and *ko* or (2) counters are newer in Japan than in Vietnam or Korea. I prefer the second interpretation.

4.2. Analysis of grade B etymologies

Grade B etymologies:

郡 'count(r)y': MK *kovol*, OJ *kuni*, EMC *gunh, OC *guns; grade Bj

梅 'plum': OJ *ume2*, EMC *may, OC *hmay; grade Bj

笛 'flute': MK *tyeh*, EMC *dek, OC *lek; grade Bk

兔 'hare': MK *twos(ki)*, OJ *usagi*, EMC *thooh, OC *hlaas; grade Bk

布 'hemp cloth': MK *pwoy*, EMC *pooh, OC　*paas; grade Bk

---

[14]Early Middle Chinese syllable-final *-y does not derive from Old Chinese syllable-final *-y.

倭 'Japan': MK *yey*, Old Korean *yeli, EMC **qwaa/qwia*, OC **qwaay/qwyay*; grade Bk

褥 'mattress': MK *zywoh*, EMC *nyuak, OC *nywak; grade Bk

尺 'measure 1': MK *cah*, EMC *chiak, OC *thyak; grade Bk

斗 'measure 2': MK *twoy*, EMC *tawq, OC *toq; grade Bk

芥 'mustard plant': MK *kas*, EMC *kraayh, OC *kraats; grade Bk

屬 'wooden sandal': MK *kyekci*, EMC **k+ak*, OC **k+ak*; grade Bk

書 'write': MK *su-*, OJ *sur-* 'rub', EMC **sy+a*, OC **st+a*; grade Bk

筆 'brush': MK *pwut*, OJ *pude*, EMC *prit, OC *prit; grade Bkj

佛陀'Buddha': MK *pwuthye*, OJ *poto2ke2*, EMC **but daa/buu doo*; **but lay/*
浮屠　　*buu daa*; grade Bkj

刹 'temple': MK *tyel*, OJ *tera*, EMC *chraat, OC *tshraat; grade Bkj

The first of the Pre-Sino-Japanese candidates, *kuni* 'country', appears to be solid on first glance. The concept of a state is foreign to Japan and a word for it would likely be an import. However, the following phonological problems force me to give a grade of 'B' instead of 'A'. *g is believed to have become zero in Old Japanese (Unger 1993: 35). If the word was *guni in pre-Old Japanese, it should be *uni, not *kuni in Old Japanese. Furthermore, there is nothing about the Chinese forms that would favor the addition of a final *-i*; I would expect a final echo vowel *-u*, not *-i*. The first of these problems is more crucial than the second. Perhaps the word was borrowed by pre-Old Japanese as *kun or even *kuni from a peninsular language which had undergone a *g > *k shift and possibly added a suffix **-i* (cf. the example of MK *pali* and OJ *pati* 'bowl' < EMC or OC *pat above). Another possibility is that the word was borrowed at the Proto-Koreo-Japonic level. If Whitman's (1991) correspondence PKJ *g : OJ *k is correct and Unger's correspondence pre-OJ *g* : OJ zero is wrong, then perhaps the word was borrowed at some pre-Old Japanese level as **gun(i)*, later becoming OJ *kuni*.

The Middle Korean word *kovol* suggested by Kim (1971) as a cognate does not resemble either the Japanese or Chinese forms and is probably not related.

The second Pre-Sino-Japanese candidate, *ume2* 'plum', is slightly problematic because of its initial *u-*. Its final *-e2* may be derived from pre-OJ *ai or *oi corresponding to EMC *ay [aj]~[əj], but where does its *u-* come

from? Note that EMC *may* [梅] has a xiesheng relationship with EMC
hayq 'sea' [海] (Leon A. Serafim; personal communication). Perhaps OJ
ume2 < pre-OJ *humoi* or *humai*, with *hum-* corresponding to the Old
Chinese voiceless nasal *hm-*. However, no *h* has ever been posited for pre-
Old Japanese or for Proto-Koreo-Japonic. Furthermore, an alternate Old
Chinese theory (Baxter 1992: 761, 776) posits *m-* for 'plum' and *hm-* for
'sea', the reverse of my claim. Unless evidence emerges for the importation of
plums from the continent into Japan, perhaps this word should be reclassified
as a grade D look-alike.

Although the Pre-Sino-Korean words here are not as obviously similar to
their Chinese counterparts as those in section 5.1, if their etymologies are
correct, they show a number of interesting correspondence patterns.

MK -*h* corresponds to EMC and OC *-k* in 'flute', 'mattress', and 'measure
1' (Kim 1971: 230). This may either (1) reflect weakening of final *-k* to -*h* in
Korean (but why in these words and not in Sino-Korean? Perhaps this
weakening is of high antiquity and is reflected in these words because they
were borrowings from Old Chinese) or (2) reflect weakening of final stops
between Late Middle Chinese and Old Mandarin, which lacks final stops. If
(2) is the case, then these words may be borrowings from some stage of
Chinese between Late Middle Chinese and Old Mandarin and are not Pre-
Sino-Korean.

The *z-* in 'mattress' corresponds to EMC *ny*, which later becomes LMC
(n)zy and Old Mandarin *(z)r-*. *z-* resembles the Late Middle Chinese and
Old Mandarin initials more than the Early Middle Chinese initial. If
hypothesis (2) above concerining the correspondence MK -*h* : Early Middle
Chinese, OC *-k* is correct, then the initial and final of 'mattress' date it (and
'flute' and 'measure 1' with the same final phenomena) as late borrowings. On
the other hand, if the grapheme [triangle], usually interpreted as *z*, is actually
a palatal nasal *ny* as claimed by Vovin (1993), then the Middle Korean initial
would be identical with the Early Middle Chinese and Old Chinese initial *ny-*
and these words may have been borrowed from Early Middle Chinese or Old
Chinese.

'Hemp cloth' (a product introduced from China?) and 'measure 2' both
have a final -*y* that does not correspond to anything in Chinese. Could this be
the same -*i* suffix that appears in OJ *kuni, pati* and MK *pali?*

'Hare' MK *twoski* has -*s-* corresponding to Early Middle Chinese qusheng
-h and OC *-s*. However, its vowel *wo* resembles EMC *oo* rather than OC
aa. Could this be proof for the vowel shift *aa* > *oo* occuring before
TONOGENESIS, in which OC *-s* > EMC qusheng *-h*:

OC *thaas* > *thoos* > EMC *thooh*

If *aa* > *oo* after tonogenesis (or if Korean borrowed the word at a very early
date), then I would expect to see MK *taski* for 'hare', since no Chinese form
thoos would have existed:

OC *thaas* > *thaah* > EMC *thooh*.

Like 'hare', 'mustard plant' has MK -s- corresponding to EMC qusheng *-h and OC *-s. But here the MK -s- may be (1) a simplification of the final cluster in OC *kraats, (2) reflect pre-EMC *kraas[15] > EMC *kraayh, or (3) reflect earlier Korean *-t, possibly from OC *-ts. Compare with Thai kaat 'mustard plant', which also shows the correspondence *-t : OC *-ts (Manomaivibool 1976: 14).

Pre-Sino-Korean words like 'hare' and 'measure 1' have Middle Korean nonaspirates corresponding to Chinese aspirates. This is proof for the late origin of Middle Korean aspirate stops as hypothesized by Ramsey (1993). The Sino-Korean equivalents of these words have aspirate initials: thwo 'hare' and chek 'measure 1'.

Most of the above words would have good motivations for borrowing. The measure words, following the trend, would be imported along with their lexical category from Chinese. Flutes, hemp cloths, mattresses, and mustard plants might be Chinese imports. However, why would 'hare' be imported? One possibility is that the word was imported along with the GANZHI (Heavenly Stem and Earthly Branch) system as a gloss for EMC *mraawq 'hare' [卯]. This may have been the case for the Korean words for 'horse' and 'chicken' as well; see below. On the other hand, the word may be a fortuitous native look-alike and may be related to OJ usa+gi, possibly through some Proto-Koreo-Japonic form like *dusaki. (But why don't we then have OJ *yusagi, with pre-OJ *d > OJ y?)

The remaining grade B Pre-Sino-Korean words are more cultural in nature than their predecessors and hence even more likely to be borrowings. But they are not without problems; otherwise they would be in grade A.

MK yey 'Japan' bears a strong resemblance to OC *qwyay 'long and winding' (Pulleyblank 1991: 321; also read OC *qwaay 'dwarf'). However, the existence of the form [倭理] in a HYANGKA, which Kim (1971) interprets as 'Old Korean' *yeli brings up other possibilities. OK *yeli may be yey < OC? plus a suffix *li or it may be the ancestor of MK yey via medial -l- loss: *yeli > MK yey. Kim (1971) claims that *yeli corresponds to Karlgren's Old Chinese form with final *-r, but Baxter (1992) does not reconstruct final *-r for Old Chinese. Still, Baxter (1992) does admit that final *-r and *-l may have existed in Old Chinese, as they did in Proto-Sino-Tibetan. If the Old Chinese form did have a final *-r, then the *i in *yeli may be the same *-i or *-y suffix or added vowel in kuni, pali, pati, etc.

Perhaps the Old Chinese form itself is an adaptation of a ethnonym like *wey or *weri belonging to some people (Japonic or otherwise—Jōmon?

---

[15]OC syllables ending in stops or stop clusters such as *-ts were exempt from the vowel shift OC *aa > *oo found in 'hare'. OC *-ts > *-s after OC *aa > *oo, so OC *kraats did not become *kraas (*ts > *s) > *kroos (*aa > *oo) > EMC *krooh.

Ainoid?) on the Japanese archipelago. The Chinese may have chosen [倭] primarily because of its sound and only secondarily because of an alternate reading with the negative connotation of 'dwarf'.[16] The lack of any known ethnonyms in Japan or Korea resembling *wey or *weri weakens this hypothesis.

But if the above is correct, the Middle Korean form may not have been from Old Chinese. Silla may have borrowed the word from other Korean peninsular languages, which in turn had borrowed it from the *wey or *weri of Japan.

Fortunately, the other cultural grade B Pre-Sino-Korean words do not involve unknown languages and peoples of early Japan. Two involve writing, which was clearly a Chinese import into the Korean peninsula. The Korean peninsular peoples in turn imported it into Japan.

The first of these words is MK *su-* 'write'. The vowel corresponds well with *+ in EMC *sy+a and OC *st+a. Middle Korean has no diphthongs like *ua* or *uo*, so nothing in the Middle Korean form corresponds to final *-a [ə] in Early Middle Chinese unless an earlier Korean form was *sö, following Whitman's (1991) PKJ *ö > MK *u* shift. Although PKJ *ö is front and rounded and EMC *+a [+ə] is central and unrounded, they are similar acoustically, Perhaps I should have given this word grade A, since the phonological match might be perfect.

Slight doubts prevent me from doing so. I suspect that MK *su-* 'write' may somehow be related to the homophonous (in New Korean[17]) word *ssu-* 'use', which has a wide semantic range. But the semantic links between 'write' and 'use' (a brush?) are almost nonexistent and if *ssu-* 'use' is MK *psu-* or the like, then this argument is invalid. MK *su-* 'write' might also be related to OJ *sur-* 'rub', but the usual Middle Korean-Old Japanese vowel correspondence (Whitman 1991) is MK *wu* : OJ *u*, not MK *u* : OJ *u*.

The second Pre-Sino-Korean word connected with writing is MK *pwut* 'brush', which may be cognate with OJ *pude*. The phonological problem which prevented these forms from received grade A was their poor vowel correspondence with the Early Middle Chinese and Old Chinese forms: MK *-wu-* : OJ *-u-* : EMC, OC *-ri-*. Compare with SK *phil* and SJ *pitu*, which show better vowel correspondences. On the other hand, Sino-Vietnamese has *bút*, which does not show the regular SV *-â-* : LMC *-i-* correspondence and should perhaps be reclassified as Pre-Sino-Vietnamese.[18] The forms MK *pwut*, OJ

---

[16]Compare the Chinese toponyms *Ou* 'vomit' for 'Europe' and *Fei* 'not' for 'Africa'.

[17]The New Korean form of MK *su-* 'write' is *ssu-*.

[18]Sino-Vietnamese has a number of character readings such as *bút* that are not derived from Late Middle Chinese. These readings are treated as SV by

pude, and SV *bút* may force me to alter the Old Chinese reconstruction from **prit* to **prwit*[19] or **prut.* Note that [筆] has a xiesheng relationship with EMC **lwit* 'law' [律], reinforcing the possibility of a medial -w- or an older -u-. (But the even older Pre-Sino-Vietnamese form *viêt* 'write', with [-iə-], may be counterevidence against this proposal.) 'Brush' is a case where Pre-Sinoxenic forms may help us to improve our reconstruction of Old Chinese. The voiced -d- in OJ *pude* remains a problem. I would expect OJ *putu,* with -t- and a non-front echo vowel. Perhaps the etymology deriving this word from *pumi* 'writing'[20] and *te* 'hand' is correct:

pumi + *te* > *pumte* > *punde* > *pude*

This etymology accounts for the final -e as well as the prenasalized medial *d,* but I find the similarity to the Pre-Sino-Korean and Pre-Sino-Vietnamese forms difficult to ignore.

The last two grade B words, 'Buddha' and 'temple', are obviously Buddhist and must have been imported along with the religion, first by the Chinese into the Korean peninsula and then by Korean peninsular peoples into Japan. The Chinese words are ultimately transcriptions of Sanskrit *Buddha* 'Buddha' and *kṣetra* 'place'. Although the Old Chinese forms, **buu daa* and **tsraat* (**ksraat?*) resemble the Sanskrit originals, the Pre-Sino-Korean and Pre-Sino-Japanese forms do not resemble the Old Chinese forms very much.

The first half of MK *pwuthye* matches the first characters of both of the Chinese transcriptions of *Buddha:* EMC **but daa* [佛陀] (cf. SK *pultha* < LMC **pxüt txaa*) and OC **buu daa* [浮屠][21]. But where does -*thye* come from? Nothing in the second character of either transcription suggests a *ye.* Perhaps the aspiration might serve as a clue. According to Whitman (1991) and Ramsey (1993), Korean aspirates derive from earlier sequences with *o* or *u.* Could *pwuthye* then derive from something like **pwuto-ye,* with **pwuto* deriving from EMC **buu doo* [浮屠], the outdated Chinese transcription of *Buddha,* and **-ye* from some kind of suffix, possibly related to the -*i/y* seen elsewhere in ths paper?

---

tradition, although they are highly irregular.

[19] Compare the pronunciation of *wuy* in some varieties of New Korean as [ü]. **prwit* may have phonetically been [prüt].

[20] Ōno et al. (1991) derives this word from a reading *Fun* of [文], but this reading would have to anachronistically derive from LMC **mbun.* LMC postdates the appearance of *pumi* in the *Man'yōshū,* written at a time when Early Middle Chinese-based Go-on was still the standard in Japan.

[21] Once sound changes rendered Old Chinese-based Sanskrit transcriptions obscure, new Early Middle Chinese-based transcriptions were created using different characters.

A proto-form like *pwutohye (with medial -h- later lost in Korean) might account for OJ poto2ke2, which bears even less resemblance to Buddha than MK pwuthye. Pre-Old Japanese would have borrowed the word from the Korean peninsula, complete with its suffix *-hye. If the proto-form were *pwutuhye with -u- instead of -o-, then -tu- would correspond perfectly with OJ -to2-, following the usual Korean u : OJ o2 pattern. However, I would expect Korean *-hye to be reflected as OJ -ke1 or OJ -ko2, not OJ -ke2. Perhaps the Middle Korean and Old Japanese forms derived from earlier Korean peninsular forms with slightly different suffixes. In any case, I would like the Middle Korean and Old Japanese forms to ultimately derived from the Chinese transcriptions rather than be imports from yet another, non-Chinese language.

The words for 'temple', MK tyel and OJ tera, do not present as many difficulties. At first, MK tyel hardly resembles EMC *chraat. However, the correspondence MK ty- : EMC c(h)- is already attested in the grade A word 'achievement' above. The correspondence MK e : EMC aa is difficult to explain unless one takes into account a sound change that affected at least some varieties of Early Middle Chinese: *-raa- > *-yaa- > *-ee- (or *-œœ-). The correspondence Korean l : EMC -t is well known and often attributed to a dialect of Chinese with final -ð or -l < *-t. The Early Middle Chinese form at the time of borrowing was therefore something like *cheel or *chœœl < *chraat < OC *tshraat or *ksraat. Compare *-ee- and *-œœ- with the vocalism of Go-on seti.

This etymology is more likely than the one preferred by Kim (1971), in which MK tyel derives from OC *teq 'residence', on both phonological and semantic grounds. I have given this latter etymology a grade of D. MK tyel and *teq look vaguely alike, but their relationship is improbable.

The OJ form, tera, was probably borrowed from Korean peninsular *tyel or *tyäl, with the added final -a possibly being an echo of -ä-. The correspondence Japanese t- : EMC c- is unknown, so the t- of tera indicates that it was borrowed through a Korean peninsular language.

4.3. Analysis of grade C etymologies

Grade C etymologies

馬 'horse': MK mol, OJ uma, EMC *mraaq, OC *mráq; grade Cpkja

熊 'bear': MK kwom, OJ kuma, EMC *wung, OC *wum or *gum; grade Cpkjx

In cases where Chinese and unrelated languages appear to have words in common, Chinese is almost always assumed to be the donor language. This assumption probably reflects Sinocentric biases, not reality. Many 'Chinese' words may actually be loans into Chinese from Tai, Austroasiatic, and Austronesian rather than loans from Chinese into those languages.

I suspect that the Chinese words for 'horse' and 'bear' are ultimately not Chinese in origin. If that is so, then the Middle Korean and Old Japanese words may be cognate to the Chinese forms but may not necessarily be borrowings from Chinese.

'Horse' may be an Altaic loan into Chinese. The Altaic peoples are notable for horse riding, whereas the Chinese are not. I suspect that the Chinese may have adopted the practice of riding horses and perhaps even the word for 'horse' from their northern neighbors.

This hypothesis is not as simple as it may seem. OC *$mraq$ is assumed to be cognate to Proto-Tibeto-Burman *$s\text{-}rang\text{~}$*$m\text{-}rang$ (Benedict 1972: 215), represented by Written Burmese $MRANGH$[22] and perhaps also by Classical Tibetan rta (Benedict 1972: 43). Furthermore, it is also assumed to be cognate to Thai $m\acute{a}a$, Written Thai MAA^2 (Manovaivibool 1976: 18).[23] I speculate that the word originated in Altaic and was borrowed by Sino-Tibetan. Proto-Koreo-Japonic inherited the word, as did Mongolian *(morin)*, while Tai borrowed it from Chinese.

This scenario does not resolve many complications, such as why all the above words for 'horse' are so different from each other. Again, I can offer only speculations. Perhaps Mongolian $morin$ is closest to the original form of the word, which was *$mVrVn$. This *$mVrVn$ was borrowed into Sino-Tibetan as something like *$mVrVng$ (but why *$\text{-}ng$?). The first V was lost in Tibeto-Burman, reducing the root to *$mrang$; *$srang$ < *$s\text{-}mrang$? The final nasal was maintained in Mongolian but lost in other Altaic branches, such as Koreo-Japonic; hence Middle Korean has mol < PKJ *$molV$? corresponding to Mongolian $morin$. Chinese may have reborrowed 'horse' from such a final nasal-less branch of Altaic, replacing *$mVrVn$, inherited from Sino-Tibetan, with *$mVrV$ (cf. the Proto-Koreo-Japonic form) > OC *$mraq$. This *mraq was borrowed into Proto-Tai as *$mraq$ > Thai $m\acute{a}a$.

But why doesn't Old Japanese have simple ma instead of uma? The existence of the Tibeto-Burman root *$srang$ < *$smrang$? made me wonder whether the OC form was *$smraq$ or *$hmraq$ < *$sm\text{-}$. The inherited word for horse in PKJ may have been supplanted in Japonic by a similar sounding word from a Korean peninsular language like *$huma$, borrowed from OC *$hmraq$.

---

[22]Capital letters denote transliterations of Indic scripts. Spellings of Southeast Asian languages are extremely conservative and provide many hints about reconstruction. Written Burmese -H is cognate to EMC *-h and OC *-s (qusheng), not EMC and OC *-q (shangsheng) as one might expect from this example.

[23]Written Thai tone 2 is cognate to EMC and OC *-q (shangsheng).

Initial *h- was lost in Japonic, resulting in OJ *uma*. Compare this with my explanation for *u-* in OJ *ume2* above. But there is no proof that Proto-Tai ever had *hm-* for 'horse', though Proto-Tai distinguished between *hm-*, *m-*, and possibly *qm-*. The *u-* in *ume2* and *uma* remains a mystery.

A mystery of greater proportions is the origin of the Chinese word for 'bear'. Forms resembling OC *wum* or *gum* are found not only in Tibeto-Burman (Written Burmese *VAM*, Classical Tibetan *dom*; Benedict [1972: 116] reconstructs Proto Tibeto-Burman *d-wam*) and Koreo-Japonic but also Ainu *(kamui)*. Graham Thurgood (1995; personal communication to Leon A. Serafim) has claimed that the Proto-Mon-Khmer word for 'bear' also resembles this root. Vietnamese has *gau* [ɣəw]; comparative Mon-Khmer evidence indicates that this derives from *(rV-)kVw* (Gage 1985: 504). Manomaivibool (1976) does not list 'bear' in his list of Sino-Thai lexical correspondences. Nevertheless, the fact remains that a kum-like word for 'bear' is widespread in Asia. I am inclined to think that the word had a northern origin, since the bear is of great importance to Ainu and Korean mythology (i.e. the story of Hwanwung). Hence the word was probably in Proto-Koreo-Japonic, which might have borrowed it from some Ainoid language. The Mon-Khmer form may just be a poor lookalike, but if Alexander Vovin is correct about an Ainu-Austroasiatic connection, this may not be the case and the word may ultimately be Austroasiatic.

The Middle Korean and Old Japanese forms for 'bear' generally match neatly, with the expected MK -*wo-* : OJ -*u-* correspondence (Whitman 1991). Old Japanese final -*a* may be a retention from Proto-Koreo-Japonic that was lost in Korean. Problems in correspondence only occur if we take OC *gum* into consideration. Although its -*u-* and -*m-* fit neatly with the Proto-Koreo-Japonic : Middle Korean : Old Japanese correspondences *u* : *wo* : *u* and *m* : *m* : *m*, its initial *g-*, if matched with PKJ *g-*, should produce MK *n-* and OJ *k-* (or zero, if Unger 1993 is correct). But of course MK *nwom* and OJ *uma* are not the attested forms.

Perhaps the original form of this word in Northern Asia (and in Mon-Khmer) was *kum* with a voiceless initial and Old Chinese borrowed it as such, only to later confound it with *wum*, a similar sounding native root with a voiced initial, creating a new blend like *gum* or *γum* (with gamma later devoicing, explaining the *h-* or *h*-derived reflexes in Mandarin *xióng* < Old Mandarin *hyung*, Cantonese *hùhng*, Taiwanese *him*, SV *hùng*, etc.).

4.4 Analysis of grade D etymologies

Grade D etymologies

築 'build': MK *tuk-*, EMC *truk*, OC *truk*; grade Dj

析 'cleave': (NK *sayki-* 'carve'), OJ *sak-*, EMC *sek*, OC *sek*; grade Dj

松 'cryptomeria': OJ *sugi2*, EMC **suong*, OC **skwong*; grade Dj

魚 'fish': OJ *uwo, iwo*, EMC **ng+a*, OC **ng+a*; grade Dj

隔 'hedge': OJ *kaki1*, EMC **krak*, OC **krak*; grade Dj

琢 'polish': (NK *takk-*), OJ *to1g-*, EMC **trok*, OC **trok*; grade Dj

秈 'rice 2': OJ *sine*, EMC **sian*, OC **syan*; grade Dj

米 'rice 3': OJ *ko2me2*, EMC **meeq*, OC **(h)meq*; grade Dj

湿 'salt': OJ *sipo*, EMC **syip*, OC **hy+p*; grade Dj

鎌 'sickle': OJ *kama*, EMC **liam*, OC **gryam*; grade Dj

絹 'silk': OJ *ki1nu*, EMC **kwianh*, OC **kwyans*; grade Dj

蚕 'silkworm': OJ *kapi1.ko1*, EMC **kep*, OC **kep*; grade Dj

氣 'spirit': Koguryo **k+al*, OJ *ke2*, EMC **kh+yh*, OC **kh+ys*; grade Dj

社 'adjust robe': MK *nyemuy*, EMC **nyimh*, OC **n+ms*; grade Dk

到 'arrive': MK *tah*, OJ *ita-r-*, EMC **taawh*, OC **taaws*; grade Dk

界 'boundary': MK *koz*, EMC **krayh*, OC **krats*; grade Dk

石 'gravel': (NK *cakal*), EMC **jiak*, OC **d+ak*; grade Dk

墨 'ink stick': MK *mek*, OJ *sumi*, EMC **mak*, OC **(h)mak*; grade Dk

楮 'mulberry tree': MK *tak*, EMC **thr+aq*, OC **thr+aq*; grade Dk

鼠 'rat': (NK *cwuy*), EMC **sy+aq*, OC **h+aq*; grade Dk

誌 'record': MK *cek-*, EMC **ciih*, OC **ciih*; grade Dk

齏 'salted food': MK *cel-* or *ces*, EMC **tsee*, OC **tee*; grade Dk

祗 'salutation': MK *cel*, EMC **cii*, OC **tii*; grade Dk

屦 'straw sandal': (NK *cipseki*), EMC **siaq*, OC **syaq*; grade Dk

臿 'spade': MK *salp* or *stapwu*, OJ *sapi1*, *sape1*, (MJ *sarapi*), EMC **chrap*, OC **tshrap*; grade Dkj

邺 'temple': MK *tyel*, OJ *tera*, EMC **teeq*, OC **teq*; grade Dkj

鳥 'chicken': MK *tolk*, OJ *to2ri*, EMC **tewq*, OC **tewq*; grade Dpkj

剝 'flay': MK *pehi-* or *pahi-*, OJ *pag-*, EMC **prok*, OC **prok*; grade Dpkj

坩 'pot': (NK *kama*), (MJ *kama*), EMC **khaam*, OC **khaam*; grade Dpkj

稗 'rice 1': MK *pye*, OJ *po2*, EMC **braayh*, OC **braats*; grade Dpkj

熱 'summer': MK *nyerom*, OJ *natu*, EMC **nyiat*, OC **nyat*; grade Dpkj

其 'that 1': MK *ku*, OJ *ko2* 'this', EMC **g++*, OC **gr++*; grade Dpkj

比 'that 2': MK *tye* (distal), OJ *so2*, EMC **tshia*, OC **thya*; grade Dpkj

時 'time': MK *cek* or *cey*, OJ *to2ki1*, EMC **j++*, OC **d++*; grade Dpkj

盆 'vessel': MK *poy*, OJ *pune*, EMC **ban*, OC **ban*; grade Dpkj

麥 'wheat': (NK *mil*), OJ *mugi1*, EMC **mrak*, OC **mrak*; grade Dpkj

鴈 'wild goose': MK *kuyreki*, OJ *kari*, EMC **k++*, OC **kr++*; grade Dpkj

I gave slightly over half of the proposed Chinese etymologies in this study—roughly percent—a grade of D. Grades A and B were largely dominated by Pre-Sino-Korean. Grade D, on the other hand, is evenly distributed among 'false' Pre-Sino-Japanese, 'false' Pre-Sino-Korean, and 'false' Pre-Sino-Koreo-Japonic. I would interpret this to mean that Korean peninsular peoples were in more intense contact with Chinese; hence the high concetration of Pre-Sino-Korean in grades A and B. On the other hand, Japonic peoples received little if any direct contact with Chinese and learned about Chinese culture only second-hand through Korean peninsular sources at a late date; hence the low concentration of Pre-Sino-Japanese in grades A and B. Any language can be assumed to have a certain number of chance look-alikes with words in another language, regardless of the presence or absence of a contact situation. Random chance would thus give Middle Korean, Old Japanese, and Proto-Koreo-Japonic roughly the same number of Chinese look-alikes.

Due to (1) the large number of items and (2) my belief that not much time and space should be wasted on probable look-alikes, I can only briefly state my reasoning for why I have given each of these words a 'D'. Keep in mind that some words are more deserving of a 'D' than others; some may upon further analysis be promoted to grade 'B' while others may be demoted to 'F'.

4.4.1. Grade D Pre-Sino-Japanese etymologies

'build':   OJ *tuk-* < EMC or OC *$*truk$*

Actually, OJ *tuk-* does look a lot like EMC *$*truk$* and OC *$*truk$*. Compare with the reading *tuku* of the homophonous character [筑] in *Tsukuba* [筑 波]. If YODAN verbs were originally vowel stems, perhaps the older verb stem was *tuku-. Perhaps this word was important along with Chinese construction technology from the Korean peninsula.

So why didn't I give it grade A or even B? First, creation of verbs from foreign stems (other than the *-suru* kind) is rare in Japanese. Second, if the Korean peninsular languages were like Japanese in that respect, then it would be unlikely that they would have a verb stem *tuk(u)-* from Chinese *$*truk$*. These factors make me hesistant to accept Chinese etymologies for Japanese ver stems; see 'cleave', 'hedge', and 'polish' below. Third, this word is probably linked to the native Japanese verb stem *tukur-* 'make'—which on the other hand may not be 'native' if it is a derivative of *tuk(u)-* < Chinese *$*truk$*. Ōno et al. (1990) list 'build' as a derivative meaning of the native Japanese verb stem *tuk-* 'penetrate'.

I know of no Chinese etymology for *tuk-* 'penetrate', although I am sure that if one goes through all the entries of Morohashi's monumental *Dai kanwa jiten*, one just might find a similar-sounding Chinese word for 'penetrate'. The huge number of monosyllables in a Chinese dictionary, including many lexical ghosts unattested outside dictionaries and many fragments of disyllabic words, insures that look-alikes will be plentiful.

'cleave': OJ *sak-* < EMC or OC *$*sek$*

The Old Japanese vowel *a* does not match the Early Middle Chinese and Old Chinese vowel *e*. But compare Go-on *syaku*, implying OC *$*syak$*. Then again, if the word were borrowed prior to Go-on (and the development of *yō-on*) as *$*siaku$*, *$*ia$* > OJ *e1*, not OJ *a*. Why borrow a word for 'cleave'? The New Korean form *sayki-* 'carve' is probably not related to OJ *sak-*.

'cryptomeria': OJ *sugi2* < EMC *$*suong$*, OC *$*skwong$*

The semantic fit is imperfect: the Chinese form means 'pine', not 'cryptomeria'. Given the vocalism *$*-uo-$* and *$*-wo-$* in Early Middle Chinese and Old Chinese respectively, why isn't the Old Japanese form *so1gi2*? Compare Kan-on *sou*. But also note Go-on *syu* with *-u*, not *-o(u)*. The final *gi2* may be related to *ki2* 'tree': *sugi2* < *$*su no2 ki2$*?

'fish': OJ *uwo, iwo* < EMC or OC *$*ng+a$*

Could initial *ng- > zero in pre-Old Japanese? Maybe, but judging from Go-on, I would expect prenasalized Ng- to correspond to Chinese ng-. Then again, this word could have been borrowed via Korean peninsular fishermen, whose reflex of Chinese initial ng- is zero (as in Sino-Korean). But if this is the case, why do we have -wo for Chinese *-+a [+ə] instead of -u (see 'write' in section 5.2)? There is nothing labial about the Chinese final. Perhaps the -w- is a glide inserted between u/i and wo to make it pronounceable. The i/u variation may reflect different attempts at imitating [+]. A foreign origin would explain the coexistence of two roots for 'fish' in Old Japanese. But why would the Korean peninsular fishermen, the source of the Old Japanese loan, borrow the word from the Chinese? Was the Chinese word, mutilated into something like [+o], part of some lost Northeast Asian fishing jargon? Although my instincts oppose a Chinese etymology, this word is a good candidate for an upgrade to 'B'.

'hedge': OJ kaki1 < EMC or OC *krak

Despite the close phonetic resemblance, I side with Kamei (1954: 13), who claims that kaki1 'is the deverbal noun of kaku (to enclose).' Kamei admits that the stem kak- itself 'rather seems to support Karlgren [who proposed the 'hedge' etymology],' but he and I see the adoption of foreign verb stems in Japanese as very unlikely.

'polish': OJ to1g- < EMC or OC *trok

The vowel matches, but what about the stem-final g-? Why not OJ to1k-? I would prefer to derive this stem from to1 'whetstone' (suggested by Unger 1993: 120) + NV + k(V): OJ to1g- < *to1Nk- < *to1NVk(V)-. NK *takk- may be related, but the correspondence Korean a : Japanese o1 is irregular according to Whitman (1991).

'rice 2': OJ sine < EMC or OC *syan

Despite the close phonetic resemblance, OJ sine is linked with ine and possibly yo2ne2. Its initial s- may be secondary via the genitive marker *-tu- (Leon A. Serafim; personal communication). OJ sine might then be the reanalyzed second half of an earlier compound *X-tu-ine.

'rice 3': OJ ko2me2 < OC *(h)meq

The phonetic resemblance between ko2me2 and OC *(h)meq is not overwhelming at first glance. However, the m- in Old Chinese may have been voiceless hm- < *hVm-. ko2m- may reflect some attempt at the Japonic or deeper levels to approximate *hm- or *hVm-. (This contradicts my earlier hypotheses about Proto-Koreo-Japonic *hum- being an attempt to approximate OC *hm- in 'plum' and 'horse'.) If OC *(h)meq is related to Vietnamese mẻ, glossed by Nguyễn (1967: 341) as 'fermented rice' and with a high register tone implying an earlier voiceless nasal and final glottal stop in Vietnamese, then this would strengthen the claim for OC *hm-, though the semantics remain questionable. Leon A. Serafim (personal communication) has also attempted to connect this root with Sanskrit vrīhi 'rice'. No Korean cognates are known; was the word transmitted to Japan via one of the dead branches of Koreo-Japonic? The evidence linking ko2me2 and OC *(h)meq (much less Sanskrit vrīhi) is scanty at best but if a link between these words can be proved in the future, it will tell us a great deal about the spread of rice agriculture in Asia.

'salt': OJ sipo < EMC *syip

The semantics are poor: EMC *syip means 'swamp', not 'salt'. Kamei (1954: 3-7) argues that sipo originally meant 'tide' and that the Japanese collected salt via seawater, not salt marshes.

'sickle': OJ kama < OC *gryam

Like 'rice 3', this word would have been loaned during the spread of agriculture to Japan. As with 'country' in section 5.2, the Chinese initial *g- poses a problem. If Ramsey and Unger's (1972) theory is correct, pre-OJ *g- > zero and 'sickle' should be OJ ama < pre-OJ *gama. The dating of Old Chinese > Early Middle Chinese initial cluster simplifiation (OC *gr- > EMC *l-) is uncertain; if it occured at an extremely early date, predating contact with Proto-Koreo-Japonic, then this etymology is impossible since it would have been borrowed by Proto-Koreo-Japonic or later languages as *ram or *ryam without an initial velar. The vocalism is also problematic: I might expect OJ ke1ma < pre-OJ *kiama < OC *gryam.

'silk': OJ ki1nu < EMC *kwianh or OC *kwyans

Silk and silk products must have been brought to Japan via the Asian continent. Silk-related vocabulary was also probably imported. Still, this word is not without problems. I would expect OJ ki2nu < pre-OJ *kuinu, OJ ke2nu < pre-OJ *kianu, or OJ ko1nu < pre-OJ *kuanu, depending on which Chinese glides and vowels the borrowers (Proto-Koreo-Japonic? Japonic?) chose to emphasize. But since a foreign origin for this word remains probable, perhaps I should upgrade it to grade B.

'silkworm': OJ kapi1(ko1) < EMC or OC *kep

The vocalism is poor. Kamei (1954: 8) claims it is 'feeding-worm', derived from kap- 'feed'.

'spirit' < OJ ke2 < EMC *kh+yh or OC *kh+ys

[気] 'spirit' is a MAN'YŌGANA for OJ ke2. Surely OJ ke2 'spirit, vapor' treated as native Japanese by Whitman (1990: 522) is connected to the Chinese word for 'spirit, vapor'. Whitman compares OJ *ke2* to Koguryo *$k+al$*[24] 'heart' [居乙]. This latter word may also be from Chinese. However, there are at least two problems. First, according to Ōno et al. (1990), *ke2* is related to the prefix *ka-* and the suffixes *-yaka* and *-raka*. The *e~a* vowel alternation suggests that *ke2* originates from earlier **ai* or **oi*. I would not expect a loan to undergo such vowel alternations, although earlier **oi* [əj?] fits well with Chinese **+y*. Second, if the Koguryo and Old Japanese forms are related, then they may not be related to Chinese, since the Koguryo **-al* does not correspond to anything in Chinese.

4.4.2. Grade D Pre-Sino-Korean etymologies

'adjust robe': MK *nyemuy* < EMC **nyimh* or OC **n+ms*

The vocalic match is poor. The Chinese word is a noun, 'skirts of robe', which unlike many other Chinese substantives, cannot be used as a verb. Why convert this noun into a verb in Korean? Since Korean has many native terms for clothes, surely native terms for adjusting clothes would already exist, so why import this word?

'arrive': MK *tah* < EMC **taawh* or OC **taaws*

Korean is not known to have syllable-final *-Vw*. Chinese *-aw* and *-aaw* appear in Sino-Korean as *-u* and *-wo*. Perhaps Korean once had *-aw* and *-aaw* as in Chinese but monophthongized them prior to the invention of *Hankul*. If that was so, then why do we have MK *a*, not *o*, corresponding to Chinese *-aaw* in 'arrive'? Could this be a borrowing from some aberrant, unattested Chinese dialectal form **taah* with MK *-h* representing pre-tonogenetic -h? But why import such a basic vocabulary item? Perhaps the word is related to OJ *itar-*.

'boundary': MK *koz* < OC **krats*

Despite the orthography, the vowels match well. OC **a* was probably phonetically [ə]. However, the final correspondence MK *-z* : OC **-ts* contradicts the earlier correspondence MK *-s* : OC **-ts* seen in 'mustard plant' in section 5.2. Kim (1971) suggests that this *-z* reflects OC **-dz* < pre-OC **ds*, but according to Baxter (1992), Old Chinese had no final voiced stops. My guess is that MK *koz* originates from some form unrelated to Chinese like **koso* or **kosu*, with intervocalic voicing of **-s-* and subsequent loss of the final vowel:

*koso > **kozo* > MK *koz*

'gravel': NK *cak(al)* < EMC **jiak* or OC **d+ak*

---

[24]Reconstructed by Whitman (1990: 522) as **kel*.

The first half of NK *cakal* resembles the Chinese forms, but where does the second half, *-al*, come from? Splitting *cakal* into *cak* and a suffix *-al* unattested elsewhere to accomodate a Chinese etymology seems *ad hoc*. *cakal* is probably a single native Korean morpheme.

'ink stick': NK *mek* < EMC **mak* or OC **(h)mak*

The vocalic match is poor, but where else could Korean have borrowed a word for 'ink stick' from? The Middle Korean form is probably not cognate with OJ *sumi*, though if they were cognate with each other and with Old Chinese, then would OJ *sumi* derive from Korean peninsular? **humi* < OC **hm+k* (using Baxter 1992's vocalism)? Note that this account contradicts earlier hypotheses in this paper concerning the loan equivalents of OC **hm-*.

'mulberry tree': MK *tak* < EMC or OC **thr+aq*

The vocalic match is poor. Since Chinese **+a* is phonetically [+ə], I would expect MK *tok* or *tuk*. But the correspondence MK *k* : OC **q* is intriguing. See 'record' and 'straw sandal' below.

'rat': NK *cwuy* < EMC **sy+aq*

Hashimoto (1977: 103-4), who proposed this etymology, defends it by noting that some modern Chinese dialects have an affricate initial *ch-* for this word. If this affricate variant initial existed at the time of borrowing, then the real problem is the final. Why would Chinese **+a* [+ə} be represented by back, rounded *wu* followed by a palatal glide *y*?

'record': MK *cek-* < EMC **ciih* or OC **ciis* (*ciiqs*?)

The vocalic match is poor, though stem-final *-k* may reflect an earlier Chinese glottal stop *q*. See 'mulberry tree' above and 'straw sandal' below.

'salted food': MK *cel-*, *ces* (< **cels*?) < EMC **tsee* or OC **tee*

Where would the final consonants in the Middle Korean forms come from?

'salutation': MK *cel-* < EMC **cii* or OC **tii*

Where would the final *-l* in Middle Korean come from?

'straw sandal': NK *(cip)sek(i)* < EMC **siaq* or OC **syaq*

This seems to be another *ad hoc* word division to accomodate a Chinese etymology, but note the correspondence of *-k* and Chinese glottal stop. See 'mulberry tree' and 'reord' above. I would not like to posit the mysterious suffix *-i/y* again.

4.4.3. Grade D Pre-Sino-Japanese via Pre-Sino-Korean etymologies

Japonic presumably borrowed the following items from Korean peninsular languages, which in turn presumably borrowed them from Chinese.

'spade': MK *salp, stapwu*, MJ *sarapi*, OJ *sapi1, sape1* < MC **chrap* or OC **tshrap*

The correspondence of MK *s* : Chinese **ch* or **tsh* is unexpected. I would expect MK *ty-* or *c-*. Where does MK *-l-* and MJ *-ra-* come from? At first, they may appear to be reflexes of Chinese **-r-* but this **-r-* is consistently ignored in Sino-Korean, Sino-Japanese, and the Pre-Sinoxenic forms covered in this paper. If MK *-l-* represented Chinese **-r-*, I would expect MK *slap*, not *salp*, unless metathesis occured to avoid the impermissible initial sequence *sl-*.

I suspect that MK *salp* and *stapwu* have nothing to do with Chinese and are doublets from different Korean peninsular languages—one native to the Silla line *(stapwu?)* and one not *(salp?)*. The Japanese forms would then be borrowed from the non-Silla peninsular word for 'spade', **salpi?* < Proto-Peninsular **stalpwuy?*

'temple': MK *tyel*, OJ *tera* < MC **teeq* or OC **teq*.

Where does MK *-l* and OJ *-r(a)* come from? My preferred etymology is in section 4.2.

4.4.4. Grade D Pre-Sino-Koreo-Japonic etymologies

These words were supposedly borrowed from Chinese by Proto-Koreo-Japonic and then genetically transmitted to Korean and Japanese.

'chicken': MK *tolk*, OJ *to2ri* 'bird' < OC **tewq* (< **telq?*) 'bird'

The vocalic match between Middle Korean and Old Japanese is imperfect, but that with Chinese is poor. The idea of OC **w* deriving from earlier **l* is appealing but has no basis in comparative Sino-Tibetan; Benedict (1972: 192) reconstructs Proto-Sino-Tibetan **tow~*dow* for 'bird'. But if the words were cognate, then MK *k* would once again correspond to OC **q*. See 'mulberry tree', 'record', and 'straw sandal' in section 5.4.2 above.

'flay': MK *pehi-, pahi-*, OJ *pag-* < OC **prok*

The vocalic match is poor. The *-g-* in Old Japanese implies earlier **-NVk(V)-*. The Proto-Koreo-Japonic stem (assuming the Middle Korean and Old Japanese forms are cognate at all) may have been something like **päNVki-*

'pot': *kama* (NK), *kama* (MJ) < OC **khaam*

The resemblance between the forms is obvious, but where does the final *-a* in *both* New Korean and Middle Japanese come from? Is this too good to be true? Should 'pot' be upgraded to B? The Old Japanese form is *kamado1*, which may either be *kama* + *to1* 'place' or *ka* 'smell' + *mado1* 'window', as proposed by Kamei (1954: 22-24).

'rice 1': *pye* (NK), *po2* (OJ) < OC **braats*
The vocalic match with Chinese is poor. The *-s* one might expect in Middle Korean corresponding to OC **-ts* is absent. Compare 'mustard plant' in section 4.2 above.

'summer': *nyerom* (MK), *natu* (OJ) < OC **nyat* 'heat'
The semantic match with Chinese is poor. Where does the final *-m* in Middle Korean come from?

'that 1': MK *ku*, OJ *ko2* 'this', *so2* 'that' < OC **gr++*
All the forms exhibit central unrounded vowels and the vowel correspondences are regular PKJ **ö* (cf. OC **+*) : MK *u* : OJ *o2*. The initials present problems. *s-* in OJ may stem from some earlier **kh* (cf. the possible relationship of OJ *s-* 'to do' and MK *ho-* 'to do'), but if PKJ **g* > zero in OJ, then why isn't "this' *o2* in Old Japanese? The semantics are imperfect. Finally, I doubt that deictics can be easily borrowed.

'that 2': MK *tye* (distal), OJ *so2* (medial) < OC **thva* 'this'
The phonetic match is good, since OJ *so2* [tsə] (Miyake, forthcoming) < **čo2* < **tyo2*? and the vowel correspondences are regular: PKJ **ä* (cf. OC **ya*) : MK *e* : OJ *o2*. However, the semantics are poor and I still doubt that deictics can be easily borrowed.

'time': MK *cek*, *cey*, OJ *to2ki1* < OC **d++*
The vocalic match between Middle Korean and Old Chinese is poor. Where does the *k* in Middle Korean and Old Japanese come from? If Proto-Koreo-Japonic borrowed this word from Old Chinese, then the initial of the Proto-Koreo-Japonic form would have been either **d* or **j*. Both **d* and **j* > OJ *y*, so the OJ form should be *yo2ki1*, not *to2ki1*.

'vessel': MK *poy*, OJ *pune* < OC **ban*
Where does the *n* in Old Japanese come from? If the Proto-Koreo-Japonic form had initial **b-*, the Old Japanese form should be *une*, not *pune*.

'wheat': NK *mil*, OJ *mugi1* < OC **mrak*
These words have nothing in common but initial *m-* and are probably not cognate to each other, though the idea of a common Northeast Asian word for 'wheat' is appealing. I should probably demote them to grade F.

'wild goose': MK *kuyreki,* OJ *kari* < OC **kr++*

These words have nothing in common but the sequence of segments *k* and *r* and are probably not cognate to each other. I should probably demote them to grade F. I have not been able to find OC **kr++* outside Kim (1971); as an uncommon word, it would be an unlikely loan source.

4.5 Analysis of grade F etymologies

Grade F etymologies

矢 'arrow': MK *sal,* EMC **syiiq,* OC **hliq;* grade F

閾 'floor': OJ *yuka,* EMC **hw+k,* OC **hrw+k;* grade F

邑 'house': (NK *cip*), OJ *ipe1,* EMC **qrip,* OC **qrip;* grade F

龜 'turtle': MK *kepwup,* EMC **kwii,* OC **krw++;* grade F

室 'village': OJ *sato1,* EMC **syit,* OC **stit;* grade F

萎 'wither': MK *ivul-,* EMC **qwia,* OC **qwyay;* grade F

竹 'bamboo': MK *tay,* OJ *take2,* EMC **truk,* OC **truk;* grade Fpkj

雁 'goose': MK *kewuy,* OJ *kari,* EMC **ngraanh,* OC **ngraans;* grade Fpkj

I will go through these etymologies at an even faster pace than those in section 4.4, for the lack of resemblance is often so great that it deserves little comment.

'arrow': MK *sal* < EMC **syiiq*

The vocalic match is poor. Where does MK *-l* come from? There is a Proto-Tibeto-Burman root **tal* 'arrow' (Benedict 1972: 207) which was once held to be cognate to the Chinese word for 'arrow', but advances in Chinese reconstruction (such as Baxter 1992's abandonment of final **-r* in OC) have rendered that previous view invalid.

'floor': OJ *yuka* < EMC **hw+k* or OC **hrw+k*

These forms only have *k* in common. If the Old Japanese initial *y-* came from pre-OJ **d-,* then this etymology will never work.

'house': NK *cip,* OJ *ipe1* < EMC or OC **qrip* 'village'

The semantics are poor. If NK *cip* and OJ *ipe1* are related, then since the former cannot be related to the Old Chinese form, neither can the latter. These words probably stem from PKJ **jip,* with devoicing in Korean and **j* > zero /_*i* in OJ.

'turtle': MK *kepwup* < EMC **krwii* or OC **krw++*

Middle Korean only shares initial *k-* with the Chinese forms.

'village': OJ *sato1* < EMC **syit* or OC **stit* 'room'

The vocalism and semantics are poor.

'wither': MK *ivul-* < EMC **qwia* or OC **qwyay*

Middle Korean only shares *i* with the Chinese forms. It probably derives from earlier **iphul* via **ibhul*.

'bamboo': MK *tay*, OJ *take2* < EMC or OC **truk*

The Middle Korean and Old Japanese forms only share *t-* with the Chinese forms. Vovin (1994: 385) derives them from Proto-Altaic **tah[V]-i*.

'goose': MK *kewuy*, OJ *kari* < EMC **ngraanh* or OC **ngraans*

The Middle Korean and Old Japanese forms share almost nothing with the Chinese forms but are probably related to each other. Except for the *u* in Middle Korean, the vowel correspondences are regular. However, the lack of *-r-* in Korean (as opposed to Japanese, where *-r-* loss is common) is difficult to explain.

5. Conclusion

Out of the roughly seventy proposed Pre-Sino-Korean and Pre-Sino-Japanese etymologies examined in this study, only a handful—seven or roughly ten percent—were regarded as definite (Grade A). Of these seven, only three actually could be classified as Pre-Sinoxenic; the others were of more recent date and belonged to the more general category of 'Naturalized Sino-Korean' Roughly twenty percent were regarded as probable (Grade B). Two etymologies turned out to be false because the words were probably inherited from Proto-Koreo-Japonic and not borrowed from Chinese. The direction of borrowing was probably *into* Chinese from Altaic or some other language family rather than the other way around (Grade C). Over half were regarded as improbable; any resemblances between the Koreo-Japonic and the Chinese forms was likely to be coincidental and not the product of borrowing (Grade D). The remaining ten percent were regarded as invalid (Grade F).

Nearly all of the Grade A and B etymologies—roughly twenty-five percent of all etymologies—involved only Korean. There were only seven Japanese words in the upper grades—one in Grade A and six in Grade B. Most, if not all of them, were probably loans through Korean peninsular languages. Many of the Grade A and B words involved the trappings of Chinese civilization and language: Buddhism, material goods, counters, measures, and writing. Agricultural and basic vocabulary clustered in Grade D.

This skewed distribution indicates that the Korean peninsular peoples were involved in much more direct contact with the Chinese than the Japonic peoples. This is exactly what we would expect based on geography, since the Korean peninsula is next door to China and Japan is not. The contact between the Korean peninsula and China resulted in the importation of Buddhism, material goods, counters, measures, writing, and the associated Chinese vocabulary. If there was much of an exchange of agricultural technologies, the Korean peninsular peoples may have borrowed the implements and the plants but not their names, since most of the proposed agricultural loans from Chinese received Grade D. Native Korean peninsular words may have undergone semantic shifts to cope with any advances in agriculture brought in from China.

Although the contact between China and the Korean peninsula was strong, it was nowhere near as intense as the contact between China and Vietnam. Vietnamese has at least a hundred known Pre-Sino-Vietnamese words, including agricultural and even basic vocabulary. This study has confirmed no more than about fifteen Pre-Sino-Korean words in Grades A and B. None of them fall into the categories of agricultural or basic vocabulary. The Vietnamese situation is no doubt due to the millenium of Chinese political domination over Vietnam; no parallel long-term occupation occured in Northeast Asia.

If Pre-Sino-Vietnamese represents one extreme of the Pre-Sinoxenic spectrum, Pre-Sino-Japanese represents the other extreme. The paucity of Pre-Sino-Japanese words in Grades A and B and the high frequency of Pre-Sino-Korean cognates for them suggest that early Japan did not absorb very much Chinese culture from Korean peninsular intermediaries. This does not mean that Japan gained nothing through its contacts with the Korean peninsula. On the contrary, Korean peninsular peoples may have left a large linguistic as well as cultural impact upon Japan. Many 'native' Old Japanese words may actually be loans from peninsular linguistic relatives. Perhaps some of the Japanese words in Grades D and F which appear to be cognate to Korean are such loans.

This study paints quite a bleak picture of Pre-Sino-Korean and Pre-Sino-Japanese. However, there may be a few more Pre-Sino-Korean and Pre-Sino-Japanese words that are yet to be discovered. Most of the words in this study were chosen on the basis of their similarities to Karlgrenian reconstructions of Old and Middle Chinese. If we search for Middle Korean and Old Japanese words on the basis of their similarities to post-Karlgrenian reconstructions of Old and Middle Chinese, we may find words that were overlooked because they looked nothing like Karlgrenian reconstructions.

An example of a post-Karlgrenian innovation that has already aided us in this study is the tonogenetic hypothesis advanced first by Haudricourt (1954) and later by Matisoff (1973). According to this hypothesis, modern Asian tonal languages were originally non-tonal. The tonal distinctions arose to compensate for the loss of earlier segmental distinctions: glottal stops conditioned rising tones and fricatives conditioned falling tones. Early loans such as Pre-Sinoxenic from non-tonal Old Chinese would reflect these earlier segmental distinctions.

Kim (1971) partly exploited this hypothesis in his search for Pre-Sino-Korean words, turning up results like 'mustard plant' MK *kas* < OC *kraats* that preserved the lost *-s*. However, he did not screen all of his Pre-Sino-Korean candidates with this process in mind. Furthermore, no one to date has exploited the tonogenetic hypothesis in searching for Pre-Sino-Japanese words. A full-scale search for Korean and Japanese words with k and s corresponding to Old Chinese $*-q$ and $*-s$ may enable us to approach the completion of our list of Pre-Sino-Korean and Pre-Sino-Japanese words.

To be honest, I am not optimistic about the prospects of finding many more examples of Pre-Sino-Korean and Pre-Sino-Japanese words. But quality may count more than quantity. We may find only five more Pre-Sino-Korean and Pre-Sino-Japanese words. But if all five of them turn out to be agricultural vocabulary—the very loanwords that have eluded us until now—then our picture of the Northeast Asian contact situation will have been further clarified and our search will have been worthwhile.

References

Baxter, William H. 1992. A handbook of Old Chinese phonology. Berlin and New York: Mouton de Gruyter.

Benedict, Paul K. 1972. Sino-Tibetan: a conspectus. James A. Matisoff, contributing editor. Cambridge: Cambridge University Press.

Gage, William W. 1985. Vietnamese in Mon-Khmer perspective. Southeast Asian linguistic studies presented to Andre-G. Haudricourt, ed. by Suriya Ratanakul et al., 493-524. Bangkok: Mahidol University.

Hashimoto, Mantarō J. 1977. Current developments in Sino-Korean studies. Journal of Chinese linguistics 5.103-22.

Haudricourt, André. 1954. De l'origine des tons en viêtnamien. Journal Asiatique 242.68-82.

Kamei Takashi. 1954. Chinese borrowings in prehistoric Japanese. Tokyo: Yoshikawa Kōbunkan.

Karlgren, Bernhard. 1926. Philology and ancient China. Oslo: H. Aschehoug.

Karlgren, Bernhard. 1957. Grammata serica recensa. Bulletin of the Museum of Far Eastern Antiquities 29.1-332.

Kim Wancin. 1971. Kwuke umwun cheykyey uy yenkwu [Studies of the Korean phonological system]. Seoul: Ilcokak.

Manomaivibool, Prapin. 1976. Chinese and Thai: Are they related genetically? Computational analyses of Asian and African languages 6.11-32.

Martin, Samuel E. 1953. The phonemes of Ancient Chinese. Supplement to the Journal of the American Oriental Society, no. 16. Baltimore: American Oriental Society.

Martin, Samuel E. 1991. Recent research on the relationships of Japanese and Korean. Sprung from some common source, ed. by Sydney M. Lamb and E. Douglas Mitchell, 205-231. Stanford: Stanford University Press.

Martin, Samuel E. 1992. A reference grammar of Korean. Rutland and Tokyo: Tuttle.

Matisoff, James A. 1973. Tonogenesis in Southeast Asia. Consonant types and tone, ed. by Larry M. Hyman, 71-95. Los Angeles: University of Southern California.

Mineya, Tōru. 1972. Etsunan kanji'on no kenkyū [Studies on the Sino-Vietnamese]. Tokyo: Tōyō Bunko.

Nguyễn Đình Hoà. 1967. Vietnamese-English Student's Dictionary. Saigon: Vietnamese American Association.

Ōno Susumu, Satake Akihiro, and Maeda Kingorō, eds. 1990 [1974]. Iwanami kogo jiten [Iwanami Classical Japanese dictionary]. Revised ed. Tokyo: Iwanami shoten.

Pulleyblank, Edwin G. 1981. Some notes on Chinese historical phonology. Bulletin de l'Ecole Française d'Extrême-Orient 69.277-88.

Pulleyblank, Edwin G. 1984. Middle Chinese: A study in historical phonology. Vancouver: University of British Columbia Press.

Pulleyblank, Edwin G. 1991. Lexicon of reconstructed pronunciation in Early Middle Chinese, Late Middle Chinese, and Early Mandarin. Vancouver: University of British Columbia Press.

Ramsey, S. Robert. 1993. Some remarks on reconstructing earlier Korean. Ehak yenkwu [Language research] 29.4.433-442.

Ramsey, S. Robert and J. Marshall Unger. 1972. Evidence for a consonant shift in 7th century Japanese. Papers in Japanese linguistics 1.2.278-95.

Ray, David Tryon. 1979. Sources of Middle Chinese phonology: A prolegomenon to the study of Vietnamized Chinese. Master's dissertation, Southern Illinois University at Carbondale.

Serafim, Leon A. 1994. A modification of the Whitman Proto-Koreo-Japonic hypothesis. Korean linguistics 8.181-205.

Serafim, Leon A. 1994. Whitman's PJK hypothesis. Handout distributed at University of Hawai'i at Mānoa No-Brownbag Roundtable 'Issues in the genetic relation of Korean and Japanese.'

Serafim, Leon A. 1995. Handouts for University of Hawai'i at Mānoa class 'The relation of language change to culture change: exploring the entry and spread of Japonic through island northeast Asia.

Thomason, Sarah Grey and Terence Kaufman. 1988. Language contact, creolization, and genetic linguistics. Berkeley, Los Angeles, Oxford: University of California Press.

Unger, J. Marshall. 1993 [1977]. Studies in early Japanese morphophonemics, 2nd ed. Bloomington: Indiana University Linguistics Club.

Vovin, Alexander. 1993. On the phonetic value of the Middle Korean grapheme [triangle]. Bulletin of the School of Oriental and African Studies 56.2.247-59.

Vovin, Alexander. 1994. Is Japanese related to Austronesian? Oceanic linguistics 33.2.323-44.

Whitman, John B. 1990. A rule of medial *-r- loss in Pre-Old Japanese. Linguistic change and reconstruction methodology, ed. by Philip Baldi, 511-45. Berlin and New York: Mouton de Gruyter.

Whitman, John B. 1991 [1985]. 'The phonological basis for the comparison of Japanese and Korean.' Updated ms. of doctoral dissertation, Harvard University.

Yi Ki-moon. 1971. Language and writing systems in traditional Korea. Papers of the International Conference on Traditional Korean Culture and Society, ed. by Peter H. Lee, 15-31. Honolulu: Center for Korean Studies.

Part III

Phonology

NN: Rendaku and Licensing Paradox*

KEIICHIRO SUZUKI
University of Arizona

1 Introduction

Ito, Mester, and Padgett (1995) propose an analysis of the "nasal underspecification paradox" in Japanese where the specificational requirement of the feature [voice] in a nasal segment varies depending on whether the nasal is a singleton segment or is in an NC cluster. They argue that such paradoxical behavior of the redundant [voice] with respect to singleton N and NC cluster is resolved by the notion of licensing under the framework of Optimality Theory (Prince and Smolensky 1993, McCarthy and Prince 1993, among others). Their analysis hinges on the assumption that the redundant feature [voice] cannot be licensed by nasals (or sonorants). Thus, [voice] is licensed only when linked to an obstruent, whether a singleton like *d* or in a cluster like *nd*, explaining the [voice] specification in NC clusters.

In this paper, I introduce additional data containing nasal geminates which are not included in Ito, Mester, and Padgett (1995). I show that a

* Thanks to Diana Archangeli, Mike Hammond, Jaye Padgett, Doug Pulleyblank, Bruce Hayes, Samuel E. Martin, and Amy V. Fountain for their comments and suggestions. I also thank the participants of the University of Arizona Phonology Summer Discussion Group, and the participants of The Sixth Annual Japanese/Korean Linguistics Conference. This work was supported by Diana Archangeli's NSF grant No. BNS-9023323.

215

nasal geminate, schematized as NN, requires a redundant [voice] specification despite there being no obstruent in the NN cluster. This complicates the "nasal underspecification paradox": N must *not* be specified for [voice]; NC must be specified for [voice]; and NN must be specified for [voice]. I argue that the requirement that NN must be specified for [voice] exceeds the requirement for the redundant [voice] to be unspecified. In particular, I demonstrate that LOCAL CONJUNCTION (Smolensky 1993, 1995), a formal operation in OT, of the grounded constraint (such as NASVOI) accounts for the NN paradigm. I also appeal to the TWO-ROOT THEORY OF LENGTH by Selkirk (1988), as opposed to the standard moraic theory of length (McCarthy and Prince 1986, Hayes 1989, Ito 1989, among others).

The organization of the paper is as follows. First, I review Ito, Mester, and Padgett's (1995) analysis of the "nasal underspecification paradox". Second, I introduce forms containing NN which cannot be accounted for by Ito, Mester, and Padgett (1995). Third, I provide an analysis of the NN paradigm, employing Local Conjunction of the grounded constraint NASVOI and the Two-Root Theory of Length (Selkirk 1988). Finally, I discuss the central implication of this analysis, predicting featural unmarkedness in phonologically long segments (geminates and long vowels).

2   The Nasal Underspecification Paradox

This section reviews Ito, Mester, and Padgett's (1995) analysis of the "nasal underspecification paradox" in Japanese. This paradox is revealed through Rendaku ('sequential voicing') where an initial obstruent of the second member of a Yamato (native) compound undergoes voicing (Martin 1952:48-49, McCawley 1968: 86-87). This is illustrated in (1).

(1)

    a.   /ori+kami/   →   ori-**g**ami   'paper folding'

    b.   /yama+tera/ →   yama-**d**era   'mountain temple'

Rendaku is limited by a phenomenon known as Lyman's Law: there can be no more than one voiced obstruent within a Yamato root (Ito and Mester 1986). Thus, as in (2), the second member of the Yamato compound contains a voiced obstruent, and Rendaku is blocked.

(2)

        /kami+kaze/   →   kami-kaze   'divine wind'

                            *kami-**g**aze

In (2), the voiced obstruent /z/ in the second member of the compound prevents Rendaku: /kami+kaze/ does not become *kami-gaze, but rather, surfaces as kami-kaze.

Based on the assumption that Lyman's Law is due to the OCP holding over the [voice] tier, the interaction between Rendaku and Lyman's Law serves as a diagnostic for whether or not a segment is specified for the feature [voice] (Ito and Mester 1986, Steriade 1987, Archangeli and Pulleyblank 1994, Ito, Mester, and Padgett 1995). If Rendaku occurs, there is no other [voice] specification in the second member of the compound, but if Rendaku is blocked, there must be another [voice] specification in the second member of the compound[1]. To illustrate, in (3a), -futa becomes -buta, there being no [voice] specification (below, "V" stands for [voice]), whereas in (3b), -fuda is unaffected by Rendaku, since there is another [voice] specification in -fuda.

(3)

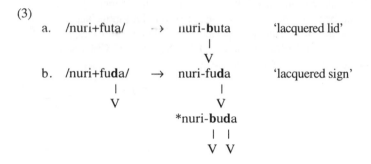

A second phenomenon, post-nasal voicing in Yamato Japanese, gives evidence of feature [voice] in NC clusters (Ito and Mester 1986, Ito, Mester, and Padgett 1995). In Yamato Japanese (which does have a voicing contrast in obstruents), the obstruents in NC clusters are always voiced (4).

(4)
a.	tombo	'dragonfly'	*tompo
b.	unzari	'disgusted'	*unsari

We are now in a position to understand the "nasal underspecification paradox", discussed extensively in Ito, Mester, and Padgett (1995). The paradox arises from two facts, illustrated in (5a) and (5b) respectively: 1) a singleton nasal does not block Rendaku, suggesting that the singleton nasal must not be specified for [voice] (5a); 2) an NC sequence blocks Rendaku, suggesting that the NC must be specified for [voice] (5b).

---

[1] Following Ito, Mester, and Padgett (1995), I assume privative voicing theory (Lombardi 1991, among others).

(5)

    a.   /haya+kane/   →   haya-**gane**   'fire bell'

                                    *haya-kane

        /širooto+kaŋgae/   →   širooto-ka**ŋg**ae   'layman's idea'

    b.   *širooto-**gaŋg**ae

In (5a), the nasal in [-kane] must not be specified for the redundant [voice], allowing Rendaku, whereas in (5b), NC cluster in [-kaŋgae] must be specified for the redundant [voice], blocking Rendaku. The paradox which Ito and Mester (1986) recognize is that [voice] is redundant in both cases, yet specified only in an NC cluster, not in a singleton N.

    While derivational accounts of the paradox (Borowsky 1986, Taub 1988) remain unsatisfactory, Ito, Mester, and Padgett (1995) convincingly argue that the paradox can be resolved from the perspective of Optimality Theory (Prince and Smolensky 1993, McCarthy and Prince 1993). Their basic idea is that because the feature [voice] is redundant in nasals (as well as sonorants), it cannot be licensed by nasals. Ito, Mester, and Padgett (1995) propose a principle of universal grammar, LICENSING CANCELLATION (6a) which regulates such segment-internal redundancy.

(6)   Licensing Cancellation: If $F \supset G$, then $\neg(F \lambda G)$

        "If the specification F implies the specification G, then it is not the case that F licenses G (Ito, Mester, and Padgett 1995: 580)".

Given the well-motivated grounded constraint NASVOI (7a), a nasal segment cannot license [voice]. Thus, any singleton nasal specified for [voice] fails to satisfy the requirement of the constraint, LICENSE[VOICE] (7b), which demands the feature [voice] to be licensed.

(7)

    a.   **NASVOI**: [nasal] $\supset$ [voice]

        "If a segment is specified for [nasal], then the segment is also specified for [voice] (Ito, Mester, and Padgett 1995: 580-582)".[2]

    b.   LICENSE[VOICE] (**LICENSE**):

        The feature [voice] must be licensed.

---

[2] Ito, Mester, and Padgett's (1995) interprestation of grounded conditions ($F \supset G$) is different from that of Archangeli and Pulleyblank's (1994): Ito, Mester, and Padgett's (1995) version makes reference to *segments* (i.e. root nodes), while Archangeli and Pulleyblank's (1994) original version is defined over *paths* (1994: 177). Since my analysis builds on Ito, Mester, and Padgett's (1995), I simply follow their formulation of the grounded constraints.

While a nasal segment cannot license [voice], an obstruent segment can. [Voice] is not redundant in obstruents, so an obstruent specified for [voice] does not violate LICENSE.

The tableau in (8) shows that the "nasal underspecification paradox" is resolved by the ranking LICENSE >> NASVOI >> FAITH, where **FAITH** stands for a set of feature faithfulness constraints which are violated whenever features and association lines are inserted or deleted (Ito, Mester, and Padgett 1995: 586).

(8)   LICENSE >> NASVOI >> FAITH

Input 1=/kami/; Input 2=/tompo/

Candidates	LICENSE	NASVOI	FAITH
a. ☞ k a m i		*	
b. k a m i | V	*!		*
c. ☞ t o m b o \ / V			* *
d. t o m p o | V	*!		*
e. t o m p o		*!	
f. t o m b o | V		*!	*

The constraint hierarchy in (8) correctly picks a winning candidate for both a singleton N and an NC sequence. For /kami/, the candidate with a redundant [voice] specification (8b), is eliminated by LICENSE. The underspecified candidate (8a) wins. For the NC case (/tompo/), candidates (8d,e,f) violate either LICENSE or NASVOI, while the candidate (8c) wins, violating neither LICENSE nor NASVOI. This is because the doubly-linked [voice] is licensed by the obstruent (not licensed by the nasal).

As shown above, Ito, Mester, and Padgett's (1995) appeal to Licensing elegantly accounts for the "nasal underspecification paradox", explaining why 1) a single N is unspecified for [voice], allowing Rendaku; and 2) NC is specified for [voice], blocking Rendaku.

3   NN must be specified for [voice]

If Ito, Mester, and Padgett (1995) are right in arguing that [voice] can be licensed only when linked to an obstruent, then it must also be the case that if [voice] is *not* linked to an obstruent, it cannot be licensed. Keeping this prediction in mind, consider the following additional data in (9) in which the second member of the compound contains a nasal geminate.[3] These data show that Ito, Mester, and Padgett's (1995) prediction with respect to geminates is false.[4]

(9)

    a.   /hana+kammuri/   →   hana-kammuri   'flower crown'
                                       *hana-gammuri

    b.   /ito+koɲɲaku/   →   ito-koɲɲaku   'thin konjak'
                                         *ito-goɲɲaku

    c.   /yaki+samma/   →   yaki-samma   'fried saury'
                                         *yaki-zamma

None of the forms with nasal geminates undergo Rendaku, indicating that NN must be specified for [voice]. Therefore, contrary to Ito, Mester, and Padgett's (1995) claim, it must be the case that [voice] is licensed without being linked to an obstruent.

---

[3] The lexical status of these words are somehow controversial. Samuel E. Martin (p.c.) told me that these words could be considered Sino-Japanese. He suggests that a Yamato word, *kanna* 'a plane', would provide more definitive argument for NN case. Bruce Hayes (p.c.) suggested to me that an experiment with some hypothetical words would also provide a clearer picture of the phenomenon. For the argument provided here, however, I assume that these examples are Rendaku/Lyman's Law sensitive, taking the above insightful suggestions into my future investigation.

[4] The recent proposal by Steriade (1995) and Pater (1995), that post-nasal voicing involves an obstruent-exclusive feature [EXP] ([expanded pharynx]) also makes false predictions with respect to NN and Rendaku. Pater (1995) suggests that Lyman's Law in Japanese is a prohibition against multiple occurrences of [EXP], not [voice]. However, if [EXP] is the crucial feature, then NN (which has no obstruents and so has no tokens of [EXP]) should allow Rendaku effects, contrary to the evidence presented here. I conclude, as do Ito, Mester, and Padgett (1995), that it is probably worth keeping the "unity and integrity of the distinctive feature [voice]" (1995: 577).

The introduction of the data in (9), thus, further complicates the "nasal underspecification paradox" discussed in Ito, Mester, and Padgett (1995), as illustrated in (10).

(10)

	NC	NN	N
Rendaku/Lyman's Law:	[voice]	[voice]	unspecified
Ito, Mester, and Padgett (1995):	[voice]	unspecified	unspecified

As shown in this extended picture of the "nasal underspecification paradox" (10), Ito, Mester, and Padgett (1995) draw the line in wrong place. Accordingly, the constraint hierarchy in (8) fails to account for the NN case, as shown in (11).

(11)   LICENSE >> NASVOI >> FAITH

Input=/koɲɲaku/

Candidates		LICENSE	NASVOI	FAITH
a. ☞ wrong winner:	k o ɲ ɲ a k u		*	
b. ‼ attested form.	k o ɲ ɲ a k u \ / V	*!		*

The candidate (11a) is incorrectly picked as a winner, since the candidate (11b) violates LICENSE. However, the actual output must be (11b) in order to have the [voice] specification to block Rendaku. Therefore, Ito, Mester, and Padgett's (1995) prediction that a nasal cannot be specified for [voice] if not linked to an obstruent is too restrictive. *NN must be specified for [voice]* even though in such cases [voice] is not licensed by an obstruent.

4   The Analysis

In this section, I provide a comprehensive analysis of the Rendaku paradigm. Building on the idea of feature licensing developed in Ito, Mester, and Padgett (1995), I argue that the requirement for NN to be specified for [voice] exceeds the requirement for a singleton nasal to be unspecified for [voice]. In other words, the requirement for the redundant [voice] to be specified is *stronger* in geminate nasals (NN) than in singleton nasals (N). This idea can be straightforwardly implemented in OT, combining Local

Conjunction (Smolensky 1993, 1995) and the Two-Root Theory of Length (Selkirk 1988) with grounded conditions like NASVOI.

4.1. Local Conjunction

LOCAL CONJUNCTION, introduced by Smolensky (1993, 1995), is based on the idea that "two constraint violations are worse when they occur in the same location: constraint interactions can be stronger locally than non-locally" (1995: 4). For example, the locally-conjoined constraint, $C^1 \&_{LC} C^2$, is violated when there is some domain D in which *both* C^1 and C^2 are violated. Local Conjunction can be self-conjoining: if $C^1 = C^2$, $C^1 \&_{LC} C^2$ is violated when there is some domain D in which C is violated *twice*. Further, it must be universally the case that the locally-conjoined constraint is always ranked above both of the component constraints: $C^1 \&_{LC} C^2 \gg C^1, C^2$ (Smolensky 1993, 1995).

In the case of NN, I argue that although the effect of the redundancy implication NASVOI is negated by a higher-ranked LICENSE[VOICE] in singleton nasals, NASVOI is active in the domain of geminate nasals. Formally, the locally self-conjoined constraint $NASVOI^2$ ($NASVOI \&_{LC} NASVOI$) (12a) expresses that two local violations of NASVOI is worse than violating NASVOI (12b) once .

(12)
    a. $NASVOI \&_{LC} NASVOI$ (**$NASVOI^2$**):
             $NASVOI^2$ is violated when NASVOI is violated twice in some domain D.
    b.   NASVOI:
             [nasal] $\supset$ [voice] (if a segment is [nasal], then it is also [voice])

$NASVOI^2$ formally expresses the idea that in nasal geminates, the requirement for nasals to be specified for [voice] is stronger than in singleton nasals. The challenge here is to define "domain D" so that the $NASVOI^2$ is *locally* violated twice in NN.

4.2 Two-Root Theory of Length

For NN, but not N, to be subject to $NASVOI^2$, the domain D must be formally defined so that the local violation of $NASVOI^2$ is assessed only in phonologically long segments. Here I adopt the TWO-ROOT THEORY OF LENGTH (Selkirk 1988) in which phonologically long segments are represented as having two root nodes which share some feature(s). This is a crucial assumption to be made, because the standard moraic representation is unable to distinguish between single segments and long segments at the root node level. In standard moraic theory of length (Hyman 1985, McCarthy and Prince 1986, Hayes 1989, Ito 1989, Katada 1990), there is only one root node and one feature for a geminate, as shown below in (13).

(13)

    a. Long Vowel   b. Geminate Consonant   c. Single Segment

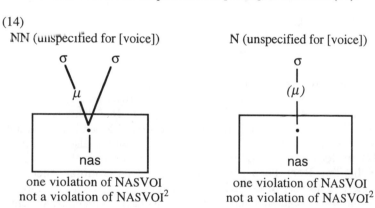

Since long segments (13a,b) and short segments (13c) have the identical structure below a root node, the only representational difference between long segments and the short ones is their prosodic structure (above the root node). Under this view, the violations of the constraint, NASVOI^2, are the same for both N and NN unspecified for [voice], as shown in (14).

(14)

    NN (unspecified for [voice])   N (unspecified for [voice])

one violation of NASVOI   one violation of NASVOI
not a violation of NASVOI^2 not a violation of NASVOI^2

For NN and N, the relevant structures for NASVOI^2 are identical (as indicated by the two boxes) in which NASVOI is violated only once. However, we know that while NN specified for [voice] is wellformed, N specified for [voice] is illformed. Under the moraic theory of length, there is no way of distinguishing between NN and N with respect to NASVOI^2.

    In the Two-Root Theory (Selkirk 1988), on the other hand, geminate entities (both long vowels and geminate consonants) involve two root nodes, sharing some feature [F], as shown in (15).

(15)

    a. Long Vowel   b. Geminate Consonant   c. Single Segment

The representation of long segments (15a,b) is different from that of singleton segments (15c) below the root node: in long segments (15a,b), the feature [F] is doubly-linked, whereas in single segments (15c), [F] is singly-linked. Thus, the NN cluster under the Two-Root Theory can be subject to the locally-conjoined NASVOI^2 by violating NASVOI twice locally, if we define 'local' as involving *the same token of [nasal]*. This is illustrated in (16).

(16)

        NN (unspecified for [voice])

    violation of NASVOI^2

In (16) where NN is unspecified for [voice], each root node is violating NASVOI, (as indicated by *1 and *2), because the two root nodes share the same token of [nasal]. This constitutes a violation of NASVOI^2, as desired.

    Since Ito, Mester, and Padgett's (1995) version of grounded constraints are defined as "if a *segment* (i.e. root node) is [F], then it is also [G]" (1995: 580-582), the locally-conjoined F⊃G^2 can refer to long segments only if we assume the Two-Root Theory of Length. Under the moraic theory of length, there is no way of computing violations for the locally-conjoined F⊃G^2, since single segments and long segments have an identical structure below the root node level.

4.3   The Final Result

The locally-conjoined grounded constraint NASVOI^2, under the Two-Root Theory, accounts for the NN paradigm, as shown in (17). For the Japanese facts, NASVOI^2 must dominate NASVOI, exactly as claimed in Smolensky (1993, 1995).

(17) $NASVOI^2$, LICENSE >> NASVOI >> FAITH

Input=/koɲɲaku (with no specification)/

Candidates	$NASVOI^2$	LICENSE	NASVOI	FAITH
a. k o ɲ ɲ a k u	*		*!*	
b. ☞ k o ɲ ɲ a k u \ / V		*		**
c. k o ɲ ɲ a k u │ V		*	*!	*
d. k o ɲ ɲ a k u │ V		*	*!	*

The above ranking accounts for the NN paradigm, capturing the generalization that the requirement of [voice] specification in nasal geminates is stronger than in single nasals.

Significantly, the optimal candidate is always the one in which [voice] is doubly-linked (17b) regardless of the specificational status in the input, since the constraint FAITH is inactive in the hierarchy. Thus, the above analysis does not destroy Ito, Mester, and Padgett's important claim that *underspecification is an emergent property of the output* (1995: 609).

This account simply builds on the account offered in Ito, Mester, and Padgett (1995), preserving their analysis of NC voicing. The difference is that the introduction of Local Conjunction allows an explanation for the data that Ito, Mester, and Padgett (1995) do not consider -- NN.

5   Conclusion

I have argued that the NN paradigm in Japanese is accounted for by locally self-conjoining the grounded constraint NASVOI. Rather than creating a new constraint to specifically refer to NN, the present analysis appeals to Local Conjunction (Smolensky 1993, 1995) which is an independently motivated constraint operation in OT (see Archangeli and Suzuki 1995, Ohno 1995, and Suzuki 1995 for other possible applications of Local Conjunction).

The significance of this analysis is its applicability to other observable cases. As Smolensky (1993, 1995) observes, Local Conjunction is an operation generalizable to the ranking scheme $F{\supset}G^2 \gg F{\supset}G$. The prediction which this ranking makes with respect to grounded constraints is that they may hold phonologically long segments even when violated in singleton segments, leading to the emergence of the unmarked in long segments (see McCarthy and Prince 1994 on Emergence of the Unmarked in general). Below, I give some examples where such emergence of the unmarked in long segments is observed.

In languages such as Japanese, Finnish, Yakut, and Lak (Maddieson 1984), there are both voiced and voiceless obstruents, but only voiceless obstruent geminates are observed. This is explained through the grounded constraint OBSVOI (If obstruent, then not [voice]). The ranking OBSVOI^2 $\gg$ LICENSE[VOICE] $\gg$ OBSVOI accounts for voicelessness in obstruent geminates, i.e. obstruent geminates are unmarked with respect to [voice]. For the redundant [voice] in vowels, there are languages which have both voiced and voiceless short vowels but only voiced long vowels (Southern Paiute (Sapir 1930), Ik, Dafla (Maddieson 1984)). This is captured by the ranking VOCVOI^2 $\gg$ LICENSE[VOICE] $\gg$ VOCVOI (VOCVOI = "if [-consonantal], then [voice]" (Ito, Mester, and Padgett 1995: 596)). In languages like Wolof (Ka 1988, Archangeli and Pulleyblank 1994) which have ATR contrast in short low vowels, such a contrast disappears in long vowels. Based on the grounded constraint LO/ATR (If [lo], then not [ATR]) proposed by Archangeli and Pulleyblank (1994), The unmarked value of [ATR] in long low vowels can be explained by having the ranking LO/ATR^2 $\gg$ LICENSE(ATR) $\gg$ LO/ATR. Further details remain to be worked out. Nonetheless, the present approach promises a formal account of the emergence of the unmarked in long segments.

References

Archangeli, Diana. and Douglas Pulleyblank (1994) *Grounded Phonology*, MIT Press, Cambridge, Mass.

Archangeli, Diana. and Keiichiro Suzuki (1995) "Menomini Harmony: Phonological Representations in OT", presentation at *the Arizona Phonology Conference: Features in OT*, University of Arizona.

Borowsky, Toni. (1986) Topics in English Phonology, Doctoral dissertation, University of Massachusetts, Amherst.

Hayes, Bruce. (1989). "Compensatory Lengthening in Moraic Phonology." *Linguistic Inquiry* 20: 253-306.

Hyman, Larry. (1985) *A Theory of Phonological Weight*, Foris, Dordrecht.

Ito, Junko. and Armin Mester (1986) "The Phonology of Voicing in Japanese: Theoretical Consequences for Morphological Accessibility", *LI* 17, 49-73.

Ito, Junko., Armin Mester and Jaye Padgett (1995) *NC: Licensing and Underspecification in Optimality Theory*, To appear in Linguistic Inquiry.

Itô, Junko. (1989) "A Prosodic Theory of Epenthesis," *Natural Language and Linguistic Theory* 7, 217-259.

Ka, Omar. (1988) *Wolof Phonology and Morphology: A Non-Linear Approach*, Doctoral dissertation, University of Illinois at Urbana-Champaign.

Katada, Fusa. (1990) "On the Representation of Moras: Evidence from a Language Game," *LI* 21, 641-646.

Lombardi, Linda. (1991) *Laryngeal Features and Laryngeal Neutralization*, Doctoral dissertation, University of Massachusetts, Amherst.

Maddieson, Ian. (1984) *Patterns of Sounds*, Cambridge University Press, Cambridge.

Martin, Samuel E. (1952) *Morphophonemics of Standard Colloquial Japanese*, Supplement to *Language*, Language Dissertation No. 47.

McCarthy, John J. and Alan. Prince (1986) *Prosodic Morphology*, ms, University of Massachusetts, Amherst and Brandeis University.

McCarthy, John J. and Alan Prince (1994) *The Emergence of the Unmarked: Optimality in Prosodic Morphology*, ms, University of Massachusetts, Amherst and Rutgers University.

McCawley, James D. (1968). *The Phonological Component of a Grammar of Japanese*. The Hague, Netherlands, Mouton.

Ohno, Sachiko (1995) "Synchronically-Unified Ranking and Distribution of Voice in Japanese", presentation at *the Arizona Phonology Conference: Features in OT*, University of Arizona.

Pater, Joe. (1995) "Austronesian Nasal Substitution and other NC Effects", paper presented at the *Utrcht Prosodic Morphology Workshop*.

Prince, Alan. and Paul Smolensky (1993). *Optimality Theory: Constraint Interaction in Generative Grammar*, ms, Rutgers University and University of Colorado at Boulder.

Sapir, Edward. (1930) "The Southern Paiute Language: Southern Paiute, a Shoshonean language," in eds., *Proceedings of the American Academy of Arts and Sciences*, 1-296.

Selkirk, Elizabeth. (1988) *A Two-Root Theory of Length*, ms, University of Massachusetts, Amherst.

Smolensky, Paul. (1993) *Optimality, Markedness, and Underspecification*, ms, Rutgers University.

Smolensky, Paul. (1995) *On the Internal Structure of the Constraint Component Con of UG (Hdt)*, ms, Johns Hopkins University.

Steriade, Donca (1987) "Redundant Values", *Papers from CLS-23*, vol. 2, 339-362.

Steriade, Donca. (1995). Underspecification and Markedness. in J. Goldsmith, ed., *The Handbook of Phonological Theory*. Cambridge, Mass, Basil Blackwell: 114-174.

Suzuki, Keiichiro. (1995) "Vowel Raising in Woleaian: Adjacency and Linear Precedence in OT", presentation at *the Arizona Phonology Conference: Features in OT*, University of Arizona.

Taub, Alison. (1988) *The Underspecification of [voice] and the Status of Nasal-Consonant Clusters in Japanese Phonology*, ms, University of Massachusetts, Amherst.

Korean Place and Sonorant Assimilations in Optimality Theory

HYEONKWAN CHO
University of Minnesota

1. Introduction

This paper provides an explicit formal analysis of Korean place and sonorant assimilations in the framework of OPTIMALITY THEORY (Prince and Smolensky 1993, McCarthy and Prince 1993). I assume that there exist two opposite forces with regard to speech production. One is a listener-oriented tendency which tries to preserve the contrasts of underlying segments in order to keep lexical items maximally distinct for the sake of perception. The other is a speaker-oriented tendency which tries to reduce the contrasts in order to make articulations easier.

In the view of Optimality Theory, consonant assimilations occur when constraints relevant to maintaining high perceptibility are violated in order to preserve constraints relevant to ease of articulation. If there is no consonant assimilation, constraints for ease of articulation are violated whereas constraints which maintain perceptual clarity are observed. A language with assimilations has a constraint ranking in which constraints for easy articulations dominate constraints for high perceptibility, and the opposite is true for a language with no assimilation.

I claim that the constraint family primarily responsible for increasing ease of articulation is CLUSTER CONDITION, which forces consonant clusters to have the same places, manners, or voicing. I also claim that the constraint family primarily responsible for maintaining perceptual clarity is PARSE, which disfavors the deletion of any elements.

I argue that underspecification is a property which can be derived from constraint interactions, and thus that underspecified representations may be unnecessary in phonological theories. Smolensky (1993) argues that the underspecification of the coronal node for coronal epenthesis can be resolved by employing a constraint ranking. I will show that underspecification for default values in assimilations can also be derived by using constraint ranking. The organization of the paper is as follows: In section 2 an overview of Optimality Theory is given. In section 3 I show that consonant assimilations are the result of constraint interactions and that the variability of assimilations can be accounted for by assigning different constraint rankings. In section 4 I discuss underlying representations and propose that constraint rankings can achieve the same results as underspecification does in regard to assimilation. In section 5 and 6 I will give an analysis of Korean place assimilation and sonorant assimilation, respectively. Section 7 gives the summary.

2. An Overview of Optimality Theory

In the development of phonological theory, there has been a shift from process-based approaches to constraint-based approaches. In a purely process-based approaches the burden of explanation for phonological phenomena has been on phonological rules and underlying representations. However, according to Prince and Smolensky, process-based theories cannot capture significant regularities on output structures which derive from well-formedness constraints on output structures. Only a few well-formedness constraints such as No Association Line Crossing and OCP on outputs have been used peripherally in process-based theories like autosegmental phonology and feature geometrical phonology.

In Optimality Theory proposed by Prince and Smolensky 1993 and McCarthy and Prince 1993, well-formedness constraints are universal. They claim that Universal Grammar consists of a set of universal constraints on representational well-formedness. Constraints are often conflicting and such conflicts are resolved by the ranking of these constraints. The satisfaction of higher ranked constraints forces the violation of lower ranked constraints. Prince and Smolensky claim that languages differ primarily in how they resolve the conflicts of constraints.

The general architecture of Optimality Theory is composed of Input, Output, the function GEN (generator), and the function H-EVAL (harmony-evaluator) as follows.

(1) Structure of Optimality-theoretic grammar
    a. Gen (Input$_k$) $\rightarrow$ {Output$_1$, Output$_2$, ...}
    b. H-eval(Output$_i$, $1 \leq i \leq \infty$) $\rightarrow$ Output$_{real}$

Gen generates a set of candidate outputs from an input, and then the candidates are assessed by H-eval. Among output candidates, the candidate that best-satisfies the constraint system is the optimal output.

The main proposal of Optimality Theory is a means for determining which candidate best-satisfies a given constraint system. The optimal output which best-satisfies is the most harmonic candidate. H-eval is a function that selects an optimal candidate out of a set of output candidates. The function H-eval is illustrated in constraint tableaux. I will introduce McCarthy and Prince's explanation of H-eval in the following section.

Assume that a grammar has two constraints, A and B, and two related candidates, $cand_1$ and $cand_2$ for a given $input_k$. If $cand_1$ satisfies A but violates B while $cand_2$ satisfies B but violates A, the two constraints are in conflict for the candidate set. If the optimal output is $cand_1$, constraint A has priority over constraint B. In other words, A dominates B (A » B). Thus, the constraint conflict is resolved by constraint ranking. The following constraint tableau shows how the optimal output is selected.

(2) constraint tableau: A » B and $input_k$

candidates	A	B
☞ $cand_1$		*
$cand_2$	*!	

Violation of a constraint is marked by '*' whereas satisfaction is indicated by a blank cell. The sign '!' stands for a fatal violation and any candidate with '!' cannot be optimal. The symbol '☞' draws attention to the optimal candidates (In this paper, the borders of a cell will be bold-faced to indicate the optimal outputs). Shading emphasizes the irrelevance of the constraint to the fate of the candidate. A loser's cells are shaded after the fatal violation. In the given tableau, $cand_2$ has a fatal violation because it violates the higher ranked constraint A whereas $cand_1$ violates the lower ranked constraint B. H-eval selects $cand_1$ as the optimal output because it is more harmonic.

In evaluating candidates, the number of constraint violations is not crucial. If $cand_1$ violates only a highest ranked constraint A and $cand_2$ violates two lower ranked constraints B and C, the optimal output is $cand_2$ even though it violates more constraints as in the following constraint tableau.

(3) constraint tableau: A » B, C and $input_k$

candidates	A	B	C
$cand_1$	*!		
☞ $cand_2$		*	*

(a single line for a ranking and a dotted line for no ranking)

Because of this kind of evaluation, constraint ranking is said to be in a STRICT DOMINANCE HIERARCHY. Each constraint has absolute priority over all the constraints lower in the hierarchy.

In sum, Optimality Theory is a purely constraint-based theory and constraints are rankable and violable. The function H-eval evaluates a set of candidates generated by the function Gen, based on constraint ranking.

3. Assimilations and Constraint Interactions

The constraint family primarily responsible for ease of articulations is Cluster Condition which forces consonant clusters to have the same place, manner, or voicing. Since Cluster Condition is a family of constraints, Cluster Condition holds of all the nodes in feature geometry as follows.[1] Adjacent consonants which have different places, manners, or voicing must violate the related constraints of Cluster Condition.

(4) Cluster Condition
   Adjacent consonants(CC) must have the same place, manner, or voicing:
   ClusterCond(place of articulation or POA), ClusterCond(sonorancy),
   ClusterCond(continuancy), ClusterCond(voicing), . . .

The constraint family primarily responsible for clarity of perception is Parse. Parse is a family of constraints, and the family has one member for each possible element. Delinking an element results in a violation of the related Parse constraint since the delinked element is not linked to its mother node.

(5) Parse: Prince and Smolensky (1993)
   Elements must be linked to the appropriate mother node:
   $\text{Parse}^{\text{segment}}$, $\text{Parse}^{\text{Place}}$, $\text{Parse}^{\text{labial}}$, $\text{Parse}^{\text{nasal}}$, $\text{Parse}^{\text{voice}}$, . . .

A general typology of possible consonant assimilations results from different constraint rankings:

(6)   Grammar A: with no consonant assimilation
        constraint ranking: Parse » Cluster Condition

   Grammar B: with consonant assimilations
        constraint ranking: Cluster Condition » Parse

However, few human languages fall into the two extremes given above. Most languages lie somewhere between these two extremes. Generally, consonant assimilations are restricted in terms of targets, triggers, and directionality. Variability of consonant assimilations results from different restrictions on targets, triggers, and the directionality of assimilation.

The variability of targets in place assimilation is the result of differences in the constraint rankings between Parse and Cluster Condition:

(7) Variability of Targets
   a. when all places of articulation are targets
      ClusterCond(POA) » $\text{Parse}^{\text{dor}}$, $\text{Parse}^{\text{lab}}$, $\text{Parse}^{\text{cor}}$
   b. when only coronals are targets
      $\text{Parse}^{\text{dor}}$, $\text{Parse}^{\text{lab}}$ » ClusterCond(POA) » $\text{Parse}^{\text{cor}}$
   c. when only coronals and labials are targets
      $\text{Parse}^{\text{dor}}$ » ClusterCond(POA) » $\text{Parse}^{\text{lab}}$, $\text{Parse}^{\text{cor}}$

When ClusterCond is higher ranked, the optimal output can violate any lower ranked Parse constraints in order to satisfy the higher ranked ClusterCond. Thus, place features like dorsal, labial, and coronal assimilate to a trigger place by delinking their original place features. However, when ClusterCond is ranked lower, the optimal output can tolerate the violation of the lower ranked ClusterCond. If Parse[dor] is ranked higher than ClusterCond, violation of Parse[dor] will be fatal. Thus, the dorsal place will not assimilate to a trigger place.

The variability of directionality is the result of differences in the rankings of featural Alignment and ClusterCond. Featural Alignment constraints disfavor extending the domains of input features. Doubly-linked features which result from feature spreading violate Alignment. I will employ BASIC ALIGNMENT (Cole and Kisseberth 1994) for featural alignment.

(8) Basic Alignment
Every sponsor of feature F is aligned with the edges of a F-domain.

The sponsor of a feature could be any node that dominates the feature in the underlying representation. I assume that root nodes are sponsors.[2] The underlying domain of a feature is from the left edge to the right edge of its sponsor node. Basic Alignment has two forms: Basic Align(F, Right, Root, Right) and Basic Align(F, Left, Root, Left). The former aligns the right edge of a feature with the right edge of the underlying sponsor root node. The latter aligns the left edge of a feature with the left edge of the underlying sponsor root node. Thus, in case of assimilation, one of those constraints must be violated. Regressive assimilation will violate Basic Align(F, Left, Root, Left) while progressive assimilation will violate Basic Align(F, Right, Root, Right), as follows.

(9)a. regressive assimilation   b. progressive assimilation

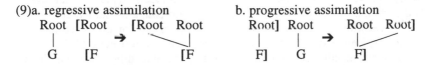

Since Basic Alignment interacts with ClusterCond, the variability of spreading is explained by the following constraint rankings. From now on, for featural alignment, I will use the term ALIGN instead of Basic Align.

(10) Variability of Directionality
a. regressive assimilation
   Align(F, Right, Root, Right) » ClusterCond » Align(F, Left, Root, Left)
b. progressive assimilation
   Align(F, Left, Root, Left) » ClusterCond » Align(F, Right, Root, Right)

When ClusterCond is ranked higher than Align(F, Left, Root, Left) but lower than Align(F, Right, Root, Right), the violation of lower ranked

Align(F, Left, Root, Left) to satisfy ClusterCond leads to the optimal solution. Thus, only regressive assimilation occurs. When ClusterCond is ranked lower than Align(F, Left, Root, Left) but higher than Align(F, Right, Root, Right), violating lower ranked Align(F, Right, Root, Right) to satisfy ClusterCond leads to the optimal solution. Thus, only progressive assimilation occurs.

Featural Alignment constraints can also explain variability of triggers. A triggering feature violates Align of the feature in the case of spreading, whereas a non-triggering feature must not violate Align of the feature. In place assimilation, the variability of triggers results from the constraint rankings of ClusterCond and Align:

(11) Variability of Triggers
   a. when all places are triggers
      ClusterCond(POA) » Align(cor), Align(lab), Align(dor)
   b. when only labials and dorsal are triggers
      Align(cor) » ClusterCond(POA) » Align(lab), Align(dor)
   c. when only dorsals are triggers
      Align(cor), Align(lab) » ClusterCond(POA) » Align(dor)

In short, consonant assimilation is the result of constraint interactions. ClusterCond, Parse, and Alignment are crucially involved in these constraint interactions. The variability of consonant assimilations is a result of the different rankings among the ClusterCond, Parse, and Alignment constraint families.

4. Underlying Representations

The degree of specification of underlying representations can influence the interpretation of consonant assimilations. In radical underspecification theory underlying unmarked coronals are underspecified for coronal nodes. Thus, when *tk* becomes *kk* as in English and Korean, a dorsal feature spread to the preceding consonant which is underspecified for the place feature. Align(dor, Left, Root, Left) is violated because the left edge of the dorsal articulator is misaligned with the left edge of the preceding consonant due to the doubly linked dorsal node:

(12) assimilation under underspecification

input /...tk.../	ClustCond(POA)	Align(dor, L)

R   R
| |
Pl   Pl
     |
    dor
	*!	

R   R
| |
Pl   Pl
  \ |
    dor
		*

If the underlying representation is fully specified, unmarked coronals must be specified for coronal nodes. Thus, the optimal output *kk* results in the violation of Parse^{cor} and Align(dor, Left):

(13) assimilation under full specification

input/...tk.../	ClustCond(POA)	Parse^{cor}	Align(dor, L)
R R | | Pl Pl | | cor dor	*!		
R R | | Pl Pl =|= \ | cor dor		*	*

In brief, both underspecification and full specification of underlying representations appear to be compatible with Optimality Theory in accounting for assimilations. Whether underspecification theory is necessary in Optimality Theory is not clear.

However, if underspecification effects can be derived from constraint interactions, it is doubtful whether underspecification is necessary in Optimality Theory. In this regard, Smolensky (1993) and Prince and Smolensky (1993) argue that underspecification of a default value for unmarked coronal can be resolved by employing a constraint ranking like *PL/Lab » *PL/Cor.

(14) Prince and Smolensky (1993)
    *Pl/Lab: Place may not dominate a labial node.
    *Pl/Cor: Place may not dominate a coronal node.

Smolensky demonstrates that the universal domination relation *PL/Lab » *PL/Cor entails that epenthetic consonants should be coronals. For example, when a consonant is epenthesized to supply an onset for an input /a/, an unmarked coronal is inserted, as in [ta]. Since the constraint ranking is *PL/Lab » *PL/Cor, [ta] is more harmonic and thus optimal. According to Smolensky, the constraint ranking *PL/Lab, *PL/Dor » *PL/Cor is the only solution needed to account for unmarkedness of coronals. Therefore, the constraint ranking with fully specified underlying representations accounts for epentheses of default features. It is no longer necessary to assume that epenthetic segments have to be underspecified and that default features are filled in later.

In underspecification theory, assimilation is feature filling by spreading since specified features spread to underspecified nodes. Thus, the directionality of spreading is predicted. This point was the most compelling evidence for underspecification theory. Smolensky was unable to account for why coronals must be targets in assimilations. He pointed out that the result of place assimilation may be apparently anti-harmonic in terms of the constraint ranking *PL/Lab » PL/Cor. The following constraint tableau shows the right output would be anti-harmonic in Smolenky's analysis. I add ClusterCond(POA) to motivate the place assimilation.

(15) place assimilation

input /..tp../	ClusterCond(POA)	*PL/Lab	*PL/Cor
R R | | Pl Pl | | cor lab	*!	*	*
R R | | Pl Pl =|= \ | cor lab		**!	
R R | | Pl Pl | / =|= cor lab			**

The question here is why [cor][lab] changes to [lab][lab] and not [cor][cor]. Both the second candidate [lab][lab] and the last candidate [cor][cor] are better than the first candidate because they do not violate ClusterCond(POA). Due to the ranking *PL/Lab » *PL/Cor, the last candidate would be the optimal output. Thus, that constraint ranking incorrectly predicts that the wrong output is optimal. Smolensky could not provide an alternative analysis of assimilation under full specification of underlying representation.

If we just reverse the order of the ranking to have *PL/Cor » *PL/Lab, [lab][lab] could be chosen as the optimal output. However, that cannot account for why coronals tend to be epenthetic consonants. The best alternative is using Parse constraints. I claim that the crucial constraints to explain those place assimilation are Parse^{lab}, Parse^{dor}, and Parse^{cor}. There is a cross-linguistic tendency that coronals assimilate to labials and dorsals. A constraint ranking like Parse^{lab}, Parse^{dor} » Parse^{cor} can correctly capture this tendency. Given this ranking, an output which violates Parse^{cor} is more harmonic than an output which violates Parse^{lab} or Parse^{dor}. Thus, we can explain why unmarked coronals are more likely to be affected in place assimilations. The following constraint tableau shows interaction of the related Parse constraints. The crucial constraint ranking responsible for the place assimilation is Parse^{lab} » Parse^{cor}, rather than *PL/Lab » *PL/Cor.

(16) place assimilation

input /..tp../	ClusterCond	Parse^lab	Parse^cor	*PL/Lab	*PL/Cor
R R | | Pl Pl | | cor lab	*!			*	*
R R | | Pl Pl =|= \ | cor lab			*	**	
R R | | Pl Pl | / =|= cor lab		*!			**

Furthermore, another effect of underspecification can also be explained by constraint interaction. In underspecification theory, the non-triggerness of [cor] was explained by underspecification of the feature. However, in fully specified representations, spreading features is a matter of featural alignment constraints. Thus, non-triggerness of [cor] must be due to a higher ranked constraint, Align(cor, L/R, Root, L/R) whereas triggerness of [lab] or [dor] must be due to lower ranked constraints, Align(lab, L/R, Root, L/R) and Align(dor, L/R, Root, L/R).

In short, epenthesis and assimilation phenomena that have provided strong supports for underspecification theory can be alternatively handled in Optimality Theory under full specification theory. The special status of coronals in epentheses and assimilation is due to the following rankings:

(17) under fully specified underlying representations
 a. coronal epenthesis: *PL/Lab, *PL/Dor » *PL/Cor
 b. coronal targetness: Parse^dor, Parse^lab » Parse^cor
 c. coronal non-triggerness: Align(cor) » Align(do), Align(lab)

Underspecification is not an inherent property since underspecification for epenthesis and assimilation can be derived from unmarked constraint rankings of related universal constraints. Thus, underspecification does not have to be invoked to account for epenthesis and assimilation.

5. Korean Place Assimilations

In Korean place assimilation, as the following data show, alveolars assimilate to labials and velars, and labials assimilate to velars. The place assimilation is always regressive.

(18) data: Cho (1990)

/pat + ko/	[pakko]	'receive and'
/kot + palo/	[kopparo]	'straight'
/kət + co/	[kəcco]	'let's uncover'
/hankaŋ/	[haŋkaŋ]	'the Han river'
/han + bən/	[hambən]	'once'
/kamki/	[kaŋki]	'a cold'
/əp + ko/	[əkko]	'carry on the back + Conj'

Additionally, velars never assimilate to coronals and labials: *məkta* *[mətta] 'eat' and *naŋpo* *[nampo] 'good news'. Labials assimilate to dorsals as in [kaŋki] and [əkko] but not to alveolars: *simta* *[sinta] 'plant'.

In Optimality Theory, Korean place assimilation will be interpreted as constraint interactions of ClusterCond(POA), Parse$^{cor/lab/dor}$, and Align(cor/lab/dor, L/R, Root, L/R). In regard to targets of assimilation, coronals and labials can undergo assimilation to satisfy ClusterCond(POA) whereas velars never undergo assimilation. Thus, Parse^{cor} and Parse^{lab} are ranked lower than ClusterCond(POA), but Parse^{dor} is ranked higher than ClusterCond(POA). Since progressive assimilation is not allowed, Align(cor/lab/dor, R, Root, R) is ranked higher than ClusterCond(POA). Even though the directionality of assimilation is regressive, coronals cannot be triggers. Thus, Align(cor, L, Root, L) is ranked higher than ClusterCond(POA), but Align(lab/dor, L, Root, L) is ranked lower than ClusterCond(POA). The whole constraint ranking is:[3]

(19) Align(cor/lab/dor/, R), Parse^{dor}, Align(cor, L) » ClusterCond(POA) »
  Parse^{lab}, Parse^{cor}, Align(lab/dor, L)

I illustrate the following constraint tableaux to show how this constraint ranking accounts for Korean place assimilation. The element within < > means that the element is delinked or underparsed. The Fill^{PL} constraint means a place node must have an articulator node and it is never violated in Korean.

(20) coronal-labial to labial-labial[4]

cor-lab	Fill^{PL}	Align (cor, R)	Parse dor	Align (cor, L)	Cluster Cond	Parse lab	Parse cor	Align (lab, L)
cor lab					*!			
<cor>lab	*!						*	
cor<lab>	*!					*		
<corlab>	**!					*	*	
cor cor		*!				*		
lab lab							*	*

(21) labial-dorsal to dorsal-dorsal

lab-dor	Fill^{PL}	Align (lab,R)	Parse dor	Align (cor,L)	Cluster Cond	Parse lab	Parse cor	Align (dor, L)
lab dor					*!			
<lab>dor	*!					*		
lab<dor>	*!		*!					
<labdor>	**!		*!			*		
lab lab		*!	*!					
dor dor						*		*

In both constraint tableaux, the first candidates violate ClusterCond(POA). The second, third, and fourth candidates resolve the violation of ClusterCond(POA), but those candidates have fatal violations because they violate the high ranked constraints, Fill^{PL}, or Parse^{dor}. The second to last candidates are the results of progressive assimilation, thus they violate the high ranked Align(cor, R) and Align(dor, R), respectively. Each of the last candidates resolves the violation of ClusterCond(POA) with no fatal violations of the higher ranked constraints. They violate only the low ranked Parse^{lab}, Parse^{cor}, Align(lab, L), or Align(dor, L). Thus, they are the optimal outputs.

On the other hand, the same constraint ranking must account for the cases that do not undergo place assimilation. In the constraint tableaux (22) and (23), the optimal outputs are identical to the inputs.

(22) labial-coronal: no assimilation

lab-cor	Fill^{PL}	Align (lab, R)	Parse dor	Align (cor, L)	Cluster Cond	Parse lab	Parse cor	Align (dor, L)
lab cor					*			
<lab>cor	*!					*		
lab<cor>	*!						*	
<labcor>	**!					*	*	
lab lab		*!					*	
cor cor				*!		*		

(23) dorsal-labial: no assimilation

dor-lab	Fill^{PL}	Align (dor, R)	Parse dor	Align (cor, L)	Cluster Cond	Parse lab	Parse cor	Align (lab, L)
dor lab					*			
<dor>lab	*!		*!					
dor<lab>	*!					*		
<dorlab>	**!		*!			*		
dor dor		*!				*		
lab lab			*!					*

In both constraint tableaux, any candidates that violate Fill^{PL} are fatal. The candidates that undergo progressive assimilation are fatal because they violate high ranked Align(lab, R) and Align(dor, R). The candidate [cor] [cor] of the first tableau and the candidate [lab] [lab] of the second tableau are the result of regressive assimilation. They satisfy ClusterCond(POA) with no violations of Fill^{PL}, Align(lab, R), and Align(dor, R). However, the former violates high ranked Align(cor, L) that is motivated to prevent coronal spreading. The latter violates high ranked Parse^{dor} that is motivated to prevent deletion of dorsals. Thus, the first candidates of both tableaux are optimal even though they violate ClusterCond(POA). The optimal outputs tolerate the violation of ClusterCond(POA) because any attempts to resolve the violation result in some fatal violations of other constraints that are ranked higher than ClusterCond(POA).

6. Korean Sonorant Assimilation

According to Hooper 1976 and Vennemann 1988, there is a condition requiring a different consonant strength between a coda consonant and an onset consonant: the strength of an onset consonant is greater than that of a coda consonant. In other words, the sonority level of a coda consonant should be greater than that of a following onset consonant. Rice and Avery (1991) and Iverson and Sohn (1994) suggest that Korean sonorant assimilation is motivated by the cross-syllable sonority restriction and thus Korean sonorant assimilation takes place to conform to the sonority restriction. I will include the sonority restriction as a constraint, which is SONORITY CONDITION in the analysis of Korean sonorant assimilation.

(24) Sonority Condition
   The sonority of a coda is not lower than that of an onset.

SonorityCond and ClusterCond(sonorancy) are similar to each other because both constraints can be satisfied when sonorant assimilation occurs. For example, if an input is /tn/, it violates both Sonority Condition and ClusterCond(sonorancy). An output /nn/ satisfies both constraints by nasal assimilation. However, the two constraints are distinguished when coda sonority is greater than onset sonority. For example, when an input is /nt/, it violates ClusterCond(sonorancy), but does not violate SonorityCond. If an optimal output is /nn/, nasal assimilation occurs to resolve the violation of ClusterCond(sonorancy).

I adopt the feature geometry of Rice and Avery (1991), which is proposed for representations of sonorants. /n/, /l/, and /r/ are represented as follows:

```
(25)    /n/              /l/                    /r/
        Root             Root                   Root
         |                | \                    | \
        SV               SV [continuant]        SV [continuant]
                          |
                        [lat]
```

There is no SV(spontaneous voicing) node for obstruents. All features are privative: features are absent or present. The feature geometry is based on underspecification theory, and thus [nasal] will be inserted later by a default rule if there is no [continuant] feature. An SV node for /r/ must lack some feature in order to distinguish it from /l/ which must have [lat]. For the representation of /r/, Rice and Avery mention R-features: a general term referring to manner features that are present in the representation of /r/, if indeed there are any. Since R-features are not defined, I will use traditional features, [-lateral] for /r/ and [+lateral] for /l/. I use plus and minus values for convenience in order to distinguish a lateral liquid and a non-lateral liquid. Thus, I assume that /n/, /l/, and /r/ are represented as follows.

(26)

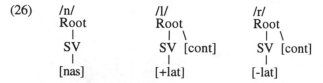

Rice and Avery (1991) and Iverson and Sohn (1994) claim that, in Korean, obligatory nasal assimilation and lateral assimilation are motivated by a need to conform to sonority restrictions across syllables, which is based on Hooper 1976 and Vennemann 1988 and others. The following data are taken from Cho 1988, Iverson & Kim 1987, and Iverson & Sohn 1994.

(27) Nasal assimilation

/kukmul/	[kuŋmul]	'soup'
/kakmok/	[kaŋmok]	'wood"
/napnita/	[namnita]	'to sprout'
/apʰnal/	[amnal]	'future'
/katʰni/	[kanni]	'to be same'
/patʰnoŋ sa/	[pannoŋsa]	'field farming'

These inputs violate SonorityCond because coda consonants are less sonorous than onset consonants. They also violate ClusterCond (sonorancy) since they have stop-nasal clusters. Regressive sonorant assimilation resolves those violations. Thus, low ranked Align(SV, Left, Root, Left) is violated to satisfy SonorityCond. If an SV node of the onset were underparsed, then the two constraints could not be violated. However, such a result is not optimal because Parse^{SV} is ranked higher. On the other hand, if the input consonant clusters consist of sonorant-obstruent like /mk/, /np/, /nt/, and /lt/, no sonorant assimilation takes place even though ClusterCond(sonorancy) is violated. Thus, Align(SV, Right, Root, Right) is ranked higher than ClusterCond(sonorancy). Therefore, the constraint ranking will be:

(28) Align(SV, R), SonorityCond, Parse^{SV} » ClusterCond(sonorancy), Align(SV, L)

When an input cluster is an obstruent-sonorant cluster as in the data above, a sonorant-sonorant cluster is optimal, as shown in the following constraint tableau (29). The first candidate violates SonorityCond, which must not be violated in Korean. The second candidate resolves the violation of SonorityCond by deleting an SV node, but it violates Parse^{SV}. The last candidate undergoes spreading of an SV node to satisfy SonorityCond. Since this candidate violates only the lowest ranked constraint Align(SV, L), it is the optimal output.

(29) sonorant assimilation

/pn/ [mn]	Align (SV, R)	Sonority Cond	Parse^{SV}	Cluster Cond	Align (SV, L)

R   R
    |
    SV
    |
    nas
		*!		*	

R   R
   =|=
    SV
    |
    nas
			*!		

R   R
 \ |
    SV
    |
    nas
					*

On the other hand, if an input is a nasal-stop cluster, no assimilation occurs. As the following constraint tableau shows, deletion or progressive spreading of an SV node results in violations of the higher ranked Parse^{SV} or Align(SV, R), respectively. Thus, the optimal output is the candidate which does not undergo any change, and this candidate tolerates violation of ClusterCond(sonorancy).

(30) no sonorant assimilation

/np/ [np]	Align (SV, R)	Sonority Cond	Parse^{SV}	Cluster Cond	Align (SV, L)
R R | SV | nas				*	
R R =|= SV | nas			*!		
R R | / SV | nas	*!				

Next, let's look at obstruent-lateral clusters (data from Iverson and Sohn 1994).

(31) obstruent-lateral clusters
a. labial or dorsal plus lateral
/pəp-lyul/　　　[pəmnyul]　'law'
/pak-lam/　　　[paŋnam]　'exhibition'
b. coronal plus lateral
/tikɨt+liɨl/　　　[tikɨlliɨl]　't..l':sequence in the Korean alphabet

These inputs violate SonorityCond, which is an undominated constraint in Korean. The outputs repair this violation, but they resolve the violation in different ways depending on the place of the preceding consonant. When C_1 is a coronal, lateral assimilation occurs by spreading a following SV node. On the other hand, when C_1 is a non-coronal, both the obstruents and the following laterals become nasals. To account for these phenomena, Rice and Avery (1991) introduce 'only copying an SV node'. After copying an SV node, a lateral node is delinked and a default feature [nasal] is inserted, as in (32).

(32) /pl/ → [mn]

```
R   R         R    R           R    R          R      R
|   |         | \  |           | \  |          | \    |
Pl  SV  copy  Pl SV SV  delink Pl SV SV default Pl SV  SV
|   |    →    |    |     →     |          →     |   |   |
lab lat       lab  lat         lab             lab nas nas
```

Copying only an SV node is a non-traditional type of structural change in theories of feature geometry. If copying is allowed, any node could be copied without copying its daughter nodes. I will analyze the sonorant assimilation in a more traditional way, as in (33).

(33) /pl/ → [mn]　　　　/kl/ → [ŋn]　　　　/tl/ → [ll]

```
R     R           R     R           R     R
|  \  |           |  \  |           |  \  |
Pl    SV          Pl    SV          Pl    SV
|    =|= \        |    =|= \        |     |
lab  lat nas      dor  lat nas      cor   lat
```

The input /tl/ violates SonorityCond, and spreading of an SV node to the obstruent resolves the violation. However, just spreading an SV node for the inputs /pl/ and /kl/ incurs violations of other constraints like feature cooccurrence restrictions that disallow lateral labials and lateral velars. In order to satisfy the undominated SonorityCond, there might be other possible resolutions like underparsing one consonant, an SV node, or an articulator node. However, they do not take place since $\text{Parse}^{\text{seg}}$, Parse^{SV}, $\text{Parse}^{\text{lab}}$, and $\text{Parse}^{\text{dor}}$ are ranked high and not to be violated due to SonorityCond. The last option is spreading an SV node and delinking a lateral node and then inserting a nasal node. Spreading an SV node is motivated not to violate SonorityCond. Deleting a lateral node is motivated to satisfy feature cooccurrence restrictions that disallows lateral labials and lateral velars. Inserting [nasal] is motivated not to violate Fill^{SV}, which requires a daughter node of an SV node. However, inserting [nasal] is not just free. Insertion of an element must violate a constraint. I employ Itô, Mester, and Padgett (1995)'s FILLFEAT constraints, which are motivated to prevent inserting features.

(34) FillFeat: Itô, Mester, and Padgett (1995)
    All features are part of the input.

Thus, Fill^{nas} can be violated to get the optimal outputs [mn] and [ŋn] with the violation of $\text{Parse}^{\text{lat}}$. The constraint ranking for (31) will be as follows:

(35) FeatureCooccur, Fill^{SV}, Parse^{SV}, SonorityCond » $\text{Parse}^{\text{lat}}$, Fill^{nas}

On the other hand, if the input consonant clusters are /lp/, /lk/, and /lt/, no assimilation takes place. These clusters already satisfy the SonorityCond, but violate ClusterCond(sonorancy). As mentioned above, since ClusterCond(sonorancy) is not ranked high enough to force violations of Parse^{SV} and Align(SV, R), the candidate with the violation of Cluster Cond(sonorancy) will be optimal. The constraint rankings of (28) and (35) are collapsed, as follows:

(36) FeatureCooccur, Parse^{SV}, Fill^{SV}, Align(SV, R), SonorityCond »
    $\text{Parse}^{\text{lat}}$, Fill^{nas}, ClusterCond(sonorancy), Align(SV, L)

The constraint tableau (37) shows how the optimal output is selected when the input consonant cluster is /pl/. The first candidate violates SonorityCond. All the other candidates resolve violations of SonorityCond. However, the last candidate violates only lower ranked constraints like $\text{Parse}^{\text{lat}}$, Fill^{nas}, and Align(SV, L) whereas other candidates violate one of the higher constraints like FeatureCooccurrence, Parse^{SV}, $\text{Parse}^{\text{lab}}$, and Fill^{SV}. Thus, the last candidate is the optimal output.

When the input is /lp/ as in the constraint tableau (38), the cluster satisfies SonorityCond, but violates ClusterCond(sonorancy). Any attempts to resolve the violation of ClusterCond end up with violations of other higher ranked constraints. The optimal output is thus the candidate which is the same as the input form.

(37) /pl/ → [mn]

/pl/	Feature Cooccur	Par SV	Fill SV	Align (SV, R)	Sonor Cond	Par lat	Fill nas	Clust Cond	Align (SV, L)
Pl SV | | lab lat					*!			*	
Pl <SV> | | lab lat		*!							
R R | \ | Pl SV | | lab lat	*!								*
R R | \ | Pl SV | =|= lab lat			*!			*			*
R R | \ | Pl SV |nas =|= lab lat						*	*		*

(38) /lp/: no change

/lp/	Feature Cooccur	Par SV	Fill SV	Align (SV, R)	Sonor Cond	Par lat	Fill nas	Clust Cond	Align (SV, L)
R R | | SV Pl | | lat lab								*	
R R =|= | SV Pl | | lat lab			*!						
R R | / | SV Pl | | lat lab	*!			*!					
R R | / | SV Pl =|= | lat lab			*!	*!		*			
R R | / | SV Pl =|= nas| lat lab				*!		*	*		

So far, ClusterCond(sonorancy) has not been playing a crucial role to motivate sonorant assimilations. However, the constraint plays a very crucial role in some lateral assimilation. It is well known that all assimilations in Korean are regressive except one kind of progressive lateral assimilation. Korean lateral assimilation has both regressive and progressive assimilation, as follows.

(39)a. coronal nasal plus lateral

/han-lyaŋ/   [hallyaŋ]   'limit'

/chən-li]   [chəlli]   'natural law'

     b. lateral plus coronal nasal

/mul+nan-li/   [mullalli]   'flood'

/səl+nal/   [səllal]   'New Year's Day'

/tɨl+namul/   [tɨllamul]   'wild vegetable'

Coronal nasal-lateral clusters undergo regressive lateral assimilation whereas lateral-coronal nasal clusters undergo progressive lateral assimilation by spreading a lateral node. Lateral assimilation in sonorant clusters is represented as follows:

(40) a.   /nl/ → [ll]   b.   /ln/ → [ll]

```
     R    R              R    R
     |    |              |    |
     SV   SV             SV   SV
     =|=  \  |           |  / =|=
     nas  lat            lat   nas
```

The motivation for regressive lateral assimilation follows from the SonorityCond, because the input /nl/ violates the constraint. On the other hand, progressive lateral assimilation has been commonly regarded as an exceptional case in Korean consonant assimilation. Since the input /ln/ already satisfies SonorityCond, the constraint cannot be the motivation of the progressive lateral assimilation.

The long-standing problem of Korean progressive lateral assimilation can be explained by ClusterCond(sonorancy) and constraint interaction. As shown in (40), the results of both lateral assimilations satisfy ClusterCond(sonorancy). ClusterCond(sonorancy) is not ranked high enough to compel violations of high ranked constraints such as Parse^{seg}, Parse^{SV}, Fill^{SV}, Align(SV, R), and SonorityCond. However, if ClusterCond(sonorancy) is ranked over Parse^{nas} but below Parse^{lat}, /nl/ to /ll/ and /ln/ to /ll/ can be explained by a constraint ranking:

(41) SonorityCond » Parse^{lat} » ClusterCond(sonorancy) » Parse^{nas}

The following constraint tableaux show how ClusterCond(sonorancy) interacts with other constraints to get the optimal output /ll/. I omit Parse^{SV}, Fill^{SV}, Align(SV,R), Parse^{seg}, and related candidates in order to save space.

(42) /nl/ → [ll]

/nl/	Sonor Cond	Par lat	Clust Cond	Par nas
SV SV | | nas lat	*!		*	
SV SV | / =|= nas lat		*!		
SV SV =|= \ | nas lat				*

(43) /ln/ → [ll]

/ln/	Sonor Cond	Par lat	Clust Cond	Par nas
SV SV | | lat nas			*!	
SV SV | / =|= lat nas				*
SV SV =|= \ | lat nas		*!		

In (42), the first candidate violates both SonorityCond and ClusterCond(sonorancy). The second and the last candidates resolve the violations of SonorityCond and ClusterCond(sonorancy) by violating Parse^{lat} and Parse^{nas}. Since Parse^{lat} is ranked over Parse^{nas}, the optimal output is the last candidate, which undergoes regressive lateral spreading and nasal deletion. In (43), the input or the first candidate satisfies SonorityCond, but violates ClusterCond(sonorancy). Both the second and the last candidates satisfy ClusterCond(sonorancy). Since the second candidate violates the lower ranked Parse^{nas} whereas the last candidate violates the higher ranked Parse^{lat}, the optimal output is the second candidate, which undergoes progressive lateral spreading and nasal deletion.[5]

Finally, let's move onto lab/dor nasal-lateral and lateral-lab/dor nasal clusters. When a non-coronal nasal comes before a lateral, the lateral becomes a nasal. When a lateral comes before a non-coronal nasal, there is no change.

(44)a. labial/dorsal nasal plus lateral
/sam-lyu/   [samnyu]   'third-rate'
/yəŋ-lak/   [yəŋnak]   'downfall'
  b. lateral plus labial/dorsal nasal
/kal-maŋ/   [kalmaŋ]   'longing'
/tal+muli/   [talmuri]   'halo'
/mil+mul/   [milmul]   'tidewater'

Both /ml/ and /ŋl/ violate undominated SonorityCond. The optimal outputs are [mn] and [ŋn], respectively. Since SonorityCond is ranked higher than Parse^{lat}, SonorityCond can force the violation of Parse^{lat}. It is ambiguous whether the nasality of the second consonant is from the preceding nasal or by independent nasal insertion. However, recall that the lateral undergoes lateral deletion and independent nasal insertion when an input is /pl/, as in (37). Thus, I assume the optimal output is the candidate that shows nasal insertion as in the following constraint tableau.

(45) /ml/ → [mn]

/ml/	Feature Cooccur	Sonority Cond	Parse lat	Cluster Cond	Parse nas	Fill nas
R R / Pl SV SV / lab nas / lat		*!		*		
R R / Pl SV SV / lab nas =|= lat	*!					*
R R / Pl SV SV / lab nas =|= lat nas			*			*

When the input is /lm/, the optimal output is the first candidate, which violates ClusterCond(sonorancy). Other candidates that undergo lateral spreading or deletion violate higher ranked FeatureCooccurrence or Parse^{lat}. Since ClusterCond(sonorancy) is ranked lower than FeatureCooccurrence and Parse^{lat}, ClusterCond(sonorancy) cannot compel the violation of Parse^{lat}.

(46) /lm/ : no change

/lm/	Feature Cooccur	Sonority Cond	Parse lat	Cluster Cond	Parse nas	Fill nas
R R / SV SV Pl / lat nas lab				*		
R R / SV SV Pl / lat =|= nas lab	*!					*
R R / SV SV Pl =|= lat nas lab			*!			
R R / SV SV Pl =|= nas lat nas lab			*!			*

7. Summary

In this paper, I have shown that consonant assimilations are the result of constraint interactions. I assume fully specified underlying representations in the analysis of assimilation, since the behaviors of unmarked features can be captured by employing constraint rankings, and thus underspecification of unmarked features is unnecessary.

In the analysis of Korean place assimilation, I argue that ClusterCond(POA) motivates place assimilation. I explain the targetness of both coronals and labials by ranking constraints so that ClusterCond(POA) is dominant over Parse^{cor} and Parse^{lab}. In order to satisfy the higher ranked ClusterCond(POA), the lower ranked Parse^{cor} and Parse^{lab} can be violated. Velars are not targets since Parse^{dor} is ranked over ClusterCond(POA) and thus ClusterCond(POA) can not compel the violation of Parse^{dor}. The triggerness of labials and velars is explained by ranking Align(lab, Left, Root, Left) and Align(dor, Left, Root, Left) lower than ClusterCond(POA). These lower ranked Alignment constraints can be violated in order to satisfy the higher ranked ClusterCond(POA). Coronals are not triggers since Align(cor, Left, Root, Left) is ranked over ClusterCond(POA) and thus ClusterCond(POA) can not force the violation of higher ranked Align(cor, Left, Root, Left). Even though labials and velars are triggers of spreading, the directionality of the spread is right-to-left not left-to-right. This directionality is explained by ranking constraints so that Align(lab/dor, Right, Root, Right) is ranked over ClusterCond(POA), which is in turn ranked ranked over Align(lab/dor, Left, Root, Left). Since ClusterCond(POA) forces the violation of lower ranked Align(lab/dor, Left, Root, Left), leftward spreading of labial and dorsal features occurs. Rightward spreading of labial and velar features is not possible since ClusterCond(POA) can not force the violation of higher ranked Align(lab/dor, Right, Root, Right).

In the analysis of Korean sonorant assimilation, SonorityCond motivates sonorant assimilation except for the progressive lateral assimilation. Obstruent-sonorant clusters which violate SonorityCond undergo sonorant assimilation since SonorityCond is undominated and thus must be satisfied by violating the lower ranked Align(SV, Left, Root, Left). Sonorant-obstruent clusters which satisfy SonorityCond do not undergo sonorant assimilation since ClusterCond(sonorancy) can not force the violation of the higher ranked Align(SV, Right, Root, Right), which prevents rightward spreading of an SV node. Among sonorant-sonorant clusters, nasal-lateral clusters resolve the violation of SonorityCond by either spreading or delinking a lateral node. A lateral node spreads when the preceding nasal is a coronal. When the preceding nasal is a non-coronal, lateral spreading is not available because non-coronal laterals are not allowed in Korean. Thus, a lateral node is delinked and then a nasal node is inserted to satisfy SonorityCond. Lateral-nasal clusters satisfy SonorityCond, but progressive lateral assimilation takes place when the nasal is a coronal. When the nasal is a non-coronal, the lateral spreading is not possible because non-coronal laterals are not allowed. Progressive lateral assimilation is explained by the following constraint ranking: Parse^{lat} » ClusterCond(sonorancy) » Parse^{nas}. ClusterCond(sonorancy) can not force the violation of the higher ranked Parse^{lat} and thus a lateral node must not be delinked. Since Parse^{nas} is ranked lower than ClusterCond(sonorancy), ClusterCond(sonorancy) forces the violation of Parse^{nas}. Thus, a nasal node can be delinked and a lateral node can spread to the following consonant.

Notes

[1] Yip(1991)'s Cluster Condition differs from mine. Her Cluster Condition is a phonotactic constraint on consonant clusters, which limits at most one place feature specification. Place assimilation might be motivated by such a phonotactic constraint. I assume that the crucial driving force of place assimilation is ease of articulation, not phonotactic constraints.

[2] Cole and Kisseberth assume features are anchored in prosodic units of timing, such as the X-slot or mora in their Optimal Domains Theory. Thus, the X-slot or mora can be sponsors for features. In this paper, I will maintain more traditional feature geometry in which a root node is required.

[3] Korean place assimilation is optional. Optionality can be interpreted in two ways in Optimality Theory. One is to posit two different constraint rankings. In case of no place assimilation, ClusterCond(POA) must be ranked lower than other conflicting constraints. Thus, the optimal outputs tolerate the violations of ClusterCond(POA). The other is to posit a constraint ranking which has a tie of two constraints. For example, if ClusterCond(POA) and Parse^{lab} are tied in constraint ranking, a violation of ClusterCond(POA) or a violation of Parse^{lab} are equal in H-eval. When ClusterCond(POA) is violated and Parse^{lab} is satisfied, a labial consonant will not undergo assimilation. When Parse^{lab} is violated and ClusterCond(POA) is satisfied, a labial must undergo assimilation.

[4] In the framework of Prince and Smolensky (1993), underparsed input features remain as floating features before they delete in order to keep the principle of Containment. It is not certain whether underparsed floating features violate Alignment constraints or not. It might be the case that Alignment constraints are violated because a floating feature is not aligned with any nodes. However, if Alignment constraints apply only when a feature is aligned with some nodes, floating features do not violate Alignment constraints. I assume that Alignment constraints apply only when a feature has a domain in the output. Thus, if there is no domain for a feature, Alignment constraints are irrelevant. An alternative is to give up the principle of Containment so that underparsed elements do not have floating status.

[5] Featural alignment constraints might give another way of looking at those assimilations. If Align(nasal, L/R, Root, L/R) is ranked higher than ClusterCond(sonorancy), which is in turn ranked higher than Align(lateral, L/R, Root, L/R), then lateral spreading will be more harmonic than nasal spreading. Thus, the optimal outputs will be the ones that violates the lower ranked Align(lateral, L/R, Root, L/R).

References

Avery, P., and K. Rice. 1989. Segment Structure and Coronal Underspecification. Phonology, 6, 179-200.

Cho, Y-M. 1988. Korean Assimilation. In the Proceedings of West Coast Conference on Formal Linguistics 7: 41-52.

Cho, Y-M. 1990. Parameters of Consonantal Assimilation. Ph.D. Dissertation. Stanford University.

Cole, J., and C. Kisseberth. 1994 a. Optimal Domains Theory of Harmony. ms., University of Illinois, Urbana Champaign.

Hooper, J. B. 1976. An Introduction to Natural Generative Phonology. Academic Press.

Itô, Junko, R. Armin Mester, and Jaye Padgett. 1995. NC: Licesing and Underspecification in Optimality Theory, LI 26.4.

Iverson, G.K., and K-H. Kim. 1987. Underspecification and Hierarchical Feature Representation in Korean Consonantal Phonology. CLS 23.2: 182-98.

Iverson, G. K., and H-S Sohn. 1994. Liquid Representation in Korean. In Y-K Kim-Renaud, eds., Theoretical Issues in Korean Linguistics. 77-100. Center for the study of Language and Information, Leland Stanford Junior University.

McCarthy, J. 1993. Generalized Alignment. In G. Booij and J. van Marle, eds., Yearbook of Morphology 1993. 79-153.

McCarthy, J., and A. Prince. 1993. Prosodic Morphology I: constraint interaction and satisfaction. ms., University of Massachusetts, Amherst and Rutgers University.

Mohanan, K. P. 1993. Fields of Attraction in Phonology. In J. Goldsmith, eds., The Last Phonological Rules. 61-116. University of Chicago Press.

Prince, A., and P. Smolensky. 1993. Optimality Theory: Constraint Interaction in Generative Grammar. ms., Rutgers University and University of Colorado.

Rice, K., and P. Avery. 1991. On the Relationship between Laterality and Coronality. In C. Paradis and J. F. Prunet, eds., The Special Status of Coronals, Phonetics and Phonology volume 2. 101-124. Academic Press, Inc.

Smolensky, P. 1993. Harmony, Markedness, and Phonological Activity. Talk presented at the Rutgers Optimality Workshop, New Brunswick.

Vennemann, T. 1988. Preference Laws for Syllable Structure. Mouton de Gruyter.

Yip, M. 1991. Coronals, Consonant Clusters, and the Coda Condition. In C. Paradis and J. F. Prunet, eds., The Special Status of Coronals, Phonetics and Phonology volume 2. 101-124. Academic Press, Inc.

Constraints on Post-Obstruent Tensification in Korean

SEOK-CHAE RHEE
University of Illinois at Urbana-Champaign

1. Introduction

This study explores constraints and their hierarchies in an account of Post-Obstruent Tensification (POT) in Korean within the framework of Optimality Theory (Prince & Smolensky 1993, McCarthy & Prince 1993ab). POT has received much attention in Korean phonology, in particular, debates have centered on the 'geminate analysis' by Han 1992, Kim 1993, and Lee 1994ab versus the 'nongeminate analysis' by Oh 1988, Baek 1991, Cho & Inkelas 1994. Previous works, however, fail to formalize the cause of POT and explain its manifestation. This paper reveals the problems in previous accounts and argues that POT is an implementation of the auditory cue that results directly from the nonrelease of an obstruent coda.

2. Data and Assumption

As illustrated in (1), plain obstruents are tensified (marked as C') after an obstruent in Korean.[1] The preceding consonant in a sequence of two is always strictly unreleased (marked as C'). Consequently, there is no release

---

[1]   Korean consonant inventory:

plain	p	t s	c	k	h
aspirate	p^h	t^h	c^h	k^h	
tense	p'	t' s'	c'	k'	
sonorant	m	n l		ŋ	

253

burst between the two consonants unlike French (Tranel 1987) where a coda can be released before an onset ([akʰ.tœʁ] 'actor'). Since Korean syllable structure allows only a single consonant in coda and onset positions, clusters consisting of maximally two C's in the surface are always divided by a syllable boundary. Thus, we can say that POT occurs in onset position after an unreleased obstruent coda. Due to POT, a neutralization occurs in onset position between plain and tense consonants. For example, /sip + p'un/ 'ten only' and /sip + pun/ 'ten minutes' are both pronounced as [sip˺.p'un]. The data in (2) show that aspirate obstruents escape POT, and the nonoccurrence of tensification after a sonorant coda is given in (3).[2]

(1) POT

/niktæ/	[nik˺.t'æ]	'wolf'
/kikpinca/	[kik˺.p'in˺.ja]	'very poor person'
/ipku/	[ip˺.k'u]	'entrance'
/təpʰkæ/	[təp˺.k'æ]	'cover'
/moksum/	[mok˺.s'um˺]	'life'
/kuksu/	[kuk˺.s'u]	'noodle'
/əkcilo/	[ək˺.c'i.ro]	'by force'
/cikcaŋ/	[cik˺.c'aŋ]	'job'

(2) An aspirate C does not undergo POT

/mokcʰəŋ/	[mok˺.cʰəŋ˺]	*[mok˺.c'əŋ˺]	'vocal cords'
/paktʰal/	[pak˺.tʰal˺]	*[pak˺.t'al˺]	'deprivation'
/əkcʰək/	[ək˺.cʰək˺]	*[ək˺.c'ək˺]	'hard headed'
/pʰoktʰan/	[pʰok˺.tʰan˺]	*[pʰok˺.t'an˺]	'bomb'
/kotcʰu/	[kot˺.cʰu]	*[kot˺.c'u]	'straight'
/sikcʰo/	[sik˺.cʰo]	*[sik˺.c'o]	'vinegar'
/cakpʰum/	[cak˺.pʰum˺]	*[cak˺.p'um˺]	'a piece of work'

(3) A sonorant coda does not induce tensification[3]

/imca/	[im˺.ja]	*[im˺.c'a]	'owner'
/kumpeŋi/	[kum˺.beŋ˺.i]	*[kum˺.p'eŋ˺.i]	'sluggard''
/pancuk/	[pan˺.juk˺]	*[pan˺.c'uk˺]	'dough'
/kyəncuta/	[kyən˺.ju.da]	*[kyən˺.c'u.da]	'to compare'
/maŋtuŋi/	[maŋ˺.duŋ˺.i]	*[maŋ˺.t'uŋ˺.i]	'goby'
/salku/	[sal˺.gu]	*[sal˺.k'u]	'apricot'
/bolki/	[bol˺.gi]	*[bol˺.k'i]	'hips'

---

[2] In some morphological and syntactic environments, tensification occurs even after a sonorant coda (/pom + pi/ → [pom.p'i] 'spring rain', /nəm + ta/ → [nəm.t'a] 'to go over'). However, this type of tensification is beyond the scope of this study.

[3] Underlying voiceless consonants are voiced after a sonorant.

The articulatory nature of the so-called tense (fortis, forced, strong, or glottalized) consonants is characterized by minimal glottal opening and muscular tension at vocal folds, pharynx, vocal tract wall, and even at the supralaryngeal articulators involved (Kim 1965, Hardcastle 1973, and Kagaya 1974). In a waveform, the closure duration of the tense consonants is two or three times longer than that of the plain consonants, especially in intervocalic positions. According to Han (1992), closure duration of a tense consonant in an intervocalic position (e.g. in /ik'i/ 'moss') is around 145 msec, whereas that of a plain consonant (e.g. in /iki/ 'to win' /k/ is voiced in the surface) is around 54 msec. Based on this phonetic length distinction, she proposed that a tense consonant is a geminate associated with two timing units on the timing tier. However, since her geminate analysis faces several serious problems from a phonological point of view (see Cho & Inkelas 1994), I discard the hypothesis and represent the tense consonants (stops) as having the feature [cg] (= [constricted glottis]) under the A_m node of Steriade (1993, 1994) (see (4a)). As for the aspirate and plain stops, representations in (4b) and (4c) will be assumed, respectively (A_o: total absence of oral airflow, A_m: maximal aperture for a consonant, [sg]: spread glottis)[4]

(4) a. tense stop   b. aspirate stop   c. plain stop

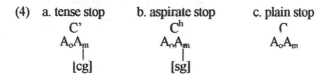

Steriade's idea on which (4) is based on is that segments are represented as positions defined in terms of oral aperture. In her aperture geometry, released stops, unreleased stops, fricatives, affricates, and approximants are represented as follows:

(5) Steriade's (1993, 1994) aperture geometry

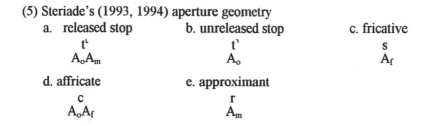

The aperture positions can function as anchoring sites for features characterizing nasality, place of articulation, and laryngeality.

---

[4] For the representations of tense, aspirate and plain fricatives and affricates, see the footnote 10.

As a general background of the analysis, I adopt the Optimality Theory (OT) framework in (6) which claims that interaction of universal, ranked, and violable constraints characterizes the grammar of a language. A language particular constraint ranking as a core part of Eval determines the surface output (out$_{real}$) from candidates generated by Gen. The computation is done in a parallel fashion. There are no rules and no step-by-step derivations.

(6) OT Grammar (McCarthy & Prince 1993a: 4)
   Gen (input$_i$) = {cand$_1$, cand$_2$, cand$_3$, ... }
   Eval ({cand$_1$, cand$_2$, cand$_3$, ... }) = out$_{real}$

3. Criticism of Previous analyses

In this paper, 'nongeminate analysis' refers to the view in which POT is regarded as an outcome of the direct insertion of [cg], as opposed to the 'geminate analysis' in which longer duration of a consonant is conceived as a primary distinctive property for tense consonants.

Though different in details, all the nongeminate analyses (Oh 1988, Baek 1991, Cho & Inkelas 1994, and others) share the assumption that an insertion of laryngeal feature specified as [ʔ] or [cg] is responsible for POT. This approach is rooted in the view that a tense consonant in Korean is a glottalized one. The feature [cg] is inserted onto the coda and spreads to the following onset, rendering the plain onset tensified ((7a) & (7b)). Alternatively, it is proposed that [cg] is directly inserted onto the onset (7c) (since whether the inserted feature is [ʔ] or [cg] is not significant in the review, I will represent it as [cg]).

(7) Nongeminate analyses of POT
   a. Oh (1988): insertion of ʔ onto the coda, then spreading & delinking

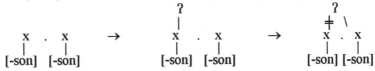

   b. Baek (1991): insertion of ʔ onto the coda, then just spreading[5]

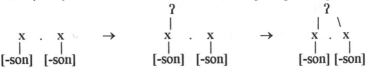

---

[5]   This is a formal and phonological reinterpretation of the Baek's phonetic analysis.

c. Cho & Inkelas (1994): direct insertion of [+cg] onto the onset

$$
\begin{array}{ccccccc}
\mu & \cdot & \mu & & \mu & \cdot & \mu \\
| & & | & & | & & | \\
[\text{-son}] & & \text{RN} & \rightarrow & [\text{-son}] & & \text{RN} \\
& & & & & & | \\
& & & & & & [\text{+cg}]
\end{array}
$$

Some questions that immediately arise regarding the above nongeminate analyses could be summarized as follows:

(8) Questions for the nongeminate analysis:
   a. What is the motivation for the insertion of [cg]?
   b. Why does the inserted [cg] spread to the following consonant? Why is the inserted [cg] delinked from the coda? If [cg] is not delinked, is the coda a tensed consonant? (regarding (7a) and (7b))
   c. Why is an aspirate onset excluded from the target of POT?

First, all the analyses in (7) fail to provide a formal explanation for the question (8a): the reason is just described informally and separately as being connected with the coda nonrelease. As pointed out by Lee (1994ab), by simply looking at the rules in (7), we cannot capture the fact that POT has a close correlation with the coda nonrelease. A more serious question to be asked at this juncture is whether or not the glottal constriction really happens at the moment the final coda is produced. Regarding this, Oh's and Baek's claim that glottal constriction cooccurs with the unreleased coda is quite impressionistic: they give no physical evidence. In some languages like English and Thai, an unreleased final stop accompanies a strong glottal constriction, sometimes in English (Kahn 1976) and always in Thai (Bennett 1995). However, according to Hirose, Park & Sawashima's (1983) electromyographic (EMG) experiment on the thyroarytenoid muscle activity (which is closely related to the glottal behaviors), no significant signal is detected indicating a glottal constriction at the unreleased final stop position in Korean. Moreover, Sawashima, Park, Honda & Hirose's (1980) fiberoptic observation confirms that no glottal constriction accompanies Korean unreleased final stop. Considering these experimental results, any approach claiming that [cg] is produced at the coda position should be rejected. Secondly, the analyses in (7a) and (7b) do not give any principled reason why inserted [cg] spreads to the right (even if we reluctantly allow such an insertion). In addition, (7a) fails to account for why [cg] is delinked from the coda after spreading. If [cg] is not delinked from the coda as in (7b), it is implied that the final coda is a tensed consonant, which is quite contrary to fact. It is certain that all these problems originate from associating an imaginary ghost [cg] with the coda.

Thirdly, (7a) and (7b) exclude the aspirate consonant from the target of POT by setting up the rule environment. However, this kind of analysis is not an explanation but a description.

By contrast, the geminate analysis (Han 1992, Kim 1993, and Lee 1994ab) builds on the idea that a tense consonant is a geminate which has two timing slots. In order to derive the tensed onset, they formalize POT as an insertion of one timing slot. Feature [cg] is inserted at a late stage of the derivation through reinforcement (Han 1992) or by default (Lee 1994ab).

Since problems for Han's approach have already been discussed in detail by Cho & Inkelas (1994), I will argue against Lee's proposal that deserves close attention on separate grounds. To the best of my knowledge, he is the first who has tried to combine the nonreleasing of a coda and POT in a formal way. His approach is based on Steriade's aperture geometry briefly introduced in the previous section. One thing crucially different from my assumption is that tense and aspirate consonants occupy two timing skeletons as represented in (9).

(9) Lee's (1994a: 12) assumption

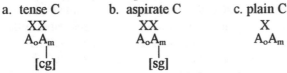

   a. tense C   b. aspirate C   c. plain C
     XX   XX   X
    $A_o A_m$ $A_o A_m$ $A_o A_m$
      | |
    [cg]   [sg]

Under the assumption in (9), POT is derived in a step-by-step way: First, A_m is delinked from the coda to obtain an unreleased coda (10a). Then, the delinked A_m is recovered by an insertion of an empty X on the timing tier (10b). Next, the inserted X is incorporated onto the following onset (10c). After that, [cg] is supplied by default onto the two-X configuration resulting in a tensed consonant (10d). Finally, the incorporated X is deleted to satisfy the Korean syllable structure (10e).

(10) Derivation for POT in Lee (1994ab)
    a. Coda nonrelease as delinking of A_m
         $X]_\sigma$ [X
          ̸   /\
       $A_o A_m$ $A_o A_m$

    b. Delinked A_m is recovered by an empty X on the timing tier
         $X]_\sigma$ X [X
         A_o $A_o A_m$

    c. X is incorporated into the following onset
         $X]_\sigma$ [XX
         A_o $A_o A_m$

d. Feature [cg] is supplied by default to the two-X configuration

$$X]_\sigma \quad [XX$$
$$A_o \qquad A_o A_m$$
$$|$$
$$[cg]$$

e. One X is deleted from the onset to satisfy the syllable structure

$$X]_\sigma \quad [X$$
$$A_o \qquad A_o A_m$$
$$|$$
$$[cg]$$

      Though he tried to connect coda nonrelease and POT in a single derivational process, his analysis raises some conceptual and empirical questions. The first question is why the delinked aperture node A_m is recovered by a timing slot X, which is entirely different from the former by definition. Even if we interpret an aperture node A_m as a portion of one segment duration, it is not feasible that this relatively small portion of a segment is recovered by a full timing slot X. As far as I know, no single case is attested in other languages showing that a suppression of a stop release is compensated for by extra length duration of the neighboring segments. The next question is why the inserted floating timing slot X is incorporated onto the following onset. In a situation like (10b) where X is inserted between two consonants, there is a chance that a double-flopping can occur (a coda links itself to the inserted X, then X once associated with the coda lengthens the preceding vowel). However, he fails to give a principled reason why Korean allows a floating timing slot to combine with the following consonant not with the preceding vowel. The third question is on what basis [cg], not [sg], is supplied by default. Under Lee's assumption, aspirate consonants also have two X's (see (9b)), therefore, insertion of [cg] cannot be determined simply by counting the numbers of X on the timing tier. Regarding this, he remarks in a footnote (Lee 1994a: 13) that '*an aspirated consonant preceded by an unreleased obstruent will be phonotactically filtered out in Korean phonology*'. Unfortunately, however, this observation is simply wrong. In Korean, an aspirate consonant does occur after an unreleased coda as seen in the examples like [mokˈcʰəŋ] 'vocal cords', [pakˈtʰal] 'deprivation', [əkˈcʰək] 'hard headed', [cakˈpʰum] 'a piece of work', and [pʰokˈtʰan] 'bomb' (already seen in (2)). Therefore, his assertion that the number of timing slots determines the default supply of [cg] should be reconsidered. Fourth, his claim that X is deleted in the last stage of the derivation in order to satisfy the syllable structure goes against the well-motivated argument that syllabification is cyclic in Korean (Cho & Inkelas 1994). Lastly and most importantly, Lee's geminate analysis cannot deal with POT given in (11), where the plain obstruent is tensified after an underlying fricative.

(11) POT in underlying sequence of fricative + plain obstruent

/saskas/	[sat'.k'at']	'conical bamboo rain-hat'
/cəskal/	[cət'.k'al']	'salted fish'
/t'ispak'e/	[t'it'.p'a.k'e]	'unexpectedly'
/sosta/	[sot'.t'a]	'to soar'
/s'ista/	[s'it'.t'a]	'to wash'
/yəspota/	[yət'.p'o.da]	'look furtively'
/pəskwa/	[pət'.k'wa]	'with a friend'

The underlying fricative /s/ becomes an unreleased [t'] in the surface coda. Note that the final /s/ in the first syllables of the given examples is not the 'linking-s' that frequently appears in the noun compounds of Korean (/koki + s + pæ/ → [ko.git'.p'æ] 'fishing boat', /næ + s + ka/ → [næt'.k'a] 'riverside', /swe + s + təŋi/ → [swet'.t'əŋ'.i] 'a mass of metal'). Therefore, tensification in (11) cannot be accounted for by the insertion of a timing slot X that, unrelated to the loss of A_m in the preceding segment, is proposed for tensification in compounds. POT in (11) cannot be handled either by invoking the X that is recovered from the delinked A_m. The reason is simple. Under Lee's assumption that a fricative is represented as having an A_f position, we cannot say that X is recovered from the delinked A_f. The A_f position in the coda is not delinked. Rather, it changes its aperture degree into A_o to satisfy the coda constraint (Rhee 1995). Because of these several reasons, it is hard to maintain Lee's geminate analysis.

4. Analysis

In this section, I will suggest some constraints and the ranking relations necessary to account for POT. Since my analysis is directly related to the coda nonrelease, one of the major properties in Korean consonantal phonology, a constraint governing the release of coda consonants is a prerequisite. Under the assumption that all aperture nodes are underlyingly present, I account for the coda nonrelease by ranking CODACOND over a faithfulness constraint PARSE-A_m. The constraints are given in (12) and (13), respectively.

(12) CODACOND
    A coda ends with A_o.

(13) PARSE-A_m
    $*<A_{max}>$

The constraint CODACOND requires a coda to end in a closed articulation. PARSE-A$_m$ forbids underparsing of the release phase of a stop. In other words, the constraints are inherently contradictory to each other. In this situation, the constraint hierarchy CODACOND >> PARSE-A$_m$ explains why a released stop in the coda position is strictly prohibited in Korean, as illustrated in (14). The relevant tableau is presented in (15).

(14) Prohibition on released coda stop in Korean

/pap/	[pap˺]	*[papˡ]	'cooked rice'
/kot/	[kot˺]	*[kotˡ]	'soon'
/kuk/	[kuk˺]	*[kukˡ]	'soup'
/napse/	[nap˺.s'e]	*[napˡ.s'e]	'tax payment'
/yəksi/	[yək˺.s'i]	*[yəkˡ.s'i]	'also'
/kotcaŋ/	[kot˺.c'aŋ˺]	*[kotˡ.c'aŋ˺]	'directly'

(15) Coda nonrelease: CODACOND >> PARSE-A$_m$

/pap/: UR	CODACOND	PARSE-A$_m$
a. ☞ p a p˺ A$_o$<A$_m$>		*
b. p a pˡ A$_o$A$_m$	*!	

The candidate (15b) loses the competition immediately, since a coda ends with an A$_m$, violating the CODACOND. Though the winning candidate disobeys PARSE-A$_m$, it is selected as an output in the hierarchy CODACOND >> PARSE-A$_m$. The reverse ranking predicts a language where a coda is always released. Keresan, an American Indian language spoken in New Mexico, is a good example.[6] According to the Spencer's description of Keresan (1946: 231), ' ... *all consonants in final position are subject to a marked release, ... and the release of consonants in terminal positions is in no way affected by the preceding sounds or by the initial phonemes in words which follow.*' Obligatory release of the coda in this language is, of course, explained by ranking PARSE-A$_m$ over CODACOND. French, briefly mentioned in the first section, is another example that is included in this type.

When an unreleased obstruent coda is followed by an onset obstruent in Korean, an A$_o$ node under the coda immediately precedes an A$_o$ or an A$_f$ node of the following segment, as depicted in (16). Needless to say, high ranking of the constraint CODACOND is responsible for the ending

---

[6]   Many thanks are due to Grover Hudson (1995 & electronic communication) who brought this language to my attention.

of a coda as A_o (underparsed $<A_m>$ is omitted in (16) to clarify an A_oA_o or an A_oA_f sequence). Recall that a CC sequence cannot be a tautosyllabic cluster in Korean. Consequently, there is always a syllable boundary between two C's.

(16) a. stop + stop   b. stop + affricate   c. stop + fricative

$C^{,}$. C	$C^{,}$. C	$C^{,}$. C
A_o A_oA_m	A_o A_oA_f	A_o A_f

The representations in (16) show that, due to the nonrelease of the coda, an A_oA_o or an A_oA_f string inevitably occurs in a CC sequence (an A_oA_o string from $A_oA_oA_m$ or $A_oA_oA_f$). One thing evident here is that a release phase A_m cannot intervene between two A_o's or between A_o and A_f, and that this makes the duration of the obstruency at a syllable boundary long. On the basis of this observation, I claim that the tenseness is closely related to the long duration of the obstruency defined in terms of the A_oA_o and A_oA_f. The constraint ATTRACT-[cg] given in (17) expresses the idea. In the following discussions, [cg] attracted by the A_oA_o or A_oA_f sequence is interpreted as an auditory cue that correlates with the tenseness of a consonant. It is not clear at this moment whether or not a glottal constriction actually occurs in these environments.

(17) ATTRACT-[cg] (tentative)
    i) Long duration of obstruency attracts [cg],
    ii) [cg] attracts long duration of obstruency.
       (Long duration of obstruency: A_oA_o or A_oA_f)

Bidirectional relation between the long duration of obstruency and the acoustic image of tenseness can be restated as follows:

(18) ATTRACT-[cg]
    LO $\leftrightarrow$ [cg]   (LO: Long duration of Obstruency, that is, A_oA_o or A_oA_f)

The implementation of acoustic image of tenseness due to the A_oA_o or A_oA_f sequence is closely linked to the increased buccal air pressure caused by the nonrelease of a coda: the buccal air pressure behind the point of closure is evidently increased, since air from the lungs continuously flows out and accumulates in a closed oral cavity which has a fixed volume in a normal pronunciation. This view is taken by Kim-Renaud (1974) and Sohn (1987) claiming that the release of the increased oral air pressure is responsible for the tenseness. The idea is supported by Kim's (1965) recording of oral air pressure behind the point of stop closure. According to him, the tense consonant has relatively higher buccal air pressure (increased pressure duration is around 141 msec) than the plain consonant (94 msec). This finding suggests that increased air pressure is one of the characteristics defining tense consonants in Korean. Especially when an unreleased coda is followed by a stop in the next syllable, the increase of buccal air pressure first generated by the nonrelease of a coda is almost, roughly speaking, doubled because of the extended A_o sequence. The consecutive A_o sequence (i.e. prolonged closure duration), which manifests itself as a long horizontal line in a waveform, suggests accumulation of more air pressure. See the closure duration in the waveforms given in (19): closure duration in (19a) is a sequence of an unreleased coda and an onset stop, whereas that in (19b) is an underlying tense consonant in an intervocalic position. (19c) is given here to show that an intervocalic plain consonant has a relatively very short period of duration with voicing.

(19) a. /ipku/ [ip'.k'u] 'entrance'

b. /ik'i/ [i.k'i] 'moss'

c. /iki/ [i.gi] 'to win'

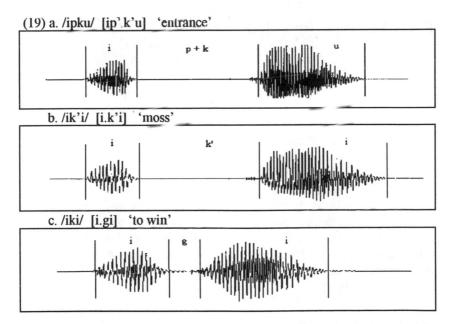

A long horizontal line between the vowels in (19a) implies that the air pressure is augmented during the period which is represented as two consecutive A_o's in my approach, and that the acoustic image of POT comes from that long duration of closure. This is confirmed by comparing the closure duration of the underlying tense consonant given in (19b) with that of a plain consonant given in (19c): the tense consonant is acoustically distinguished from the plain consonant by the long closure duration. Hence, it is not surprising that the similar closure duration in (19a)

incurred by successive A_o's is perceived as tense, not as a plain consonant. This is why POT occurs in (19a).

Though I share the idea with Han (1992) and Lee (1994ab) that length correlates with tenseness, my view is crucially different from theirs in that long closure duration is defined in terms of the sequence of aperture positions not of timing slots. Thus, my approach does not need several procedures that are related to the time slot such as X-insertion, X-incorporation, and X-deletion (recall (10)). At this point, I want to make it sure that the tense consonant in Korean is not underlyingly geminate. Rather, the long closure duration of the underlying tense consonant as seen in (19b) results from the satisfaction of the constraint ATTRACT-[cg].[7]

Now, let us consider how satisfaction or violation of the constraint ATTRACT-[cg] is determined in a given environment. In short, ATTRACT-[cg] is violated in a form like (20a), but satisfied in (20b).

(20) a. Violation of ATTRACT-[cg]   b. Satisfaction of ATTRACT-[cg]

       * n i k'. t   æ   n i k'. t'   æ

            A_o A_oA_m A_o A_oA_m

                                          |

                                     [cg]

(20b) satisfies ATTRACT-[cg], because a sequence of consecutive A_o's incurred by the nonrelease of the coda renders [cg] implemented at the onset of the following syllable that has a release phase.[8] By contrast, (20a) is a violation of ATTRACT-[cg], since [cg] is not attracted in spite of the existence of the A_oA_o sequence. Under the view that the ATTRACT-[cg] is bidirectionally defined, the constraint is also violated in cases where [cg] is inserted into an environment where a long obstruency duration does not exist. Thus, (21a) and (21b) below also violate ATTRACT-[cg]. In (21a), an intervening A_m position breaks up the obstruency duration. In (21b), the A_oA_o sequence is not an obstruency duration, since the first A_o is associated with [nas].

---

[7] Muscular tension characterizing the tense consonant (Kim 1965) also plays a role in lengthening the closure duration.

[8] Regarding the anchoring site of the feature [cg], the following FEATURE APERTURE COOCCURRENCE (FAC) constraint is assumed:

FAC(F, A), where F is a feature and A is an aperture node
F cooccurs with A.

For example, FAC([cg], A_x x>0) requires that [cg] cooccurs with an aperture node whose degree is larger than A_o. Hence, the attracted [cg] feature realizes itself under the A_m or A_f node.

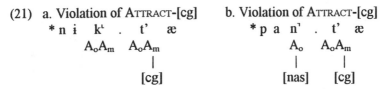

(21) a. Violation of ATTRACT-[cg]   b. Violation of ATTRACT-[cg]

Notice here that a satisfaction of ATTRACT-[cg] in (20b) causes a violation of a faithfulness constraint *INSERT-[cg] given in (22).

(22) *INSERT-[cg]
    Do not insert [cg].

     Discussions so far are summarized in the tableau given in (23), which shows that an obstruent sequence CC results in a string of an unreleased coda and a tensified onset (C'.C') due to the dominance relation whereby CODACOND and ATTRACT-[cg] outrank PARSE-A_m and *INSERT-[cg]. Under the given hierarchy, an underlying form /niktæ/ 'wolf' surfaces as [nik'.t'æ].

(23) POT in /niktæ/ 'wolf'

/niktæ/: UR	CODA CUND	ATT-[cg]	PAR-A_m	*INS-[cg]
a. ☞ n i k' . t' æ A_o<A_m> $A_o A_m$ | [cg]			*	*
b. n i k' . t æ A_o<A_m> $A_o A_m$		*!	*	
c. n i k^L . t' æ $A_o A_m$ $A_o A_m$ | [cg]	*!	*!		*
d. n i k^L . t æ $A_o A_m$ $A_o A_m$	*!			

The winning candidate (23a) satisfies both CODACOND and ATTRACT-[cg], sacrificing two faithfulness constraints PARSE-A_m and *INSERT-[cg]. The candidate (23b) is out because of the critical violation of ATTRACT-[cg].

Candidates (23c) and (23d) where the codas are released also drop out because of the CodaCond violation. Since there is no supporting evidence at this moment, I assume that there are no strict ranking relations between CodaCond and Attract-[cg], and between Parse-A$_m$ and *Insert-[cg].[9] Note that candidates like *[nikt.æ] and *[ni.ktæ] in which a consonant cluster occurs in the syllable margin are not considered in (23). They are sifted out very "early" in the competition because of the constraint *Comp(lex)Margin given in (24) that is never violated in Korean. The active role of *CompMargin will be assumed in the discussion that follows.

(24) *CompMargin
   Do not allow consonant clusters at the syllable margin.

Under the aperture geometry introduced in (4), the ranking hierarchy CodaCond, Attract-[cg], (and *CompMargin) >> Parse-A$_m$, *Insert-[cg] also explains why both the underlying C^{h}C and C'C obstruent sequences surface as C'.C' (neutralization and POT). The following tableaus (25) and (26) demonstrate this: /təp^{h}kæ/ 'cover' in (25) and /nak'si/ 'fishing' in (26) come out as [təp'.k'æ] and [nak'.s'i] respectively.

(25) Nonoccurrence of aspirate C in the coda and POT

/təp^{h}kæ/: UR	Coda Cond	Att-[cg]	Par-A$_m$	*Ins-[cg]
a. ☞ tə p' . k' æ 　　A$_o$<A$_m$> A$_o$A$_m$ 　　　|　　　　| 　　[sg]　　　[cg]			*	*
b. tə p' . k æ 　A$_o$<A$_m$> A$_o$A$_m$ 　　　| 　　[sg]		*!	*	
c. tə p^h . k' æ 　A$_o$A$_m$　A$_o$A$_m$ 　　|　　　　| 　[sg]　　　[cg]	*!	*!		*
d. tə p^h . k æ 　A$_o$A$_m$ A$_o$A$_m$ 　　　| 　　[sg]	*!			

---

[9]　In later discussion, however, it will be shown that CodaCond outranks Attract-[cg].

(26) Nonoccurrence of tense C in the coda and POT[10]

/nak'si/: UR	CODA COND	ATT- [cg]	PAR- A_m	*INS- [cg]

a. ☞   n a   k'   .   s'   i
     $A_o<A_m>$ A_f
       | |
      [cg]   [cg]
			*	*

b.   n a   k'   .   s   i
     $A_o<A_m>$ A_f
       |
      [cg]
		*!	*	

c.   n a   k'   .   s'   i
     A_oA_m A_f
      | |
     [cg]   [cg]
	*!	*!		*

d.   n a   k'   .   s   i
     A_oA_m A_f
      |
     [cg]
	*!			

Features like [sg] and [cg] in the coda cannot survive in the optimal output leading to a coda neutralization. It's because their mother node A_m should be underparsed to obey the inviolable constraint CODACOND. Observe that any candidates in (25) and (26) that hold the laryngeal feature in the coda position are winnowed out by the CODACOND. From the candidates that pass

---

[10] Under the Steriade's (1993, 1994) aperture geometry, plain /s/ and tense /s'/ in words like /si/ 'poem' and /s'i/ 'seed' can be represented as follows (there is no underlying and surface aspirate fricative):

tense s	plain s
s'	s
A_f	A_f
|	
[cg]	

That is, the feature [cg] can appear under the A_f position as well as under the A_m position of a stop. Similarly, tense, aspirate, and plain affricates can be represented in the following way:

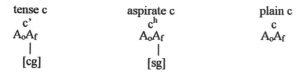

tense c	aspirate c	plain c
c'	c^h	c
A_oA_f	A_oA_f	A_oA_f
|	|	
[cg]	[sg]	

the CODACOND, candidates (25a) and (26a) are picked out, since the other candidates (25b) and (26b) violate the ATTRACT-[cg].

Although a plain obstruent in the second position of CC, C^{h}C, and C'C becomes tensified along with the neutralization of the preceding obstruent, an aspirate consonant in the same position avoids the effect of POT, but still with the neutralization of the preceding consonant. This is shown in (27) below.

(27) Neutralization and nonoccurrence of POT in an aspirate onset

/k'it^{h}p^{h}an/	[k'it'.p^{h}an']	*[k'it'.p'an']	'last stage, finale'
/ap^{h}c^{h}æ/	[ap'.c^{h}æ]	*[ap'.c'æ]	'a front outbuilding'
/kyət^{h}c^{h}æ/	[kyət'.c^{h}æ]	*[kyət'.c'æ]	'a side outbuilding'
/mokc^{h}ən/	[mok'.c^{h}ən']	*[mok'.c'ən']	'vocal cords'
/pakt^{h}al/	[pak'.t^{h}al']	*[pak'.t'al']	'deprivation'
/cakp^{h}um/	[cak'.p^{h}um']	*[cak'.p'um']	'a piece of work'
/kakc^{h}uk/	[kak'.c^{h}uk']	*[kak'.c'uk']	'competition'

In the pronunciation of the consonant sequences given above, an A_oA_o string inducing an auditory image of [cg] occurs in the syllable boundary, since here again the A_m position of the coda consonant is underparsed due to the constraint CODACOND. So, the nonoccurrence of POT in (27) suggests that some constraints ranked higher than the ATTRACT-[cg] play an active role to prevent tensification of the aspirate consonant. On the grounds that only aspirate consonants resist the implementation of [cg], we can deduce that the acoustic image of the feature [sg], characterized by a strong puff of air, is stronger than that of the [cg]. To explain this, the following constraints are needed: FEATURE COOCCURRENCE and PARSE-[sg].

(28) FEATURE COOCCURRENCE
    *[cg, sg]

(29) PARSE-[sg]
    *<[sg]>

Under the view that the FEATURE COOCCURRENCE constraint *[cg, sg] is inviolable in Korean (this constraint is probably universally inviolable), ranking PARSE-[sg] over ATTRACT-[cg] accounts for why an aspirate onset is not tensified in Korean. The tableau in (30) clarifies this point, demonstrating the nonoccurrence of POT in /pakt^{h}al/ 'deprivation' (in (30), I omit the underparsed A_m, and do not consider the lowly ranked constraints PARSE-A_m and *INSERT-[cg]).

(30) Nonoccurrence of POT in an aspirate onset

/pakt^{h}al/: UR	*[cg, sg]	CODA COND	PAR- [sg]	ATT- [cg]
a. ☞ p a k' . t^h a l A$_o$ A$_o$A$_m$ | [sg]				*
b. p a k' . t$'^h$ a l A$_o$ A$_o$A$_m$ /\ [cg] [sg]	*!			
c. p a k' . t' a l A$_o$ A$_o$A$_m$ /\ [cg] <[sg]>			*!	
d. p a k^t . t^h a l A$_o$A$_m$ A$_o$A$_m$ | [sg]		*!		

The candidate (30b) does not obey the constraint *[cg, sg], thus loses the competition immediately. Selection of (30a) over (30c) shows that dominance of PARSE-[sg] over ATTRACT-[cg] is crucial. If the ranking between the two constraints is reversed, (30c) will be picked out incorrectly. The fact that candidate (30d) drops out makes it clear that CODACOND plays an important role in Korean. If the coda obstruent is released as in (30d), ATTRACT-[cg] is vacuously satisfied, and all other constraints are also satisfied. Thus, without the active role of CODACOND, (30d) will be selected, resulting in a wrong output.

One thing to be noted at this moment is the ranking relation between CODACOND and ATTRACT-[cg]. In previous discussion, I have assumed that there is no dominance relation between the two constraints. However, in a situation where *[cg, sg] and PARSE-[sg] outrank ATTRACT-[cg], there emerge two seemingly possible ways to place the CODACOND in the hierarchy. One is to put both CODACOND and ATTRACT-[cg] in the same rank, keeping the original assumption. In this scenario, in order to maintain the proved hierarchy *[cg, sg], PARSE-[sg] >> ATTRACT-[cg], the whole ranking relation would be like this: *[cg, sg], PARSE-[sg] >> CODACOND, ATTRACT-[cg]. But, this is not desirable in the sense that *[cg, sg] and PARSE-[sg] outrank the CODACOND that is never violated in Korean. In other words, to say that an inviolable constraint is dominated by some other constraints does not fit the idea of OT. Therefore, the CODACOND should rank the same with *[cg, sg] and PARSE-[sg], dominating ATTRACT-[cg], as given in the above tableau (30).

Finally, let us see why a sonorant, for example, a nasal in the coda position does not induce the tensification of the following onset. The examples given in (3) are reproduced as (31) below.

(31) No tensification after a sonorant (nasal)

/imca/	[im'.ja]	*[im'.c'a]	'owner'
/kumpeŋi/	[kum'.beŋ'.i]	*[kum'.p'eŋ'.i]	'sluggard''
/pancuk/	[pan'.juk']	*[pan'.c'uk']	'dough'
/kyəncuta/	[kyən'.ju.da]	*[kyən'.c'u.da]	'to compare'
/maŋtuŋi/	[maŋ'.duŋ'.i]	*[maŋ'.t'uŋ'.i]	'goby'

Like obstruents, nasals in the coda do not allow releasing of the closed oral articulators as seen in (32). Obviously, this is an effect of the CODACOND that is inviolable in Korean.

(32) Nonrelease of a coda nasal

/cam/	[cam']	*[camˡ]	'sleep'
/san/	[san']	*[sanˡ]	'mountain'
/saŋ/	[saŋ']	*[saŋˡ]	'table'
/yaŋsaŋ/	[yaŋ'.saŋ']	*[yaŋˡ.saŋˡ]	'aspect'
/piŋpʰan/	[piŋ'.pʰan']	*[piŋˡ.pʰanˡ]	'icy place'

Even though the oral cavity is strictly closed at the point of articulation, airstream continuously flows out through the nasal cavity for a production of a nasal sound. Thus, in a candidate where [cg] appears in an NC cluster as NC', the constraint ATTRACT-[cg] is violated in the sense that the [cg] is inserted into an environment where there is no motivation (i.e. long obstruency duration). Hence, in a grammar where ATTRACT-[cg] is highly ranked, NC' cannot survive as an optimal output (see (34a) below).

The nonoccurrence of tensification after a sonorant verifies that POT is closely related to increased oral air pressure: air pressure behind the closure point is not increased during the pronunciation of the nasal sound, since air goes out through the nasal cavity. Another thing to be briefly addressed here (though not related to POT) is the sharing of the [voice] feature in the NC cluster, as fully discussed in Itô, Mester & Padgett (1995) and Pater (1995). In this paper, however, I simply assume that a constraint like SHARE-[voc] given in (33) is inviolable in Korean, and that that's why a candidate containing, for example, an [nt] sequence cannot be chosen as an output.

(33) SHARE-[voc]

```
    N C
     \ /
    [voc]
```

The tableau given in (34) illustrates why tensification does not occur in the NC cluster and why an underlying /nt/ surfaces as [nd] in an example /pantæ/ 'opposition'.

(34) No tensification after a nasal

/pantæ/: UR	CODA COND	SHA-[voc]	ATT-[cg]	PAR-A$_m$	*INS-[cg]
a. p a n' . t' æ A$_o$<A$_m$> A$_o$A$_m$ / \ | [nas] [voc] [cg]		*!	*	*	*
b. p a n' . t æ A$_o$<A$_m$> A$_o$A$_m$ / \ [nas] [voc]		*!		*	
c. ☞ p a n' . d æ A$_o$<A$_m$> A$_o$A$_m$ / \ / [nas] [voc]				*	
d. p a n^l . t' æ A$_o$A$_m$ A$_o$A$_m$ / \ | [nas] [voc] [cg]	*!	*!	*		*
e. p a n^l . d æ A$_o$A$_m$ A$_o$A$_m$ / \ / [nas] [voc]	*!				

As seen in (34), nonoccurrence of the tensification in NC cluster is explained in terms of the ranking hierarchy established so far. Observe that the winning candidate (34c) satisfies the constraints such as CODACOND, SHARE-[voc] and ATTRACT-[cg], whereas the other candidates are sifted out by them. Though not illustrated here, no tensification in an onset after a liquid coda (/salku/ → [sal'.gu], *[sal'.k'u] 'apricot'; /bolki/ → [bol'.gi], *[bol'.k'i] 'hips') will be explained in a similar way.

5. Summary

In this paper, I have revealed the problems in previous accounts of POT, and proposed a set of constraints and their ranking relations in order to explain POT without recourse to rules. Occurrence and nonoccurrence of POT in different environments result from the ranking relations summarized in (35). Constraints in the first column are the highest ones, probably inviolable in Korean, and those in the rightmost column are ranked lowest.

(35) Constraint Ranking

CODACOND	>>	ATTRACT-[cg]	>>	PARSE-A_m
*COMPMARGIN				*INSERT-[cg]
*[cg, sg]				
PARSE-[sg]				

High ranking of the CODACOND and the *COMPMARGIN makes it suboptimal for the intervocalic obstruent strings other than the C".C to appear. Ranking ATTRACT-[cg] over *INSERT-[cg] is directly responsible for POT which occurs as an acoustic image of the A_oA_o or the A_oA_f sequence. Finally, dominance of ATTRACT-[cg] by *[cg, sg] and PARSE-[sg] explains why an aspirate consonant is not tensified.

References

Baek, E-J. 1991. Unreleasing in Korean: A phonetic Explanation. *Harvard Studies in Korean Linguistics* IV. 29-35.

Bennett, J. F. 1995. *Metrical Foot Structure in Thai and Kayah Li: An Optimality-Theoretic Study of Prosodic Phonology in Two Southeast Asian Languages.* Doctoral dissertation, University of Illinois at Urbana-Champaign.

Cho, Y-M. & S. Inkelas. 1994. Post-Obstruent Tensification in Korean and Geminate Inalterability. *Theoretical Issues in Korean Linguistics,* ed. by Kim-Renaud, 45-60. Stanford: CSLI.

Han, J-I. 1992. On the Korean Tensed Consonants and Tensification. *CLS* 28. 206-23.

Hardcastle, W.J. 1973. Some Observations on the Tense-Lax Distinction in Initial Stops in Korean. *Journal of Phonetics* 1. 263-72.

Hirose, H., H-S. Park & M. Sawashima. 1983. Activity of the Thyroarytenoid Muscle in the Production of Korean stops and Fricatives. *Vocal Fold Physiology: Biomechanics, Acoustics and Phonatory Control,* eds. by Titze, I. R. & R. C. Scherer, 105-12.

Hudson, G. 1995. Consonant release and the syllable. *Linguistics* 33. 655-72.

Itô, J., A. Mester & J. Padgett. 1995. NC: Licensing and Underspecification in Optimality Theory. to appear in *LI*

Kagaya, R. 1974. A fiberscopic and Acoustic Study of the Korean Stops, Affricates and Fricatives. *Journal of Phonetics* 2. 161-80.

Kahn, D. 1976. *Syllable-based Generalization in English Phonology.* Doctoral dissertation, MIT.

Kim, C-W. 1965. On the Autonomy of the Tensity Feature in Stop Classification. *Word* 21. 339-59.

Kim, S-H. 1993. Process and Rule in Phonology: Phonological Phenomena between Korean Obstruents. *Linguistic Journal of Korea* 18.2. 201-31.

Kim-Renaud, Y-K. 1974. *Korean Consonantal Phonology.* Doctoral dissertation, University of Hawaii.

Lee, S. 1994a. Obstruent Unreleasing and Tensification in Korean. ms., University of Southern California.

Lee, S. 1994b. Neutralization and Tensification in Korean. *Japanese Korean Linguistics* 4. 511-20. Stanford: CSLI.

McCarthy, J. & A. Prince. 1993a. Prosodic Morphology I: Constraint Interaction and Satisfaction ms. University of Massachusetts, Amherst, & Rutgers University, New Brunswick, NJ.

McCarthy, J. & A. Prince. 1993b. Generalized Alignment. ms., University of Massachusetts, Amherst, & Rutgers University, New Brunswick, NJ.

Oh, J-R. 1988. Kwuke hwutwuum chungyel uy cenglip (On Korean Laryngeal Tier). *Cwusikyeng hakpo.* 2. 130-53.

Pater, J. 1995. Austronesian Nasal Substitution and other NC effects. to appear in the Proceedings of the Utrecht Prosodic Morphology Workshop.

Prince, A. & P. Smolensky. 1993. Optimality Theory. ms., Rutgers University, New Brunswick, NJ. & University of Colorado, Boulder.

Rhee, S-C. 1995. A Constraint on Coda Aperture and Neutralization. to appear in *Linguistic Journal of Korea.* 20.4.

Sawashima, M., H-S. Park, K. Honda, & H. Hirose. 1980. Fiberscopic study on laryngeal adjustments for syllable-final applosives in Korean. *Ann. Bull. RILP* 14. 125-38.

Sohn, H-S. 1987. *Underspecification in Korean Phonology.* Doctoral dissertation, University of Illinois at Urbana-Champaign.

Spencer, R. F. 1946. The phonemes of Keresan. *International Journal of American Linguistics* 12. 229-36.

Steriade, D. 1993. Closure, Release, and Nasal Contours. *Phonetics and Phonology 5: Nasals, Nasalization, and the Velum*, eds. by Huffman, M. K. & R. A. Krakow, 401-70. Academic Press.

Steriade, D. 1994. Complex Onsets as Single Segments: The Mazateco pattern. *Perspectives in Phonology*, eds. by Cole, J. & C. Kisseberth, 202-91. Stanford: CSLI.

Tranel, B. 1987. *The Sounds of French: an Introduction*. Cambridge University Press.

Perception of Japanese Pitch Accent by Koreans and its Implications for Understanding Phonological Structures

YASUHIKO SUKEGAWA AND SHIGERU SATO
Tohoku University, Japan

Abstract: The minimum units for recognition and production of speech sounds are understood to be a mora and a syllable for Japanese and Korean, respectively. This paper reports a perception experiment on Korean learners of Japanese to identify the accentual pattern of words synthesized with various pitch heights assigned for the moras. The experiment used two-mora nonsense words of the /CV-CV/, /CV-H/, and /CV-N/ types, and showed that detection of pitch change in a word of two consecutive CV moras is more difficult than that in a two-mora-one-syllable word of the /CV-H/ or /CV-N/ type. The implication of the present paper is that speakers of a syllabic language may find it difficult to learn the change in pitch heights between the adjacent syllables in a word.

Introduction

In the speech of foreign learners of Japanese, unnatural word accentuation often occurs, possibly due to the lack of training for detection of relative pitch heights between syllables. There are differences in the degrees of naturalness among learners according to the native language his or her speech production is based on. The authors have observed for instance that for a Bantu speaker with a similar accentuation system in his/her own language, acquisition is easier than for Korean or Chinese speakers, who constitute the majority of learners. For detection of pitch in adjacent moras, the learner must first recognize the autonomous CV-mora, and then the auxiliary moras, /Q/, /N/, /H/, and /I/, which , although phonologically independent, are merely the sounds playing supplementary roles in making syllables in other languages (Minakawa 1995). It is a time-consuming process for a learner to understand that Japanese speech is a concatenation of moras, that the moras are hierarchically aligned, and that they have inherent pitch heights in utterance.

Word accentuation in Japanese is closely related to perception of moras, and its acquisition is the key to realization of sentence intonation(Pierrehumbert et al. 1988, Kubozono 1993), and thus overall natural prosody of Japanese .

This paper reports on a pitch accent perception experiment conducted on 57 Korean learners of Japanese using two-mora nonsense words of the /CV-CV/, /CV-H/, and /CV-N/ types. Korean learners have been reported previously to have difficulties both in segmental and in prosodic production of Japanese speech (Oonisi 1990, Sukegawa 1993). It is assumed that these difficulties may partly be due to insufficient perception of moras and their pitch heights (Sukegawa et al. 1995).

Methods

57 Korean high school teachers of Japanese were employed as the subjects, of whom 38 are males and 19 females. Their ages range from 26 to 47 with the average of 32.5. They had studied Japanese for the period of 4 to 10 years. Their dialectal background was that in addition to 32 others, there were 25 from Kyongsang Province where they are said to retain relative pitch accent in their dialect.

A speaker of Tokyo dialect uttered the three nonsense words [nene], [ne:] and [nen], the moraic structure of each being /CV-CV/, /CV-H/, and /CV-N/, respectively. They were used to make synthesized sample words with 'flat', 'rising', and 'falling' pitch patterns as shown in Table 1.

Mora Type	Accentual Pattern
CV-CV	[nene] Flat
	[nene] Rising
	[nene] Falling
CV-H	[ne:] Flat
	[ne:] Rising
	[ne:] Falling
CV-N	[nen] Flat
	[nen] Rising
	[nen] Falling

Table 1. Stimuli

A	B	X
Flat	Falling	Flat
Flat	Falling	Falling
Flat	Rising	Flat
Flat	Rising	Rising
Falling	Flat	Falling
Falling	Flat	Flat
Falling	Rising	Falling
Falling	Rising	Rising
Rising	Flat	Rising
Rising	Flat	Flat
Rising	Falling	Rising
Rising	Falling	Falling

Table 2. Stimulus combinations

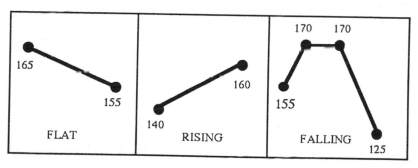

Fig. 1. Synthesized pitch contours (Unit: Hz)

Each stimulus word is of 420 ms duration and of one of the pitch patterns given in Figure 1. We used the ABX method to present the stimuli to the subjects. Figure 2 is a temporal organization of an ABX series of stimuli. As in Table 2, there are 12 combinations of stimuli, but the accentual constraint in Tokyo dialect is that no rising pattern exists in the transition from a CV-mora to an H-/N-mora. In Table 3 are the actual patterns used. The triplets were presented five times in random order, and the subject was asked to make 20 choices, corresponding to each one of the 20 presentations (4 patterns X 5 presentations).

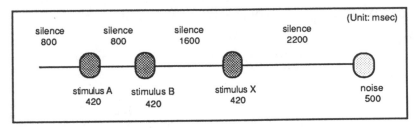

Fig 2. Temporal organization of an ABX stimulus

Pattern	A	B	X
1	Falling---------- Flat-------------- Flat
2	Falling---------- Flat-------------- Falling
3	Flat-------------- Falling---------- Flat
4	Flat -------------- Falling---------- Falling

Table 3. Presentation patterns

Results and discussions

The correctness of responses given by the 57 subjects was analyzed statistically. Table 4 shows the average values and standard deviations of the scores. The control group was formed by five speakers of Tokyo dialect, for whom full scores were marked for all the patterns.

An analysis of variance (ANOVA) comparing the scores of correct answers shows that there is a significant difference in the perception of the three phonological types [$F(2, 168)=16.419$, $p<0.0001$], and that the scores are significantly lower for /CV-CV/ than the other two types, but that no significant difference is seen between /CV-H/ and /CV-N/. The analyses within each of the four patterns (Patterns 1-4) show that Patterns 1-3 have similar results as the above [Pattern 1: $F(2, 168)=5.419$, $p=0.0052$; Pattern 2: $F(2, 168)=7.421$, $p=0.0008$; Pattern 3: $F(2, 168)=15.789$, $p<0.0001$], indicating significantly lower values for /CV-CV/ than the other two patterns. For Pattern 4, however, this relationship does not hold true [F(2, 168)=2.708, p=0.0696].

Pattern	Mora Type	Mean	S.D.
ALL	/CV-CV/	15.404	2.915
	/CV-H/	17.737	2.629
	/CV-N/	17.842	2.094
1	/CV-CV/	4.070	0.923
	/CV-H/	4.561	0.627
	/CV-N/	4.561	0.780
2	/CV-CV/	3.772	1.210
	/CV-H/	4.368	1.080
	/CV-N/	4.333	0.951
3	/CV-CV/	3.193	1.329
	/CV-H/	4.246	1.154
	/CV-N/	4.246	0.950
4	/CV-CV/	4.368	0.919
	/CV-H/	4.561	0.682
	/CV-N/	4.684	0.540

Table 4. Correct scores in accentual perception

Significant dialectal influences were anticipated for the 25 pitch sensitive speakers of Kyongsang dialect. Table 5 contains the scores according to dialectal difference. ANOVA reveals the same tendency for each of the two groups as for the entire body in the comparison of the results [Kyongsang: F(2,72)=10.997, p<0.0001; non-Kyongsang: F(2,93)=7.825, p=0.0007], exhibiting significantly lower values for /CV-CV/ than the other two types. Significant difference in the correct answers of Kyongsang speakers from those of non-Kyongsang speakers was sought for each of the three moraic types, but t-tests failed to reach significance for /CV-CV/ and /CV-N/ [p=0.3438 and p=0.0752, respectively], whereas for /CV-H/, which is phonetically [ne:], Kyongsang subjects marked a significantly higher score [p=0.0354], which may well be affected accidentally by analogy to the frequently used word in Korean.

Dialect	Mora Type	Mean	S.D.
Kyongsang	/CV-CV/	15.760	2.619
	/CV-H/	18.560	2.599
	/CV-N/	18.400	1.803
Non-Kyongsang	/CV-CV/	15.031	3.032
	/CV-H/	17.094	2.506
	/CV-N/	17.406	2.227

Table 5. Correct perception: dialectal difference

In identifying the pitch pattern in a two-mora word, the native speaker of Japanese makes an instant attempt first to locate the moras and then to detect the relative pitch heights of the adjacent moras. From the results above, we observe that Koreans may be using a scale of a totally different nature. For Koreans, comparison of the pitches in two autonomous CV-moras seems difficult, whereas the other two types (/CV-H/ and /CV-N/) may allow the subject to perceive the absolute pitch change in these moraic types that are phonetically similar to existing syllables in Korean.

Figure 3 is a schematic diagram of the relevant syllable structures shown with corresponding Japanese moras. It should be noted that in Korean, /CV-H/ and /CV-N/ are regarded as single syllables, but that /CV-CV/ is counted as two syllables.

Conclusions

An accent perception experiment was performed on Korean learners of Japanese using two-mora nonsense words of the /CV-CV/, /CV-H/, and /CV-N/ types. The results show that detection of pitch change in a word of two consecutive CV moras is more difficult than that in a two-mora-one-syllable word of the /CV-H/ or /CV-N/ type. A comparison between non-Kyongsang and pitch

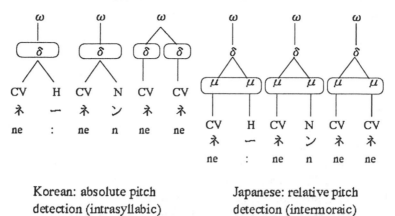

Korean: absolute pitch
detection (intrasyllabic)

Japanese: relative pitch
detection (intermoraic)

Fig.3. Syllable structures and pitch detection (δ : syllable μ : mora)

sensitive Kyongsang subjects was also attempted in anticipation of significant difference in accent perception between these groups, but it rendered negative results. The implication of the present paper is that speakers of a syllabic language may find it difficult to learn pitch detection between adjacent syllables in a word. The findings are: (1) that detection of relative pitch change between consecutive CV-moras is difficult for the Korean subjects, and (2) that if a multimoraic construction is construed phonologically as a single syllable in Korean, the pattern becomes easier to recognize. The phonological implications of the experiment are: (1) for speakers of a language where intersyllabic accentuation is not utilized, perception of pitch change between adjacent moras becomes difficult when the moras fall segmentally within their own multisyllable types, and (2) recognition of nonautonomous moras and their phonological formation may not be necessary for identifying the accentual pattern of a multi-mora-one-syllable word.

Acknowledgments

This work was supported in part by Scientific Research Grant (No. 07780193) of the Ministry of Education of Japan. The authors gratefully acknowledge discussions with Kikuo Maekawa on experimentation and the assistance of Hyunchoel Choi in data processing.

References

Kubozono, Haruo. 1993. The Organization of Japanese prosody. Tokyo: Kurosio Publishers.

Minakawa, Yasuyo. 1995. Eigo, kankokugo wasya no nihongo tyoo'on tikaku. Paper presented at the 10th Tokyo Onsei Gengo Kenkyuukai.

Oonisi, Haruhiko.1990. Kankokuzinno nihongono akusentoni tuite. Kokusai Gakuyuukai Nihongo Gakkoo Kiyoo 12. 52-60.

Pierrehumbert, Janet and Mary Beckman. 1988. Japanese tone structures. Cambridge: MIT Press.

Sukegawa, Yasuhiko. 1993. Bogobetuni mita hatuonno keikoo: ankeeto tyoosano kekka kara. Nihongo Onsei to Nihongo Kyooiku, Kakenhi Zyuuten Ryooiki 'Nihongo Onsei' Group D1 Report. 187-222.

Sukegawa, Yasuhiko, Hyunchoel Choi, Kikuo Maekawa, and Shigeru Sato. 1995. Kankokuzin nihongo gakusyuusyani yoru akusento tikaku to onsetu koozooni kansuru koosatu. Inst. Elect., Info., and Comm. Eng.Tech. Rep. SP95-9.

Umlaut In Kyungsang Korean: The Optimal Domains Theoretic Account[1]

SEUNG-HOON SHIN
Indiana University

1. Introduction

Umlaut in Korean is a type of vowel harmony in which a vowel is fronted when followed by an underlyingly high front vowel. The front harmony seems to have a very narrow harmonic domain, and some words do not undergo this harmony. Also, umlaut applies to only native Korean words (Hankeul), not to Sino-Korean words, ideophones and loanwords. The goal of this paper is to examine Kyungsang Korean umlaut within the framework of OPTIMAL DOMAINS THEORY (ODT) proposed by Cole and Kisseberth (1994a, b, c). In this paper, I argue that umlaut is a domain-based process, and that the harmony domain and the feature realization are derived from the interaction of alignment constraints with Faithfulness constraints (see Prince and Smolensky 1993 and McCarthy and Prince 1993 a, b for relevant discussion). I then propose some constraints which account for the disharmony derived from intervening geminates, long vowels,

---

[1]I am especially grateful to Stuart Davis for his many helpful comments. I would like to also thank Jennifer Cole, Elizabeth Hume, No-Ju Kim and Minsu Shim for their comments and Haejin Koh, Borim Lee and Hyunsook Kang for their assistance.

prefixes and different classes of Koreans morphemes such as Sino-Korean, ideophones and loanwords.

I will proceed as follows. In the following sections, I briefly review the ODT and describe Korean umlaut. I then give an account for the harmony, focusing on its domain and the interaction between alignment constraints and Faithfulness constraints.

2. Optimal Domains Theory (ODT)

In the past few years, there have been several attempts to analyze vowel harmony within the theoretical framework of Optimality Theory, where vowel harmony is analyzed by some language specific alignment constraints and additional Faithfulness constraints (see Akinlabi 1994a, b, c, Kirchner 1993, Pulleyblank 1993, 1994 among others).

Given that the realization of an active harmonic feature in vowel harmony has a specific domain, Cole and Kisseberth (1994a, b, c) propose ODT, which states that the harmonized features are parsed on all relevant anchors in DOMAINS. The theory is similar to others in that it accounts for harmony by means of alignment constraints. However, it is different from other accounts of harmony, such as that of Pulleyblank's and Kirchner's, in that it accounts for the harmony in terms of harmonic domains which can be strong or weak PROSODIC UNITS depending on the properties of the harmony instead of handling harmony in terms of simple alignment constraints such as left-alignment, right-alignment and NoGapping.

Consequently, under the ODT account of harmony, harmony is described as in (1).

(1) Harmony in ODT
- ●Harmony is the requirement that a feature [F] be uniformly realized on anchors in an F-domain.
- ●F-domains are explicit aspects of phonological structure, with the same status as structures for the syllable, foot, word, etc.
(quoted from Cole and Kisseberth 1994a: 3)

In the theory, the F-domain and feature realization are derived from the universal constraints, based on language-particular properties. Those harmonic domains tend to satisfy the so-called principle of EXTENSION, which 'extend(s) a feature over longer stretches of sound in order to maximize Perceptibility and Articulator Stability' (Cole and Kisseberth 1994a: 4). This Extension principle is then satisfied by the sets of constraints, that they call WIDE SCOPE ALIGNMENT (WSA), which 'extend(s) an F-domain to the edge of a morphological (e.g. stem) or prosodic constituent (like word or foot)' (Cole and Kisseberth 1994a: 4). WSA is defined in (2).

(2) Wide Scope Alignment (WSA)
        a) WSA-left   Align(F-domain,L; P-Cat/M-Cat,L)
        b) WSA-right   Align(F-domain,R; P-Cat/M-Cat,R)

Within the domain, an active harmonic feature is realized in terms of the constraint EXPRESSION in (3), but a language will not undergo harmony if the potentially harmonic feature is aligned only with the feature-bearing unit since BASIC ALIGNMENT requires a feature to be limited to a single anchor or segment.

(3) Expression: [F] must be affiliated with every anchor in an F-domain.
(4) Basic Alignment:
        a) BA-left   Align(F-domain,L; Sponsor, L)
        b) BA-right   Align(F-domain,R; Sponsor, R)

If both BA-left and BA-right are highly ranked and unviolated then a language will not undergo harmony since the domain of the relevant feature would be limited to its anchoring source.

    These constraints can also be strong or weak, depending on the properties of a sponsor and an anchor as shown in (5).

(5) Expressing prosodic strength distinctions
        a) Strong F-domain (F-domain$^+$): A domain for a feature
          (F) whose underlying sponsor is *strong*.
        b) Strong WSA (WSA$^+$):
          Align-L/R (F-domain$^+$; M-Cat/P-Cat)
        c) Strong Expression (Express$^+$): Express [F] on a *strong*
          anchor in an F-domain.

As a consequence, in ODT, neutrality is derived from the ranking of two constraints. That is, opaqueness is accounted for by ranking the WSA constraint lower than Express[F], while transparency is captured by ranking WSA higher than Express[F].

    As mentioned earlier, with respect to vowel harmony, ODT is different from other accounts in that it is a domain- and strength-based approach. For instance, ODT does not have several universal constraints regarding Faithfulness such as Lex-Feat, Lex-Link (Kirchner 1993) RecP or RecF (Pulleyblank 1993, 1994), but instead, the relevant domain plays an important role. Compared to other optimality theoretic accounts of harmony, ODT provides a more concise analysis. First, it needs fewer constraints, which thus provides a simple and empirical account. Second, it does not need feature insertion or additional constraints, both of which are required for a feature to be realized far from the source in other theories. When the harmonic feature is realized in a very narrow domain in some languages, the ODT approach seems to be more systematic because alignment limits the harmonic domain to a small prosodic structure such as a syllable or a foot. In ODT, WSA and Express substitute for several feature cooccurrence constraints and other constraints such as RecF and RecP. That is, strong or weak Expression constraints take the places of both surface feature constraints and Parse-Feat, and the specific domain of the harmony takes the places of Align-L, Align-R and RecF or Lex-Link, NoGapping and so on.

In the following sections, I will describe Korean front harmony and propose an account for the harmony and disharmony within the framework of ODT.

3. Front harmony in Kyungsang Korean

Umlaut is a type of partial front harmony, which is optional. In terms of umlaut, a back vowel is fronted when it is followed by a high front vowel /i/. In this paper, I assume that the sponsor /i/ is underlyingly specified as [+front].

(6) and (7) illustrate several examples of umlaut in Kyungsang Korean.

(6) Umlaut in Kyungsang Korean: Nouns

a) əmi	~	ɛmi	'mother'
b) nampi	~	nɛmpi	'kettle'
c) aki	~	ɛki	'baby'
e) tulumaki	~	turumɛki	'traditional coat'
f) sonaki	~	sonɛki	'shower'
g) kyətɨlaɲi	~	kyətɨrɛɲi	'armpit'
h) paŋmaɲi	~	paŋmɛɲi	'bat'

(7) Umlaut in Kyungsang Korean: Verbs

a) pəli -	~	pɛli -	'to spoil'
b) s'ɨli -	~	s'ili -	'to be painful'
c) kɨli -	~	kili -	'to draw'
d) tali -	~	tɛli -	'to iron'
e) səmki	~	simki-	'to respect'
f) tɨli -	~	tili -	'to let someone come into, to hire'

In addition to the examples above, front harmony can be triggered by many suffixes. As Lee (1993) observes in Seoul Korean, some suffixes such as the nominalizer /i/, passive marker /hi:/ and causative marker /-i/ trigger the harmony, while other suffixes such as the nominative /i/, adverbial /hi/ and /i/, gerundive /ki/ and copula /ita/ do not. However, in the Kyungsang dialect, where the front harmony is far more productive than in any other dialect, even nominative /i/, gerundive /ki/ and copula /ita/ may trigger umlaut (adverbial /hi/ and /i/ still do not). This is shown in (8).

(8) Umlaut triggered by suffixes
  a) Nominative /-i/ (N + /-i/)
    salam + i   salami ~ salɛmi   'man' + nominative /-i/
  b) Copula /-ita/ (N + /-ita/)
    pəp + ita   pəpita ~ pɛpita   'law' + copula /-ita/
  c) Nominalizer /-ki/ (V + /-ki/)
    po + ki   poki   ~   piki   'seeing'
    nəmki   nəmki   ~   nɛmki   'turning'
  d) Passive morpheme /-hi:/
    mək + hi: məkʰi: ~   mikʰi: 'to be eaten'
  e) Infinitive suffix /-ita/
    cuk + ita   cukita   ~   cikita   'to kill'
      (N refers to a noun, while V refers to a verb stem.)

However, in a combination of two roots, the high front vowel does not trigger harmony as shown in (9).

(9) Disharmony at phrasal level
    sinpal 'shoe' + kili 'length'   ~   sinpal kili (*sinpɛl kili)
                                          'length of a shoe'

In (9) the first vowel of the first word, /a/, is not fronted even though it is followed by a high front vowel /i/ in the second root. Consequently, umlaut does not apply at the phrasal level.

3.1. Disharmony by intervening geminates

In addition to the general properties of front harmony in Kyungsang Korean as shown above, it also has some special cases which do not undergo harmony. The first example to be discussed is the blocking effect by means of a geminate.

Geminates between a sponsor /i/ and an anchor block the front harmony. For instance, although as shown in (8), the nominalizer /-ki/ normally triggers the harmony, it blocks the harmony when it is preceded by a syllable that ends in a coda /k/, which instead produces a geminate with the /k/ of the nominalizer /-ki/. Compare the examples in (10).

(10) Disharmony by geminates vs. harmony

	Disharmony	Harmony
/mək-/ 'to eat'	mək + ki (nominalizer) -> mək-ki ~ *mɛk-ki	mək + ita (copular) --> mək-ita ~ mɛk-ita
/sak-/ 'to mitigate'	sak + ki (nominalizer) --> sak-ki ~ *sɛk-ki	sak + ita (copular) --> sak-ita ~ sɛk-ita

In the *Disharmony* column, the nonfront vowels /ə/ and /a/ are not fronted due to the geminate that is produced by the suffixation. In the *Harmony* column, however, the same vowels in the same roots agree with the following vowel /i/ and therefore undergo harmony.

As is expected, umlaut does not occur over an underlying geminate. Compare examples in (11) with in (7).

(11) Disharmony by geminates
a) alli-	~	alli	*ɛlli	'to inform'
b) kəlli-	~	kəlli	*kɛlli	'to be hung'
c) p'alli	~	p'alli	*pɛlli	'to be sucked'
d) malli	~	malli	*mɛlli	'to dry'

(data from Davis and Lee 1994: 456)

3.2. Disharmony by long vowels

In addition to geminates, long vowels in Kyungsang Korean also do not harmonize in frontness. If a root contains a long vowel, it undergoes harmony depending on the suffixation. Compare the examples in (12).

(12) Disharmony by long vowels vs. harmony by short vowels

	Disharmony	Harmony
/na:m-/ 'to remain'	na:m + ki (nominalizer) --> na:mk'i[2] ~ *nɛ:mk'i (*ɛnk'i)	na:m + ki (causative morpheme) + ta (ending marker) ---> namkita ~ nɛmkita
/tə:p-/ 'to be hot'	tə:p + ki (nominalizer) --> tə:pk'i ~ *tɛ:pk'i (*tɛpk'i)	tə:p + hi (passive morpheme) + ta (ending marker) ---> təpʰita ~ tɛpʰita

The nominalizer /ki/ normally triggers harmony. However, if the root contains a long vowel, as in the *Disharmony* column, the word (i.e., the root plus nominalizer /ki/) does not undergo harmony. Second, adding both the causative morpheme /ki/ or passive morpheme /hi/ and the ending marker /ta/ to the same root, as in the *Harmony* column, changes the long vowel to a short vowel. Therefore, with the long vowel eliminated, there is nothing preventing the blocking of harmony. The only difference between the *Disharmony* and *Harmony* columns is the length of the vowel in the word, even though it is the same root. In the same way, all other words which have long vowels do not undergo the harmony. As a consequence, I suggest that long vowels are disharmonic for the harmony.

3.3. Disharmony by intervening coronal consonant

As the literature on Korean phonology has noted, coronal consonants between an anchor and a sponsor block the harmony just as geminates do. This is shown in (13) and (14).

(13) Disharmony by palatal consonants
a) mačita	~	*mɛčita	'to finish'
b) tačita	~	*tɛčita	'to be injured'
c) tocita	~	*tɛcita	'worsening of an illness'
d) hucita	~	*hicita	'to be old-fashioned'
e) pʰəcita	~	*pʰɛcita	'to spread out'

(data (c) - (e) from Hume (1990: 232))

---

[2]Causative morpheme 'ki' is tensified in the output by menas of so-called 'tensification' (see Cheun (1985), Choi (1991), Han (1992), Shin (1995b)).

(14) Disharmony by alveolar consonants[3]

a) masita	~	*mɛsita	'to drink'
b) k'asi	~	*k'ɛsi	'thorn'
c) kasita	~	*kɛsita	'to go' (honorific)
d) kasina	~	*kɛsina	'girl' (slang)

(15) Disharmony by nasals[4]

a) əməni	~	*əmɛni	'mother'
b) cuməni	~	*cumɛni	'pocket'
c) halməni	~	*halmɛni	'grandmother'
d) maŋnani	~	*maŋnɛni	'rogue'
e) acuməni	~	*acumɛni	'aunt'
f) əkɨmni	~	*əkɨmni	'back tooth'

Thus, as is expected, in (13), intervening palatal consonants block the harmony, and in (14) and (15), alveolar obstruents and nasals, respectively, also block the harmony.

3.4. Prefixes and suffixes

In Kyungsang Korean, the front vowel /i/ in prefixes is not harmonic in frontness. The front vowel /i/ in suffixes, however, does trigger the harmony. This means that prefixes are not in the domain of the harmony, while suffixes are. Compare the examples in (16) and (17).

(16) Sequence of a prefix and a root

a) **kalaŋ** + ip	~	*kalɛŋip	'leaf'
b) **kalaŋ** + pi	~	*kalɛŋpi	'drizzle'
c) čam + kilɨm	~	*čemkilɨm	'sesame oil'

(17) Root word having a sequence of /a/ and /i/

kalaŋi	~	kalɛŋi	'crotch'

---

[3]As many examples in the previous sections show, I assume that the lateral /l/ in Kyungsang Korean is not specified for coronal, following Shin (1994).

[4]Among most Korean verb and noun roots (approximately sixty) that end in -ni according to the *A Reverse Dictionary of Modern Korean*, I could not find any word which undergoes umlaut. Only one word, *tani-* 'walk around', is considered as harmonic (Lee 1993, for Seoul Korean), but as a native speaker of Kyungsang Korean, I do not think the word undergoes umlaut in Kyungsang Korean.

In (17), while /a/ in *kalaɲi* harmonizes with the following vowel /i/, *kalaŋ-* in (16a) and (16b) does not since in (16a) and (16b) *kalaŋ-* is a prefix, whereas in (17) *kalaɲi* consists of one root. However, as mentioned above, the front harmony applies within a suffix as in (18).

(18) Sequence of a root and a suffix

a) sikol-t'ɨki	~	sikol-t'iki	'rural area'	+	'person'
			'a country bumpkin'		
b) səul-naki	~	səul-nɛki	'Seoul'	+	'origin'
			'person who was born in Seoul'		
c) ap-capi	~	ap-cɛpi	'front'	+	'holder'
			'a guide'		
d) tol-təŋi	~	tol-tɛŋi	'stone'	+	'lump'
			'rock'		
e) kal-capi	~	kal-cɛpi	'knife'	+	'holder'
			'a warrior'		
f) kəcitmal-caŋi	~	kəcitmal-cɛŋi	'lie'	+	'person'
			'liar'		

In (18), the second element of each word is a suffix, and therefore the nonfront vowels in the suffix are harmonized with the following front vowel /i/. This harmony by a suffix and this disharmony by a prefix provides evidence that suffixes are in the domain of the harmony, while prefixes are not. Therefore, there is no difference between a root and a suffix regarding front vowel harmony since they share the same domain.

3.5. Opaqueness of front mid vowel /ɛ/

Contrary to the front vowel /i/, the front mid vowel /ɛ/ does not trigger harmony and is opaque as is shown in (19).

(19) Opaqueness of front vowel /ɛ/

a) kalmɛki	~	*kɛlmɛki	'sea gull'
b) caktɛki	~	*cɛktɛki	'rod'
c) maktɛki	~	*mɛktɛki	'stick'
d) t'ɨnɛki	~	*t'inɛki	'wanderer'

As will be shown later, this opaqueness results from the domain of the harmony.

3.6. Summary of Kyungsang Korean optional front harmony

From the above description of Korean front harmony, the following generalizations can be summarized.

> i) The active harmonic feature of Korean front harmony is
> [+front], and vowels are underlyingly specified for the feature.
> ii) Only the syllable that immediately precedes the front high
> vowel is harmonic, thereby limiting the domain of harmony.
> iii) Umlaut cannot occur between different roots nor between a
> prefix and a root.
> iv) Geminates between an anchor and a sponsor block the
> harmony.
> v) Long vowels do not undergo the harmony.
> vi) Coronal consonants between an anchor and a sponsor block
> the harmony.
> vii) The front mid vowel /ɛ/ is opaque for the harmony.

In the following sections, we will see how these characteristics of Korean front harmony can be analyzed within ODT[5].

4. Kyungsang Korean front harmony and relevant constraints within ODT

Based on ODT described earlier, let us now examine Kyungsang Korean front harmony. An ODT analysis must consider the following four properties of the harmony: range of the domain, strength of the domain (if it is applicable), strength of an anchor (if it is applicable), and opaqueness or transparency in the domain. In this section, these four properties of Kyungsang Korean harmony and the relevant constraints will be discussed.

---

[5]With respect to the Korean front harmony, there are many words which do not undergo harmony even though they are properly conditioned for the harmony. Shin (1995a) suggests that there are two types of /i/s in Kyungsang Korean: (1) a coronal, [+front] which triggers umlaut and (2) a dorsal, [-back] which does not trigger umlaut. This assumption is supported by several phonological processes such as /k/-palatalization, ideophone vowel harmony and vowel coalescence. However, the possibility that Kyungsang Korean has two types of /i/s is a matter that require further investigation.

4.1. Disharmony by means of geminates and long vowels

In section 3, it was shown that front harmony applies only to the syllable that immediately precedes the sponsor. Therefore, in ODT, the two syllables that undergo the harmony form the strong domain of the harmony. However, the fact that geminates and long vowels in the strong domain block the harmony requires us to limit the harmonic domain. That is, the lack of the harmony here results from the fact that geminates and long vowels have different moraic status from that of a single segment and of a short vowel, respectively. As a consequence, it is plausible that the front harmony has a bimoraic foot as its strong harmonic domain as shown in Figure 1.

Figure 1. Harmonic domain for *aki* 'baby'

This bimoraic harmony domain seems to account for the blocking effect of both geminates and long vowels. That is, syllables with geminates and long vowels do not satisfy the bimoraic foot, thus being disharmonic for the harmony. According to previous discussion, when a sponsor is a long vowel (that is, /i:/), the syllable immediately preceding the long vowel should not undergo harmony. This is because the long vowel already has two moras and thus the vowel consists of a bimoraic foot on its own. However, (20) shows that this is a wrong prediction and requires us to reconsider the domain.

(20) Front vowel harmony by a long vowel
    a) /cap-/   'to catch'
        i) /cap + hi:+ ta/   cap^{h}i:ta ~ cɛp^{h}i:ta 'to be caught'
    b) /mək-/   'to eat'
        i) /mək + hi: + ta/   mək^{h}i:ta ~ mɛk^{h}i:ta 'to be eaten'
    (/hi:/ is a passive marker and /ta/ is an ending marker.)

As in (20), when the bimoraic foot is the strong domain of the harmony, a discrepancy arises in that even when the sponsor is long, the preceding syllable undergoes the harmony. In order to account for all the relevant facts, I propose that the strong domain of the harmony be an IAMBIC FOOT, where the second element of the foot is either light or heavy, but the first element necessarily light, as shown in (21).

(21) Strong F-domain of the harmony: iambic foot
    a) $(\sigma_\mu \sigma_\mu)$ or $(\sigma_\mu \sigma_{\mu\mu})$
    b) $*(\sigma_{\mu\mu} \sigma_\mu)$

This — having a light first element — accounts for the disharmony by geminates and by long vowels. That is, geminates are generally considered moraic cross-linguistically (Hayes 1989), and thus the harmonic feature cannot be realized in a vowel that precedes the geminate since the domain of the harmony ends before the vowel. Futhermore, long vowels cannot be in the strong domain since an iambic foot requires a light syllable as its first element. Since the second element can be either light or heavy, a long vowel triggers vowel harmony. In sum, the strong domain for the front harmony in Kyungsang Korean can be described under the framework of ODT as in (22).

(22) WSA$^+$-left
    Align(F-domain$^+$,L, Iambic foot, L)
    : The leftmost edge of the strong F-domain should align with the
      leftmost edge of an iambic foot.

The constraint in (22) means that the F-domain extends leftwards from the sponsor until the domain becomes an iambic foot. Also, vowels in the strong domain (in the iambic foot) must undergo harmony by means of Expression described in section 2.

Regarding the disharmony by long vowels and by geminates, we still need another constraint which blocks the harmonic feature on the second mora of a long vowel. As a consequence, I propose that there is another constraint that prevents the harmonic feature from being realized on only one mora of a bimoraic segment.

(23) LONGV-FT
    Moras of a long vowel must be in the same foot.

The constraint in (23) means that moras of a single segment should be placed in the same foot. That is, the strong domain, which refers to an iambic foot, cannot have only one mora of a bimoraic single segment as the initial element of the foot. This is illustrated in Figure 2.

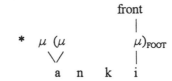

Figure 2. Disharmony by long vowels

In Figure 2, the foot boundary intervenes between the two moras of the long vowel, thereby violating the constraint.

These two constraints, however, do not address all possibilities. Specifically, with no further constraints, the harmonic feature can still be realized on the mora of a geminate. In order to rule out this improbable harmony, I propose a constraint 'NoHarmonicC', given in (24).

(24) NoHarmonicC
A harmonic feature from a vowel cannot be realized on a consonant.

Since F-realization is a constraint on an anchor in a domain, Express$^+$ can also account for the disharmony if Express$^+$ limits the harmonic feature to be realized only on strong anchors, which are vowels. However, in this paper, I used NoHarmonicC instead of limiting the Express [F] constraint since in harmony, it is very natural that an active harmonic feature be realized only on vowels. Thus, it would be somewhat awkward to divide the anchors into two groups, consonants and vowels. This is illustrated in Figure 3.

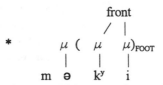

Figure 3. Disharmony by geminates

In Figure 3, the harmonic feature from a vowel is realized on a consonant and results in a wrong output. It shows that even if the harmonic feature is realized in a domain, it must be ruled out if it violates NoHarmonicC.

Of interest here is that a long vowel in a verb root can still be harmonic in frontness when it underparses one mora and becomes a weak anchor.

Figure 4. Front Harmony within a domain

In Figure 4, one mora was eliminated from the underlying bimoraic vowel /a/, thus satisfying the template so that the harmonic feature is realized on the vowel.

4.2. Disharmony by means of intervening coronals

In the traditional account, the blocking of front harmony by coronal consonants can be accounted for in terms of the so-called No Crossing Line Constraint since the trigger of the umlaut is a front vowel, and front vowels are coronal. This constraint will be adopted here.

(25) NoCrossingLine
Association lines cannot be crossed.

4.3. Behaviour of affixes in harmony

In section 3.5, it was shown that prefixes are not harmonic in frontness even though suffixes are, and also that /i/s in the suffixes trigger the harmony. In order to account for this asymmetry, I assume that prefixes behave as if they are in their own prosodic domain, unlike suffixes, following Kang (1992), rather than positing a new constraint. That is, prefixation is a type of compounding process phonologically so that the harmonic feature cannot be realized on a prefix and thus does not appear in the domain of harmony.

5. Constraint interaction

In section 4, I proposed some constraints, which account for both harmony and disharmony with respect to Korean front harmony. The ranking of the constraints proposed so far is given in (26).

(26) Ranking of relevant constraints
BA-right, NoHarmonicC, LongV-Ft, NoCrossingLine >> Express [+front], WSA+-left >> *Insert [front] >> BA-left

The table in (27) examines front harmony by means of the constraint ranking. Constraints are arranged in the tables from left to right in order of domination.

(27) Korean front vowel harmony (umlaut)

Input: holulak + i   'whistling sound' + nominalizer 'whistle'

|
front

Candidates	BA-right LongV-Ft NoCrossingL NoHarmonicC	Express WSA⁺-left	*Insert	BA-left
a. h o l u (l a k i) μ μ (μ μ)_FT | front		*! Express		*
b. h o l u l a (k i) μ μ μ (μ)_FT | front		*! WSA⁺- left		
c. (h ɛ l i l a k i) (μ μ μ μ)_FT \ \ | front		*!** Express WSA⁺- left	**	***
d. h o (l i l ɛ k i) μ (μ μ μ)_FT \ \ | front		*! WSA⁺- left	**	**
e. h o l u (l a k i) μ μ (μ μ)_FT | front		*! Express		*
f. ☞ h o l u (l ɛ k i) μ μ (μ μ)_FT \ | front			*	*
g. h o (l u l ɛ k i) μ (μ μ μ)_FT \\| front		*!* Express WSA⁺- left	*	**

In the table, candidates (a), (c), (e) and (g) are ruled out since the harmonic feature is not realized on a mora within a domain. Candidates (b) and (d) are also ruled out since the harmonic domain is not an iambic foot. Again, the so-called GAPPED CONFIGURATION, candidate (c) is ruled out by Expression.

As mentioned in section 2, the constraint WSA-left is different from WSA⁺-left in that it has an entire prosodic word as the domain of harmony, thus having the same effect as Align-L and Align-R by Pulleyblank (1993, 1994) and Akinlabi (1994a, b, c), while WSA⁺-left has a limited domain of harmony. If BA-left in a language is higher than WSA⁺-left there would not be evidence for a harmonic domain on the left side of the trigger since BA-left is an alignment constraint which aligns the leftmost edge of an anchor with the leftmost edge of an F-domain.

(28) and (29) illustrate how geminates block the harmony and how long vowels are disharmonic with respect to frontness.

(28) Blocking effect by geminates

Input: mək + ki   'to eat' + nominalizer
|
front

Candidates	NoHarmonicC	Express WSA⁺-left	*Insert	BA-left
a. (m ɛ k i) (μ μ μ)FT \ | front		**! Express WSA⁺-left	*	**
b. m ə (kʸ i) μ (μ μ)FT \ | front	*! NoHarmonicC		*	*
c. (m ɛ kʸ i) (μ μ μ)FT \ \ | front	*! NoHarmonicC	* WSA⁺-left	**	**
d. ☞ m ə (k i) μ(μ μ)FT | front		*		*

Even though candidate (b) has correct strong F-domain and feature realization, it cannot be optimal since the harmonic feature is realized on the mora of a geminate, rather than on the mora of a vowel, thereby violating NoHarmonicC, the highest constraint. Candidate (c) is similarly ruled out by the constraint NoHarmonicC. Candidate (a) is ruled out since it violates WSA⁺-left, and the optimal output is therefore (d). The table also provides evidence that Express cannot be undominated.

(29) Disharmony by long vowels

  Input: a n + ki 'to hug' + nominalizer
     |
    front

Candidates	LONGV-FT	Express WSA⁺-left	*Insert	BA-left

a. (a n k i)
 μ(μ μ)_FT
    |
   front
	*!	*
		Express
				*

b. (ɛ n k i)
 (μμ μ)_FT
  ∨ |
   \ |
   front
		*
		WSA⁺-left
			*!	**

c. (a n k i)
 (μμ μ)_FT
    |
   front
		**!*
		Express
		(**)
		WSA⁺-left
		(*)
				**

d.☞ a n (k i)
 μμ (μ)_FT
    |
   front
		*
		WSA⁺-left		

As mentioned previously, a long vowel is disharmonic since it has two moras, which conflicts the WSA⁺-left requirement of an iambic foot, while LONGV-FT requires both moras of a long vowel to be placed in the same foot. Consequently, in (29), candidate (a) violates LONGV-FT since the two moras of a long vowels are split by a foot, and candidates (b) and (c) are also ruled out in terms of WSA⁺-left since the foot is not iambic. Thus, candidate (d) is the optimal output.

6. Disharmony in other types of Korean morphemes

Similar to what Itô and Mester mention (1995a, b) in describing Japanese grammar, the Korean lexicon also has four different morpheme classes: native Korean (Hankeul), Sino-Korean, ideophones and loanwords. Unlike native Korean, Sino-Korean, ideophones and loanwords have different phonological properties as shown in Table 1, and not surprisingly, they do not undergo umlaut. For the three classes which do not undergo harmony, I propose that the constraint BA-left outranks all other alignment constraints as shown in Table 2.

Hankeul	Sino-Korean	Ideophones	Loanwords
Umlaut	*	*	*
Palatalization	Palatalization	*	*
Verbal Morphology	Verbal Morphology	Vowel Harmony	*
-Vowel Harmony	- Vowel Harmony		
Vowel Merger	*	*	*

Table 1. Phonological phenomena found in four different morpheme classes

Ranking	Outcome	Korean Classes
BA-left >> WSA⁺-left	CVCi | front ☞ CV(Ci) | front	Sino-Korean Loanword Ideophone
Express, WSA⁺-left >> *Insert >> BA-left	CVCi | front ☞ (CVCi) \\ | front	Hankeul

Table 2. Constraint ranking for four different morpheme classes

7. Summary

In this paper, I offered an analysis of umlaut in Kyungsang Korean using a domain-based approach to harmony, which also accounted for instances of disharmony. This analysis has led to three principle characteristics of umlaut. First, I suggested an alternative explanation for umlaut in Kyungsang Korean: that is, umlaut is a result of the interaction of domain-based alignment constraints. More specifically, I proposed that the harmonic domain and the feature realization are determined by the interaction of alignment constraints with Faithfulness constraints. Second, I posited that the iambic foot, a strong F-domain for umlaut, accounts for both harmony and disharmony, depending on the position and the moraic status of the anchor. And third, for Sino-Korean, Ideophones and Loanwords, I proposed that BA-left outranks all other alignment constraints, and hence none of these morpheme classes undergo umlaut.

References

Akinlabi Akinbiyi. 1994a. Featural Alignment, Unpublished ms., Rutgers University, New Brunswick.

Akinlabi Akinbiyi. 1994b. Alignment Constraints in ATR Harmony. To appear in *Studies in the Linguistic Sciences*. 24.

Akinlabi Akinbiyi. 1994c. Kalabari Vowel Harmony. Unpublished ms., Rutgers University, New Brunswick.

Cheun, Sang-Buom. 1985. Tensification Phenomena in Modern Korean. *Korean Journal*. 33-40.

Cole, Jennifer and Charles Kisseberth. 1994a. An Optimal Domains Theory of Harmony. To appear in *Studies in the Linguistic Sciences* 24.2.

Cole, Jennifer and Charles Kisseberth. 1994b. Paradoxical Strength Conditions in Harmony Systems. To appear in the proceedings of *NELS* 25.

Cole, Jennifer and Charles Kisseberth. 1994c. Nasal Harmony in Optimal Domains Theory. To appear in the proceedings of *WECOL* 1994.

Davis Stuart and Jin-Seong Lee. 1994. Infixal Reduplication in Korean Ideophones. *Japanese/Korean Linguistics* IV. 447-461

Han, Jeong-Im. 1992. On the Korean Tensed Consonants and Tensification. *CLS* 28.1. 206-223.

Hayes, Bruce. 1989. Compensatory Lengthening in Moraic Phonology. *Linguistic Inquiry*. 20. 253-306.

Hume, Elizabeth. 1990. Front Vowels, Palatal Consonants and the rule of Umlaut in Korean. *NELS* 20. 230-243, Amherst: GLSA,University of Massachussets, Amherst, Massachussetts.

Itô, Junko and Armin Mester. 1995a. The Core-Periphery Structure of the Lexicon and Constraints on Reranking. In Jill Beckman, Suzanne Urbanczyk, and Laura Walsh eds., *UMOP* 18: Papers in Optimality Theory. 181-209. Amherst, Messachusetts: Graduate Linguistic Student Association

Itô, Junko and Armin Mester. 1995b. Japanese Phonology. In J. Goldsmith eds., *The Handbook of Phonological Theory*. 817-838.

Kang, Ongmi. 1992. Prosodic Word-Level Rules in Korean. *Harvard Studies in Korean Linguistics* V. 147-163.

Kirchner, Robert. 1993. Turkish Vowel Harmony and Disharmony: An Optimality Theoretic Account. (paper presented at Rutgers Optimality Workshop I, Oct 22-24, 1993).

Lee, Yongsung. 1993. *Topics in the Vowel Phonology of Korean.* Doctoral dissertation. Indiana University, Bloomington, Indiana.

McCarthy, John and Alan Prince. 1993a. Prosodic Morphology: Constraint Interaction and Satisfaction. Unpublished ms., University of Massachusetts, Amherst, and Rutgers University, New Brunswick.

McCarthy, J. and Alan Prince. 1993b. Generalized Alingment. In Geert Booij and Jaap van Marle eds., *Yearbook of Morphology.* 79-153, Dordrecht: Kluwer.

Prince Alan and Paul Smolensky. 1993. Optimality Theory: Constraint Interaction in Generative Grammar. Unpublished ms., Rutgers University, New Brunswick, and University of Cororado, Boulder.

Pulleyblank, Douglas. 1993. Vowel Harmony and Optimality Theory. To appear in the *Proceedings of the Workshop on Phonology.* University of Coinbra, Portugal.

Pulleyblank, Douglas. 1994. Neutral Vowels in Optimal Theory: A Comparison of Yoruba and Wolof. Unpublished ms., University of British Columbia.

Shin, Seung-Hoon. 1994. Location of the Feature [Lateral] in Feature Geometry. Unpublished ms., Indiana University, Bloomington, Indiana.

Shin, Seung-Hoon. 1995a. Two Types of /i/s in Kyungsang Korean. Unpublished ms., Indiana University, Bloomington, Indiana.

Shin, Seung-Hoon. 1995b. The Status of Tensed Consonants in Korean; Based on the Duration of the Consonant Closure. Unpublished ms., Indiana University, Bloomington, Indiana.

Generalized Alignment and Prosodic Subcategorization in Korean*

HYUNSOOK KANG AND BORIM LEE
Hanyang University and Wonkwang University

0. Introduction

It has been convincingly argued that morphological and phonological constituents are not necessarily isomorphic and that some phonological rules are sensitive to phonological constituents, not morphological constituents (Nespor and Vogel 1986, Selkirk 1988, Inkelas 1989, etc.). Some Korean phonologists like Ongmi Kang (1993) have also argued for prosodic constituents in Korean to explain neutralization in a coda position.

In this paper, we will argue that prosodic constituents which are different from morphological ones are necessary for Sino-Korean words. We will show that the phonetic realizations of Sino-Korean morphemes with an initial [l] depend on their positions in a prosodic constituent. Based on phonological evidence, we will argue that prosodic affixes as well as prosodic stems are necessary in Sino-Korean words. This paper is organized as follows: Section 1 shows the traditional explanation for [l]-[r]-[n] alternation. Section 2 shows some recent analyses which introduce prosodic constituents. We will address some problems with these analyses. In section 3 we suggest a new analysis using prosodic constituents.

* We thank Ki-Jeong Lee, Jong-Shil Kim, Hyung-Yeob Kim, and Youngsoon Kang for their help. Needless to say, all errors are our own.

1. [l]-[r]-[n] Alternation

Sino-Korean morphemes with an initial [l] show the following alternations in (1).

(1)

a. ko-lak	[korak]	'pain and pleasure'
b. lak-wə n	[nakwə n]	'paradise'
c. kɨk-lak	[kɨŋnak]	'heaven'
d. pal-tal	[palt'al]	'development'
e. an-lak	[allak]	'comfortableness'
f. thal-lak	[thallak]	'dropout'

In (1a) [l] in /-lak/ is pronounced as [r] in an intervocalic position. If an [l] appears either at the beginning of a word as in (1b) or after a consonant other than [n] as in (1c), [l] changes into [n]. In (1d), /l/ appears as [l] in a syllable final position. In addition, when [l] is adjacent to another morpheme ending in [l] or [n], a geminate [l] surfaces as in (1e, f).

The surface form of an underlying /l/, then, can be determined depending on its position in a word as in (2).

(2) /l/-alternation rules (cf. K-H Kim)
a. /l/ ---> [r] / V ____ V
b. /l/ ---> [n] / \$ ____ (or) {#____, C____}
c. /l/ ---> [l] / elsewhere

The non-alternating syllable initial /l/ in (1e,f) can be explained by [n]-lateralization rule given in (3a) (cf. K-H Kim) and the OCP triggered merger in (3b).

(3)
a. [n]-lateralization (stem level)

```
% C   C         C C
   |   |         ≠\ /
   n   l ---->   n l
```

b. The OCP triggered merger

```
  C   C         C C
  |   |          \ /
  l   l ----->    l
```

A sample derivation for (1e) is given in (4).

(4)
a. U.R.   an-lak
b. /n/-lateralization (3a)   allak
c. /l/-alternation (2c)   allak
d. S.R.   allak

In (4c) [l] does not undergo rule (2b) because of the inalterability of a geminate consonant. (cf. linking constraints in Hayes 1986).

The alternation of /l/-/r/-/n/, however, is more complicated than it appears in (1). Consider a Sino-Korean morpheme /lo/. It surfaces as expected in (5a-c). However, it does not surface as expected in (5d).

(5)
a. to-lo   [toro]   'street'
b. lo-sən   [nosən]   'line'
c. sən-lo   [səllo]   'railroad track'
d. sin-mun-lo   [sinmunno]   'sinmun street'
e. kyo-cha-lo   [kyocharo]   'crossing street'

In (6) we have shown the expected, but incorrect derivation for (5d).

(6)
a. U.R.   sin-mun-lo
b. n-lateralization (3)   sin-mul-lo
c. /L/-alternation (2c)   sin-mul-lo
d. S.R.   *sinmullo

Some other examples which show similar surface forms to those in (5) are given in (7). /-lyo/ is a Sino-Korean morpheme which means 'substance'.

(7) -lyo 'substance'
a. cæ - lyo   [cæryo]   'material'
b. wən-lyo   [wəllyo]   'raw material'
c. hyaŋ-sin-lyo   [hyaŋsinnyo]   'spice-adding condiment'
d. co-mi-lyo   [comiryo]   'condiment'

Again, in (7c) [n]-lateralization does not take place although [n] and [l] are juxtaposed. In (8) we have shown again the expected but incorrect derivation.

(8)
a. U.R.   hyaŋ-sin-lyo
b. /n/-lateralization (3)   hyaŋ-sil-lyo
c. /l/-alternation (2c)   -------
S.R.   *hyaŋsillyo

The unexpected surface forms in (5d, 7c), we argue, should be explained with their phonological structures which are different from their morphological structures.

Before we discuss the morphological and phonological structures of Sino-Korean words in detail, we should be acquainted with some basic characteristics of Sino-Korean morphemes. Many linguists (cf. Han 1994) have noted that Sino-Korean morphemes are not stems themselves. Only when a Sino-Korean morpheme is concatenated with another Sino-Korean morpheme, can it become a stem. In addition, another Sino-Korean morpheme can be also added to stems consisted of more than two roots. Examples are given in (9).

(9) roots: /san/, /bon/, /doŋ/, /lo/
a. san-bon   'name of a place'
b. san-bon-dong   'San-Bon district'
c. san-gon-dong-lo   'A street of San-Bon district'

2. Previous Analyses

Kang Ongmi (1994) argues that different phonological structures should explain different surface froms of /l/-initial Sino-Korean morphemes. She argues that /sə n-lo/ and /shin-mun-ro/ should be prosodically structured as (10). In (10), $\underline{w}$ is a phonological word and $\emptyset$ is a phonological phrase.

(10) $_w$(sə n-lo)
          $\emptyset$($_w$(sin-mun) $_w$(lo))

That is, Kang Ongmi (1994) argues that a morphological stem should be analyzed as a phonological word and that when another Sino-Korean root is added to it, it becomes a phonological word by itself.

Relevant rules which should apply to (10) are given as (11) in Kang Ongmi (1994).

(11)
Within prosodic word boundary
a. /n/-lateralization
b. /l/-nasalization : /l/---> [n] / {$_w$(__), $_w$(...C__ ...)}

Some derivations are given in (12).

(12)
U.R.	sən-lo	sin-mun-lo
Prosodic Structuring	ᵥᵥ(sə n-lo)	ø(ᵥᵥ(sin-mun) ᵥᵥ(lo))
PW-domain		
n-lateralization	səl-lo	--------------
l-nasalization	------------	ø(ᵥᵥ(sin-mun) ᵥᵥ(no))
S.R.	səllo	sinmunno

Kang Ongmi's (1994) analysis seems to work with examples in (12). However, a problem occurs when /-lo/ appears after a vowel final base as in /kyo-cha-lo/ in (5e). Recall that Kang Ongmi (1994) assigns a prosodic word category to a Sino-Korean root if it is added to a phonological word as shown /sin-mun-lo/. The expected, but an incorrect surface form of /kyo-cha-lo/ is given in (13).

(13)
U.R.	kyo-cha-lo
Prosodic Structure	ø(ᵥᵥ(kyo-cha) ᵥᵥ(lo))
PW-domain	
/n/-lateralization	--------------
/l/-nasalization	ø(ᵥᵥ(kyo-cha) ᵥᵥ(no))
S.R.	*kyochano

Note that the problem comes from /l/-nasalization applying at the prosodic word level. However, as shown in (12), /l/-nasalization is necessary in prosodic word level to explain the surface form of /sin-mun-lo/.

While discussing the /n/-insertion rule in Korean, Han (1994) argues for the similar prosodic structures for the left-branching Sino-Korean words. Han (1994) uses a prosodic stem to refer to a prosodic word category in Kang Ongmi's analysis. Han (1994) argues that /sik-yoŋ-yu/ should be analysed as (14). In (14), s̱ refers to prosodic stem, and ṟ a root.

(14) [[sik-yoŋ] yu]

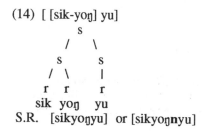

S.R.   [sikyoŋyu] or [sikyoŋnyu]

In (14) two roots, namely /sik/ and /yoŋ/, are combined and become a stem. When another root /yu/ is added to a stem /sik-yoŋ/, it becomes a stem first and then added to a stem /sik-yoŋ/ on its leftside, resulting in another stem.

The motivation for this structure is an /n/-insertion rule. Han (1994) argues that /n/ is inserted in the following environment. PS refers to a phonological stem and U refers to an utterance in (14).

(15) /n/-insertion (Han 1994)[1]
$\emptyset$ ---> n / [...[..C]$_{ps}$ ___ [i/y...]$_{ps}$..]U

Han (1994) argues that since /n/ is optionally inserted between /sikyoŋ/ and /yu/, both should be analyzed as prosodic stems. Han (1994) also argues that words with right branching structures should have different prosodic structures from those with left branching structures in (14) since they do not undergo n-insertion rule.

Consider a word in (16) with a right branching structure; /n/ is not inserted between /kyəŋ / and /yaŋsik/. If /kyəŋ-yaŋ-sik/ is prosodically structured as two prosodic stems, the following incorrect surface form would occur.

(16)
morphological structure	[kyəŋ [yaŋ-sik]]
prosodic structure	$_s$(kyəŋ) $_s$(yaŋsik)
n-insertion	$_s$(kyəŋ) **n** $_s$(yaŋsik)
S.R.	*kyəŋnyaŋsik

Han (1994) argues that words with right branching structures should be analyzed as root compounds as shown in (17). Since it is a root compound, /n/ cannot be inserted between /kyəŋ / and /yaŋsik/.

(17)

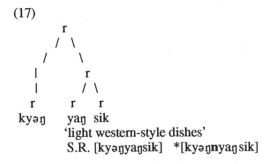

kyəŋ   yaŋ sik
'light western-style dishes'
S.R. [kyəŋyaŋsik] *[kyəŋnyaŋsik]

We agree with Kang Ongmi (1994) and Han (1994) in that prosodic structures are important in analyzing Sino-Korean words. We will argue, however, that different prosodic structures are necessary than those proposed

---

[1] Some examples which undergo /n/-insertion are as follows.
a. mæŋ-caŋ-yəm   [mæŋcaŋyəm] or [mæŋcaŋ nyəm]
b. hwi-bal-yu   [hwi-bal-yu] or [hwiballyu]

by Kang Ongmi (1994) and Han (1994) in order to explain the phonetic alternations of /l/-/r/-/n/ for /l/-initial Sino-Korean words.

3. A New Analysis

In this section, we will examine phonetic alternations of /l/-/r/-/n/ for /l/-initial Sino-Korean words in detail. First, let us reconsider the /l/-alternation rules given in (2). (2b) says that /l/ changes into /n/ word initially and postconsonantally. K-H Kim (1987) argues that these two environments can be collapsed into one as syllable initial. However, we would like to suggest that rules changing /l/ to /n/ in these two environments are different rules and therefore, cannot be collapsed into one. First, consider some loanwords recently borrowed from other languages.

(18)
a. ramyon   [ramyon]
b. radio   [radio]
c. lucky   [rəki]
d. Timely Cafe   [taimni kafe]
e. Comry   [komni]

In (18a-c), /r/ rather than expected /n/ by rule (2b) appears word-initially: the rule changing a non-nasal sonorant /l/ to /n/ in the word-initial position is violated. However, if /l/ appears after a consonant, as we see in a hypothetical English shop name in (18d), no exceptions to /l/-->/n/ arise. The surface realization of word initial /l/ is different from that of postconsonantal /l/ for loanwords in that exceptions are allowed only in word initial position.

Also consider North Korean dialect. Again, /l/ shows up as /n/ postconsonantally but not word initially.

(19)
a. /kyəŋ-lo/ [kyəŋ-no]   'respect for old people'
b. /lo-doŋ/ [ro-doŋ]   'labor'

If we argue that the rule which changes /l/ to /n/ in those two environments is one and the same rule, it would be difficult to explain why we get different surface forms in these two environments for loanwords and North Korean dialect. Therefore, we suggest that /l/ --> /n/ rule in the word-initial position is different from /l/-alternation rule in the postconsonantal position. Following Korean traditional grammarians, we suggest the word-initial /l/-->/n/ alternation rule in (20a). In addition, we provide another kind of Du-im Law which might become necessary in our discussion later. Another Du-im Law deletes /n/ before /i, y/ given in (20b). Some examples are given in (21).

(20) Du-im Law (Law of initial sounds)
a. /l/-nasalization
/l/---> /n/ / pw(___
b. n-deletion rule
n---> ø / pw(___ /i, y/

(21)
a. ca+nyə ----> canyə   'child'
b. nyə+ca ----> yəca   'woman'

    With Du-im Law (20) in hand, we may have a modified /l/-alternation
rules as in (22). We argue that /l/ alternation rules in (22) are post-lexical
level rules. Note that a segment which alternates between /l/-/r/-/n/ needs to
be specified only as a non-nasal sonorant underlyingly. We will represent
this archiphoneme as /L/ from now on.

(22) /L/-alternation rules
a. /L/ ---> [+nasal]   / C   C
                        |
                         ____

c. /L/ ---> [r] /   C
                 |
            σ[___
c. /L/ ---> [+lateral] / elsewhere

A sample derivation is given in (23).

(23)
U.R.	sən-lo
Prosodic Structuring	σ(sən-lo)
/n/-lateralization (3)	səl-lo
/L/-alternation (22a)	D.N.A. (by Inalterability)
(22b)	D.N.A. (by Inalterability)
(22c)	səllo
S.R.	səllo

    Now we are ready to tackle /l/-/r/-/n/ alternations. We have already
pointed out why we coule not take the phonological structure of
[w(sin-mun) w(lo)] and phonological rules (11) suggested by Kang Ongmi
(1994) (cf. 13). Rather, we argue that the phonological structure for /sin-
mun-lo/ should be as in (24) which is similar to the one suggested by Kang
Ongmi (1994) but the relevant phonological rules, namely [n]-lateralization
(2) and /L/-alternation rules (22) apply in different phonological structures:
[n]-lateralization (2) is a prosodic stem internal rule and /L/-alternation rules
(22) are post-lexical.

(24)

a. $_W$ ($_S$(sin-mun) $_S$(lo))

b.
```
            w
          /   \
        s       s
        |       |
       (r)      |
       / \      |
      r   r     |
      |   |     |
     sin mun   lo
```

(25)

Within prosodic stem boundary
    /n/-lateralization
Post lexically
    /L/-alternation rules (22)

The derivations are given in (26).

(26)

a. U.R.   sin-mun-lo

prosodic structure $_W$($_S$(sin-mun) $_S$(lo))

/n/-lateralization (stem level)   ------------

Du-im Law (word level)

      /L/--->/n/ / $_W$(___   ------------

/L/-alternation (post-lexical)

         /L/ --> /n/   sin-mun-no

         /L/--->/r/   ----------------

         /L/--->/l/   ----------------

S.R.   sinmunno

b. U.R.   kyo-cha-lo

Prosodic Structuring $_W$($_S$(kyo-cha) $_S$(lo))

n-lateralization (stem-level)   ------------

Du-im Law (word-level)

      /L/--->/n/ / $_W$(___   ------------

/L/-alternation

         /L/ --> /n/   ------------

         /L/--->/r/ $_W$($_S$(kyo-cha) $_S$(ro))

         /L/--->/l/   ------------

S.R.   kyo-cha-ro

c. U.R.   sən-lo

Prosodic Structuring $_s$(sə n-lo)

n-lateralization (stem level) $_s$(sə l-lo)

Du-im Law

         /L/--->/n/ / $_w$(___   -----------

/L/-alternation

                /L/ --> /n/   -----------

                /L/--->/r/   -----------

                /L/--->/l/ $_w$, $_s$(sə l-lo)

S.R.   səllo

The phonological structure in (24) is different from the morphological structure for the same word given in (27).

(27)

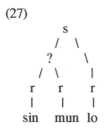

As we have said earlier, a Sino-Korean morpheme cannot be a stem by itself in Korean morphology. Therefore, /-lo/ cannot be assigned a morphological stem category. However, it is assigned a phonological stem categoty in (24). We suggest that the phonological structure (24) can be given by the following alignments within the Generalized Alignment Theory (McCarthy and Prince (1994) and the assumption that a root cannot be attached to a prosodic stem unless it becomes the same type of prosodic category.

(28)

a. align (morphological stem, right, prosodic stem, right)

b. align (morphological stem, left, prosodic stem, left)

c. align (prosodic stem, right, prosodic stem, left)

By assuming the prosodic structure in (24) and different phonological levels for phonological rules as in (25), the surface forms of /l/-initial Sino-Korean words are well explained. There are, however, other examples which seem to be problematic. Consider (29).

(29)   /-lo/: work

a. kin-lo   [killo]   'work'

b. lo-doŋ   [nodoŋ]   'labor'

c. kwa-lo   [kwaro]   'overwork'

d. mu-lo-doŋ   [mu-no-doŋ]   'no work'

The examples in (29 a,b, c) show that Du-im Law (20) and /L/-alternation rules (22) apply as expected. However, (29d) shows that something else is going on in this word. One thing to note is that /mu-no-doŋ/ has a right-branching morphological structure.

We have noted earlier that Han (1994) suggests the prosodic structure (17) for the right-branching Sino-Korean words because of /n/-insertion rule. We repeat (17) in (30) for convenience.

(30)

```
      r
     / \
    /   \
   |     r
   |    / \
   r   r   r
  kyəŋ  yaŋ sik
  [kyəŋyaŋsik]
```

Though the structure (28) may explain the non-application of /n/ insertion as Han (1994) argues, it cannot produce the right surface forms for /L/-initial Sino-Korean words as (31) shows.

(31)

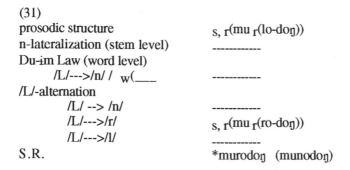

prosodic structure	₅, ᵣ(mu ᵣ(lo-doŋ))
n-lateralization (stem level)	-----------
Du-im Law (word level)	
/L/--->/n/ / w(___	-----------
/L/-alternation	
/L/ --> /n/	-----------
/L/--->/r/	₅, ᵣ(mu ᵣ(ro-doŋ))
/L/--->/l/	-----------
S.R.	*murodoŋ (munodoŋ)

In order to explain the phonological behavior of [munodoŋ] we suggest that some Sino-Korean morphemes like /mu-/ behave like prefixes which are subcategorized for prosodic word. We suggest the following prosodic structure for the words like (29d).

(32)
a. w(mu w,s(lo-doŋ))
b.

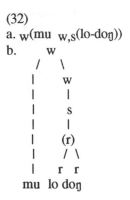

```
          w
        /   \
       |     w
       |     |
       |     s
       |     |
       |    (r)
       |    / \
       |   r   r
      mu  lo  doŋ
```

The generalized alignments necessary for /mu-/ is given in (33) followed by sample derivations in (34).

(33)
Align (/mu-/, right, prosodic word, left)

(34)
a. mu-lo-doŋ   'no work'
prosodic structure   w(mu w,s(lo-doŋ))
n-lateralization (stem level)   ------------
Du-im Law (word level)
    /L/--->/n/ / w(____   w(mu w,s(**no-doŋ**))
    /n/---> ø / w(__ i,y   ------------
/L/-alternation
    /L/ --> /n/   ------------
    /L/--->/r/   ------------
    /L/--->/l/   ------------
S.R.   munodoŋ

b. sə n-li-ca   'interest in advance'
prosodic structure   w(sə n w,s(li-ca))
n-lateralization   ------------
Du-im Law
    /L/--->/n/ / w(____   w(sə n w,s (**ni**-ca))
    /n/---> ø / w(__ i,y   w(sə n w,s(**i**-ca))
/L/-alternation
    /L/ --> /n/   ------------
    /L/--->/l/   ------------
    /L/--->/r/   ------------
S.R.   sə nica

However, not all bases with the right branching structures have the prosodic structures. Consider (35).

(35)
a. [so-[lip-ca]]   [soripca]   'elementary particle'[2]
b. [so-[lip-ca]]   [soipca]   'a small particle'[3]

/lip/ and /ca/ in (35a, b) are same morphemes. Two /so/s in (35a, b), even though pronounced same, are represented by distinct Chinese characters and have different meanings. Both words in (35), however, have the right branching morphological structures. Note that only (35b) undergoes Du-im Law even though both (35a) and (35b) have a constituent starting with /l/. We suggest that two /so-/s have different alignment structures given in (36). Prosodic structures for (33a, b) are given in (35a, b), respectively.

(36)
a. /so-/$_1$: particle
Align (/so/$_1$, right, root, left)
b. /so-/$_2$: small
Align (/so/$_2$, right, prosodic word, left)

(37) prosodic structures for (35),

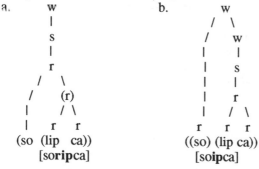

a.
```
      w
      |
      s
      |
      r
    /   \
   /    (r)
  |    /  \
  |   r    r
 (so (lip  ca))
    [soripca]
```
b.
```
      w
    /   \
   /     w
   |     |
   |     s
   |     |
   |     r
   |    /  \
   r   r    r
 ((so) (lip ca))
     [soipca]
```

---

[2] A few stems with similar characteristics of [soripca] are as follows.
a.   [su-ryu-than]]   'a hand grenade'
     cf. yu-than   'a howitzer shell'
b.   [a-nyə -ca]]   'children and women'; 'women'
     cf. yə -ca   'women'

[3] We have used this particular word to contrast it with (35a). One may not have this word in lexicon. In that case, generate a word with this meaning using the three Sino-Korean roots we used and see what is the surface form. Clear examples with the same structure as (35b) are already given in (34) so that even if one cannot generate [soipca] due to blocking should not refuse the following argument.

The derivations are given in (38).

(38)
a. [soripca]   'elementary particle'
prosodic structure $_{w,s}((so)(lip-ca))$
Du-im Law
    /L/--> /n/   ------------------
    n-deletion   ------------------
/L/-alternation $_{w,s}(so\ r(\textbf{rip}-ca))$
S.R.   so-rip-ca

b. [soipca]   'small particle'
prosodic structure $_w(so\ _{w,s}(lip-ca))$
Du-im Law
    /L/--> /n/ $_w(so\ _{w,s}(\textbf{nip}-ca))$
    n-deletion $_w(so\ _{w,s}(\textbf{ip}-ca))$
/L/-alternation   ---------------
S.R.   so-ip-ca

    When a word which is an exceptin to Du-im Law is concatenated with another word as in (39), two surface forms occur. If there is no pause between two words, /shin/ and /ramyə n/, it is pronounced as [shinnamyə n]. If there is a pause between two words, it is pronounced as [shin ramyə n].

(39)   sin + Lamyə n --> [si**nn**amyə n]
                           [sin ramyə n]

In (40), we have shown derivations.

(40)
a. sin + Lamyə n
Phonological structure $_w(_w(sin\ _w(Lamyə n))$
Du-im Law[4]   ----------
/L/-alternation rules
    /L/ --> /n/ $_w(_w(sin\ _w(namyə n))$
    /L/--->/r/   -----------
    /L/--->/l/   -----------
S.R.   sinnamyə n

---

    [4] Du-im Law does not apply since /Lamyə n/ is a recent loanword. (cf.19).

b. sin + Lamyə n

Phonological structure	$\emptyset_w$(sin) $\emptyset_w$(Lamyə n)
Du-im Law[5]	---------- (exception)
/L/-alternation rules	
/L/ --> /n/	-----------
/L/--->/r/	$\emptyset_w$(sin) $\emptyset_w$(ramyə n)
/L/--->/l/	-----------
S.R.	sin ramyə n

One more case we should consider in relation to /l/ alternations is given in (41).

(41) a. tal + nala [tallara] 'moon world'
   b. tol + noli   [tollori]   'playing with a stone'

As is shown in (39), when /n/-initial words are concatenated with /l/-final words, another /n/-lateralization applies, making an /l##n/ sequence a geminate /ll/. However, the lateralization across word boundary is not bidirectional as we have shown in (40). Across word boundary, only progressive lateralization applies. Therefore, any attempt to collapse the lateralization rules which apply in (41) and (2) is ill-fated. In Korean, we have to acknowledge two lateralization rules: The regressive lateralization applies only stem internally whose effect is shown only in Sino-Korean words. In native Korean words, the effect has already been realized and thus we cannot observe it. The progressive lateralization, on the other hand, is a phrase internal rule and applies whenever its environment is met.

4. Conclusion

In this paper, we have argued that prosodic constituents are indeed necessary in Korean phonology. With the introduction of phonological constituents, we can explain not only coda neutralization and /n/-insertion rule which are argued by some phonologist like Kang Ongmi (1994) and Han (1994) but also /l/-/r/-/n/ alternations for Sino-Korean words.

In particular, we have argued that there are not only prosodic stems but prosodic affixes which should be subcategorized for prosodic words in Korean. We have also argued that there are two /n/-lateralization rules in Korean; regressive lateralization applies only stem internally but progressive lateralization phrase internally.

---

[5] Du-im Law does not apply since /Lamyə n/ is a recent loanword. (cf.19).

References

Ahn, Sang-Cheol. 1985. The Interplay of Phonology and Morphology
in Korean. Doctoral dissertation, University of Illinois at
Urbana-Champagne.

Han, Eunjoo. 1994. Prosodic Structures in Compound, Doctoral
dissertation, Standford University.

Hayes, Bruce. 1986. Inalterability in CV phonology, Language 62. 321-
351.

Inkelas, Sharon 1989. Prosodic Constituency in Prosodic Phonology.
Doctoral dissertation, Stanford University.

Kang, Ongmi. 1993. Morphology and prosodic phonology in Korean,
Doctoral dissertation. University of Washington.

Kang, Ongmi. 1994. Prosodic Analysis for /l/-nasalization, /n/-deletion
and /n/-lateralization in Korean. Linguistic Journal of Korean 19.
1-26.

Kim, Jong-Shil. 1992 Word Formation, the Phonological Word, and
Word Level Phonology in Korean. Doctoral dissertation,
University of Texas, Ausin.

Kim, Kee-Ho. The Phonological Representation of Distinctive
Features: Korean Consonantal Phonology. Doctoral dissertation,
University of Iowa.

McCarthy, John and Alan Prince. 1993. Prosodic Morphology I:
Constraint Interaction and Satisfaction. To appear. Cambridge,
MA: MIT Press.

McCarthy, John and Alan Prince 1994. The emergence of the
unmarked: Optimality in Prosodic Morphology. In Merce
Gonzales, ed., NELS 24. Amherst, MA: Graduate Linguistic
Student Association. 333-379

Nespor, Marina and Irene Vogel. 1986. Prosodic phonology, Dordrecht:
Foris.

Selkirk, Elisabeth 1984. Phonology and Syntax: The Relation Between
Sound and Structure. Cambridge, MA: MIT Press.

Selkirk, Elisabeth and Tong Shen. 1988. Prosodic Domains in Shanghai
Chinese. Sharon Inkelas and Draga Zec, ed. The phonology-Syntax
Connection 1990. Chicago: University of Chicago Press

Aspiration in Korean Phonology

MIRA OH
Yeajoo Technical College, Korea

1. Introduction

Obstruents are aspirated whether they are preceded or followed by /h/ in Korean. There has been a dispute in the literature about Korean aspiration. First of all, it is not clear whether Korean aspiration consists of one rule or two rules. B. Lee (1976), C. Kim (1967), and Moon (1974) treat both progressive and regressive aspiration as one rule employing the mirror image rule convention. On the other hand, Kim-Renaud (1974) and S. Kim (1976) take progressive and regressive aspiration processes as two independent rules since they are ordered differently with respect to other phonological rules, e.g., syllable-final neutralization, within the linear phonological framework. As phonological theory develops in nonlinear fashion, K. Kim (1987) and Iverson and Kim-Renaud (1994) argue for one rule analysis making use of feature geometry. However, there is one difference between these two analyses. That difference has to do with the second issue in the literature: the directionality of aspiration. K. Kim (1987) argues that aspiration takes place bidirectionally depending on where /h/ is located with respect to the targeting obstruent. Laryngeal spreading occurs first in either direction and then supralaryngeal spreading takes place. In contrast, Iverson & Kim-Renaud (1994) contend that aspiration applies monodirectionally. Thirdly, aspiration has also been analyzed differently in terms of its nature: metathesis (Martin 1951), coalescence (S. Kim 1976), assimilation (Kim-Renaud 1974, K. Kim 1987, Iverson & Kim-Renaud 1994). Likewise, aspiration in Korean has drawn much attention from many phonologists but a satisfactory analysis has not been given so far.

In this study we explored these issues aiming at reviewing previous analyses and providing a more satisfactory analysis to aspiration. This paper argues for one rule analysis and the coalescence analysis of aspiration as opposed to assimilation. It also argues for the bidirectional analysis as opposed to the monodirectional one in order to account for the interaction between palatalization and aspiration.

2. Korean Aspiration

2.1. A Review of Previous Analyses on Aspiration

Previous analyses on aspiration are compared in (1).

(1)

Literature	Nature
Martin (1951)	Metathesis
Kim-Renaud (1974)	Assimilation (progressive) & Coalescence (regressive)
S. Kim (1976)	Coalescence
K. Kim (1987)	Assimilation
Iverson & Kim-Renaud (1994)	Assimilation

(continued)

Literature	Directionality	Long consonants
Martin (1951)	bidirectional	
Kim-Renaud (1974)	bidirectional	by assimilation
S. Kim (1976)	bidirectional	by insertion
K. Kim (1987)	bidirectional	by assimilation
Iverson & Kim-Renaud (1994)	monodirectional	by assimilation & emphatic lengthening

Martin (1951) accounts for aspiration as metathesis in structuralist accounts. Metathesized cluster is then equated with the class of phonemically aspirated stops. On the other hand, S. Kim (1976) takes the position of the coalescence analysis which merges the two input segments, /h/-plus-stop or stop-plus-/h/, into a single aspirated stop directly. Then aspiration is a laryngeal gesture inherent in the articulation of the stop itself. Aspiration is represented by a feature rather than a segment in this analysis. Under this account, a long stop like [kk^h] in [cokk^{h}ol] (< /coh ı ku/ 'good and') results from inserting a segment before the derived aspirated stop. In both analyses, aspiration is considered to be bidirectional in that only /h/, whether the feature or the whole segment, is combined with the adjacent obstruent to produce a single aspirated stop. Another analysis put forth by K. Kim (1987) and Iverson & Kim-Renaud (1994) is assimilation. Under that account, /h/-plus-stop and stop-plus-/h/ result in the bisegmental representation. However, there is one difference between these two analyses. K. Kim (1987) argues that aspiration apply bidirectionally depending on where the /h/ is located with respect to the targeting obstruent. Laryngeal spreading occurs first in either direction and then supralaryngeal spreading takes place. In a contrary opinion, Iverson & Kim-Renaud (1994) contend that aspiration spreads material specified in the left segment into positions underspecified in the right segment retaining the bisegmental structure of the input representation. In other words, aspiration applies monodirectionally, i.e., rightwards.

2.2. Iverson & Kim-Renaud's (1994) Analysis

Iverson & Kim-Renaud (1994) criticize the previous analyses on aspiration and propose the monodirectional assimilation analysis. Next, we will review Iverson & Kim-Renaud's analysis in detail before proposing an integrated analysis.

2.2.1. Monodirectional Analysis

Iverson & Kim-Renaud (1994) define aspiration as shown in (2).

(2) Aspiration adjustment: In a heterosyllabic cluster containing /h/ and a lax consonant, spread marked features from the coda to the onset.

Under their assimilation analysis, aspiration spreads material specified in the left segment into positions underspecified in the right segment. For example, the specified [spread glottis] feature of /h/ extends into the unmarked laryngeal node of a following /k/, as given in (3a), and the specified oral cavity features of /k/ spread into a following /h/, which is not marked for those features, as shown in (3b).

(3) (Iverson & Kim-Renaud 1994)

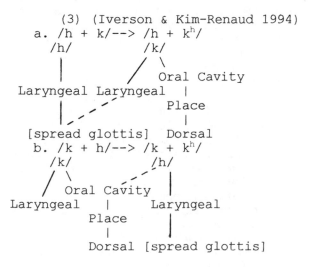

The /k/ acquires the aspiration in an /h + k/ sequence by spreading the [spread glottis] property rightwards as shown in (3a), while the /h/ acquires the oral properties of /k/ in a /k + h/ sequence as shown in (3b). That is to say, aspiration is taken to be the result of monodirectional, i.e., rightward, assimilation. For example, all the specified features and structures of the left segment illustrated in (4), spread into the underspecified portions of the right one.

(4) /coh/+/ko/   ---> /cohk^{h}o/ --->
  'good' 'and' aspiration   neut.
  [cokk^{h}o] --> [cotk^{h}o]--> [cok^{h}o]
     place assim. gem. reduction

The resulting bisegmental representation in (4) is then subject to independently motivated adjustments, including the obligatory neutralization of syllable-final /h/ to [t] in careful speech (/coh+k^{h}o/-->/cotk^{h}o/), the optional regressive assimilation of place of articulation in stop clusters (/cot+k^{h}o/--> /cok+k^{h}o/), and the stylistically governed optional simplification of long segments (/cokk^{h}o/--> [cok^{h}o]) in casual speech.

Iverson and Kim-Renaud (1994) argue that underlying sequences of either stop-plus-/h/ or /h/-plus-stop may surface with either long or short aspirated stops depending on the style of speech as illustrated in (5).

(5) Variation   Emphatic   Formal   Casual
 i. /ip+hak/   -->   [ipp^{h}ak]   [ip^{h}ak]
  'entering school'
   /cap+hi/   -->   [capp^{h}i]   [cap^{h}i]
  'catch' pass.
   /k'oc+hi/ -->   [k'otc^{h}i]   [k'oc^{h}i]
  'stick in' pass.
   /sok+hi/   -->   [sokk^{h}i]   [sok^{h}i]
  'quick' adv.
 ii. /coh+ko/   --> [cotk^{h}o] [cokk^{h}o]   [cok^{h}o]
  'good' 'and'
   /nah+ta/   --> [natt^{h}a] [nat^{h}a]
  'give birth' ind.

2.2.2. Weaknesses in Iverson & Kim-Renaud's Analysis

There are a few weaknesses in Iverson & Kim-Renaud's analysis. Firstly, the intervocalic stop gemination is derived from two separate processes

under their analysis. As for the two underlying
segments, aspiration assimilation, coda
neutralization and place assimilation apply as
illustrated in (4), while a single laryngeal
consonant is lengthened intervocalically: /ap'a/-->
[app'a] 'daddy'. Emphatic gemination is considered
to insert a homorganic stop before a laryngeal
consonant. Then the question arises as to if they
anyway take emphatic lengthening for a single
lexical laryngeal consonant, wouldn't it be possible
to account for stop gemination in terms of
coalescence followed by emphatic lengthening without
coda neutralization? The answer is 'no' for them.
The alternant of [cotk^{h}o] in (6a) cannot be accounted
for under the coalescence analysis. If the [h]
found in (6a) first coalesces with the /k/ to
produce [k^h], then /h/ would no longer be available
to be neutralized into [t].

(6) a. /coh+ko/-->cotk^{h}o->[cokk^{h}o]~[cok^{h}o],
        also [cotk^{h}o]
        /cap+hi/-->capp^{h}i-->[capp^{h}i]~[cap^{h}i],
        but not *[catp^{h}i]
    b. /ap'a/-->[ap'a] (base) ~ [app'a] (expressive),
       'daddy'   but not *[atp'a]

Although Iverson & Kim-Renaud claim that there
exists such an alternant as [cotk^{h}o] as in (6a),
informal phonetic study conducted by the author
suggests that the alternant does not exist even in
emphatic reading.

Furthermore, Iverson & Kim-Renaud's emphatic
gemination/gemination reduction analysis of speaking
style variation as shown in (5) predicts that bare
laryngeal consonants and geminate laryngeal
consonants are neutralized, but may be realized
either as geminates or as singletons depending on
speaking style. However, Johnson & Oh (1995) claim
that there is no evidence in favor of analyzing
speaking style variation in Korean using categorical
rules like emphatic gemination and geminate
reduction by demonstrating that the intervocalic
lexical laryngeal consonants remained geminate
regardless of speech rate.

Secondly, their analysis contains some
inconsistency in blocking aspiration between /s/
and sonorants. /coh+so/ surfaces as [coss'o] but not
*[cots^{h}o] due to the violation of Structure

Preservation. In other words, the aspirated /s^h/ is not phonemic in Korean. However, they extend the application of aspiration adjustment in (2) to the sequence of sonorant and /h/ as shown in (7).

(7) /an+ha+ko/->[an^{h}ago]~[ann^{h}ago]=[an̮n̮ago]~[an̮ago]
    'not' 'do' 'and'
    /maL + ha + ta/ -->[malhada]~[mall^{h}ada]=
    'language' 'do'   ind.   [mall̮ada]~[mar̮ada]

Although aspirated sonorants are not phonemic either, aspiration still applies to sonorants in their analysis. Then their analysis would predict *[sunom] for /suh+nom/ as shown in (8).

(8) /suh+nom/-->/suhn^{h}om/-->|sutn^{l}om]-->[sunn^{h}om]=
    'male animal'   *[sunn̮om]~*[sun̮om]

In order to get the correct output, i.e.,[sunnom], they apply neutralization before aspiration as shown in (9).

(9) /suh+nom/ --> /sut+nom/ > [sunnom]
              Neut.   Assim.

Notice that this extrinsic rule ordering which applies neutralization prior to aspiration is opposite to their rule application for obstruents: neutralization is preceded by aspiration as for obstruents as shown in (4). Likewise, although they extend aspiration adjustment to the sequence of sonorant and /h/, the sequences of /son+h/ and /h+son/ are not treated in the same way.

Thirdly, contrary to their extrinsic rule ordering between aspiration and neutralization, aspiration is not always preceded by neutralization: aspiration should apply cyclically to account for the output in (10).

(10)   /pu∂k^h ## hanke/ -->[pu∂k^{h}ange]
        'kitchen' 'one'

If aspiration involves the rightward spreading of the specified into the unspecified structure, aspiration cannot apply in the first place since /k^h/ as well as /h/ has a specified structure to begin with. Iverson & Kim-Renaud account for aspiration in terms of the linking constraint to exclude the case where the aspirated consonants also trigger aspiration: the only association the rule need refer to relative to this feature is the single line between the root element and the laryngeal node in /h/, not the multiple lines of association involved in the representation of an aspirated stop, e.g., /k^h/. To account for the example shown in (10), neutralization first applies in the word level and aspiration applies later. Therefore, aspiration applies cyclically.

Finally, the interaction between aspiration and palatalization testifies that their analysis is not working. T-palatalization in Korean is shown in (11).

(11) t-palatalization: (t,t^h--> c,c^h / ____{i,y})
/pat^h + i/ --> [pac^{h}i]
'field' nom.
cf. /titita/ --> [tidida]
'to tread on' *[cijida]

As shown in (11), /t/ is palatalized when followed by /i/ across a morpheme boundary. However, /t/ and /i/ in (12) are not adjacent to each other but palatalization still applies.

(12) /kut + hi + ta/-->[kuc^{h}ida] 'stabilize'
'hard' pass. ind.

Here, we assume that aspiration precedes palatalization. Otherwise, the palatalization rule itself has to specify that /h/ does not block palatalization as in (13).

(13) palatalization: C + (h)i--> C hi
[-back]

However, the rule in (13) does not explain why only /h/ is transparent to aspiration, while the least marked consonant /t/ is not, as shown in (14).

(14) /mut + ti/ --> [mutt'i] *[muc'i]
'bury' que. (retrospective)

If natural rule ordering is adopted, i.e., a rule applies whenever its structural description is met, the rule ordering between aspiration and palatalization naturally falls out. Whenever /h/ is adjacent to a stop, aspiration takes place. And then whenever coronal stops are adjacent to /i,j/ across a morpheme boundary, palatalization applies. Then what does the example in (12) mean? In Iverson & Kim-Renaud's (1994) view, /pat+hita/ becomes /pat tʰida/ via aspiration and it undergoes palatalization resulting in [pacʰida]. This account is in line with Iverson's (1989) Revised Alternation Condition account for Korean palatalization since the /tʰ/ is phonologically derived via aspiration. However, his original account is confined to one derived morphologically. In contrast, this way of account appears to be at odds with Oh's (1995) analysis on Korean palatalization, which argues that only the unsyllabified stem-final coronal stops undergo palatalization. The /tʰ/ after the application of aspiration in (12) occurs at the onset under Iverson & Kim-Renaud's analysis and is syllabified and would be no longer subject to palatalization contrary to the fact.

Let us examine the effects on aspiration of these two different approaches to palatalization Iverson & Kim-Renaud (1994) only accepts the monodirectional aspiration, rightward spreading. Then the /h + t/ and the /t + h/ sequences result in /h + tʰ/ and /t + tʰ/, respectively. Then the derived aspirated stops are predicted to undergo palatalization when adjacent to /i,y/ across a morpheme boundary since they are phonologically derived. However, the data in (15) shows that the derived aspirated stops behave differently with respect to palatalization. It depends on where the stop has been located in the first place as opposed to the location of the /h/.

> (15) a. /pat+hi+ta/-->pattʰita->[pacʰida] * [patʰida]
>   'be struck' asp.   pal.
>   b. /coh + ti/ --> cottʰi-->[cotʰi] * [cocʰi]
>   'good' que. asp.

The stop in the sequence of /t+h/ undergoes palatalization as well as aspiration. Bur when the stop is in the sequence of /h+t/, it undergoes aspiration excluding palatalization. This kind of asymmetry cannot be explained by Iverson & Kim-Renaud's account since they treat both /C + h/ and /h + C/ in the same way. Then how can it be resolved in our account? The next section will deal with this problem.

3. Aspiration as Bidirectional Coalescence

The main argument for taking progressive and regressive aspiration as two independent processes is derived from the ordering relationship of progressive and regressive aspiration with respect to h-unreleasing (Kim-Renaud's (1974) term). The data in (16) provides for the two process argument by Kim-Renaud (1974)[1].

(16) a. /suh + tweci/-->[sutt^{h}weji] 'male pig'
     h   t^h progressive
                  aspiration
       t   t^h h-unreleasing
   b. /suh + holaŋi/-->[sut^{h}oraŋi] 'male tiger'
     t   h-unreleasing
     t^h regressive
                  aspiration

Progressive aspiration precedes h-unreleasing, while regressive aspiration follows it in (16). However, given that aspiration is cyclic as shown in (10), aspiration fails to apply in (16b). The structural description of aspiration is not met but it applies after coda neutralization (h-unreleasing) in the prosodic word level.[2] Therefore progressive and regressive aspiration need not be independent of each other. Then aspiration in Korean is one process rather than two separate processes.

The next issue concerns the directionality of aspiration. This paper supports bidirectionality since it correctly accounts for the different behavior of derived aspirated consonants with respect to palatalization. The application of aspiration depends on where the /h/ is put in the

---

[1] Kim-Renaud (1974) takes progressive aspiration as assimilation but regressive aspiration as coalescence.

[2] Korean profixes, as opposed to suffixes, behave like phonologically independent words, and t-palatalization whose domain is a prosodic word does not apply in prefix-final /t/ before stem-initial /i,y/.
    /hot^h+ibul/-->[hodibul][honnibul]*[hoc^{h}ibul]
    ' single layer comforter'

first place as shown in (15). For explication, (15) is given in (17) again.

(17) a. /pat+hi+ta/-->patt^{h}ita->[pac^{h}ida]*[pat^{h}ida]
      'be struck' asp.   pal.
    b. /coh + ti/ -->cott^{h}i-->[cot^{h}i] *[coc^{h}i]
      'good' que. asp.

The asymmetry between the stops in the sequence of /t+h/ and the stop in the sequence of /h+t/ with respect to palatalization can be accounted for by bidirectional coalescence. Wherever /h/ is originally located, it coalesces with the adjacent stop to produce /t^h/. The direction matters in that case. If the stem-initial /h/ coalesces with the stem-final /t/, the derived aspirated consonant is put stem-finally, i.e., extraprosodic, and it undergoes palatalization as illustrated in (17a).If the stem-final /h/ coalesces with the stem-initial /t/, the derived aspirated consonant ends up in stem-initial position. It is no longer extraprosodic, and it cannot undergo palatalization as shown in (17b)

Another issue is concerned with the nature of aspiration. Iverson & Kim-Renaud (1994) argue for assimilation analysis, which retains the bisegmental skeletal structure of the input representations based on the data in (18).

(18) /coh+ko/-->cotk^{h}o-->[cokk^{h}o]~[cok^{h}o],also
      'good and'   [cotk^{h}o]
  cf. /cap + hi/-->capp^{h}i-->[capp^{h}i]~[cap^{h}i],
      'be caught'   but not*[catp^{h}i]

If the coalescence analysis which merges the two input segments into a single aspirated stop directly is taken, the alternant [cotk^{h}o] in (18) cannot be accounted for. The coalescence analysis would be at stake: As discussed earlier, if the /h/ coalesces with the /k/ to produce /k^h/ in /coh + ko/, then /h/ would no longer be available to be neutralized into [t]. However, as mentioned earlier, informal phonetic study conducted by the author indicates that such an alternant as [cotk^{h}o] is not possible even in emphatic reading. Thus the coalescence analysis is taken for Korean aspiration.

Then the final question arises as to how to derive both [cokkʰo] and [cokʰo] alternants from /coh+ko/. In Iverson & Kim-Renaud's (1994) view, two different processes are involved to derive geminates or long stops like the [kkʰ] in [cokkʰo] (</coh + ko/). One process for the two underlying segments consists of aspiration, coda neutralization and place assimilation as shown in (19a). The other process for a single lexical laryngeal segment involves emphatic lengthening as shown in (19b).

(19) a. two underlying segments
/coh+ko/-->[cotkʰo]-->[cokkʰo]~[cokʰo]
'good and'
/cap+hi/-->[cappʰi]-->[cappʰi]~[capʰi]
'be caught'
b. a single lexical segment
/ap'a/-->[ap'a](base)~[app'a](expressive)
'daddy'

Emphatic lengthening in (19b) can be said to insert a segment homorganic to the following stop. Given that the alternant like [cotkʰo] does not exist, as discussed above, the alternants with gemination in (19a) and (19b) can be accounted for in the same way. Johnson & Oh (1995) support that claim by showing that both aspirated and tensed consonants are lengthened intervocalically and there is little difference in emphatic lengthening between a single lexical laryngeal consonant and two underlying consonants intervocalically. Taking the coalescence analysis as opposed to assimilation for aspiration, and following Johnson & Oh's (1995) argument, we contend that the derived aspirated consonants as well as the underived aspirated consonants are geminated intervocalically. Then the lengthening effect of aspirated consonants are explained in the same way regardless of how they are derived.

4. Conclusion

We explored first how many processes are involved in aspiration. Next we explored the directionality of aspiration, and thirdly we explored the nature of aspiration. This paper argues for one bidirectional rule analysis based on the different behavior between the /t + h/ and /h + t/ sequences with respect to palatalization and aspiration. It also takes the coalescence analysis of aspiration as opposed to the assimilation since the alternant like [cotk^{h}o] (</coh + ko/) does not exist. The lengthened aspirated consonants in the intervocalic position are claimed to be the result of gemination based on Johnson & Oh's (1995) observation.

References

Iverson, Gregory. 1989. The Revised Alternation Condition in Lexical Phonology. Nordic Journal of Linguistics 10.151-64.

Iverson, Gregory & Youngkey Kim-Renaud. 1994. Phonological Incorporation of the Korean Glottal Approximant. Presented at the Ninth International Conference of Korean Linguistics.

Johnson, Keith & Mira Oh. 1995. Intervocalic Consonant Sequences in Korean. Working Papers in Linguistics 45.87-97.

Kim, Chinwu. 1967. Some Phonological Rules in Korean.munyenkwu (Phonological Study) 5.153-77.

Kim, Keeho. 1987. The Phonological Representation of Distinctive Features: Korean Consonantal Phonology. Doctoral dissertation, University of Iowa.

Kim-Renaud, Youngkey. 1974. Korean consonantal Phonology. Doctoral dissertation, University of Hawaii.

Kim, Sookon. 1976. Palatalization in Korean. Doctoral dissertation, University of Texas at Austin.

Lee, Byunggun. 1976. Hyen-tay Han-kwuk-e-uy Sayng-seng Um-wun-lon (Generative Phonology of Modern Korean). Seoul: Il-ci-sa.

Marin, Samuel. 1951. Korean Phonemics. Language 21.511-33.

Oh, Mira. 1995. A Prosodic Analysis of Non-Derived-Environment Blocking. Journal of East Asian Linguistics 4:4.

Part IV

Syntax

Future Based Account of Complementizer Deletion*

HIROTAKA MITOMO
Yokohama National University

0. Introduction

Some verbs in English allow their complement clauses to appear without a complementizer *that* as in (1).

(1)　a.　Ben knew [$_{S'}$ (**that**) the teacher was lying]
　　　b.　Louise announced [$_{S'}$ (**that**) she was angry **at** me]

However, if the embedded clause is in subject position or topicalized, the presence of *that* is obligatory as

*I would like to thank Christopher Tancredi for checking the English and giving grammaticality judgements, valuable comments and helpful suggestions. I would also like to thank Yoshio Endo, Yoshio Nakamura, Kunitoshi Takahashi, Miyuki Yamashina and Makiko Nakayama for helpful comments and suggestions. Remaining errors, of course, are all mine.

illustrated in (2) and (3) respectively.

(2)   a.   [$_{S'}$ *(That) the teacher was lying] was hardly obvious

        b.   [$_{S'}$ *(That) Louise was angry at me] came as no surprise

(3)   a.   [$_{S'}$ *(That) the teacher was lying]$_i$ Ben already knew [e]$_i$

        b.   [$_{S'}$ *(That) she was angry at me]$_i$ Louise forgot to mention [e]$_i$

Stowell (1981) proposes to account for the above contrast in terms of the Empty Category Principle (ECP) with respect to the empty element that may appear in the complementizer position of a tensed clause.

Similar phenomena are seen in certain dialects of Japanese. Saito (1986) observes that some verbs allow their S' complements to appear without an overt complementizer as in (4).

(4)   a.   John-ga   [$_{S'}$ pro Kobe-ni iku (te)]   yuuta
              John-NOM   Kobe-to go **(that)** said
              'John said that he was going to Kobe'

        b.   John-ga   [$_{S'}$ zibun-ga tensai-ya (te)]
              John-NOM   self-NOM genius-cop. COMP
              omooteru (koto)
              think   fact
              'John thinks that he is a genius'

Saito also observes that once the S' is scrambled, it can no longer appear without an overt complementizer as in (5).

(5)   a.   [$_{S'}$ pro Kobe-ni iku *(te)]$_i$ John-ga t$_i$ yuuta

        b.   [$_{S'}$ Zibun-ga tensai-ya *(te)]$_i$ John-ga t$_i$
             omooteru (koto)

In section 1, I review Stowell's analysis and pose a problem for the analysis. In section 2, I give an alternative account for the facts in English in terms of feature-checking. Finally in section 3, I extend this analysis to the above examples in Japanese.

1. Previous Analysis

Since Stowell (1981) argues that COMP is the head of S', the examples in (1a) and (2a) in the case where there is no overt complementizer are analyzed as follows.

(6) Ben $[_{V'}$ $[_V$ knew] $[_{S'}$ [e] the teacher was lying]]

(7) *$[_S$ $[_{S'}$ [e] the teacher was lying] $[_{I'}$ $[_I$ INFL-was$_i$] $[_{VP}$ t$_i$ hardly obvious]]]

His formulation of the ECP is given below.

(8) The Empty Category Principle:
    $[_\alpha$ e] must be PROPERLY GOVERNED

(9) Proper Government:
    α properly governs β if and only if
    (i) α GOVERNS β, and
    (ii) α is lexical, and
    (iii) α is co-indexed with β.

(10) Government:
    In the configuration $[_\gamma \ldots \beta \ldots \alpha \ldots \beta \ldots]$, α governs β, where
    (i) $\alpha = X^0$, and $\gamma = X^i$ (i.e. γ is an X-BAR PROJECTION of α), and
    (ii) for each MAXIMAL PROJECTION of δ, $\delta \neq \alpha^n$,

if δ DOMINATES β, then δ also dominates α.

Note that in (9) the lexical requirement of the proper governor in (ii) and the co-indexing requirement in (iii) are conjunctive. Therefore under this formulation, a proper governor must be co-indexed with its target empty category even if the empty category is LEXICALLY GOVERNED. Stowell assumes that co-indexing can result from THETA-ROLE assignment as well as from movement. According to his analysis, a subcategorized object assigns its referential index to a slot in the THEMATIC GRID of the verbal matrix.

Consider now (6). Since the S' complement of *knew* is assigned a theta-role from the verb, the S' is co-indexed with *knew*. Since *knew* governs the S', the S' is properly governed by the matrix verb. If we adopt Stowell's assumption that COMP is the head of S', since there is no maximal projection distinct from S' which dominates the empty category and does not dominate *knew*, the requirements of Government in (10) are satisfied. However, for the empty complementizer to be properly governed, it must be co-indexed with the matrix verb in addition. Stowell does not mention how this co-indexing comes about. We can either assume that the index of the S' percolates down to its head COMP or that it is not the subcategorized object itself but its head that assigns the referential index to a slot in a thematic grid.

Next, consider (7). If we assume that *was* is base generated under V and raised to be adjoined to INFL, the embedded S' is not in the X-bar projection of *was*. Since the S' is not governed by a lexical element, it cannot be properly governed. Therefore the empty complementizer cannot be properly governed. The sentence is ruled out as a violation of the ECP.

Stowell explains the obligatoriness of the presence

of *that* in the sentence in (3) in the same way. It is analyzed as in (11) when it lacks an overt complementizer.

(11) *[$_{S'}$ [e] [The teacher was lying]]$_i$ Ben already knew [e]$_i$

In topic position, the S' is not governed by a lexical element.[1]

As seen above, though we found that Stowell's account can rule out the bad examples in (2) and (3) under his formulation of the ECP, we need to add an appropriate mechanism by which a verb and an empty complementizer in the subcategorized S' are co-indexed.

Now consider the following example.

(12) Men differ from animals in *(that) they can think and speak

This sentence is analyzed as in (13) when it lacks an

---

[1] Stowell further rules out the following data in terms of the ECP.

(i)   It surprised me [*(that) [you had heard about Roger]]
(ii)   I distrust [the claims [*(that) Bill had left the party]]
(iii) Bill muttered [*(that) Denny was playing too much poker]

These examples are, however, clearly better than the examples in (2) and (3) when they lack an overt complementizer. I leave the problem of how the weak unacceptability in (i-iii) comes about to future research.

overt complementizer.

(13) *Men differ from animals [PP in [S' [e] they can think and speak]]

If this sentence is to be ruled out as a violation of the ECP, the empty category in (13) must not be properly governed.   There is, however, an example which suggests that it is properly governed. Consider (14).

(14) What$_i$ do men differ from animals in t$_i$

The grammaticality of this sentence suggests that t_i is properly governed.   In this case, since the empty category is a trace left behind by WH-movement, COMP, to which the index of *what*$_i$ percolates, is a potential proper governor.   However, COMP does not govern t_i because the maximal projection PP which dominates t_i does not dominate COMP.   Thus, this configuration fails to satisfy the condition for government in (10ii). Since the sentence is grammatical, t_i must be properly governed by some other potential proper governor.   The only other potential proper governor is t_i's theta-role assigner.

Stowell (1981) attributes the success in the proper government of t_i in the following similar preposition stranding construction to REANALYSIS.[2]

(15) [Which income]$_i$ do you depend on the government for t$_i$

Here, the verb *depend* and the preposition *for* are

---

2 Stowell (1981) argues that reanalysis applies only to arguments of verbs. If this is correct, the PP headed by *in* in (12) must be an argument of the verb.

reanalyzed as a complex verb which can assign a theta-role, though there is an intervening PP argument. If we adopt the same analysis for (14), the proper governor of t_i will be the complex verb [differ-from-animals-in]. If so, the same complex verb properly governs the S' complement and its head in (13). Therefore, Stowell's ECP account says nothing about the ungrammaticality of the sentence in (12).

Now we have two options to take. One is to maintain Stowell's ECP account and look for an independent constraint on complementizer deletion in PP. The other is to give up Stowell's ECP account and give an alternative analysis which gives an account for the data in a uniform way. I will take the second option since the notion of government which Stowell's ECP account is based on plays no role in explanation in the Minimalist Program of Chomsky (1992), which I follow here.

2. Feature Based Account

The obligatoriness of *that* in CPs in subject position as in (2) and the optionality of *that* in the object position as in (1) is reminiscent of the EXTENDED PROJECTION PRINCIPLE (EPP), which forces a clause to have a subject even if there is no theta-role to assign to it.

(16) *(It) [[seems]   [that John is honest]]
       | --theta-role-- ↑

Since *seems* does not have a theta-role to assign to its subject, the THETA-CRITERION, which requires a one-to-one relation between theta-roles and arguments, could be satisfied even if the expletive *it* were not present. Take (2a), repeated here in (17), for example.

(17)   [*(That) the teacher was lying] was hardly

   ↑ ----------------theta-role--------------------

obvious

---- |

In (2) as well, the one-to-one relation between theta-roles and arguments holds regardless of whether the embedded finite clause has an overt complementizer. As the examples in (1) suggest, finite clauses can be arguments even if they lack an overt complementizer, when they appear in the object position. In spite of the fact that the theta-criterion is satisfied like (16), the sentences in (2) are ungrammatical when they lack an overt complementizer. Therefore, some defect in the subject position seems to cause ungrammaticality in the same way as (16). Apparently, (2) satisfies the EPP because there is a clause in subject position. In the Minimalist Program, however, since the EPP is recaptured based on features of lexical items, what is important is whether the subject contains a relevant feature or not rather than whether the subject position is occupied or not. For example, in (16), the nominative Case feature on *it* is checked against the STRONG N-FEATURE in T(ENSE). If the expletive *it* is not inserted in (16), the strong N-feature, which is visible but uninterpretable at PF, does not participate in checking with a corresponding feature and will remain illegitimate at PF, causing the derivation to CRASH.

   Now, return to the examples in (2). I will argue that the complementizer *that,* like *it,* bears a nominative Case feature which has to be checked when the CP is in the relevant position to have its Case checked.[3] If so, since the complementizer is the head

---

3 The idea that the Case feature on CP is attributed to the property of a lexical item *that* is hinted at by Christopher Tancredi.

of the subject clause CP, the feature percolates to the maximal projection, and when the CP is raised to the Spec of AGRsP, the Case feature is checked against the N-feature in T adjoined to AGRs. In this way, all the features that need to be checked are checked, which makes the derivation CONVERGE. This is illustrated in the structure of sentence (2a) given in (18).

(18) $[_{AGRsP}$ $[_{CP}$ **that** the teacher was lying$]_i$ $[_{AGRs'}$ $[_{AGRs}$

[nom]$\leftarrow$-------------**check**--------------------

was$_j$-T$_k$-AGRs] $[_{TP}$ t$_k$ $[_{AGRoP}$ $[_{VP}$ t$_j$ $[_{AP}$ t$_i$ hardly

-------[N]

obvious]]]]]]

On the other hand, when the overt complementizer is not present, the strong N-feature in T does not participate in checking since the subject clause does not have a corresponding nominative Case feature.[4,5] As a result, the N-feature causes the derivation to crash. This is indicated in (19).

---

4 Under the VP (or predicate) internal subject hypothesis, (19) is also ruled out as a violation of the principle of Greed (see (24)) since the subject clause is raised into the Spec of AGRsP without thereby satisfying any morphological requirement of its own such as Case checking.

5 Makiko Nakayama points out that according to this argument, if we insert *it* into the subject position of the sentences without *that* in (2) under the VP-internal subject hypothesis, we predict that the sentences should be grammatical. The ungrammaticality seems to be due to subjects' staying in the internal position.

(19)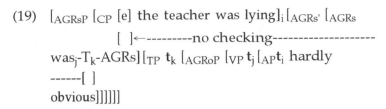

In this analysis, we can rule out (19) without resorting to the empty complementizer's violation of the ECP. Hereafter I will assume that the empty complementizer is immune to the ECP.

So far, we have looked at subject finite clauses. However, finite clauses can also be seen in object position as in (1). In this case, I will assume that *that* bears an accusative Case feature which is checked against an accusative Case feature on a verb. I illustrate with (1a) below.

(20)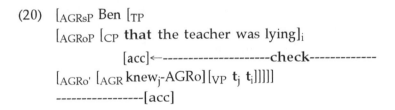

In (20), the embedded CP has raised to the Spec of AGRoP at LF to have its Case checked against the accusative Case feature on the verb which is adjoined to AGRo. This derivation does not leave any feature unchecked which needs to be checked, as seen in (20).

In contrast with (2), (1) is also grammatical if the complementizer is not overtly present. In order to rule in these examples, I will assume that there are two variants for verbs like *know*. One has an accusative Case feature, namely the one in (19), the other does not. The embedded CP without *that* in (1) is paired with the latter variant. This is shown in (21) for the example in (2a).

(21) $[_{AGRsP}$ Ben $[_{TP}$
    $[_{AGRoP}$ $[_{AGRo'}$ $[_{AGRo}$ knew$_i$-AGRo$]$ $[_{VP}$ t$_i$ $[_{CP}$ [e] the
                [ ]   [ ]
    teacher was lying$]]]]]]$

In this case, the embedded CP stays in the complement position of the matrix VP throughout the derivation to LF, resulting in no unchecked features.

Next, I will consider complementizer deletion in a prepositional phrase as in (12). I will assume that *that* in (12), like *that* in a CP which occupies an object position of a verb, has an accusative Case feature. I will further assume that the preposition *in*, unlike verbs such as *know*, always has an accusative Case feature which must participate in checking with a corresponding feature on its complement and that failure to check this feature causes the derivation to crash because the feature is uninterpretable at LF. The structure of the sentence in (12) is analyzed in (22).

(22) a.   Men differ from animals
        $[_{PP}$ in $[_{CP}$ that they can think and speak$]]$
        [acc]-- →[acc]
    b.   Men differ from animals
        $[_{PP}$ in $[_{CP}$ [e] they can think and speak$]]$
        [acc]-- × →[ ]

In (22a), since the Case feature of *that* is checked against the Case feature of *in*, there is no violating feature. On the other hand, in (22b), since the accusative Case feature of *in* checks nothing, it will cause the derivation to crash.

Finally, I will consider the examples in (3), where an embedded CP occupies topic position. Following a suggestion in Chomsky (1992), I assume that topicalization is triggered by checking of a topic feature which is assigned arbitrarily. The topic feature is checked when a maximal projection with a corresponding topic feature occupies the relevant checking position. I will assume further that *that* can be assigned a topic feature whereas the empty complementizer can not. I take no stand on what category checks the topic feature, though this category must be located in the topmost position of the matrix clause. Take (3a) for example.

(23) $[_{XP}$ $[_{CP}$ That the teacher was lying$]_i$ $[_{X'}$ X $[_{IP}$ Ben
      $[top]\leftarrow$------------check--------------------|
      already knew $t_i]]$

In this case, the preposing of the CP is driven by morphological necessity, which satisfies the principle of GREED proposed by Chomsky (1992).

(24) Greed: ...Move-α applies to an element α
                   only if morphological properties of α
                   itself are not otherwise satisfied.

On the other hand, if the complementizer is empty, the preposing violates the principle of Greed since the embedded CP does not have any feature that can be checked in that position. As a result, the sentence will be ungrammatical.

3. Complementizer Deletion in Japanese

Saito (1986) argues that the contrast between the Japanese sentences in (4) and (5) is accounted for in exactly the same way as the contrast between the English sentences in (1) and (3) based on Stowell's (1981) ECP account of the *that*-deletion phenomena. According to Saito, under the assumption that scrambling involves adjunction to S, the structures of (4a) and (5a), when they lack an overt complementizer, will be as in (25a) and (25b) respectively.

(25) a.   [$_S$ John-ga [$_{VP}$ [$_{S'}$ [$_S$ pro Kobe-ni iku] e]
          yuuta]]

     b.   [$_S$ [$_{S'}$ [$_S$ pro Kobe-ni iku] e]$_i$ [$_S$ John-ga [$_{VP}$ t$_i$
          yuuta]]]

The empty complementizer in (25a) is properly governed by the verb *yuuta* 'said'. Thus (4a) satisfies the ECP.[6] On the other hand, the empty category in (25b) is not governed by the verb *yuuta*, since the S' is scrambled out of the VP and hence is no longer governed by that verb. Thus, the empty complementizer in (25b) violates the ECP.

If Saito's perspective is correct, that is, if topicalization in English and scrambling in Japanese should be analyzed in the same way; then under the analysis of complementizer deletion phenomena proposed in the previous section, scrambling should be treated as movement motivated by checking of morphological features, as proposed by Miyagawa (1994). It is known that clause internal IP-adjunction scrambling, which may include the preposing of S' in (5), shows both A and A'-movement properties. Miyagawa proposes that A-scrambling is motivated by Case/Agreement and A'-scrambling is motivated by focus. Since we do not know whether scrambling of the embedded finite clause seen in (5) is A-movement or A'-movement, we have to rule out both possibilities when the complementizer is not overt.

First, let us examine the case of A-scrambling. Miyagawa motivates the movement due to Case/Agreement based on the following assumptions.

---

6 Saito's formulation of the ECP is different from Stowell's. The difference, however, is not relevant here.

(26) a. Subject Agreement in Japanese is strong (Miyagawa 1993).

   b. Object Agreement (AGRo) in Japanese is weak (Tada 1992, Ura 1993)

   c. Japanese allows layered-specifier structure (Ura 1993)

(26a) results in the nominative subject moving to Spec of AGRsP in the overt syntax; (26b) means that the accusative object raises to the Spec of AGRoP at LF. Therefore, the derivation results in the following structure.

(27) [$_{AGRsP}$ Subj$_i$ [$_{AGRs'}$ [$_{AGRoP}$ [$_{VP}$ t$_i$ [$_{v'}$ Obj verb]]]]]

   ↑ ---------------- | (LF)

In addition, Miyagawa proposes that if the AGRo head incorporates into AGRs, AGRo may take on the strong feature of the AGRs, thereby making it necessary to check the accusative Case in the overt syntax. This is possible since the IP-adjunction position counts as a Spec position due to (26c). Therefore, the derivation results in the structure in (28) at the point of SPELL-OUT.

(28) [$_{AGRP}$ Obj$_j$ [$_{AGRP}$ Subj$_i$ [[$_{VP}$ t$_i$ t$_j$ ...] AGRo-..-AGRs...

   I assume that the Japanese complementizer *te* always bears an accusative Case feature and that Japanese verbs such as *yuuta*, like English verbs such as *know*, have an accusative Case feature optionally. Now consider (4a). When the overt complementizer is present, the derivation has the following structure at some stage in LF.

(29)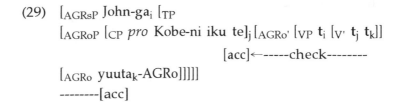

Here, the accusative Case feature of *yuuta* checks the Case feature of the CP. Since there are no violating features and the raising of the CP satisfies the principle of Greed, it will be grammatical. On the other hand, when the complementizer is not overt, I will assume that the verb does not have an accusative Case feature, which is shown in (30).

(30) $[_{AGRsP}$ John-ga$_i$ $[_{TP}$
$[_{AGRoP}$ $[_{AGRo'}$ $[_{VP}$ t$_i$ $[_{V'}$ $[_{CP}$ *pro* Kobe-ni iku [e]] t$_k$]]
[ ]
$[_{AGRo}$ yuuta$_j$-AGRo]]]]]
[ ]

In this case, there are no unchecked Case features and no movement violating Greed since the embedded CP stays in the Spec of the VP throughout the derivation. So this will be grammatical again.

Turn now to the examples of IP-adjunction scrambling in (5). Take (5a) for example. When the complementizer is overt, the structure will be as in (31) at the point of Spell-Out.

(31)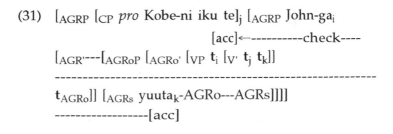

This is an instance of the schematic structure in (28). Here, the accusative Case feature on the embedded CP is checked in the overt syntax mediated by AGRo which is incorporated into AGRs. We can see neither violating features nor ill-formed movement.

On the other hand, when the complementizer is not overtly present, the embedded CP is assumed not to have an accusative Case feature. If we assume that the verb *yuuta* also has no accusative Case feature, there are no unchecked Case features. In this case, however, it follows that this preposing operation of the CP is not motivated by Case/Agreement since the CP does not have a Case feature.

If there were another appropriate motivation of this preposing, the sentence would be ruled in. It is possible to count this preposing as A'-scrambling as stated above. We can, however, make this option unavailable when the preposed finite clause lacks an overt complementizer, leaving the possibility that preposing of the finite clause headed by *te* is an instance of A'-scrambling motivated by focus suggested by Miyagawa.[7] Here again, following Chomsky's (1992) suggestion, I will assume that focus movement is drived by the necessity of checking of focus features which are assigned optionally and have to be checked when the maximal projection to which the feature percolates occupies the relevant checking position which is located higher than AGRsP.[8] I will further assume that focus

---

[7] Miyagawa (1994) does not present any formulation of focus movement.

[8] If A'-scrambling is motivated exclusively by focus, the checking position of long distance VP adjunction scrambling remains a problem for Miyagawa (1994).

features, like topic features, can be assigned to the overt complementizer *te* whereas they cannot be assigned to the empty complementizer. If so, in (5), the preposing of the embedded clause can count as an instance of A'-scrambling when the complementizer is overtly present. On the other hand, when the complementizer is not overtly present, the preposing is not motivated by focus. Accordingly, in this case, preposing of the embedded finite clause in (5) is ruled out as a violation of the principle of Greed because it has neither Case/Agreement nor focus feature.

4. Conclusion

In this paper, I proposed to give an account for complementizer deletion phenomena in terms of feature-checking. In particular, the analysis on Japanese in this term supports Miyagawa's (1994) view of scrambling that it is an instance of obligatory movement.

References

Chomsky, Noam. 1992. A Minimalist Program for Linguistic Theory. MIT Occasional Papers in Linguistics Vol. 1.

Miyagawa, Shigeru. 1993. LF Case-checking and Minimal Link Condition. Case and Agreement II, MIT Working Papers in Linguistics, ed. by Colin Phillips.

Miyagawa, Shigeru. 1994. Scrambling as an Obligatory Movement. Proceeding of the Nanzan Conference on Japanese Linguistics and Language Teaching. Nagoya, Japan: Nanzan University.

Saito, Mamoru. 1986. Three Notes on Syntactic Movement in Japanese. Issues in Japanese Linguistics, ed. by Imai, T. and Saito, M. , 301-50. Dordrecht: Foris.

Stowell, Timothy. 1981. Origins of Phrase Structure. Doctorial dissertation, MIT.

Tada, Hiroaki. 1992. Nominative Objects in Japanese. Journal of Japanese Linguistics Vol. 14, 91-108.

Ura, Hiroyuki. 1993. L-relatedness and Parametric Variation. MIT Working Papers in Linguistics 19, 377-99.

Tense in the Subject Raising Construction*

KAORU OHTA
University of Washington

0. INTRODUCTION

In this paper, I will discuss the subject raising (hereafter, SR) construction in Japanese and its implications for the theory of tense. Examples of SR are the (b) sentences of (1)-(2).

(1)   a. Baisinin-tati-wa <u>sono otoko-ga</u>   hannin-da-to
           juror-pl.-top.   that man-nom. criminal-be-quot.

           sinzi-te-i-ru.
           believe-TE-exist-pres.

           'Jurors believe that that man is a criminal.'

---

* I would like to thank Tim Stowell and Anoop Mahajan for their helpful comments and suggestions, which played major role in developing this paper. Also, I would like to express my gratitude to George Bedell, Kuo-ming Sung, Akira Nakamura, Matsuzo Izutani, and participants at the conference for their valuable comments. All of the errors, however, are mine.

    b. Baisinin-tati-wa <u>sono otoko-o</u>   hannin-da-to
        juror-pl.-top.   that man-acc. criminal-be-quot.

        sinzi-te-i-ru.
        believe-TE exist-pres.

        'Jurors believe that man to be a criminal.'

(2)   a. Yamada-wa <u>Mary-ga</u>   kawaii-to omot-ta.
             -top.   -nom. cute-quot. think-past

        'Yamada thought Mary was cute.'

    b. Yamada-wa <u>Mary-o</u>   kawaii-to omot-ta.
            -top.   -acc. cute-quot. think-past

        'Yamada thought Mary was cute.'

In the (a) sentences of (1) and (2), the embedded subject is marked in the nominative (as indicated by the nominative marker -*ga*). In contrast, the same NP in the (b) sentences of (1)-(2) is marked with the accusative marker -*o*. This alternation of the embedded subject has been considered to be the result of the rule of SR (Kuno 1976, and Sakai 1994, among others).[1]

    As the grammaticality of both the (a) and (b) sentences in (1)-(2) shows, for the Japanese SR construction, SR of the embedded subject appears to be optional. This property is not shared by the English SR construction, often referred to as the ECM construction (cf. Chomsky 1981) exemplified by the sentences in (3). Raising of the embedded subject is obligatory in English, as the ungrammaticality of the sentence in (4) shows.

(3)   a. Mary believed him to be innocent.

    b. Mary considers herself to be the prettiest.

    c. The girls found them to be in danger.

    d. I expect him to win the championship.

(4)   a. *Mary believed he to be innocent.

    b. *Mary considers she to be the prettiest.

    c. *The girls found they to be in danger.

---

[1] For a different approach to this alternation, see Sells 1990.

      d. *I expect he to win the championship.

I will argue that the apparent optionality of SR in Japanese can be attributed to the property of Tense in the embedded clause involved in SR. More specifically, the optionality of the Japanese SR construction results from the optionality of the head T in the embedded clause, not the optionality of the rule. Finally, I will show that this account is consistent with the English SR construction.

1. PROPERTIES OF JAPANESE SR

In English, the matrix verb of SR sentences must be the "B-type" (Postal 1974), as shown in (5). Other types of matrix verbs are involved in the control structure, as shown in (6).

(5)   a. Mary believed him to be innocent.

        b. Mary considers herself to be the prettiest.

        c. The girls found them to be in danger.

        d. I expect him to win the championship.

(6)   a. Mary convinced him PRO to leave.

        b. Vicky persuaded him PRO to take her to the theater.

        c. Debbie advised them PRO to find a new job.

        d. Tracy reminded him PRO to turn the lights on.

In Japanese, too, it appears that the matrix clause of SR sentences must involve "B-type" verbs. For instance, verbs expressing internal feeling or thinking such as *dantei-suru* 'to judge, to draw a conclusion', *omo-u* 'to think', *sinzi-ru* 'to believe', and *syoomei-suru* 'to prove' allow SR.[2]

---

[2] It appears that some native speakers accept SR sentences containing verbs of saying as matrix verbs although Kuno 1976 states that such verbs do not allow SR.

(7) a . Gakusei-tati-wa <u>Yoko-ga</u>   kawaii-to   omot-ta.
        student-pl.-top.   -nom. pretty-quot. think-past

     'The students thought that Yoko was pretty.'

     b. Gakusei-tati-wa <u>Yoko-o</u> kawaii-to   omot-ta.
         student-pl.-top.   -acc. pretty-quot. think-past

     'The students thought that Yoko was pretty.'

(8) a . Keizi-wa   <u>sono otoko-ga</u>   hannin-da-to
        detective-top. that   man-nom. criminal-cop.-quot.

        dantei-si-ta.
        judgment-do-past.

     'The detective judged that man to be a criminal.'

     b. Keizi-wa   <u>sono otoko-o</u>   hannin-da-to
         detective-top. that   man-acc. criminal-cop.-quot.

        dantei-si-ta.
        judgment-do-past.

     'The detective thought that man to be a criminal.'

Although both the English and Japanese SR constructions require the same type of matrix verb, these two languages crucially differ with respect to the type of embedded clause involved in SR sentences. In English, the embedded clause must be infinitival. In contrast, the embedded clause in the Japanese SR construction is tensed. This is obvious because the complement clause in the SR construction is headed by the complementizer-like element -*to*.[3]

Note also that the embedded clause generally contains a "stative" predicate as Kuno 1976 points out. Thus, application of SR to a sentence such as (9a) whose embedded clause contains the

---

[3] Infinitival complement clauses in Japanese must be subject to "Predicate Raising" to form complex predicates. For instance, the infinitival clause involved in (i) becomes a part of a complex predicate in the process of causative sentence formation to derive (ii)

(i)   Taroo [Hanako nihon ik] sase Tense
                    Japan go Caus.

(ii)   Taroo-wa Hanako-ni   nihon-e ika-se-ta.
             -top.   -dat. Japan-to go-Caus.-past

       'Taro let Hanako go to Japan.'

eventive predicate *nihon-ni ik-u* 'to go to Japan' results in ungrammaticality as shown in (9b).

(9) a. Keizi-wa   sono otoko-ga   nihon-ni ik-u-to
         detective-top. that   man-nom. Japan-to. go-pres.-quot.

         omot-ta.
         think-past

         'The detective thought that the man went to Japan.'

     b. *Keizi-wa   sono otoko-o   nihon-ni ik-u-to
         detective-top. that   man-acc. Japan-to. go-pres.-quot.

         omot-ta.
         think-past

         '*The detective thought that man to have gone to Japan.'

The second way that the Japanese SR construction differs from the English is that while SR is obligatory in English, it is optional in Japanese. Hence, for Japanese, both SR and non-SR sentences are grammatical as in (10), but for English, only SR sentences are grammatical as in (11).

(10) a. Yamada-wa <u>Mary-ga</u> kawaii-to omot-ta.
              -top.   -nom. cute-quot.   think-past

          'Yamada thought Mary was cute.'

      b. Yamada-wa <u>Mary-o</u> kawaii-to omot-ta.
              -top.   -acc. cute-quot. think-past

          'Yamada thought Mary to be cute.'

(11) a. Mary believed him to be innocent.

      b. *Mary believed he to be innocent.

The apparent optionality of SR for Japanese poses two theoretically significant questions: First, within the "minimalist" framework (cf. Chomsky 1992, 1995 and Lasnik 1993, among others), all required syntactic movement must be forced. This means that no syntactic rule is optional. If SR in Japanese is optional, this fact would cast doubt on the minimalist framework. Secondly, assuming that the SR structure is derived via raising-to-object, the movement of the embedded subject violates the minimality condition. Recall that movement involved in SR moves the embedded subject out of a clause headed by the complementizer-like element -*to*, which is assumed to constitute the head of CP. This sort of movement clearly violates the minimality condition as it moves "across" CP.

2. THE TENSE SYSTEM OF JAPANESE

As mentioned earlier, the Japanese SR construction involves a tensed stative predicate in its embedded clause. In section 3 below, I will show that embedded clauses in the Japanese SR construction are subject to a tense restriction. In this section, I will argue that the present tense in Japanese stative predicates is optional whereas the past tense is obligatory. This accounts for the optionality of SR in Japanese.

Let's examine the tense system of Japanese in comparison with that of English. Stative predicates show a peculiar property in their tense interpretation both in English and Japanese. First of all, consider the examples in (12).

(12)   Taroo-wa [Hanako-ga Rosu-ni i-ta   to]   it-ta.
              -top.   -nom. LA-in   exist-past quot. say-past

'Taro said that Hanako had been in LA.'

In (12), the embedded predicate is stative. Notice that the embedded clause is in the past tense and that it is under the matrix past. The time relation between the matrix and embedded tense is that the event time of the embedded clause must precede the time referred to by the matrix predicate. This interpretation is known as the past-shifted reading (PSR).

It is well-known that Japanese does not force the "sequence of tense phenomenon (hereafter SOT)" (Ogihara 1989, Stowell 1993, 1995, and Nakamura 1993 among others). Compare the English examples in (13) where the embedded past tense under the matrix past tense allows both the PSR and an interpretation in which the event time of the embedded clause is cotemporaneous with that of the matrix clause, an interpretation I will refer to as the "past-cotemporaneous reading (PCR)".

(13)   Mary said that Bill was sick.

Stowell 1993 argues that the availability of SOT in English is perhaps due to the fact that past tense is actually a past polarity item occurring under the ZP (*Zeit* phrase) in the complement position of TP. This PRO-like element allows the PCR interpretation when licensed by the matrix semantic tense. Japanese past tense, on the other hand, is not a polarity item: it is a tense element and therefore must receive the past tense interpretation. Because tense in Japanese is not a polarity item, therefore, only the PSR, but not the PCR interpretation is available.

Another interesting contrast between English and Japanese is the interpretation of the present tense under the matrix past. Consider the sentences in (14) and (15).

(14) Taroo-wa [Hanako-ga   Rosu-ni i-ru   to]   it-ta.
      -top.   -nom. LA-in   exist-pres. quot. say-past

'Taro said that Hanako was (*lit.* =is) in LA.'

(15) Bill said that Mary is pregnant.

In the Japanese sentence in (14), the embedded stative predicate only allows the "simple-simultaneous reading (SSR)". Under SSR, the event time of the embedded clause is contemporaneous with the matrix event time.

In contrast, along with the SSR interpretation, the English sentence in (15) allows an interpretation often referred to as the "double-access reading (DAR)". Under DAR, the time referred to by the embedded clause encompasses the utterance time as well as the present time. Hence, Mary's pregnancy holds true both of the time of the utterance as well as of the time of Bill's original utterance. No such reading is available for the Japanese sentence in (14). In (14), no mention was made regarding Hanako's existence in LA at the time of utterance; Hanako's existence in LA holds true only of the time of Taro's original utterance.

In order to account for the availability of SSR and DAR in English, Stowell 1993 proposes that the English present tense is an anti-past polarity item. Being an anti-past polarity item, it scopes out of the domain of the semantic past by leaving a trace in its original position. The availability of both SSR and DAR is now attributed to the trace and the position in which the anti-past polarity item ultimately lands. In contrast, the Japanese present tense, just like the past tense, is neither a polarity nor an anti-

polarity item. I propose that the Japanese present tense is in fact
an optional element. Therefore, SSR results from the non-existence
of the present tense; since it does not project its head, the matrix
past forces SSR.

These differences between English and Japanese can be
schematically represented as in (16) and (17).

(16) English
    a.   [Past T [Past   ]   ]
                                  [polarity]   ... PSR/PCR

    b.   [Past T [Present   ]   ]
                                  [anti-polarity]

    b'. Present [Past T [t   ]   ]
        ↑_____| ...SSR/DAR

(17) Japanese
    a. [[Past   ] Past T]
                    [non-polarity]   ...PSR only

    b. [[Present   ] Past T]
                    [optional]   ...SSR only

Now, in order to see the optionality of the present tense in
Japanese, compare the sentences in (18) and (19), where simplex
sentences involve stative predicates.

(18) Taroo-wa nihon-ni i-ru.
             -top. Japan-in exist-pres.

    'Taro is in Japan.'

(19) Taroo-wa nihon-ni i-ta.
             -top. Japan-in exit-past

    'Taro was in Japan.'

The time referred to in the past tense sentence in (19) never
refers to the utterance time. On the other hand, the present tense
sentence in (18) refers to the present time. Note that the present
time relevant to a sentence such as (18) is identical to the utterance
time. Being an optional element, the present tense may or may not
project. If the present tense does not project, the present time
reading would be forced by the utterance time. In contrast, if the

present tense does project, the present tense reading follows from the interpretation of the tense element.

Recall that no DAR is available in the Japanese structure in (17b) where the present tense occurs under the matrix past. Even if the present tense is optionally projected in the embedded clause, since it is not an anti-polarity item it cannot scope out, and only SSR results. Therefore, it is plausible to assume that the Japanese present tense is optional.

3. THE MECHANISM OF SR

Now let's return to SR. In section 2 above, I pointed out two theoretically significant issues in connection to Japanese SR: the potential minimality violation and the optionality of application of SR. In this section, I will answer these questions in a principled manner.

First, I hypothesize that the complementizer-like element -to incorporates to the matrix verb in LF in the manner illustrated in (20).

(20) a. [[CP... [TP [NP ...] ø] to] V]

b. [... [CP... [TP [NP ...] ø] t_i] to_i-V]

The effect of this incorporation is twofold: it causes the S-bar deletion effect as it erases the CP projection, while also enabling raising of the embedded subject without violation of the minimality condition.[4]

---

4 Note that there are a number of cases in which the complementizer-like element -to is morphologically incorporated. For instance, in idiomatic expressions such as those in (i), the complementizer-like element -to cooccurs with verbs with the complementizer-like function of the element -to being lost.

(i) a. Yamada to-yuu otoko
quot.-say man   'a man called Yamada'

b. To-suru-to, sono hanasi-wa uso-da.
quot.-do-if that   story-top. lie-be=pres.

'If so, this story is a lie.'

In idiomatic expressions such as those in (20), the complementizer-like element -to is inseparable from governing verbs such as -yu-u 'to say' and -suru 'to do'. In addition, the verbs involved in these expressions lose their original semantic property with the entire expression being re-interpreted as a unit.

Earlier, I showed that the present tense of stative predicates optionally projects the head of TP in Japanese. Recall that the embedded clause of the SR construction is typically stative. This means that the embedded tense of the SR construction may not be projected. Assuming that the nominative Case is assigned by the head of TP, when the embedded tense is not projected the embedded subject cannot receive Case, thereby motivating raising of the embedded subject. As I have argued, this movement does not violate the minimality condition, since CP does not block this movement after incorporation.

Furthermore, I have also argued that the past tense of Japanese stative predicates must project the head T. This hypothesis is borne out by the observation originally pointed out by Kuno 1976, who shows that Japanese SR sentences normally result in lower acceptability when the embedded clause is past tense. Consider the examples in (21).

(21) a. (=Kuno's 1976 (89))
　　　?Yamada-wa zibun-o oroka-na　otoko dat-ta-to
　　　　　-top.　self-acc. stupid-NA man　be-past-quot.

　　　omot-ta.
　　　think-past

　　　'Yamada thought that he had been a stupid man.'

　　b. ??Baisinin-tati-wa sono otoko-o　　hannin-dat-ta
　　　　juror-pl.-top.　　　that man-acc. criminal-be.-past

　　　-to　　sinzi-te　　i-ru.
　　　-quot. believe-TE exist-pres.

　　　'Jurors believe that man to have been criminal.'

　　c. ??Gakusei-tati-wa Yoko-o　　kawaikat-ta-to　omot-ta.
　　　　student-pl.-top.　　　-acc. pretty-past-quot. think-past

　　　'The students insisted that Yoko was pretty.'

Obviously, the sentences in (21) are marginally acceptable although there is a significant difference in acceptability between the cases where the present tense is involved. Recall that the

---

Given incorporation, it naturally follows that these idiomatic expressions are formed by incorporating -to into the verb. Therefore, it seems plausible to assume that the complementizer-like element -to incorporates into the matrix verb.

optionality of the present tense "motivates" the embedded subject to undergo raising to receive Case. Then, the lower acceptability of cases with past tense embedded clauses such as those in (21) can be attributed to the fact that SR is not forced since the embedded subject can receive Case.

To summarize, the Japanese SR construction is derived in the manner illustrated in (22).

(22) a. [... [CP... [TP [NP ...] ø] to] V]

   b. *-to* incorporates
       [... [CP... [TP [NP ...] ø] t_i] to_i-V]

   c. S-bar deletion effect
       [... [TP [NP ...] ø] to-V]

   d. raising-to-object
       [... NP$_j$ [TP [t_j ...] ø] to-V]

The advantages of this analysis of SR are threefold: (i) the optionality of SR can be attributed to the optionality of Tense, not the optionality of the "rule" of SR; (ii) this analysis indirectly accounts for why SR only applies when complement clauses are stative; (iii) it naturally follows that SR constructions involving past tense embedded clauses are less acceptable than those involving present tense embedded clauses.

Note that Kuno 1976 points out that there is a construction in which what appears to be the embedded subject is marked only in the accusative. This construction involves *-no koto* '(someone's) matter', as shown in (23).

(23) a. (=Kuno's 1976(97)))
       Yamada-wa musuko-no-koto-o   baka da-to
            -top. son-gen.-matter-acc. fool be=pres.-quot.

       omot-te i-ru.
       think-TE exist-pres.

       'Yamada thought that his son was a fool.'

b. Gakusei-tati-wa <u>Nicole-no   koto-o</u>   kiree-da-to
   student-pl.-top.   -gen. thing-acc. pretty-cop.-quote

omot-ta.
think-past

'The students thought that Nicole was pretty.'

Note that the phrase NP-*no-koto* cannot be marked in the nominative as the ungrammaticality of the sentences in (24) shows.

(24) a. *Yamada-wa <u>musuko-no-koto-ga</u>   baka da-to
          -top.   son-gen.-matter-nom. fool be=pres.-quot.

omot-te i-ru.
think-TE exist-pres.

'Yamada thought that his son was a fool.'

b. *Gakusei-tati-wa <u>Nicole-no   koto-ga</u>   kiree-da
     student-pl.-top.   -gen. thing-nom. pretty-cop.

-to   omot-ta.
-quote think-past

'The students thought that Nicole was pretty.'

In (24), the NPs *musuko-no-koto* and *Nicole-no-koto* are marked in the nominative, and these sentences are ungrammatical. In contrast, the sentences in (23), which involve the accusative NPs (*musuko-no-koto* and *Nicole-no-koto*), are grammatical. In both cases, the embedded clause is present tense. Kuno 1976 claims that -*no koto* is optionally inserted after SR raises the embedded subject.

I propose, however, that the accusative NP is base-generated in the matrix object position without undergoing SR. As Kuno himself shows, phrases with *no-koto* are always limited to the object position of verbs of feeling, thinking and saying.[5] Compare the sentences in (25) with (26), cited from Kuno 1976 (his (92)-(96)).

(25) a. Yamada-wa <u>Tanaka-no-koto-o</u>   nikun-de i-ru.
          -top.   -gen.-matter-acc. hate-TE exist-pres.

'Yamada hates Tanaka.'

---

[5] Also, objects to which -*no koto* is attached to must be [+human]. (Kuno 1976).

b. Yamada-wa <u>Hanako-no-koto-o</u>   aisi-te i-ru.
   -top.   -gen.-matter-acc. love-TE exist-pres.

'Yamada loves Hanako.'

c. Yamada-wa <u>Hanako-no-koto-ga</u>   suki-rasii-yo.
   -top.   -gen.-matter-nom. like-seem-SP

'It seems that Yamada likes Hanako.'

(26)   a. *Yamada-wa [<u>musuko-no-koto-ga</u>   baka-na] koto-o
          -top. son-gen.-matter-nom. fool-NA   fact-acc.

sira-na-i.
know-neg.-pres.

'Yamada does not know that his son is fool.'

a'. cf. Yamada-wa [musuko-ga baka-na] koto-o
          -top. son-nom.   fool-NA fact-acc.

sira-na-i.
know-neg.-pres.

b. *Yamada-wa [<u>musuko-no-koto-ga</u>   rikoo-na] koto-o
   -top. son-gen.-matter-nom. clever-NA fact-acc.

zimansi-ta.
brag-past

'Yamada bragged of the fact that his son is bright.'

b'. cf. Yamada-wa [musuko-ga rikoo-na] koto-o
          -top. son-nom.   clever-NA fact-acc.

zimansi-ta.
brag-past

As mentioned above, Kuno 1976 claims that -*no koto* is incorporated after SR raises the embedded subject into the matrix object position. However, there is evidence showing that the object NP-*no koto* in SR-like sentences such as those in (23) are base-generated in the matrix object position. Compare the sentences in (27) and (28).

(27) Gakusei-tati-wa <u>Nicole-no-koto-o</u>   kiree-dat-ta
      student-pl.-top.   -gen.-matter-acc. pretty-be-past

      -to   omot-ta.
      -quot. think-past

      'The students thought that Nicole had been pretty.'

(28) ??Gakusei-tait-wa <u>Nicole-o</u>   kiree-dat-ta-to
        student-pl.-top.   -acc. pretty-be-past-quot.

      omot-ta.
      think-past

      'The students thought Nicole to have been pretty.'

Embedded clauses in this type of construction can be past tense as
the grammaticality of the sentence in (27) indicates. This contrasts
clearly with the SR construction where a past tense embedded
clause causes marginal status.

Assuming that the sentence in (27) does not involve SR, the
contrast between (27) and (28) can be easily accounted for. Since the
embedded clause of (28) is past tense, SR of the embedded subject
violates the minimality condition, resulting in marginal
acceptability. In contrast, no such violation occurs in (27) as what
appears to be the embedded subject is base-generated in the matrix
object position, resulting in a fully grammatical sentence.

As only the SR sentence is affected by the existence of past
tense embedded clause, the comparison between (27) and (28)
indicates that SR is subject to the tense effect.

4.   CROSS-LINGUISTIC IMPLICATIONS

Finally, this analysis is consistent with the tense
interpretation available for the English SR construction. Stowell
1982 shows that the tense interpretation of SR complements is
largely determined by the semantics of the governing verb. For
instance, in English SR sentences such as (29), the present tense
interpretation is available in (29a), the future tense is understood
for the embedded clause in (29b), and the embedded clause is
interpreted in the past tense in (29c).

(29) a. The girls consider themselves to be the smartest.

   b. I expect him to win the competition.

   c. I remember her to be the smallest.

These facts show that the SR complement does not project its own TP. By assuming that SR occurs only if the embedded clause does not project its own TP, both English and Japanese SR facts can be accounted for by one principle.

REFERENCES

Chomsky, Noam. 1981. *Lectures on Government and Binding*. Dordrecht: Foris.

Chomsky, Noam. 1992. A Minimalist Program for Linguistic Theory. reproduced in Noam Chomsky. 1995. *The Minimalist Program*. Cambridge, MIT Press: 167-218.

Chomsky, Noam. 1995. The Minimalist Program. MIT Press: Cambridge, MA.

Enç, Mürvet. 1987. Anchoring Condition for Tense. *Linguistic Inquiry* 18: 633-657.

Fukui, Naoki. 1986. *A Theory of Category Projection and Its Applications*. Doctoral dissertation. MIT.

Kuno, Susumu. 1976. Subject Raising. In M. Shibatani (Ed.), *Syntax and Semantics 5: Japanese Generative Grammar* New York: Academic Press: 17-49.

Lasnik, Howard. 1993. *Lectures on Minimalist Syntax*. Cambridge, MA: MIT Working Papers in Linguistics.

Lasnik, Howard and Mamoru Saito. 1991. On the Subject of Infinitives. In Lynn Nichols Lisa M. Dobin and Rosa M. Rodriguez (Eds.), *Papers from the 27th Regional Meeting of the Chicago Linguistics Society*: 324-343.

Nakamura, Akira. 1993. On Some Temporal Constructions in Japanese and the Theory of Tense. ms., University of California, Los Angeles.

Ogihara, Toshiyuki. 1989. *Temporal Reference in English and Japanese*. Doctoral dissertation, University of Texas, Austin.

Ogihara, Toshiyuki. 1995. The Semantics of Tense in Embedded Clause. *Linguistic Inquiry* 26: 663-680.

Ohta, Kaoru. 1994. *Verbal Nouns in Japanese*. Doctoral dissertation. University of California, Los Angeles.

Postal, Paul. M. 1974. *On Raising: One Rule of English Grammar and its Theoretical Implications*. Cambridge, MA: MIT Press.

Sakai, Hiromu. 1994. Raising Asymmetry and Derivational Uniformity. a paper presented at the Theoretical East-Asian Linguistics Workshop, UC Irvine.

Sells, Peter. 1990. Is There Subject-to-Object Raising in Japanese? in K. Dziwirek, P. Farell, and E. M. Bikandi (Eds.) Grammatical Relations: A Cross Theoretical Perspective. Stanford, CA: CSLI.

Stowell, Timothy. 1982. The Tense of Infinitives. *Linguistics Inquiry* 13: 561-570.

Stowell. Timothy. 1993. Syntax of Tense. ms. UCLA.

Stowell, Timothy. 1995. What Do the Present and Past Tense Mean? a paper presented at the Cortona Conference on Tense and Aspect Meeting.

Two Types of Synthetic Compounds and Move-Affix in Korean*

CHUNG-KON SHI
Korea University

0. Introduction

In this paper I would like to propose a new analysis of Korean synthetic compounding to account for questions concerning the morphology-syntax interfacing, discussing the two different types of synthetic compounds, lexical (e.g., *tonpeli* type) and syntactic synthetic compound (e.g., *mwulpati* type).

Since many linguists believe root compounds are lexically generated one might conclude that synthetic compounding is a lexical process. On the other hand, one could argue that both synthetic and root compounding are syntactic processes. In this paper, however, I will demonstrate that certain aspects of synthetic compound formation are lexical, while other aspects are the result of syntactic processes.

This paper begins §1 by giving a brief overview of the issues and basic observations of synthetic compounds. In §2, I will review and discuss previous analyses. In §3, I will propose a new analysis. § 2-3 will be the main body of my proposal. After arguing my new analysis, I will return in

* I would like to thank Susumu Kuno, Kwang-Soo Sung, Peter Sells, Youngjun Jang and Denny Smith for many valuable comments and observations. However, remaining shortcomings are mine.

§4 to how the new analysis can be extended to other examples. In §5, I will summarize my discussion.

1. Issues and Basic Observations
1.1 Issues

In many respects compounding represents the interface between morphology, syntax and phonology. This is particularly true of synthetic compounds. The term SYNTHETIC COMPOUND is conventionally used to denote complex morphological forms such as the following:

(1)a. truck-driver, oven-cleaner, peace-making, etc. : English
   b. ton-pel-i(making money), hay-tot-i(sunrise), mwul-pat-i(waterspout), etc. : Korean

The above examples indicate that their structures are composed of [N-V-Affix]. However, such constructions raise a number of questions concerning word formation. The first question about these structures which we need to answer is the following :

(2) Where does the formation take place: lexicon, syntax or both ?

Another question, concerning the structure of synthetic compounds, is the following:

(3) Does affixation precede compounding? (see a and b below)
   a. [N + [V + Affix]]
   b. [[N + V] + Affix]

1.2 Basic Observations

There are a number of observations shared by synthetic compounds which need to be explained. The first observation is that permissible and impermissible verbal compounds are related to grammatical and ungrammatical sentences, as illustrated in (4)-(5).

(4) a. truck-driver   (He drives a truck)
       *house-driver   (*He drives house)
    b. oven-cleaner (She cleans the oven)
       *oven-folder   (*She folds oven)
    c. peace-making (She makes peace)

*peace-thinking (*She thinks peace)[1]

(5) a. ton-pel-i   (Kwu-ka   ton-ul   pel-un-ta)
              He-Nom   money-Acc   makes
              'He makes money'

    b.*os-pel-i   (*Kwu-ka   os-ul   pel-un-ta)
              He-Nom   cloth-Acc   makes
              '*He makes clothes'

    c. hay-tot-i   (Hay-ka   tot-nun-ta)
              sun-Nom   rises
              'The sun rises'

    d.*tal-tot-i   (*Tal-i   tot-nun-ta)
              moon-Nom   rises
              '*The moon rises'

    e.mwul-pat-i   (Kwu-ka   mwul-ul   pat-nun-ta)
              He-Nom   water-Acc   receives
              'He receives water'

    f.*palam-pat-i   (*Kwu-ka   palam-ul   pat-nun-ta)
              He-Nom   wind-Acc   receives
              '*He receives wind'

The above examples show us that the verb's argument and semantic structure are satisfied by the noun

The second is that some synthetic compounds such as *tonpeli* go through T-EPENTHESIS (hereafter t-E)[2] and hence tensification takes place. Others such as *haytoti* and *mwulpati* do not go through t-E, as illustrated in (6).

(6)   t-E and tensification

     a. 'ton-pel-i' ---> [tonp'əri]   (*[tonbəri])   O
     b. 'hay-tot-i' ---> [haedoci]   (*[haet'oci])   X
     c. 'mwul-pat-i' ---> [mulbaci]   (*[mulp'aci])   X

---

[1] The sentence is from Roeper and Siegal (1978:208). However, for some speakers, it may be permissible.

[2] In the literature on Korean phonology (Choi 1937), t-E has been referred to as the SAISSOLI-PHENOMENON, where the consonant -s is inserted between the two elements of a compound. It has been controversal among linguists whether /t/ is a morpheme or just phonologically inserted. Traditional grammarians such as Choi(1937) analyzed /t/ as a reflex of Middle Korean genitive case marker while Martin(1954) has taken the latter position. In this paper, I take the former position according to Choi(1937). This can be suported in the sense that there is a meaning distinction between *namwu-pay* ([namubae]:boat made from wood) and *namwuspa* ([namup'ae]:boat for shipping wood).

What need to be explained here is how we can make this distinction between synthetic compounds.

The third is that all structures of [V-Affix] in English can exist as independent nouns while ones in Korean can not.

			Independent Noun
(7) a. truck-driver	-->	[drive+er]	O
b. oven-cleaner	-->	[clean+er]	O
c. peace-making	-->	[make+ing]	O
(8) a. ton-pel-i	-->	[pel+i]$_N$	O
b. 'hay-tot-i'	-->	*[tot+i]$_N$	X
c. 'mwul-pat-i'	-->	*[pat+i]$_N$	X

(9) peli : peli-kam (thing for making money)
   peli-cali (place for making money)

In examples (7)-(9), we see that the derived nominals in English are formed from [V+ Affix], unlike Korean.[3]

2. Previous Analyses and Problems

Synthetic compounding has become a focal point of recent works such as Ahn(1985), Sohn(1987), Kim(1990), to name a few.[4] In this chapter, I will review the previous analyses and show the problems which their analyses raise.

Ahn(1985)[5] proposed that synthetic compounds are formed in the lexicon and the structure must be reanalyzed in LF as illustrated in (10).

Reanalysis

(10) [[hay]$_N$+ [tot$_V$ + i]$_N$]$_N$ (Lexicon) --> [[hay$_N$+ tot]$_V$+i]$_N$ (LF)

However, his proposal has some problems in a sense that the formation of (10) does not keep his linear-ordered lexical model(Sub-compounding --> Co-

---

[3] This paper follows the basic assumptions of Aronoff(1976)'s word-based morphology, which Scalise(1984:40) spells out, as follows:
   i) The words which will be the bases of WFRs must be existing words.
   ii) WFRs can take as a base only a single word, no more (e.g., phrase) and no less (e.g., bound forms).
[4] For English synthetic compounding, there are many proposed theories; Roeper and Siegal(1978), Allen(1978), Selkirk(1982), Lieber(1983), and Pesesky(1985) etc. For such proposals, the particular argument here can not be made.
[5] We have a lot of works of Korean linguists based on the constituent analysis of synthetic compounds, not theoretical approaches. See 4.3 of Shi (1994).

compounding --> Derivation --> Inflection) and there is not any reason why affixation precedes compounding because *[tot-i]$_N$ in *haytoti* is not a independent word.

Rejecting Ahn(1985)'s the linear-ordered lexical model, Sohn(1987) suggests MOVE-AFFIX in LF, as illustrated in example (11).

Move-affix

(11) [[hay]$_N$+ [tot$_V$ + i]$_N$]$_N$ (Lexicon) ---> [[hay$_N$+ tot]$_V$+i]$_N$ (LF)

In the above example, she argues that argument structure of the verb can be satisfied with the noun by her proposal. As in Ahn(1985), however, what must be explained here is the reason why affixation precedes compounding and why t-E does not take place in *[hay-tot-i]$_N$* unlike *[ton-pel-i]$_N$*. [6]

Like Sohn(1987), Kim(1990) also proposes move-affix in LF to satisfy the argument structure of the verb. And he attempts to capture the distinction of t-E between *[ton-pel-i]$_N$* and *[hay-tot-i]$_N$*. He argues that the move-affix rule applies to *[hay-tot-i]$_N$*. but not to *[ton-pel-i]$_N$* as shown in example (12).

Move-affix

(12) a. [[hay]$_N$+ [tot$_V$ + i]$_N$]$_N$ (Lexicon) ---> [[hay$_N$+ tot]$_V$+i]$_N$ (LF)
    b. [[ton]$_N$+ [pel$_V$ + i]$_N$]$_N$ (Lexicon) -X → [[ton$_N$ + pel]$_V$+i]$_N$ (LF)

However, his proposal has the same problems as seen in Ahn(1985) and Sohn(1987). In addition, his proposal has to explain why the move-affix applies to *[hay-tot-i]$_N$* but not *[ton-pel-i]*.

3. A New Analysis
3.1. Two types Synthetic Compounds

This paper proposes the two different types of synthetic compounds, such as *tonpeli* and *mwulpati* type. They are different in the sense that the former is driven by the process of affixation--> compounding in lexicon, while the latter by the process of compounding--> affixation in syntax   as seen in (13)-(14).

(13) [[pel]$_V$+ i]$_N$]$_N$ --- derivational affixation   (Lexicon)
    [[ton]$_N$+ [[pel]$_V$+ i]$_N$]$_N$ --- compounding

---

[6] Kang(1989) suggests that a class of exceptions to t-E is synthetic compounds. However, Kang(1989) has a problem in a sense that she can not explain the t-E of *tonpeli* type.

(14) [[mwul]$_N$ + [pat]$_V$]$_V$ --- compounding (by head movement) (Syntax)

[[[mwul]$_N$ + [pat]$_V$]$_V$ + i]$_N$ ---affixation (by head movement)

Under this assumption, we can naturally account for the distinction of t-E illustrated in the basic observations, because this analysis implies that word formation can take place in syntax as well as in lexicon. Note that t-E can be applied only to 'N+N' root compound (especially subcompound)[7] in lexicon as seen in (15)-(16)(c.f. Chung 1980, Ahn 1985, Sohn 1987, Kim 1990, and Shi 1994), where each Ns should be the independent nouns. On the other hand, t-E can not be applied to syntactic compound.[8]

(15)a. ton + cwumeni ---> [ton]$_N$ t [cwumeni]$_N$ ---> [tonc'um∂ni]
    'money' 'pocket'   (*[toncum∂ni])
                                          'a purse'

   b. an + pang   ---> [an]$_N$ t [pang]$_N$ ---> [anp'ang] (*[anbang])
     'inside' 'room'   'a living room'

   c. kaul + palam---> [kaul]$_N$ t [palam]$_N$ ---> [kaulp'aram] (*[kaulbaram])
     'fall'   'wind'   'fall wind'

(16) a. khun + cip   ---> [khuncip] (*[khunc'ip])
     'big-pres' 'house'   'the head house'

   b. kwun + pam   ---> [kunbam] (*[kunp'am])
     'burn-pres' 'chestnut' 'a roast chestnut'

   c. tal + po-ki   ---> [talbogi] (*[talp'ogi])
     'moon' 'seeing'   'seeing the moon'

In addition, there is good empirical evidence for this analysis that [V+i]$_N$ *peli* in *tonpeli* is an independent word, while *pati* in *mwulpati* is not.

(17) peli : peli-s-kam (thing for making money),
      peli-s-cali (place for making money)

---

[7] There are some exceptions for t-E even in subcompounds. If the first constituents of subcompounds mean the possessor, shape or material for the second ones, t-E can not apply to them such as *kay-koki* (dog meat) --> [kaygogi](*[kayk'ogi]), *saca-pawy* (a rock like a lion)-->[sacabawy](*[sacap'awy]) and *kwum-pinye* (a golden hairpin)-->[kwumbinye](*[kwump'inye]).

[8] Tensification takes place in the modifier structure such as *mek-ul kes*(something to eat). However, this paper distinguishes this tensification from t-E. This paper assumes that the underlying form of the modifier is *-ul?* in a sense that there are some strong evidences in ancient and middle korean: *kal? kil* (a road to go) (in middle korean) (see Sohn 1987, Oh 1988 and Shi 1994)

3.2 Word Interpretation and Move-Affix at LF

In this paper, I assume that syntactic synthetic compounds are formed from noun incorporation in syntax. The term NOUN INCORPORATION (henceforth NI) is generally used to refer to a particular type of compounding in which a V and N combine to form a new V. That is, a N stem is compounded with a V stem to yield a larger, derived, intransitive V stem, as seen in (18) (c.f. Mithun 1984).

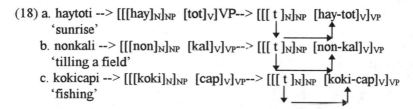

(18) a. haytoti --> [[[hay]$_N$]$_{NP}$ [tot]$_V$]VP--> [[[t]$_N$]$_{NP}$ [hay-tot]$_V$]$_{VP}$
      'sunrise'
   b. nonkali --> [[[non]$_N$]$_{NP}$ [kal]$_V$]$_{VP}$--> [[[t]$_N$]$_{NP}$ [non-kal]$_V$]$_{VP}$
      'tilling a field'
   c. kokicapi --> [[[koki]$_N$]$_{NP}$ [cap]$_V$]$_{VP}$--> [[[t]$_N$]$_{NP}$ [koki-cap]$_V$]$_{VP}$
      'fishing'

In (18a), a N *hay*, which functions as the subject of the verb, is compounded with a V *tot* and in (18b,c) Ns *non* and *koki*, which functions as the objects of the verb, are compounded with Vs *kal* and *cap* respectively.[9] In (18), all Ns should be left adjoined to Vs. Let's see how this proposal is supposed to work for a concrete case such as *haytoti*. If we apply NI and head movement, then we will obtain (19).

(19) a.   b.

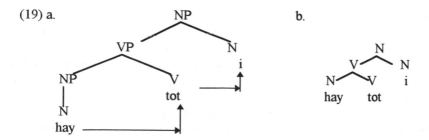

In this construction, N bears a specific semantic relationship to its host V-mainly as THEME.[10] That is to say, the argument structure and semantic

---

[9] Unlike Korean, it is impossible for the non-head to function as the subject of the verb in English : *child driver(on the reading 'child who drives'), *girl-swimming, *weather-changing.

[10] There are a few examples in Korean that the themathic roles of Ns are location or instrument. For instances, the N *son* in *soncapi* (grip) bears *instrument* while the N *cheka* in *chekasali* (living in one's wife's home) *location*.

structure of the verb must be satisfied in such compounds.[11] This means that such synthetic compounds must be interpreted properly, if not, we can not obtain the right word form: *os-pel-i, *palam-pat-i, *namwu-cap-i.

I assume that such compounds are able to be interpreted properly by theta-govern in LF. Under this assumption, we can easily recognize the semantic relation, such as 'argument+predicate' and hence account for the relationship between the verb and noun illustrated in the basic observations.

Let's see how the word interpretation of *mwulpati* takes place in LF. In example (20) we see that the semantic relation in *[[mwul-pat]-i]* can be interpreted in LF because the verb *pat* governs and hence assigns a theta role to its complement *mwul,* on the other hand, the one in *[ton-[pel-i]]* can not because the verb *pel* does not govern its complement *ton*: this role is 'trapped' inside the deverbal head as seen in (21).

(20)　　　　　　　　　　　(21)

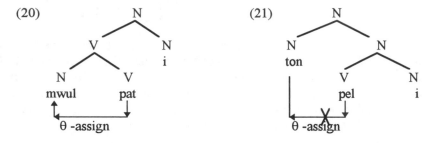

In (21), the noun *ton* has to be interpreted as the object of the verb *pel.* What has to be explained here is how the verb of *tonpeli* can assign a theta role to its complement *ton.* Notice that this structure is an example of a bracketing paradox, because the morphological constituent structure is *[ton-[pel-i]]* while the morpho-syntactic constituent structure must be *[[ton-pel]-i].*

For this purpose this paper assumes move-affix in LF. According to Peseskey(1985), this paper suggests that the mapping from S-structure to LF can be for the derivation of words as well as sentences to produce a proper LF word interpretation. If we apply move-affix to (21) in LF, we will obtain the LF representation shown in (22)

---

[11] The semantic relationship between N and V is discussed in some of the earlier works (e.g. Lieber 1983, Di Sciullo & Williams 1987, Roeper 1987 in English, Sohn 1987, Kim 1990 in Korean). They are mainly focused on how the argument structure of the verb can be satisfied in such compounds, however, they are not how the semantic structure of the verb must be satisfied.

(22) (LF)

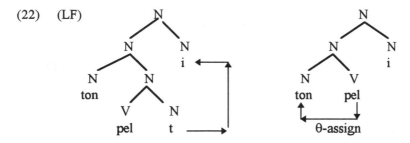

In the (22), this paper assumes that the traces must be removed because they are meaningless in LF. Then, the representation of (22) gives us the right morpho-syntactic constituent structure such as *[[ton-pel]-i]* so that the noun *ton* can be interpreted as the object of the verb *pel* because the verb *pel* can assign a theta role to its complement *ton*.

4. Empirical Consequences

This analysis can be extended to synthetic compounds which are combined with another suffix *-um* as well as *-i* : *pal-kel-um* (step), *kyewul-ca-m* (hibernation), etc.[12]

These examples show us the same observations as *tonpeli*. First, permissible and impermissible verbal compounds are related to grammatical and ungrammatical sentences as illustrated in (23).

(23) a. pal-kel-um (Kwu-ka   pal-lo   ket-nun-ta)
                        He-Nom feet-with   walks
                        'Lit., He walks with feet'

   b. *tol-kel-um (*Kwu-ka   tol-lo   ket-nun-ta)
                        He-Nom stone-with   walks
                        'Lit., *He walks with stone'

(24) a. kyewul-ca-m (Paym-i   kyewul-ey ca-un-ta)
                        Snake-Nom winter-at sleeps
                        'Lit., He sleeps at winter.'

   b.. *hanul-ca-m (*Paym-i   hanul-eyse ca-un-ta)
                        Snake-Nom sky-at   sleeps
                        'Lit., *Snake sleeps at sky.'

Second, they go through t-E like *tonpeli,* so that tensification takes place as seen in (25).

---

[12] There are some more supporting examples such as *twy-s-patchi-m* (support), *twy-s-kel-um-cil* (stepping backward).

(25) a. pal-kel-um   ---> [palk'əlum]   (*[palgəlum])
   b. kyewul-ca-m ---> [kyəulc'am]   (*[kyəulcam])

Third, all [V+ Affix]_N are independent nouns, so that they can participate in another compounding. Let us see below.

(26) a. kelum-kel-i (gait), kelum-ma (toddling),
      kelum-say (the way one walks), etc.
   b. nac-cam (day sleep), pam-cam (night sleep), cam-cali (bed), etc.

These observations show that such compounds are also examples of bracketing paradox like *tonpeli*, because the morphological structure must be *[keywul-[ca-m]], [pal-[kel-umi]]*   to satisfy t-E, while LF structure *[[keywul-ca]-m], [[pal-kel]-um]* to satisfy word interpretation. We can also apply move-affix to them in LF as seen below.

(27)   (LF)

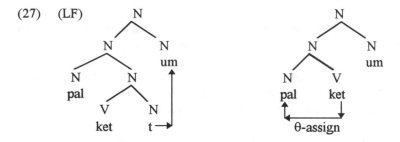

In (27) we can obtain the right LF word structure such as *[[pal-ket]-um]*. so that the verb *ket* can assign a theta role to its complement *pal*.

5. Summary

In this paper I have proposed a new analysis of Korean synthetic compounding. The basic observations have provided us with some properties of Korean synthetic compounds concerning morphology-syntax and morphology-phonology interfacing. To account for such properties, this paper has proposed the two different types of synthetic compounds, such as lexical (e.g., *tonpeli*) and syntactic (e.g., *mwulpati*) synthetic compounds.

This new analysis is conceptually and empirically preferable to the previous analyses. First, this paper can naturally account for the distinction of t-E, illustrated in the basic observations, because this analysis implies that word formation can take place in syntax as well as in the lexicon. Second, this analysis can easily capture the semantic relation, such as 'argument+predicate' and hence account for the correspondence illustrated in the chapter 1. However, in *tonpeli* type, the move-affix is required at LF to satisfy the word interpretation. Third, this analysis can be extended to another synthetic compounds which are combined with suffix *-um* not *-i*.

Therefore, in this paper, unlike the previous approaches, I assumed that synthetic compounding is a lexical & syntactic process. This means, theoretically, this paper can support 'everywhere morphology'.

References

Ahn, Sang-Cheol. 1985. *The Interplay of Phonology and Morphology in Korean,* the doctoral dissertation in University of Illinois of Urbana. Seoul : Hanshin Publishing Company.

Chomsky, N. 1981. Lectures on Government and Binding, Dordrect:Foris Publications.

Chung, Kook. 1980. *Neutralization in Korean : a functional view,* the doctoral dissertation in University of Texas of Austin. Seoul: Hanshin Publishing Company.

Kim, Hyeong-Yep. 1990. *Voicing and Tensification in Korean :A Multiple-Face Approach,* the doctoral dissertation in University of Illinois of Urbana. Seoul:Hanshin Publishing Company.

Lieber, T. 1983. "Argument linking and compounding in English. *Linguistic Inquiry* 14. 251-86.

Oh, Jeong-Rhan. 1988. *Kyengumuy Kwukesacek Yenkwu(The Historical Research of Tensification in Korean),* Seoul:Hanshin Publishing Company.

Pesesky, D. 1985. "Morphology and Logical Form." *Linguistic Inquiry* 16. 193-246.

Roeper, T. 1988 "Compound syntax and head movement. *Year book of Morphology* 1. 187-228.

Sohn, Hayng-Sook. 1987. *Underspecification in Korean Phonology,* the doctoral dissertation in University of Illinois of Urbana. Seoul:Hanshin Publishing Company.

Spencer, A. 1991. *Morphological Theory.* Basil Blackwell, Inc., Cambridge

Kang, Okmi . 1989. "Conditions on -/t/-insertion in Korean Noun Compounds." in *Harvard Studies in Korean Linguistics III*, edited by Susumu Kuno, 101-116, Seoul: Hanshin Publishing Company.

Mithun, M. 1984. "The evolution of noun incorporation." *Language* 60-4. 847-894.
Shi, Chung-Kon. 1994. *Kwueuy Tanehyengseng Wenli (The Principle of Wordformation in Korean)*, Seoul:Kwukhak Publishing Company.

80-39 Chenyen-dong Sedaymun-gu
Seoul, 120-040 Korea
e-mail: chungkon@kuccnx.korea.ac.kr

Numeral Classifiers as Adverbs of Quantification

YUKIKO SASAKI ALAM
Texas A&M University

The present paper concerns a general feature of Japanese referred to as the subject-object asymmetry in `quantifier floating'. It also deals with two types of recently discovered counterexamples to the generalization. The claim made here is that the subject-object asymmetry and the counterexamples, though they appear to be contrasting, are both effects of a universal principle in event quantification that has been exposed in recent years. Object noun phrases measure out the event more often than subject noun phrases, and hence the numeral classifiers are often event modifiers, entitled to have greater freedom in their positions in the sentences. By contrast, subject noun phrases do not measure out the event as often as object noun phrases, and thus tend to be quantifiers over entities with more restricted positions. In addition, there exist such object noun phrases that do not measure out the event while there exist such subject noun phrases that do measure out the event. These object and subject noun phrases give rise to counterexamples to the generalization.

1. Introduction

In the literature of numeral classifiers in Japanese it has been known that there exists a subject-object asymmetry in numeral classifier position:

(1) The Subject-Object Asymmetry in Numeral Classifier Position
     The object NP (noun phrase) can be related to its NC (numeral classifier) when the subject NP intervenes between them, whereas the subject NP cannot be related to its NC when the object NP intervenes between them (Haig 1980, Kuroda 1980).

Example sentences are given below:[1]

(2) a. *San-nin-no*   *gakusei-ga*   *hon-o*   *katta.*
         3-NC-GEN   student-SUBJ   book-OBJ   bought
         `Three students bought a book/books.'
     b. *San-nin*   *gakusei-ga*   *hon-o*   *katta.*
         3-NC   student-SUBJ   book-OBJ   bought
     c. ?**San-nin*   *hon-o*   *gakusei-ga* *katta.*
         3-NC   book-OBJ   student-SUBJ bought
     d. *Gakusei-ga*   *san-nin*   *hon-o*   *katta.*
         student-SUBJ   3-NC   book-OBJ   bought
     e. *Gakusei*   *san-nin-ga*   *hon-o*   *katta.*
         student   3-NC-SUBJ   book-OBJ   bought
     f. ?**Gakusei-ga* *hon-o*   *san-nin*   *katta.*
         student-SUBJ   book-OBJ   3-NC   bought

(3) a. *Gakusei-ga*   *san-satsu-no* *hon-o*   *katta.*
         student-SUBJ   3-NC-GEN   book-OBJ   bought
         `A student/Students bought three books.'
     b. *Gakusei-ga*   *san-satsu*   *hon-o*   *katta.*
         student-SUBJ   3-NC   book-OBJ   bought
     c. *San-satsu*   *gakusei-ga*   *hon-o*   *katta.*
         3-NC   student-SUBJ   book-OBJ   bought
     d. *Gakusei-ga*   *hon-o*   *san-satsu*   *katta.*
         student-SUBJ   book-OBJ   3-NC   bought
     e   *Gakusei-ga*   *hon*   *san-satsu-o* *katta.*
         student-SUBJ   book   3-NC-OBJ   bought
     f. *Hon-o*   *gakusei-ga*   *san-satsu*   *katta.*
         book-OBJ   student-SUBJ   3-NC   bought

---

[1]There seems to exist a subtle difference in meaning among these different quantificational constructions (cf. Note 2). But I will not go into details. However, because the main concern of this paper is to find out what causes the asymmetry in NC position, there will be a discussion as to functional or semantic differences of NCs immediately following the case-marked NPs (like 2d and 3d) and 'floated' NCs (like 3f).

In (2a), (2b), (2d), and (2e) when the NC is adjacent to the subject NP, the sentences are grammatical, whereas in (2c) and (2f), when the object NP intervenes between the subject NP and its NC, the sentences are ungrammatical. By contrast, as (3c) and (3f) show, the intervention of the subject NP between the object NP and its NC does not affect the construal of the NC as that for the distant object NP.

The subject-object asymmetry in NC position has been discussed under the rubric of `quantifier floating', and the solution has been sought from various theoretical backgrounds: by postulating impossible scrambling operations (Haig 1980); by assuming the trace theory (Saito 1985, Miyagawa 1989); by positing the quantifier floatability hierarchy of Case (Shimozaki 1989); and by resorting to the thematic hierarchy (Yatabe 1990). There is no general agreement yet as to the underlying principles that cause this subject-object asymmetry in `quantifier floating'.[2]

However, in recent years the above generalization on the subject-object asymmetry in `quantifier floating' has been challenged. Kitahara (1993) introduces a type of counterexamples to the generalization which do not allow the subject intervention between the object NP and its NC. Furthermore, Kawashima and Kitahara (1993) present another type of counterexamples to the generalization which permit the object intervention between the subject NP and its NC. As a result, the explanation for `quantifier floating' phenomena must cover both the general tendency of subject-object asymmetry and the two types of counterexamples to the generalization.

The present paper attempts to shed light on the underlying principles of the `quantifier floating' phenomena by examining them from the perspective of which may be quantified by NCs. First, in Section 2.1 we will examine Kitahara's (1993) analysis of those examples that do not permit the subject intervention between the object NP and its NC. Next, in Section 2.2 we will look into

---

[2] I use quotation marks to cite *quantifier floating* to avoid commitment to the theory that quantifiers have moved away from the original positions adjacent to the NPs. There is a strong reason to believe that quantifiers have been generated in the same positions where they appear on surface, because their positions affect the interpretation of quantification. Takano (1984, 1986) observes that adnominal NCs such as that of 2a and postnominal NCs such as that of 2d differ in the implication of definiteness and partitivity. Downing (1993) reports that text counts of Japanese numeral classifier constructions reveal different pragmatic profiles of different constructions. Junker (1990) argues that the 'floated' quantifiers *chacun/each* force the distribution of the event.

Kawashima and Kitahara's (1993) solution to those examples that allow the object intervention between the subject NP and its NC. Finally, in Section 3 I will present an alternative analysis of the `quantifier floating' phenomena.

2. Two Types of Counterexamples

2.1. Impermissible Subject Intervention

Kitahara (1993) brings to our attention the existence of sentences that do not allow the intervention of the subject NP between the object NP and its NC. These sentences are counterexamples to the hitherto widely held generalization that the subject NP can intervene between the object NP and its NC. Observe the following structurally same sentences:

(4)   a. ***San-satsu***   *Taro-ga*   ***gengogaku-no***   ***hon-o***   *yonda.*
        3-NC   -SUBJ   linguistics-GEN book-OBJ read
        `Taro read three linguistics books.'

    b. ?****San-nin***   *Taro-ga*   ***Harvard-no***   ***gakusei-o***   *matta.*
        3-NC   -SUBJ   -GEN   student-OBJ waited
        `Taro waited for three Harvard students.'

In (4a), the NC *san-satsu* `three (used for counting bound objects)' is related to the object NP *gengogaku-no hon* `linguistics book' across the subject NP *Taro*, and the intended construal obtains, as predicted by the generalization on `quantifier floating'. By contrast, in (4b), though it has the same structure as that of (4a), the NC *san-nin* `three (used for counting people)' cannot be related to the object NP *Harvard-no gakusei* `Harvard student' across the subject NP *Taro*. (4b) is a counterexample to the generalization. Using a test to examine specificity, Kitahara detects difference in specificity between *gengogaku-no hon* `linguistics book' and *Harvard-no gakusei* `Harvard student': namely, *gengogaku-no hon* `linguistics book' is a nonspecific NP while *Harvard-no gakusei* `Harvard student' is a specific NP.

The diagnostic test used for specificity is based upon the theory that the empty pronoun coindexed with a nonspecific NP may refer to a different member of the set named by the nonspecific NP, whereas the empty pronoun coindexed with a specific NP must denote the same member referred to by the specific NP. Test sentences are provided below:

(5) a. *(Watashi-wa) Taro-ga* **gengogaku-no   hon-o   san-satsu**
         I-TOP   -SUBJ linguistics-GEN book-OBJ 3-NC
     yonda-to   kiiteita-kedo Hanako-mo   ø   yonda-rashii-yo.
     read-COMP heard-while   -too   read-seem-SP
     'While I have heard that Taro read three linguistics
     books, it seems that Hanako read (three linguistics
     books), too.'

     b. *(Watashi-wa) Taro-ga* **Harvard-no gakusei-o   san-nin**
         I-TOP   -SUBJ   Harvard-GEN student-OBJ 3-NC
     matta-to   kiiteita-kedo Hanako-mo   ø   matta-rashii-yo.
     waited-COMP heard-while   -too   waited-seem-SP
     'While I have heard that Taro waited for three
     Harvard students, it seems that Hanako waited for
     (three Harvard students), too.'

In (5a), the three books referred to by the empty pronoun differ from
the three books referred to by the antecedent NP. This suggests
that *gengogaku-no hon* 'linguistics book' is a nonspecific NP. By
contrast, in (5b) the three Harvard students referred to by the
empty pronoun are the same students referred to by the antecedent
NP. This indicates that *Harvard-no gakusei* 'Harvard student' is
a specific NP. Based upon the above observation, Kitahara
proposes a hypothesis stated below:

(6)   Extraction out of a specific DP [3] is prohibited while
         extraction out of a nonspecific DP is allowed.[4]

However, Kitahara's claim is unwarranted. (7) and (8) show a
possible 'extraction' of the NC from a specific DP:

(7) a. **Ni-hon** *tomodachi-ga* **eiga-o**   *mite-kita.*
        2-NC   friend-SUBJ   movie-OBJ   seeing-came
     'My friend saw two movies.'

     b. *ø Omoshiro-soona-node,   boku-mo   ø   miru-koto-ni-shita.*
        interesting-seem-because I-too   see-to-decided
     'As (they) seem to be interesting, I have decided to see
     (the two movies).'

---

[3]A DP consists of a determiner phrase and an NP.

[4]This is similar in spirit to Diesing's hypothesis (1992: 103):
Extraction cannot take place out of a presuppositional NP.

(8) **Sono-hon-o**   gakusei-ga   **san-satsu**   katte-itta.
     the-book-OBJ   student-SUB   3-NC   buying-went
     `Students bought three copies of the book.'

The referent of the object DP in (7a), which consists of *ni-hon* `two (used for counting cylindrical objects)' and *eiga* `movie' is the same as that of the two empty pronouns in (7b), and therefore the object DP should be specific. Yet `extraction' from the specific object DP is possible, as evidenced by the intervention of the subject DP *tomodachi* `friend'. In addition, (8) shows that although the object DP is specific, `extraction' from the specific object DP takes place. Thus, Kitahara's hypothesis stated in (6) is not viable.

2.2. Possible Object Intervention

Another type of counterexamples to the generalization on the subject-object asymmetry in `quantifier floating' concern a possible object intervention between the subject NP and its NC (Kawashima and Kitahara 1993). (9) is such an example sentence:

(9) *Watashi-wa*   *[imamadeni Metropolitan-no*   *auction-de*
     I-TOP   up-to-now   -GEN   -at
     nihonjin-ga   Gogh-no   e-o   **san-nin**
     Japanese-SUBJ   -GEN painting-OBJ   3-NC
     rakusatsu-shita-to]   kiita.
     bid-successfully-COMP   heard
     `I heard that up to now, three Japanese bid successfully for paintings by van Gogh at the Metropolitan Auction.'

Kawashima and Kitahara account for this possible object intervention, based on the following two assumptions:

(10)   This object intervention between the subject NP and its NC
       is possible because:
       a. *Nihonjin-ga san-nin* `three Japanese (subject)' in
          (9) is a nonpresuppositional DP, and
       b. A nonpresuppositional subject DP allows the
          object intervention between the subject NP and its
          NC.

To determine the presuppositionality of a DP, they use a diagnostic test which is based upon the hypothesis stated below:

(11) Antecedent Constraint (Bennis 1986, Diesing 1992)
     An empty DP can refer to its (potential) antecedent
     DP iff the antecedent DP receives a presuppositional
     interpretation.

As shown in (12), Kawashima and Kitahara demonstrate that the
split subject DP in (9) is a nonpresuppositional DP, since the subject
DP in (12a), which is a variant of (9) with the unsplit subject DP,
cannot be the antecedent of the empty pronoun in (12b):

(12) a. *Watashi-wa [imamadeni   Metropolitan-no   auction-de*
         I-TOP   up-to-now   -GEN   -at
         nihonjin-ga   san-nin   Gogh-no   e-o
         Japanese-SUBJ 3-NC   -GEN   painting-OBJ
         rakusatsu-shita-to]   kiita.
         bid-successfully-COMP   heard
         `I heard that up to now, three Japanese bid successfully
         for paintings by van Gogh at the Metropolitan Auction.'

      b. *#Louvre-no auction-de-mo ø Gogh-no   e-o*
            -GEN   -at-too   -GEN   painting-OBJ
         rakusatsu-shita   rashii,
         bid-successfully seem
         `It seems that ø bid successfully for paintings by van
         Gogh at the Louvre Auction, too.'

Furthermore, they demonstrate that the removal of the temporal
expression *imamadeni* `up to now' from (12a) and the preposing of
the subject DP of (12a) change the subject from a
nonpresuppositional DP to a presuppositional DP, as shown in (13),
because the preposed subject DP *nihonjin ga san-nin* `three Japanese'
of (13a), unlike the counterpart of (12a), can be the antecedent of
the empty pronoun in (13b):

(13) a. *Watashi-wa [nihonjin-ga   san-nin Metropolitan-no*
         I-TOP   Japanese-SUBJ 3-NC   -GEN
         auction-de Gogh-no e-o   rakusatsu-shita-to]
            -at   -GEN painting-OBJ bid-successfully-COMP
         kiita.
         heard
         `I heard that three Japanese bid successfully for
         paintings by van Gogh at the Metropolitan Auction.'

b. *Louvre-no   auction-de-mo ø Gogh-no e-o*
    -GEN   -at-too   -GEN painting-OBJ
rakusatsu-shita rashii.
bid-successfully seem
    `It seems that ø bid successfully for paintings by van
    Gogh at the Louvre Auction, too.'

They point out that (13a), which has a presuppositional subject DP,
does not allow the object intervention, as is illustrated in (14b):

(14) a. (= 13a)
        Watashi-wa [nihonjin-ga   san-nin Metropolitan-no
        I-TOP   Japanese-SUBJ   3-NC   -GEN
        auction-de   Gogh-no e-o   rakusatsu-shita-to]
                  -at   -GEN painting-OBJ bid-successfully-COMP
        kiita.
        heard

      b. ?**Watashi-wa   [nihonjin-ga Gogh-no e-o   san-nin*
        I-TOP   Japanese-SUBJ -GEN painting-OBJ 3-NC
        Metropolitan-no auction-de   rakusatsu-shita-to]
                  -GEN   -at   bid-successfully-COMP
        kiita.
        heard
           `I heard that three Japanese bid successfully for
           paintings by van Gogh at the Metropolitan Auction.'

Based upon these data, they propose the following descriptive
generalizations on the admissibility of the object intervention
between the subject NP and its NC:[5]

(15) a.   If a subject DP receives a presuppositional
        interpretation, an object DP cannot intervene between
        the subject NP and its NC.
      b.   If a subject DP receives a non-presuppositional
        interpretation, an object DP can intervene between the
        subject NP and its NC.

However, Kawashima and Kitahara's claim is untenable, as
shown in the following examples:

---

[5]The statement in (15a) conforms to Diesing's (1992) hypothesis cited
in Note 4.

(16) a. *Yoshiko-ni*   *damasareta*   **otoko-ga**   *kinoo*
         -by   cheated   man-SUBJ   yesterday
      Yoshiko-no   *uchi-o*   ***san-nin***   *otozureta.*
         -GEN   house-OBJ   3-NC   visited
      `Three men who were cheated by Yoshiko visited her
      house yesterday.'

    b. *Shikashi,*   *Yoshiko-ga*   *uchi-ni*   *inakatta-node*
      but   -SUBJ   house-at   was-not-because
      ø shitsubooshite   *kaette-itta.*
      being disappointed   returning-went
      `But because she was not at home, they went back with a
      broken heart.'

The subject DP *Yoshiko-ni damasareta otoko-ga san-nin* `three men who were cheated by Yoshiko' is the antecedent of the empty pronoun in (16b), and therefore it should be presuppositional. Yet the object intervention between it and its NC is possible, as shown in (16a). This example is against Kawashima and Kitahara's hypotheses, in particular, the one stated in (15a).[6] In the next section, I propose an alternative analysis of `quantifier floating' phenomena. It will also be shown why (15a) is not viable, but (15b) is.

3. The Analysis

3.1. What Is Quantified?

     In this section I argue that a decisive factor in `quantifier floating' hinges on the reading of the event described by the predicate. When the predicate is interpreted **distributively** or **as a quantified event**, `quantifier floating' is permissible, because in this case the NC is a quantifier over event, entitled to have wide scope over beyond the NP. By contrast, when the predicate is interpreted **as an integrated mass** or in the `totalization' mode,

---

    [6] Kawashima and Kitahara's analysis is based upon several hypotheses including Diesing's (1992) Mapping Hypothesis, and often leads to assumptions of three different structures at D-structure, S-structure, and LF for sentences with numeral classifiers. Their analysis, in my opinion, complicates the grammar of Japanese which does not grammaticalize configuration as much as English. However, I will not go into this topic, as it is in itself a major issue.

`quantifier floating' is not allowed.[7] For instance, recall the sentences in (4), which are repeated:

(17) a. **San-satsu** Taro-ga   **gengogaku-no hon-o**   *yonda.*
    3-NC   -SUBJ   linguistics-GEN book-OBJ   read
    `Taro read three linguistics books.'

    b. ?***San-nin** Taro-ga   **Harvard-no gakusei-o**   *matta.*
    3-NC   -SUBJ   -GEN students-OBJ   waited
    `Taro waited for three Harvard students.'

(17a) and (17b) are structurally the same, but differ from each other in terms of predicate type. A clear difference emerges when the temporal expression *san-ji-kan* `for three hours' is added:

(18) a. #*Taro-ga*   *gengogaku-no hon-o*   *san-satsu*
    -SUBJ   linguistics-GEN book-OBJ   3-NC
    san-ji-kan   *yonda.* (<- 17a)
    for 3 hours   read
    `Taro read three linguistics books for three hours.'

    b. *Taro-ga*   *Harvard-no gakusei-o*   *san-nin*
    -SUBJ   -GEN students-OBJ   3-NC
    san-ji-kan   *matta.* (<- 17b)
    for 3 hours   waited
    `Taro waited for three Harvard students for three hours.'

As is well documented in the literature of aspect (Vendler 1967, Dowty 1979 to name a few), a temporal expression of duration cannot modify a dynamic event that denotes a terminal point (i.e. a telic event), but it can modify a dynamic event that does not (i. e. an atelic event). The verb of (18a) *yomu* `read' can form an atelic predicate together with the object DP meaning an unspecified amount of reading material, while it can form a telic predicate with the object DP denoting a specified amount of reading material. Because (18a) has *san-satsu* `three (for counting bound objects)', it denotes a telic event consisting of three completed events. Thus, *san-ji-kan* `for three hours' is not compatible with (18a). By contrast, the verb of (18b) *matsu* `wait' inherently denotes an atelic

---

[7] See Verkuyl 1994 for the clarification of the terms *distributive* and *totalization.*

event with no indication of an endpoint or an intermission. The process of waiting is a homogeneous event throughout the interval, because it continues without any internal change. Namely, the event is conceptualized in the `totalization' mode in which three students are taken together. Thus, (18b) is compatible with the temporal expression of duration.

This amounts to saying that the NC *san-satsu* `three (for counting bound objects)' in (18a) is a quantifier over an event (of reading a book by Taro), whereas the NC *san-nin* `three for people' in (18b) is a quantifier over an entity (which is a Harvard student). That is to say, *san-satsu* `three (for bound objects)' is **an adverb of quantification**, thus having wide scope and exhibiting a relative freedom in its position in the sentence, and *san-nin* `three (for people)', which quantifies over an entity, has narrow scope and is restricted within the domain of the entity.[8]

The present analysis is closely related to Krifka's (1992) observation on quantifiers. He argues that quantifiers induce two types of readings, i.e. the object-related reading and the event-related reading. For instance, (19) has two readings:

(19) Four thousand ships passed through the lock last year.
      A: There are four thousand ships which passed
          through the lock last year. (**Object-related** reading)
      B: There were four thousand events of passing through
          the lock by a ship last year. (**Event-related** reading)

The object-related reading presupposes the existence of (at least) four thousand ships, whereas the event-related reading does not unless specified to this effect. The four thousand events of lock traversals may include those events by the same ships.

Using Krifka's terminology, we can restate the proposed analysis of (17a) and (17b). (17a) has an event-related reading with focus on the number of completed events, although in this case, pragmatics forces the interpretation that the three books Taro read are different books. The quantifier for an event-related reading is a measure function of event, thus entitled to have scope over beyond the related NP. By contrast, (17b) has an object-related reading, thus forcing the NC to be adjacent to the NP. As

---

[8]In this sense, traditional linguists' views are insightful. Martin (1975) calls the NCs located after case-marked NPs adverbialized NCs in his reference grammar of Japanese. Ikegami (1971) introduces in his entry about Japanese numerals Yamada's (1936) viewpoint that numerals not only denote numbers but also have adverbial-like functions of measuring or counting.

san-nin `three (for counting people)' has an object-related reading, *Harvard-no gakusei san-nin* `three Harvard students' has the presuppositional reading.

The object-related reading of the quantifier presupposes the existence of the specified number of the entities. Therefore, if the existence of the quantified entities is not presupposed, it can be said that the quantifier has an event -related reading and may `float' from the NP. Usually the event-related reading of the quantifier does not presuppose the existence of the specified number of the entities, but it may not preclude the possibility of such presupposition, as is evidenced in (17a), in which pragmatics induces the reading of the occurrence of each different event and hence the existence of each different entity. Therefore, the following formula obtains:

(20) Object-related reading $\longrightarrow$ Presuppositional DP

Event-related reading $\diagup\!\!\!\diagup\!\!\!\longrightarrow$ Nonpresuppositional DP

Next let us recapitulate the relation between quantificational constructions and the semantics. As understood from the pair of sentences in (4), despite the fact that they have the same structure, *gengogaku-no hon-o san-satsu* `three linguistics books (object)' in (21a) is a nonspecific DP while *Harvard-no gakusei-o san-nin* `three Harvard students (object)' in (21b) is a specific DP:

(21) a. *Taro-ga*   **gengogaku-no** **hon-o**   **san-satsu** *yonda.*
      -SUBJ   linguistics-GEN book-OBJ 3-NC   read
      `Taro read three linguistics books.'

    b. *Taro-ga*   **Harvard-no**   **gakusei-o san-nin** *matta.*
      -SUBJ   -GEN   student-OBJ 3-NC   waited
      `Taro waited for three Harvard students.'

In addition, the following example sentence in (22), which is similar to Krifka's (19), has both an object-related reading and an event-related reading, as is the case with (19):

(22) *Moo*   *kuruma-ga hyaku-dai*   *kono-michi-o*   *tootta.*
     already car-SUBJ   100-NC   this-road-OBJ passed
     `One hundred cars have already passed this road.'

Therefore the following relation holds between quantificational constructions and the semantics:[9]

(23)   Object-related reading $\longrightarrow$ NP-Subj/Obj + NC

Event-related reading $\longleftrightarrow$ NP-Subj/Obj .... NC

NC .... NP-Subj/Obj

In view of this relation between presuppositionality and NC constructions, let us reexamine Kawashima and Kitahara's hypothesis in (15), which is repeated below:

(24) a.   If a subject DP receives a presuppositional interpretation, an object DP cannot intervene between the subject NP and its NC.
      b.   If a subject DP receives a non-presuppositional interpretation, an object DP can intervene between the subject NP and its NC.

Because a presuppositional subject DP with the NC in an event-related reading permits the intervention of the object DP, the statement in (24a) is too strong. But (24b) seems to be a correct assumption, because if a DP receives a nonpresuppositional interpretation, the NC has an event-related reading and can have scope over beyond the NP, thus allowing the intervention of other elements.

In the literature of NCs in Japanese, it has been noted that an addition of temporal expressions such as *imamadeni* and *koremadeni* `so far/up to now' licenses `quantifier floating' (Miyagawa 1989, Yatabe 1990), as shown below:

(25) a. ?**Gakusei-ga*   *hon-o*   **san-nin**   *katta.*
          student-SUBJ   book-OBJ   3-NC   bought
          `Three students bought a book.'

      b. *Gakusei-ga*   *hon-o*   **imamadeni**   *san-nin   katta.*
          student-SUBJ   book-OBJ   **up-to-now**   3-NC   bought
          `So far three students bought a book.'

---

[9]As (2) and (3) show, there are other quantificational constructions. How object-related and event-related readings relate to those constructions is not explored in this paper. See Note 10 for a passing comment on this subject.

The present analysis is able to account for the change of grammaticality. The change takes place because the temporal expression induces a distributive reading of the event by creating a context that expects the input of the number of occurrences of a delimited event. (25) reads that up to now three events of buying a book by a student took place.

3.2. The Origin of the Subject-Object Asymmetry

In the beginning of this paper I discussed the generalization that there is a subject-object asymmetry in `quantifier floating': the object NP can be related to the NC when the subject NP intervenes, whereas the subject NP cannot be related to the NC when the object NP intervenes. Namely, `floating' of the NC from the subject NP is more restricted than that from the object NP.

I argue that this subject-object asymmetry is due to functional differences in event semantics between subject and object NPs, of which Tenny (1989, 1992) has exposed several underlying principles. She proposes the following principle stated in (26), which I call the Event Role of the Internal Argument:

(26)   The Event Role of the Internal Argument (Tenny 1992: 6-7)
       All direct internal arguments undergoing change in the
       event described by the verb measure out the event. ...
       With some verbs (*perform, translate, destroy, redden, ripen*)
       the direct internal argument measures out and delimits the
       event. With other verbs (*push*) the direct internal argument
       measures out the event and an indirect internal argument may
       delimit it.

In her theory, the direct INTERNAL ARGUMENT means not only the object of a transitive verb, but the subject of an UNACCUSATIVE VERB (i.e. a nonagentive, telic intransitive verb). When the internal argument is a count noun, the event is delimited. On the other hand, when the internal argument is a mass noun, the event is nondelimited. Example sentences are given:

(27)   a. *Charles drank **a mug of beer**.*   (*??for an hour/in an hour*)
                                         (**delimited** event)

       b. *Charles drank **beer**.*   (*for an hour/#in an hour*)
                                         (**nondelimited** event)

She goes on to note that there are no classes of verbs for which countness of the EXTERNAL ARGUMENT translates into delimitedness of the event. As is evidenced by (28), whether the external arguments in block are mass or count nouns does not change the delimitedness of the event:

(28) a. *The heater melted the candle.*   (**delimited** event)
      b. *Heat melted the candle.*   (**delimited** event)

In my opinion, this difference in the function of measuring out the event between internal and external arguments is responsible for the subject-object asymmetry in `quantifier floating' in Japanese. The NCs for object NPs are relatively free in their positions in the sentences, because object NPs often measure out the events and the NCs function as measure of the event. They quantify over events, thus receiving the right to wide scope beyond the NPs. When object NPs do not measure out the events, their NCs are quantifiers over entities, and therefore their positions are restricted. The scarcity of instances of `quantifier floating' from subject NPs is due to the paucity of instances of their functioning as measure of the event. In other words, the NCs for subject NPs tend to receive an object-related reading while the NCs for object NPs tend to have an event-related reading, and these general tendencies of theirs are due to the different roles their host NPs play in event semantics.[10]

4. Conclusion

In this paper I have presented an analysis of linguistic phenomena relating to quantificational asymmetry in Japanese.

---

[10]Event semantics seems to offer an answer to Okutsu's (1969) puzzle as to why NCs can follow the case-marked subject or object ARGUMENTS, but not the case-marked oblique arguments:

Kono e-wa	fude	ippon-de	kaita.
this painting-TOP	brush	1-NC-with	painted

`I painted this painting with one brush.'

#Kono e-wa	fude-de	ippon	kaita.
this painting-TOP	brush-with	1-NC	painted

According to this theory, the reason is that NCs for oblique arguments receive purely an object-related reading (without any suggestion of contribution to the quantification of the event) and hence are located within the NPs, avoiding the NP-Case-NC construction used both for an object-related and an event-related readings (cf. 23). Inoue (1978) presents such counterexamples that have NCs located immediately after the case-marked oblique arguments:

Watashi-wa	yadoya-ni	ni-san-gen	atatte-mita.
I-TOP	inn-DAT	2-3-NC	inquired

`I inquired at two or three inns.'

The NC in this example contributes to the quantification of the event. It indicates the occurrence of two or three events of inquiring at an inn. Event semantics is at work here, too.

The proposed theory is able to explain that the seemingly conflicting facts are in fact the effect of universal principles of event quantification exposed by Tenny (1989, 1992) and Krifka (1990). Namely, the subject-object asymmetry in `quantifier floating' and the counterexamples to the asymmetry are both the effect of different functions of NCs: i.e. measure functions of events or entities. Object NPs' greater permissibility for NC position is due to the fact that object NPs measure out the event more often than subject NPs. At the same time we have observed that not all object NPs measure out the event while some subject NPs measure out the event. In addition, we have seen that distributive readings of event are also induced by adverbials such as *imamadeni* `up to now'. These instances comprise counterexamples to the generalization of the subject-object asymmetry. It also proves that earlier linguists' intuitive treatment as adverbialization is correct. It also shows that there are certain correlations between quantificational constructions and presuppositionality, but that they are not pervasive. Nonpresuppositional quantificational constructions allow `quantifier floating' because of the event-related reading, but presuppositional counterparts seem to divide depending upon whether the reading is object-related or event-related. In addition, specificity participates in event quantification. For instance, a subject or object NP which is specific in terms of reference, quantity, or both often contributes to measuring out the event because of the sense of delimitedness it has.

References

Bennis, Hans. 1986. Gaps and dummies. Dordrecht: Foris.

Diesing, Molly. 1992. Indefinites. Cambridge, MA: MIT Press.

Downing, Pamela. 1993. Pragmatic and semantic constraint on numeral quantifier position in Japanese. J. Linguistics 29. 65-93.

Dowty, David. 1979. Word meaning and Montague grammar. The semantics of verbs and times in generative semantics and in Mongague's PTQ. Dordrecht: Reidel.

Haig, John H. 1980. Some observations on quantifier float in Japanese. Linguistics 18.1065-1083.

Ikegami, Akihiko. 1971. Suushi. Nihon Bunpoo Daijiten, ed. by Akira Matsumura, 347-348. Tokyo: Meiji Shoten.

Inoue, Kazuko. 1978. Nihongo-no Bunpoo Kisoku. Tokyo: Taishukan.

Junker, Marie-Odile. 1990. Floating quantifiers and Georgian distributivity. CLS 26.211-219.

Kawashima, Ruriko and Hisatsugu Kitahara. 1993. On the distribution and interpretation of subjects and their numeral classifiers. Proceedings for SALT 3, ed. by Utpal Lahiri and Adam Zachary Wyner, 97-116. Cornell University Dept. of Modern Languages and Linguistics.

Kitahara, Hisatsugu. 1993. Numeral classifier phrases inside DP and the specificity effect. Japanese/Korean Linguistics Volume 3, ed. by Soonja Choi, 171-186. Stanford: CSLI.

Krifka, Manfred. 1990. Four thousand ships passed through the lock: object-induced measure functions on events. Linguistics and Philosophy 13.487-520.

Kuroda, S.-Y. 1980. Bun-koozoo no hikaku. Nichieego Hikaku Kooza 2: Bunpoo, ed. by Tetsuya Kunihiro, 23-61. Tokyo: Taishukan.

Martin, Samuel E. 1975. A reference grammar of Japanese. New Haven: Yale University Press.

Miyagawa, Shigeru. 1989. Syntax and semantics 22: structure and case marking in Japanese. New York: Academic Press.

Okutsu, Keiichiro. 1969. Suuryooteki Hyoogen-no Bunpoo. Nihongo Kyooiku. 14.

Saito, Mamoru. 1985. Some asymmetries in Japanese and their theoretical consequences. Doctoral dissertation, MIT.

Shimozaki, Minoru. 1989. The quantifier float construction in Japanese. Gengo Kenkyu 95.176-205.

Takano, Yasukuni. 1984. The lexical nature of quantifiers in Japanese. Linguistic Analysis 14.289-311.

Takano, Yasukuni. 1986. The lexical nature of quantifiers in Japanese part II. Linguistic Analysis 16.41-59.

Tenny, Carol. 1992. The aspectual interface hypothesis. Lexical matters, ed. by Ivan A Sag and Anna Szabolcsi, 1-28. Stanford: CSLI. (Originally in Lexicon project working paper 31 (1989). MIT Center for Cognitive Science.)

Vendler, Zeno. 1967. Linguistics in philosophy. New York: Cornell University Press.

Verkuyl, Henk. 1994. Distributivity and collectivity: a couple at odds. Dynamics, polarity, and quantification, ed. by Makoto Kanazawa and Christopher J. Piñón, 49-80. Stanford: CSLI.

Yamada, Takao. 1936. Nihon Bunpoogaku Gairon. Tokyo: Hinbunkan.

Yatabe, Shuichi. 1990. Quantifier floating in Japanese and the theta-hierarchy. CLS 26.437-451.

Opacity and Subjunctive Complements in Japanese

ASAKO UCHIBORI

University of Connecticut

0. Introduction

The primary concern of this paper is to investigate what characterizes opaque domain for some syntactic phenomena such as long-distance A-scrambling and long-distance binding of local anaphora in Japanese. It has been commonly held that opaque domain for A-movement and anaphor binding is induced by the category CP. The Japanese data discussed in this paper reveal that this is not necessarily the case: a certain type of CP complement do not constitute an opaque domain for those syntactic phenomena. This is shown by taking a closer look at SUBJUNCTIVE complements. I argue that either a subjunctive suffix attached to a verb or a

*I am deeply grateful to Keiichiro Kobayashi, Howard Lasnik, Masao Ochi, Toshifusa Oka, Satoshi Oku, Mamoru Saito, Daiko Takahashi, and Hiroyuki Ura for their invaluable comments and suggestions on the materials presented here. All remaining inadequacies are mine.

modal auxiliary morphologically marks an embedded predicate to be sub-junctive in such a CP complement that is not opaque. Thus, opacity is induced not by clausal category of a domain, but by the existence of a certain modality in the domain, which must be distinct from indicative. It will be also demonstrated that neither finiteness nor the existence of an overt subject marked with nominative Case does not induce opacity.

In the next section, I will present the data indicating that a certain type of complement is transparent for A-scrambling and anaphor binding, and argue that it is a CP subjunctive complement. In section 2, reexamining the so-called control complement with *-yoo(ni)*, I will show that it is regarded as another instance of subjunctive complement. A discussion on a subjunctive complement with an overt nominative subject will be given in section 3. I conclude this paper by giving a brief comment on the complement headed by *-koto* in section 4.

1. CP Complements with the Subjunctive Suffix

In English, the CP complement disallow NP raising out of it and binding of a local anaphor within it from the matrix clause.

(1) a. *$John_i$ seems [$_{CP}$ that it is told t_i that Mary will win the race.]

b. *$John_i$ [$_{CP}$ that Mary recommended $himself_i$.]

It has been claimed that such an opacity is created by CP also in Japanese (see Nemoto 1991 and Saito 1992, for example). The bridge-verb CP complement, which involves tense morphology on the embedded predicate, allows neither A-scrambling out of it; nor binding of a local anaphor within it from the matrix clause, as shown by the examples in (2) below.

(2) a. *$Karera_i$-o [$otagai_i$-no   sensei]-ga [$_{CP}$ Hanako-ga t_i suisenshi
 $They_i$-acc *each other*-gen teacher-nom   -nom   recommend
 -ta   to]   omot-ta.
 -past comp think-past
 '*$Them_i$, each $other_i$'s teachers thought that Hanako recommended.'

b. *$Taro_i$-ga [$_{CP}$ $iinkai_j$ -ga zibun-$zishin_j$/kare-$zishin_i$-o
          -nom   committee-nom self-self / he-self   -acc
 suisenshi -ta   to]   omot-ta.
 recommend-past comp think-past
 '*$Taro_i$ thought that the committee recommended $himself_i$.'

There are certain types of complement which are actually CP, yet transparent, however. Let us consider a complement subcategorized by a verb which depicts ordering, asking, advising, and so forth.[1,2]

(3) Koochyoo-ga sono sensei$_i$ -ni [e$_i$ Hanako-o suisenshi -ro to]
Principal-nom that teacher-dat   -acc recommend-subj comp
meiji/motome/susume-ta.
order/require/urge   -past
'The principal ordered/required/urged the teacher to recommend Hanako.'

This type of complement is to be regarded as CP, if -to, which heads the complement in (3), is the same one as the complementizer -to introducing the bridge-verb complements in (2). It has been sometimes claimed that the complement clause such as in (3) is a quotation of actual speech with the quotation marker -to (Shibatani 1978), however. It is true that verbs selecting a subjunctive complement as in (3) may take a quotation, as shown in the example in (4).[3]

(4) Taro-ga   Jiro-ni   'saa omae(-ga) sono heya-o   hak -e -yo'
       -nom   -dat int you(-nom) that room-acc sweep-subj-part
to meiji-ta.
qm order-past
'Taro said to Jiro, "hey, you, sweep that room."'

The existence of the interjections saa and the particle -yo in (4) indicates that the clause containing these elements is a quotation. But, the complement in (3) crucially differs from such a quotation in the following two respects: First, a wh-element in a complement as in (3) can have its scope over the matrix clause, as shown in the example in (5).

---

[1]   Whether the embedded subject in (3) is PRO or pro does not matter at this point. It must be controlled by the matrix object. The following example indicates that it is not a trace; that is, this construction does not involve a subject-to-object raising structure. The matrix verb assigns an independent theta-role to the object noun phrase, which must be agentive.
   (i)*Taro-ga   ame$_i$-ni [e$_i$ hur-e   to]   meireishi-ta.
        -nom rain-dat   fall-subj comp command-past
   '*Taro ordered rain to fall.'

[2]   This verb ending -ro is called 'subjunctive' for reasons I will directly return below.

[3]   The abbreviations used here are; int = interjection; part = particle; qm = quotation marker.

(5) Taro-ga Jiro$_i$-ni [$_{CP}$ e$_i$ doko-o   hak -e   to]   meiji-ta no?
     -nom   -dat   where-acc sweep-subj comp order-past Q
     'Where did Taro order Jiro to sweep?'

Secondly, an element in this type of complement can be scrambled out of it, as shown by the example in (6).

(6) Sono heya-o$_j$ Taro-ga   Jiro$_i$-ni [$_{CP}$ e$_i$ t$_j$ hak -e   to] meiji-ta.
     That room-acc,   -nom   -dat   sweep-subj   order-past
     'That room, Taro ordered Jiro to sweep.'

On the other hand, quotations allow neither of them, as shown by the ungrammatical examples in (7) and (8).

(7) *Taro-ga Jiro-ni "saa omae(-ga) doko-o   hak -e -yo to"
         -nom   -dat int you(-nom) where-acc sweep-subj-part qm
     meiji-ta   no?
     order-past Q
     '*Where did Taro said to Jiro "Hey, you, sweep."'

(8) *Sono heya-o$_i$ Taro-ga   Jiro-ni "saa omae(-ga) t$_i$ hak -e   -yo
     That room-acc,   -nom   -dat int you(-nom)   sweep-subj-part
     to" meiji-ta.
     qm order-past
     '*That room, Taro said to Jiro "Hey, you, sweep."'

That is, the complement in (3) is not an instance of real quotation headed by the quotation marker -to.

In fact, there is empirical evidence indicating that -to, which introduces the complement at issue, is the same entity as the complementizer -to in the bridge-verb CP complements. It is a well-known fact that Osaka Japanese allows deletion of a complementizer -te, which is an equivalent to -to in this language (Saito 1986).[4] This is exemplified in (9) .

(9) Taro-ga [$_{CP}$ Hanako-ga ashita   Kobe-ni ik-u   (te)] yuu-ta.
     -nom   -nom tomorrow   -to go-pres comp say-past
     'Taro said (that) Hanako would go to Kobe the next day.'

Here, the complement clause is not a quotation, because scrambling out of it and embedding a wh-phrase which takes the matrix scope within it are

---

[4]   Tokyo Japanese does not allow deletion of the complementizer -to in principle. There is one exceptional case, however. See fn 11 and fn 14.

both possible even if -*te* is deleted. The grammatical examples in (10) and (11) show this point.

(10) Taro-ga [$_{CP}$ Hanako-ga ashita   doko-ni   ik-u   (te)]
     -nom   -nom tomorrow where-to go-pres comp
yuu-ta-n?
say-past-Q
'Where did Taro say that Hanako will go tomorrow?'

(11) Kobe-ni, Taro-ga [$_{CP}$ Hanako-ga   ashita   ik-u   (te)]   yuu-ta.
     -to   -nom   -nom tomorrow go-pres comp say-past
'Kobe, Taro said that Hanako will go tomorrow.'

Interestingly, Osaka Japanese also permits -*te* to be deleted from a subjunctive complement, as shown by the example (12).

(12) Taro-ga Jiro$_i$-ni [$_{CP}$ e$_i$ sono heya-o   hak -e   (te)] yuu-ta.
     -nom   -dat   that room-acc sweep-subj comp say-past
'Taro told Jiro to sweep that room.'

It is therefore natural to say that -*te* in this type of complement is also a complementizer. It should be noted here that a quotation prohibits a deletion of -*te* even in Osaka Japanese, as shown by the example in (13).

(13) Taro-ga   Jiro-ni   "ora omae(-ga) sono heya-o   hak -e -yo
         -nom   -dat   int you(-nom) that room-acc sweep-imp-part
*(te)" yuu-ta
'Taro said to Jiro, "hey, you, sweep that room.'

In sum, -*to*, which introduces the complement in (3) above,, is the complementizer -*to*; hence, the complement is CP.

    Given both the common assumption that CP induces opacity and our conclusion that the clausal status of the complement in (3) is CP, it is expected that such complements like the bridge-verb complement allow neither long-distance A-scrambling nor long-distance binding of a local anaphor. It may come as a surprise to find that this prediction is not born out, as the grammatical examples in (14-15) indicate.

(14) Karera$_i$-o   koochyoo-ga [otagai$_i$ -no sensei]$_j$ -ni [$_{CP}$ e$_j$ t$_i$ suisenshi
     Them -acc principal -nom *e.o.* -gen teacher-dat   recommend
-ro to]   meiji/motome/susume-ta.
-subj comp order/require/urge   -past

'*Them$_i$, the principal ordered/required/urged each other$_i$'s teachers to recommend.'

(15) Taro$_i$-ga iinkai$_j$ -ni [$_{CP}$ e$_j$ zibun-zishin$_{i/*j}$/kare-zishin$_{i/*j}$-o suisenshi
    -nom committee-dat   self-self / he-self   -acc recommend
    -ro to] meiji/motome/susume-ta.
    -subj comp order/require/urge   -past
    '*Taro$_i$ ordered/required/urged the committee to recommend himself$_i$.'

In the example in (14), the NP *karera*, 'them', is scrambled to the sentence initial position, and it can bind the anaphor *zibun-zishin* 'self-self' or *kare-zishin* 'he-self', in the matrix indirect object position. This means that A-scrambling out of the complement is possible. In the example in (15), the matrix subject can bind the anaphor in the complement. That is, contrary to the expectation, this type of CP complement does not induce opacity regardless of the existence of an overt subject in the complement. It follows that the CP status of a complement is not a crucial factor for opacity.

What differentiates the complement of this type from the bridge-verb complement such as in (2)? The verb in the complement in question is followed by the special morphology, e.g. *-ro*, but the verb in the bridge-verb complement is not. This morphology seems to correspond to the so-called imperative suffix that appears in an imperative sentence, which denotes a speaker's command, as shown in (16) below.

(16) (Omae-ga) Hanako-o   suisenshi -ro.
    (You-nom)   -acc recommend-subj
    '(You,) recommend Hanako.'

The term 'imperative' is not appropriate to refer to the form which also appears in the complement at issue, however. As we have seen above, the complement with this form is not a direct quotation of an imperative speech.[5] It is evident from the English translations of the examples above that the meaning of the complement is command, request, wish, advise, and so on. It generally expresses unreality or possibility of the state of affair, which is certain modality. The semantics of the modality is carried by the main verb like *meiji* 'order', *motome* 'require', and *susume* 'urge', etc.

---

[5]   It has been reported that an imperative sentence usually does not occur as a subordinate clause in many languages. Palmer (1986) suggests that what seems to be a subordinate imperative is a direct speech (or a non-clausal element such as a noun phrase). As shown in (4), an imperative sentence with a quotation marker can be a direct (reported) speech also in Japanese.

Since this form is not exclusively used to denote a speaker's command, the term 'imperative' is not only misleading, but also inadequate.

Furthermore, this form used in the main clause is not always interpreted as imperative, but also to be optative, which denotes a speaker's wish, as shown in (17) below.[6]

(17) a. (Kami-yo) hitobito-ni saiwai ar-e.   b. Ame-yo hur-e.
     (God -voc) people-dat happy be-subj   Rain-voc fall-subj
     '(God) may people be happy.'   'May it rain.'

Thus, it is preferable to use a single term that covers these functions of this form whether it is used in the main clause or in a subordinate clause.

A similar case can be found in other languages. For example, in Latin, the distribution of the subjunctive mood is not limited to a subordinate clause, and some of its meaning are in common to the meanings of what I here call 'subjunctive' in Japanese. According to Lakoff (1968), at least eight meanings of the subjunctive can be recognized, i.e. imperative, optative, jussive, concessive, potential, deliberative, purposive, and relative purposive. Moreover, the subjunctive plus the complementizer *ut* is used as a complement of verbs of ordering, requesting and so on (Palmer 1986). The same applies to the subjunctive in Japanese, as we have already seen above. Accordingly, this form is regarded as the subjunctive suffix.

We now find out that a certain morphology on the embedded verb that is closely related to a certain modality plays an important role in inducing opacity. Given the above observation that the subjunctive complement does not constitute an opaque domain regardless of the fact that it is CP, it follows that it is the subjunctive morphology that characterizes opacity with respect to long-distance A-scrambling and binding of local anaphora. In the next section, I will demonstrate that the complement in which the modal auxiliary -*yoo(ni)* appears is not opaque either, which will further support the analysis proposed here.

2. Complement Headed by Modal Auxiliary: Another Instance of Subjunctive Complement

Nemoto (1991) points out that the so-called control complement, where an embedded verb is followed by the special morphology,

---

[6]   The abbreviation -voc is for a vocative marker.

-yoo(ni(-to)), does not create opacity.[7] The sentence in (18) below exemplifies this type of complement.[8]

(18) Koochyoo-ga sensei$_i$-ni [e$_j$ seito-o   home -ru   -yoo(ni(-to))[9]]
Principal-nom teacher-dat   student-acc praise-nonpast
meiji/motome/susume-ta.
order/require/urge   -past
'The principal ordered/required/urged the teachers to praise the students.'

The verbs selecting the complement headed by *-yoo(ni(-to))* are the same as those taking the subjunctive complement discussed in section 1. The meaning of the complement headed by *-yoo(ni(-to))* is also almost same as that of the subjunctive complement marked with the subjunctive suffix, i.e. wish, advice, request, and so on, which depends on the semantics of the main verb.[10] Both A-scrambling and binding of local anaphor are allowed to take place across the so-called control complements, as shown below.

(19) a. Karera$_i$-o koochyoo-ga [otagai$_i$-no sensei]$_j$-ni [e$_j$ t$_i$ suisensu
Them-acc principal-nom   e.o. -gen teacher-dat   recommend
-ru   -yoo(ni(-to))] meiji/motome/susume-ta.
-nonpast   comp order/require/urge   -past
'*Them$_i$, the principal ordered/required/urged each other$_i$'s teachers to recommend t$_i$.'

b. Taro$_i$-ga iinkai$_j$ -ni [e$_j$ zibun-zishin$_{i/*j}$/kare-zishin$_{i/*j}$-o suisenshi
-nom committee-dat self-self / he-self   -acc recommend
-u   -yoo(ni(-to))] meiji/motome/susume-ta.
-nonpast   comp order/require/urge -past
'*Taro$_i$ wanted/adviced/orderd the principal to recommend himself$_i$.'

---

[7]   See also Saito (1994) for discussion on A-scrambling out of this type of complements.

[8]   The empty subject in the complement is controlled by the matrix object. For general discussions on the control properties of this type of complements, see Sakaguchi (1990). See also Watanabe (1995), for an analysis of control complements from a crosslinguistic perspective.

[9]   The morpheme *ni* alone cannot be omitted if the morpheme *-to* appears. That is, either *ni-to* or *-to* can be dropped off. Some of Kansai dialect speakers report to me that the whole sequence *-yoonito* sounds unnatural. I have no explanation about this.

[10]   There is a slight difference in meaning between *-yooni* and the subjunctive suffix. See fn 13.

Under the theory of BARRIERS (Chomsky 1986), Nemoto claims that this type of complement clause does not yield opacity because it is not CP, but VP, and that the embedded subject is PRO controlled by the matrix object. According to Nemoto, the examples in (19) are thus fine due to the nonexistence of CP-boundary.

Contrary to Nemoto, I am claiming that the clausal status of this complement does not concern opacity. That is, at least when the complement is headed by the complementizer -to, it projects CP. In fact, both the example in (19a) above, where A-scrambling takes place out of the complement, and the example in (10) below, where wh-phrase in the complement takes the matrix scope, prove that -to in the complement at issue is not a quotation marker, and it also shows that it is a complementizer.[11]

(20) Koochyoo-ga sensei$_i$-ni [$_{CP}$ e$_j$ dare-o   hame -ru   -yoo(ni(-to))]
    Principal-nom teacher-dat   who-acc praise-nonpast   comp
    meiji/motome/susume-ta -no?
    order/require/urge   -past-Q
    'Who did the principal order/require/urge the teachers to praise?'

In short, the complement headed by -yoo(ni-) behaves exactly like the complement marked with the subjunctive suffix with respect to opacity. Both of them do not constitute an opaque domain. I pointed out in section 1 that, when there is a special marking of certain modality that is distinct from indicative in a complement, the complement is not opaque. This suggests a possibility that -yoo(ni) is another way of signifying certain non-indicative modality.

What is -yoo(ni), then? There is evidence that -yoo(ni) is not a complementizer. Consider the following example, where this form appears in a main clause to express direction, duty, advice, and so on.

(21) Hon-o   takusan yom-u   -yoo(ni)   (*-to).
    Book-acc many   read-nonpast-modal aux   comp
    'You should read many books.'

The fact that -yoo(ni) appears in the main clause indicates that it is not any kind of subordinate marker. Since it is attached to an amalgam of a verb and inflectional suffixes like a negative suffix, a tense suffix and so on, it is assumed to be a modal auxiliary that appears at the end of a clause in

---

[11]   It is not clear why the complementizer -to can be omitted only if it follows -yooni even in Tokyo dialect, though. See fn 14, for a brief discussion about this.

Japanese.[12] Furthermore, since *-to* cannot follow *-yoo(ni)* in this case, *-to* must be a subordinate marker. This again supports the above claim that *-to* is the complementizer when the clause headed by *-yoo(ni(-to))* is a complement.

One should notice here that the meaning of the sentence in (21) is similar to that of a sentence with a verb marked with the subjunctive which functions as the imperative.[13] In addition to this, a main clause with this form signifies a speaker's wish, as shown in the following example.

(22) Hanako-ga   shiken-ni ukar-u   -yoo(ni)   (*-to).
     -nom exam-dat pass-nonpast-modal aux -comp
     'May Hanako pass the exam.'

This is also analogous to the use of the subjunctive suffix to express a speaker's wish (i.e. the optative). Recall that the main verbs selecting the complement with *-yoo(ni)* overlap with those taking the subjunctive complement discussed in section 1. That is, *-yoo(ni)* serves to signify modality of the kind expressed by the subjunctive suffix whether it is used in the main clause or it is in a complement clause. I therefore consider *-yoo(ni)* to be a modal auxiliary, i.e. another instance of subjunctive morphology.[14]

Another piece of supporting evidence is the fact that a purposive clause is marked by *-yoo(ni(-to))*, as shown below

(23) Sensei-ga [seito -ga   hon-o   takusan yom-u   -yoo(ni
         -nom student-nom book-acc many   read-nonpast-modal aux
     (-to))] zoosyo   -o   kurasu-ni kifushi-ta.
     -comp one's library-acc class   -dat donate-past
     'The teacher donated his library to the class so that the students should read many books.'

---

[12]   For example, the modal auxiliary *-daroo* 'it is possible that .../I think that ... ', which expresses a speaker's judgment, follows a verb with inflectional suffixes.

[13]   They are slightly different in that *-yoo(ni)* sounds weaker.

[14]   As Mamoru Saito pointed out to me, in Italian, a complementizer *che* cannot be omitted with indicative complements, but it can be with a subjunctive complement. The deletablity of the complementizer *-to* from *-yoo(ni(-to))* are very much like the Italian case. However, it is unclear why *-to* cannot be deleted from the subjunctive complement as discussed in section 1. I leave this problem to future research.

The modal auxiliary -*yoo(ni)* follows a tensed verb. Here, -*to* functions as a subordinate marker that is attached to a non-complement subordinate clause. A similar way of indicating purposive clauses is found in Latin. A clause with the subjunctive mood plus the complementizer *ut* is also used to express 'in order that ...' (Palmer 1986).

I have argued so far that the so-called control complement headed by -*yoo(ni(-to))* is another instance of subjunctive complement, i.e. (CP) control complements marked by the modal auxiliary. The fact that it does not induce opacity confirms the claim that opacity depends on subjunctive marking in a complement.

3. Subjunctive Complement with Overt Nominative Subject

One might claim that the tense morphology is equally or more important to determine opacity, since a nonfinite clause is not an opaque domain for both A-movement out of it and binding of a local anaphor within it in English, as shown in (24) below.

(24) a. John$_i$ seems [$_{IP}$ to be told t$_i$ that Mary will win the race.]
   b. John$_i$ seems [$_{IP}$ t$_i$ to recommend himself$_i$.]

In Japanese, the embedded verb marked with the subjunctive suffix never carries any tense suffix such as the past -*ta* or the nonpast -*(r)u*,[15] whereas the embedded verb in the bridge-verb complement does. In fact, this is expected, because a possible temporal interpretation of the unrealized event expressed by a subjunctive complement is rather restricted. Tense in the subjunctive complement is defective in this sense. This might indicate that the subjunctive complement is nonfinite and does not induce opacity.

It is not the case, on the contrary, since an overt nominative subject can appear in the complement whose predicate is marked with the subjunctive suffix, as shown in (25).

(25)   Taro-ga [Hanako-ga   shiken-ni   ukar-e   to]
         -nom   -nom exam -dat pass-subj comp
       nenji/inot/setsubooshi-ta
       wish/pray/desire   -past
       'Taro wished/prayed/desired that Hanako would pass the exam.'

---

[15]   Aspectual suffixes, for example, a perfective -*teshimaw*, can precede the subjunctive suffix.

The main verb in (25a) subcategorizes a subjunctive complement, but not an NP object.[16] This example indicates that, in the complement clause, there must be an element necessary to license nominative Case marking on the embedded subject. According to Takezawa (1987), such an element is tense in Japanese as well as in English. It follows that this type of subjunctive complement is finite, even though tense is not so rich as in an indicative complement.[17,18]

Given the analysis presented in section 1 and 2, it is predicted that, even if an overt subject appears within a CP subjunctive complement, the complement is transparent; that is, both A-scrambling out of it and binding of local anaphor within it from the matrix clause are possible. This prediction is born out by the following examples.

(26) Karera$_i$-o [otagai$_i$ -no sensei]$_j$ -ga [$_{CP}$ koochyoo-ga t$_i$ susisenshi
Them -acc *e.o.* -gen teacher-nom principal-nom recommend
-ro to] nenji/inot/setsubooshi-ta
-subj comp wish/pray/desire-past
'*Them$_i$, each other$_i$'s teacher wished/prayed/desire the principal to recommend t$_i$.'

(27) Taro$_i$-ga [$_{CP}$ iinakai -ga zibun-zishin$_{i/*j}$/kare-zishin$_{i/*j}$-o suisenshi
-nom committee-nom self-self / he-self -acc recommend
-ro to] nenji/inot/setsubooshi-ta
-subj comp wish/pray/desire -past
'*Taro$_i$ wished/prayed/desired the committee to recommend himself$_i$.'

Opacity does not depend on whether an overt subject appears or not.

Let us turn to the subjunctive complement marked with *-yoo(ni)*. The null subject in the complement with *-yooni* can alternately become

---

[16] In contrast, the main verb as shown in section 1 alternatively selects a subjunctive complement of this type together with an object NP, which controls the embedded subject. In this case, some speakers disallow the embedded overt subject in the complement. Generally speaking, when an controller overtly shows up, an embedded controllee is preferred to be null. See Hasegawa (1984) for relevant discussions, for example. For similar cases, see fn 20 and fn 22.

[17] Then, an empty subject in this type of subjunctive complements is *pro*.

[18] One might reject this, claiming that what licenses nominative Case marking on the subject in Japanese might turn out to be not Tense, but Agreement, for example, and that tense morphology plays a crucial role in determining opacity. But, there is evidence against such a claim. We will see certain complements which are not opaque regardless of the existence of tense morphology soon below.

overt, if the complement is selected by a verbs of the kind listed in (25) above.[19] Consider the example in (28) below.[20]

(28) Sensei -ga   [$_{CP}$ Hanako-no ronbun-ga   saikoo -ten -o
Teacher-nom   -gen paper -nom highest-mark-acc
tor-u   -yoo(ni   (-to))] nenji/inot/setsubooshi-ta
get-nonpast-modal aux-comp wish/pray/desire-past
'The teacher wanted/requested Hanako to get the highest mark (on her paper).'

An element licensing nominative Case marking on the embedded subject, i.e. tense, must exist in the complement clause. In fact, the embedded verb of this type must be immediately followed by the suffix *-ru*, which is regarded as the nonpast suffix that is often used to express a future event, as shown below.

(29) Watashi-wa [$_{CP}$ [$_{IP}$ ashita   ame-ga hur-u]   to]   omo-u.
I   -top   tomorrow rain-nom fall-nonpast comp think-nonpast
'I think that it will rain tomorrow.'

Accordingly, *-yoo(ni)* is not an infinitival marker, and the complements headed by *-yoo(ni(-to))* is finite.[21] Although tense is not so rich in the sense that only the nonpast can appear, it is not surprising because the event denoted by the complements is an unrealized one that might happen in the future.

Even when an embedded subject is overt, this type of complements do not induce opacity, as shown by the following examples.

(30) a. Karera$_i$-o   [otagai$_i$ -no sensei]$_j$-ga [$_{CP}$ koochyoo-ga
-acc e.o. -gen teacher-nom   principal -nom
suisensu   -ru   -yoo(ni   (-to))] nenji/inot/setsubooshi-ta
recommend-nonpast-modal aux-comp wish/pray/desire   -past

---

[19]   There are some verbs which take both types of subjunctive complement; namely, those with an overt matrix object and a null embedded subject and those with an overt embedded subject. For example, *nozom* 'want' and *motome* 'require' take any of them.

[20]   Again, some people do not allow an embedded overt subject if the main verbs as discussed in section 2 also take an object NP.

[21]   This indicates that, even if it might turn out that the subjunctive complement marked with the subjunctive suffix is nonfinite, we cannot classify these non-opaque complements all together in terms of nonfiniteness.

'*Them, the principal wanted/requested each other's teachers to recommend.'

b. Taro$_i$-ga [$_{CP}$ iinkai   -ga   zibun-zishin$_{i/*j}$/kare-zishin$_{i/*j}$-o
        -nom   committee-nom self-self / he-self   -acc
      suisensu -ru   -yoo(ni) (-to))] nenji/inot/setsubooshi-ta
      recommend-nonpast-modal aux-comp wish/pray/desire   -past
'*Taro$_i$ wanted/requested the committee to recommend himself$_i$.'

These examples show that the complement with the modal auxiliary -yoo(ni) is not opaque whether the complementizer -to and/or an overt nominative-marked subject appear. We therefore cannot maintain the assumption that the finiteness of the embedded complement and/or the existence of a nominative marked subject determines opacity with respect to long-distance A-scrambling and long-distance binding of a local anaphor in Japanese.

4. Conclusion: -*Koto* Complements

Let us make a brief comment on another type of complement subcategorized by the kind of verb we are considering in this paper. This type of verb also selects a complement headed by -*koto*, which is attached to an inflected verb just like -*yoo(ni)*, as shown below.[22]

(31) Sensei -ga   (Hanako$_i$-ni) [kanojyo$_i$-no ronbun-ga   saikoo -ten
      Teacher-nom   -dat   she   -gen paper -nom highest-mark
      -o   tor-u   -koto] nozon/motome-da/ta
      -acc get-nonpast   want/request -past
      'The teacher wanted/requested Hanako to get the highest mark on her paper.'

Interestingly enough, A-scrambling out of it (see Nemoto 1993a) and binding of an anaphor within it are permitted, as shown below.

(32) a. Karera$_i$-o [otagai$_i$-no sensei]-ga (koochyoo$_j$-ni) [kanojyo$_j$-ga t$_i$
        They-acc e.o. -gen teacher-nom principal -dat   she -nom
        suisensu -ru   koto]-o   nozon/motome-da/ta.
        recommend-nonpast   -acc want/request -past

---

[22]   The pronoun in the embedded subject position in (31) has the referential property as described in fn 16. If the matrix object appears, the pronoun in the embedded subject position must be coreferential with it. If not, it refers to any person. In the former case, some speaker do not allow the overt embedded subject.

'*Them$_i$ each other's$_i$ teacher wanted/requested the principal/her to recommend.

b. Taro$_i$-ga (sono iin$_j$ -ni) [knojyo$_j$-ga   zibun-zishin$_{i/j}$
   -nom that committee-dat she -nom   self-self
/ kare-zishin$_{i/*j}$-o   suisensu -ru   -koto]-o   nozon/motome-da/ta.
/he-self   -acc recommed-nonpast   -acc want/request -past
'*Taro$_i$ wanted/requested the member of the committee/her to recommend himself$_i$.'

It has been questioned in the literature whether the morpheme -*koto* is a noun or a complementizer. Whichever it is, the significant similarity in opacity among the three types of the complement of these verbs is straightforwardly captured by assuming that -*koto* is also a subjunctive marker,[23] and that they are all subjunctive complements.

To summarize, I provided the evidence showing that neither the category CP, the existence of tense, nor the existence of an overt nominative-marked subject, characterizes opacity. Our observation leads us to the conclusion that the existence of the embedded subjunctive morphology is the decisive factor, and strongly points to the necessity for an alternative theory of opacity. George and Kornfilt (1981) reports that opacity in Turkish is not triggered by the complement with the tensed predicate, but by the complement with the predicate marked by an agreement morphology. I will leave the issue as to why such a morphology characterizes opacity to future research.[24]

---

[23]   Based on the study of control property of the -*koto* complements, Watanabe (1995) also suggests that -*koto* is a subjunctive complementizer

[24]   See Uchibori (in progress) for discussions on this issue as well as on the question of what derives the long-distance binding under the framework of the minimalist program (Chomsky 1995). What is of particular interest concerning anaphor binding is the fact that a morphologically complex local anaphor like *zibun-zishin/kare-zishin* is long-distantly bound in a subjunctive complement, which is conflict with the claim that anaphora which allow long-distance binding are morphologically simple across languages (Progovac 1993, Koster and Reuland 1991).

References

Chomsky, Noam. 1986. Barriers. Cambridge, Mass.: MIT Press.

Chomsky, Noam. 1992. Minimalist program for linguistics theory. The View from Building 20, eds. by Kenneth Hale and Samuel J. Kayser, 1-52. Cambridge, Mass.: MIT Press.

Chomsky, Noam. 1995. The minimalist program. Cambridge, Mass.: MIT Press.

George, Leland, and Jaklin Kornfilt. 1981. Finiteness and boundedness in Turkish. Filters and control, ed. by Frank Heny, 105-127. Cambridge, Mass.: MIT Press.

Hasegawa, Nobuko. 1984. On the so-called 'zero-pronoun' in Japanese. TLR 4:289-341.

Koster, Jan. and Eric. Reuland (eds.) 1991. Long-distance anaphora. Cambridge: Cambridge University Press.

Lakoff, Robin. 1968. Abstract syntax and Latin complementation. Cambridge, Mass.: MIT Press.

Nemoto, Naoko. 1993a. Notes on control constructions in Japanese. Journal of Japanese Linguistics 13:125-137.

Palmer, F. R. 1986. *Mood and modality*. Cambridge: Cambridge University Press.

Progovac, Ljiljana. 1993. Long-distance reflexives: Movement-to-Infl versus relativized SUBJECT. LI 24:755-772.

Saito, Mamoru. 1986. Three notes on syntactic movement in Japanese. Issues in Japanese linguistics, eds. by Takashi Iamai and Mamoru Saito, 301-350. Dordrecht: Foris.

Saito, Mamoru. 1992. Long-distance scrambling in Japanese, JEAL 1:69-118.

Saito, Mamoru. 1994. Improper Adjunction. Formal approaches to Japanese linguistics. vol 1. 263-293. MITWPL 24. MITWPL, MIT.

Sakaguchi, Mari. 1990. Control structures in Japanese. Japanese and Korean linguistics, ed. by Hajime Hoji, 303-317. Stanford, Calif.: CSLI.

Shibatani, Masayoshi. 1978. Nihongo no bunseki [Analyses of Japanese]. Tokyo: Taisyuukan syoten.

Takezawa, Koichi. 1987. A configurational approach to Case marking in Japanese. Doctoral dissertation, University of Washington.

Uchibori, Asako. in progress. The syntax of subjunctive complements. Doctoral dissertation, University of Connecticut.

Watanabe, Akira. 1995. Nominative-Genitive conversion and AGR in Japanese: A crosslinguistic perspectives. ms., Kanda University of International Studies.

NPIs Outside of Negation Scope

DAEHO CHUNG AND HONG-KEUN PARK
University of Southern California

1. Introduction

It is generally taken for granted that **negative polarity items** (henceforth, NPIs) must be in the (immediate) **scope** of their licensing trigger, although there is controversy on what constitutes the trigger, e.g., a downward entailing element (Ladusaw 1980) or an element with a negative implicature (Linebarger 1980). In this paper, however, we claim that there may exist some discrepancy between the NPI licensing **domain** of a trigger and its scope. In particular, we claim that NPIs are not necessarily in the scope of a trigger, although a certain locality has to be fulfilled between such NPIs and their licenser. We have a predecessor in claiming the discrepancy. Suh (1990) also claims that NPIs can be licensed outside of the **negation scope**. Unfortunately, however, we do not agree with her grammatical judgment on the crucial data.

Our claim that NPIs are not necessarily in the **scope** of their trigger is based on the following two sets of Korean data: (I) there is a certain kind of NPIs that cannot be in the scope of **negation** (section 2), and (II) there is a certain kind of negative predicates that cannot have scope over a position taken by NPIs (section 3).

In section 4 we discuss a locality condition on NPI licensing in Korean. In section 5 we speculate on the reason why NPIs in Korean can have a wide scope over negation.

2. NPIs Taking a Negative Proposition

A certain kind of NPIs in Korean cannot be in the scope of negation. Sentential adverbs like *kyelkho/celtaylo* `absolutely' are such NPIs.

2.1. An NPI Property

The negative orientation of these adverbs is evidenced in the fact that they require a clause mate negation:[1]

(1)   a. Ku-nun <u>kyelkho/celtaylo</u> kukos-ey ga-ci <u>ani</u> ha-ess-ta.
           He-Top absolutely   there-to go-CI Neg do-Pst-DE.
           `It is <u>absolute</u> that he did <u>not</u> go there.'
     b. *Ku-nun <u>kyelkho/celtaylo</u> kukos-ey ga-ess-ta.
           He-Top absolutely   there-to go-Pst-DE.
           `It is <u>absolutely</u> true that he went there.'

(1a) is grammatical, but (1b) is not. The only difference between these two sentences is that (1a) has a **negation morpheme** *ani*, whereas (1b) does not. This indicates that such adverbials are NPIs.

---

[1]In Chung (1993) such adverbial NPIs are classified as the strongest NPIs in the sense that they are licensed only in the sentential negation unlike *to*-NPIs, which are licesned in BEFORE clauses as well, as observed by Lee (1993).

2.2. Scopal Facts

The interpretation of (1a), however, tells us that such NPIs are not in the **negation scope**. In other words (1a) has the reading (2a) but not (2b).

(2)   a. It is <u>absolutely</u> true that he did <u>not</u> go there.
        b. #It is <u>not</u> the case that he <u>absolutely</u> went there.

These adverbial NPIs are similar to adverbs of speaker's attitude toward assertion, such as English *truly, verily, assuredly, unfortunately, most definitely*, etc., in the sense that they take a proposition as their **scope**. As paraphrased in (2a), the adverbial NPI *celtaylo* `absolutely' takes the rest of the sentence as its scope. Similarly, *unfortunately* in (3) below also takes the rest of the sentences as its scope:

(3)   a. Unfortunately, he came late.
        b. Unfortunately, he did not come late.

The sentential adverbial NPIs, however, cannot be simply equated with the adverbs of speaker's attitude since there are at least two differences between them. First, these NPIs must take a negative proposition in their (immediate) scope as was seen in (1), whereas the latter allow a positive proposition as well as a negative one as illustrated in (3). A second difference is that the adverbs of speaker's attitude toward assertion cannot be embedded as they are root adverbs, whereas no such restriction applies to the adverbial NPIs. Compare the following contrast in grammaticality:

(4)   a. *John met a person who <u>unfortunately/assuredly</u> came late.[2]
        b. *If John <u>most definitely</u> comes late, he will be punished.

---

[2]These sentential adverbs may appear in a nonrestrictive relative clause as shown in (i) below:

(i) John met a person, who <u>unfortunately/assuredly</u> came late.

For some reasons, non-restrictive relative clauses behave like root clauses.

(5)　　a. na-nun [celtaylo/keylkho ic-ci　　　mos-ha-l] salam-ul
　　　　　I-Top　absolutely　　　　　forget-NMZ not-do-Fut man-Acc
　　　　　manna-ess-ta.
　　　　　meet-Pst-DC
　　　　　`I met a man who I would never forget.'
　　　　b. [John-i celtaylo/kyelkho o-ci　　　mos-myen] ney-ka　　taysin
　　　　　J.-Nom absolutely　　　　come-NMZ cannot-if　you-Nom instead
　　　　　hay-ela.
　　　　　do-Imp
　　　　　`If John could not come definitely, you do it instead.'

The sentential adverbs *unfortunately/assuredly/most definitely* are not allowed
in a relative clause or in a conditional as in (4), whereas Korean adverbial NPIs
like *celtaylo/kyelkho* are allowed in those contexts as in (5).

3. Types of Negation, Negation scope, and NPI Licensing Domain

It is generally accepted that Korean has two types of **negation**: **short
forms** and **long forms**. In this section, we propose to classify the so-called
suppletion form of negation as a third type since negation of this type shows
different scopal facts from the other two types. As will be seen, **negation scope**
of the third type is restricted to the predicate into which the negation force is
incorporated. Negation of this type, however, may license clause mate NPIs just
like the other two types of negation do. This indicates again that NPIs are
licensed outside of the negation scope.

3.1. Suppletion forms as a Third Type of Negation

It is well-known that Korean has two forms of negation at least on the
surface:[3] the so-called **short form negation** and the so-called **long form
negation**. The short form negation is formed by prefixing *ani* `not' (or its
contracted form *an*) to a verb, whereas the long form negation is formed by

---

[3] In his series of work, Song (1971, 1973, 1988), however, tries to unify the two forms
into one. He analyzes the so-called long form negation v-*ci ani-ha* simply as a
nominalization of an embedded verb, v, followed by negation of main verb *ha*. Verb *ha*
in his sytem is a main verb, not an auxiliary one.

suffixing a nominalizer *ci* to a verb stem and adding a dummy verb *ha* `do' prefixed with *ani* or *an*.   The two forms of **negation** are schematically represented in (6) and exemplified in (7):

(6)   a. **short form negation**: *ani*-Verb
                                                        Neg
        b. **long form negation**: Verb Stem-*ci*   *ani-ha*
                                                        NMZ Neg-do

(7)   a. John-i <u>ani-o-ess-ta</u>.
           J.-Nom Neg-come-Pst-DC
           `John did not come.'
        b. John-i <u>o-ci   ani-ha-ess-ta</u>.
           J.-Nom come-NMZ Neg-do-Pst-DC
           `John did not come.'

Any verb can conjugate with a **long form**, but not all verbs can take a **short form**. In general, verbs with one or two syllables may take a **short form negation**: e.g., *ani-ka* `not go', *ani-tali* `not run', etc. But verbs with three or more syllables generally do not take a short form negation: e.g., *ani-kongpwuha `not study', \**ani-alumtap* `not be beautiful'. (See Ahn 1990).

Interestingly, verbs like *al* `know' and *iss* `exist' are mono-syllabic but do not take a short form negation: *ani-ul, and *an-iss.[4] Instead they take a **suppletion form** of negation: *molu* `not;know', and *eps* `not;exist'. Negation or negative force in suppletion forms is incorporated into the predicate so that the predicate cannot be analyzed into a core predicate and a **negation morpheme**.

A question that arises is whether short forms and suppletion forms are two different types of negation or just two different instances of the same type of negation with different information in the area of morphology.

---

[4]In fact, the verb *iss* may take a short form negation, that is, *an-iss*, in certain contexts, especially when it means `to stay', as opposed to `to exist'.

(i)   cip-ey   <u>an-iss-ko</u>   eti ka-ni?
        house-at Neg-exist-and where go-QE
        `Where are you going, not staying at home?

Negation in (i) cannot be replaced by a suppletion form, *eps-ko*.

Suppletion forms do not necessarily show syntactic or semantic differences from regularly conjugated forms in grammar. Let us consider past conjugations in English. Past tense is formed in various ways: by adding -ed to the verb stem (e.g., *look/looked*), by altercating stem vowels (e.g., *run-ran*), or by adopting a suppletion form (e.g., *go-went*), among other modes. The formal variation, however, does not make any functional difference. The so-called irregular forms do not show any difference from the regularly conjugated forms in their syntactic or semantic behaviors. For example, irregular verbs convey the past meaning as the regular past forms and license the same types of time adverbials as the regular forms do.

Let's turn back to the question of the relation between **short form negation** and suppletion form negation in Korean, i.e., the question of whether **negation** in the suppletion forms shows any difference from that in the short form apart from their difference in morphology, a specific morphological information added for the former. As will be argued in the next subsection, the answer should be affirmative. Unlike the suppletion forms in English past tense, the suppletion form negation in Korean does show a syntactic difference from the short form negation. More specifically, the two forms of negation differ from each other in scope interpretation.

Thus, as far as the factual claim to be made in the next subsection is correct, Korean has three types of negation: short forms, **long forms**, and suppletion forms.

3.2. Types of Negation and Negation scope

Due to De Morgan's theorem, negation is an **anti-morphic**, i.e., **anti-multipliticative** and **anti-additive**, function on its **scope** (argument). Relevant notions are defined below:[5]

---

[5]The defintions in (8) are cited from Nam (1993:1, his (2)).

(8)   Let $<A, \leq>$ and $<B, \leq>$ be two Boolean algebras.
        a. $f \in [A \rightarrow B]$ is *anti-multipliticative* iff
           for all $\alpha, \beta \varepsilon A$, $f(\alpha \wedge \beta) = f(\alpha) \vee f(\beta)$.
        b. $f \in [A \rightarrow B]$ is *anti-additive* iff
           for all $\alpha, \beta \varepsilon A$, $f(\alpha \vee \beta) = f(\alpha) \wedge f(\beta)$.
        c. $f \in [A \rightarrow B]$ is *anti-morphic* iff
           f is anti-additive and anti-multiplicative.

Anti-multiplicity extends over the conjunctions in sentences with short or **long form negation** but not in those with **suppletion form negation**.[6]

The **negation** in suppletion forms shows different scopal facts from the negation in short forms and in long forms. Specifically, the negation scope of suppletion forms is confined to the predicate to which negation morpheme is incorporated, whereas the negation scope of short or long forms may extend over any elements in the clause.[7]

Consider the following structures:

(9)   a. ...[A-*kwa* B]... *ani*-Verb-Tense-SE (SE=sentence ender)
            and   Neg
        b. ...[A-*kwa* B]... Verb-*ci*   *ani-ha*-Tense-SE
            and   NMZ Neg-do
        c. ...[A-*kwa* B]... Verb/[+neg]-Tense-SE

---

[6]We avoid testing **anti-additivity** since the so-called disjunction morpheme in Korean, *ina* 'or', can have a conjunctive reading as well as a disjunctive reading. For example, *ina* is compatible with distributor *ta* 'all' as in (i):

(i) John-ina Mary-ka ta mikwuk salam-i-ta.
    J.-or   M.-Nom   all America man-be-DC
    'Both John and Mary are all Americans.'

[7]We agree with Song (1988) in claiming that short form negation and long form negation can have a wide **scope** over conjunctions in the same clause. Suh(1990), however, claims differently. According to her, scope of a short form negation is confined to the predicate to which the negation is attached. In contrast, scope of a long form negation extends over an object position, but not over a subject position.

Our argument for the existence of NPIs outside of **negation scope** in the text is not weakened even if Suh's claim is correct.

and

(9a) represents the **short form negation**, (9b) **long form negation**, and (9c) **suppletion form negation**. Negation or negative force in suppletion forms is incorporated into the predicate so that the predicate cannot be analyzed into a core predicate and a **negation morpheme**.

The negation in suppletion forms can not have **scope** over conjunctions whereas the negation in short or long forms may. Consider sentences in (10), (11), and (12) below:

(10)   a. [John-<u>kwa</u> Mary]-ka <u>ani-o-ess-ta.</u>
          J.-and   M.-Nom Neg-come-Pst-DC
          'John and Mary did not come.'
    b. [John-<u>kwa</u> Mary]-ka <u>o-ci</u>   <u>ani-ha-ess-ta.</u>
          J.-and   M.-Nom come-NMZ Neg-do-Pst-DC
          'John and Mary did not come.'

(11)   a. [chayk-<u>kwa</u> yenphil]-i   chayksang-wiey <u>eps-ta.</u>
          book-and   pencil-Nom desk-on   not;exist-DC
          'There is no book or pencil on the desk.'
    b. [chayk-<u>kwa</u> yenphil]-i   chayksang-wiey <u>iss-ci</u>   <u>ani-ha-ta.</u>
          book-and   pencil-Nom desk-on   exist-NMZ Neg-do-DC
          'There is no book or pencil on the desk.'

(12)   a. John-un [Susan-<u>kwa</u> Mary]-lul <u>molu-n-ta.</u>
          J.-Top   S.-and   M.-Acc   not;know-PRES-DC
          'John does not know Susan and Mary.'
    b. John-un [Susan-<u>kwa</u> Mary]-lul <u>al-ci</u>   <u>mos-ha-n-ta.</u>[8]
          J.-Top   S.-and   M.-Acc   know-NMZ Neg-do-PRES-DC
          'John does not know Susan and Mary.'

The short form negation in (10a) may have scope over the conjunction. Similarly the long form negation in (10b), (11b), or (12b) also may have scope over the conjunction. The suppletion form negation in (11a) or (12a), however, does not have scope over the conjunction. This is evidenced in the fact that both (10a) and (10b) imply (13), (11b) but not (11a) implies (14), and (12b) but not (12a) implies (15).

---

[8]Negation in the long form negation of *al* 'to know' is *mos* 'unable, cannot'.

(13) John did not come OR Mary did not come.

(14) There is no book on the desk OR there is no pencil on the desk.

(15) John does not know Susan OR John does not know Mary.

The conjunctions in (11a) and (12a) are not under the **scope** of the **suppletion form negation**. Thus, the sentences are compatible with the readings in (16) and (17) below, respectively:

(16) Books are not on the desk AND pencils are not on the desk, either.

(17) John does not know Susan AND John does not know Mary.

Notice that the conjunctions remain conjunctive, not turning into disjunctive, when the predicate is distributed over each conjunct. In other words, **anti-multiplicity** of the negation of the suppletion forms does not apply to the conjunctions, which indicates that the conjunctions are outside of the **negation scope**.

Tests with quantifiers show in the same direction. The negation in suppletion forms does not have scope over a universal quantifier in the sentence, whereas the negation in **short forms** or **long forms** may have scope over a universal quantifier in the sentence. Let us take a look at the following sentences:

(18)   a. <u>motwu-ka</u>   <u>ani-o-ess-ta</u>.
          everyone-Nom Neg-come-Pst-DC
          `Everyone did not come.'

        b. <u>motwu-ka</u>   <u>o-ci</u>   <u>ani-ha-ess-ta</u>.
          everyone-Nom come-NMZ Neg-do-Pst-DC
          `Everyone did not come.'

(19)   a. <u>motun mwulken-i</u> chayksang-wiey <u>eps-ta</u>.
          all   thing-Nom desk-on   not;exist-DC
          `All things are not on the desk.'

        b. <u>motun mwulken-i</u> chayksang-wiey <u>iss-ci</u>   <u>ani-ha-ta</u>.
          all   thing-Nom desk-on   exist-NMZ Neg-do-DC
          `All things are not on the desk.'

(20)   a. John-un <u>motun salam-ul</u> <u>molu-n-ta</u>.
         J.-Top all   man-Acc not;know-PRES-DC
         `John does not know all the people.'
        b. John-un <u>motun salam-ul</u> <u>al-ci</u>   mos-ha-n-ta.
         J.-Top all   man-Acc know-NMZ Neg-do-PRES-DC
         `John does not know all the people.'

The universal quantifiers have a wide **scope** over **suppletion form negation** in (19a) and (20a), whereas those in the other sentences have a wide scope over or a narrow scope under **negation**. (19a) has the reading in (21a) but not that in (21b), and similarly (20a) has the reading in (22a) but not (21b):

(21)   a. For all x, x a thing, x is not on the desk.
        b. It is not the case that all things are on the desk.
(22)   a. For all x, x a person, John does not know x.
        b. It is not the case that John knows all the people.

In contrast, (19b) is ambiguous between the two readings in (21a,b) and similarly (201b) is ambiguous between the two readings in (22a,b). Both (18a) and (18b) are ambiguous between the following two readings in (23):

(23)   a. For all x, x a person, x did not come.
        b. It is not the case that all the people came.

It was argued in Chung (1993) that the **ambiguity** of these sentences is caused by the relative hierarchy between quantifiers and NEGP. Quantifiers may remain in-situ or may be scrambled to a position higher than NEGP. When a quantifier remains in-situ, it is c-commanded by negation which is in a higher position in the base, and it has narrow scope. When it is scrambled out of NEGP, then it has a wide scope over negation.

That negation may have a wide scope over conjunctions or universal quantifiers in **short forms** and **long forms**, but not in **suppletion forms** is further evidenced in a compatibility test as follows.

Let's first discuss the cases where conjunctions and negation interact. Consider the following sequence of sentences:

(24) a. [John-kwa Mary]-ka <u>ani-o-ess-ta</u>.   John-man o-ess-ta.
      J.-and   M.-Nom Neg-come-Pst-DC J.-only   come-Past-DC
      `It is not the case that John and Mary came. Only John came.'

      b. [John-kwa Mary]-ka <u>o-ci   ani-ha-ess-ta</u>. John-man
      J.-and   M.-Nom come-NMZ and-do-Pst-DC J.-only
      o-ess-ta.
      come-PAST-DC
      `It is not the case that John and Mary came. Only John came.'

(25) a.*[chayk-<u>kwa</u> yenphil]-i   chayksang-wiey <u>eps</u>-ta.
        book-and   pencil-Nom desk-on   not;exist-DC
      chayk-man iss-ta.
      book-only exist-DC
      `Books and pencils are not on the desk. Only books are there.'

      b. [chayk-<u>kwa</u> yenphil]-i   chayksang-wiey <u>iss-ci   ani-ha</u>-ta.
        book-and   pencil-Nom desk-on   exist-NMZ Neg-do-DC
      chayk-man iss-ta.
      book-only exist-DC
      `Books and pencils are not on the desk. Only books are there.'

(26) a. *John-i [Susan-<u>kwa</u> Mary]-lul <u>molu-n-ta</u>.   Susan-man
      J.-Nom S.-and   M.-Acc   not;know-Pres-DC S.-only
      al-n-ta.
      know-PRES-DC
      `John does not know Susan and Mary. He knows Susan only.'

      b. John-un [Susan-<u>kwa</u> Mary]-lul <u>al-ci   mos-ha-n-ta</u>.
      J.-Top S.-and   M.-Acc   know-NMZ Neg-do-Pres-DC
      Susan-man al-n-ta.
      S.-only   know-PRES-DC
      `John does not know Susan and Mary. He knows Susan only.'

All the first sentences above involve an NP conjunction. The second sentences are identical to the first sentences except that the NP conjunction is replaced with the first conjunct with a particle *man* `only' and the negative predicate is replaced with the positive one. The first sentence has **short form negation** in (24a), **long form negation** in (24b), (25b), and (26b), and **suppletion form negation** in (25a) and (26a). The second sentences are compatible with the first ones in **short form negation** and **long form negation** but not in **suppletion form negation** as abstractly represented in (27) below.[9]

(27)   a. ...[A-*kwa* B]... *ani*-Verb... A-*man* Verb...
              and   Neg-Verb   only
    b. ...[A-*kwa* B]... Verb-*ci*   *ani-ha*... A-*man* Verb...
              and   NMZ Neg-do   only
    c. *...[A-*kwa* B]... Verb/[+neg]... A-*man* Verb...
              and   only

The contrast between the short form negation and the long form negation on the one hand and the suppletion form negation on the other hand with respect to the compatibility test can be explained in the following way. Suppose that a (abstract) quantifier BOTH exists over conjunctions as illustrated below.

(28)   a. ... BOTH [A-*kwa* B]... *ani*-Verb...
              and   Neg-Verb
    b. ... BOTH [A-*kwa* B]... Verb-*ci*   *ani-ha*...
              and   NMZ Neg-do
    c. ... BOTH [A-*kwa* B]... Verb/[+neg]...
              and

Since **negation** in short forms or long forms may have **scope** over any element, it can be associated with the quantifier BOTH, which results in partial negation of the conjunctions. The partial negation of the conjunctions is compatible with the partial affirmation of the conjunctions. This explains the grammaticality of

---

[9]Some native speakers including Suh (1990) say that the two sentences in (25a) are contradictory, but others including us do not. The contrast between (28a) and (28b) on the one hand and (28c) on the other becomes clearer when the two sentences are combined into one by changing the verbal conjugation of the first sentences appropriately. For example, if (25a) is changed to (i) below, we clearly secure the reading that we want.

(i)   [John-kwa Mary]-ka <u>ani-o-ko</u>   John-man o-ess-ta.
        J.-and   M.-Nom Neg-come-and J.-only   come-Past-DC
        `It is not the case that John and Mary came but only John came.'

the sentences like (24a), (24b), (25b), and (26b). In contrast the **negation scope** of suppleltion forms being restricted to the predicates, the association of the **negation** and the quantifier BOTH is impossible. Thus, the conjuncts distribute over the negative predicate in **suppletion form negation**. No partial negation of the conjunctions is possible, which in turn blocks the reading of partial confirmation. Therefore, sentences like (25a) and (26a) are contradictory.

In brief, we have seen in this subsection that the negation scope of **short forms** or **long forms** may extend over the entire clause in which the negative predicate appears, whereas the negation scope of **suppletion forms** is confined to the predicate to which the negation force is incorporated.

3.3. NPI Licensing

Having seen the scopal discrepancy between suppletion negation vs. short/long form negation, let us now consider whether the scopal discrepancy affects the licensing **domain** of NPIs. To say the conclusion first, there is no difference in NPI licensing domain.

NPIs in object positions are licensed by a suppletion form of negation as well as short or long form negation, as exemplified below:

(29) a. John-i amwu-kes-to   ani-mek-ess-ta.
      J. Nom any-thing-even Neg-eat-Pst-DC
      `John did not eat anything.'
   b. John-i amwu-kes-to   mek-ci ani-ha-ess-ta.
      J.-Nom any-thing-even eat-NMZ Neg-do-Pst-DC
      `John did not eat anything.'
   c. John-i amwu-kes-to   molu-ess-ta.
      J.-Nom any-thing-even not;know-Pst-DC
      `John did not know anything.'

The negation is a short form in (29a), a long form in (29b), and a suppletion form in (29c). NPI *amwu-kes-to* `any-thing-even' in object position is licensed by any of the three forms of negation.

NPIs in subject positions are also licensed by suppletion form negation as well as by short or long form negation, as exemplified below:

(30)   a. <u>amwu-to</u> sakwa-lul <u>ani-mek-ess-ta</u>.
             any-even apple-Acc Neg-eat-Pst-DC
             `No one ate apples.'
          b. <u>amwu-to</u> sakwa-lul <u>mek-ci   ani-ha-ess-ta</u>.
             any-even apple-Acc eat-NMZ Neg-do-Pst-DC
             `No one ate apples.'
          c. <u>amwu-to</u> John-ul <u>molu-ess-ta</u>.
             any-even J.-Acc   not;know-Pst-DC
             `No one knows John.'

NPI *amwu-to* `anyone-even' is licensed by **short form negation** *ani-mek-ess-ta* `Neg-eat-Pst-DC' in (30a), by **long form negation** *mek-ci ani-ha-ess-ta* `eat-NMZ Neg-do-Pst-DC' in (30b), and by **suppletion form negation**   *molu-ess-ta* `not;know-Pst-DC' in (30c).

Despite the **scope** difference as was observed in the previous subsection, all the three types of **negation** do not show any variation in NPI licensing. In particular, NPIs may be licensed by a suppletion form negation, although the **scope** of this form of negation is confined to the predicate to which negation force is incorporated. This indicates that NPIs can be licensed outside of the scope of negation.

4. A Locality Condition in NPI Licensing

In section 2 we observed that some NPIs, i.e., adverbial NPIs like *kyelkho* `ever' and *celtaylo* `absolutely' necessarily have scope over negation. In section 3, we also observed that suppletion form negation cannot have scope over the positions taken by NPIs. Thus, there is some discrepancy between the negation scope and NPI licensing **domain**. Does this mean that NPIs have nothing to do with negation? Of course the answer is negative. In this section, however, we observe that NPIs must have a certain kind of local relation with a negation expression.

4.1. A Clause mate condition

Choe (1987) observes that NPIs in Korean require a clause mate **negation morpheme**. Thus the structures in (31) are not allowed in Korean:

(31)   a. ...[s... NPI...] ...Neg...
         b. ...NPI... [s ... Neg...] ...

In (31a) an NPI is embedded while a **negation morpheme** is in a higher clause. Conversely, in (31b), an NPI is in a higher clause, while **negation** is embedded. The structure in (31b) seems to be bad universally. The illicitness of the structure in (31a) is language specific. The structure in (31b) is allowed in English, but not in Korean, as exemplified in (32) below.

(32)   a. John does <u>not</u> think [that Mary saw <u>anyone</u>].
         b. *John-un [Mary-ka <u>amwuto</u> po-ess-ta-ko] sangkakha-ci
            J.-Top   M.-Nom anyone see-Pst-DC-C think-NMZ
            <u>ani</u>-ha-n-ta.
            Neg-do-Pres-DC

Apparently sentences like (33) below are allowed, questioning the validity of the **clause mate condition**, as was discussed in Chang (1992):

(33)   Mary-ka [<u>amwuto</u> hwulyungha-ta-ko] sayngkakha-ci <u>ani</u>-ha-n-ta.
         M.-Nom anyone great-DC-C   think-NMZ   Neg-do-Pres-DC
         `Mary does not think that anyone is great.'

Chung (1995) argues that the NPI **in** (33) is raised to the matrix clause whose predicate is an exceptional case marking (henceforth, ECM) verb, satisfying the clause mate condition. The raising analysis receives support from the following two facts. First, no embedded adverbial can precede the NPI: *...[s ADV... NPI...] ... Neg... Assuming that adverbs do not move, especially across a clause boundary, the NPI in this structure is not in the same clause as negation is, explaining the illicitness of the structure. Second, NPI and its potential licenser cannot be separated by two or more clause boundaries: *...[s ... [s NPI...]... V_1...] ... Neg...V_2... Even if V_1 is an ECM verb, raising to the immediately higher clause does not help since Neg is in a still higher clause.

Thus we concluded that NPI licensing in Korean must satisfy the clause mate condition.

4.2. A Checking Condition

We argue in this subsection that the **clause mate condition** is just a manifestation of a stricter condition. In other words, the clause mate condition is not sufficient in explaining the distribution of Korean NPIs. As was discussed in Chung (1995), Korean NPIs must be theta-related (or Case-related for the ECM cases) to a negated predicate. Thus structures like (34) are not allowed as exemplified in (35):

(34)　　*... [$_{XP}$... NPI...] ... Neg...
　　　　where NPI is properly contained in XP.

(35)　　a. *[amwuto-(uy) hyeng]-i　　　ani-o-ess-ta.
　　　　　　anyone-Gen　brother-Nom Neg-come-Pst-DC
　　　　　　`*Anybody's brother did not come.'
　　　　　　(Intended) `Nobody's brother came.'

　　　　b. *na-nun [amwuto(-uy) hyeng]-ul　ani-po-ess-ta
　　　　　　I-Top　anyone-Gen　brother-Acc Neg-see-Pst-DC
　　　　　　`I did not see anybody's brother.'

(36)　　a. *John-i [amwuto-eykey] ton-ul　　　ani-cwu-ess-ta.
　　　　　　J.-Nom anyone-to　　　money-Acc Neg-give-Pst-DC
　　　　　　`John did not give money to anyone.'

　　　　b. *[amwu kos-to]-ey　ton-i　　　eps-ta.
　　　　　　any place-even-at　money-Nom not;exist-DC
　　　　　　(Intended) `There is no money in any place.'

As illustrated in (35) and (36), NPIs cannot be embedded within an NP or a PP while negation is outside of the NP or the PP. In this sense the clause mate condition is just a subcondition of (34), where XP is a CP or a clause.

For sentences in (35) and (36) to be correct, -to must appear at the right edge of the bracketed phrases. For example, (35a,b) become grammatical if *[amwuto hyeng]-ka/ul* is replaced by *[amwu salam-uy hyeng]-to* as shown in (37) below.[10]

---

[10]We assume that *amwu* NPIs have the following form: *amwu N-to*, e.g., *amwu salam-to* `any person-even', *amwu kes-to* `any thing-even', *amwu chayk-to* `any book-even', etc. Thus we analyze *amwuto* as being derived from *amwu* [+human]-*to* by deleting nouns like *salam* `man'.

(37)   a. [amwu salam-uy hyeng]-to   ani-o-ess-ta.
           anyone-Gen   brother-even Neg-come-Pst-DC
           `*Anybody's brother did not come.'
           (Intended) `Nobody's brother came.'
        b. na-nun [amwu salam-uy hyeng]-to   ani-po-ess-ta
           I-Top   anyone-Gen   brother-even Neg-see-Pst-DC
           `I did not see anybody's brother.'

It seems that *to* decides the range of NPIs. Thus the whole subject in (37a) and the whole object in (37b), instead of just *amwu* N, are NPIs. If so construed, the sentences in (37) do not violate the locality condition in (34). Similarly the sentences in (36) become grammatical if *amwuto-eykey* and *amwu kos-to-eyse* are replaced by *amwu-eykey-to* and *amwu kos-eyse-to*.

5. A Negation Typology and NPI Licensing

In section 2 and 3, we observed some discrepancy between the NPI licensing **domain** and the **negation scope**. In section 4, we observed a locality condition that NPIs have in relation to their licensing negation expression. In this section, we try to locate the source of the tension between these two statements based on Chung's (1995) idea of negation typology and NPI licensing.

It is argued in Chung (1995) that the locality condition in Korean is derived from the projectional status of its negation expression. Korean **negation morpheme** *ani* is always prefixed to a verb, an x^0, unlike English *not*, which is arguably an XP (Rizzi 1990). Negative expressions, *ani*-Verb in Korean and *not* in English, raise to the **checking domain** of the functional category NEG, which is represented as [+neg], to discharge the abstract feature. Due to the chain uniformity condition (Chomsky 1992), *ani*-V, as an x^0, adjoins to NEG, while *not*, as an XP, goes to SPEC of NEGP, as schematically represented below.[11]

---

[11]In fact it is not clear whether *not* is based generated at the SPEC of NEGP or moved there from a lower position.

(38)   a. Korean   b. English

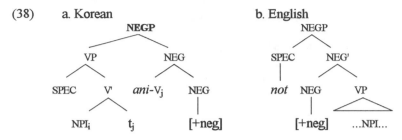

With these structures in mind let us discuss why the locality condition applies to Korean NPI licensing but not to English NPIs licensing. In grammar, for an element to be syntactically related to a head, the former must be located in the local (**checking**) **domain** of the latter. In contrast, a **maximal element** may have a long distance relation to another maximal element, a typical example being binding. Now that NPIs are licensed directly by negation expressions (rather than by [+neg]), Korean NPIs have to move to the checking domain of negative expression *ani*-V, an x^0, whereas English NPIs do not have to (and must not, for economy reason,) move since a binding option is available, as schematically represented below:

(39)   a. Korean   b. English

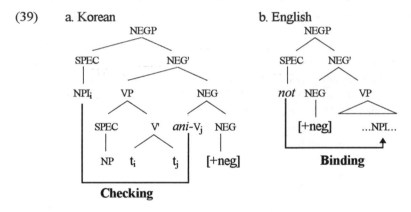

Now let us discuss why Korean NPIs may be located outside of the **negation scope**, whereas NPIs in English are under the **scope of negation**. This follows from the difference in the structures under the assumption that the scope of an element is defined as its c-command **domain**. The **scope domain** of *ani*-V in (39a) is VP. Notice that NPIs are outside of VP. The NPIs which are in SPEC of NEGP are outside of the **negation scope**. The **scope domain** of *not* in (39b) is NEG' within which NPIs are located. Therefore NPIs in English are in the negation scope.

6. Implications

We would like to conclude this paper by mentioning two theoretical implications that the theory proposed here makes. One is syntactic and the other semantic.

First, we argued that Korean NPIs are licensed by a **checking** relation, while English NPIs are licensed by a binding relation. Since binding does not restrict the number of bindees, e.g., unselective binding of multiple *wh*-phrases in situ, a prediction is that more than one NPI could be licensed by the same trigger in English. This seems to be borne out in English, as the following examples illustrate:

(40) a. John did not give <u>anything</u> to <u>anybody</u>.
      b. John did not say to <u>anybody</u> that Mary likes <u>anyone</u>.

The two internal arguments of verb *give* are NPIs in (40a). In (40b) one NPI is in the matrix clause and the other is in the embedded clause. Such multiple occurrence of NPIs is disallowed in Korean, which was observed by Nam (1993). Korean sentences corresponding to (40) are bad:

(41) a. *John-i <u>amwukes-to</u> <u>amwu-eykey-to</u> ani-cwu-ess-ta.
         J.-Nom anything-even anyone-to-even Neg-give-Pst-DC
         'John did not give anything to anybody.'
      b. *John-i <u>amwu-eykey-to</u> Mary-ka <u>amwukes-to</u> cohaha-n-ta-ko
         J.-Nom anyone-to-even M.-Nom anything-even like-Prs-DC-C
         malha-ci ani-ha-ess-ta.
         say-NMZ Neg-do-Pst-DC

The ungrammaticality of these sentences could be attributed to the restriction on **checking** relation. That is, agreement is a one-to-one relation.[12]

---

[12] In fact some native speakers allow sentences like (40a). Probably multiple

Since we have argued that Korean NPIs are outside the **negation scope** while English NPIs are within the negation scope, the former are interpreted as universal quantifiers, while the latter are as existential quantifiers. Carlson (1980) take the modifiability by ALMOST as one of the diagnostics to determine whether a quantifier is a universal one or not.[13] The prediction again seems to be correct., when we consider the fact that Korean NPIs can be modified by *keuy* `nearly' in contrast with English NPIs, as exemplified below:

(42) a. John-i <u>keuy</u> <u>amwu-to</u> ani-manna-ess-ta.
        J. -Nom nearly anyone-even Neg-meet-Pst-DC
        `John saw almost noone.'
     b. * I did not see almost anyone.

References

Ahn, Heedon. 1990. *Light Verbs, VP-Movement, Negation, and Clausal Architecture in Korean and English*. Ph.D. dissertation. University of Wisconsin-Madison.

Carlson, Greg N.1980. Polarity *Any* is Existential. *LI* 11.799-804.

Chang , Kyungsun.1992. Negation in Korean. ms. USC.

Choe, Hyunsook.1987. Successive-cyclic Rightward Movement in Korean. Kuno et al (eds.) *Harvard Studies in Korean Linguistics*, Vol. 2. 40-56.

Chomsky, Noam.1992. A Minimalist Program for Linguistic Theory. *MIT Occasional Papers in Linguistics*, NO.1.

Chung, Daeho.1993. Negative polarity items in Korean. ms. USC.

Chung, Daeho.1995. A Negation Typology and Distribution of NQs and NPIs. a paper presented at LSA annual meeting Jan. 5-8, 1995.

SPECs are available for those speakers. The parametric difference between English and Korean, i.e., the binding vs. checking distinction, still should be preserved for the contrast between (39b) vs. (40b).

[13] The other diagnostics discussed in Carlson (1980) are not relevant for independent reasons to the determination of properties of Korean NPIs.

Ladusaw, William. 1980. *Polarity Sensitivity as Inherent Scope Relations.* New York: Garland Press.

Lee, Young-Suk.1993. Licensing and Semantics of *Any* Revisited. Kuno et al (eds.) *Harvard Studies in Korean Linguistics,* Vol.5. 577-592.

Linebarger, Marcia, C.1980. *The Grammar of Negative Polarity.* Ph.D. dissertation. MIT.

Nam, Seungho.1993 (in Press). Another Type of Negative Polarity Itmes. CLSI.

Rizzi, Luigi. 1990. *Relativized Minimality,* MIT Press.

Song, Seok Choong. 1971. A Note on Negation in Korean. *Linguistics* 76:59-76.

Song, Seok Choong. 1973. Some Negative Remarks on Negation in Korean. *Language Research* 9.2:252-263.

Song, Seok Choong 1988. *Explorations in Korean Syntax and Semantics.* Korean Research Monograph 14. Institute of East Asian Studies. University of California:Berkeley.

Suh, Jinhee 1990. *Scope Phenomena and Aspects of Korean Syntax,* Ph. D. dessertation, USC.

Argument Selection of Sino-Korean Verbal Nouns

YUNSUN JUNG
Harvard University

1. Introduction*

In this paper I will discuss the selective nature of the transitive Sino-Korean verbal nouns (VNs) with respect to their genitive modifier. It is not well known that VNs are selective in terms of the θ-role they assign to their primary genitive modifier [1]: some VNs such as *cungo* 'hate', or *kyengmyel* 'contempt' assign only an external θ-role (Agent) to the genitive modifier and thus it is always interpreted as an agent, as illustrated below:

(1)   a.   Mary-uy <u>cungo</u>
                gen hate
           'Mary's$_{ag}$ / * Mary's$_{th}$ hate'
      b.   John-uy <u>kyengmyel</u>
                gen contempt
           'John's$_{ag}$ / * John's$_{th}$ contempt'

---

* I would like to thank Wesley Jacobsen, Peter Sells, and especially Susumu Kuno for their indispensable advice and guidance. I am also grateful to the participants of J/K conference for their comments.

[1] I will deal with only a primary genitive modifier, which appears when the VN takes only one genitive modifier.

As the glosses indicate, *Mary* or *John* in (1) is interpreted only as an agent, not a theme. On the other hand, some VNs such as *wanseng* 'completion', or *phokpha* 'explosion' assign only an internal θ-role (Theme) to the genitive modifier, and it is interpreted only as such.

(2)　a.　kulim/*John-uy　<u>wanseng</u>
　　　　　picture/John-gen completion
　　　　　lit. 'the picture's/John's completion'
　　b.　kongsa/*John-uy　<u>cwungci</u>
　　　　　construction -gen　stop
　　　　　lit. 'construction's/John's stop'

Finally, another type of VN such as *phyencip* 'edit' or *selkyey* 'design' seems to assign either Agent or Theme to its genitive modifier.

(3)　a.　Bill /capci-uy　<u>phyencip</u>
　　　　　　magazine-gen editing
　　　　　'Bill's/ magazine's editing'
　　b.　John/kenmwul-uy <u>selkyey</u>
　　　　　　building-gen　design
　　　　　'John's/building's design'

I will refer to the first type of VN as Type I, the second as Type II, and the third as Type III. The following table gives representative members of each type.

(4)

Type I	Type II	Type III
conkyeng 'respect'	phakoy 'destruction'	piphan 'criticizing'
sinloy 'trust'	hayko 'dismissal'	yenkwu 'research'
tongceng	phokpha 'explosion'	selkyey 'design'
'sympathy'	phamyen 'firing'	phyencip 'editing'
hyemo 'dislike'	kamkum 'locking up'	ceswul 'writing'
cungo 'hate'	wanseng 'completion'	cosa 'investigation'
chongay 'adoration'	cenghwa 'purification'	kongpwu 'study'
cilthwu 'envy'	hwakcang 'expansion'	yencwu 'playing'
sayngkak 'thought'	phason 'breaking'	kanho 'care'

I will argue that (i) the prenominal genitive modifiers are base-generated where they are and (ii) the difference among three types of VNs is aspectual. This analysis will consequently support the claims that (i) the abstract nouns assign a specific θ-role to their genitive modifier (Kim

1990) and (ii) aspectual level mediates between the argument structure and syntactic structure, and this intermediate level constrains the kinds of arguments that can appear in certain constructions (Grimshaw 1990, Pustejovsky 1991, Tenny 1992).

2. NP-Movement Analysis

Anderson (1979) discusses a phenomenon in English similar to the one illustrated in (1) and (2). Consider the following sentences:

(5) a. the destruction of the city/ the city's destruction
     b. the renovation of the room/ the room's renovation
     c. the explosion of the bomb/ the bomb's explosion

(6) a. love of music/ *music's love
     b. fear of dogs/ *dogs' fear
     c. knowledge of Latin/ *Latin's knowledge

While the nominalized verbs such as *destruction* and *renovation* etc. allow the Theme as a prenominal genitive modifier, those such as *love* and *fear* do not allow it to appear prenominally.

Anderson argues that the semantic notion of AFFECTEDNESS contributes to the difference in the D-structure between (5) and (6). The objects of *love* and *knowledge* are not affected (i.e., they do not undergo change of state or location) by the action expressed by the derived nominal. On the other hand, the objects of nouns like *destruction* and *renovation* are clear cases of affected objects. Anderson suggests that while the derived nominals in (5) take an NP-complement, those in (6) take a PP-complement, headed by the lexical preposition *of*. According to her analysis, the object cannot appear prenominally since this preposition *of* blocks its movement to the prenominal position.[2] The D-structure representation of *the destruction of the city* will be as in (7), whereas that of *knowledge of Latin* will be as in (8).

(7) [$_{NP}$ [$_{N'}$ destruction [$_{NP}$ the city]]]

(8) [$_{NP}$ [$_{N'}$ knowledge [$_{PP}$ of [$_{NP}$ Latin]]]]

In (7), since *destruction* cannot assign Case to *the city*, though it assigns θ-role, the object must move to prenominal position to get Case from the

---

[2] Anderson (1979:47-54) states that the stranded preposition as a result of the NP preposing is not interpreted at LF, and thus filtered out by the interpretive rule.

genitive Case marker 's. In (8), on the other hand, the lexical preposition *of* assigns Case to the object NP.

Anderson (1983:9-10) further stipulates that assigning a subject θ-role must be optional to allow NPs like (9).

(9) the destruction of Rome

Although Anderson does not specifiy, however, the assignment of an object θ-role must be optional too, because there are examples like the following:

(10) the destruction (was devastating)

Then, under the assumption that the derived nominal optionally assigns a θ-role, how does Anderson's analysis account for the following examples?[3]

(11)   a. *enemy's $_{ag}$ destruction
       b. John's $_{ag}$ love

Destruction does not allow the prenominal subject to appear alone, whereas *love* does. To explain the discrepancy in (11), there must be an ad hoc stipulation for (11a) that the object has a priority for the prenominal position and that subject cannot apear without the object appearing. [4]

The following examples also pose a problem to Anderson's analysis:

(12)   a. John's rebuttal
       b. John's supervision

The prenominal genitive modifier of some English derived nominals as in (12) are interpreted as either the subject or the object (Hamano 1989). [5] In order to obtain *John's rebuttal* with *John's* having an object θ-role, it must be assumed that *rebuttal* takes a bare NP as *destruction*, according to Anderson's view. If *rebuttal* and *supervision*, like *destruction*, do not have *of* in their D-structure, we must explain why *John* can be interpreted as a subject with these VNs, while the prenominal genitive NP of *destruction* cannot, as in (11a). On the other hand, if they do have *of* at D-structure as *love*, the object interpretation of *John* will be impossible.

---

[3] This problem in Anderson's analysis was suggested to me by S. Kuno.

[4] Note that Anderson's extended version of Burzio's (1981) proposal, stated below, cannot explain (11a).
(i) If some NP governed by N is assigned no case then the N' which N is the head assigns no θ-role.
It does not apply to (11a) because there is no NP governed by N.

[5] I thank P. Sells for bringing Hamano's work to my attention.

The movement analysis of prenominal genitive modifiers also cannot extend to a similar phenomenon in other languages, such as Korean and Japanese. Since Korean and Japanese are head-final languages, the complement always precedes the head. Hence, blocking the object from appearing before the derived nominal as a primary modifier would result in an overly complicated analysis.

3. An Analysis

In this section, I propose that the primary genitive modifier in Korean, whether it has a subject θ-role or an object θ-role, is base-generated in the prenominal position and governed by the aspectual property of the VN. I show that aspectual property can be affected by various factors, such as delimitability of the object and lexical specification.

To see the aspectual differences among VNs, it is necessary to introduce the traditional verb classification by Vendler (1967). Vendler classifies verbs into following four categories on the basis of aspect:

(13) a. STATES are represented by mostly psych-verbs and mental stative verbs. *love, want, know, think.*
   b. ACTIVITIES denote actions which do not involve a terminal point or climax. *run, walk* etc.
   c. ACHIEVEMENTS, being typically instantaneous events, involve a point in time, although this is not the terminal point of any activity or process as in the case of accomplishments. *recognize, run a mile*, etc.
   d. ACCOMPLISHMENTS involve a clear end point and thus can be analyzed as being composed of an activity plus an achievement. *write a book , build a house*, etc.

As we saw in (4), what distinguishes Type I VNs from other VNs is that they do not denote the change which the object undergoes as a result of the activity of the subject. In other words, Type I VNs represent states in (13). Thus, Type I VNs seem to be the same category as *love* and *knowledge* in (6). But here I adopt an approach proposd by Tenny (1992), which is different from Anderson's. Tenny interpretes the affectedness in the following way: the affected object of the verbs 'measures out' the action denoted by the verb. Consider the following sentence:

(14) John eats an apple.

An apple is affected by the activity of eating, and it marks an endpoint or a terminal point of the event of eating. Someone who eats an apple progresses through the process of eating it in increments, until it has been completely consumed. On the other hand, the unaffected object of some verbs such as psych-verbs does not mark an endpoint of the event as *an apple* does in (14).

According to this view, Type I VNs are significantly different from other VNs in that the activity denoted by them is not delimited ('measured out' in Tenny's terms) by the object. Then, how is this difference reflected on the genitive modifier? Tenny proposes a mechanism which mediates between syntax and lexical semantics:

(15) *Aspectual Interface Hypothesis*
  The mapping between thematic structure and syntactic argument structure is governed by aspectual properties. A universal aspectual structure associated with internal (direct), external and oblique arguments in syntactic structure constrains the kinds of event participants that can occupy these positions. Only the aspectual part of thematic structure is visible to the syntax.

According to this view, the syntax proper does not need to "see" thematic roles. It only "sees" certain syntactic/aspectual structures with which the thematic roles are associated. We can extend this hypothesis so that only the object which aspectually delimits the event denoted by the verb is aspectual and consequently visible to some syntactic constructions, one of which is the primary genitive modifier. The constraint on this correspondence may be stated as:

(16) Condition on the primary genitive modifier (tentative)
  The primary genitive modifier of a VN is constrained so that if the object does not delimit the process denoted by the VN, it cannot be a primary genitive modifier.

The object of activity, accomplishment and achievement verbs registers the temporal end of the event and thus it can be a primary genitive modifier. With this aspectual analysis of the genitive modifier, we can generalize the discrepancy seen in types of VN other than Type I, which is not based on affectedness.

Let us now see why a subject cannot appear as a primary genitive modifier in Type II. Here, I assume that the verbal form of the VN, the VN followed by the light verb *hata*, inherits its argument structure from the VN, following Grimshaw and Mester (1988). I also assume that the

VNs and the corresponding verbal form VN + *hata* are associated with the same event structure. I follow Dowty, 1979, Pustejovsky 1991 among others to assume that each agentive verb has an event structure associated with it, which, when combined with elements in the clause, provides an event structure for an entire sentence. The event structure represents the aspectual analysis of the clause. The event structure of the transitive agentive VNs that I will adopt is the "bisentential" analysis argued for by Dowty (1979). The event structure of the transitive agentive VNs consists of two subparts mediated by CAUSE. An Agent argument has a standard representation in such an analysis: it will always be associated with the first subevent, which is causally related to the second subevent. Each of the arguments of the verb is associated with each subevent: the Agent is associated with the first subevent, and the Theme with the second subevent. (17) illustrates how the argument structure of *phason* 'breaking' is represented and subsequently mapped onto the event structure (ES) representation and how it is realized as a subject and an object of the sentence.

(17) Argument structure (AS) of *phason* 'breaking' : X Y

Event Structure: $[[x$ *does something*$]$ CAUSE $[$BECOME $\sim[y$ *is broken*$]]]$

X -ka Y-lul phason-hayssta.
nom acc breaking-did
'*X* broke *Y*.'

An important characteristic of Type II VN is that they all lexically specify the second subevent. For example, in *phason* 'breaking', the first syllable *pha* denote the state of being broken.[6] Likewise, either or both of the two syllables of the change of state VNs as in (18), which constitute a large part of Type II, implies the result state.

(18) *phason* 'breaking', *haytong* 'thawing', *yencang* 'lengthening', *nayngtong* 'freezing', *phyopayk* 'whitening', *kenco* 'drying'

For example, each syllable of *nayngtong* 'freezing', *nayng* and *tong*, respectively means 'cold' and 'frozen'.

Since they always specify the second subevent, a resultative adverb sounds redundant when it appears with this type of VN:

---

[6] Most VNs consist of two syllables, each of which has its own meaning.

(19) a.? Koki-lul *chakapkey* nayngdong-hata.
      meat-acc coldly   freezing-did
      lit. 'to freeze the meat cold'
   b. ? Os-ul   *hayahkey* phyopayk-hata.
      cloth-acc white   whitening-did
      lit. 'to whiten the cloth white'

On the other hand, many of Type II VNs lack the specification of the causing event. For example, *wanseng* 'completion' specifies the result state of the object, which is complete, but leaves the causing event unspecified. In *John-i kulim-ul wanseng-hayssta* 'John completed the picture', it is only the change in the state of the picture that is specified by the verb: John could have brought this change about by any of a wide variety of activities. [7] A wider variety of subjects may appear with these VNs than Type I and III:[8]

(20) a. Pwultoce-ka   ku the-lul   hwakcang-hayssta.
      bulldozer-nom the place-acc expansion-did
      'Bulldozer expanded the area.'

   b. Phokphwung-i ku kenmwul-ul phason-hayssta
      storm-nom   the building-acc breaking-did
      'The storm broke the building.'

This implies that in Type II VNs, the first subevent is not lexically as specified as the second one.

    Another piece of evidence supporting the present analysis comes from Japanese. In Japanese, each counterpart of the VNs in (18) such as *cenghwa* 'purification,' and *hwakcang* 'expansion,' also allows only a Theme as a primary genitive modifier. *Zooka* is the counterpart of *cenghwa* 'purification' and *kakutyoo* is that of *hwakcang* 'expansion'.

---

[7] Levin and Rappaport (1991) discussed the semantic distinction between *clear* and *wipe*: "while the meaning of a *clear* verb does not make explicit how the removal of a substance from a location is effected, the meaning of a *wipe* verb does. The *wipe* verbs further differ from the *clear* verbs in not specifying the effect that the action they denote has on the location. According to Talmy (1985), these verbs *lexicalize* a resultant state."

[8] In English counterparts, a variety of subjects, inanimate as well as animate, can appear with the change of state verbs. Levin and Rappaport attribute this to the lack of specification of the first subevent.
   (i) a. The hot wind dried the wet clothes very quickly.
      b. A stone broke his arm.

(21) a. mizu-no zyooka
         water-gen purification
         lit. 'water's $_{th}$ purification'
      b.*Taro-no zyooka
         gen purification
         'Taro's $_{ag}$ purification'

(22) a. mise-no kakutyoo
          shop-gen expansion
          'the shop's $_{th}$ expansion'
      b. *Taro-no kakutyoo
          gen expansion
          'Taro's $_{ag}$ expansion'

Korean counterparts of these VNs with the light verb *hata* are only used
transitively. However, in Japanese, they are used intransitively as well as
transitively, as is illustrated below (Jacobsen 1992):

(23) a. mizu-ga   zyooka-sita
          water-nom purification-did
          'Water was purified.'
      b. mizu-o   zyooka-sita
          water-acc purification-did
          '(I) purified the water.'

(24) a. Mise-ga kakutyoo-sita
          shop-nom expansion-did
          'The shop was expanded.'
      b. Mise-o kakutyoo-sita
          shop-acc expansion-did
          '(I) expanded the shop.'

It has been argued that unaccusative verbs are ones with the first subevent
unspecified (Grimshaw 1990, Levin &Rappaport 1995). The fact that
some of Type II VNs are unaccusative in Japanese supports the analysis
that in these type of VNs, the first subevent is not lexically specified. Note
that a movement analysis like Anderson's needs a separate explanation for
the instability of this type of VNs.[9]

---

[9] The condition on the detransitivization in Japanese would be as follows:
    (i) The transitive VNs may be detransitivized when the first subevent is not
        lexically specified (also see Levin and Rappaport 1995).
On the other hand, those VNs do not seem to be detransitivized in Korean.

The difference of Type II VNs from Type III VNs is that neither syllable of Type III VNs lexicalizes the second subevent. How is this lack of specification of a given subevent interpreted at the aspectual level? I suggest that a given subevent of the event structure of a VN is visible to the syntactic structure of the genitive modifier only when it is fully lexicalized (that is, denoted by both syllables). The following event structure illustrates the lexical specification of Type II. The subevent which is not fully specified is parenthesized:

(25) a. John-i   kulim-lul   wanseng-hayssta.
         nom picture-acc completion-did
         'John completed the picture.'

b. AS of *wanseng*:

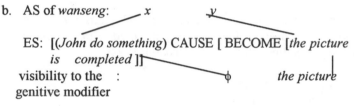

ES: [(*John do something*) CAUSE [BECOME [*the picture is completed*]]
visibility to the   :   φ   *the picture*
genitive modifier

Hence, an argument in the first subevent is not realized as a primary genitive modifier, as illustrated below:

(26) a. * John-uy wanseng
                 gen completion
          lit. 'John's completion'
      b. kulim-uy   wanseng
          picture-gen completion
          'picture's completion'

Let us turn to Type III. They represent activities, achievements and accomplishments VNs excluding Type II. What these VNs have in common is that although the object is affected by the action denoted by the VN, it is not specified how it is affected, as in Type II. For example, in *He designed a building*, it is not specified how the building is affected by the activity of designing. On the other hand, the lexical specification of the first subevent is quite clear. In fact, both syllables of all Type III VNs denote the activity of the subject, not the resulting state. For example, in *piphan* 'criticizing', *pi* and *phan* have the meaning 'compare' and 'judge' respectively. In other words, in Type III VNs, only the first subevent is lexically specified. Thus, it would be formalized as follows:

(27) a. John-i   kenmwul-ul <u>selkyey</u> hayssta.
       nom building-acc design did
       'John designed a building.'

    b.   AS of *selkyey:* *x*   *y*

       ES: [[*John designed*] CAUSE [BECOME [*a building is*
       affected]]
       visibility to the SS : *John*   *a building*
       of the genitive modifier

Hence the primary genitive modifier of *selkyey* is interpreted as either Agent or Theme:

(28) a. John-uy <u>selkyey</u>
         gen design
      'John's design'

    b. kenmwul-uy <u>selkyey</u>
       building-gen design
       'building's design'

To recapitulate, as for Type II, the subject is not realized as a primary genitive modifier because the first subevent it belongs to is not fully lexicalized. As for Type III, the object delimits the event and the subject is also fully specified. It is clearly the aspectual property of the VN that constrains the syntactic realization. It seems appropriate to revise the tentative condition in (16) to accommodate the observation made here. I refer to the argument which has the aspectual property to be a primary genitive modifier as 'aspectually prominent' in the condition:

(29) Condition on the primary genitive modifier of VNs (final)
      Only an aspectually prominent argument can be a primary genitive
      modifier. An argument is aspectually prominent if
      i) it delimits the activity denoted by the VN, or
      ii) the VN lexically specifies only the subevent to which it belongs.

The argument of each type of VNs which is realized as the genitive modifier is summarized below. *X* is an external and *Y* is an internal argument:

(30)

Type I	Type II	Type III
X	Y	X Y

In this section, I argued that the syntactic visibility of semantic arguments is determined by aspectual properties of the VN and there are differing aspectual constraints on internal and external arguments. The rest of this paper will address other constructions which show the same sensitivity to the aspectual interface as the primary genitive modifiers.

4. Other Constructions with VNs

4.1. Passives

Korean has two kinds of VN passives with the verbal suffixes *tangha* and *toy*, respectively.

(31)   John-i   piphan-   **toy/tangha**-essta.
                nom criticizing-TOY/TANGHA-past
        'John was criticized.'

Many VNs are compatible with either of the suffixes. *Tangha* literally means that 'have adverse effect on' and thus is used only when the subject is so affected. Hence, VNs like *senen* 'announcement' or *phyencip* 'editing' do not take the *tangha* suffix because they do not connote adversity on the subject.

(32)   Kayhoy-ka   senen-toy/*tangha-essta.
                opening-nom announcement-TOY/TANGHA-past
        'The opening (of the ceremony) was announced.'

Because of the literal meaning of *tangha*, it usually appears with a human subject. There is a counterpart of *tangha*, which usually goes with a human subject as *tangha* but lacks its adverse connotation: *pat*. It literally means 'receive' and usually connotes a favorable effect on the subject.[10]

(33) a. Sensayngnim-i haksayng-tul-eykey conkyong -**pat**-nunta
        teacher-top   student-pl-by   respect - PAT-pres

---

[10] *Pat* does not always have a favorable connotation, as the following examples illustrate:
    i) a. piphan pat-ta
            criticizing PAT
            'be criticized'
        b. swusayk pat-ta
            search   PAT
            'be searched'

'Teachers are respected by students.'

    b. John-i   chingchan pat-assta
           nom praise   PAT-past
    'John was praised.'

Also, there are VNs which are compatible with either *toy* or *pat*:

(34) a. Haksayng-tul-un sensayngnim-eykey kyoyook -pat/toy-(n)unta.
        student-pl-top   teacher-by   education- PAT/TOY-pres
        'Students are educated by teachers.'

      b. John-i   Bill-eykey piphan   pat/toy-essta.
           nom   by   criticizing PAT/TOY-past
      'John was criticized by Bill.'

It is intriguing that although the *toy* passive is not semantically selective as is *tangha* or *pat*, some VNs are not compatible with *toy* .

(35)   a. John-i   cungo-tangha/*toy-yessta.
             nom   hate-TANGHA/TOY-past
       'John was hated.'

      b. John-i   tongceng - pat/*toy-yessta.
           nom sympathy- PAT/TOY-past
       'John was sympathized.'

I find that all these VNs which do not take the *toy* passive are Type I VNs, of which the internal argument is not aspectual, as the following genitive forms illustrate:

(36) a. John-uy cungo
          gen hate
      'John's $_{ag/*th}$ hate'

      b. John-uy tongceng
           gen sympathy
      'John's $_{ag/*th}$ sympathy'

This demonstrates that the *toy* passive is sensitive to the aspectual property of the VN, as is the genitive modifier. The condition on the *toy* passive is formalized as follows:

(37) The *toy* passive passivizes only an aspectually prominent argument.

4.2. Causatives

In this section I show that the causative in Korean isolates Type II. Korean has two forms of causative constructions with VNs. The following examples illustrate each causative construction:

(38) a. John-i   hwasal-ul _myengcwung_-**sikhi**-essta.
         nom arrow-acc hit-SIKHI-past
      'John hit the target with the arrow.'

   b. John-i   Mary-lul <u>siksa</u> **hakey ha**-yssta.
         nom   acc dine-HAKEY HA-past
      'John forced Mary to have a meal.'

One form of causative suffix is *-sikhita* with VNs, while the other form is *-hakey ha*. I will refer to the former as SIKHI causative and the latter, HAKEY causative.

While the passive is sensitive to the visibility of the internal argument, *sikhi* causative is sensitive to the visibility of the external argument. Whereas the *toy* passive requires the visibility of the argument, the *sikhi* causative requires the invisibility of the argument.

It is well known that the causative suffix introduces a new external argument to the original argument structure of the verb, as is shown below (Miyagawa 1989, Kim 1990):

(39) a. Hwasal-i   kwanyek-ey <u>myengcwung</u>-hayssta
         arrow-nom target-at   hit-did
      'The arrow hit the target.'

   b. John-i   hwasal-ul _myengcwung_-sikhi-essta
         nom arrow-acc hit-SIKHI-past
      'John hit the target with the arrow.'

A new external argument *John* in (39b) is introduced in the argument structure of *myengcwung* in (39a) as a result of causativization. It is schematized as follows:

(40) V: ϕ (y) --> V + Cause : x (y)

This type of causativization is most compatible with unaccusative VNs such as *hoycen* 'rolling,' and *myengcwung* 'hit,' since the slot of the external argument is originally empty for those VNs, as in (40).

However, there is another role of *sikhi* suffix. In some cases, the causative suffix can subsititute for -*hata* 'do', seemingly without a siginificant difference in the argument structure. [11]

(41) a. John-i   koki-lul <u>nayngtong-*ha/sikhi*-yessta</u>.
            nom met-acc freezing   HA/SIKHI-past
        'John froze the meat.'

      b. Sacang-i   John-ul <u>hayko-*ha/sikhi*-yessta</u>
         president-nom   acc firing-HA/SIKHI-past
         'The president fired John.'

Only Type II VNs are found with this type of causativization. Type I and III are unacceptable with *sikhita* in this usage. [12]

(42) a. John-i Mary-lul <u>tongceng-ha/*sikhi*-essta</u>
             nom   acc sympathy-HA/SIKHI-past
          'John sympathized Mary.'

      b. John-i Mary-lul <u>kwuco-ha/*sikhi*-essta</u>
             nom   acc rescue-HA/SIKHI-past
          'John rescued Mary.'

I suggest that the reason that sentences in (41) are acceptable is that in the process of causativization, the *sikhi* causative cannot "see" the original external argument, because it is not aspectually prominent. That is, the external argument must be invisible to the *sikhi* causative, after filtered out at the aspectual interface. Thus the causative have an empty argument position to introduce a new argument to. On the other hand, Type I or III VNs do not have the position which the new argument can fill in, because their external argument is aspectually prominent. It results in the incompatibility with the *sikhi* causative. I propose the following condition on the *sikhi* causative:

---

[11] Not all of Type II VNs are compatible with *sikhita*. For example, *sicak* 'start' and *pwunsil* 'loss', do not go with *sikhita*. Thus the visibility of the Agent seems to be a necessary, but not a sufficient condition.

[12] There are some VNs other than unaccusative and Type II which allow the *sikhi* causativization.

    i) Sensayngnim-i Bill-ul <u>kongpwu</u> sikhi-essta
       teacher-nom   acc study   SIKHI-past
    'The teacher forced Bill to study.'

I assume that this type of causativization undergoes a different process from one discussed above and refer readers to Levin and Rappaport (1995:110-119).

(43) The *sikhi* causativization is possible only when the external argument is not aspectually prominent.

This condition can capture the generalization between the unaccusative and Type II VNs.

The fact that the aspectual analysis can account for the syntactically related constructions such as passives and causatives in the uniform way demonstrates the validity of this analysis.

5. Summary and Remaining Issues

I have argued that the genitive modifiers of VNs are controlled by the intermediate aspectual level between thematic structure and syntactic structure. Only parts of the argument structure filtered by aspectual level are visible to the syntax. I have shown that the effect of the aspectual interface is reflected in other constructions as well, such as the *toy* passive and the *sikhi* causative.

Many untouched issues remain, however. Examination of the wider range of VNs, including those with a more complicated argument structure, is essential for further development of this topic. Comparative study of abstract nominals across languages with respect to the syntactic phenomena discussed here also awaits further research.

References

Anderson, M. 1979. *Noun Phrase Structure*. Ph.D. dissertation. University of Connecticut.

Anderson, M. 1983. Prenominal Genitive NPs. *The Linguistic Review* 3:1-24.

Burzio, L. Intransitive Verbs and Italian Auxiliaries. Ph.D. dissertation. MIT.

Dowty, D. R. 1979. *Word Meaning and Montague Grammar*. D. Reidel Publishing Company.

Grimshaw, J. 1990. *Argument Structure*. Cambridge, Mass.: MIT Press.

Grimshaw, J. and A. Mester. 1988. Light Verbs and θ-Marking. *Linguistic Inquiry* 19:205-232.

Hamano, S. 1989. Thematic Role Assignment of the Single Argument of (De)verbal Nouns. ESCOL.126-137.

Jacobsen, W.M. 1992. *The Transitive Structure of Events in Japanese*. Kurosio Publishers. Tokyo.

Kim, Y-J. 1990. *The Syntax and Semantics of Korean Case: The Interaction between Lexical and Syntactic Levels of Representation.* Ph.D. dissertation. Harvard University.

Levin, B., and M.R. Hovav. 1991. Wiping the Slate Clean: A Lexical Semantic Exploration. *Cognition* 41:123-51.

Levin, B., and M.R. Hovav. 1995. *Unaccusativity.* Cambridge, Mass.: MIT Press.

Miyagawa, S. 1989. *Syntax and Semantics 22: Structure and Case Marking in Japanese.* New York: Academic Press.

Pustejovsky, J. 1991. The syntax of event structure. *Cognition,* 41:47-81.

Talmy, L. 1985. Lexicalization Patterns: Semantic Structure in Lexical Forms. In *Language Typology and Syntactic Description 3: Grammatical Categories and the Lexicon,* ed. T. Shopen, 57-149. Cambridge: Cambridge Unviersity Press.

Tenny, C. 1992. The Aspectual Interface Hypothesis. in *Lexical Matters* , ed. I. A. Sag and A. Szabolsci, 1-27. Stanford, Calif.: CSLI Publications.

Vendler, Z. 1967. *Linguistics in Philosophy.* Cornell University Press. Ithaca, New York.

Argument Structure Changes in the Korean Benefactive Construction[1]

SEOK-HOON YOU
University of Hawaii at Manoa

0. Introduction

In Korean, there are two means of expressing the benefactive function. One is to attach an adverbial phrase, either *-(l)ul wiha-ye(-se)* 'for, in the favor of' or *-ttaymun-ey* 'for the sake of, because of', after a beneficiary NP. (See (1).) The other is to attach a benefactive verbal form *-e cwuta*[2] 'to do something for someone' (lit. 'to give (the benefit of)') after non-final verb(s). (See (2) and thereafter.) The goal of this paper is to investigate the change in argument structure that occurs in

---

[1] Abbreviations:

Ag/<a>: Agent/Agent Role Marker	Ac: Accusative Case Marker
AS: Argument Structure	Dat: Dative Case Marker
DO: Direct Object	Go/<g>: Goal/Goal Role Marker
IO: Indirect Object	Loc/<loc>: Location/Location Role Marker
Nm: Nominative Case Marker	Pst: Past Tense Marker
SE: Sentence Ending	SU: Subject
Th/<th>: Theme/Theme Role Marker	th$_{cs}$: Complement Sentential Theme

[2] This plain form *-cwuta* is interchangeable with an honorific counterpart *-tulita*. When the speaker requests some kind of favor done for himself or herself, a command ending in either polite (*-cwuseyyo*) or non-polite (*cwe*) form can be used.

the process of grammaticalizing the verb 'give' form to benefactives in -*e cwuta* in the latter construction. Consider the following examples.

(1) Phrasal benefactive construction in Korean
Yumi-ka   John-*ul wihaye(se)* chayk-ul   sa-Ess-ta.
Yumi-Nm   John-Ben   book-Ac   buy-Pst-SE
'Yumi bought a book FOR John.'

(2) Complex benefactive construction in Korean
Yumi-ka   John-eykey chayk-ul *sa-E cwu*-Ess-ta.
Yumi-Nm   John-Go   book-Ac buy give-Pst-SE
'Yumi bought a book FOR John.'

In section 1, I will discuss the basic usage, and the structural and functional characteristics of -*E cwuta* construction. Section 2 is a review of previous studies paying special attention to Shibatani (1994). In section 3, an analysis about the argument structure change based on both structural and functional aspects of the construction is presented. Section 4 presents the concluding remarks.

1. Basic usage, structure and functions

The first usage of -*E cwuta* construction is for sequential DONATORY actions meaning 'to do something AND give it to someone.' The second usage is a BENEFACTIVE one meaning 'to do something (represented by non-final verb(s)) FOR someone (speaker (the first person) or hearer (the second person) or the third person)'. This benefactive usage is derived from the donatory meaning of the verb. Consider the following example.

(3)   Yumi-ka   Sumi-eykey chayk-ul   sa-E   cwu-Ess-ta[3]
        Yumi-Nm Sumi-Go   book-Ac   buy   give-Pst-SE

  (i) 'Yumi bought a book AND gave it to Sumi.'
  (ii) 'Yumi bought a book FOR Sumi.'

I will assume the following as a tentative underlying D-structure of the benefactive sentence in (3ii). The underlying structure of the donatory sentence in the sense of (3i) is assumed to be something like (5).

(4)[4]

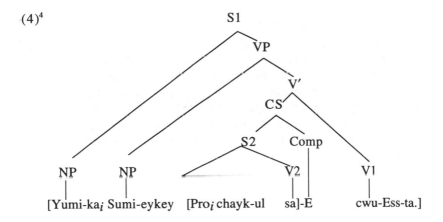

[Yumi-ka$_i$ Sumi-eykey [Pro$_i$ chayk-ul   sa]-E   cwu-Ess-ta.]

In (4), I assume an embedded complement sentence (CS) construction. In other words, S2 which contains V2 as its main verb is a subordinate sentence embedded within S1 which contains V1 as its main verb. The COMPLEMENTIZER (COMP) -E connects two sentences. Compare (4) with the following.

---

[3] Depending on the quality of a vowel in the stem of a verb, the complementizer -E can be realized in the following ways:

  $-E \rightarrow \emptyset / a$ __   (where C, Lv, Dv, and HA mean a consonant, a light

  $-E \rightarrow a$ / CLvC __   vowel (a, ya, o, and yo), a dark vowel ($\varepsilon, y\varepsilon, e, ye, wu$,

  $-E \rightarrow e$ / CDvC __ ywu, u, and i), and HA- verb respectively.)

  $-E \rightarrow y(e)$ / HA __

[4] For brevity's sake, specific tree information is omitted on purpose.

(5)

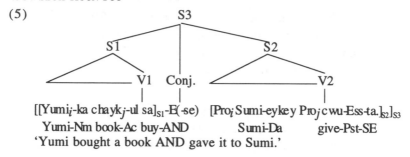

[[Yumi$_i$-ka chayk$_j$-ul sa]$_{S1}$-E(-se) [Pro$_i$ Sumi-eykey Pro$_j$ cwu-Ess-ta.]$_{S2}$]$_{S3}$
Yumi-Nm book-Ac buy-AND   Sumi-Da   give-Pst-SE
'Yumi bought a book AND gave it to Sumi.'

The structural difference between the two is very clear. Contrary to the embedded construction in (4a), construction (5) is a typical example of COORDINATION as shown clearly by the use of a coordinate conjunction -E(-se) which coincidentally has an identical form with the complementizer -E after an optional omission of -se. Besides, the meanings in the two constructions are completely different from each other. The benefactive meaning is not allowed in sentence (5) which only expresses a sequence of two events connected by -E(se) with the second event being a donatory action of giving represented by a verb cwuta. In contrast, sentences in (4) uniformly deliver benefactive meaning.

2. Previous studies

Previous formal approaches were not quite successful in providing a proper explanation for the benefactive construction. Aissen (1983) and Baker (1988) tried to provide a uniform and structural analysis about the inability of INTRANSITIVE constructions to undergo change to BENEFACTIVE constructions. However, their approaches are inappropriate in various respects. First, it is not only intransitive verbs, but a large number of transitive verbs that do not allow their clausemate goal NP to convert to a benefactive NP. It is shown clearly in the following examples.

(6) a. Sumi-ka Yumi-eykey yo-lul   kkal-E cwu-Ess-ta.
         Sumi-N   Yumi-Go   mattress-Ac spread give-Pst-SE
         'Sumi spreaded the mattress FOR Yumi.'

b. ?*Sumi-ka Yumi-eykey yo-lul   kay-E cwu-Ess-ta.
Sumi-N   Yumi-Go   mattress-Ac fold   give-Pst-SE
'Sumi folded up (put away) the mattress FOR Yumi.'

(7) a.   Sumi-ka Yumi-eykey mun-ul   yel-E cwu-Ess-ta.
Sumi-N Yumi-Go   door-Ac   open give-Pst-SE
'Sumi opened the door FOR Yumi.'

b. *Sumi-ka Yumi-eykey mun-ul   tat-E cwu-Ess-ta.
Sumi-N   Yumi-Go   door -Ac close give-Pst-SE
'Sumi closed the door FOR Yumi.'

(8) a.   Sumi-ka Yumi-eykey kwutwu-lul   takk-E cwu-Ess-ta.
Sumi-N Yumi-Go   shoes-Ac   polish give-Pst-SE
'Sumi cleaned the shoes FOR Yumi.'

b. *?Sumi-ka Yumi-eykey chang-ul   takk-E cwu-Ess-ta.
Sumi-N   Yumi-Go   window-Ac clean give-Pst-SE
'Sumi cleaned the windows FOR Yumi.'

In spite of the fact that all the (b) sentences in (6), (7), and (8) carry a transitive verb as a main verb in subordinate sentence as do (a) sentences, they are not still quite acceptable.

Second, even some intransitive verbs in Korean easily convert to benefactive constructions while some do not. The following examples show this point clearly.

(9) a.   Sumi-ka Yumi-eykey ka-E cwu-Ess-ta.
Sumi-N Yumi-Go   go   give-Pst-SE
'Sumi went to Yumi (FOR Yumi).'

b. *?Sumi-ka Yumi-eykey nol-E cwu-Ess-ta.
Sumi-N   Yumi-Go   play   give-Pst-SE
'Sumi played with Yumi (FOR Yumi).'

According to Shibatani (1994), these facts prove that both Aissen's stipulation prohibiting the OBLIQUE TO 3 ADVANCEMENT and

Baker's Case theoretic explanation, which predicts that intransitive verbs fail to convert to benefactives because they cannot assign Case to their object NP's, have nothing to say about the unacceptable transitive-based benefactives. Baker's approach is strictly restricted to just one type of benefactive constructions in which the goal/beneficiary NP is realized as a direct object. But more significantly, the central problem is not really concerned with the transitivity of the verb base. The grammaticality is not simply as categorical as these formal analyses suggest. Furthermore, even the same verb shows a measurable difference in the acceptability scale depending on the situations.

Among other studies, Shibatani (1994) is the most recent, comprehensive, and relevant to the topic. Insightful as it may be, his approach, the so-called 'CONSTRUAL BY THE GIVE-SCHEMA THEORY' does not explain the full spectrum of the phenomena related to the construction. Diagram (10) shows Shibatani's basic schema of the construction:

(10)

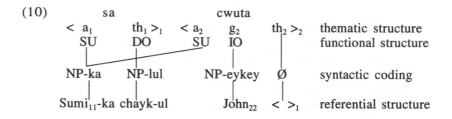

It is not totally clear how Shibatani's approach shown above can capture some crucial facts of the following sorts. First, the THEMATIC STRUCTURE assumed by Shibatani does not fully reflect the meaning and behavior of the arguments carried by the benefactive verb (the GOAL meaning vs. the 'do/be for' meaning). Despite an identical argument valency, there is a big difference in the meaning between DATIVE CONSTRUCTION and BENEFACTIVE CONSTRUCTION. Second, the *Give*-schema that drives the theory accounts for some aspects of the benefactive construction but not others. In other words, even though the schema explains some aspect of the semantics of the relevant construction, it does not tell anything about pragmatic factors that will be discussed later. Third, Shibatani's coindexing interpretation module, especially $< >_1$ (e.g., (10)) in the referential structure, is unable to account adequately for sentential themes because it does not have any distinction between lexical argument vs. sentential complement argument. Finally, Shibatani's approach does not fully reflect the DIACHRONIC aspect of the phenomena although he touches on it to a certain extent. In order to explain the full range of phenomena, it is indispensable for us to explain not only the SYNCHRONIC but also its diachronic aspect.

3. Analysis

In this section, I will present an analysis that will explain various aspects of the constructions in question, including both synchronic and diachronic aspects. My analysis is two-fold. I basically claim that the constructions actually reflect different stages of an on-going gradual GRAMMATICALIZATION process along the cline from a full donatory to a full benefactive construction. I also claim that both structural and functional factors are deeply involved in the process. As was already pointed out in the previous section, the problems with other approaches are in their basic assumption that all of these phenomena are purely synchronic and structural. For these theories, it would not be easy to explain both the discrepancies in argument structure found among the same type of verbs with identical categorical status and some grammaticalized forms that are discussed in You (1995).

3.1. Grammaticalization in *-E cwuta* and Valency Discrepancies in Argument Realization

As alluded to thus far, I propose that the benefactive *cwuta*, a so-called AUXILIARY VERB, has been grammaticalized from the donatory *cwuta*, an independent verb. The grammaticalization has taken place only when *cwuta* occurred after a complement clause that ends in the complementizer *-E* which itself developed from the conjunctive suffix *-E(se)* 'and then' with the deletion of *-se*. Thus, *-E cwuta* has the original ungrammaticalized meaning 'and then give something to' as in (5) and the grammaticalized benefactive meaning 'give the benefit/act of doing/being for' as in (4). I thus claim that the donatory *cwuta* and the benefactive *cwuta* have different argument structures as in the following:

(11) a. donatory *cwuta*: $< a\ g\ th >$
    b. benefactive *cwuta*: 1. $< a\ g\ th_{cs} >$
                       2. $< a\ th_{cs} >$

Notice the progressive argument structure change effected as the grammaticalization gets mature. The NP theme (th) which refers to an object in the donatory *cwuta* is changed to a clause theme (th$_{CS}$) which refers to an event in the benefactive *cwuta*. Furthermore, goal (<g>) which is an obligatory argument in the case of the donatory *cwuta* becomes obsolete in the benefactive *cwuta* except when its appearance is allowed under a variety of grammatical, semantic, and pragmatic conditions to be discussed in 3.2. To indicate such restrictiveness of the occurrence of *g*, I propose < a *g* th$_{CS}$ > for the argument structure of the benefactive *cwuta*.

As a result of the grammaticalization involved in *-E cwuta*, VALENCY DISCREPANCIES occur in the realization of arguments in benefactive constructions. The valency discrepancies in argument structure[5] are caused when more than two verbs combine to make a complex verb. In the following, th$_\alpha$ is a short form of th$_{CS\alpha}$.

(12)   Yumi-ka Sumi-eykey   chayk-ul sa-E   cwu-Ess-ta.
          sa$_{V1}$ + cwu$_{V2}$ → sa-cwuta$_{V1\text{-}V2}$
    AS: <a$_1$ th$_1$>$_{V1}$ + <a$_2$ g$_2$ th$_2$>$_{V2}$ → <a$_{12}$ g$_2$ th$_{12}$>$_{V1\text{-}V2}$
    (i)   'Yumi bought-gave a book to Sumi.'
    AS: [<a$_1$ th$_1$>$_{V1}$]$_\alpha$ + <a$_2$ **g**$_2$ th$_\alpha$>$_{V2}$ → <a$_{12}$ g$_2$ th$_1$>$_{V1\text{-}V2}$
    (ii) 'Yumi bought a book FOR Sumi.'

(13)   Yumi-ka Sumi-eykey   kukes-ul iyakiha-E cwu-Ess-ta.
          iyakiha$_{V1}$ + cwu$_{V2}$ → iyakihay-cwuta$_{V1\text{-}V2}$
    AS: [<a$_1$ g$_1$ th$_1$>$_{V1}$]$_\alpha$ + <a$_2$ **g**$_2$ th$_\alpha$>$_{V2}$ → <a$_{12}$ g$_1$ th$_1$>$_{V1\text{-}V2}$
          'Yumi told the fact to and FOR Sumi.'

(14)   Yumi-ka halapeci-kkey   yo-lul kkal-E   tuli-Ess-ta.
          kkala$_{V1}$+ tuli$_{V2}$ → kkala-tulita$_{V1\text{-}V2}$
    AS: [<a$_1$ th$_1$>$_{V1}$]$_\alpha$ + <a$_2$ **g**$_2$ th$_\alpha$>$_{V2}$ → <a$_{12}$ g$_2$ th$_1$>$_{V1\text{-}V2}$
          'Yumi spread a mattress FOR her grandfather.'

(15)   Yumi-ka (*Sumi-eykey) kukcang-ey ka-E   cwu-Ess-ta.
          ka$_{V1}$ + cwu$_{V2}$ → ka-cwu$_{V1\text{-}V2}$
    AS: [<a$_1$ loc$_1$>$_{V1}$]$_\alpha$ + <a$_2$ **g**$_2$ th$_\alpha$>$_{V2}$ → <a$_{12}$ loc$_1$>$_{V1\text{-}V2}$
          'Yumi went to the theater FOR Sumi.'

---

[5] By 'valency discrepancies in argument structure', I mean the differences in argument structure between input and output constructions as shown in examples (12) through (15).

Examples (12) through (15) show both input and output argument structures of each sentence with regard to its component verbs. The sum of the argument structure of component verbs on the input side does not necessarily match that of complex verbal form on the output side. The gradual grammaticalization process has affected the valency of ARGUMENT STRUCTURE in the relevant verbal complex. The valency is mostly determined by the transitivity of a verb. Thus, an intransitive verb takes just a single argument, usually an AGENT or an EXPERIENCER argument. A TRANSITIVE verb takes two arguments, usually an agent or an EXPERIENCER and a THEME argument. Finally, a DITRANSITIVE verb can take up to three arguments, an agent or an experiencer, a theme, and a GOAL argument. Case markers attached to the end of each argument NP reflect an output argument structure of a verb. The following is the observation from the above examples:

(16) a. Agent sharing (12-15) and Theme sharing (12i)
   b. Suppression of Benefactive Goal in the presence of embedded Goal (13)
   c. Suppression of Benefactive Goal when CS lacks *th* (15)
   d. Contrast between the Goal meaning and Benefactive meaning for an identical Goal argument ((12i) vs. (12ii))

THEME SHARING is very widespread in serial verbal constructions like (12i). Observing this pervasiveness, Baker (1988) proposes the so-called THEME-SHARING HYPOTHESIS in the INCORPORATION process of CAUSATIVES and other constructions. However, (12ii) through (15) make obsolete the predictability of the hypothesis. A theme does not need to be a lexical item, but rather it can be a sentential complement. Observation (16c) says that not all the component arguments need to be included in the argument structure of an output verbal complex. Observation (16d) is relevant to the functional aspect of the construction. Depending on both structure and context, an identical argument can carry different meanings.

3.2. Functional filters

For proper explanation of various benefactive constructions, we need to have a set of devices to filter only acceptable sentences. I propose the following functional filtering devices.

3.2.1. Theme referent-transferability condition

As has already been mentioned, Shibatani's unified 'GIVE-schema' approach does not fully provide a clear explanation for the valency discrepancies of the argument structures in target sentences. The first problem is related to example (12) which is repeated in the following:

(17) Yumi-ka Sumi-eykey chayk-ul sa-E cwu-Ess-ta.

$sa_{V1} + cwu_{V2} \rightarrow sa\text{-}E\text{-}cwu_{V1\text{-}V2}$

(i) 'Yumi bought-gave a book TO Sumi.'

AS: $<a_1\ th_1>_{V1} + <a_2\ g_2\ th_2>_{V2} \rightarrow <a_{12}\ g_2\ \textbf{\textit{th}}_{12}>_{V1\text{-}V2}$

(ii) 'Yumi bought a book FOR Sumi.'

AS: $[<a_1\ th_1>_{V1}]_\alpha + <a_2\ g_2\ th_\alpha>_{V2} \rightarrow <a_{12}\ g_2\ \textbf{\textit{th}}_1>_{V1\text{-}V2}$

Comparison of the argument structures ((17i) and (17ii)) reveals that the argument structure is sensitive to the semantics of the sentence. The interpretation (17i) is for the dative construction while (17ii) is for the benefactive one. In this distinction, the properties of the theme object argument is crucial. Only a physical, tangible, and transferable object can be employed as a theme object for a dative interpretation. This becomes evident if we compare the argument structure in (17i) with the following:

(18) Yumi-ka Sumi-eykey kaps-ul kkak-E cwu-Ess-ta.

$kkak_{V1} + cwu_{V2} \rightarrow kkak\text{-}E\text{-}cwu_{V1\text{-}V2}$

(i) *'Yumi gave a discount TO Sumi.'

AS: $<a_1\ th_1>_{V1} + <a_2\ g_2\ th_2>_{V2} \rightarrow <a_{12}\ g_2\ \textbf{\textit{th}}_{12}>_{V1\text{-}V2}$

(ii) 'Yumi gave a discount **FOR** Sumi.'

AS: $[<a_1\ th_1>_{V1}]_\alpha + <a_2\ g_2\ th_\alpha>_{V2} \rightarrow <a_{12}\ g_2\ \textbf{\textit{th}}_1>_{V1\text{-}V2}$

A theme argument *kaps* 'price' is a non-transferable object, thus the first dative interpretation (18i) turns out to be unacceptable. The following are further examples with benefactive-only interpretation. For these examples, dative interpretation is not possible at all:

(19) Yumi-ka Sumi-eykey kukes-ul iyakiha-E cwu-Ess-ta.
iyakiha$_{V1}$ + cwu$_{V2}$ → iyakiha-E-cwu$_{V1\text{-}V2}$
AS: [<a$_1$ g$_1$ th$_1$>$_{V1}$]$_\alpha$ + <a$_2$ g$_2$ th$_\alpha$>$_{V2}$ → <a$_2$ g$_1$ *th$_1$*>$_{V1\text{-}V2}$
'Yumi talked to Sumi about it (**FOR** Sumi).'

(20) Yumi-ka Sumi-eykey chingchanha-E cwu-Ess-ta.
chingchanha$_{V1}$ + cwu$_{V2}$ → chingchanha-E-cwu$_{V1\text{-}V2}$
AS: [<a$_1$ th$_1$>$_{V1}$]$_\alpha$ + <a$_2$ g$_2$ th$_2$>$_{V2}$ → <a$_{12}$ g$_2$>$_{V1\text{-}V2}$
'Yumi praised Sumi (**FOR** Sumi).'

3.2.2. Temporal/Spatial immediacy condition

The second condition is closely related to the discourse situation. One of the most important discourse factors that affects the grammaticality of relevant sentences is 'TEMPORAL/SPATIAL IMMEDIACY CONDITION'. This pragmatic condition requires a goal NP referent (mostly a beneficiary) to be present at the event scene. Otherwise, the sentence turns out to be unacceptable due to a violation of felicity code in the given situation. Consider the following example:

(21) Yumi-ka halapeci-kkey yo-lul kkal-E tuli-Ess-ta.
kkala$_{V1}$+ tuli$_{V2}$ → kkal-E-tuli$_{V1\text{-}V2}$
AS: [<a$_1$ th$_1$>$_{V1}$]$_\alpha$ + <a$_2$ g$_2$ th$_\alpha$>$_{V2}$ → <a$_{12}$ g$_2$ *th$_1$*>$_{V1\text{-}V2}$
'Yumi spread a mattress for her grandfather.'

This sentence is perfect in an ordinary situation but if the situation changes, i.e., if Yumi's grandfather is absent at the moment of speaking, the acceptability of the sentence dramatically degrades.

3.2.3. Appropriateness condition

For some other examples, different kinds of conditions or constraints are needed. The first one is an 'APPROPRIATENESS CONDITION'. A sentence should be appropriate to the context in order for the goal argument (beneficiary) to appear on the surface. Consider the following.

(22) a. Yumi-ka   sensayngnim-kkey kwutwu-lul   takk-E tuli-Ess-ta.
       Yumi-Nm   teacher-Dat   shoes-Ac   clean   Give-Pst-SE
    AS: $[<a_1 \text{ th}_1>_{V1}]_\alpha + <a_2\, g_2 \text{ th}_\alpha>_{V2} \rightarrow <a_{12}\, g_2\, \textbf{\textit{th}}_1>_{V1\text{-}V2}$
    'Yumi polished the shoes for her teacher.'

   b. ?*Yumi-ka sensayngnim-kkey yulichang-ul takk-E tuli-Ess-ta.
      Yumi-Nm   teacher-Dat   glass-Ac   clean   Give-Pst-SE
      'Yumi cleaned window panes for her teacher.'

(23) a. Yumi-ka   sensayngnim-kkey mwun-ul   yel-E   tuli-Ess-ta.
       Yumi-Nm   teacher-Dat   door-Ac   open   Give-Pst-SE
    AS: $[<a_1 \text{ th}_1>_{V1}]_\alpha + <a_2\, g_2 \text{ th}_\alpha>_{V2} \rightarrow <a_{12}\, g_2\, \textbf{\textit{th}}_1>_{V1\text{-}V2}$
    'Yumi opened the door for her teacher.'

   b. ?*Yumi-ka sensayngnim-kkey mwun-ul   tat-E   tuli-Ess-ta.
      Yumi-Nm   teacher-Dat   door-Ac   close   Give-Pst-SE
      'Yumi closed the door for her teacher.'

Despite the fact that all non-final verbs in the sentences in (22) and (23) are uniformly transitive, the grammaticality judgment of (b) sentences is bad. The (b) sentences do not fit into appropriate situations in the normal context while (a) sentences do. In order to improve acceptability of (b) sentences, additional contextual elaboration is needed. Consider the following examples:

(24) (Sensayngnim-kkeyse pwuthakhasiesski ttaymwuney)
      (Since her teacher asked Yumi to do so,)
      Yumi-ka   sensayngnim-kkey yulichang-ul   takk-E tuli-Ess-ta.
      Yumi-Nm   teacher-Dat   glass-Ac   clean   Give-Pst-SE
      'Yumi cleaned window panes for her teacher.'

(25) (Sensayngnim-kkeyse puthakhasiesski ttaymuney)
(Since her teacher asked Yumi to do so,)
Yumi-ka   sensayngnim-kkey mun-ul   tat-E tuli-Ess-ta.
Yumi-Nm teacher-Dat   door-Ac close Give-Pst-SE
'Yumi closed the door for her teacher.'

3.3. Other filters

3.3.1. Intransitivity filter

When an intransitive verb is employed as a non-final verbal complement in a benefactive construction, it triggers another type of filter — the so-called 'INTRANSITIVITY FILTER'. Consider the following example:

(26=15) Yumi-ka   (*Swumi-eykey) kucang-ey ka-E cwu-Ess-ta.
Yumi-Nm Swumi-Dat   theater-Loc go   Give-Pst-SE
AS: $[<a_1 \text{ loc}_1>_{V1}]_\alpha + <a_2 \text{ } g_2 \text{ th}_\alpha>_{V2} \rightarrow <a_{12} \text{ } loc_1>_{V1\text{-}V2}$
'Yumi went to the theater (for Swumi).'

The 'Intransitivity Filter' suppresses the surface realization of a goal argument. This suppression is an obligatory process. If it does not apply, then the output sentence becomes unacceptable as marked in (26). This process also affects the meaning of a sentence. Since a goal argument never surfaces, the beneficiary just remains understood. The only way to express the goal argument on surface is to put it in an adjunct position as in (27) in the following:

(27) *Swumi-lul wihay*[6] Yumi-ka   kucang-ey ka-E cwu-Ess-ta.
Swumi-Ac for   Yumi-Nm theater-Loc go   Give-Pst-SE
'For Swumi, Yumi went to the theater.'

3.3.2. Animate-object constraint

When an animate object is selected as a complement of an embedded verb, it exerts similar effect as in 'intransitivity filter' on the

---

[6] Subject to scrambling.

beneficiary argument. Thus the goal NP is suppressed and does not surface. Consider the following examples.

(28) a. (emeni-kkeyse puthakha-si-Ess-ki ttaymuney)
     (mother-Nm   ask-Hon-Pst-because)

     Swumi-ka Yumi-lul tow-E $\begin{cases} \text{cwu} - \text{Ess} - \text{ta.} \\ \text{*tuli} - \text{Ess} - \text{ta.} \end{cases}$

     Swumi-Nm Yumi-Ac help   give-Pst-SE

   AS: $[<a_1\ th_1>_{V1}]_\alpha + <a_2\ g_2\ th_\alpha>_{V2} \rightarrow <a_{12}\ th_1>_{V1\text{-}V2}$

     'Swumi helped Yumi (because her mother asked to do so).'

  b. Swumi-ka (*Yumi-eykey) Yumi-lul   tow-E cwu-Ess-ta.
     Swumi-Nm Yumi-Dat   Yumi-Ac help give-Pst-SE
     'Swumi helped Yumi for Yumi (because her mother asked to do so).'

  c. Swumi-ka (*emenim-kkey) Yumi-lul tow-E $\begin{cases} \text{cwu} - \text{Ess} - \text{ta.} \\ * \text{tuli} - \text{Ess} - \text{ta.} \end{cases}$

     Swumi-Nm mother-Dat   Yumi-Ac help   give-Pst-SE
     'Swumi helped Yumi for her mother (because her mother asked to do so).'

The forced realization of a goal argument renders the sentence bad as shown in (28b,c). Again, the only way to represent a goal argument on the surface is to adjoin it in an adverbial position within a sentence as in the following:

(29) (emeni-kkeyse   puthakha-si-Ess-ki ttaymuney)
     (mother-Nm   ask-Hon-Pst-because)
     Yumi-lul wihay Swumi-ka Yumi-lul tow-E cwu-Ess-ta.
     Yumi-Ac for   Swumi-Nm Yumi-Ac help give-Pst-SE
     'For Yumi, Swumi helped her (Yumi) (because her mother asked to do so).'

3.3.3. Internal Argument Primacy Condition

Another condition which is crucial in determining the grammaticality of a sentence is an 'INTERNAL ARGUMENT

PRIMACY CONDITION.' When an argument of an embedded sentence and that of a higher sentence are identical, this condition gives primacy only to an embedded (or internal) argument in the realization in an output sentence. Consider the following examples:

(30) a. (emeni-kkeyse puthakha-si-Ess-ki ttaymuney)
   (mother-Nm ask-Hon-Pst-because)
   Yumi-eykey piano-lul kaluchy-E cwu-ess-ta.
   Yumi-Dat piano-Ac teach   give-Pst-SE
  AS: $[<a_1\,g_1\,th_1>_{V1}]_\alpha + <a_2\,g_2\,th_\alpha>_{V2} \rightarrow <a_{12}\,g_1\,th_1>_{V1\text{-}V2}$
   'For Yumi, Sumi taught her (Yumi) playing piano (because her (Yumi's) mother asked to do so).'

  b. (emeni-kkeyse puthakha-si-Ess-ki ttaymuney)
   (mother-Nm ask-Hon-Pst-because)
   *emeni-kkey piano-lul kaluchy-E cwu/tuli-ess-ta.
   mother-Dat piano-Ac teach   give-Pst-SE
   'For Yumi, Sumi taught her (Yumi) playing piano (because her (Yumi's) mother asked to do so).'

Only *Yumi*, the argument of an internal verbal *kaluchi-* 'teach', realizes in sentence (30a).

4. Concluding Remarks

The basic usages, structures, and functions of *-E CWUTA* benefactive construction in Korean is discussed. I have also discussed problems in current analyses with regard to the same construction. The following problems were discussed:

 a. Structure- and category-oriented approaches do not predict the acceptability profile of the sentences in (6-8), (15), (18), (23), and (28) correctly.

 b. Insightful as it may be, Shibatani's 'Construal by the *Give*-schema theory' does not completely predict the semantics and pragmatics of benefactive construction.

c. Shibatani's 'Construal by the *Give*-schema theory' lacks crucial devices such as various structural and contextual filters.

d. Shibatani's coindexing interpretation module does not explicitly account for complement sentential theme.

Acknowledging these problems, I suggested various filters including THEME REFERENT-TRANSFERABILITY CONDITION, TEMPO-RAL/SPATIAL IMMEDIACY CONDITION, INTRANSITIVITY CON-STRAINT, APPROPRIATENESS CONDITION, ANIMATE-OBJECT CONSTRAINT, and INTERNAL ARGUMENT PRIMACY CONDITION. And also an interesting aspect in the change of argument structure in relevant construction with various configurations has been observed. The following is the summary.

Table 1. Stages of Grammaticalization toward Benefactive -*E cwuta*

Stage	Meaning	Condition	AS	Exs.
I	to give something to someone (for him/her/them)	(1) theme referent-transferability condition	$<a, g, th>$	(2); (3); (12i)
II	to give the benefit of doing something to someone	(2) lack of (1) (3) temporal/ spatial immediacy condition (i.e., beneficiary's presence at event scene)	$<a, g, th_{cs}>$	(3ii); (4); (6a); (7a); (8a); (9a); (12ii); (13-15); (17ii); (18ii); (19-21); (22a); (23a)
III	to do/be for (an understood but un-specifiable person)	(4) lack of (1) and (3) (5) intransitivity constraint (6) appropriateness condition (7) animate-object constraint (8) internal argument primacy condition	$<a, th_{cs}>$	(26) (22-25) (28-29) (30)

Table (1) provides several significant points: First, it shows the difference in meaning between stages (in the Meaning column). Second, it shows the conditions to be met, whether they are syntactic, semantic, pragmatic, or discourse ones (in the Condition column). Third, it also shows the change of argument structure of the benefactive verb (in the AS column). Finally, it captures the nature of GRAMMATI-CALIZATION in a systematic manner. In other words, GRAMMATI-CALIZATION results from the superimposition of various specific conditions. One crucial point in this approach is that the more a construction (in this particular case 'benefactive construction' V-*E cwuta*) becomes grammaticalized, the more its argument valency reduces. A final incidental observation is that adverbial benefactive phrases like *-(l)ul wiha-ye(-se)* have begun to take over the function of the defunct goal argument in stage III. As a final word, this analysis is applicable to many other auxiliary verbal constructions with V1 + -E + V2 configuration.

REFERENCES

Aissen, J. 1983. Indirect Object Advancement in Tzotzil. In D. Perlmutter ed., *Studies in Relational Grammar 1*. 272-302. Chicago: University of Chicago Press.

Baker, M. 1988. *Incorporation: A Theory of Grammatical Function Changing*. Chicago: University of Chicago Press.

Grimshaw, J. 1990. *Argument structure*. Cambridge, Massachusetts: MIT Press.

Heine, Bernd, Ulrike Claudi, and Friederike Hunnemeyer. 1991. *Grammaticalization: a conceptual framework*. Chicago: University of Chicago Press

Hopper, Paul J. and Elizabeth Closs Traugott. 1993. *Grammaticalization*. London: Cambridge University Press.

Jackendoff, R. 1972. Semantic interpretation in generative grammar. Cambridge: MIT Press.

Jackendoff, Ray. 1983. *Semantics and cognition*. Cambridge, Massachusetts: MIT Press.

Jackendoff, Ray. 1987. The status of thematic relations in linguistic theory. *LI*. 18.369-411.

Kim, Young-joo. 1990. *The syntax and semantics of Korean case: The interaction between lexical and syntactic levels of representation*. Ph.D Dissertation. Harvard University.

Shibatani, M. 1979. Where Analogical Patterning Fails. *Papers in Japanese Lingusitics*. 6:287-307.

Shibatani, M. 1994. Benefactive Constructions: A Japanese-Korean Comparative Perspective. *Japanese Korean Linguistics*. 4:39-74.

Sohn, Ho-min. 1994. *Korean*. London and New York: Routledge.

You, Seok-Hoon. 1995. Teaching Benefactive Construction to KFL Learners: A Contrastive Perspective. *Korean Language in America*. Vol. 1: 137-152.

Incorporation in Syntax and LF: The Case of Light Verb Constructions and Temporal Constructions in Japanese[1]

HIROTO HOSHI
Univeristy of London

1. INTRODUCTION

Larson (1988) proposes that θ-roles can be assigned in the course of the derivation, based on the properties of the dative complement construction and the dative shift construction. Chomsky (1992) argues that it is desirable to eliminate the internal interface level between the lexicon and the computational system, D-structure, from the grammatical model, because there is no conceptual necessity. Consequently, he argues for Larson's theory of θ-marking.

In this paper, through a study of the light verb construction (henceforth, LVC) and the temporal affix construction (henceforth, TAC), I argue that to analyze those constructions, we cannot maintain D-structure, and support Larson's theory of θ-role assignment and Chomsky's proposal

---

[1] Earlier versions of this paper were presented at Quinto Coloquio de Grammatica Generativa (April 5-7, 1995), the British Association of Japanese Studies Annual Conference (April 19-21, 1995), and the Sixth Japanese/Korean Linguistics Conference (August 9-11, 1995). I profited from the comments and criticisms of the audience of each conference. Here, I would like to thank them all. I am also grateful to Jun Abe, Mona Anderson, Howard Lasnik, Diane Lillo-Martin, Naoko Nemoto, Javier Ormazabal, Myriam Uribe-Etxebarria, and especially to Mamoru Saito for their valuable criticisms and comments on this paper. Needless to say, all the shortcomings in this paper are my own.

that D-structure does not exist. In doing so, I also argue for Chomsky's (1986, 1992) proposal on the economy of derivation, in particular, last resort/greed.

The Japanese verb *su* functions exactly as the English main verb *do* in examples such as (1).

(1) Mary-ga [$_{NP}$ (suugaku-no) syukudai]-o **sita** (= *su* + *ta* (past))
       -Nom   (math -Gen) homework -Acc did   (HVC)
    'Mary did the (math) homework'

As the translation of (1) indicates, this type of *su* has clearly semantic content, and is called the heavy verb *su*.

The Japanese verb *su* can be "devoid of meaning" as well. This is shown in examples in (2).

(2)a. Mary-ga John-to (kyonen) kekkon -**sita**
        -Nom   -with (last year) marriage-did (married)
      'Mary married John (last year)'

   b. Mary-ga John-to (kinoo) taidan   -**sita**
        -Nom   -with (yesterday) conversation-did (talked)
      'Mary talked with John (yesterday)'

In (2a) and (2b), the incorporated nouns, *kekkon* 'marriage' and *kaiwa* 'conversation,' assign θ-roles to the clausal arguments *Mary* and *John-to*, and *su* functions merely as a "category changing affix."

Compare now (2a-b) with examples in (3a-b).

(3)a. *Mary-ga John-to* (kyonen) [$_{NP}$ kekkon]-o **sita**   (LVC)
        -Nom   -with (last year)   marriage -Acc did
      'Mary married John (last year)'

   b. *Mary-ga John-to* (kinoo) [$_{NP}$ taidan   ]-o **sita**   (LVC)
        -Nom   -with (yesterday)   conversation -Acc did
      'Mary talked with John (yesterday)'

Here, the arguments of the θ-role assigning nouns, *Mary* and *John-to*, appear as clausal arguments, as in (2a-b). If they were within a projection of a noun, *kekkon* or *kaiwa*, they must be accompanied by the genitive case marker *no*. This is illustrated in examples (4).

(4)a. [_{NP} Mary-*(no) John-to -*(no) kekkon]
    -*(Gen)   -with-*(Gen) marriage
'Mary's marriage with John'

b. [_{NP} Mary-*(no) John-to -*(no) taidan   ]
    -*(Gen)   -with-*(Gen) conversation
'Mary's conversation with John'
                        (Saito 1982, Fukui 1986, Murasugi 1991, others)

Notice, however, that in (3a-b), the θ-role assigning nouns, *kekkon*
and *kaiwa*, are not adjoined to the light verb *su* in contrast with (2a-b).
Those nominal θ-markers are, instead, attached with accusative Case *o*, and
appear as the objects of *su*. The construction exemplified by (3a) and (3b)
is called the Japanese LVC.

Interestingly, Sells (1988) and others observe that the TAC,
exemplified in (5a) and (5b), has similar properties.

(5)a. *Mary-ga John-to* (kyonen) kekkon -go , Susan-ga
      -Nom   -with (last year) marriage-after,   -Nom

    amerika-ni itta (rasii)
    America-to went (seems)
    '(It seems that) Susan went to America, after Mary married John
    (last year)'

b. *Mary-ga John-to* (kinoo) taidan   -go , Susan-ga
      -Nom   -with (yesterday) conversation-after,   -Nom

    amerika-ni itta (rasii)
    America-to went (seems)
    '(It seems that) Susan went to America, after Mary talked with
    John (yesterday)'

In these examples, the temporal nominal affix *go* 'after' is used.
Importantly, the arguments of the θ-marking nouns, namely *Mary* and *John-
to*, appear as clausal arguments as was the case in LVCs (3a-b). Observe
further that there does not appear to be any verb in a temporal clause, but
that even adverbial phrases such as *kyonen* and *kinoo* are licensed in the
clause.

In this paper, to explain these similarities between LVCs and

TACs, I propose that the nominal θ-marker undergoes incorporation in both of these constructions. I derive the differences between them, which I will show later, from a single minimal distinction. Namely, incorporation is forced for morphological reasons in TACs, whereas incorporation is triggered for θ-role assignment in LVCs. In the following section, I first show that Grimshaw and Mester's (1988) Argument Transfer analysis nicely accounts for interesting properties of LVCs. In section 3, after examining the nature of one of the constraints which Grimshaw and Mester assumed for their Argument Transfer account, I present an LF incorporation analysis which Hoshi and Saito (1993) and Saito and Hoshi (1994) proposed. There, I argue that there is no such lexical operation as Argument Transfer, and that the LF incorporation theory explains a wide range of data without any stipulation. In section 4, I set forth a unified analysis of LVCs and TACs based on our incorporation analysis. I show in that section that the proposal captures the similarities between LVCs and TACs. In section 5, I demonstrate that the proposed analysis coupled with Chomsky's (1986) last resort principle can also explain the differences between LVCs and TACs. In section 6, I will conclude the discussions of this paper.

2. RESTRICTIONS ON ARGUMENT TRANSFER

The intriguing property of the LVC is that some of the arguments of the θ-role assigning noun can remain within the projection of the noun, while others appear as clausal arguments. The example (6) illustrates this point.

(6) Mary-ga Susan-kara [$_{NP}$ hooseki-no ryakudatu]-o sita   (LVC)
      -Nom   -from   jewelry-Gen plunder   -Acc did
      'Mary stole the jewelry from Susan'

In (6), the theme argument *hooseki* 'jewelry' is within the NP headed by the θ-role assigning noun *ryakudatu* 'plunder,' as indicated by the presence of the genitive case marker. The agent and source arguments, *Mary* and *Susan-kara* 'from Susan,' on the other hand, appear as clausal arguments, outside the projection of *ryakudatu*, because there is no genitive case marker attached to these arguments. Given this fact, Grimshaw and Mester (1988) propose that the θ-role assigning noun can transfer some (and possibly all) of its θ-roles to the light verb *su*.

Roughly put, when *ryakudatu* 'plunder' transfers its agent and source θ-roles to *su*, we obtain the lexical entry in (8) from those in (7).

(7)a. *ryakudatu* (agent (source (theme)))

  b. *su* ( ) <acc>

↓

↓ by Argument Transfer

↓

(8) *ryakudatu* (theme) + *su* (agent (source)) <acc>   (for 6)

This argument transfer analysis, thus, accounts for the interesting properties of example (6), where *Mary* and *Susan-kara* appear in positions normally occupied by the arguments of a verb.

Developing their theory of Argument Transfer, Grimshaw and Mester make theoretically important discoveries that Argument Transfer needs to be constrained in a systematic way. If Argument Transfer is completely unconstrained, we predict that the arguments of the θ-role assigning noun can be realized either within the NP headed by the noun, or outside it at the clausal level quite freely. This is so since any θ-role of the noun can optionally be transferred to *su*.

However, Grimshaw and Mester note rather surprising restrictions on the LVC. One of them is give in (9).

(9) If a θ-role T is assigned outside the NP, then all θ-roles that are higher than T in the thematic hierarchy must also be assigned outside the NP.

If theme is the lowest in the thematic hierarchy as in (10), constraint (9) implies that for example, when the theme argument is realized at the clausal level, all other θ-roles must also be realized at this level.

(10) (Agent (Experiencer (Goal/Source/Location (Theme))))

(Grimshaw 1990)

Let us see now how this prediction is borne out. It should be first noted that when the theme θ-role is realized outside the NP at the clausal level, the sentence becomes marginally ungrammatical, as shown in (11).

(11)a.??*Mary-ga Susan-kara hooseki-o ryakudatu-o   sita
        -Nom   -from jewelry-Acc plunder -Acc did
    'Mary stole the jewelry from Susan'

  b. *ryakudatu* ( ) + *su* (agent, source, theme) <acc>

This is because of the two accusative NPs within the sentence. The relevant constraint is Harada's (1973) double-*o* constraint (12).[2]

(12) the double-*o* constraint:
  A simple sentence cannot contain more than one *o*-marked phrases.
      (Harada 1973, Kuroda 1978, Poser 1980, Saito 1982, 1985, etc.)

  Example (6), repeated here as (13a), is correctly predicted to be grammatical under Grimshaw and Mester's Argument Transfer analysis. This is because in (13a), the lowest argument in the thematic hierarchy, i.e. theme argument, is untransferred and is inside the nominal projection of *ryakudatu*, and, the highest arguments, agent and source, are transferred and are realized as clausal arguments.

(13)a. Mary-ga Susan-kara [$_{NP}$ hooseki-no ryakudatu]-o   sita   (= 6)
       -Nom   -from   jewelry-Gen plunder   -Acc did
     'Mary stole the jewelry from Susan'

   b. *ryakudatu* (theme) + *su* (agent (source)) <acc>   (= 8)

  Notice, however, when the theme argument appears outside the NP and some other argument occurs inside, the result is hopeless as shown in (14a).

(14)a. *Mary-ga hooseki-o [$_{NP}$ Susan-kara-no ryakudatu]-o   sita
        -Nom jewelry-Acc   -from-Gen plunder   -Acc did
     'Mary stole the jewelry from Susan'

---

  [2] Precisely speaking, there are in fact two types of double-*o* constraint, the surface double-*o* constraint and the abstract double-*o* constraint. See Harada (1973), Kuroda (1978), Poser (1980), Saito (1982, 1985), among others, for relevant discussion of the differences of these constraints.

  Sells (1988) argues that examples such as (11a) are in violation of the surface double-*o* constraint, not in violation of the abstract double-*o* constraint. Here, I assume that he is indeed correct and that the surface double-*o* constraint (12) rules (11a) out. The reader is also referred to Hoshi and Saito (1993) and Saito and Hoshi (1994) for detailed discussion of the nature of the ungrammaticality of (11a).

b. *ryakudatu* (source) + *su* (agent, theme) <acc> → * due to (9)

In this example, the source argument *Susan-kara* appears NP-internally and the theme argument *hooseki* at the clausal level. Thus, the sharp contrast in grammaticality between (13a) and (14a) and the contrast between (11a) and (14a) clearly shows the validity of Grimshaw and Mester's constraint. (13a) is grammatical, since it does not violate any condition. (11a), however, is marginally ungrammatical, since it is in violation of the double-*o* constraint (12). (14a) is worse than (11a), since it violates constraint (12) in addition to (9).

A question, however, arises as to why Argument Transfer must apply in an outside-in fashion in the thematic hierarchy. Grimshaw and Mester (1988) state that this is because the basic hierarchy among arguments is preserved even after Argument Transfer. However, if the basic hierarchy among arguments of the nominal θ-marker is always preserved, it is only natural to consider that the nominal θ-marker should be the only θ-marker in LVCs. This idea, however, immediately faces the problem of how the nominal θ-marker assigns its θ-roles to its arguments, given the strict locality condition of θ-marking (Chomsky 1981). In fact, it was the locality of θ-marking at D-structure that led Grimshaw and Mester to propose the Argument Transfer analysis. As a result, they had to stipulate constraint (9).

3. LF INCORPORATION

Based on these considerations, in Hoshi and Saito (1993) and Saito and Hoshi (1994), we reinterpreted Grimshaw and Mester's discoveries under Chomsky's (1992) new grammatical model which discarded D-structure. There, we argued that we do not need any stipulation to account for the properties of the LVC. Specifically, we proposed that there is no such lexical operation as Argument Transfer, and that there is only one θ-marker, the nominal θ-marker, in the LVC. That nominal θ-marker assigns a θ-role within its maximal projection NP, if there is an argument in it. In LF, it raises to the light verb *su*, and assigns its θ-roles to its arguments at the sentential level. Under this proposal, the hierarchical order of the arguments which the nominal θ-marker licenses follows from the standard assumption that θ-markers assign their θ-roles from the bottom-up in accordance with the thematic hierarchy (Larson 1988, Chomsky 1992, etc.)

Let us see now how this LF incorporation analysis explains the data in (11a), (13a), and (14a). (11a) is repeated here as (15).

(15)??*Mary-ga Susan-kara hooseki-o* ryakudatu-o sita   (= 11)
    -Nom   -from jewelry-Acc plunder -Acc did
   'Mary stole the jewelry from Susan'

The structures which Hoshi and Saito and Saito and Hoshi proposed for (15) are given in (16a-b).[3]

(16)a.   b.   (LF)

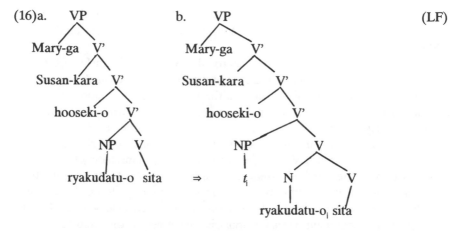

(15) violates the double-*o* constraint (12), since it contains two NPs marked with *o*, *hooseki-o* and *ryakudatu-o*. Besides this, there is no violation in (15). As illustrated in (16b), in LF, the nominal θ-marker *ryakudatu* raises up to the light verb *sita*. Then, it assigns all of its θ-roles from the bottom up, observing the order of the arguments in the thematic hierarchy.

    (13a), repeated here as (17), is assigned structures in (18).

(17) *Mary-ga Susan-kara* [$_{NP}$ hooseki-no ryakudatu]-o   sita   (= 13)

---

[3] In this paper, I assume Saito's (1982, 1985) theory of Case assignment in Japanese: nominative case *ga* is structurally assigned to an NP which is immediately dominated by IP; accusative Case *o* is assigned to an object; as for the dative marker *ni*, it is assigned to an argument of a verb which cannot surface with either the nominative *ga* or accusative Case *o*. Thus, strictly speaking, the external argument *Mary* must move into the SPEC of IP to be assigned nominative case *ga* in (16). Just for ease of exposition, however, the IP projection above the VP is suppressed in structures such as (16) in this paper.

-Nom   -from   jewelry-Gen plunder   -Acc did

'Mary stole the jewelry from Susan'

(18)a.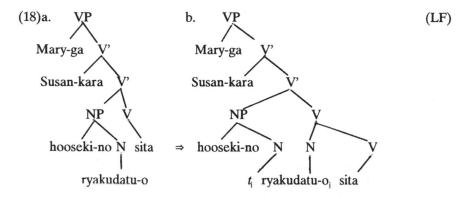

In (18a), the nominal θ-marker first assigns its theme θ-role to *hooseki* within the NP. In LF, the nominal θ-marker raises and adjoins to the LV, as in (18b). In that position, it first assigns the source θ-role to *Susan-kara* and then, the agent θ-role to *Mary*. This derivation violates no constraint and thus, (17) is correctly ruled in.

Consider now the grammatical example (14a), repeated here as (19), and the structures (20a-b) for it.

(19) *Mary-ga hooseki-o* [NP Susan-kara-no ryakudatu]-o sita   (= 14)

-Nom jewelry-Acc   -from-Gen plunder   -Acc did

'Mary stole the jewelry from Susan'

(20)a. *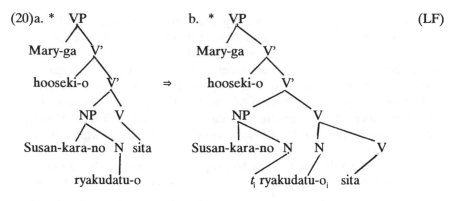

The double-*o* constraint (12) is violated in (19), because this example contains two *o* marked NPs, *hooseki-o* and *Susan-kara-no ryakudatu-o*. Observe that in addition to this, there is another violation involved in (19), as illustrated in (20a-b). In (20a), the nominal θ-marker first assigns its source role to *Susan-kara* within the NP. After raising to *sita* in LF, it assigns its theme θ-role to *hooseki-o*. This is an impermissible order of θ-marking, because according to the thematic hierarchy shown in (10), the nominal θ-marker *ryakudatu* must first assign its theme role, and then, its source role. Due to the violation in the order of θ-marking, (19) is, thus, predicted to be completely out, as desired.

4. A UNIFIED ANALYSIS OF TEMPORAL AFFIX CONSTRUCTIONS AND LIGHT VERB CONSTRUCTIONS

Given this incorporation analysis of LVCs, let us compare the TAC (21a) and the LVC (17), repeated here as (21b).

(21)a. *Mary-ga Susan-kara* hooseki-no ryakudatu-go ,   (TAC)
      -Nom   -from jewelry-Gen plunder -after,

    Bill-ga   yattekita (rasii)
      -Nom came by   (seems)
   '(It seems that) after Mary stole the jewelry from Susan, Bill came
    by'

  b. *Mary-ga Susan-kara* [$_{NP}$ hooseki-no ryakudatu]-o   sita   (LVC)
      -Nom   -from   jewelry-Gen plunder   -Acc did   (= 17)
    'Mary stole the jewelry from Susan'

In both (21a) and (21b), the theme argument *hooseki* is inside the NP, since it is accompanied by the genitive case marker *no*. The agent and the source arguments, *Mary* and *hooseki-kara*, on the other hand, appear as clausal arguments. And these similarities seem to demand a similar explanation for both TACs and LVCs. I, therefore, propose that the nominal θ-marker undergoes incorporation in both TACs and LVCs, and that incorporation is forced for morphological reasons of nominal θ-markers in TACs, whereas incorporation is triggered for θ-role assignment in LVCs as argued in our previous work.

Assuming that there is an IP projection selected by the temporal affix *go*, and that the head of the IP projection selects a VP shell, I propose a unified analysis of TACs and LVCs. Specifically, I propose the structures in (23a-b) for the TAC (21a), repeated in (22).

(22) *Mary-ga Susan-kara* hooseki-no ryakudatu-go ,   (TAC)
      -Nom   -from jewelry-Gen plunder -after,   (= 21a)

    Bill-ga yattekita (rasii)
      -Nom came by (seems)
    '(It seems that) after Mary stole the jewelry from Susan, Bill came
    by'

(23)a.

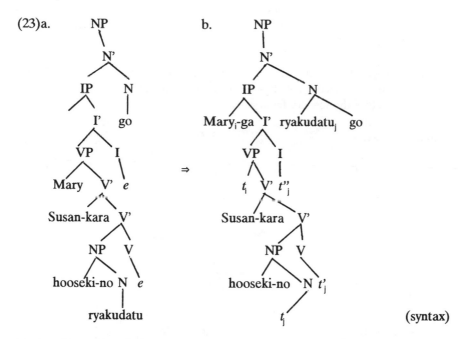

(syntax)

Under this proposal, the nominal θ-marker first assigns a θ-role to the
theme argument *hooseki* as in (23a). Since the nominal θ-marker *ryakudatu*
is a stem, it has to attach to some element in syntax (Lasnik 1981).[4] It,
thus, moves up and adjoins to the temporal affix *go* as illustrated in (23b).
In the course of the movement up to the temporal affix *go*, it moves into

---

[4] Lasnik's (1981) constraint requires that a morphologically realized
affix be a syntactic dependent of a morphologically realized category at S-
structure.

the empty V position and assigns θ-roles to the agent *Mary* and the source *Susan-kara.*

The TAC (24a), which corresponds to the LVC (15), repeated here as (24b), is assigned the structures (25a-b).

(24)a. *Mary-ga Susan-kara hooseki-o ryakudatu-go ,*　　　　　(TAC)
　　　　-Nom　　-from jewelry-Acc plunder -after,

　　Bill-ga yattekita (rasii)
　　　-Nom came by (seems)
　'(It seems that) after Mary was stealing the jewelry from Susan,
　　Bill came by'

　b.?? *Mary-ga Susan-kara hooseki-o ryakudatu-o sita*　　　(LVC)
　　　　-Nom　　-from jewelry-Acc plunder -Acc did　　　　　(= 15)
　　'Mary stole the jewelry from Susan'

(25)a.

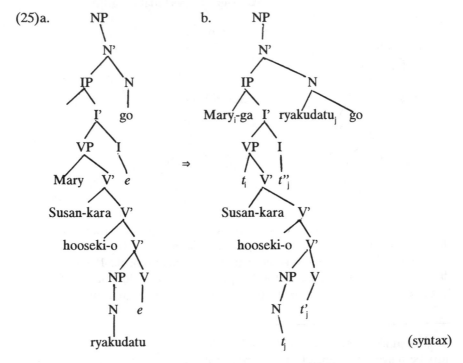

In the course of the movement up to *go,* the θ-marking noun *ryakudatu*

assigns its θ-roles to *hooseki*, *Susan-kara*, and *Mary*, from the bottom-up in accordance with the thematic hierarchy. In contrast with (24b), (24a) is perfectly grammatical, simply because it does not violate the double-*o* filter (12).

Recall here that the example (19), which is repeated here as (26), is ungrammatical. Given the unified analysis, it is thus predicted that the TAC which corresponds to the LVC (26) is ungrammatical. This prediction is borne out. Sells (1988) and others observe the ungrammaticality of the TAC (27).

(26) **Mary-ga hooseki-o* [NP Susan-kara-no ryakudatu]-o sita   (LVC)
     -Nom jewelry-Acc   -from-Gen plunder -Acc did   (= 19)
  'Mary stole the jewelry from Susan'

(27) **Mary-ga hooseki-o* Susan-kara-no ryakudatu-go ,   (TAC)
     -Nom   -Acc   -from-Gen plunder -after,   (cf. 22)

  Bill-ga yattekita (rasii)   (Sells 1988, etc.)
     -Nom came by (seems)
  '(It seems that) after Mary was stealing the jewelry from Susan, Bill
    came by'

Given the proposed structures (28a-b) for (27), we can straightforwardly account for this. This is so, because the nominal θ-marker first assigns the source role to *Susan-kara* within its own projection as in (28a). After moving into the empty V position, it cannot license the theme argument *hooseki* by its θ-role, as illustrated in (28b), since it is an impermissible order of θ-marking.

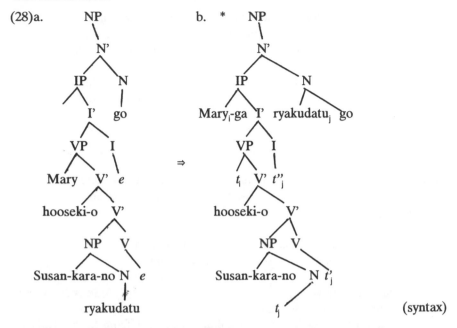

(28)a. ... (syntax)

5. DIFFERENCES BETWEEN TEMPORAL AFFIX CONSTRUCTIONS AND LIGHT VERB CONSTRUCTIONS

So far, I have argued that TACs and LVCs are explained in a unified way by an incorporation analysis. However, there are differences between them, and they appear to pose a problem for the proposed analysis.

Consider the examples in (29a-b). Grimshaw and Mester (1988) observe that (29a), in which only an external argument is realized at the sentential level, is ungrammatical with the light verb construction interpretation. Importantly, however, the corresponding TAC (29b) is grammatical.

(29)a. *Mary-ga [NP Susan-kara-no hooseki-no ryakudatu]-o   sita
          -Nom   -from-Gen jewelry-Gen plunder   -Acc did
      'Mary stole the jewelry from Susan'   (Grimshaw and Mester 1988)
                                    (?? with the heavy verb interpretation)

  b. Mary-ga Susan-kara-no hooseki-no ryakudatu-go ,
        -Nom   -from-Gen jewelry-Gen plunder -after,

Bill-ga yattekita (rasii)
-Nom came by (seems)
'After Mary was stealing the jewelry from Susan, Bill came by'

To account for the ungrammaticality of (29a), Grimshaw and Mester stipulated another constraint for Argument Transfer, which is given below:

(30) At least one internal θ-role of the nominal θ-marker must be assigned to an argument outside the NP.

Here, I argue that the contrast between (29a-b) is not a problem for the proposed analysis, but under my analysis, it is in fact straightforwardly explained by Chomsky's (1986, 1992) Last Resort Principle.

Roughly put, the Last Resort Principle states that movement applies only when it is necessary for the moved item. Thus, the movement in (31a) is possible, but that in (31b) is disallowed.

(31)a. Mary$_i$ seems [t_i to be intelligent]

b. *John$_i$ seems to t_i [that Mary is intelligent]   (Chomsky 1986)

In (31a), *Mary* needs to move to the IP SPEC position to have its Case checked. But in (31b), *John* is already in a Case position before movement, and hence, there is no need for this NP to move into the SPEC of IP. Hence, the Last Resort Principle only allows the movement in (31a).

The contrast in (32a-b) is explained in a similar way.

(32)a. There seems to be a man in the corner

b. *There seems to a man [that Mary is intelligent]   (Chomsky 1986)

The expletive *there* cannot be present at LF, and hence, must be replaced, due to the Principle of Full Interpretation. In (32a), the NP a man needs to have its Case checked, and hence, must move to the IP SPEC position in LF. Thus, *there* is successfully replaced. But in (32b), *a man* is already in a Case position, and consequently, there is no reason for this NP to move to IP SPEC. As a result, the expletive remains at LF in violation of Full Interpretation. These examples clearly show that movement takes place only to fulfill a need of the moved item.

Given this, let us consider the ungrammatical example (29a), which is repeated in (33), with the assumption that the external θ-role of a noun does not have to be assigned.

(33) *Mary-ga [$_{NP}$ Susan-kara-no hooseki-no ryakudatu]-o sita
    -Nom   -from-Gen jewelry-Gen plunder   -Acc did   (= 29a)
'Mary stole the jewelry from Susan'

(?? with the heavy verb interpretation)

This assumption is motivated by the NPs in (34b).

(34)a. *(The barbarians) destroyed the city

   b. the barbarians'/the destruction of the city

Structures in (35) are what Hoshi and Saito (1993) and Saito and Hoshi (1994) assigned for the ungrammatical example (33).

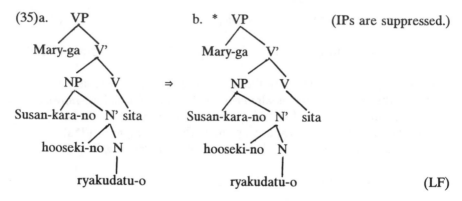

(35)a. VP   b. * VP   (IPs are suppressed.)

                            (LF)

In (35a), the nominal θ-marker assign θ-roles to *Susan-kara* and *hooseki* within its maximal projection. As illustrated in (35b), the nominal θ-marker *ryakudatu* cannot raise and adjoin to the light verb in LF. This is so, because as we argued in our previous work, nouns do not have to assign their external θ-roles (cf. 34b). Consequently, the Last Resort Principle prevents *ryakudatu* from incorporating to the LV *sita*. As a result, the subject *Mary* can't receive any θ-role at any point of the derivation, and hence, example (33) is in violation of the Principle of Full Interpretation (Chomsky 1986).

Consider again the TAC (29b), repeated in (36).

(36) Mary-ga Susan-kara-no hooseki-no ryakudatu-go ,   (TAC)
    -Nom   -from-Gen jewelry-Gen plunder -after,   (= 29b)

Bill-ga yattekita (rasii)
  -Nom came by (seems)
'(It seems that) after Mary stole the jewelry from Susan, Bill came
by'

The proposed unified analysis of LVCs and TACs assign the
structures (37a-b) for (36).

(37)a.

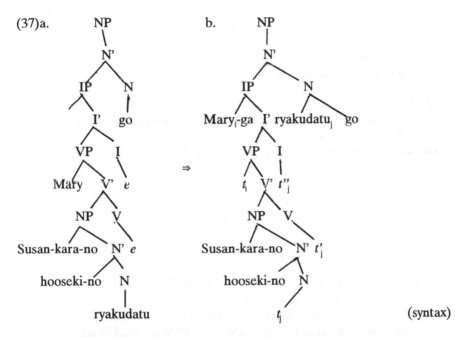

(syntax)

The nominal θ-marker in (37), in contrast with the one in (35), must raise
and adjoin to the temporal affix *go*, crucially because *ryakudatu* is a stem
from of a noun. In the course of the movement up to *go*, *ryakudatu*
succeeds in assigning the external θ-role to the subject *Mary*. Hence, the
TAC example (36) is correctly predicted to be grammatical (cf. *(33)).
Importantly, the contrast between (29a-b) is now straightforwardly explained
by the proposed analysis together with the Last Resort Principle.

5. CONCLUSIONS

In this paper, I have proposed that the nominal θ-marker undergoes incorporation in both TACs and LVCs. I also argued that incorporation is forced for morphological reasons of the nominal θ-marker in TACs, whereas it is triggered for θ-role assignment in LVCs, as argued in Hoshi and Saito (1993) and Saito and Hoshi (1994).

The proposed analysis shows that θ-roles need not be assigned at D-structure or S-structure, but can be discharged at LF. Thus, it provides strong support for Chomsky's proposal to eliminate D-structure as a pure representation of GF-θ relations, together with the Projection Principle, and consequently, for the Minimalist Program. I have also argued that incorporation in TACs and LVCs is subject to the Last Resort Principle, which was initially motivated for movement of maximal projections. The proposed analysis, thus, broadens the empirical scope of this principle, and provides support for Chomsky's (1986, 1992) general approach based on the Economy of Derivation as well.

REFERENCES

Chomsky, Noam. 1981. *Lectures on Government and Binding.* Foris Publications. Dordrecht.

Chomsky, Noam. 1986. *Knowledge of Language: Its Nature, Origin and Use.* Praeger. New York.

Chomsky, Noam. 1992. A Minimalist Program for Linguistic Theory. *MIT Occasional Papers in Linguistics Number 1.*

Fukui, Naoki. 1986. *A Theory of Category Projection and its Applications.* PhD dissertation. MIT.

Grimshaw, Jane. 1990. *Argument Structure.* MIT Press. Cambridge. Massachusetts.

Grimshaw, Jane and Armin Mester. 1988. Light Verbs and Theta-Marking. *Linguistic Inquiry* 19. 205-232.

Harada, S.-I. 1973. Counter Equi NP Deletion. *Annual Bulletin* 7. Research Institute of Logopedics and Phoniatrics. University of Tokyo. 113-147.

Hoshi, Hiroto and Mamoru Saito. 1993. The Japanese Light Verb Construction: a Case of LF Theta Marking. in Mamoru Saito (ed.), *Japanese Grammar (II),* Second Annual Report for the Research Project, *Development of a Formal Grammar of Japanese.* University of Connecticut. 45-62.

Kuroda, S.-Y. 1978. Case Marking, Canonical Sentence Patterns, and Counter Equi in Japanese. in J. Hinds and I. Howards (eds.). *Problems in Japanese Syntax and Semantics.* Kaitakusya. Tokyo.

Larson, Richard. 1988. On the Double Object Construction. *Linguistic Inquiry* 19. 335-391.

Lasnik, Howard. 1981. Restricting the Theory of Transformations: a Case Study. in N. Hornstein and D. Lightfoot (eds.), *Exploration in Linguistics*. Longman. Inc.. 152-173.

Murasugi, Keiko. 1991. *Noun Phrases in Japanese and English: A Study in Syntax, Learnability, and Acquisition.* PhD dissertation. University of Connecticut.

Poser, William. 1981. The 'Double-*o* Constraint': Evidence for a Direct Object Relation in Japanese. ms. MIT.

Saito, Mamoru. 1982. Case Marking in Japanese: A Preliminary Study. ms. MIT.

Saito, Mamoru. 1985. *Some Asymmetries in Japanese and Their Theoretical Implications.* PhD dissertation. MIT.

Saito, Mamoru and Hiroto Hoshi. 1994. Japanese Light Verb Construction and the Minimalist Program. ms. University of Connecticut.

Sells, Peter. 1988. More on Light Verbs and θ-Marking, ms. Stanford University.

Part V

Semantics

Verb Lexicalization Patterns in Korean - with Focus on Motion Conflation in Complex Verb Constructions

YOUNG-JOO KIM
Hong-Ik University

1. Introduction

Korean abounds in complex verb constructions which consist of two or more component verbs as illustrated in (1):

(1) a. *ttwi-e-   nem-*
        jump-CONN-move:over
        'jump over'

     b. *tul-   i-   e-   o-*
        move:in-CAUSATIVE-CONN-come
        'bring something into a place toward the speaker'

     c. *kel- e-   na-   ka-*
        walk-CONN-move:out-go
        'walk out of a place away from the speaker'

Complex verb constructions in Korean are not limited to motion expressions, but exhibits a wide variety of semantic relations. Much research has been carried out on these complex verb constructions from traditional descriptive and semantic perspectives, while more recent research has analyzed these complex verbs as serial verb constructions primarily from a syntactic point of view (S. Lee 1992; Chung 1993).

The present paper approaches the semantic aspect of the internal structure of complex motion verbs, applying Talmy's (1975, 1985) model of analysis in particular. The two questions that I will address in this paper are summarized as follows.

Questions

(i) Is there a unified internal semantic structure of Korean complex motion verbs? When single verbs expressing different semantic categories are combined to form a complex motion verb, is there a principled ordering among the component verbs?

(ii) Which component of a complex verb expresses the main motion of the event? That is, what is the characteristic motion-conflation pattern in Korean complex motion verb constructions?

2. Previous research – general and specific

2.1. Talmy (1975, 1985, 1991)

Talmy (1985) identifies basic components of a motion event as follows:

(2) *John   walked/ran/crawled into   the room*
[Figure] [Motion+Manner]   [Path] [Ground]

"Motion" indicates the main action/state most identified with the verb root; "Figure" is the salient moving or stationary object in a Motion event; "Ground" is the reference-frame in a Motion event, with respect to which the Figure's path/site is reckoned; "Path" is the course followed by or site occupied by the Figure object; "Manner" or "Cause" refers to a subsidiary action or state that the Figure manifests concurrently with its main action or state.

Talmy (1985) gives a typology of how different languages characteristically lexicalize motion events. Languages such as English and Chinese typically lexicalize in the verb the Manner or Cause rather than any other aspects of motion. Romance Languages, on the other hand, typically lexicalize the Path of motion in the verb, while leaving it to syntactic context to specify other aspects of motion events. In still other languages such as Atsugewi, the Figure (i.e., the moving object) of the motion is lexicalized in the verb. According to Talmy, any language of the world uses only one of the three basic patterns for lexicalizing motion events.

Talmy's (1985) typological generalization is summarized below:

Typology of Motion-Conflation Patterns (Talmy, 1985)

(I) Conflation of Motion with Manner or Cause: Indo-European (except Romance), Chinese

> e.g., *The rock slid/rolled/bounced down the hill*
> *I knocked/pounded/hammered the nail into the*
> *board with a mallet*

(II) Conflation of Motion with Path: Romance, Semitic, etc.

> e.g., *La botella entró   a la cueva*
> the bottle moved:in to the cave

(III) Conflation of Motion with Figure: Atsugewi, Navajo

> e.g., *It rained in through the bedroom window*
> *I spat into the cuspidor*

Talmy (1991) provides a two-category typology concerned only with whether the path is expressed in the verb or in the "satellite" (=the grammatical category of any constituent other than a nominal complement that is in a sister relation to the verb root). "Verb-framed" languages express the Path in the verb, and they include Romance, Semitic, Japanese, Tamil, Polynesian, most Bantu, most Mayan, Nez Perce, and Caddo. "Satellite-framed" languages express the Path in the satellite, and they include most Indo-European minus Romance, Finno-Ugric, Chinese, Ojibwa, and Walpiri.

2.2. Wienold and Schwarze (1989); Wienold (1990, 1992)

Wienold and Schwarze (1989) and Wienold (1990, 1992) have proposed, mainly observing the behavior of simplex verbs, that Korean and Japanese belong to the second class of Talmy's (1985)·types -- that Korean and Japanese lexicalize the path of the motion in the verb. Therefore, both Talmy's original proposal and Wienold *et al.*'s application of Talmy's proposal to Korean and Japanese were intended for the analysis of simplex verb roots.

2.3. Choi and Bowerman (1991)

Choi & Bowerman (1991), on the other hand, have applied Talmy's analysis to Korean complex motion verbs as well. They proposed, observing the behavior of complex as well as simplex motion verbs, that Korean exhibits different motion conflation patterns for expressing spontaneous and caused motion: the motion conflates with a path element in transitive clauses for caused motion, whereas the motion conflates with the deictic element in intransitive clauses for spontaneous motion – a pattern not described by Talmy. Observe the following examples:

Choi and Bowerman's (1991) analysis

Spontaneous motion

(3) *Yumi-ka   pang-ey   ttwi-e-   tul-   e-   o-   ass- ta*
         NOM room-LOC run- CONN enter-CONN-come-PAST-DEC
    [Figure] [Ground] [Manner] [Path]   **[Motion+Deixis]**
    'Yumi ran into the room'

Caused motion

(4) *Yumi-ka   selap- ey   yelsoy-lul   neh-   ess- ta*
         NOM   drawer-LOC key-   ACC   put:in-PAST-DEC
         [Ground]   [Figure]   **[Motion+Path]**
    'Yumi put the key into the drawer'

Caused-motion verbs that Choi and Bowerman list are: (i) "cause to ascend/descend verbs" such as *ol-li-* 'cause something to ascend' and *nayli-* 'cause something to descend'; (ii) "join/separate" verbs such as *neh-* 'put in', *puth-i-/ttey-* 'join/separate a flat surface to/from another flat surface', and *'pus-* 'pour liquid into a container'; (iii) clothing verbs such as *ip-* 'put clothing item onto one's trunk of body' and *pes-* 'take off clothing'; and (iv) carrying verbs such as *an-* 'carry a person/an object in arms' and *ep-* 'carry a person on back'.

3. A proposal – Internal structure of complex motion verbs

I propose that Korean employs basically the same motion- conflation pattern for expressions of spontaneous and caused motion. There seems to be a unified internal structure of Korean complex motion verbs. When single verbs expressing different semantic categories are combined to form a complex verb, the most frequently obeyed ordering is that of manner/cause verbs preceding path verbs, which in turn precede deictic verbs, or any subpart of the sequence. Hence for expressions of spontaneous motion, *ttwi-e-tul-e-o-* (run-CONN-move:in-CONN-come) [Manner][Path][Deixis] 'run into a place toward the speaker' stands in contrast with ungrammaticalities of **ttwi-e-o-a-tul-* [Manner][Deixis][Path], **o-a-tul-e-ttwi-e.* [Deixis][Path][Manner], **tul-e-ttwi-e-o-* [Path][Manner][Deixis] and all other combinations. The same principle applies for expressions of caused motion, as we see in *kwul-li-e-nay-ka-* (roll-CAUS-CONN-move:out-go) [Manner][Path][Deixis] 'roll something out of a place away from the speaker' contrasted with ungrammaticalities of *kwul-li-e-ka-nay- [Manner][Deixis][Path], *ka-kwul-li-e-nay- [Deixis][Manner][Path], *nay-kwul-li-e-ka- [Path][Manner][Deixis] and all other combinations. There are certain exceptions to this generalization. The position of the deictic verb, however, if it occurs at all, is invariably final. Moreover, whereas more than one path verb may occur in a row in certain compounds (e.g., tul-i-pak- (enter-CAUS-drive:into) [Path][Path] 'drive into'), the number of deictic verb is restricted to one. The following section provides specific evidence showing that Korean employs basically the same motion conflation pattern for spontaneous- and caused-motion expressions.

3.1. Morphologically Related Verb Pairs Expressing Spontaneous and Caused Motion Conflated with Path

As is well known, Korean abounds in morphologically related verb pairs for spontaneous and caused motion expressions. Korean adds the causative morpheme -i- (in 7 allomorphic variations -i-/-hi-/-li-/-ki-/-wu-/-kwu-/-chwu-) or -ttuli- to derive a causative expression if the verb root expresses spontaneous motion, and the inchoative/passive morpheme -ci- or -i- (in 4 allomorphic variations i/hi/li/ki) to derive an expression for spontaneous motion from an inherently causative root. Instead of enumerating a very large set of such verb pairs found in Korean adult grammar, I pulled out relevant examples from the lexicon of very young Korean-speaking children. The data come from five children's spontaneous speech up through 24 months.[1] The children spontaneously produced, by the age of 24 months, either or both forms of each verb pair listed in Table 1. Data like these show not only that Korean employs basically the same motion-conflation pattern for spontaneous- and caused-motion expressions along a Path, but also that Korean children from the earliest stage of language acquisition learn such a language-specific motion conflation pattern. The logic behind using acquisition data is that they provide even stronger evidence for the proposed verb lexicalization pattern although they are not necessary for the purpose of making a typological generalization of Korean adult grammar.

---

[1] Kim (in press) provides a detailed description of these longitudinal data. I gratefully acknowledge Pat Clancy for allowing me to use W's and H's data, and Seungbok Lee for J's data.

Table 1. Path-Conflating Expressions for Spontaneous and
          Caused Motion in Five Children's Utterances Up
          Through 24 Months

olu- 'move up'; *ol-li-* 'cause to move up'
!*nayli-* 'move down'; *nayli-* 'cause to move down'
na- '(eruption, sweat, blood) move out/break out';
!*nay-* 'cause to move out'
!*tah-* 'reach'; *tay-* 'hold something against a surface'
puth- 'a surface sticks to another surface';
puth-i- 'join a surface to another surface'
mut- 'liquid/soil sticks to a surface/ !*mut-hi-* 'put
          liquid substance onto a surface'
mac- 'one two or three dimensional object fits another';
mac-chwu- 'fit one two or three dimensional object to
          another' (building blocks, puzzle pieces)
!*phul-e-ci-* '(button, knot) come undone'; *phul-* 'undo
          (button, knot)'
!*ttut-e-ci-* 'fall off'; *ttut-* 'tear off' (chocolate pack,
          band-aid, seam)
ppa-ci- (i) 'fall out'; *ppay-* 'unfit'
          (ii) 'fall into'; !*ppa-ttuli-* 'cause to fall
               into, drop' (water, swimming pool,
               container, gap)
ttel-e-ci- (i) !'fall out'; *ttey-* 'take off, separate a
               flat surface from another flat surface'
               (band-aid, tape, poster)
          (ii) 'fall'; !*ttel-e-ttuli-* 'drop'
ssot-a-ci-; *ssot-* 'pour out' (rain, liquid, a large
               quantity of objects)
ephcill-e-ci-; *ephcilu-* 'spill'
tha- 'get on' (car, airplane, horse, seesaw);
!*thay-wu-* 'cause to get on'
pes-ki-e-ci- 'come off'; *pes-* 'take off (clothing)'
!*an-ki-* '(voluntarily) get held in arms' (= 'move into a
          person's arms'); *an-* 'hold someone in arms'
!*ep-hi-* '(voluntarily) get carried on one's back' (=
          'ride pickaback on someone'); *ep-* 'carry someone
          on back'
tal-li- 'get attached'; !*tal-* 'attach'
pikhi- 'step aside'; !*pikhi-* 'move something aside'

(Note: ! indicates that children's production of the verb
form before 24 months may have been an imitation of
adults' preceding utterances or/and that the spontaneous
production of the form has not been observed by 24
months.)

Note that all these verbs express motion conflated with
Path, in expressions of spontaneous motion and caused
motion alike.

    Acquisition data and adult Korean grammar concur to
show that lexical independence between forms for
spontaneous and caused motion (e.g., *tul-e-ka* 'go in' vs.
neh- 'put in') may not be a general phenomenon with

motion verbs. More importantly, I will argue in Section 4 that even morphologically unrelated verb pairs such as *tul-e-ka-* 'go in' and *neh-* 'put in' exhibit the same motion-conflation pattern, showing that motion is expressed in the path verb *tul-* 'move:in' rather than in the deictic verb *ka-* 'go' in *tul-e-ka-* 'go into', for example.

If we extend our attention to a wider range of motion verbs, including those that do not entail change of location, and to verbs expressing change of state, children produce even more verbs that belong to this morphological category, not to speak of adults. This morphological parallelism reaches far beyond motion verbs (Wienold 1990). Table 2 lists relevant verbs selected from children's speech. It shows again that children from the earliest stage produce a good number of verbs that participate in this derivational process. Some of the verbs in Table 2 are expressions of "contained" motion that result in no overall change of location, others are Manner-conflating motion verbs, and still others are verbs expressing change of state.

Table 2. More Examples of Morphologically Related Pairs
of Spontaneous and Caused-Motion Verbs and
Spontaneous and Caused State-of-Change Verbs -
from the Speech of Five Children Up Through 24
Months

nem-e-ci- 'fall down'; !*nem-e-ttuli-* 'cause to fall down'
!*yel-li-*; *yel-* 'open'
!*tat-hi-*; *tat-* 'close'
!*tol-* 'turn around [intrans]'; *tol-li-* 'turn around
    [trans]'
ttu-; 'float, rise' (boat, airplane); !*ttuy-wu-* 'make
    float'
hulu- 'run out, flow'; !*hul-li-* 'let (liquid) flow''
mo-i- 'gather'; *mou-* 'collect'
!*camk-i-* 'get locked'; *camku-* 'lock'
!*ket-hi-* 'lift up (cloud, fog); *ket-* 'lift up, roll up
    (curtain, sleeve)'
!*cep-hi-* 'get folded'; *cep-* 'fold' (collar, umbrella,
    paper)
!*kke-ci-* '(light) go off'; *kku-* 'turn off'
!*khye-ci-* '(light) turn on'; *khye-* 'turn on'
nalu-; !*nal-li-* 'fly'
anc- 'sit down'; *anc-hi-* 'make sit down'
nwup- 'lie down'; !*nwup-hi-* 'make lie down'
!*huntul-li-* '; *huntul-* 'shake'
kkay-ci-; *kkay-* 'break' (glass, mirror)
puswu-e-ci-; *puswu-* 'break' (furniture, wall)
pule-ci-; !*pule-ttuli-* 'break' (long and slim object)
!*call-a-ci-*; *calu-* 'break, cut'
!*kkunh-e-ci-*; *kkunh-* 'cut' (string, thread, telephone
    line)
ccic-e-ci- 'become torn apart'; *ccic-* 'tear apart'
    (blanket, toy pack, letter)
eps-e-ci- 'disappear'; !*eps-ay-* 'make disappear, get rid
    of'

(Note: ! indicates that children's production of the verb
form before 24 months may have been an imitation of
adults' preceding utterances or/and that the spontaneous
production of the form has not been observed by 24
months.)

These verb pairs show that expressions of
spontaneous and caused motion, and those of state change
in Korean characteristically share the same verb root,
and therefore the same motion-conflation pattern.

3.2. More Examples of Spontaneous-Motion Expressions without a Deictic Verb

Verbs in Table 1 clearly show that many verbs of
spontaneous motion along a Path do not contain a deictic
element. If we attend to general verb lexicalization
patterns in Korean, there are a large number of verbs
which express spontaneous motion but which do not contain

a deictic element. Table 3 shows simplex verbs that express directed motion, that is, verbs which entail change of location but which do not contain a deictic element.

Table 3. Simplex Directed Motion Verbs without a Deictic Element – Expressions for Spontaneous Motion

tatalu- 'arrive'
ilu- 'arrive'
ttena- 'depart'
nem- 'move:over (fence)'
kenne- 'move:across (river)'
cina- 'pass:by'

Such examples are also found in complex verb constructions:

Table 4. Complex Directed Motion Verbs without a Deictic Element – Expressions for Spontaneous Motion

ttwi-e-olu- 'jump-CONN-move:up' (= 'jump up') (chair-LOC)
ttwi-e-nayli- 'jump-CONN-move:down' (= 'jump down')
            (ground-LOC)
ki-e-olu- 'crawl-CONN-move:up' (= 'crawl up')
tt-e-olu- 'float-CONN-move:up' (= 'rise onto a surface')
kala-anc- 'sink down'
sumi-e-tul- 'penetrate-CONN-move:in' (='penetrate into')
            (liquid into fabric)
tu-na-tul- 'move:in-move:out-move:in' (= 'move in and
            out')
nem-na-tul- 'move:over-move:out-move:in' (= 'move in and
            out over a boundary')
tul-lak-na-lak-ha- 'move in and out frequently'
tul-lang-keli- 'keep moving in and out'
pikhi-e-na- 'step:aside-CONN-move:out' (= 'step aside')
pikhi-e-se- 'step:aside-CONN-stand' (= 'stand aside')
may-tal-li- 'tie-hang-PASS' (= 'cling to, hang onto')
oll-a-tha- 'move:up-CONN-ride' (= 'get on (vehicle)'
ttwi-e-nem- 'jump-CONN-move:over' (= 'jump over')
kenn-e-ttwi- 'move:across-CONN-jump' (= 'jump across')
tul-i-chi- 'move:in-CAUS-hit' (= 'hit into' (e.g., "Rain
            hit into the window")
tul-i-tak-chi- 'move:in-CAUS-approach-hit' (= 'hit into')
                (e.g., "Unexpected visitors hit into the
                house")
cina-chi- 'pass:by-hit' (= 'go past')

These simplex and complex verbs for directed spontaneous motion, in addition to those in Table 1, do not contain a deictic verb.

3.3. Caused-Motion Expressions Containing a Deictic Verb

The occurrence of deictic verbs is not restricted to expressions of spontaneous motion - certain caused-motion verbs also contain a deictic element.

(5) a. I   cim-   ul i-   chung-ey ol-   li-
       this package ACC second floor LOC move:up CAUS
       e-   ka-la
       CONN go IMP
       'Move this package up to the second floor away from me.'

   b. Yumi-ka papsang-   ul pang-ey tul-   i-
         NOM dining.table ACC room LOC move:in CAUS
         e-   o-   ass-ta
         CONN come PST DECL
         'Yumi moved the dining table into the room, toward me (=the speaker).'

   c. Inho-ka Yumi-lul cip- ey teyli-   e- ka-ss-
         Nom   ACC house LOC accompany CONN go PST
         ta
         DECL
         'Inho took Yumi home, away from me.'

Some of the verbs that belong to this category appear in Table 5:

Table 5. Directed Caused-Motion Expressions Containing a
          Deictic Verb

ol-li-e-ka- (move:up-CAUS-CONN-go) 'move an object up
            away from the speaker';
ol-li-e-o- (move:up-CAUS-CONN-come) 'move an object up
            toward the speaker'
nayli-e-ka- (move:down:CAUS-CONN-go) 'move an object down
            away from speaker';
nayli-e-o- (move:down:CAUS-CONN-come) 'move an object
            down toward the speaker'
tul-i-e-ka- (move:in-CAUS-CONN-go) 'move an object into
            a place away from the speaker';
tul-i-e-o- (move:in-CAUS-CONN-come) 'move an object into
            a place toward the speaker'
nay-ka- (move:out:CAUS-go) 'move an object out of a place
            away from the speaker';
nay-o- (move:out:CAUS-CONN-come) 'move an object out of
            a place toward the speaker)
nall-a-ka- (carry-CONN-go) 'carry an object away from the
            speaker';
nall-a-o- (carry-CONN-come) 'carry an object toward the
            speaker'
teyli-e-ka- (accompany-CONN-go) 'take a person away from
            the speaker';
teyli-e-o- 'bring a person toward the speaker'
mosi-e-ka- (accompany:NON.SUBJ.HON-CONN-go) 'take a
            person who is higher in the social hierarchy
            than the speaker away from the speaker';
mosi-e-o- 'bring a person who is higher in the social
            hierarchy than the speaker toward the speaker'
kaci-e-ka- (have-CONN-go) 'take an object away from the
            speaker';
kaci-e-o- 'bring an object toward the speaker'
ppay-as-a-ka- (take:out-snatch-CONN-go) 'snatch an object
            away from the speaker';
ppay-as-a-o- (take:out-snatch-CONN-come) 'snatch an
            object toward the speaker'
ppay-nay-ka- (take:out-move:out-go) 'draw out an object
            away from the speaker';
ppay-nay-o- (take:out-move:out-come) 'draw out an object
            toward the speaker'

These path-conflating caused-motion verbs show that
deictic verbs may occur not only in complex verbs
expressing spontaneous motion but also in those
expressing caused motion. Therefore, they further support
my proposal that there is a unified motion-conflation
pattern common to spontaneous and caused-motion verbs.

To sum up, Korean characteristically employs the
same verb root for expressions of spontaneous and caused
directed motion, and therefore the two types of
expressions share the same motion-conflation pattern.
This conclusion may be less straining from a typological
perspective, too, since the mixed motion-conflation

pattern across the causation boundary does not fit Talmy's typological generalization.

I proposed that when single verbs expressing different semantic categories are combined to form a compound, the most frequently obeyed ordering is: manner/cause verbs < path verbs < deixis verbs, or any subpart of the sequence.

4. Motion-Conflation Pattern in Complex Motion Verbs along a Path

Another substantial question to be asked at this point is this: Which component of a complex verb expresses the main motion of the event? Consider *tul-e-ka-* (move:in-CONN-go) 'go in(to)', for example. Is the main motion conflated with Path or Deixis? In English *go in(to)*, it is apparent that the motion is conflated with Deixis, Path being independently expressed by the preposition. In Korean simplex verbs such as *ka-*, *olu-/ol-li-*, *ttwi-*, and *neh-*, and so on, the motion of the Figure is unambiguously expressed in the verb, whether it be a deictic verb, a path verb or a manner verb. In Korean complex motion verbs, in contrast, each component of a complex verb is a verb, and therefore has a potential to express the main motion. Some previous research (e.g., Choi & Bowerman, 1991) assumed that the final component of a complex motion verb expresses the main motion. In their analysis, motion is expressed not in the path verb but in the deictic verb in *tul-e-ka-* 'enter', for example.

There is evidence, however, which shows that in complex motion verbs along a Path, motion is conflated with Path rather than with Deixis, and that the deictic verb only provides an additional piece of information as to the direction relative to the speaker, of the main motion that occurred. The first piece of evidence for my proposal that motion is conflated with Path in a [path verb][deictic verb] compound comes from the *Se*-Insertion Test.

4.1. *Se*-Insertion

K.-D. Lee (1976) distinguishes two kinds of verbs that come in the final position of complex verbs:

(6) a. *Ku-nun ku congi-lul ccic-e   PELI-*
       he-TOP the paper-ACC tear-CONN throw:away-
       ess- ta
       PAST-DECL
       'He tore the paper and threw it away'

b. *Ku-nun ku swul-ul masi- e PELI-*
   he-TOP the wine-ACC drink-CONN-throw:away-
   ess- ta
   PAST-DECL
   'He drank up the wine'

In both (6a) and (6b), *peli-* 'throw away' appears in the complex-verb-final position, but the meanings are different. In (6a), *peli-* may carry the literal meaning expressing motion of the agent, whereas in (6b), it can only express an aspectual meaning - completion of an action.[2] To support this distinction, Lee provides the test of inserting *-se-* 'by means of' between component verbs:

(7) a. *Ku-nun ku congi-lul ccic-e- se PELI-*
       he-TOP the paper-ACC tear-CONN SE throw:away-
       ess- ta
       PAST-DECL
       'He tore the paper and threw it away'

   b. *Ku-nun ku swul-ul masi- e- *se PELI-*
       he-TOP the wine-ACC drink-CONN-SE throw:away-
       ess- ta
       PAST-DEC
       'He drank up the wine'

According to K.-D. Lee, *Se*-Insertion is not allowed before an auxiliary verb. Extending that insight, S. Lee (1992) suggests that there are two types of serial verb constructions in Korean: Type 1 serial verbs such as (6b) contain aspectual verbs which do not fully project their original argument structures - these aspectual verbs modify the event meaning expressed by preceding verb(s) by virtue of adding aspectual meanings such as completion, duration, retention, direction, and so on. Type 2 serial verbs such as (6a), in contrast, fully realize argument structures of component verbs. S. Lee proposes on the basis of the *Se*-Insertion Test that *ka-* 'go' and *o-* 'come' in serial verb constructions should be divided into two types - aspectual verbs and motion verbs:

(8) a. [Type 1: *ka-* expresses direction]

   *Ku-nun san- ey ol- a- *se ka-ss- ta*
   he-TOP mountain-LOC move:up-CONN-SE go-PAST-DEC
   'He went up the mountain.'

---

[2] *Peli-* in (6a) is ambiguous: It may express either the literal meaning or the aspectual meaning.

b. [Type 2: *ka-* expresses motion]

Ku-nun cip- ey kel- e-   se ka-ss- ta
he-TOP house-LOC walk-CONN-SE go-PAST-DEC
'He walked home.'   (S. Lee, 1992)

According to S. Lee, *ka-* in (8a) adds the aspectual meaning of direction to the motion event of 'climbing up the mountain', whereas *ka-* in (8b) expresses the original meaning of motion.

What this distinction between two types of deictic verbs in serial verb constructions implies for the discussion of the present paper is this: the complex-verb-final deictic element in directed motion verbs such as *tul-e-ka/o-* 'go/come into', *na-ka/o-* 'go/come out', *oll-a-ka/o-* 'go/come up', and *nayli-e-ka/o-* 'go/come down' do not express the main motion of the event, but provides additional information about the direction of the motion event relative to the speaker. Rather, the motion seems to be expressed in the preceding path verb.

The second piece of evidence indicating that the main motion of a complex motion verb is expressed in the path verb rather than in the deictic verb comes from the scope interpretation of negation.

4.2. Scope of Negation

S. Lee (1992) points out the long-form negation *ci anh-* can negate only the first verb of Type 2 serial verbs, whereas the scope of negation ranges over the entire string of Type 1 serial verbs. Observe the following examples:

(9) a. *Congi-lul ccic-e- peli-   ci-nun anh-*
       paper-ACC tear-CONN-throw:away-CI-CONTR do:not-
       ass-ciman peli-   ki-nun hay-ss- ta
       PAST-but   throw:away-KI-CONTR do- PAST-DEC
       'Although (I) did not tear the paper and throw it away, I threw it away.
                                          [Type2]

   b. *Swul-ul masi- e- peli-   ci-nun anh-*
      wine-ACC drink-CONN-throw:away-CI-CONTR do:not-
      *ass-ciman *peli-   ki-nun hay-ss- ta*
      PAST-but   throw:away-KI-CONTR do- PAST-DEC
      'Although (I) did not drink up the wine, I threw it away.'
                                          [Type1]

The contrast between (9a) and (9b) shows that the long-form negation has a scope over the whole [V1-e-V2] complex when V2 is aspectual in nature, whereas it can have a scope only over V1 when V2 expresses motion of the main event. The negation test applied to complex verbs with a deictic element yields the same result:

(10) a. *Hakkyo-eyse kel- e-   o-ci-nun   anh-*
school-from walk-CONN come-CI-CONTR do:not-
ass- ciman (hakkyo-eyse) o-   ki-nun   hay-ss-
PAST-but school-from come-KI-CONTR do- PAST-
ta
DEC
'Although (he) did not come from school on
foot, he came (from school).'

[Type2]

b. *Pang-eyse na-   o-   ci-nun   anh-   ass*
room-from move:out-come-CI-CONTR do:not-PAST
*ciman *(pang-eyse) o-   ki-nun   hay-ss-   ta*
but   room-from come-KI-CONTR do- PAST-DEC
'Although (he) did not come out of the room,
he came from the room.'

[Type1]

The contrast between (10a) and (10b) provides supporting
evidence for the proposal that in complex verbs
expressing directed motion, the motion is expressed not
in the complex-final deictic verb but in the preceding
path verb. Therefore, the motion-conflation pattern in
verb pairs which do not share the same root should be
described as follows:

(11) Motion-conflation pattern for morphologically
unrelated verb pairs for spontaneous and caused
motion:

a. <u>spontaneous motion</u>

tul-   e- ka-
[Motion+Path]   [Deixis]

b. <u>caused motion</u>

neh-
[Motion+Path]

The motion-conflation pattern proposed in (11) has
surprising implication for the status of Korean in the
general typology of motion-conflation pattern: it shows
that even when Korean verbs expressing spontaneous and
caused motion do not share the same morphological root,
they share the same motion-conflation pattern. That is,
it indicates that directed motion in Korean is
consistently conflated with Path regardless of whether
the motion is spontaneous or caused. This saves linguists
trouble to modify Talmy's allegedly exhaustive
typological classification on the basis of Korean
grammar. In contrast, it supports his generalization even
more strongly, because the common pattern of motion-
conflation emerges out of what seems to be radically

different in surface morphological forms.

5. Conclusion

In this paper, I proposed within Talmy's (1975, 1985) framework, an analysis of (i) the internal structure and of (ii) the motion-conflation pattern in Korean complex motion verbs. There seems to be a unified internal structure of complex verb formation, regardless of whether the verb expresses a spontaneous or a caused motion. When single verbs expressing different semantic categories are combined to form a complex verb, the most frequently obeyed ordering is that of manner/cause verbs preceding path verbs, which in turn precede deictic verbs, or any subpart of the sequence. I proposed that the existence of lexically different expressions for spontaneous and caused motion in Korean may not be general enough to render the entire language typologically unique. More importantly, I argued that even when verbs for spontaneous and caused motion are lexicalized in morphologically unrelated forms, they exhibit the same motion-conflation pattern, that is, [Motion+Path], fitting into Talmy's typological generalization without modification. By doing this, I hope to have suggested a possibility of comparing the behavior of Korean motion verbs with that of other "verb-framed" (Talmy, 1991) languages on a more equal footing, to yield many linguistically interesting results in future research without being misled by surface differences that conceal underlying regularities.

REFERENCES

Choi, S., & Bowerman, M. (1991). Learning to express motion events in English and Korean: The influence of language-specific lexicalization patterns. *Cognition, 41,* 83-121.

Chung, T. (1993). *Argument structure and serial verbs in Korean.* Unpublished doctoral dissertation, The University of Texas at Austin.

Kim, Y. (1995). Verb lexicalization patterns in Korean and some issues of language acquisition. *Language Research, 31.3,* 501-543.

Kim, Y. (in press). The acquisition of Korean. In D. I. Slobin (Ed.) *The crosslinguistic study of language acquisition* (Vol. 4). Hillsdale, NJ: Lawrence Erlbaum Associates.

Lee, K.-D. (1976). Cotongsa-uy uymi punsek (Semantic analysis of auxiliary verbs). *Munpep Yenkwu (Grammar Research)* 3, 215-236.

Lee, S. (1992). *The syntax and semantics of serial verb constructions*. Unpublished doctoral dissertation, University of Washington.

Talmy, L. (1975). Semantics and syntax of motion. In J. Kimball (Ed.), *Syntax and semantics* (Vol.4). New York: Academic Press, 181-238.

Talmy, L. (1985). Lexicalization patterns: Semantic structure in lexical forms. In T. Shopen (Ed.), *Language typology and semantic description: Grammatical categories and the lexicon* (Vol.3). Cambridge: Cambridge University Press, 36-149.

Talmy, L. (1991). Path to realization: A typology of event conflation. *Proceedings of the Seventeenth Annual Meeting of the Berkeley Linguistics Society*, 480-519. Berkeley, CA: Berkeley Linguistics Society.

Wienold, G. (1990). Semantic functions of Korean motion verbs expressing a path in typological perspective. In E.-J. Baek (Ed.), *Papers from the Seventh International Conference on Korean Linguistics*, 477-492.

Wienold, G. (1992). Up and down: On some concepts of path in Korean motion verbs. *Language Research*, *28.1*, 15-43.

Wienold, G., & Schwarze, C. (1989). Lexical structure and the description of motion events in Japanese, Korean, Italian and French. Fachgruppe Sprachwissenschaft, Universitat Konstanz, Arbeitspapier Nr.5.

On the Primacy of Progressive Over Resultative State: The Case of Japanese -*teiru**

YASUHIRO SHIRAI
Daito Bunka University

1. Introduction

In categorization studies in psychology, consistent patterns have been found regarding the internal structures of categories. The following is a quotation from Glass and Holyoak (1986:165), a textbook for cognitive psychology:

a. People reliably rate some category members as more typical than others (Rips et al. 1973, Rosch 1973). For example, people rate robins as more typical than geese for the category bird.

---

*This is a revised version of the paper presented at the 6th Japanese/Korean Linguistics Conference held in August 1995 at the University of Hawaii at Manoa. An earlier version of this paper was presented at the 4th Conference of the International Cognitive Linguistics Association held in July 1995 at the University of New Mexico. I would like to thank the following for helpful comments and suggestions: Östen Dahl, Seiko Fujii, Kevin Gregg, Young-joo Kim, Kaoru Ohta, Charles Quinn, Tim Stowell, and Foong Ha Yap. Any shortcomings are of course my own. The study is supported by a grant from the Japanese Ministry of Education, Science, and Culture (No. 05851078).

b. When people are asked to list instances of a category, they reliably produce some items both earlier and more frequently than others (Battig & Montague 1969). Furthermore, items that are produced most readily tend to be those that people also consider most typical of the category (Rosch 1973).

c. Both of these measures (typicality ratings and frequency of production) predict the speed with which people classify instances as members of a category. For example, people can verify the truth of the sentence *A robin is a bird* more quickly than they can verify *A goose is a bird.* (Glass et al. 1974, Rips et al. 1973, Rosch 1973, Wilkins 1971)

In a nutshell, these studies show that prototypical members of a category are (1) rated as more typical in typicality ratings, (2) produced earlier and more frequently in free elicitation, and (3) classified more easily in reaction time experiments.

The present study is an attempt to replicate this type of study using a polysemous linguistic category. Although "prototype" has been argued to be an important notion in both cognitive and functional linguistics (e.g. Lakoff 1987, Givón 1984, 1989), there appears to be no standard measure or method to determine prototypes, nor have systematic attempts been made to determine prototypes of various linguistic categories.[1] The aims of this paper are to propose and discuss a method of eliciting prototypes of polysemous linguistic categories, and to report an experimental study on the Japanese aspectual marker *-tei*. Based on the results of the study and related research, I argue that progressive is a cognitive reference point which serves as an axis for grammaticization.

As discussed above, psychological studies on categorization have evidenced the convergence of three experimental measures: typicality rating, free elicitation, and reaction time. For this study, the free elicitation method was chosen because the typicality rating method and the reaction time method do not work: it is impossible to control the test items for intervening factors. Let's say we want to investigate the progressive in English. If typicality rating is used, exemplars such as *He is walking to the store* (action in progress), *He is leaving tomorrow* (futurate), or *He*

---

[1]It should be noted that psychological literature abounds in studies on the prototype and/or internal structure of various natural and artificial categories. The point here is that there have not been many data-based psycholinguistic studies on polysemous linguistic categories.

is going to school by bus these days (habitual) will have to be included in the test items, and the subjects will be asked to determine which is more typical of the use of 'be +Ving.' Here, the choice of the arguments as well as adjuncts would affect the typicality rating, because some verbs, or nouns, and even verb-argument combinations are more common than others, and some may be more often used with progressive than others. Therefore, it is impossible to control for the typicality of these experimental items. The situation is basically the same for the reaction time method.[2] The free elicitation method, on the other hand, does not suffer from this drawback. If it is possible to give native speaking subjects an unbiased cue which makes sense to them, this method can elicit prototypical exemplars of the target category.

One study that used free elicitation, among other measures, to investigate a polysemous linguistic category is Caramazza and Grober (1976). They investigated the polysemy of the lexical item *line*. The sense of *line* most frequently produced, such as in *We were told to line up* and *The shortest distance between the two points is a straight line*, was 'unidimensional extension.' They also elicited acceptability ratings and typicality ratings of sentences that include different senses of *line*, and found that the frequency in production task was significantly correlated with acceptability rating ($r= .63$, $p< .001$) and typicality rating ($r= .40$, $p< .05$). The study shows that the frequency of production in a free elicitation task reliably reflects the prototypical structure of a polysemous category.

To my knowledge, no study has investigated the prototypical structure of an aspectual category using an experimental method. The present study considers the Japanese aspectual marker *-tei*, and investigates the internal structure of this polysemous category by the experimental method of free elicitation.

2. The study

2.1 Subjects

The subjects in this study were 37 undergraduate students, all of whom are native speakers of Japanese majoring in Chinese as a foreign language at a Japanese university. All the students were

---

[2] Previous studies that investigated the internal structure of polysemous categories often used statistical measures such as multidimensional scaling or cluster analysis (Carammaza & Grober 1976, Colombo & D'Arcais 1984, Kellerman 1978), which involves similarity ratings of exemplars. However, the choice of exemplar often influences the outcome, and therefore these studies suffer the same problem as typicality rating and reaction time studies.

expected to be familiar with the Japanese term 'doosi' ('verb') through their formal education up to high school.

2.2 Materials and procedures

The experiment was conducted as part of a normal class in general linguistics. All the instructions were given in Japanese. The procedures were as follows:

Step 1) A one-page questionnaire was distributed to each subject, face down. The subjects were instructed to write their name on the blank side of the sheet.

Step 2) The subjects were told that they would be given three minutes to complete the questionnaire.

Step 3) The subjects were told to turn the paper over. They read the instruction in Japanese at the top of the page, which was 'Please write as many complete sentences as you can that include verb + *teiru*.' When time was up, the questionnaires were collected.[3]

As discussed earlier, it is important to give an unbiased prompt to elicit prototypical exemplars from the subjects. However, this is not always easy. For example, in investigating the progressive form in English, the template 'be + Verb-ing' must be used. This may be somewhat opaque for some subjects. Then it becomes necessary to use *is* instead of *be*. This, in turn, constrains the choice of the sentential subject. To make the prompt bias-free, 'is/are/am' has to be used. Even then, however, the order favors *is*, and therefore, third person singular subject. For other languages, there may be other problems. One way to get around this kind of problem is to use three different versions of the questionnaire, and examine if there are any differences. Fortunately, it was relatively easy to give an unbiased prompt in Japanese; thus it was possible to have bias-free elicitation for -*teiru*, the nonpast imperfective marker.[4]

---

[3] The subjects were actually given four minutes, because three minutes was not enough for them to produce a number of tokens for the purpose of the quantitative analysis.

[4] The choice of non-past form -*teiru*, (instead of -*teita*, past form) in fact, could be a factor which biases the subjects, and should be tested in a replication study using -*teita*. A terminological note should be made here: In this paper I treated -*tei* as an imperfective marker; however there is no consensus among linguists regarding how the morpheme should be called, nor whether it should be segmented as -*tei* or -*te-i*.

2.3 Data Analysis

The present study is similar to Battig and Montague (1969), which elicited exemplars of categories, such as sport, color, precious stone, furniture, etc. from native speakers of English. In their study, they counted the frequency of the exemplars produced by the subjects, as well as the frequency of the exemplars that were mentioned first. Below are the results from Battig and Montague with the prompt category 'weapon':

	total frequency	1st mention frequency
1. knife	405	59
2. gun	394	312
3. rifle	163	29

The most frequently produced was 'knife', but more subjects (312) produced 'gun' as their first item. This shows that the most frequently produced items are not necessarily the most readily accessible ones, although for some categories they match. Following Battig and Montague, I will also report both results: overall frequency and first-mention frequency.[5]

The sentences produced by the subjects in the present study were classified into one of five possible categories, based on the aspectual meaning of *-teiru*, namely (1) unitary progressive, (2) iterative progressive, (3) resultative state, (4) experiential, and (5) habitual. These categories are a modification of Yoshikawa's (1978) classification, which is a standard classification of the different senses that the polysemous category *-tei* can have.[6] However, no token of experiential sense was produced by any of the subjects, and it will not be discussed further.[7]

Let us look at the examples of each of the remaining four categories. The examples below are sentences actually produced by the subjects.

---

[5] Caramazza and Grober (1976) unfortunately did not give details about either the procedure or the analyses of free elicitation task except that the subjects were instructed to "produce as many sentences with different senses of the word <u>line</u> as they could" (Caramazza & Grober 1976: 187).

[6] The details of the conditions under which *-tei* has these senses are beyond the scope of this paper. See, for example, Jacobsen (1982, 1992), Takezawa (1991) and Yoshikawa (1978).

[7] An example of 'experiential' is:

Kare-wa syoosetu-o takusan kai-tei-ru.
he-TOP   novel-ACC lots   write-ASP-NONPAST
'He has written many novels.'

(1) Kare-wa   eiga-o   mi-tei-ru.
    he-TOP   movie-ACC   see-ASP-NONPAST
    'He is watching a movie.'

Progressive (unitary)

(2) Booru-o   ket-tei-ru.
    ball-ACC   kick-ASP-NONPAST
    '(He) is kicking a ball.'

Progressive (iterative)

(3) Miti-ni   gomi-ga   oti-tei-ru.
    Street-LOC   trash-NOM   drop-ASP-NONPAST
    'There is trash on the street.'

Resultative

(4) Watasi-wa saikin tenisu bakari si-tei-ru.
    I-TOP   lately tennis only   do-ASP-NONPAST
    'I have been doing nothing but play tennis lately.'

Habitual

2.4 Results

Table 1 shows the distribution of the first sentence produced by the subjects (i.e. what is most readily accessible to the subject):

progressive (unitary)	33	(89.2%)
progressive (iterative)	0	(0.0%)
resultative state	3	(8.1%)
experiential	0	(0.0%)
habitual	1	(2.7%)
Total	37	(100%)
unclear cases	2	

Table 1. The frequency distribution of the <u>first</u> sentences with *teiru* produced by subjects, by sense type

Although there were 39 subjects, two cases were impossible to categorize, and were excluded. From this table it is clear that unitary progressive is the most frequent, and in fact most of the first sentences produced were unitary progressive.

Table 2 below shows the overall frequency of the sentence types produced by the subjects:

progressive (unitary)	362	(77.5%)
progressive (iterative)	9	(1.9%)
resultative state	87	(18.6%)
experiential	0	(0.0%)
habitual	9	(1.9%)
Total	467	(100%)
unclear cases	56	

(average N of sentences produced = 13.4 per subject)

Table 2. The frequency distribution of all sentences with *teiru* produced by subjects, by sense type

Here, too, the trend is very clear; unitary progressive is by far the most frequent of all 5 types, even though the percentage is a little lower compared to the first sentences produced.

Therefore, if we follow the standard argument in the categorization studies in psychology, the prototype of the linguistic category -*teiru* is unitary progressive. It should be noted here that this kind of prototype analysis can be done at different levels of specification, depending on the purpose of the research. For example, one can also do more detailed analysis of the semantics of verbs used (in terms of punctuality, telicity, etc.), types of arguments (for example, +/- human, first/second third person), presence of adverbials, and so forth. the level of specification that I have chosen for the purpose of the study is the different senses of the polysemous category -*teiru*.

3. Discussion

The results clearly show that the prototypical meaning of the polysemous category -*tei* is unitary progressive. If we accept this, the next question is where the prototype comes from. One possible source is the frequency in discourse. Therefore, I checked the frequency distribution of different senses of -*teiru* in a naturally occurring spoken discourse. The corpus (Ide et al. 1984) consists of conversations of various types on various topics recorded during a one-week period. 37 tokens of -*teiru* were randomly sampled from the corpus, and their distribution is shown in Table 3 below.

progressive (unitary)	8	(21.6%)
progressive (iterative)	0	(0.0%)
resultative state	24	(64.9%)
experiential	0	(0.0%)
habitual	5	(13.5%)
Total	37	(100%)

Table 3. The frequency distribution of the sentences with *teiru* used in daily conversation (Ide et al. 1984), by sense type

It is clear from the table that the resultative state sense is much more frequent than progressive.[8] This is in sharp contrast to the predominance of the progressive over resultative state in the free elicitation experiment.

This discrepancy between prototype and frequency of use in discourse is not surprising. In an earlier study (Shirai 1990), I investigated the prototype of the polysemous basic verb PUT and its use in discourse, and found that the prototype, in this case, defined as PTRANS (=physical transfer, Schank & Abelson 1977) based on an elicitation from native English speakers, was not so frequent either in spoken or written discourse. More recently, Johnson (1995) reported that 48.6% of children's use of the verb *see* involved a straightforward visual-perception sense of *see*, while only 22.8 percent of the caretakers' speech was used for this sense, which is presumably the prototypical sense of *see*. It thus appears that there often is a discrepancy between prototypical senses and frequent senses in the polysemous basic verbs.

If frequency is not the reason, where does the prototype come from? One possibility is that it comes from the central tendency of the various uses of the linguistic item in question. Rosch et al. (1976) have demonstrated that, in learning artificial categories, subjects learn categories by inducing prototypes based on the exemplars they encounter, and that the frequency of the prototypical exemplars itself is not very important. Specifically, in one of their experiments, subjects were trained on atypical instances of the categories more frequently than on typical instances, and their performance was still better with prototypical instances. Applied to the present study, even though the resultative state sense of *-teiru* is the most frequent in discourse, the central tendency of all the uses of *-teiru* is induced by native speakers to be progressive.

---

[8] Shirai (1995) also reports the same relative frequency in the speech of a native Japanese speaker in an interview.

Another possibility is that there is a kind of universal cognitive prominence for the prototype of some linguistic categories. This may be particularly true in the case of highly grammaticizable categories such as tense and aspect. In relation to the present study, there are two suggestive pieces of evidence in first language acquisition and grammaticization. First, Shirai (1993) specifically investigated whether progressive meaning is acquired earlier than resultative meaning in the acquisition of -teiru by a Japanese child. It was found that there is a short period of time when progressive meaning is predominant, and soon after this period, the frequencies for progressive and resultative meanings become about the same. Although the study of only one child cannot provide conclusive evidence, it suggests the prominence of progressive meaning as the prototype of the category. In this connection, it should be noted that it has been found that in the acquisition of the English progressive marker, the action-in-progress meaning is acquired first (Shirai 1991, Shirai & Andersen 1995), although this finding is not surprising. One hypothesis that can be tested is that in any language, when a polysemous inflection denotes progressive sense plus some other senses, such as immediate future, process leading up to the endpoint, habitual, resultative state, etc. progressive sense is the sense acquired first by children.[9]

Another piece of suggestive evidence for the prominence of progressive meaning is the universal paths of grammaticization proposed by Bybee et al. (1994). They claim that the progressive sense occurs early in the process of grammaticization, and sometimes develops into the more general imperfective marker, by acquiring such meanings as habitual and developing-state. Moreover, they claim that the original meaning of the progressive is strongly associated with action in progress at the reference time. To quote from Bybee et al., (1994:136) the original meaning of progressive is 'An agent is located spatially in the midst of an activity at reference time.'

Interestingly, Japanese has already developed two periphrastic progressive forms based on -teiru, that is, -teiru-

---

[9] Although the title of this paper is 'On the primacy of progressive over resultative state,' I do not claim that progressive is universally more easily grammaticized than result-state. Both 'progressive' and 'change of state' are highly grammaticizable notions (Slobin 1985). The point here is in cases where progressive and result state is expressed by the same morpheme, progressive is more grammaticizable. In fact, as Bybee et al. (1994) have shown, progressive and result-state/perfect are normally grammaticized in two separate forms.

tokoro[10] and *-teiru-saityuu*. Since the semantic space denoted by *-teiru* is so general, new periphrases have developed to express more specific meanings. These expressions cannot be used to refer to resultative states. Resultative state meanings are blocked by adding *tokoro* or *saityuu*. For example, if you add *tokoroda* to the resultative sentence (3), you obtain **gomi-ga otiteiru-tokoro-da*, which is ungrammatical because *tokoroda* blocks resultative meaning. Moreover, it is normally anomalous to say **Ame-ga futteiru-tokoro-da* (It is raining + *tokoro-da*) or **Kawa-ga nagareteiru-tokoro-da* (The river is flowing + *tokoro-da*). This is probably because the original meaning of progressive, as claimed by Bybee et al., is strongly associated with agency, and rivers and rain typically cannot be agents. It is important to note that these periphrastic expressions denote progressive, not resultative states. Japanese does not yet have productive periphrastic forms based on *-teiru* to denote resultative states. This also suggests the primacy of progressive as an axis for grammaticization.

To conclude, I argue that the special status the progressive in the semantic representations of native speakers, in first language acquisition, and in universal grammaticization processes, suggests the possibility that progressive is a cognitive reference point which humans very frequently pay attention to in the acquisition and use of language. Further study is needed, however, to confirm the validity of the claim made here. In fact, the present study poses many more questions than it answers. However, these questions relate to an important issue: How are prototypes of polysemous linguistic categories acquired? Although linguists often talk about prototypes, especially in cognitive and functional linguistics, this question has not been addressed systematically.[11] The methodology used in this study to determine the prototype of *-teiru* can easily be applied in many languages, and for various polysemous linguistic items. I believe further studies along this line would contribute to better understanding of prototypes, which is one of the key notions in cognitive and functional linguistics.

---

[10] See Ohara (1995) for a detailed discussion of the constructions involving the grammatical noun *tokoro*.

[11] In July 1995, I checked LLBA on CD-ROM, giving the command FIND 'prototype' AND 'acquisition,' and got only two citations. One was Shirai (1990) cited earlier, and the other was an irrelevant reference which happens to contain the words 'acquisition' and 'prototype,' not the acquisition OF prototype.

References

Battig, William F., and William E. Montague. 1969. Category norms for verbal items in 56 categories: A replication and extension of the Connecticut category norms. Journal of Experimental Psychology Monograph, 80, (3), Part 2.

Bybee, Joan L., Revere Perkins, and William Pagliuca. 1994. The evolution of grammar: Tense, aspect, and modality in the languages of the world. Chicago: The University of Chicago Press.

Caramazza, Alfonso, and Ellen Grober. 1976. Polysemy and the structure of the subjective lexicon. Georgetown University Round Table on Languages and Linguistics 1976, ed. by Clea Rameh, 181-206. Washington, D.C.: Georgetown University Press.

Colombo, Lucia, and Giovanni B. Flores D'Arcais. 1984. The meaning of Dutch prepositions: A psycholinguistic study of polysemy. Linguistics 22.51-98.

Givón, T. 1984. Syntax: A functional-typological introduction, vol. 1. Amsterdam: John Benjamins.

Givón, T. 1989. Mind, code and context: Essays in pragmatics. Hillsdale, NJ: Lawrence Erlbaum.

Glass, Arnold Lewis, and Keith James Holyoak. 1986. Cognition. 2nd ed. New York: Random House.

Glass, Arnold L., Keith J. Holyoak, and Carla O'Dell. 1974. Production frequency and the verification of quantified statements. Journal of Verbal Learning and Verbal Behavior 13.237-54.

Ide, Sachiko, Shoko Ikuta, Akiko Kawasaki, Motoko Hori, and Hitomi Haga. 1984. Syuhu no issyuukan no danwa siryoo [One week's discourse data of a housewife]. Tokyo: Japan Women's University.

Jacobsen, Wesley M. 1982. Vendler's verb classes and the aspectual character of Japanese te-iru. BLS 8.373-83.

Jacobsen, Wesley M. 1992. The transitive structure of events in Japanese. Tokyo: Kuroshio.

Johnson, Christopher. 1995. Metaphor vs. conflation in the acquisition of polysemy: The case of *see*. Paper presented at the 4th Conference of the International Cognitive Linguistics Association, University of New Mexico, Albuquerque, July 19.

Kellerman, Eric. 1978. Giving learners a break: Native language intuitions as a source of predictions about transferability. Working Papers on Bilingualism 15.59-92.

Lakoff, George. 1987. Women, fire, and dangerous things: What categories reveal about the mind. Chicago: The University of Chicago Press.

Ohara, Kyoko Hirose. 1995. What's in a place? Extended uses of a physical-world noun in Japanese. BLS 21.

Rips, Lance J., Edward J. Shoben, and Edward E. Smith. 1973. Semantic distance and the verification of semantic relations. Journal of Verbal Learning and Verbal Behavior 12.1-20.

Rosch, Eleanor. 1973. On the internal structure of perceptual and semantic categories. Cognitive development and the acquisition of language, ed. by Timothy E. Moore, 111-44. New York: Academic Press.

Rosch, Eleanor, Carol Simpson, and R. Scott Miller. 1976. Structural basis of typicality effects. Journal of Experimental Psychology: Human Perception and Performance 2.491-502.

Schank, Roger C., and Abelson, Robert P. 1977. Scripts, plans, goals and understanding: An inquiry into human knowledge structures. Hillsdale, NJ: Lawrence Erlbaum.

Shirai, Yasuhiro. 1990. Putting PUT to use: Prototype and metaphorical extension. Issues in Applied Linguistics 1.78-97.

Shirai, Yasuhiro. 1991. Primacy of aspect in language acquisition: Simplified input and prototype. Doctoral dissertation, UCLA, Los Angeles, CA.

Shirai, Yasuhiro. 1993. Inherent aspect and the acquisition of tense/aspect morphology in Japanese. Argument structure: Its syntax and acquisition, ed. by Heizo Nakajima and Yukio Otsu, 185-211. Tokyo: Kaitakusha.

Shirai, Yasuhiro. 1995. Tense-aspect marking by L2 learners of Japanese. Proceedings of the 19th Annual Boston University Conference on Language Development, vol. 2, ed. by Dawn MacLaughlin and Susan McEwen, 575-86. Somerville, MA: Cascadilla Press.

Shirai, Yasuhiro, and Roger W. Andersen. 1995. The acquisition of tense-aspect morphology: A prototype account. Language 71.743-62.

Slobin, Dan I. 1985. Crosslinguistic evidence for the Language-Making Capacity. The crosslinguistic study of language acquisition, vol. 2: Theoretical issues, ed. by Dan I. Slobin, 1157-1249. Hillsdale, NJ: Lawrence Erlbaum.

Takezawa, Koichi. 1991. Dyudoobun, nookakubun, bunri hukanoo syoyuukoobun to teiru no kaisyaku [Passives, ergatives, and inalienable possession sentences in the interpretation of teiru]. Nihongo no voisu to tadoosei [Voice and transitivity in Japanese], ed. by Yoshio Nitta, 59-81. Tokyo: Kuroshio.

Wilkins, Arnold J. 1971. Conjoint frequency, category size, and categorization time. Journal of Verbal Learning and Verbal Behavior 10.382-85.

Yoshikawa, Taketoki. 1978. Gendai nihongo doosi no asupekuto no kenkyuu [Research on the aspect of verbs in Modern Japanese]. Nihongo doosi no asupekuto [Aspect in Japanese verbs], ed. by Haruhiko Kindaichi, 155-328. Tokyo: Mugi Shobo.

Groups as Event-Oriented Entities

Eun-Joo Kwak
Brown University

1. Introduction

Since plural NPs are considered in semantics, it has been generally agreed that the domain of individuals should be sorted with atomic and plural individuals. Link (1984), however, argues that this domain is not rich enough to deal with the interpretations of plural NPs, and proposes that plural NPs are ambiguous between sums and groups, i.e., higher-ordered entities consisting of sums of individuals. Schwarzschild (1992) argues against the ambiguity of plurals, claiming that group readings are pragmatically driven readings. I argue that a pragmatic account cannot deal with all group readings, and that Schwarzschild's argument against groups is induced by the fact that lists of people or plurals in general are not construed as groups without any context. Thus I consider whether previous analyses of groups account for this tendency, and propose that groups are event-dependent entities.

2. Domain of Individuals

The consideration of plurals complicates the domain of individual, raising an ontological question, i.e., how the denotations of plural NPs are different from those of singular NPs. Earlier accounts on this problem such as Bennett (1974), Hausser (1974), and Hoeksema (1983) are based on set theory. A singular is assumed to denote a set of individuals, while a plural denotes the power set of its singular counterpart as exemplified in (1).

(1) a. $[[\text{ring}]] = \{x, y, z\}$
     b. $[[\text{rings}]] = \{\{x\}, \{y\}, \{z\}, \{x,y\}, \{y,z\}, \{x,z\}, \{x,y,z\}\}$

In the set-theoretic account, plurals, typed <e,t>, are higher-order entities than singulars. The different types of singulars and plurals lead to the proliferation of predicate types, and the discrepancy of types in the conjunction of a singular and a plural NPs, e.g., *Mary and her rings*.

To cope with problems around plurality, Link (1983) suggests a lattice structure for the domain of individuals. [1] A lattice is a partially ordered set with a join operation + and a part-of relation ≤. A join operation + maps any two elements to their sum, inducing a partial order among the three elements. Link (1983) proposes that the domain of individuals is a complete join semilattice without a bottom element <E, +, ≤>, i.e., a partially ordered set in which any subset has a supremum but not necessarily an infimum. The lattice structure for three individuals x, y, and z may be represented in (2).

(2)

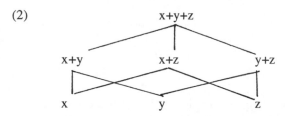

In the lattice-theoretic structure, plurals are first-ordered entities like singulars. Thus it does not induce the proliferation of predicate types nor the type discrepancy of conjoined NPs. Given the merits, I adopt a lattice-theoretic structure for the domain of individuals.

3. The ambiguity of Plurals

In this section, I consider whether the domain of atomic individuals and sums is sufficient enough to deal with the interpretations of plural NPs. I will summarize Link (1984) and Landman (1989a)'s arguments for higher-ordered entities of 'groups' and review Schwarzschild (1992)'s argument against it. I will argue for groups, considering the plural morphology of Korean.

3.1 Motivations for Groups

---

[1] Link (1983) was not the first to use a lattice structure for the study of plurality. His predecessors include Massey (1976), Wald (1977), Sharvy (1980), and Simons (1983).

In the domain of atomic individuals and sums, plurals are unambiguously interpreted as sums. There are several constructions, however, which show that this domain is not rich enough to deal with a full range of plural interpretations. First, there are some cases in which the general property of plurals does not hold. Quine (1960) observes that plurals have a 'cumulative' reference property, i.e., if there are two entities to which a plural term applies, this plural applies to their sum as well. For instance, if Brown and Smith have the property of accepting the proposal, and Kim and Jones also have the same property, then the property of accepting the proposal takes a sum of the four individuals in its denotation. Link (1984) and Landman (1989a) argue that according to this property, it is predicted that (3c) and (3d) are not true in the situation that (3a) and (3b) are true, and Committee A consists of Brown, Smith, Kim, and Jones.

(3)   a.   Brown, Smith, and Kim accepted the proposal.
      b.   Jones did not accept the proposal.
      c. # Brown, Smith, Kim and Jones accepted the proposal.
      d.   Committee A accepted the proposal.

Without mentioning that Jones also has the property of accepting the proposal, the predicate *accept the proposal* cannot apply to a sum of the four individuals. Hence the awkwardness of (2c) follows. Interestingly, *Committee A*, which has Brown, Smith, Kim, and Jones as its members, is not subject to the cumulative reference property, as shown by the acceptability of (2d). This implies that Committee A needs another interpretation in addition to a sum of its members.

A second argument concerns an ambiguity test by Zwicky and Sadock (1975). They argue that when an authentically ambiguous item is placed in a coordinate structure, it must take the same reading as to both conjuncts or have the flavor of joke. Given the test, let us consider two different descriptions of a plural like *the Talking Heads*.

(4)   a.   The Talking Heads is a pop group.
      b.   The Talking Heads are pop stars.

If *the Talking Heads* unambiguously denotes a sum of its members, the predicates of (4a) and (4b) may be conjoined without changing the acceptability. However, this is not the case.

(4)   c. * The Talking Heads is a pop group and are pop stars.

The oddness of (4c) shows that *the Talking Heads* is ambiguous as to the predicates, and needs another interpretation in addition to its sum reading. [2]

A third argument is provided by predicates referring to the internal structure of plurals. Under the assumption that plurals unambiguously denote sums, the subject NPs of (5) denote the same individual, i.e., a sum of cards in a deck.

(5)   a.   The cards below seven and the cards from seven up are separated.
       b.   The cards below ten and the cards from ten up are separated.

This implies that (5a) and (5b) are equivalent. However, in one of the readings, (5a) and (5b) are not equivalent: the cards below seven are separated from the cards from seven up in (5a), and the cards below ten are separated from the cards from ten up in (5b). Thus the sum readings of the subject NPs are not sufficient to deliver the distinct readings of the sentences.

Based on these arguments, Link (1984) and Landman (1989a) argue that we need another type of entity for a plural which behaves like a singular and is rather independent of its parts. They call this a 'group'. Then plurals are assumed to be ambiguous between plural readings of sums and singular readings of groups.

3.2 Argument against Groups

Some researchers including Schwarzschild (1992) do not agree on the status of groups, but argue that sums are enough for the interpretations of plurals. The argument of Schwarzschild (1992) is based on two observations. First, those predicates that provide evidence for group interpretations are 'inherently reciprocal' predicates. This may be shown by the equivalence of (6a) and (6b) in their group readings.

(6)   a.   The cows and the pigs were separated.
       b.   The cows and the pigs were separated from each other.

---

[2] Landman brings up the examples of (4), and then rejects this as an argument for 'group'. He attributes this as a syntactic problem of a number mismatch. But I claim that this is groundless. When we change (4c) to (i), in which there is no syntactic problem, the sentence sounds still odd.

(i)   The Talking Heads and the Beatles are pop groups and pop stars.

Thus I argue that *the Talking Heads* turns out ambiguous according to the ambiguity test.

This implies that the semantics of predicates taking groups may be reduced to that of a reciprocal. Second, grouping in a reciprocal sentence may be available only through context in some cases. For example, the most natural interpretation of (7) is that pigs belonging to Smith should be separated from pigs belonging to Jones.

(7) Farmer Smith and Farmer Jones said that although their cows could stay together, the pigs should be separated.

Since the ownership of the pigs is not represented by the subject NP but delivered by context, the grouping of pigs is decided by context in (7). This means that the group reading of the predicate may be available without resorting to the group reading of the NP. Given that, the group readings of plurals are less supported by inherent reciprocal predicates.

Now the question is whether contextual information will be sufficient to deliver a group reading in general. If it is the case, there is no point to posit a higher order entity and complicate the domain of individuals. In the non-ambiguity hypothesis, the subject NPs of (8) are equivalent.

(8) a. The cows were separated.
    b. The old cows and the young cows were separated.

Schwarzschild attributes the non-equivalence of (8a) and (8b) to the Gricean maxim. If the sentence does not concern the separation of old cows from the young cows, the choice of the subject in (8b) violates the maxim of quantity 'to be brief'. Thus the subject NPs are semantically equivalent, however, they are distinguished pragmatically. And the group reading of (8b) is due to the pragmatic constraint.

Another source of group specification is the occurrence of an adverbial such as *by age* of (9a).

(9) a. The cows were separated by age.
    b. (?) The old cows and the young cows are separated by age.

Given the equivalence of (8b) and (9a), it seems that the occurrence of the adverbial in (9a) contributes the same information as the choice of the subject NP in (8b). This is further attested by the fact that when the partition of the adverbial matches the choice of the subject NP as in (9b), some redundancy arises, which leads to the oddness of the sentence.

I agree to Schwarzschild in that the group readings of NPs may be affected by context or pragmatics to some extent. However, I am not quite convinced that all group readings may be replaced by the partition of a sum in accord with context or pragmatics. Suppose that the faculty of the math department consists of professors p_1, p_2, and p_3, and that of the applied math department is comprised of p_3, p_4, and p_5. In this situation, how can we derive the group reading of (10) from the sum interpretation of the subject NP, i.e., $p_1+p_2+p_3+p_4+p_5$?

(10)   The professors in the math department and the professors in the applied math department disagreed about the conference room.

The first way to cut this sum into two groups is to partition it, i.e., to divide the sum into subsums without allowing any element to be in the intersection of any two sets. Then it is impossible to partition the sum $p_1+p_2+p_3+p_4+p_5$ into two faculty members, since p_3 cannot be included in both of the partitioned parts. The second method is to get a cover reading of the sum, i.e., to divide the sum into subsums, allowing overlapping elements. Then the sum of the professors may be divided into $p_1+p_2+p_3$ and $p_3+p_4+p_5$. And (10) is interpreted that professors $p_1+p_2+p_3$ disagreed with professors $p_3+p_4+p_5$ about the conference room. At first glance, the cover reading of the sum seems to work for the group interpretation, under the assumption that the context determines proper covers. However, remember that sums have the cumulative reference property. According to this property, the sum interpretation of $p_1+p_2+p_3$ in (11a) entails (11b-d).

(11)   a. p_1, p_2, p_3 disagreed with p_3, p_4, p_5 about the conference room.
        b. p_1 disagreed with p_3, p_4, p_5 about the conference room.
        c. p_2 disagreed with p_3, p_4, p_5 about the conference room.
        d. p_3 disagreed with p_3, p_4, p_5 about the conference room.

Moreover, $p_3+p_4+p_5$ is also a sum and further subject to the cumulative reference property. This will give a reading such that each of the math department professors disagreed with each of the applied math department professors as to the conference room. Problematically, a part of this reading is that p_3 disagreed with p_3 about the conference room, which is the self-contradictory reading of p_3. However, (8) has no flavor of contradiction. This implies that even the cover reading is not sufficient to deliver the appropriate group interpretation of the NP. Thus the domain of sums only is not rich enough to deal with the interpretations of plurals.

3.3 Morphological Evidence for Groups in Korean

If the group readings of plurals are a pragmatic problem but not a semantic issue, we may not expect that there is any language which distinguishes between the sums and groups morphologically or syntactically. However, the plural morphology of Korean provides evidence against this prediction. The plural morphology of Korean is more flexible than that of English. A plural NP such as *ai* 'children' may occur either with or without the nominal plural marker '-*tul*'.

(12) ney-myeng-uy ai-<u>tul</u>   four-Class-Poss child-NPM
      ney-myeng-uy ai   four-Class-Poss child
      'four children'
      (where *Class* stands for classifier, *Poss* for possessive, and *NPM* for nominal plural marker)

It has been assumed that these two plural forms do not make any significant difference in semantics. Diverse tests for plural forms as in (13), however, show that *ai-tul* is understood as a sum of children, while *ai* denotes a group of children.

(13)
a. Ney-myeng-uy ai-<u>tul</u>-i/*ai-ka   tokki-lul-<u>tul</u> capassta.
   four-Class-Poss child-NPM-Nom/*child-Nom rabbit-PM   captured
   (where PM stands for plural marker)
   'Four children captured a rabbit each.'
b. Ney-myeng-uy ai-<u>tul</u>-i/??ai-ka   han-myeng-ssik ttenassta.
   four-Class-Poss child-NPM-Nom/?? child-Nom one-Class-each left
   'Four children left one by one.'
c. Ney-myeng-uy ai-<u>tul</u>-i/??ai-ka   (selo)
   four-Class-Poss child-NPM-Nom/??child-Nom (each other)
   talun   kyelkwa-lul etessta.
   different result-Acc   got
   'Four children got different results (from each other).'
d. Ney-myeng-uy ai-<u>tul</u>-i/*ai-ka   motwu tokki-lul capassta. [3]
   four-Class-Poss child-NPM-Nom/??child-Nom all   rabbit   captured
   'Four children all captured a rabbit.'

The predicates of (13) are strongly biased to distributive readings, which refer to parts of the denotations of the subject NPs. The unacceptability of *ai* in (13) shows that it does not have proper subparts to induce the distributivity of the predicates. Thus it is concluded that *ai* is construed as a group, which does not have proper subparts.

The distinction of sums and groups is further shown by conjoined plural NPs.

(14)
a. Ney-mari-uy so-<u>tul</u>-kwa yel-mari-uy toayci-<u>tul</u>-i nanuiecessta.
   four-Class-Poss cow-NPM-and ten-Class-Poss pig-NPM-Nom separated
b. Ney-mari-uy so-wa yel-mari-uy toayci-ka nanuiecessta.

---

[3] As for the distributivity of floated quantifiers such as *all*, *motwu*, etc., see Dowty (1986), Link (1986), Roberts (1987), and Kwak (1995).

more flexible than that of English. A plural NP such as *ai* 'children' may occur either with or without the nominal plural marker '*-tul*'.

(12)   ney-myeng-uy ai-<u>tul</u>   four-Class-Poss child-NPM
        ney-myeng-uy ai   four-Class-Poss child
        'four children'
        (where *Class* stands for classifier, *Poss* for possessive, and *NPM* for nominal plural marker)

It has been assumed that these two plural forms do not make any significant difference in semantics. Diverse tests for plural forms as in (13), however, show that *ai-tul* is understood as a sum of children, while *ai* denotes a group of children.

(13)
a. Ney-myeng-uy ai-<u>tul</u>-i/*ai-ka   tokki-lul-<u>tul</u> capassta.
   four-Class-Poss child-NPM-Nom/*child-Nom rabbit-PM   captured
   (where PM stands for plural marker)
   'Four children captured a rabbit each.'
b. Ney-myeng-uy ai-<u>tul</u>-i/??ai-ka   han-myeng-ssik ttenassta.
   four-Class-Poss child-NPM-Nom/?? child-Nom one-Class-each left
   'Four children left one by one.'
c. Ney-myeng-uy ai-<u>tul</u>-i/??ai-ka   (selo)
   four-Class-Poss child-NPM-Nom/??child-Nom   (each other)
   talun   kyelkwa-lul etessta.
   different result-Acc   got
   'Four children got different results (from each other).'
d. Ney-myeng-uy ai-<u>tul</u>-i/*ai-ka   motwu tokki-lul capassta. [3]
   four-Class-Poss child-NPM-Nom/??child-Nom all   rabbit   captured
   'Four children all captured a rabbit.'

The predicates of (13) are strongly biased to distributive readings, which refer to parts of the denotations of the subject NPs. The unacceptability of *ai* in (13) shows that it does not have proper subparts to induce the distributivity of the predicates. Thus it is concluded that *ai* is construed as a group, which does not have proper subparts.

The distinction of sums and groups is further shown by conjoined plural NPs.

(14)
a. Ney-mari-uy so-<u>tul</u>-kwa yel-mari-uy toayci-<u>tul</u>-i nanuiecessta.
   four-Class-Poss cow-NPM-and ten-Class-Poss pig-NPM-Nom separated
b. Ney-mari-uy so-wa yel-mari-uy toayci-ka nanuiecessta.

---

[3] As for the distributivity of floated quantifiers such as *all, motwu*, etc., see Dowty (1986), Link (1986), Roberts (1987), and Kwak (1995).

'Four cows and ten pigs were separated.'

Given the observation of (13), the subject of (14a) denotes a sum of cows and pigs, accompanied by the NPM, while that of (14b) is understood as a sum of a cow group and a pig group. This means that the subject of (14a) does not involve any internal grouping, whereas the subject of (14b) clearly addresses grouping by species. Thus when an adverbial like *nai pyello* 'by age' occurs with the subject of (14a), the sentence sounds awkward due to the mismatch of the internal structure.

(15)
a. Ney-mari-uy   so-tul-kwa   yel-mari-uy   toayci-tul-i
    four-Class-Poss cow-NPM-and   ten-Class-Poss pig-NPM-Nom
    nai pyello nanuiecessta.
    age by   separated
b. * Ney-mari-uy so-wa yel-mari-uy toayci-ka nai pyello nanuiecessta.
    'Four cows and ten pigs were separated by age.'

Thus Korean plural morphology provides more support for the semantic distinction of sums and groups.

4. Previous Analyses

In this section, I critically review two previous analyses of groups, Link (1984) and Landman (1989b), pointing out that they do not account for the different degree of group interpretations between lists of people and collection terms.

4.1 Link (1984)

To get the ambiguity of plurals, Link (1984), which is further elaborated by Landman (1989a), proposes two monadic functions, i.e., a group formation function '↑' and a member specification function '↓'. ↑ maps a sum to a group, and ↓ maps a group to a sum of its members. Given these functions, we will have a structure like (16) in the situation that John, Mary, and Kim constitutes the thesis committee and the editorial board.

(16)

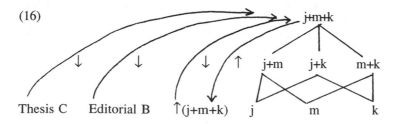

First there is a sum of j+m+k in the domain, given three individuals John, Mary and Kim. This sum is mapped to a group $\uparrow$(j+m+k) by the group formation function, and the group of $\uparrow$(j+m+k) is related to j+m+k by the member specification function. Independently, the domain includes two established groups, *the thesis committee* and *the editorial board*, and these groups are related to j+m+k by the member specification function. Thus the domain includes sums and groups, and they are related by the functions.

4.2 Problems with Link (1984)

Though Link's intuition about groups is on the right the track, the domain of individuals defined by $\uparrow$ and $\downarrow$ has several problems. First, in his domain, both an established group like *Committee A* and a derived group like *Brown, Smith, Kim and Jones* are primitive groups. Then it is predicted that both of them have the same chance to be exempted from the cumulative reference property of sums. In the situation of (17a) and (17b), however, (17c) is subject to that property, while (17d) is not.

(17)   a.   Brown, Smith, and Kim accepted the proposal.
     b.   Jones did not accept the proposal.
     c. #   Brown, Smith, Kim and Jones accepted the proposal.
     d.   Committee A accepted the proposal.

Thus Link's analysis does not give an explanation for the fact that a list of people is less likely to be interpreted as a group than a collection term like *committee*. Second, since Link postulates different groups for an established and a derived groups that have the same members, e.g., *the thesis committee* and $\uparrow$(j+m+k) in (16), there is no direct mapping relation between the two groups. However, if the context provides enough information for the group reading of (16a) that John, Mary and Kim met as the thesis committee and passed the thesis, (18a) is equivalent to (18b).

(18)   a.   John, Mary, and Kim passed the thesis.
     b.   The thesis committee passes the thesis.

Thus we need some identity relation between the two groups, which is not captured in the domain of (16). Third, when two distinct groups are generated from the same members, Link's analysis cannot distinguish them as separate groups. In the situation that John, Mary and Kim constitutes both the thesis committee and the editorial board, the group of John, Mary, and Kim acts as the thesis committee in (17a), but as the editorial board in (17b).

(19)

a.   John, Mary and Kim passed the thesis.
b.   John, Mary and Kim discussed papers submitted to the journal.

According to Link, however, there is only one group for the plural, i.e., $\uparrow$(j+m+k). The identity of the groups in (19) leads to a more serious problem, when two predicates taking different groups are conjoined.

(20)   John, Mary and Kim passed the thesis and discussed papers submitted to the journal.

In (20), the first conjunct provides the property of a group of John, Mary and Kim as the thesis committee, while the second conjunct concerns the property of the group as the editorial board. Then the subject NP cannot take the property of the conjoined predicates as a property of the thesis committee or the editorial board, raising a group mismatch problem.

4.3 Landman (1989b)

Landman (1989b) argues that the extensional domain defined by Link (1984) is not sufficient to deal with problems around groups. In a situation that all the judges, i.e., John and Bill, work also as a hangman, the truth of (21a) does not necessarily entail the truth of (21b), because (21a) asserts that the judges John and Bill are on strike as judges, but may not as hangmen.

(21)   a.   The judges are on strike.
         b.   The hangmen are on strike.

In the extensional domain, the denotation of the *judges* is identical to that of *the hangmen* as shown in (22), so (21a) is equivalent to (21b).

(22) $\uparrow(\iota x[judges'(x)]) = \uparrow(\iota x[hangmen'(x)]) = \uparrow(j+b)$

Landman maintains that the non-equivalence of (21a) and (21b) are attributed to the restrictive aspects of groups. For example, the group of *the judges* in (21a) is not construed simply as a group of John and Bill, who are the members of the group. Rather, it is a group of John and Bill as judges. Thus he argues that the problem of Link's analysis may be resolved in the intentional domain.

In Thomason (1980)'s intentional logic, basic types are the type e of individuals and the type p of propositions. So propositions are taken as primitives rather than functions from possible worlds to truth values, and properties are propositional functions of type <e,p>. By the same token, *John* is a generalized quantifier, denoting a set of properties that John has. Based on this, Landman argues that individuals may be restricted by some aspects or properties. For example, *John as a judge* denotes a set of properties that John has as a judge rather than all the properties he has. Thus he defines a restrictive term like *John as a judge* as follows.

(23)   a.   If x is a term of type e and P is a predicate of type <e,p>, then x⇑P is an expression of type <<e,p>,p>.
      b.   x⇑P is interpreted as a set of properties that x has under the aspect of P.

An individual may be restricted by some property, which is represented by the operator ⇑, and a restricted individual denotes a set of properties that the individual has under the aspect of the restricting property. Given the notion of a restricted individual, the group of the judges in the intentional domain denotes a set of properties that the group of the judges has under the aspect of judges. Thus we may have different groups that are generated from the same members.

(24)   a. $[[\text{the judges}]] = {\uparrow}(\iota x[\text{judges}'(x)]){\Uparrow}(\lambda x[\text{judge}'(x)])$
            $= {\uparrow}(j+b){\Uparrow}(\lambda x[\text{judge}'(x)])$
      b. $[[\text{the hangmen}]] = {\uparrow}(\iota x[\text{hangmen}'(x)]){\Uparrow}(\lambda x[\text{hangman}'(x)])$
            $= {\uparrow}(j+b){\Uparrow}(\lambda x[\text{hangman}'(x)])$

Although both the group of the judges and the group of the hangmen take John and Bill as members, they are restricted by different properties. Therefore (21a) and (21b) are not equivalent.

4.4 Problems with Landman (1989b)

The intentional account of Landman, however, solves only half of the problems with Link (1984). When a plural NP does not have a salient property to restrict its group aspect, it is not easily mapped to an intentional entity. Or we have to assume an implicit restriction for this NP. Then two distinct groups which consist of the same members but do not have an overt restrictor, as in (25), will be incorrectly mapped to an identical group.

(25)   a.   John, Mary and Kim passed the thesis.
      b.   John, Mary and Kim discussed papers submitted to the journal.

If we assume that the implicit restrictor of the subject of (25a) is 'the thesis committee' and the restrictor of the subject of (25b) is 'the editorial board', the two groups may be identified as distinct. However, notice that the identification of these restrictors comes from the properties of predicates. Thus when the predicates of (25) are conjoined as in (26), Landman's analysis has the same problem as Link's.

(26) John, Mary and Kim passed the thesis and discussed papers submitted to the journal.

If the subject NP is restricted by either the thesis committee or the editorial board, then it takes an incorrect property from one of the conjuncts. Or if it is restricted by both of the groups, it is interpreted that passing the thesis is a property of both the thesis committee and the editorial board, and similarly for discussing papers. Thus Landman does not account for the group mismatch problem.

Another problem is that sometimes a restrictive property of an NP may not accord with the property of the predicate.

(27) a. The judges are on strike as hangmen, not as judges.

Landman provides a meaning postulate that a restrictive term x⇑P takes P as a property. Given that, (28a) should be false, because the judges denotes a set of properties that they have as judges, but the property of the predicate is not a property of judges. Contrary to the prediction, (28a) is acceptable. Notice that when the subject is explicitly restricted by the property of judges, the sentence is awkward as shown in (28b).

(28) b. The judges, as judges, are on strike as hangmen, not as judges

The acceptability contrast between (28a) and (28b) casts strong doubt on Landman's proposal that the intentionality of a group comes from a restrictive property.

5. Proposal

In this section, I propose that groups are event-dependent individuals, and show how problems around groups are explained in this proposal.

5.1 Groups as Event-Dependent Individuals

I consider the semantics of groups in the framework of event semantics, in which a predicate denotes a relation between nominal arguments and an event argument.

(29) John buttered the toast.
   a. Classical account: $\text{butter}'(t)(j)$
   b. Event semantics : $\exists e[\text{butter}'(t)(j)(e)]$

In the classical theory, butter denotes a relation between two individuals that stand in the buttering relation. According to Davidson (1967), however, predicates are assumed to have an extra argument slot of an event. Based on this, I consider the philosophical argument of groups. Simons (1987) proposes the constitution condition of groups.

(30)   Constitution Conditions of Groups
        a.   A group consists of integrated parts.[4]
        b.   A group is involved in (regular) events.

According to Simons, to function as a group, a plural must consist of integrated parts and be involved in (regular) events. To identity as the thesis committee, the group members should hold a meeting and do some activity as a group. Without the group activity, an abstract entity like group cannot be assumed as an individual in the domain. Following Simons' philosophical argument, I propose that the domain of individuals includes two sorts of groups, i.e., well established groups like *committee* and temporary groups like a group of John, Mary and Kim. Since the identity as a group is partly decided by its activity as a group, an established group can be understood that it is involved in regular events and finally gains an identity, independent of a sum of its members. On the other hand, a temporary group does not acquire an independent identity yet, but may be mapped to some group with the salient group implication of its predicate. To put it in other words, the plural NP *John, Mary and Kim* is usually identified as a sum, but may act a group, only if its predicate has a strong implication of the action of a group.

        Given that, the group formation $\uparrow$ is redefined as a function from individual to a function from event to individual, and thus the denotation of *John, Mary and Kim* is ambiguous between a sum and an event-dependent NP, group.

(31)   a.   [[John, Mary and Kim]] = j+m+k (typed e)
        b.   [[John, Mary and Kim]] = $\lambda e[\uparrow(j+m+k)(e)]$ (typed <ε, e>)

The denotation of a derived group such as $\lambda e[\uparrow(j+m+k)(e)]$ is partly decided by an event. Depending on which event is taken, the denotation of the derived group may be different. In accord with the ambiguity of NPs, predicates also systematically ambiguous between taking an ordinary individual or an event-dependent entity.

---

[4] Here are conditions for the integrity.

(i)   Conditions of Integrity (Rescher and Oppenheim (1965))
a.   A group must possess some attribute in virtue of its status as a group.
b.   The parts of a group must stand in some special and characteristic relation of dependence with one another.
c.   The group must possess some kind of structure.

(32)
a. [[pass the thesis]] = $\lambda x \lambda e[\text{pass\_thesis}'(x)(e)]$ (typed $<e, <\varepsilon, t>>$)
b. [[pass the thesis]] = $\lambda f \lambda e[\text{pass\_thesis}'(f(e))(e)]$
(typed $<<\varepsilon, e>, <\varepsilon, t>>$)

According to the ambiguity of NPs, we can provide the sum and the group interpretations of the subjects in (33) as in (34), following a non-Boolean conjunction. [5]

(33)
a. Ney-mari-uy   so-<u>tul</u>-kwa   yel-mari-uy toayci-<u>tul</u>-i nanuiecessta.
   four-Class-Poss cow-NPM-and ten-Class-Poss pig-NPM-Nom separated
b. Ney-mari-uy so-wa yel-mari-uy toayci-ka nanuiecessta.
   'Four cows and ten pigs were separated.'

(34)   a.   [[Ney-mari-uy so-tul-kwa yel-mari-uy toayci-tul]]
             $= c1+ \ldots +c4+p1+ \ldots +p10$

        b.   [[Ney-mari-uy so-wa yel-mari-uy toayci]]
             $= \lambda e[\uparrow(c1+ \ldots +c4)(e)] \wedge \lambda e[\uparrow(p1+ \ldots +p10)(e)]$
             $= \lambda e[\uparrow(c1+ \ldots +c4)(e) + \uparrow(p1+ \ldots +p10)(e)]$

---

[5] In the domain of plural individuals, the denotation of *and* is ambiguous between the generalized conjunction and the join operator. Hence Hoeksema (1988), Krifka (1990), Lasersohn (1995), and Bayer (1996) propose a non-Boolean conjunction taking e as a base type. Here is the definition of e-conjoinable types.

(i)   a. e is an e-conjoinable type.
       b. For all a, $<a,t>$ is a predicative e-conjoinable type.
       c. If b is a predicative e-conjoinable type, then for all a, $<a,b>$ is a predicative e-conjoinable type.

Given the e-conjoinable types, the e-conjunction is defined as follows.

(ii)   a. $x \& y = x+y$ for x,y of type e.
       b. $f \& g = \{x+y | f(x) \wedge g(y)\}$ if f, g are of type $<e,t>$.
       c. $f \& g = \{<x+y, f' \& g'> | f(x) = f' \wedge g(y) = g'\}$ if f, g are of type $<e,b>$ for any b other than t.
       d. $f \& g = \lambda z[f(z) \& g(z)]$ otherwise.

(iia), as a base operation, says that the conjunction of any two functions typed e is the sum of the functions, which is basically the sum formation of two individuals. Otherwise, each argument of the functions is abstracted over to a variable which is the sum of the arguments.

So-tul and *toayci-tul* are sums of individuals, which drive their conjunction to a sum of fourteen animals. Contrastingly, *so* and *toayci* of (33b) are event-dependent individuals, so their conjunction amounts to a sum of two groups as shown in (34b). Thus the truth conditions of (33a-b) are given in (35a-b), on the assumption of the existential closure of events at a sentential level.

(35) a. $\exists e[separate(c_1+ \ldots +c_4+p_1+ \ldots +p_{10})(e)]$

   b. $\exists e[separate(\uparrow(c_1+ \ldots +c_4)(e) + \uparrow(p_1+ \ldots +p_{10})(e))(e)]$

Since the argument of (35a) does not involve any grouping, the separation of the animals is vague, and may be clarified by the occurrence of an adverbial such as *nai pyello* 'by age'. On the other hand, (35b) entails the separation of the cow group from the pig group, so it cannot occur with adverbials that do not match with this grouping.

5.2 Solving the Problems

I consider how the present proposal provides an account for the problems around groups. According to Link (1984) and Landman (1989b), groups and members are defined by the monadic operators of $\uparrow$ and $\downarrow$. Thus it is not explained why lists of people such as *John, Mary and Kim* are less likely to be interpreted as groups than collection terms like *committee*. Under the present proposal, collection terms are groups typed e, while lists of people may be understood as groups, only when their predicates have strong implications of group readings. In other words, lists of people may function as derived groups, when their predicates take event-dependent entities as arguments. Therefore it is naturally predicted that lists of people are more restricted to be interpreted as groups than collection terms.

   Second, the identity of a derived group such as a group of John, Mary and Kim depends on the property of the event. When its predicate concerns the activity of the thesis committee, the group $\lambda e[\uparrow(j+m+k)(e)]$ is mapped to the established group of the thesis committee. On the other hand, when the predicate is about the editorial board, $\lambda e[\uparrow(j+m+k)(e)]$ is mapped to the editorial board.

(36) a. $\uparrow(j+m+k)(e_1) = \iota x[thesis\_committee'(x)]$
       (if e_1 concerns the role of the thesis committee)

   b. $\uparrow(j+m+k)(e_2) = \iota x[editorial\_board'(x)]$
       (if e_2 concerns the role of the editorial board)

Therefore, (37a) and (37b) are equivalent, while (37b) and (37c) are not.

(37) a. The thesis committee passed the thesis.
   b. John, Mary and Kim passed the thesis.

   c. John, Mary and Kim discussed papers submitted to the journal.

Thus we can solve the identity problem and the problem of multiple groups at the same time.

     Finally, the present proposal provides a clear account for the group mismatch problem.

(38)   John, Mary and Kim passed the thesis and discussed papers submitted to the journal.

Under the non-Boolean conjunction (cf. footnote 5), the conjoined predicates denotes a set of events that consist of two subevents, namely an event of passing the thesis and an event of discussing papers. Thus, a derived group $\lambda e[\uparrow(j+m+k)(e)]$ depends on a different event in each conjunct, and is mapped to the thesis committee in the first conjunct, and to the editorial board in the second conjunct.

(39) $\exists e[\exists e_1 \exists e_2[e = e_1 + e_2 \wedge \text{pass\_thesis}'(\uparrow(j+m+k)(e_1))(e_1) \wedge$
     $\text{discuss\_papers}'(\uparrow(j+m+k)(e_2))(e_2)]]$

Thus it does induce a group mismatch problem. According to the present proposal, an authentic mismatch case is that one of the conjoined predicates takes a sum as an argument and the other conjunct is predicated of a group. Since the present proposal posits different types for these predicates, they end up with the discrepancy of types. As predicted by the proposal, this kind of conjunction is not allowed as shown in (40).

 (40)
a.   Ney-myeng-uy pyencipca-tul-i/pyencipca-ka hoiuy-lul hayessta.
    four-Class-Poss editor-NPM-Nom/editor-Nom meeting-Acc held
    'Four editors held a meeting.'
b.   Ney-myeng-uy pyencipca-tul-i/??pyencipca-ka cemsim-ul mekessta.
    four-Class-Poss editor-NPM-Nom/editor-Nom lunch had
    'Four editors had lunch.'
c.   Ney-myeng-uy pyencipca-tul-i/??pyencipca-ka cemsim-ul mek-ko
    hoiuy-lul hayessta.
    'Four editors had lunch and held a meeting.'

Thus it is concluded that the current proposal properly accounts for the problems around groups.

6. Conclusion

I have reviewed Link (1984) and Landman (1989a)'s arguments for groups, and Schwarzschild (1992)'s argument against groups. I show that the pragmatic account for group readings cannot cover a full range of group interpretations, and support for the semantic distinction of sums and groups with the plural morphology of Korean. I have proposed that groups are event-dependent entities, providing account for why lists of people are less likely to be construed as groups than collection terms. I have also shown how the present proposal can deal with other problems around groups.

* I am grateful to my advisor Pauline Jacobson for supporting this research, and to Emmon Bach for helpful comments on an earlier draft of this paper. I also thank Sam Bayer, Young-Suk Lee and Chris Kennedy for discussions on events and plurals. I am alone responsible, however, for any remaining errors.

References

Barker, C. (1992) "Group terms in English: Representing groups as atoms", *Journal of Semantics* 9 pp. 69-93.

Bayer, S. (1996) Confessions of a Lapsed Neo-Davidsonian, Ph. D. thesis Brown Univ.

Bennett, M. (1975) Some Extensions of a Montague Fragment of English, Ph. D. thesis, UCLA, IULC, Bloomington.

Davidson, D. (1967) "The Logical Form of Action Sentences", in *The logic of Decision and Action*, N. Rescher (ed.) Univ. of Pittsburgh Press, Pittsburgh.

Dowty, D. (1986) "Collective predicates, distributive predicates, and *all*", *ESCOL 86*, pp. 97-115.

Hoeksema, J. (1983) "Plurality and conjunction", in A. ter Meulen et al. (eds.), *Studies in Model-theoretic Semantics*, Foris, Dordrecht, pp. 63-83.

Hoeksema, J. (1988) "The semantics of non-boolean And", *Journal of Semantics* 6 pp. 19-40.

Krifka, M. (1990a) "Boolean and non-boolean and", in L. Kalman and L. Polos (eds.) Papers from the Second Symposium on Logic and Language, Akademiai Kiado, Budapest.

Kwak, E. (1995) "Korean and English Floated Quantifiers as Evidence for Event Semantics", L. Gabriele et al. (eds.), in *the Proceedings of Formal Linguistics Society of Mid-America*, pp. 127-137, Bloomington, Indiana.

Landman, F. (1989a) "Groups I", *Linguistics and Philosophy 12* pp. 559-606.

Landman, F. (1989b) "Groups II", *Linguistics and Philosophy 12* pp.723-744.

Lasersohn, P.(1988) *A Semantics for Groups and Events*, Ph.D. thesis, Ohio State University.

Lasersohn, P. (1995) *Plurality, conjunction and events*, Kluwer, Dordrecht.

Link, G.(1983) "The logical analysis of plurals and mass terms: a lattice-theoretic approach", in R. Bauerle et al. (eds.), *Meaning , Use, and Interpretation of Language*, Walter de Gruyter, Berlin and New York.

Link, G. (1984) "Hydras. On the logic of relativ constructions with multiple heads", in *Varieties of Formal Semantics*, F. Landman and F. Veltman (eds.), Foris Dordrecht.

Link, G. (1986) "Generalized Quantifiers and Plurals", in P. Gardenfors (ed.), *Generalized Quantifiers* , Reidel Publisher, pp. 151-180.

Roberts, C. (1986) *Modal Subordination, Anaphora and Distributivity*, Ph.D. thesis, Univ. of Massachusetts, Amherst.

Schwarzschild, R. (1992) "Types of plural individuals", *Linguistics and Philosophy 15* pp. 641-675.

Simons, P (1987) *Parts, A Study in Ontology*, Oxford University Press, Oxford.

Thomason, R. (1980) "A model theory for propositional attitudes", *Linguistics and Philosophy 4*.

Zwicky, A. and Sadock, J. (1975) "Ambiguity test and how to fail t hem", in *Syntax and Semantics vol. 4*, Academic Press, New York.

Topic and Focus in Korean: The Information Partition by Phrase Structure and Morphology*

HYE-WON CHOI
Stanford University

1 Introduction

The topic marker *nun/un* is known to encode a topic or contrastive reading, and the subject or nominative case marker *ka/i* to encode a presentational or focus reading in Korean, in parallel with *wa* and *ga* in Japanese.[1] This is shown in (1).

(1) a. Mary-nun John-ul manna-ko iss-ta.
    Mary-Top John-Acc meet-Inf be-Dcl
    'As for Mary, she is meeting John.'   [topic]
    'Mary (but not others) is meeting John.'   [contrastive]

  b. Mary-ka   John-ul manna-ko iss-ta.
    Mary-Nom John-Acc meet-Inf be-Dcl
    'Mary is meeting John.'   [presentational]
    'It is Mary who is meeting John.'   [focus]

---

*An earlier version of the paper was presented at the Workshop on Theoretical East Asian Linguistics, March 1995, University of California at Irvine. I am grateful to the audience there for their questions and comments. I also would like to thank Joan Bresnan, Jongbok Kim, Yookyung Kim, Peter Sells, and Henriëtte de Swart for their valuable discussions and comments on this and the earlier versions of the paper.

[1]The choice between *nun* and *un* or that between *ka* and *i*, or later the choice between *lul* and *ul*, is determined phonologically: the former is chosen when the preceding syllable ends in a vowel, and the latter, when it ends in a consonant. I will hereafter use the forms *nun*, *ka*, and *lul* respectively for convenience.

The subject *nun*-phrase in (1a) most prominently gets a topic reading, where the *nun*-phrase is interpreted as what the sentence is 'about', i.e. the topic or theme of the sentence (Reinhart 1982; Kuno 1972). This *nun*-phrase can also get a contrastive reading, where it is implied that 'Mary, but not others, is meeting John.'[2] On the other hand, the presentational reading conveyed by the *ka*-phrase in (1b) is parallel to the 'neutral description' reading in Kuno (1972, 1973) in the sense that "the entire sentence conveys new information" (1972:273). This is identifiable with Vallduví's (1993) 'all-focus' or 'no-topic' reading or the 'presentational focus' reading in Rochemont (1986) and in Herring (1990). The focus reading in (1b) is comparable with the 'exhaustive listing' reading in Kuno (1972, 1973).[3] It is a focus in the sense that it is the new or highlighted information while the rest of the sentence is given or presupposed information (Kim 1990).[4]

   This paper shows how each reading demonstrated in (1) is achieved in Korean by the morphological marking on one hand and the phrase structural configuration on the other. Section 2 discusses the readings encoded by *nun* and concludes that *nun* is a contrast marker which carries a presupposition of existence of other comparable entities in the discourse. Section 3 shows that topichood is encoded by scrambling in Korean, not by the topic marker *nun*. Section 4 follows up the problem raised in section 3 that focus is also encoded by scrambling and suggests that scrambling in Korean is a mechanism which gets a phrase out of the new-information domain.

2   Contrast Marking by *nun*

2.1   *Nun*-phrase in-situ

Though *nun* is often called a 'topic' marker, a *nun*-phrase in the base position only conveys a contrastive reading.   The in-situ object NP

---

[2]I use topic and contrastive as descriptive terms here. Each reading will be more carefully discussed and renamed later in section 2 when I discuss the difference between contrastive topic and contrastive focus.

[3]Kuno describes the focus reading carried by a *ga*-phrase in Japanese as exhaustive listing in the sense that the entity denoted by a *ga*-phrase is the all and only entity that satisfies the description of the sentence. However, the focus reading conveyed by a *ka*-phrase in Korean is not necessarily exhaustive listing since for example, *John-kwa Mary-ka ttokttokha-ta.* 'John and Mary are smart.' can infer *Mary-ka ttokttokha-ta.* 'Mary is smart.' See Szabolcsi (1981) for inference relations between exhaustively focused sentences.

[4]Here again, I use presentational and focus only as descriptive terms. Each reading will be identified as presentational focus and contrastive focus later in section 3.

John in (2b) and the locative PP *to Boston* in (3b), for example, only carry a contrastive reading.

(2) a. Mary-ka   ecey   John-ul   manna-ss-ta.
     Mary-Nom yesterday John-Acc meet-Pst-Dcl
     'Mary met John yesterday.'

   b. Mary-ka   ecey   John-un   manna-ss-ta.
     Mary-Nom yesterday John-Top meet-Pst-Dcl
     'Mary met John (but not others) yesterday.'

(3) a. Mary-ka   ecey   Boston-ey ka-ss-ta.
     Mary-Nom yesterday Boston-to go-Pst-Dcl
     'Mary went to Boston yesterday.'

   b. Mary-ka   ecey   Boston-ey-nun ka-ss-ta.
     Mary-Nom yesterday Boston-to-Top go-Pst-Dcl
     'Mary went to Boston yesterday (but not to other places).'

(2b) implies that 'Mary met John yesterday, but she did not meet anybody else.' and (3b) implies that 'Mary went to Boston, but she did not go to any other place.' In this sense, the contrastive reading here is 'exhaustive' (Han 1995).

A similar effect occurs in the existential construction, where the base position of the subject is not sentence-initial as shown in (4).[5]

(4) a. chayksang-wuyey chayk-i   iss-ta.
     desk-on   book-Nom be-Dcl
     'There is/are (a) book(s) on the desk.'

   b. chayksang-wuyey chayk-un iss-ta.
     desk-on   book-Top be-Dcl
     'There is/are (a) book(s) on the desk (but nothing else).'

A *nun*-marked NP in this position always gets a contrastive reading as in (4b), while a *ka*-marked NP in (4a) gets a neutral existential reading.

Now, let's look at the sentence-initial subject case again. As we have seen in the introduction, a subject marked with *nun* can get a topic reading as well as a contrastive reading as in (5).[6]

(5) Mary-nun John-ul   manna-ss-ta.
    Mary-Top John-Acc meet-Pst-Dcl
    'As for Mary, she met John.'
    'Mary (but not others) met John.'

---

[5]See Kuno (1973) for detailed arguments for the base order of the Japanese existential construction.

[6]It is true that the topic reading is predominant for the sentence-initial subject and that the contrastive reading requires some stress on the subject phrase. I think it is due to the fact that the sentence-initial subject is a default topic.

Let us assume that a sentence-initial subject is structurally ambiguous: in the base position versus in a scrambled position.[7] In accordance with the observation that a *nun*-phrase in the base position only receives a contrastive reading, let's assume that subject gets a contrastive reading when it is in the base position and that it receives a topic reading when it is in a scrambled position. In other words, the two readings in (5) are structurally distinguished.[8]

In distinction from the traditional belief that *nun* is a topic marker, it only encodes a contrastive reading of a phrase in the base position and a topic reading is possible only in a scrambled position. Then, we can hypothesize that the so-called topic marker *nun* in Korean is not a topic marker but a 'contrast' marker and moreover, that scrambling is the actual encoder of topichood. I will support this claim in the following sections by showing that i) even a scrambled *nun*-phrase retains a 'contrastive' interpretation (section 2); ii) a phrase which is marked with a particle other than *nun* can also convey topichood when it is scrambled (section 3).

2.2   What is Contrastive Reading?

Before we go into the discussion of the scrambling of *nun*-phrases, let us look more closely at the meaning of contrastiveness. The term 'contrastive' is often used indistinguishablly to cover two separable notions, CONTRASTIVE TOPIC and CONTRASTIVE FOCUS. Szabolcsi (1981:518-519) characterizes the difference between the two such that "by using a sentence with a contrastive topic, one suggests (or implicates) that the claim he is making need not be true of something else, whereas by using a contrastive focus one asserts that the claim he is making is in fact not true of anything else". Vallduví (1993) makes a similar observation. He distinguishes link(topic)-contrastive[9] from focus-contrastive and presents the following sentences in (6) as an example for each.

(6) a. **John** swept (and Mary mopped).
    b. JOHN swept (not Mary).

Differentiated by accent, *John* in (6a) is a contrastive topic and *John* in (6b) is a contrastive focus. While (6a) conversationally implicates that

---

[7] I use the term 'scrambling' in a broader sense that any phrase which is not in its default or canonical position is scrambled though the phrase may well be base-generated in that alternative position.

[8] Kim (1990) draws a similar generalization regarding the distribution of the neutral and contrastive readings of *nun*.

[9] He uses the term 'link' instead of 'topic'. We can identify 'link' with 'topic' for purposes of the present discussion.

'someone else did something other than sweeping (hence the appropriate continuation *and Mary mopped*)', (6b) implicates that 'no relevant person other than John swept (hence the appropriate continuation *not Mary*)'.

When we examine the sentences with *nun* marking in section 2.1 again with this distinction of contrast in mind, we see that a *nun*-phrase in the base position encodes 'contrastive focus'. The relevant examples are repeated in (7).

(7) a. Mary-ka   ecey   John-un manna-ss-ta.
    Mary-Nom yesterday John-Top meet-Pst-Dcl
    'Mary met John (but not others) yesterday.'

  b. Mary-ka   ecey   Boston-ey-nun ka-ss-ta.
    Mary-Nom yesterday Boston-to-Top go-Pst-Dcl
    'Mary went to Boston yesterday (but not to other places).'

  c. chayksang-wuyey chayk-un iss-ta.
    desk-on   book-Top be-Dcl
    'There is/are (a) book(s) on the desk (but nothing else).'

Each sentence in (7) implies that the claim it is making is not true of anything else than the entity marked by *nun*, i.e. a contrastive focus reading as Szabolcsi and Vallduví define it.

2.3 Scrambling of a *nun*-phrase

The object *nun*-phrase *John* in situ in (8a) receives a contrastive focus reading as described in section 2.2. When the *nun*-marked phrase *John* is scrambled leftward as in (8b) or (8c), however, it gets a contrastive topic reading.

(8) a. Mary-ka   ecey   John-un manna-ss-ta.
    Mary-Nom yesterday John-Top meet-Pst-Dcl
    'Mary met John yesterday (but nobody else).'

  b. Mary-ka   John-un ecey   manna-ss-ta.
    Mary-Nom John-Top yesterday meet-Pst-Dcl
    'Mary met John yesterday (and Bill today).'

  c. John-un Mary-ka   ecey   manna-ess-ta.
    John-Top Mary-Nom yesterday meet-Pst-Dcl
    'As for John, Mary met him yesterday (and as for Bill, Jane met him today).'

The *nun*-phrase *John* in (8c) is the topic of the sentence in the sense that it is what the sentence is 'about'. But it is also 'contrastive' in the sense that it implies that the claim that the sentence is making need not be true of something else or that some other claim may be true of something else, and thus make the continuation in the parenthesis in (8c) appropriate. Contrastive topic is also called SHIFTED TOPIC as opposed to CONTINUING TOPIC (Herring 1990; Aissen 1992). A contrastive or shifted topic, which is often signaled by left dislocation or an *as for* phrase in English, is used to "turn the attention of the hearer to some identifiable participant in the discourse, and then to assert something of that participant until some other entity is introduced as topic" (Aissen 1992:50). It can bring a new topic to the discourse or reactivate an old topic.

(8b) is interesting in that the scrambled phrase has an intermediate status as a topic. In (8b), the *nun*-phrase *John* is scrambled to a medial position of the sentence and it achieves a relative topichood, so to speak, with respect to the rest of the sentence. Furthermore, it is contrastive in the sense that the existence of some other entity or entities are implied, so the phrases in the parenthesis in (8b) can be a possible continuation. It seems that topichood of a *nun*-phrase is gained gradually as it moves along to the initial position of the sentence. To put it in a different way, as a *nun*-phrase moves forward, the rest of the sentence left behind becomes 'comment' to that moved phrase. It seems that topichood is in a continuum with an increasing degree from the base position to the sentence-initial position.[10]

Similar points can be made with the scrambling of a locative phrase in (9) and of a subject in the existential construction in (10).

(9) a. Mary-ka   ecey   Boston-ey-nun ka-ss-ta.
     Mary-Nom yesterday Boston-to-Top go-Pst-Dcl
     'Mary went to Boston yesterday (but not to other places).'

   b. Mary-ka   Boston-ey-nun ecey   ka-ss-ta.
      Mary-Nom Boston-to-Top yesterday go-Pst-Dcl
      'Mary went to Boston yesterday (and to San Francisco, today).'

   c. Boston-ey-nun Mary-ka   ecey   ka-ss-ta.
      Boston-to-Top Mary-Nom yesterday go-Pst-Dcl
      'To Boston, Mary went yesterday (and to San Francisco, John went today).'

(10) a. chayksang-wuyey chayk-un iss-ta.
      desk-on   book-Top be-Dcl
      'There is/are a book(s) on the desk (but nothing else).'

---

[10] Henriette de Swart (p.c.) pointed out that this phenomenon is close to the scale of communicative dynamism adopted by the Prague School.

b. chayk-un chayksang-wuyey iss-ta.
  book-Top desk-on   be-Dcl
  'The book(s) is on the desk (and the pencil(s) on the floor).'

The in-situ *nun*-phrase in (9a) or (10a) is a contrastive focus while the scrambled *nun*-phrase in (9b), (9c), or in (10b) is a contrastive topic.

To sum up, I argue that *nun* is a contrast marker, not a topic marker. *Nun* is contrastive in that it implies the existence of other comparable entities in the discourse.[11] In other words, it invokes a C(ontext)-set in Rooth's (1992) sense. In the base position, a *nun*-phrase has a strong 'focus' property enough to make the *nun*-phrase 'exhaustive', while it loses the 'focus' property as it scrambles leftward and gains a 'topic' property instead. In other words, it is the leftward movement part, not the marker *nun* itself, which gives a *nun*-phrase its topicality. On the other hand, it is the contrastive marker *nun* which makes a scrambled topic phrase retain a meaning of contrastiveness even in the sentence-initial position.

3 Scrambling and Discourse Effects

3.1 Presentational and Focus Reading

Now let us turn our attention to the two readings encoded by *ka*, i.e. a presentational and a focus reading, as shown in (1b) in the introduction and repeated here as (11).

(11) Mary-ka   John-ul   manna-ko iss-ta.
    Mary-Nom John-Acc meet-Inf   be-Dcl
    'There's Mary meeting John.'   [presentational]
    'It is Mary (not others) who is meeting John.' [focus]

A presentational reading involves the introduction of a referent into a discourse, so it involves 'new' information in the discourse. The whole sentence is 'new' in the first reading in (11). A focus reading, on the other hand, does not necessarily involve new information, though it can. Its major function is to "highlight a constituent in a sentence in contradistinction to a parallel phrase" (Herring 1990:164). In the second reading in (11), *Mary* is singled out as a focus.

Now let's see whether these two readings can be structurally distinguished. It is often noted that the subject of an individual-level

---

[11] Han (in this volume) also argues that a *nun*-phrase X-*nun* carries a presupposition, $\exists x(x \neq X)$. However, she proposes it to be only relevant to VP-internal *nun*-phrases or in-situ *nun*-phrases in my sense.

predicate cannot receive a presentational reading, but only gets a focus reading in Korean (Kim 1990).

(12) Mary-ka   ttokttokha-ta.
Mary-Nom smart-Dcl
'It is Mary who is smart.'

An individual-level predicate has been argued to be distinct from a stage-level predicate in that its subject only takes an external position, i.e. Spec of IP as opposed to Spec of VP, for instance (Kratzer 1989; Diesing 1992). If we assume that this external position is an automatically scrambled position distinct from the default subject position in Korean, then we can argue that a focus reading is achieved by scrambling.

The example in (13), in contrast, is a construction which forces a presentational reading, in parallel with the presentational *there*-construction in English.

(13) a. yeysnal-ey han maul-ey Swuni-lanun ai-ka   sal-ass-ta.
past-in   one village Swuni-named child-Nom live-Pst-Dcl
'Once upon a time, there lived a child named Swuni in a village.'

b. #Swuni-lanun ai-ka   yeysnal-ey han maul-ey sal-ass-ta.
Swuni-named child-Nom past-in   one village live-Pst-Dcl
'Once upon a time, it is a child named Swuni who lives in
a village.'

The subject *ka*-phrase in the unmarked order in (13a) gets a presentational reading. When we scramble the subject phrase as in (13b), the sentence becomes odd. If scrambling generates a focus reading as we assumed above, the oddness of (13b) is easily explained: the construction itself forces a presentational reading whereas the scrambling pushes for a focus reading, thus causing an interpretational clash.

Similarly, the in-situ *ka*-phrase in (14a) yields a presentational reading, while the scrambled *ka*-phrase in (14b) yields a focus reading.

(14) a. chayksang-wuyey chayk-i   nohi-e iss-ta.
desk-on   book-Nom lie-Inf be-Dcl
'There is/are (a) book(s) lying on the desk.'

b. chayk-i   chayksang-wuyey nohi-e iss-ta.
book-Nom desk-on   lie-Inf be-Dcl
'It is (a) book(s) that is/are on the desk.'

To sum up this section, the distributional generalization seems to be that a *ka*-marked phrase gets a presentational reading when it is in the base position, and gets a focus reading when it is scrambled.

3.2 Topic Marking by *ka*

The so-called topic marker *nun* and the nominative case marker *ka* in Korean show a striking parallelism with the Japanese correlates *wa* and *ga* respectively. The former encodes a topic or contrastive focus reading and the latter encodes a presentational or focus reading (Kim 1992; Kuno 1972, 1973). However, *ka* in Korean is different from *ga* in Japanese in that a *ka*-phrase in Korean can provide a topic of a sentence unlike the case in Japanese (see Haig (1982) for detailed comparison). Let's look at (15).

(15) a. yeysnal-ey han maul-ey Swuni-lanun ai-ka   sal-ass-ta.
        past-in   one village Swuni-named child-Nom live-Pst-Dcl
        'Once upon a time there lived a child named Swuni in a village.'

     b. Swuni-ka   halwu-nun   yeph maul-ey   nolleka-ss-ta.
        Swuni-Nom one day-Top next village-to visit-Pst-Dcl
        'One day, Swuni visited the next-door village.'

The *ka*-marked phrase *Swuni-lanun ai* 'a child named Swuni' in (15a) is a presentational focus: it is newly introduced into the discourse. The *ka*-marked phrase *Swuni* in (15b), however, is no longer new information because it is carried over from the preceding discourse. It is also a topic because it is what the sentence (15b) is about. These two characteristics make it a 'continuing topic' as defined by Herring (1990) or Aissen (1992). A continuing topic should be distinguished from a contrastive or shifted topic. Remember that a scrambled *nun*-phrase was argued to be a contrastive or shifted topic in section 2.[12]

Similarly, the *ka*-marked phrase *cicin* 'earthquake' in (16) behaves as a continuing topic: it consistently marks old information except for the first occurrence in the first sentence, where it gets a presentational reading.

(16) a: Kobe-eyse cicin-i   na-ss-e.
        Kobe-in   earthquake-Nom break out-Pst-Dcl
        'There was an earthquake in Kobe.'

---

[12]The following sentence with the subject marked with *nun* is also possible as a continuation of (15a).

(i) Swuni-nun halwu-nun   yeph maul-ey   nolleka-ss-ta.
    Swuni-Top one day-Top next village-to visit-Pst-Dcl
    'One day, Swuni visited the next-door village.'

Though *Swuni* here is given or old information because it is mentioned in the preceding discourse, the *nun* marking seems to refresh the hearer's attention and thus *Swuni* gets reintroduced or reactivated into the discourse. In this sense, *Swuni* is a contrastive or shifted topic rather than a continuing topic.

    b: cicin-i   encey na-ss-e?
      earthquake-Nom when break out-Pst-Int
      'When did the earthquake happen?'

    b': #cicin-un   encey na-ss-e?
      earthquake-Top when break out-Pst-Int
      'When did the earthquake happen?'

    c: cicin-i   ecey   na-ss-e.
      earthquake-Nom yesterday break out-Pst-Int
      'The earthquake happened yesterday.'

    c': #cicin-un   ecey   na-ss-e.
      earthquake-Top yesterday break out-Pst-Int
      'The earthquake happened yesterday.'

It is notable that the *nun* marking is not very natural in this case. Since *nun* marks a contrastive or shifted topic, it is not appropriate in this context.[13]

I have argued in section 3.1 that a presentational reading is generated in the base position and a focus reading is produced in a scrambled position. Then where does a continuing topic reading come from? I argued in section 2 in discussing the distribution of *nun* that scrambling, not *nun*, is the actual encoder of topichood. Then the default expectation would be that a *ka*-phrase also gets a topic reading in a scrambled position. This indeed is the case. The *ka*-marked phrase *Mary* in (17) as a subject of an individual-level predicate can get a topic reading. The only difference from a *nun*-marked topic is that it lacks contrastiveness. It can get a focus reading as well, as we have seen in section 3.1.

(17) a. Mary-ka   cham ttokttokha-ta.
      Mary-Nom really smart-Dcl
      'Mary is really smart.'

    b. Mary-ka   yeyppu-ko ttokttokha-ta.
      Mary-Nom pretty-and smart-Dcl
      'Mary is pretty and smart.'

    c. Mary-ka   elkwul-i yeyppu-ta.
      Mary-Nom face-Nom pretty-Dcl
      'Mary has a beautiful face.'

---

[13] Haig (1982) presents similar examples in Korean and compares them with parallel sentences in Japanese. Interestingly, the corresponding Japanese examples with *ga* marking are not acceptable. *Ga* should be replaced by *wa* in Japanese.

Likewise, a scrambled *ka*-phrase in an existential construction can also get a (continuing) topic reading as well as a focus reading, while an in-situ *ka*-phrase gets a presentational reading as shown in (18).

(18) a. chayksang-wuyey chayk-i   nohi-e iss-ta.
       desk-on   book-Nom lie-Inf be-Dcl
       'There is/are (a) book(s) lying on the desk.'

    b. chayk-i   chayksang-wuyey nohi-e iss-ta.
       book-Nom desk-on   lie-Inf be-Dcl
       'The book(s) is/are lying on the desk.'
       'It is (a) book(s) that is/are on the desk.'

To recapitulate the discussion regarding the distribution of a *ka*-phrase, a *ka*-phrase in situ carries a presentational reading, whereas a scrambled *ka*-phrase conveys either a focus or a topic reading.

3.3 Scrambling of a *lul*-phrase

If the discourse effect of topic and focus on the subject *ka*-phrase is really induced by scrambling as we argued in 3.1 and 3.2, then we can predict that the same effect is achieved with object scrambling too. And this prediction is well borne out. Look at the examples in (19).

(19) a. Mary-ka   ecey   John-ul   manna-ss-ta.
       Mary-Nom yesterday John-Acc meet-Pst-Dcl
       'Mary met John yesterday.'

    b. Mary-ka   John-ul   ecey   manna-ss-ta.
       Mary-Nom John-Acc yesterday meet-Pst-Dcl
       'Mary met John yesterday.'
       'Mary met John (among other people) yesterday.'

    c. John-ul   Mary-ka   ecey   manna-ss-ta.
       John-Acc Mary-Nom yesterday meet-Pst-Dcl
       'John, Mary met yesterday.'
       'It is John (among other people) who Mary met yesterday.'

The object phrase, *John* with accusative case marking as in (19a) gets a presentational focus reading in the base position in the sense that it is newly introduced in the discourse. As the object phrase *John* moves to a medial position as in (19b), it gets partial topicality with respect to the rest of the sentence, though the topic of the whole sentence is the subject *Mary*. Accordingly, *John* here is not presented as new information as it is in (19a), but as sort of old information with respect to the rest of the predicate. In addition, the scrambled object in the medial position gets a focus reading although this focus is not as strong as it is in the initial position as in (19c). In (19c), *John* now is the topic of the whole sentence including the subject *Mary*. Here the subject *Mary*, as well as the other elements of the sentence, is given as new information. Recall that object scrambling with *lul* marking is quite comparable to that with *nun* marking except that the *nun* marking consistently carries contrastiveness. There too, leftward movement gradually enforces the topicality of a moved phrase. Finally, the scrambled object *lul*-phrase in the initial position, just like a scrambled subject *ka*-phrase, gets a focus reading.

Now we can generalize for all the discussion above that scrambling or leftward movement out of a base position can give a moved phrase a topic reading, in addition to a focus reading, whether it is subject or object, whether it is marked *nun*, *ka*, or *lul*.

4   Topic and Contrastive Focus

(20) is the summary of the the distribution of the readings which an in-situ and a scrambled phrase can have in Korean.

(20)

	scrambled	in-situ
nun	contrastive topic	contrastive focus
ka, lul	continuing topic	presentational focus
	contrastive focus	

As shown in section 3, scrambling of a non-*nun*-phrase not only encodes topichood of a phrase, but also encodes a focus reading. This means that a phrase can be interpreted as topic or as focus in the same structural configuration. This phenomenon immediately raises a question why the same structural position or the same syntactic mechanism would yield such different readings as topic and focus; it is generally believed that topic and focus are distinct and even opposite notions in terms of informational status: topic is 'old' information and focus is 'new' information.

To answer this question, it should be noted, first of all, that 'focus' is not a uniform notion. Herring (1990:164) suggests that there are two types of focus, i.e. PRESENTATIONAL and CONTRASTIVE, and argues that "the information status of contrastive focus and presentational focus differs, in that arguments presented for the first time (e.g. as participants in a narrative) are completely new, while contrastively focused arguments are already explicitly or implicitly present in the discourse context". She takes an expression introduced by a *there*-construction and an *it*-cleft construction in English as a typical example of presentational and contrastive focus respectively, as shown in (21).

(21) a. Once upon a time, there was a beautiful princess.
     b. It's John (not Sidney) that I love.

Similarly, Rochemont (1986) and Rochemont and Culicover (1990) argue that a contrastive focus, unlike a presentational focus, does not have to be new information. For example, *JOHN* or *HIM* in (21b) is focused, but it is not new information since it is already mentioned in the prior discourse as in (22a). It is 'contrastively' focused.

(22) a. Who does John's mother like?
     b. John's mother likes JOHN/HIM.

Using the notion of C-CONSTRUABILITY, which is defined to be 'under discussion' or to 'have a semantic/pragmatic antecedent in the discourse' (Rochemont 1986:47; Rochemont and Culicover 1990:20), they define a presentational focus as 'not c-construable', but they don't define a contrastive focus to have such restriction.[14] In short, a presentational focus is discourse-new, but a contrastive focus is not.

Now let us look at a focus reading again. According to the distinction described above, it is a contrastive focus rather than a 'new-information' type of focus. Recall that an in-situ *nun*-phrase also encodes a contrastive focus. Though a contrastive focus encoded by scrambling is a bit different from a contrastive focus encoded by the morphology *nun* in that in the former case, the non-focused material is presupposed (Kim 1990), we can generalize both as not being purely new in the discourse.

It is true, however, that a contrastively focused material can be 'new' in a sense. Let's look at (23).

(23) a. chayksang-wuyey mwues-i   iss-ni?
        desk-on   what-Nom be-Int
        'What is there on the desk?' [presentational focus]

---

[14]Rochemont (1986:52) defines the presentational focus and the contrastive focus as follows:

(i) Presentational Focus:
    An expression P is a Presentational Focus in a discourse δ, $\delta = \{\varphi_1, ..., \varphi_n\}$, if, and only if,
    (i) P is an expression in φ_i, and
    (ii) at the time of utterance of φ_i in δ, P is not c-construable.

(ii) Contrastive Focus:
    An expression P is a Contrastive Focus in a discourse δ, $\delta = \{\varphi_1, ..., \varphi_n\}$, if, and only if,
    (i) P is an expression in φ_i, and
    (ii) if P/φ_i is the result of extracting P from φ_i is c-construable, and φ_i is not c-construable.

    a'. mwues-i chayksang-wuyey iss-ni?
       what   desk-on   be-Int
       'What is it that is on the desk?' [contrastive focus]

    b. chayksang-wuyey chayk-i   iss-e.
      desk-on   book-Nom be-Dcl
      'There is/are (a) book(s) on the desk.' [presentational focus]

    b'. chayk-i   chayksang-wuyey iss-e.
      book-Nom desk-on   be-Dcl
      'It is (a) book(s) that is/are on the desk.' [contrastive focus]

(23b), with the base word order, is the usual answer to the question in (23a). Here, *chayk* 'book' in the base position is a presentational or new-information focus. Actually, (23b') can be an answer, if not the best answer, to the same question (23a) as well: thus the scrambled *chayk* 'book' can be 'new' information in the sense that 'book' is an answer to 'what', the unknown part, and the rest of the sentence is given or old information. But this is not purely new. The sentence (23b') has a connotation that 'among the things we are talking about, it is (a) BOOK(s), not other things, that is/are on the desk'. In other words, (23b') has an impression that 'books', with other things, are implicitly, if not explicitly, present in the discourse. This discourse property of (23b') makes it not the best way to answer (23a). In fact, (23b') makes a better answer to the question where *mwues* 'what' is also scrambled to the initial position as in (23a'). In (23a'), the scrambled *mwues* 'what' has the same connotation as the scrambled phrase *chayk* 'book' in (23b'). Interestingly, (23b) is odd as an answer to the question (23a'). It is because the question phrase is a contrastive focus while the answer phrase is a presentational focus, which causes an informational clash.

    Let's look at a topic reading case in (24) in comparison with the contrastive focus case in (23).

(24) a. chayk-i   eti-ey   iss-ni?
       book-Nom where-at be-Int
       'Where is/are the book(s)?' [topic]

    b. chayk-i   chayksang-wuyey iss-e.
      book-Nom desk-on   be-Dcl
      'The book(s) is/are on the desk.' [topic]

    b'. #chayksang-wuyey chayk-i   iss-e.
       desk-on   book-Nom be-Dcl
       'There is/are (a) book(s) on the desk.' [presentational focus]

While (24b) is an appropriate answer to the question (24a), (24b')
is not. The reason is, as predicted, that while the scrambled phrase
chayk 'book' in (24b) is a topic, especially, a continuing topic, the
non-scrambled phrase *chayk* 'book' in (24b') is not a topic but a presentational focus. A topic is something that is 'under discussion' by
definition and thus c-construable in the sense of Rochemont (1986) or
Rochemont and Culicover (1990). In other words, a topic is certainly
not 'new' information while a presentational focus is 'new' information.
Therefore, just like (23), (24) is another case where old information
clashes with new information.

Now, let's try to answer the question of why the apparently different
notions of topic and contrastive focus are encoded by the same syntactic mechanism, i.e. scrambling in Korean. Or what is it that is common between topic and contrastive focus? As shown in (23) and (24),
topic and contrastive focus have it in common that they are distinct
from presentational focus in that they are NOT 'new' in the discourse.
Both topic and contrastive focus are the entities which are implicitly
or explicitly present in the discourse. In this sense, we can argue that
scrambling in Korean, as well as the morphological *nun* marking, is a
mechanism to get a phrase out of the presentational focus domain, i.e.
the base position, and thus to make it a topic or a contrastive focus.
Accordingly, I propose (25) as the discourse constraint on scrambling
in Korean.

(25) A scrambled phrase in Korean is not discourse-new.

5 Conclusion

In this paper, I first examined the distribution of the two readings of
nun, topic and contrastive, and argued that the so-called topic marker
nun in Korean does not actually mark topichood but marks contrastiveness of a phrase in the sense that it presupposes that there are other
entities than the entity marked with *nun* in the discourse. Thus, the
topic reading which a scrambled *nun*-phrase gets is a contrastive topic
(as opposed to a continuing topic), while the contrastive reading that
an in-situ *nun*-phrase receives is a contrastive focus.

Then, I proposed that scrambling is the real encoder of topichood. I
first showed that a *ka*-phrase in Korean, unlike a *ga*-phrase in Japanese,
can mark topichood. Then I generalized that any phrase in Korean,
regardless of its morphological marking, can get a topic reading when
it is scrambled.

Finally, I tried to answer the question of why a scrambled phrase
not only gets a topic reading in Korean but also receives a contrastive

focus reading. I argued that topic and contrastive focus have it in common that they are not purely new information in the discourse, and that scrambling in Korean is the mechanism to get a phrase out of the domain of purely new information.

References

AISSEN, JUDITH. 1992. Topic and focus in Mayan. *Language* 68.43–80.

DIESING, MOLLY. 1992. *Indefinites*. Cambridge, MA: MIT Press.

HAN, CHUNG-HYE, 1995. A syntactic account of the ambiguity of the topic marker *-(n)un* in Korean. Presented in the 6th Japanese/Korean Linguistics Conference, to appear in the proceedings.

HERRING, SUSAN C. 1990. Information structure as a consequence of word order type. In *Proceedings of BLS*, 163–174.

KIM, KWANG-SUP. 1990. Where do the constrastive and focus readings come from? In *Japanese/Korean Linguistics*, ed. by Hajime Hoji, 395–412.

KRATZER, ANGELIKA. 1989. Stage and individual level predicates. In *Papers on Quantification*. NSF Grant Report, Department of Linguistics, University of Massachusetts, Amherst.

KUNO, SUSUMU. 1972. Functional sentence perspective: A case study from Japanese and English. *Linguistic Inquiry* 3.269–320.

——. 1973. *The Structure of the Japanese Language*. Cambridge, MA: MIT Press.

REINHART, TANYA, 1982. Pragmatics and linguistics: An analysis of sentence topics. MS. Distributed by the Indiana University Linguistics Club.

ROCHEMONT, MICHAEL S. 1986. *Focus in Generative Grammar*. Amsterdam: John Benjamins.

——, & PETER W. CULICOVER. 1990. *English Focus Constructions and the Theory of Grammar*. Cambridge: Cambridge University Press.

ROOTH, MATS EDWARD. 1992. A theory of focus interpretation. *Natural Language Semantics* 1.75–116.

SZABOLCSI, ANNA. 1981. The semantics of topic-focus articulation. In *Formal Methods in the Study of Language*, ed. by T. M. V. Jannsen & M. B. J. Stokhoj, 513–540. Amsterdam: Mathematisch Centrum.

VALLDUVÍ, ENRIC, 1993. Information packaging: A survey. MS. Centre for Cognitive Science and Human Communication Research Centre, University of Edinburgh.

Part VI

Discourse

An Exploration of Sentence-Final Uses of the Quotative Particle in Japanese Spoken Discourse

MAKOTO HAYASHI

Univeristy of Colorado at Boulder

1. Introduction: The phenomenon[*]

Examining my corpus of spontaneous spoken Japanese, I have encountered a number of occurrences of the quotative particle *to* sentence-finally. This syntactic pattern is of interest because it is in a sense deviant from the 'canonical' occurrences of the particle. According to traditional Japanese grammar, the quotative particle *to* occurs following the 'quoted' clause and preceding the main-clause predicate (typically, verbs of saying or thinking). Consider the following invented examples (the quoted clause is shown in square brackets; abbreviations used for the interlinear gloss are found in Appendix 1):

(1)   a. [*'Kenji wa   daidokoro ni iru yo'*]-*to Mari wa   itta.*
             Kenji TOP kitchen   in be FP TO Mari TOP said
             'Mari said, "Kenji is in the kitchen".'

     b. *Kenji wa [Mari ga   kita] -to omotta.*
            Kenji TOP Mari SUBJ came TO thought
            'Kenji thought that Mari had come.'

---

[*] I wish to thank Barbara Fox, Zygmunt Frajzyngier, Bob Jasperson, Lise Menn, Laura Michaelis, Yuriko Suzuki, and Sandy Thompson for their helpful comments on earlier drafts. Thanks also go to Pat Clancy, whose feedback at the conference inspired substantial rethinking of the material for the present study.

In spontaneous spoken discourse, however, it is observed that *to* sometimes occurs at the end of the sentence. The following excerpt shows such a sentence-final use of *to* (in the arrowed turn):[1]

(2) (Girlfriend 30)

    C: *dakara ore <u>ga:</u> aitaku   naru   to:- au n da na.*
        so   I   SUBJ meet:want become when meet NR be FP
        'So, when I want to meet her, I meet her.'

        (so)re dake no   koto da na.
        that just GEN matter be FP
        'That's it.'

        (1.1)

--> K: *a ja   mukoo   ga   ojihi de atte kureru **to**.*
       oh then the.other.side SUBJ mercy with meet give   TO
       'Oh, so, it's that she is merciful enough to meet you.'

Although sentence-final uses of the quotative particle as seen in (2) are recurrently attested in my corpus of spoken Japanese, they have rarely been described or analyzed in the past literature. In the present study, then, I will examine various instances of sentence-final uses of *to* (and *(t)te*), and explore their workings in spoken discourse.[2]

2. The data

Instances of sentence-final uses of *to* for this study are culled from transcripts of spoken Japanese, most of which represent naturally-occurring conversations (the participants include speakers of the Tokyo and Kansai varieties of the language). Some instances are taken from radio and TV broadcasts.

3. Exploring the workings of sentence-final *to*

As suggested by the term 'quotative', uses of *to* in general appear to involve 'quotation' in one sense or another, and thus are inherently associated with REPORTED SPEECH. Now, when the particle is deployed sentence-finally in spoken discourse, various aspects of its being a marker of

---

[1] I am grateful to Ryoko Suzuki and Tsuyoshi Ono for the use of their conversational data for this study. For transcript notations, see Appendix 2.

[2] *(T)te* is often described as a colloquial variant of *to* (cf. *Nihon Kokugo Daijiten*), and in this study, they are treated as different realizations of essentially the same particle. Thus, when the text refers to 'sentence-final *to*', it includes reference to *(t)te* occurring sentence-finally. Note, however, that Mayes (1991) proposes a possible scenario for two different origins for these particles.

reported speech are highlighted so as to manage interactional concerns between the speaker and hearer(s). In particular, I will argue that *to* deployed sentence-finally emerges as a device to invoke 'another voice' in one's utterances, and thereby to deal in some contexts with the attribution of RESPONSIBILITY (in the sense used in the works in Hill & Irvine 1993) for the utterance made in talk in social interaction.

In the ensuing subsections, I will examine various sorts of sentence-final uses of *to* in spoken discourse. For convenience, I classify the instances of sentence-final *to* into four types, and discuss them one by one. Note however that they are by no means discrete categories; they are best understood to be gradient ones.

3.1 Marking direct quotes of speech fragments

Let us first examine sentence-final uses of *to* in a prototypical case of reported speech, i.e. *to* serving as a marker of direct quotes of speech fragments produced by some speaker. One might argue that this type of sentence-final *to* results from 'omitting' a verb of saying that would follow it in a 'canonical' sentence (see (1) above). As it happens, all the instances of this type of sentence-final *to* in my database contain explicit mentions of verbs of saying in immediately preceding discourse (in boldface in (3) and (4)).[3] The presence of such verbs appears to help the recipient(s) interpret the clause marked by sentence-final *to* as being another fragment of speech/writing/etc. Consider the following excerpts (the square brackets in the transcript indicate the clauses that *to* (or *tte*) marks):

(3) (TI 351)
>   T: *DAtte:: .hh aha [imootosan desu ka] tte*   **yutte** *sonoTSUGI*
>   because   sister   be Q QUOT said   very.next

-->   *ni deta   kotoba [sokkuri   d(h)esu ne:] tte.*
         PT came.out   word   just.alike be   FP TO

         .hh chotto ga::nto kite sh(h)imatt(h)a yo.
         just   shocked come finished   FP

---

[3] It is not clear if the presence of verbs of saying in the immediate linguistic contexts is a necessary condition for this use of *to*. The following (made-up, single-sentence) example cited in Martin (1975:918) appears to be intuitively acceptable without a verb of saying in its proximity:

>   (i) *Kare wa   mata   kuru   to sa.*
>   he   TOP   again   come   TO PT
>   "(He said) that he will come again."

'Because, (he) **said**, "Are you his sister?" and the very next word
that came out, "You look just like him!" -- I was just dazed!"'

(4) (Surprise 56)
    M: *atashi mo sono toki **kaichatta*** *wa yo:.* (1.3) *ichioo*   *daka(ra)*
          I   also that time have.written FP FP   basically so

         [*SANgatsu ne:?*=
         March   FP

    K: =*u:n.*=
         uh.huh

    M: =*gejun ni atashi mo* *keikosan mo* *yasumi da* *kaRA::* //.hh
         end   at I   also Keiko   also break be because

-->   *kitaRA::*]   ***tte.***=
       why.not.come TO

    K: *un.*
         uh.huh

    M: =*demo satokoyan ga*   *kuru to*   *wa omoenai*   *kara*
         but   Satoko   SUBJ come QUOT TOP cannot.think because

         [*atashitachi mo ikoo*   *to*   *wa*   *omou kedo:* .h//hh
         we   also will.go QUOT TOP think but

    K: *un:.*
         uh.huh

    M: *demo* (0.6) *yooroppa no*   *koto mo arushi* *ne:*
         but   Europe   GEN thing also exists FP

         shikinmen   *de:* .hh *mondai* *ga*   *aru*   *kara*   *maa*
         financial.aspect in   problem SUBJ exist because well

-->   *imanotokoro hatena*   *maaku desu*] ***to***.
       for.now   question mark   be   TO

'So I **wrote** (to Satoko). Like, "Around the end of March both
Keiko and I will have holidays, so why don't you come." But I
don't think Satoko will come, so "We too want to come (to your
place) but since we have a plan to go to Europe and that'd cause us
a financial problem, (our visit to your place) is a question mark for

now.'" (K's brief responses are omitted from the translation.)

In (3), T is describing her encounter with her brother's old friend -- let's call him 'A' for convenience -- whom she met for the first time. In this excerpt, she is recounting what A said to her at that occasion. A's first utterance reproduced by T, 'Are you his sister?', is followed by *tte* and a verb of saying (*yutte* 'said'). T then produces what appears to be a 'quotation-framing' phrase (*sono tsugi ni deta kotoba* 'the very next word that came out'), followed by a clause corresponding to 'You look just like him!'. Obviously, the previous sentence as well as the quotation-framing phrase help the recipient understand that this clause is another report of what A said to her. Nonetheless, it is important to observe that *tte* (and only *tte*) appears after the direct quote and serves to indicate that what preceded it is a fragment of reported speech.

Similarly, in (4), M describes what she wrote in her letter to 'Satoko'. At the beginning of this excerpt, M utters the verb *kaichatta* 'have written'. What she wrote in the letter, which she subsequently reports, is marked only by the quotative *to* or *tte*. The clause corresponding to 'Around the end of March, both Keiko and I will have a break, so why don't you come' is followed only by *tte*, and the one corresponding to 'We too want to come (to your place) but since we have a plan to go to Europe and that'd cause us a financial problem, (our visit to your place) is a question mark for now' is followed only by *to*. Again, these two sentence final quotative particles serve to mark direct quotes of speech fragments (in this case, ones produced by the speaker herself in the past).

These excerpts of naturally-occurring conversations suggest that *to* (or *tte*) is deployed sentence-finally in the context in which the speaker is introducing 'another voice' (which could be of his/her own produced on another occasion) in his/her utterance. To use Goffman's (1981) terms, *to* and *tte* observed in (3) and (4) emerge sentence-finally in the FOOTING where the speaker casts him/herself in the role of ANIMATOR, an individual who merely utters a sentence whose authorship may not belong to him/herself.[4] In this sense, the deployment of sentence-final *to* can be seen to serve to invoke 'double-voiced' utterances.

---

[4] Goffman (1981) distinguishes several possible realizations of a 'speaker'; as an 'animator', as an 'author', and as a 'principal'. The 'animator' is 'an individual active in the role of utterance production'; the 'author' is 'someone who has selected the sentiments that are being expressed and the words in which they are encoded'; and the 'principal' is 'someone whose position is established by the words that are spoken, someone whose beliefs have been told, someone who is committed to what the words say' (p.144).

3.2 Marking hearsay

There is a collection of instances of sentence-final *(t)te*[5] which appears to be closely related to that discussed in the previous subsection, and yet the focus of whose function appears to be somewhat different from them. Perhaps because of the strong association of the quotative particle with reported speech, the particle has come to be employed as an independent evidential marker indicating that the source of knowledge is hearsay (cf. Aoki 1986, Martin 1975). This use of *(t)te* then focuses not so much on quoting speech fragments produced by some speaker, as on displaying the sources of evidence for knowledge as located outside the actual speaker. Consider the following excerpts:

(5) (TI 54)
    H: *are wa ichiji   kaijoo de ichiji   han ni hajimaru*
       that TOP one.o'clock opening be one.o'clock half at start

-->   *n   //da **tte**:.*
       NR be TO

       'About that (=a party), (they say/I hear) that the place opens at one o'clock and (the party) starts at one-thirty.'

    T: *.hh a HOMMA:.*
         oh really
        'Oh, really!?'

(6) (TI 448)
    H: *de yuukosan te   sa:.*
       and Yuko   QUOT FP
       'And Yuko,'

    T: *un.=*
       uh.huh

--> H: *=amerika de umaeten **te**: (hh) (hh)*
       America in was.born TO
       '(I hear) that (she) was born in America.'

---

[5] In my database, *to* does not appear in this type of sentence-final quotative. It is not clear whether *(t)te* has completely replaced *to* in this context. Although I have not done any research on this, I have the impression that older speakers and/or speakers of some dialects might use *to* sentence-finally for marking hearsay evidential.

I: *A! SOO:::::::::.*
    oh right
    'Oh! Is that right!'

In (5) and (6), the clauses that are marked by sentence-final *(t)te* are not direct quotations of somebody's speech or writing. Rather, the particles in these cases appear to be concerned more with indicating the sources of evidence for the utterance as hearsay. In other words, sentence-final *(t)te* serves to invoke or allude to additional sources for knowledge, thereby shifting AUTHORITY for the claim (and responsibility for its consequences) away from the speaker.[6] In (5) and (6), thus, by deploying *(t)te* sentence-finally, the speaker attributes authority and responsibility for the utterance to some party other than him/herself.

3.3 From quoting thought to 'hedging'

As seen in (1) above, the quotative particle is employed to quote not only the content of 'speech', but also the content of 'thought'. The type of sentence-final *to* discussed in this subsection consists of the instances in which *to* is deployed sentence-finally to present a statement as a 'report of the content of thought'. The following excerpt contains an utterance in which the speaker reports what he thought on a particular occasion in the past:

(7) (Skiing 22)
    H: *de sa:, (0.6) toppu ni odoridete ore wa   sa*
        and FP   top to jump.up I   TOP FP
        'And, I jumped up to the top, and I...'

    ((3 lines omitted in which a waiter brings food for H))

--> H: *doonika   sa: (.) katsun ja   nai ka to.*
        manage.to FP   win   be   not Q TO
        '(I thought) that I could manage to win.'

        (0.7)

    T: *amain   da.*
        optimistic be
        'Too optimistic.'

---

[6] See Du Bois (1986) and Clifford & Fox (1990) for discussions of the relationship between authority and evidential marking.

In this excerpt, H is telling T about a card game he played during a ski trip. In the arrowed line, H deploys *to* sentence-finally, thereby indicating that he is presenting what he thought at a particular moment during the card game. In other words, sentence-final *to* in (7) serves as the device to quote or report the content of thought.

In some contexts, this type of *to* appears to serve further as a 'hedging' device. As discussed in 3.1, *to* as inherently associated with reported speech emerges when the speaker takes on the role of the 'animator', i.e., when the speaker invokes 'another voice'. Now, when the speaker is taking on the 'animator' role and is merely reporting the words of another, he/she is in a sense not speaking in his/her own right, and thus is distancing him/herself from taking full responsibility for the content of the claim he/she utters. Considering in this light the cases in which the speaker presents an utterance as a report of his/her thought, we can see how sentence-final *to* can serve as a hedging device. Namely, by deploying *to* sentence-finally, the speaker presents an utterance as a 'mere report' of a thought and nothing more, and thereby distances (or claims to distance) him/herself from responsibility for possible consequences of the utterance, such as disagreement or challenge from other participants.

Let us consider examples. Excerpt (8) is taken from a conversation in which Y argues that the advent of new technology like facsimile and computer networks will soon replace the existing media such as TV and newspaper. Y's statement in lines 1, 2, 4, and 6 expresses this opinion:

(8) (FH 1226)
```
1    Y: ... ima   aru   media  to     yuu no wa   nakanaka moo
          now  exist  media QUOT say NR TOP  pretty      now

2        korekara
         from.now

3    M: m::::::m.
         uh.huh

4 --> Y: chotto  kurushiin  de  wa  nai  ka to.
         a.little  difficult    be  TOP  not  Q  TO

5    M: m::::::::m.
         uh.huh

6    Y: aru   koto  wa   arimasu    kedo ne.
         exist  thing  TOP  exist:POL  but   FP
```

'The media that exist today will have a pretty hard time in the future, (I think).' (Lines 1, 2, and 4)
'They won't completely disappear, though.' (Line 6)

Notice that Y's statement expressed over lines 1, 2, and 4 ends with sentence-final *to*. When *to* occurs after the string of morphemes *de wa nai ka*, there is strong anticipation, because of frequent collocation, that it will be followed by a verb of thinking, such as *omou* 'to think' (the resulting expression would roughly be equivalent to *I suspect* in English). Thus, the deployment of *to* sentence-finally makes the whole utterance into a report of a thought (and a mitigated one, for that matter). And by means of taking on the role of 'reporter', the speaker claims, in effect, that 'This is just my thought, and yours may well be different', thereby distancing himself from taking responsibility for the consequences of the claim, e.g. disagreement, challenge, etc.

   Consider another excerpt, which is taken from the beginning of a phone conversation. Prior to this phone call, K called H, who was at that time talking to another friend on another line. H promised K to call back. A while later, H did so, and the conversation in excerpt (9) took place.

(9) (TK 4)
--> K: ... *nanka iso- isogashite shimatta ka na: //to.*
        well   press   finished   Q FP TO
        '... well, (I wondered) if I pressed (you to quit the conversation with your friend).'

   H: *A ie ie a:no: betsuni   taishita   yoo   demo*
       oh no no uhm   not.particularly important matter be:PT

       n//akattashi.
       not

       'Oh, no, no, uhm, it wasn't really important.'

   K: *a/ ho:ntoni:. yokatta.*
       oh really   good
       'Oh, really. Good.'

In the first utterance in the excerpt, K attempts to see if she pressed H to finish his previous phone conversation in order to call her. Note that K builds this utterance in such a way as to make a question into a quotation of her thought by adding *to* at the end. Since a question asking if the questioner caused the answerer inconvenience or trouble could put the answerer in an interactionally difficult situation (e.g., it is difficult to say 'yes' in such a situation even if the answerer does think that the questioner caused him/her trouble), adding *to* and presenting the question as simply a report of her thought serves to at least partially make the inquiry indirect, thereby avoiding a possible direct conflict with the recipient.[7]

3.4 From reporting situations to distributing responsibility

The collection of instances of sentence-final *to* discussed in this subsection also involves 'reporting', but this time, what is reported is neither speech fragments nor the content of thoughts. Sentence-final *to* of this type appears to be employed to report some 'situation', both actual or hypothetical. Again, *to* in these instances emerges when the 'footing' of the talk invokes the role of the 'animator', whose central job is voicing other voices.

Let us consider examples. In excerpt (10), G, who is a victim of a train derailment accident, is telling an interviewer what happened in the accident.

(10) (FNN - report on a train accident)
    G: ... *ma taoreta shunkan: watashi ano:: ikkaiten ijoo*
          well turn.over moment I   uhm one.roll more

      shimashite: .hhh densha to tsuchi no aida ni ashi
      did:and   train and ground GEN between in leg

      o hasande kega o shite shimatta to.
      OBJ caught.in injury OBJ do finished TO

      '... well, the moment the train turned over, I rolled more than once, got my legs caught between the train and the ground, and got injured.'

In this excerpt, the speaker is describing some situation he actually witnessed. G explains the course of events that happened to him in the accident, but he does so not in an upset manner (which might be expected from a victim of such a disaster), but rather in a detached manner. It appears that the deployment of sentence-final *to* serves to present the whole utterance as a 'report' of the situation he witnessed, rather than a vivid, emotional narration of it. Thus, although the accident itself must be vivid in his memory, G casts himself in the role of a mere 'reporter' (rather than a victim loaded with emotion), and distances himself from the event. The detachedness of his manner in describing the accident may have been responsive to the fact that he was being interviewed in front of a TV camera,

---

[7] As with English indirect questions such as those beginning with *I wonder*, the type of indirect question found in (9) is so conventionalized that it can virtually serve as an unmarked question in certain contexts. Indeed, H in (9) starts talking before K produces *to* sentence-finally.

but it is nonetheless instructive to observe that the deployment of sentence-final *to* is invoked in this particular mode of talking.

Let us consider another excerpt. In (11), M describes for H the story of a movie he recently saw. Obviously, M is not quoting speech fragments he heard either in the movie or from someone talking about it; rather, he is reporting what he saw in the movie. It is worth noticing then that M describes the development of the story by deploying *to* sentence-finally at several occasions, as if he marks each step in the story with sentence-final *to*.

(11) (FM 513)
1 M: *roshiajin no: torakku no   untenshu ga::*
        Russian GEN truck   GEN driver   SUBJ

   H: *un.*
        uh.huh

   M: *koo   sono: (0.7) uranbaatoru yattakke=sono mongoru   no*
        well uhm   Ulan.Bator was:Q   uhm Mongolia GEN

        shuto   made dokka   kara   kootto   nimotsu hakondekuru
        capital to   somewhere from   like.this load   carry:come

        tochuu DE::
        on.the.way

   H: *un.*
        uh.huh

--> M: *chotto maa   jidoosha ga   koshoo   shite shimatta* **to**.
          just   well   car   SUBJ out.of.order do   finished   TO

   H: *hm hm hm hm.*
        uh.huh

'A Russian truck driver, who was carrying a load from somewhere to Ulan Bator - was it Ulan Bator? - anyway, to the capital of Mongolia, had his truck break down on the way.'   ---- (1)

2 M: *soko e   tamatama   toorigakatta nanka sono::* (1.1)
        there to accidentally passed   like   uhm

        yuubokumin demo nai //kedo:: soogen   ni
        nomad   be   not   but   grassland in

    pao   *o*   *kamaeteru:*
    Mongolian.tent.house OBJ   have

H: *m::∶m.*
     uh.huh

    (0.6)

M: *tsch! (o)cch//an ga*   *to*   *nanka*
                  guy   SUBJ with like

H: *u:n.*
     uh.huh

    (1.7)

--> M: *shiriai*   *ni* *natta*   ***to***.
          acquaintance to became TO

    'There (comes) a guy - he may or may not be a nomad - who lives in a
    Mongolian tent house in the glassland, and (the truck driver) became
    friends with him.'   ---- (2)

3 --> M: *nde:*   (0.5) *soko no*   *ie*   *e*   *manekareta* ***to***.
       and   there GEN house to   invite:PASS TO

    'And (the driver) was invited to his house.'   ---- (3)

Prior to this portion of the conversation, turn-by-turn talk between M and H
was observed. After a brief introduction of the title, producer, etc., of the
movie, M shifts the footing to one of 'reporting the content of the movie',
and the turn-taking operation is suspended. In this interactional context, M
casts himself in the 'animator' role, voicing the story on behalf of the
movie (as it were), and deploys *to* sentence-finally at several junctures in the
story. H also participates in this shift by taking on the role of the recipient
of an extended turn at talk.

    The next excerpt involves a reporting of a hypothetical, rather than
actual, situation. In this excerpt, Y, who works for a broadcasting
company, discusses the factors that affect business organizations' decisions
in choosing which TV channel they want to put their commercials on. He
simulates the course of a possible decision-making process that appears
likely to take place in such an occasion.

(12) (FH 487)

    Y: ... *tatoeba*   *terebi* *yattara,*
              for.example TV   be:if
           '... for instance, (in the case of) TV,'

    M: *u::n.*
        uh.huh

--> Y: *kantere*   <u>*wa*</u> *wakai* *yatsu* *ga*   *miteru*   ***to.***
          Kansai.TV TOP young folk   SUBJ be.watching TO
          'Youngsters watch Kansai TV.'

--> Y: *nna* *kantere*   <u>*ni*</u> (0.5) *uchidasoo* ***to.***
          then Kansai.TV on   put.ad   TO
          'Then, let's put our ad on Kansai TV.'

    M: *kantere*   *wakai* *yatsu* *ga*   *miten*   *no?*
        Kansai.TV young folk SUBJ be.watching FP
        'Do youngsters watch Kansai TV?'

In (12), Y speculates on a hypothetical situation of some company's decision-making process, and casts himself in the role of the 'reporter' of that process. In other words, by deploying *to* sentence-finally, Y shifts the footing of the talk to one in which he plays the 'animator' role, speaking, as it were, on behalf of some hypothetical corporate executive making such a decision.

The three excerpts we examined so far in this subsection suggest that sentence-final *to* may emerge in the talk in interaction when the participants (primarily the speaker) invoke 'reportive frames', or the footing of talk where the participants perform 'reporting'. Through the deployment of sentence-final *to*, the speaker takes on the 'animator' role, voicing other voices in his/her utterances.

Now, there is a collection of instances which suggest that the type of sentence-final *to* being discussed in this subsection may further serve as what I would call a 'responsibility-distributing device'. That is, by voicing another voice and playing the role of a 'mere reporter' with sentence-final *to*, the speaker attempts to evade or diffuse responsibility for a claim that might be reprehensible.

Excerpt (13) is taken from a TV interview with a politician right after the resignation of the then prime minister Morihiro Hosokawa. Hosokawa's resignation caused political chaos in Japan, and there emerged confrontations among the parties that had constituted the coalition government. In this excerpt, politician S, who is a leader of one of the parties that was in the coalition government, is explaining the political

situation in which his party is situated after Prime Minister's resignation.
(brief responses from the interviewers are omitted from the excerpt):

(13) (FNN - Ichikawa)
--> S: *tada: sono::: seeken   no ne, yakuwari ga,   kawatta to.*
      but   uhm administration GEN FP role   SUBJ changed TO
      'But uhm the role of the administration has changed.'

--> S: *seeji   kaikaku wa   owatta to.*
      politics reform TOP ended TO
      'The political reform has been done.'

    S: *desukara sooyuu imi de wa   ne, e::: hurui gooi   de* (.)
      so   such   sense in TOP FP uhm old   agreement with

-->   *ee   yattekeru naigai   no joosee de wa nai to.*
      uhm proceed   domestic.foreign GEN situation be TOP not TO

    'So in that sense, the old agreement doesn't allow us to deal with
    the present domestic and international situations.'

In this interview, S suggests that his party may break the 'old agreement'
that was made when the coalition government was formed, and ally itself
with some other parties to survive the situation. What he does with his
utterances in (13) then is to describe (what he conceives as) current political
situations to justify his party's move. These descriptions can be highly
controversial and may be disagreed on or challenged especially by opposing
parties. Notice then that S produces sentence-final *to* at the end of each
description. This deployment of *to* indicates (or claims to indicate) that he
is doing 'being an animator' and instructs the hearers to hear it as such. In
other words, S appears to suggest that he is merely voicing what people out
there (i.e. outside himself) commonly understand as the current political
situation. By so doing, S diffuses or distributes responsibility for the
descriptions, thinning it out by alluding to additional sources for the
utterance. In this sense, sentence-final *to* appears to serve to invoke
'collective' responsibility, thereby distancing the 'animator' who merely
'animates' the claims from taking full responsibility for the utterance.
    The following excerpt, a reproduction of (2) above, provides an
example of the 'responsibility-distributing device' used as a tool to protect
the speaker when making a sarcastic comment. In the conversation from
which (14) is taken, K, who is in her early twenties, asks C, a teenage boy,
about his relationship with his girlfriend. Throughout the conversation, C
reveals his self-centered attitude toward his girlfriend, and excerpt (14)
contains an example of his expression of such an attitude.

(14) (Girlfriend 30)

    C: *dakara ore* <u>*ga:*</u>   *aitaku*   *naru*   *to:-*   *au*   *n*   *da na.*
        so   I   SUBJ meet:want become when meet NR be FP
        'So, when I want to meet her, I meet her.'

      (so)re dake no   *koto* *da* *na.*
      that just GEN matter be FP
      'That's it.'

      (1.1)

--> K: *a ja*   *mukoo*   *ga*   *ojihi*   *de*   *atte* *kureru* **to**.
      oh then the.other.side SUBJ mercy with meet give   TO
      'Oh, so, it's that she is merciful enough to meet you.'

In response to C's self-centered statement in his turn, K makes a sarcastic interpretation of the situation C just described. Notice that she produces sentence-final *to*, and invokes the 'reporter' or 'animator' role. By deploying *to* sentence-finally, K claims to indicate that 'what I am doing is just reporting what you were saying', and thereby protecting herself from responsibility for the consequences of the utterance, such as accusations from C of being sarcastic. Here again, the deployment of sentence-final *to* serves to attribute responsibility for an utterance to 'another voice' on behalf of whom the animator merely voices an utterance, and thereby distances the actual speaker from being charged as responsible for a potentially reprehensible claim.

    In this section, we examined the workings of various types of sentence-final *to* and *(t)te* in spoken discourse. In the next section, we will summarize our observations and discuss their implications.

4. Summary and discussion

    In section 3, we observed that various aspects of reported speech, with which *to* and *(t)te* are inherently associated, are exploited in the sentence-final deployment of those particles in spoken discourse. Some uses of sentence-final *to* are involved in invoking direct voices of others, or 'animating' them, in one's utterances. Other uses are concerned with allocating the sources of claims to some party other than the actual speaker, and distancing him/her from authority for the utterance. In still other uses, the speaker casts him/herself in the role of the 'reporter' of some thoughts or situations, thereby evading or diffusing responsibility for the consequences of the utterance.

    What emerges out of these observations of the workings of sentence-final *to* is that its deployment is a way a speaker claims, in effect, that the utterance he/she is producing is not constructed solely by him/herself, but 'co-constructed' by multiple voices invoked in the utterance. Through this co-construction of an utterance with other voices, the actual speaker may then shift the locus of authority and responsibility for the utterance away from him/herself and distribute it onto some alluded-to parties. Inasmuch as such a negotiation of authority and responsibility for a claim always occurs in particular social contexts with particular co-participants, the deployment of sentence-final *to* appears to be inherently a social phenomenon. It may well be the case, then, that precisely because of this nature of sentence-final *to* being inherently responsive to the social context of the utterance, such a phenomenon has rarely been investigated or even acknowledged in the past literature, a great deal of which has based its inquiry on examination of decontextualized made-up sentences.

Elucidation of sentence-final uses of *to* as inherently a social phenomenon further provides a useful angle towards reconsidering the traditional analysis of the quotative particle *to*. It has been claimed that when *to* is used as a complementizer, the *to*-marked clause does not presuppose the truth or factuality of the proposition expressed in the clause (cf. Kuno 1973). I would like to propose that this observation (based probably on examination of isolated invented sentences) stems from the fundamental workings of *to* in social interaction, i.e. invoking 'dual voice' in the utterance and shifting authority and responsibility for the proposition from the speaker who utters it. Since *to* allows the speaker to evade responsibility for a proposition it marks and attribute it to some other 'voice', it can be irrelevant whether the truth of the proposition holds or not. If this analysis is essentially correct, it then suggests that what appears to be a purely grammatical or semantic fact may be a reflection of interactional processes in which the use of a grammatical element is situated. To put it differently, it may turn out that many properties of grammatical items can usefully be seen as having the workings of social interaction profoundly embedded in them.

5. Conclusion

In this paper, we explored sentence-final uses of the quotative particle in Japanese, and observed that the deployment of sentence-final *to* is a grammatical practice in social interaction whereby participants invoke 'double-voiced' utterances, and distance themselves from taking full responsibility for the consequences of the utterances. We also pointed out that inasmuch as grammar operates in the first place in social interaction, examination of participants' grammatical practices in naturally-occurring, situated talk is essential for understanding how grammar operates as it does. I hope that the present study contributes to underscore the importance of investigating the intricately intertwined nature of grammar and interaction.

References

Aoki, Haruo. 1986. Evidentials in Japanese. Evidentiality: The linguistic coding of epistemology, ed. by Wallace Chafe and Johanna Nichols, 223-238. Norwood, NJ: Ablex.

Clifford, Joseph, and Barbara A. Fox. 1990. Evidentiality and authority in English conversation. ms. University of Colorado, Boulder.

Du Bois, John W. 1986. Self-evidence and ritual speech. Evidentiality: The linguistic coding of epistemology, ed. by Wallace Chafe and Johanna Nichols, 313-336. Norwood, NJ: Ablex.

Goffman, Erving. 1981. Footing. Forms of talk, 124-159. Philadelphia: University of Pennsylvania Press.

Hill, Jane H. and Judith T. Irvine, eds. 1993. Responsibility and evidence in oral discourse. Cambridge: Cambridge University Press.

Kuno, Susumu. 1973. The structure of the Japanese language. Cambridge: The MIT Press.

Martin, Samuel E. 1975. A reference grammar of Japanese. New Haven and London: Yale University Press.

Mayes, Patricia. 1991. Grammaticization of *to* and *tte* in Japanese. ms. University of California, Santa Barbara.

Nihon Kokugo Daijiten [The dictionary of the Japanese language]. 1975. Tokyo: Shogakkan.

Appendix 1: Abbreviations used in Interlinear Gloss

FP	final particle	GEN	genitive
NR	nominalizer	OBJ	object marker
PASS	passive	POL	politeness marker
PT	other particle	Q	question marker
QUOT	quotative particle ('canonical' use)	SUBJ	subject marker
TO	sentence-final *to*	TOP	topic marker

Appendix 2: Notational Conventions in Transcripts

The following notational conventions are used in the transcripts.

//	point at which the current utterance is overlapped by the next utterance produced by another speaker.
(0.0)	length of silence in tenths of a second.
(.)	micro-pause
underlining	relatively high pitch
CAPS	relatively high volume

An Expanded Concept of Speakerhood in Japanese Discourse

University of Hawaii at Manoa

I. Introduction

Much of the work that has been done on the encoding of speaker's role or speaker's perspective in Japanese has focused on issues of epistemic stance and information accessibility (Iwasaki 1993; Kamio 1979, 1994, Kuroda 1973; Maynard 1993; Oishi 1985). Several proposals define the role of the speaker based on the speaker's authority for or access to a certain licensed domain of information, a domain that might be best characterized as SPEAKER KNOWLEDGE. These proposals argue that the role that a speaker may create for him/herself in discourse is dependent on the distinction between information that is accessible or available to the speaker, and information that is not. On the whole, these approaches treat the indexing of the domain of speaker knowledge as a fundamentally epistemological phenomenon which may have derived pragmatic meanings related to power, politeness, intimacy, etc. (Kamio 1991; Maynard 1993; Oishi 1985).

In conjunction with this research there has been an ongoing effort to identify those linguistic markers which index information that is uniquely accessible to the speaker. Here the various approaches diverge somewhat with various items being nominated to carry out the epistemic function of indexing speaker knowledge. Items that have been proposed include the bare verb (Cook 1990; Kamio 1994), sentence-final particle *yo* with *ne* (Oishi 1985) or without *ne* (Maynard 1993), and clauses with high transitivity features (Iwasaki 1993:22). The inability of researchers to identify a coherent and limited set of epistemological indexes to mark the domain of speaker knowledge suggests that the limits of this domain and its nature have not yet been fully identified nor clearly defined.

In this paper, I will argue that the lack of agreement on the set of linguistic markers that index speaker knowledge is a result of the fact that researchers have failed to recognize that speakers are not limited to a domain of proposition-based speaker knowledge, but also have access to a domain of speaker affect (or, for the purposes of consistency in terminology, affect-based speaker knowledge, i.e., 'I know how/what I feel.').[1] I will demonstrate that two of the linguistic markers researchers have identified as indexing proposition-based speaker knowledge, *yo* and *ne*, have been mislabeled, and are, in fact, indexes of speaker affect. Moreover, I will argue that sentence-final particle *yo*, one of the most commonly-identified indexes of a speaker's evidential stance, does not, as is commonly-argued, index proposition-based information uniquely accessible to the speaker, but rather indexes an affective stance of the speaker that is relevant to the speaker's communicative goals at the given moment in discourse.

I will show that there is further merit in clearly distinguishing between a speaker's unique knowledge of proposition-based information and a speaker's unique access to his/her affective stance, by introducing the theoretical concept of SPEAKERHOOD. Within the construct of speakerhood, the idea of speaker knowledge is expanded to include both what one knows and what one feels, and both of these are shown to be communicative resources for the speaker.

In addition to the division of speaker's knowledge into epistemic-based and affect-based domains, I also demonstrate that the speaker-hearer dichotomy (or continuum, as it appears in more recent works, cf. Kamio 1994, Maynard 1993, Oishi 1985), a characteristic common to most theories of speaker knowledge, is more accurately reflected in Japanese by a self-shared dichotomy, with no continuum between the two poles. The four-cell paradigm resulting from the three variables of evidential stance, affective stance and the dichotomy of self or shared stance is argued to be a model that more closely accomodates the sociocultural values described in the literature for Japanese interpersonal interaction in the literature (Maynard, 1989); it is also shown to be more effective than current proposals in accounting for the pragmatic effects of the linguistic indexes included in the model (outlined in Figure 1 below).

II. Review of the Literature

I will begin by briefly reviewing the development of our understanding of the concept of speaker knowledge and summarizing the current state of theories regarding this concept. Kuroda's (1973) work on epistemological phenomena in Japanese was an important first step in

---

[1] For an excellent discussion of the centrality of affect in language, see Ochs and Schieffelin 1989.

recognizing the limitations imposed on speaker knowledge by the language. Kuroda pointed out that Japanese distinguishes between speech that assumes an embodied speaker, the reportive style, and speech produced without such an assumption, the nonreportive style. Reportive speech, he showed, could not directly report others' internal states, emotions, etc. as first-hand knowledge. One segment of Kuroda's work (1973:384) makes use of sentence-final particle yo as a means of testing for the presence of reportive speech; although Kuroda identifies this function of yo as reportive, its function as an indicator of reportive speech suggests that yo can be more broadly viewed as an index of the presence of an identifiable speaker (that is, one that knows and feels, unlike the literary convention of an omniscient narrator).

Based on his well-known work on the speaker's territory of information (Kamio 1979), Kamio (1994) expands the domain of speaker's knowledge to include such categories as geographical knowledge and vocational knowledge among others. This expansion of the speaker's domain of knowledge, however, is not absolute, but rather relative to the domain of knowledge claimed by the addressee. For Kamio, the speaker's knowledge is defined by two variables: epistemic concerns of first-hand and second-hand knowledge (labelled direct form and indirect form by Kamio (1994:86)), and the degree of overlap with the hearer's territory.

Kamio's contribution is to recognize that there is some variable apart from epistemic stance that governs the way a speaker frames his/her knowledge in discourse. However, although the label 'territory' is an attempt to suggest some type of innate psychological judgement (1994:68), the concept itself remains only roughly defined as 'information close to the speaker/hearer' (1994:82). Moreover, subsequent treatment of data within the framework seldom makes a clear distinction between epistemic phenomena and territory phenomena.

Several researchers have taken issue with Kamio's earlier (1979) version of the theory of speaker's territory. In the earlier version, territory was conceived of as a dichotomous variable rather than a more-less continuum, as it is currently depicted. Oishi's (1985) proposal to view speaker's territory as a continuum also differs from Kamio's work in the set of linguistic markers he claims index territory. While Kamio (1979) argues that it is sentence-final particle ne that indexes territory, Oishi claims that sentence-final particle yo, alone or in combination with sentence-final particle ne, is also an index of territory.

Like Oishi, Maynard (1993), opts for a scalar approach to speaker knowledge, and identifies yo and ne as the relevant linguistic markers (although she does not account for the sentence-final combination of yo and ne). Assuming a framework of discourse modality, she argues that 'information accessibility' rather than territory is the variable that defines the limits of speaker knowledge. Unfortunately neither 'information' nor 'accessibility' are well-defined. However, Maynard does shed new light on the pragmatic effects of a speaker's claims for information accessibility. She points out that *yo* indexes the speaker's primary focus as information exchange (1993:208), in contrast to *ne*, which indexes the speaker's primary focus is interpersonal interaction (1993:208). Maynard also recognizes that these primary discourse functions may also have secondary, context-dependent ones; she points, in particular, to the use of *yo* as an index of a speaker's 'power and dominance' (1993:208).

Iwasaki's (1993) approach to speaker knowledge parallels Maynard's in its focus on information accessibility; however, Iwasaki frames his discussion in terms of speaker subjectivity rather than discourse modality. Iwasaki's goal is to demonstrate a principled relationship between epistemic perspective and grammar (tense form variation and switch reference, in particular). His argument is that a speaker uses grammar to reflect his/her degree of first-hand involvement, volition and control in the event or condition reported in his/her talk. This aspect of Iwasaki's work echoes Kamio's (1994:77) conceptualization of the conditions governing speaker's territory (e.g., information obtained through the speaker's direct experience and information about the speaker's plans, actions and behavior).

One notable point in Iwasaki's work is his introduction of the concept of S-perspective (i.e., self-perspective) which is the perspective where the speaker is both the experiencer and the reporter of some condition or event. The type of experiences indexed by S-perspective go beyond the speaker's internal state (as discussed by Kuroda and Kamio), to include the speaker's sense of the strength of his/her volition and/or control in a given context. These variables, although classified as epistemic in nature by Iwasaki, are the type of speaker knowledge that I believe can be better accounted for by a broader and clearer understanding of speakerhood.

In sum, there have been several proposals to account for the domain of speaker knowledge and the pragmatic effects of the speaker's indexing of that domain. These accounts have recognized that speaker knowledge is defined dynamically, based on the relationship between speaker and hearer and the context of their interaction. However, these approaches have consistently been couched in epistemic or quasi-epistemic terms, a fact that has led to two significant limitations on the explanatory power of the approaches proposed.

The first limitation consistently imposed by researchers is that the data to be explained is restricted to declarative utterances, a point stated explicitly by Iwasaki (1993:17). This limitation on utterance types is recognized as problematic by Kamio (1994:99) who states, in a footnote, that 'the place of interrogative utterances within the theory of territory of information...must be seriously investigated.' Maynard (1993:191-2) includes a brief discussion of interrogative and imperative utterances (cf. exx 3-6), but does not explain how a theory of information accessibility can account for utterances that are traditionally deemed to have no propositional (i.e., informational) content. It is my contention that a broader conceptualization of speakerhood -- in other words, one which includes both proposition-based speaker knowledge and speaker affect -- will account for all utterance types, especially since there is no reason to believe that the speaker's capacity for self-expression varies across utterance type.

The second limitation relates to the types of pragmatic effects that have been identified as stemming from the speaker's indexing of his/her knowledge. Oishi (1985:172ff, esp. 177) reports that his subject avoided the use of *yo*, the particle that, for Oishi, indexes a strong claim of speaker's territory, and even eliminated the softer, but similarly functioning, *yo ne*, to 'avoid touching off [the addressee's] tendencies'. Kamio (1994:96ff) reports the existence of an 'optional *ne*', used by the speaker to attribute more information to the hearer than s/he actually is licensed to have in his/her territory. And Maynard (1993:208) explains that *ne* 'is a marker by which the speaker solicits the addressee's confirmatory attitude and/or requests the addressee's transfer of information;...*interaction is foregrounded...and...information exchange is backgrounded.*' (emphasis added). These pragmatic effects highlight the role of speaker volition and the centrality of speaker-addressee rapport in the indexing of the domain of speaker knowledge; yet none of these approaches offer an explanation for the interplay between the domain of speaker affect (i.e., volition and rapport) and the domain of speaker knowledge (i.e., proposition-based information). Here again, it is my contention that a broader conceptualization of speakerhood will provide a consistent and logical account of the relationship between the use of a linguistic index, such as *yo* or *ne*, and the pragmatic effects that that index has in natural discourse.

It is clear from the above discussion that previous research has not fully explored the limits of speaker knowledge, nor has definitive evidence been provided that this domain is uniquely epistemic in nature. The two limitations outlined above necessitate 1) broadening of the types of utterances considered to include non-declarative utterances, and 2) clarifying the relationship between the indexing of speaker knowledge and the derivative pragmatic effects of such indexing (especially those pragmatic effects that entail the indexing of speaker affect). In the remainder of this paper, I will address these and related concerns.

III. A Reanalysis of *yo*

In this section I will focus on the sentence-final particle *yo*, which is commonly identified either as a linguistic index of speaker knowledge (Maynard 1993; Oishi 1985; in Kamio 1994:86 *yo* is used for this function optionally), or as an index of the function of reporting or telling information

(Iwasaki 1993:36; Kuroda 1973:384).[2] I will expand the analysis of sentence-final particle *yo* to utterances without semantic content (e.g., imperatives, interrogatives and performative utterances, such as requests and hortatives), as a means of demonstrating the inadequacy of previous analyses of *yo* that focus on its evidential qualities.

In the expanded data set below, it is clear that the index of *yo* is not the speaker's epistemic stance towards the content of the utterance, but rather the speaker's attitude towards a) the addressee, b) the content of the utterance or c) the act of performing the utterance itself. This type of speaker meaning, which falls under the category of AFFECT (Ochs and Schiefflin, 1989), is a well-recognized component of language that has been poorly accounted for in Japanese (but cf. Cook, 1992). The existence of an affective domain of speaker knowledge, not recognized heretofore in the literature, is the fundamental motivation for the concept of speakerhood proposed in this work. (The model of speakerhood will be elaborated in Section IV below.)

III.1 The analysis of *yo* in imperatives

The occurrence of *yo* in imperative and hortative utterances has been noted by several researchers (Maynard, 1993; Tanimori, 1994; Uyeno, 1975). With respect to imperatives, *yo* is said to have the effect of softening the forcefulness of the command (Tanimori, 1994; Uyeno, 1975).

The following constructed example is given by Tanimori:

Example 1 (Tanimori 1994:308)

1 speaker; Chanto shiro yo.
          Do it right, okay?

Yo serves here to soften the abruptness and forcefulness of the blunt imperative form. If this utterance is made by a supervisor to an employee, then it detracts from the social power and authority inherent in the utterance of a speaker in a higher status role to an addressee in a lower status one. In so doing, the use of *yo* highlights the bond of confident trust that exists between this supervisor and employee, who have a relationship that is not governed solely by the authority inherent in the higher status party's position. This reading is consistent with Tanimori's comment that the use

---

[2] In accounts of *yo* that do not assume a framework of speaker knowledge, a performative analysis is often proposed (Uyeno 1971, Givon 1982, Tsuchihashi 1983). In such analyses, *yo* is said to indicate the speaker's insistence (Uyeno 1971:99) or the speaker's a) high confidence/certainty in his/her utterance, b) lack of willingness to admit challenge to his/her knowledge and c) the lack of influence of the hearer's agreement on the force of the utterance (Tsuchihashi 1983).

of *yo* may be used to decrease the authoritativeness of one's command towards someone with whom the speaker has a close relationship.[3]

Not all researchers are in agreement with this reading of *yo* (i.e., as a softening device). Makino and Tsutsui (1986:544) state that *yo* attached to a command or a *kudasai*-request has exactly the opposite effect; that is, it 'makes the sentence more forceful'. Maynard (1993:194) argues that *yo*, rather than *ne*, attaches to an abrupt command form because, in such an utterance, 'the speaker denies any negotiating room for the addressee'. Maynard's argument is used as evidence for her claim that *yo* indexes the speaker's exclusive access to/possessorship of the information contained in a *yo*-marked clause.

While it is clear that the pragmatic effects of bluntness/forcefulness described above can be subsumed under the category of speaker attitude, Maynard's claim that this effect is achieved by virtue of the speaker's claim to sole access to the information in the command, would, at first glance, appear to contradict the analysis of *yo* being proposed here. However, as mentioned above, commands do not have proposition-based informational content, so the only information that the speaker can index here is information about his/her own state of mind/heart, in other words, affective information. The idea that the forcefulness of an imperative followed by *yo* (as in Example 1) is rooted in the speaker's expression of an affective stance is supported by Uyeno's (1971) description of the pragmatic consequences that stem from uttering such a turn: the use of *yo* by a higher status speaker to make an utterance more blunt constitutes a display of unbridled emotion, and, as such, undermines the authority which is inherent in the speaker's social position.

Thus, while the use of *yo* may highlight the speaker's attitude, or render the utterance itself more forceful, the increased forcefulness can only be viewed in affective terms, in that the forcefulness stems from the speaker's intense emotional state or attitude (outrage, exasperation, etc.). Moreover, in no way does the use of *yo* index the speaker as having greater authority or license for his/her command in some type of epistemic sense. There can be no increased authority or forcefulness derived from the speaker's license to know since there is no proposition-based information in the utterance to be known.

Both of these points contradict Maynard's ultimate reading of *yo* as 'backgrounding the concern regarding the participants' emotional involvement' and as pointing to the speaker as 'exhibiting power' because the speaker is the 'possessor of more information' (1993:208). In this way, the proposed account is shown to provide a more consistent and economical

---

[3] This example replaces the original example 1 presented at the conference. I am indebted to Sam Martin for pointing out my error in interpreting the original example.

account of the indexical meaning and pragmatic functions of *yo*.

III.2 The analysis of *yo* in hortatives and requests

In contrast to utterances in the blunt command form, utterances in the hortative express the speaker's volition in a softer, less abrupt way. Hortatives most commonly express the speech act of suggestion, as in Example 2 below.

Example 2   (Tanimori, 1994:309)

1 speaker: Eiga o mi ni ikoo yo.
            Let's go and see a movie.

If we assume that Example 2 is uttered in the context of two friends deciding what to do, then the pragmatic effect of *yo* is ambiguous in that, depending on the speaker's tone of voice (whiny or enthusiastic), *yo* may either shift the force of the utterance from a relatively soft suggestion to a strong expression of the speaker's desired goal ('Let's go see a movie' -- I really want to see one.), or, it may index that the speaker's suggestion has the addressee's well-being in mind ('Let's go see a movie' -- I think you'd like that.) As with example 1 above, the attitude indexed may relate to the speaker's internal emotions or to the speaker's close rapport with the addressee. In either case, *yo* acts as an index of the speaker's attitude -- here, towards the context of the utterance or towards the addressee.

The pragmatic effect of *yo* is similar in utterances with *-te kudasai*, where the speaker's volition is conveyed in the form of a request. Requests in this form are typically deemed to be polite, and leave the option of compliance to the addressee. However, when *yo* is appended, the request takes on a sense of urgency, reflecting the intensity of the speaker's volition that is involved in the act of requesting:

Example 3 (from a samurai television drama)

> The servant's master has just been stabbed, possibly fatally, by a mysterious assailant. The servant falls to his knees by the master's body.

1 servant: danasama, ikite kudasai yo!
            Master, please don't die!

The speaker's use of *yo* with *-te kudasai* results in a request that approaches the force of a command. However, it would be inappropriate to label the force as a command given the servant's use of the title *dana-sama* and the polite request form *kudasai*; these serve as evidence that the servant's social position is lower than that of the addressee, his master. A consistent translation of this request then, might be 'I'm imploring you' (which indexes the servant's heartfelt emotion) rather than 'I order you' (which would index power and authority that the servant does not, and is not licensed, to have).

In example 3, we see the two indexes of *yo* described above -- the speaker's close relationship to the addressee and the speaker's expression of (intense) internal emotion -- unified in one utterance. The increased forcefulness of the request comes, not from the social power of the speaker's position, but rather from the the intensity of his loyalty to his master. Hence, rather than labeling the pragmatic effect of *yo* an increase of forcefulness (which has connotations of power and authority), it is more accurate to attribute the shift in pragmatic force to the the servant's emotional investment in his relationship with his master. *Yo* indexes the heartfelt imploring of the devoted servant. clearly a domain of speaker affect.

III.3 The analysis of *yo* in interrogatives and in co-occurrence with the interrogative particle *ka*

Having addressed the function of *yo* in imperatives and other types of performative utterances, I now turn to the use of *yo* in interrogatives and with the interrogative marker *ka*, areas not addressed in previous research. Since interrogatives, like imperatives and requests, have no semantic content, we can expect that the index of *yo* will be related to speaker attitude, as was demonstrated in examples 1-3 above.

While *yo* cannot join with *ka* to form a true interrogative, *yo* does occur in wh-questions without compromising the interrogative force of the utterance as in Example 4.

Example 4 (D-M148/F53)

The family is completing their dinner and getting ready to view a nearby fireworks display.

1 m; otoosan kyou doko yaro?
2 f; kyou are ya, ano: Biwako ya
3 m; ame ga futte n no kashira n kedo, sugoku hidoi
$$|$$
4 s;   mi ni ikoo ka
5 d1; mi ni ikoo
6 d2; o, ikoo. iku zo:
7 d1; yo:shi
8 f; doko ni mi ni iku n yo
9 d1; ((already on her way out)) soto

1 m; Father, where will it [the fireworks display] be today?
2 f; Today it'll be at that place, uh: Lake Biwa.

2 f; Today it'll be at that place, uh: Lake Biwa.
3 m; It might rain, that would be really terrible.

|

4 s;   Shall we go see?
5 d1; Let's go see.
6 d2; Oh, let's go. I'm going.
7 d1; Off we go.
8 f; Where are you going to watch [the fireworks]?
9 d1; Outside.

It is clear from the daughter's response in line 9 that the father's question represents a true interrogative (of the type *doko iku no?*'). The addition of *yo*, however, shifts the focus of the father's question, suggesting that he is not simply asking for information's sake, but is somewhat irritated that the children (two 10-year-old twin girls and their 18-year-old brother) are running out without telling him or the mother where they are going. The father's use of *yo*, then, indexes his attitude towards the situation at hand: he is both taken by surprise by the children's sudden departure, and somewhat vexed that he has to ask them where they are headed.

In contrast to wh-questions, when *yo* occurs with *ka* the result is a rhetorical question rather than a true interrogative.

Example 5 (Makino and Tsutsui, 1986:544, ex. 1a)

1 speaker: yomu ka yo.
         You think he's gonna read it?
         (implied: I bet he isn't going to read it.)[4]

---

[4] Makino and Tsutsui point out that the formal version of this utterance (i.e., with the verb in the *-masu* form) cannot be interpreted as a rhetorical question. Work by Cook and Kasper (1995), which posits that the *-masu* form indexes the disciplined, sociocentric self (as opposed to the spontaneous, egocentric self) may provide an explanation for this phenomenon.

If we assume that a speaker's expression of affect is more or less spontaneous, depending on the degree of speaker control (Yoshimi, in progress), and if the degree of speaker control for rhetorical questions is assumed to be low (i.e. more spontaneous expression of affect), then the conflict in the meaning of the two indexes in example 5 -- *-masu* for disciplined self and *yo* for low control/high spontaneity -- may explain the anomolous nature (i.e., pragmatically infelicitous) of the example. Such an analysis would highlight the contribution of affect to the discourse meaning of rhetorical utterances, thereby providing further support for the concept of speakerhood, and for the proposal that *yo* functions primarily as an index of speaker affect.

Rhetorical questions are commonly used to express the speaker's attitude towards some person or situation without overtly stating it. Here, the rhetorical question reveals the speaker's lack of confidence in the individual referred to in the utterance. The function of *yo*, then, is to index the speaker's cynical attitude towards the individual/event mentioned in the utterance. The utterance may also be said to express the speaker's confidence in his prognostication; however, since example 5 is a performative utterance without propositional content, *yo* cannot be said to index epistemic certainty of knowledge.

What is clear from the above examples is that *yo* is very much related to the domain of the speaker, but in an affective rather than an epistemic sense. In examples 1-5, *yo* has been shown to index:

-the speaker's paternalistic care for the addressee (ex. 1),
-the speaker's enthusiasm/sincerity (ex. 2),
-the speaker's loyal dedication to the addressee (ex. 3),
-the speaker's irritation or impatience with the addressee
(exx 2, 4), and
-the speaker's cynicism (ex. 5).

From these examples we can conclude that the function of *yo* is to indicate that the speaker's attitude is a relevant aspect of the meaning of the utterance. Since *yo* by itself does not index any specific attitude, but rather indexes that some speaker attitude is relevant to the communicative goal of the moment, I will conclude here that *yo* is an index of the speaker's affective stance.

IV. A proposal for an expanded notion of Japanese speakerhood

In light of the above discussion, it is clear that limiting the domain of speaker knowledge to proposition-based information in declarative utterances fails to capture an important aspect of a Japanese speaker's conversational resources. Since the function of *yo* in the examples discussed above was shown to align with a speaker's affective stance rather than his/her epistemic stance, it is clear that the concept of speaker knowledge must be expanded to include both proposition-based knowledge and knowledge dependent on the speaker's affective stance. Taking these facts into account, I propose the following definition of speakerhood for Japanese:

(i)   SPEAKERHOOD: The domain of a speaker's conversational resources that enables the speaker to index his perspective as distinct from or harmonious with the perspective of the addressee. These resources include the speaker's epistemic and affective stances, and the linguistic markers which index those stances.

Speakerhood recognizes that a speaker does indeed have a uniquely accessible domain to mark in conversation and use as a strategic resource in interaction. However, speakerhood also recognizes that, in conversational interaction, a speaker has more at stake than territorial claims to proposition-based knowledge; the affective domain of emotion, desire and volition that makes up much of the information shared in interaction must also be included among the speaker's conversational resources. Finally, speakerhood assumes that the motivation for putting these resources into action is not merely to demarcate the limitations of speaker as ego (i.e., the center of subjective feeling and judgment and objective knowing), but rather, to signal whether the orientation of communication is to be determined by self's perspective alone, or whether it is to be constructed from the shared perspectives of speaker and addressee.[5]

IV.1 Speakerhood, independent self and group orientation

This latter point is central to the conceptualization of speakerhood as it relates to Japanese conversation. Much has been made of the claim that Japanese have a weak concept of ego because they are so strongly group-oriented (cf. Doi, 1973:173). This claim is evident in the many works that argue for a Japanese cultural norm of harmony in conversation, evidenced by a preference for agreement with co-present interlocutors over individualized self-expression (cf. Maynard 1989, among others). At least one researcher (Rosenberger, 1989), however, has taken issue with this conceptualization of the Japanese self, arguing that the Japanese self can exhibit both individual expression and harmony-oriented group expression, and that the self shifts between these modes based on the normative social expectations of the context in which the individual is interacting.[6]

---

[5] This formulation of a speaker's communicative orientation may serve to clarify Maynard's dichotomy of foregrounding information exchange and foregrounding interaction (functions she attributes to *yo* and *ne*, respectively). In the model of speakerhood proposed herein, a speaker may indicate that orientation of communication is to be determined by self (Maynard's focus on information exchange) or by the shared perspectives of speaker and hearer (Maynard's foregrounding of interaction). In contrast to Maynard's model, however, the notion of speakerhood assumes that the linguistic indexes for communicating these orientations are distinct for proposition-based and affect-based domains of knowledge. (See figure 1.)

For a similar conceptualization of the speaker's communicative orientation and its relationship to the indexical functions of discourse markers in English, see Schiffrin (1987).

[6] Evidence for a domain of self-expression accessible only to the subjective self is available in the grammar of Japanese as well. As has often been pointed out (Aoki, 1986; Iwasaki, 1993; Kuroda, 1973), Japanese morphology provides a special index of second-hand knowledge, *-garu*, to report the internal states and desires of non-first person subjects. Moreover, restricted use of non-first person

The notion of speakerhood addresses precisely this type of variability, which is, in fact, readily evident in Japanese conversational behavior. Despite cultural norms valuing indirectness, harmony, and the like, Japanese speakers do express stance independent of, and even contrary to, the perspectives of others,[7] and, in the appropriate context, this expression is socially-acceptable. Speakerhood accounts for these contexts, as well as for contexts in which speakers collaborate with other conversational participants in aligning themselves with a stance shared by all participants. Most importantly, the notion of speakerhood does not imply (as Rosenberger's model does) that a speaker must remain with his/her chosen orientation (individual-oriented or group-oriented) for the duration of a given context/activity. Quite to the contrary, this concept was developed to account for the moment-to-moment shifts in communicative orientation

---

subjects when speaking of others' thought processes (cf. Iwasaki, 1993:14 on *omou/omotte iru*) or intentions (cf. Iwasaki, 1993: 13-4 on *-oo, -mai and -te miru*) provides further evidence that Japanese, at least at the morphological level, has established an inaccessible domain of a speaker's subjective experiences. Finally, the description of *yo* as an index of speaker affective stance not only complements the function of *-garu* (*-garu* indexes the inaccessible affective/experiential domains of others; *yo* indexes the inaccessible affective/experiential domain of self), but also provides additional support for the claim that there is a place for individual self-expression in Japanese interactions.

I do not find counterevidence for my argument in the fact that *-garu* may also be used to refer to one's own feelings when they occurred in the distant past. Ochs et al. (1992) observe that in relating past events in a narrative, co-present interlocutors may attribute feelings to the primary teller or even challenge the primary teller's first-hand account of 'the facts', even though the co-present interlocutor was not present when the narrative events occurred. This suggests that the spatial and temporal distance between the primary teller and the events that s/he is reporting tends to objectify the individual (as s/he is portrayed in the story).

The use of *-garu* for one's own feelings (as they were felt in the distance past) suggests that temporal and spatial distance have a similar effect on the Japanese speaker. Thus, a speaker who relates feelings from the distant past may use *-garu* to index that s/he no longer has unique access to the original motivation for or intensity of that feeling.

[7] The preference for harmony, then, should be seen as a goal of interaction rather than as a directive that holds for each utterance in an interaction. Steverson (1995:68ff) describes an interaction between a husband and wife which begins as an overt conflict of opinions, but ends with the wife validating the husband's perspective. Importantly, this harmony-oriented move by the wife extends over the course of several turns, with each turn indicating less resistance to the position taken by the husband. The reconciling moves, however, are generated by the wife's initially taking a stance that is independent of and overtly in conflict with the husband's.

that are readily evident in Japanese conversational interactions.

In promoting the importance of both individual and shared stances in Japanese communication, I would also appeal to the work of Japanese psychiatrist, T. Doi (1973), whose discussion of the role of *amae* in Japanese relationships is often mentioned in the same breath as the preference for harmonious interaction. Doi (1973:19) points out that there is a

> 'close connection between *amae* and the awareness of the self as expressed in the Japanese word *jibun*...this awareness of a *jibun* presume[s] the existence of an inner desire to *amaeru*, and [makes] itself felt in opposition to that desire. To put it briefly, a man who has a *jibun* is capable of checking *amae*, while a man who is at the mercy of *amae* has no *jibun*.'

Doi goes on to say that people considered 'normal' from a psychological perspective are those who have a self (*jibun ga aru*), and as such, are capable of checking *amae*. Hence, it is quite clear that when developing a model of Japanese interaction, and speaker-related speech phenomena in particular, we must be able to account both for the expression of self as an independent actor, and as a member acting in harmony with one or more other interlocutors.

IV.2 A model of Japanese speakerhood

I have argued that speakerhood incorporates both evidential and affective stances and that understanding the linguistic means for the self-expression of ego in interaction is as important as understanding that for the achievement of harmony in interaction. However, apart from the discussion of *yo*, I have not identified the other linguistic markers associated with the remaining aspects of speakerhood. In fact, it is my contention that the other indexes of speakerhood, and their functions, have already been identified in the literature, but lacking a coherent theoretical framework, their systemic relationship has not been recognized.

The proposed model of Japanese speakerhood, including the relevant linguistic indexes, is drawn in figure 1, with the three variables of speakerhood (epistemic stance, affective stance and self-shared perspective) combining to create a four-cell paradigm:

	Epistemic Stance	Affective Stance
Self	zero-form	*yo*
Shared	*no*	*ne*

Figure 1. A proposed model of Japanese speakerhood

Evidence for the selection of *yo* as the index of the speaker's affective stance was provided above, and additional support will be offered below.

With regard to the selection of the zero-form and *no* as the indexes of the speaker's individual and shared epistemic stances, respectively, I draw primarily on Cook (1990), which argues that the evidential functions of the zero-form and *no* are best accounted for by the concept of authority for knowledge (Du Bois, 1986). Cook's proposal that the zero-form indexes individual authority for knowledge while *no* indexes group authority for knowledge[8] is consistent with the functions of indexing self's epistemic stance and indexing shared epistemic stance attributed to the zero-form and *no*, respectively, in the proposed model. Moreover, Cook's division of individual-group (as opposed to speaker-hearer), which includes the speaker in the epistemic perspectives indexed by the zero-form and by *no*, is consistent with the goals of the speakerhood model -- to demonstrate how the speaker uses conversational resources to index his/her perspective as distinct from or harmonious with the perspective of the addressee (cf. the definition of speakerhood above).

As for the selection of *ne* as the index of shared affective stance, there are many researchers who have argued that the function of *ne* is related to agreement, confirmation or other forms of mutual exchange. However, these characterizations tend to miss the mark by focusing on the exchange of proposition-based information that underlies these types of interactions. Cook (1992), however, argues that *ne* indexes affective common ground; she recognizes not only that the particle indexes a shared perspective, but also focuses on its affective qualities. From the perspective of speakerhood, *ne* enables the speaker to align his/her affective perspective harmoniously with that of the addressee, a stance that is frequently preferred (from the perspective of sociocultural norms), and may even serve as a default stance, in Japanese discourse.

Having elaborated the model of Japanese speakerhood and the place of *yo* within that model, I now turn to examining the meanings that may be created when two indexes of speakerhood co-occur. Following the direction of my discussion thus far, I will limit my discussion to the co-occurrence of other indexes of speakerhood with *yo*. Moreover, by focusing on the relationship of speaker affect to the speaker's communicative goals, his/her social role and his/her relationship to the other interlocutors, I will further clarify the contribution of speakerhood to an understanding of the expression of self in Japanese discourse.

---

[8] Rudolph (1993:149) offers a similar proposal for the indexical meaning of *no*, arguing that '*no* indexes the domain of expertise which a speaker assumes him/herself to share with all the other members of his/her speech community, i.e., "common sense" in the true sense of the phrase.'

V. The co-occurrence of *yo* with other indexes of speakerhood[9]

In my discussion of the use of *yo* in non-declarative utterances (Section III), I demonstrated that the interpretation of speaker affect is heavily dependent on the context in which *yo* is uttered. *Yo* was shown to index a wide range of affective stances ranging from heartfelt loyalty to cynicism. In this section, I will demonstrate that, while the possible range of affective stances indexed by *yo* is, in effect, limitless, there are also constraints on the appropriate use of *yo* as an index of self's affective stance. These constraints on expression of self's affect are closely tied to the speaker's social role and topic, and can often be circumvented through the use of speakerhood markers that index a shared stance.

In the examples below, I examine a 45-minute interaction between a professor and his graduate student. An analysis of the participants' use of markers of speakerhood in the interaction reveals that, while there is not a single instance of *yo* as the only non-zero index of speakerhood by the student, the student does make regular use of the particle in conjunction with other non-zero indexes of speakerhood. In contrast, while the professor makes fairly liberal use of *yo* in his talk with the student, he tends to reserve the use of *yo* for talk that is not closely related to academic matters (e.g., personal stories and reminiscences). When the topic is oriented towards academic topics, the professor regularly uses *yo* in conjunction with other indexes of speakerhood.

A look at the professor's use of *yo* in Examples 6, 7 and 8 -- examples in which *yo* occurs alone, and in conjunction with *no* and *ne*, respectively -- will clarify the relationship of social role, utterance content and the speaker's expression of speakerhood.

Example 6

The student has presented the results of her statistical tests and an interpretation of them. The professor, finding fault with her analysis, reinterprets the student's results in his own way.

1 p; de, maa iwaba, nokori mitai na kanji de, ano, dete kuru to
2   omou yo. ((continues))

1 p; So, well, I'm pretty sure you'll get something that looks
2   like residuals so to speak. ((continues))

The professor is an expert in statistical analysis; yet, despite this fact, he

---

[9] This section has been shortened: in the conference paper I presented nine examples illustrating the use of *yo* by family members at dinnertime and by professors during office hours with graduate student advisees.

makes use of the evidential hedge *to omou* in line 2. The use of this hedge is appropriate since he is engaged in an impromptu analysis of the student's data, which he is seeing for the first time. In using the hedge, he avoids authoritatively stating 'the correct analysis' (which would be indexed by the speakerhood marker for self's evidential stance, the zero-form). Nonetheless, being an expert in statistics, the professor also indicates, through his use of *yo*, that his lack of certainty should in no way be taken as a sign that his analysis is open for criticism or challenge from the student. Thus, the professor uses an evidential hedge to frame his expertise responsibly -- he cannot be completely certain of his analysis after such a brief exposure to the data -- and, using an index of his affective stance, he indicates that his judgment is not to be questioned.[10]

The pragmatic effect of this utterance, then, is to communicate to the student that she must correct her previously-stated analysis in view of the fact that it conflicts with the analysis offered by the professor. Regardless of the professor's degree of certainty, his authority, deriving from his social role as professor, remains unchanged, and hence, his right to assert his opinion vis-a-vis the student's work (and expect compliance with his point-of-view) also remains unchanged.

This interpretation also clarifies the scope of *yo* as an index of speakerhood: it is clear that *yo* acts on all semantic content in the preceding utterance, and its pragmatic effect is unaffected by any epistemic hedges on that semantic content. This should not be surprising given the findings in Section III that *yo* has a pragmatic effect on utterances without any semantic content whatsoever. In example 6, then, the discoursal effects of the evidential hedge *to omou* and the affective index *yo* can be clearly separated, with *to omou* providing an index of the speaker's evidential stance toward the propositional content of the utterance and *yo* providing an index of the speaker's affective stance towards the uttering of the turn itself and toward the addressee as well.

The differential in scope between the epistemic index *to omou* and the affective index *yo* also holds with the epistemic index of speakerhood *no*, as can be seen in example 7 below:

Example 7

Professor and student talk about the process of topic selection for

---

[10] This interpretation suggests that the reportive 'I tell you' interpretation so often attributed to *yo* (Kuroda 1973, Martin 1975:918ff) does in fact exist; however, it is not tied to the speaker's assertion of the correct analysis ('You'll get something that looks like residuals'), but rather to his pragmatic assertion that the analysis provided is to be taken as authoritative (and not to be questioned by the student, as the professor's comments so often are). Givon's (1982) variable of 'non-challengeability' is also evident in this analysis.

an M.A. thesis. The student has asked what would happen if a
student brought in two topics, as she had done.

1 p; ma: (2) gakusei ga futatu: no teema o motte kita toki ni wa boku wa
2   dou shite ru ka na: ((laughs))
3 s; ((laughs)) yappari imasen ka sou iu hito wa
4 p; iya: inai koto wa nai no yo?
5 s; hai.

1 p; Well: (2) I wonder what I'd do when a student brought in two
      topics ((laughs))
2 s; Of course there isn't anyone like that
3 p; No: I wouldn't say that
4 s; Oh.

In line 4, the professor rebuts the student's assumption that no one ever
comes in with two topics, and supports this rebuttal in the discourse that
follows with a story about just such a two-topic student. The two indexes
of speakerhood used in his rebuttal, *no* for shared epistemic stance and *yo*
for non-shared affective stance, appear to index conflicting perspectives.
However, if the difference in scope of *no* and *yo* is taken into account, the
conflict is easily resolved.

The professor marks the semantic content of his utterance, the
rebuttal to the student, with *no*, thereby indicating that both he and the
student know better than to think that no one ever brings in two topics.
Given the fact that the discussion is initiated with the student's reminiscing
that she originally brought in two topics, the professor's selection of shared
epistemic perspective is hardly surprising. He knows that they both know
better than to think that such an occurrence is impossible.

The professor's use of *yo* indicates that, although they both have
access to the same facts, he assumes that his affective take on those facts is
different. This is evident in the differing treatments given the shared
information (i.e., that the student brought in two topics) by student and
professor. The student demonstrates a cavalier attitude towards the
information by using *yappari* and a postposed subject (line 3); from her
stance, it is clear that she sees her case as an anomaly which she and the
professor share as a private joke. This stance has the inadvertent effect of
diminishing the professor's years of experience in advising students by
uttering a judgment about his extensive experience ('Of course you never
see anyone who comes in with two topics.') through her very inexperienced
eyes. The student's highly personalized interpretation of his experience
appears to rankle the professor, thereby prompting him not only to rebut her
remark, but also to use *yo* to index that he does not share her affective
perspective. Thus, the apparent conflict between the co-occurrence of *no*
and *yo* is easily resolved: the professor bases his rebuttal on shared facts

(marked by *no*), but, by using *yo*, he adds additional pragmatic force to his fact-based rebuttal by indexing that he does not share the student's light-hearted take on his experience. The effect of the professor's use of *no yo* is to curtail the student's casual tone and return her to her context-appropriate role of obedient social lower, as is reflected in her use of *hai* as a response token.

In example 8, another common pairing of speakerhood indexes, *yo ne*, occurs:

Example 8

> The professor has been critiquing the student's work and the student seems to be following the criticisms. Her two previous turns, in which she has contributed to the professor's line of critique, have been evaluated positively by the professor, who continues to provide feedback.

1 p; soo iu koto soo iu koto. un. dakara, kore-

2 s;   a jya-

3 p; un.

4 s; ((embarrassed laugh)) heh heh, kasetsu wa shiji sarenai?

5 p; ((breathing in)) n: shiji sarenai tte iu ka sono kasetsu made iu no wa

6   chotto, kai-, ano:, shuchou ga tsuyosugiru yo ne? () un.

1 p; That's right, that's right. Yeah. So, this-

2 s;   oh then-

3 p; Go ahead.

4 s; ((embarrassed laugh)) Heh heh. The hypothesis isn't supported?

5 p; ((breathing in)) Um: I don't know whether you can say it's not supported, [but] to go as far as stating that hypothesis it's a little, um:, your claims are too strong (you know). () right.

The co-occurrence of *yo*, index of non-shared affective stance, and *ne*, index of shared affective stance, seems even more contradictory than the co-occurrence of *no* and *yo*: does the professor's turn index that he shares an affective stance with the student or not? In resolving this question, I will take the same step-by-step approach to analysis that was taken in examples 6 and 7.

In the interaction which encompasses example 8, the student is engaged in the problem-solving activity of determining why the professor finds her work unacceptable. At the same time, the professor is engaged in the delicate task of critiquing the student's work without dampening her enthusiasm or disparaging her efforts. The student's high level of involvement is evident in her use of the plain form (line 4), which is normally a sociolinguistically inappropriate form to use with a professor[11]. The professor's care in criticizing the student's work is evident in his prefatory remark (in which he both acknowledges and subtly challenges the student's perspective) and in the two hedges (*chotto* and *ano:*) that precede his identification of the problem he perceives.

As the student has already acknowledged several of the professor's points of criticism, the interaction can be considered a cooperative one: through their talk, professor and student establish a shared perspective that something is wrong with the student's analysis and it needs to be fixed. However, at line 6, the professor reaches a point in the interaction where his turn directly challenges the very assumptions of the student's work. Although the surface form of the utterance simply indicates disagreement or dissatisfaction with the nature of the student's claims ('*shuchou ga tsuyosugiru yo*'), the pragmatic effect of the professor's contradictory stance derives force from his position as academic advisor and statistical expert (as in example 6). The professor's use of *yo*, then, creates an authoritative challenge to the validity of the student's work, a challenge that the professor hesitates to utter, but which is a necessary step in the ongoing problem-solving activity.

However, unlike the use of *yo* in example 6, the authoritativeness of the profesor's uterance in example 8 is tempered by the co-occurrence of *ne* (index of shared affective stance). By using *ne*, the professor further indexes his turn as a constructive link in the ongoing joint problem-solving activity. The use of *ne* recasts the pragmatic force of the portion of the turn that precedes *ne*, changing the function of the turn from an unmitigated and, from the student's perspective, unchallengeable critique to a cooperative step in the problem-solving activity of professor and student. Furthermore, the use of *ne* indexes the professor's desire to sustain the shared focus of the ongoing collaborative efforts with the student[12].

---

[11] Use of the plain form by lower status interlocutors with higher status addressees is sociolinguistically acceptable when intense and/or spontaneous emotion is expressed. It is likely that the professor recognizes the student's high involvement in the ongoing problem-solving task and ignores her breech of sociolinguistic norms.

[12] Because of the assumption of shared affective stance indexed by *ne*, there is an implicit weakening of the authoritativeness of *yo* when it co-occurs with *ne* in situations such as the one in example 8. This weakening effect is described by Oishi (1985) in terms of the speaker's territory of information, and is assumed to be the definitive quality of *yo ne*. In this paper, however, I have shown that the interpretation of indexes of speakerhood is a highly contextualized process, and hence, I would argue that the weakening effect of *ne* on *yo* is not absolute, but rather will depend on the context of the utterance, and, more importantly, on the

Through the analysis of examples 7 and 8, both of which contain co-occurring markers of speakerhood, I have demonstrated the robustness of the model of speakerhood proposed in Figure 1. I have shown that that a) co-occurring markers of speakerhood can and should be interpreted according to the functions indicated in Figure 1 and that b) the interpretation of co-occurring markers is sequential, with the pragmatic effect of a given marker extending to all turn-internal linguistic content that precedes it.

The fact that there is a fixed sentence-final ordering for the linguistic items shown to mark speakerhood in Japanese highlights an interesting match of structure-based rules and sociocultural norms. The fixed sentence-final ordering is such that indexes of shared perspective follow non-shared ones, and affective indexes follow epistemic ones. This ordering enables a speaker to convert any utterance marked with a non-shared stance to one with a shared stance (*no* capping off a zero-form and *ne* capping of a *yo*), much in the same way that the verb-final characteristic of Japanese enables speakers to strategically change the polarity of the verb at utterance's end. Similarly, assertions of epistemic certainty (shared or not) can be softened (or strengthened) through the strategic addition of affective stance markers. Overall, the Japanese system of marking speakerhood enables the speaker to frame his/her utterance in a socioculturally-favorable light.

VI. Conclusion

In this work I have presented a model of speakerhood for Japanese. Linguistic indexes for each of the four stances included in the model were proposed, and the viability of the proposed indexical meanings was demonstrated based on the analysis of excerpts from natural discourse. The analysis also showed that the indirect meanings of the proposed indexes are closely related to the context-based role of the speaker. As such, these indexes clearly provide an important linguistic means through which the speaker achieves self-expression of her socially-situated self. Future attempts to incorporate other linguistic indexes of speaker stance into this model will provide a test of its strength and explanatory power.

References

Aoki, Haruo. 1986. Evidentials in Japanese. *Evidentiality: The linguistic coding of epistemology*, ed. by Wallace Chafe & Johanna Nichols, pp 223-238. Norwood, NJ: Ablex.
Cook, Haruko. 1990. An indexical account of the Japanese sentence-final particle *no. Discourse Processes* 13.401-439.
Cook, Haruko. 1992. Meanings of non-referential indexes: A case study

---

nature of the relationship of the interlocutors.

of the Japanese sentence-final particle *ne*. *Text* 12.507-39.

Cook, Haruko and Gabriele Kasper. 1995. Paper presented to the ESL Spring 1995 Lecture Series. University of Hawaii at Manoa.

Doi, Takeo. 1973. *The anatomy of dependence*. Tokyo: Kodansha International.

Du Bois, John W. 1986. Self-evidence and ritual speech. *Evidentiality: The linguistic coding of epistemology*, ed. by Wallace Chafe & Johanna Nichols, pp 313-333. Norwood, NJ: Ablex.

Givon, Talmy. 1982. Logic vs. pragmatics, with human language as the referee: toward an empirically viable epistemology. *Journal of Pragmatics* 6:81-133.

Iwasaki, Shoichi. 1993. *Subjectivity in grammar and discourse*. Philadelphia: John Benjamins.

Kamio, Akio. 1979. On the notion of speaker's territory of information: A functional analysis of certain sentence final forms in Japanese. *Explorations in linguistics: Papers in honor of Kazuko Inoue*, ed. by G. Bedell, E. Kobayashi, & M. Muraki, pp 213-231. Tokyo: Kaitakusha.

Kamio, Akio. 1991. *The theory of territory of information*. Unpublished manuscript, Dokkyo University.

Kamio, Akio. 1994. The theory of territory of information: The case of Japanese. *Journal of Pragmatics* 21.67-100.

Kuroda, S.-Y. 1973 Where epistemology, style and grammar meet: A case study from Japanese. *A festschrift for Morris Halle*, ed. by Stephen R. Anderson & Paul Kiparsky, pp 377-391. New York: Holt, Rinehart and Winston.

Makino, Seiichi and Tsuitsui, Michio. 1986. *A Dictionary of Basic Japanese Grammar*. Tokyo: The Japan Times.

Martin, Samuel. 1975. *A Reference Grammar of Japanese*. New Haven: Yale University Press.

Maynard, Senko. 1993. *Discourse modality: Subjectivity, emotion and voice in the Japanese language*. Philadelphia: John Benjamins.

Ochs, Elinor and Bambi Schieffelin. 1989. Language has a heart. *Text* 9.7-25.

Oishi, Toshio. 1985. A description of Japanese final particles in context. Doctoral dissertation, University of Michigan.

Rosenberger, Nancy R. 1989. Dialectic balance in the polar model of self: The Japan case. *Ethos* 17.88-113.

Rudolph, Dina. 1993. Getting past politeness: The role of linguistic markers of evidentiality and informational domains in Japanese student-teacher interactions at the graduate level. Doctoral dissertation, University of Southern California.

Schiffrin, Deborah. 1987. *Discourse Markers*. Cambridge: Cambridge University Press.

Steverson, Misako. 1995. The Mother's Role in Japanese Dinnertime Narratives. M.A. thesis, University of Hawai'i-Manoa.

Tanimori, Masahiro. 1994. *Handbook of Japanese Grammar*. Rutland, VT: Tuttle.

Tsuchihashi, Mika. 1983. The speech act continuum: an investigation of Japanese sentence final particles. *Journal of Pragmatics* 7:361-387.

Uyeno, Tazuko. 1971. A study of Japanese modality -- A performative analysis of sentence particles. Doctoral dissertation, University of Michigan.

Yoshimi, Dina R. In progress. Framing responsibility in Japanese conversation: evidentiality and affect. Ms., University of Hawaii at Manoa.

Japanese *Kedo*: Discourse Genre and Grammaticization

Toshihide Nakayama & Kumiko Ichihashi-Nakayama

University of California, Santa Barbara

1.   Introduction[1]

The Japanese particle *keredo(mo)* or its shortened form *kedo* is commonly characterized as a concessive or contrastive conjunctive particle corresponding to the English 'although' or 'but' (e.g. Martin 1975; Makino and Tsutui 1986). As a concessive conjunctive particle, it connects two finite clauses by attaching to the end of the first clause and expresses a contrastive relationship between two propositions such that the second proposition states an 'unexpected' or 'surprising' result in the light of the first proposition. Example (1) would be a canonical example of this usage: based on the fact of 'being small in size' stated in the first clause, the person in quesion is usually expected not to be physically strong, but the second clause expresses this unexpected fact.

[1] We would like to thank Sandra Thompson and Patricia Clancy for their comments on an earlier version of this paper. We are also grateful to Tsuyoshi Ono and Ryoko Suzuki for some of the conversational data used in this study.

(1)   (Martin 1975:977)[2]
karada wa chiisai **kedo**, chikara   wa tsuyoi.
body   TOP small   physical.strength TOP strong
'Although (he) is small in size, (he) is mighty in strength.'

This 'basic' function of *kedo* corresponds to the historical origin of the particle. *Kedo* originated as a combined form of the inflectional ending *kere* and the old concessive particle *do(mo)* (Doi 1969:415). It started to be used from around the end of Muromachi period and gradually took over the function of *do(mo)*.

In modern Japanese, however, as described in the literature (e.g. Alfonso 1966; Doi 1969; Maynard 1990), clauses connected by *kedo* do not necessarily indicate contrastive meaning, that is, the second proposition may not in any way be contradictory or unexpected in view of the first proposition, nor does the particle necessarily even connect two clauses. In fact, in our spoken Japanese data, the NON-CONTRASTIVE usage of *kedo* accounts for about 47% of the total usage of the particle. Also, 27% of the uses of *kedo* appear without any 'main' clause following.

In this paper, we focus on non-contrastive uses of *kedo* and examine them in two discourse genres, namely, narrative and conversation. It will be shown that non-contrastive *kedo* is used in quite different ways in the two genres. We will then argue that the non-contrastive functions of *kedo* have been GRAMMATICIZED from its 'basic' function as a contrastive conjunctive particle, and that the functional differences in the use of *kedo* across genres reflect different pathways of grammaticization motivated by different communicative goals.

2.   *Kedo* in Narratives

First, we look at the usage of *kedo* in narratives. The narrative data considered in this study consist of three speeches (total length 15 min.) given at a wedding reception. The speakers, two male and one female, were college classmates of the bride and groom and were in their late 20s. The speeches may have been premeditated since all three speakers were asked in advance to give a speech. The speeches, however, were made without any written scripts, and we consider them to be natural and spontaneous. Out of 49 tokens of *kedo* (or *keredo(mo)*) in the speeches, 32 are used to express non-contrastive meanings.

In the majority of these non-contrastive uses, the clauses followed by *kedo* ('*kedo*-clauses') function to provide a context, or to set up a frame of reference or evaluative undercurrent for the events sequentially reported in the main clauses. In many cases, the *kedo*-clause describes the background situation in which a particular incident occurs.

---

2 The abbreviations used in the glosses are: ACC: accusative; DAT: dative; GEN: genitive; LOC: locative; NEG: negative; NOM: nominative; NOM-IZER: nominalizer; PRT: particle; QUOT: quotative; TOP: topic marker.

In (2), for example, the *kedo*-clause states the fact that the speaker and the groom, together with two people called Satoh and Takahashi, used to hang around together. Having given this general frame, the speaker proceeds to speak about individual occasions, which are here introduced by the expression of instantiation *tatoeba* 'for example'.[3]

(2)   satoo-kun takahashi-kun nanka to,
         Mr. Satoh Mr. Takahashi etc.   with

         e=,
         well

         yoku tsurundetandesu   **kedo**,
         often hang.around.together

         tatoeba,
         for.example

         %atarashii deai   o   motomete itta= nonimokakawarazu,
         new   meeting ACC seek   went   in.spite.of

         tada hiyake dake shite kaettekita koozushima no tuaa toka
         only sun.tan only got   came.back Koozu.Island GEN tour or

                  desu ne,
                  be   PRT

         'We used to hang around quite a lot with Mr. Satoh, Mr.
         Takahashi, and others — for example, we made a trip to the Koozu
         Island where we hoped to meet someone but only got a sun tan ...'

There is no contrastive relation between the two facts reported here, their hanging around together and their trip to the Koozu Island. The *kedo*-clause here gives the background situation in which the specific event, the trip to the Koozu Island, took place.

Kedo-clauses are also used to introduce a referent which is necessary for the main story line. Example (3) is a segment reporting an event which happened in a rehearsal for a theatrical play. In this segment, the *kedo*-clause functions to introduce one of the important elements in the event, *serifu* 'line', into the context, and the speaker develops the story based on it.

---

[3] The transcription of data is based on the conventions described in Du Bois et. al. (1993). Each line represents an INTONATION UNIT (Chafe 1987, 1994), 'a sequence of words combined under a single, coherent intonation contour' (1987:22).

(3)   *'Kathy, I love you'*,

tte   iu   serifu ga   attandesu **kedo**,
QUOT say line   NOM existed

sore ga   desu ne,
that NOM be   PRT

nankai   yatte mo   dekinaindesu ne,
how.many.times did   even is.not.able.to PRT

'(He) had a line that said 'Kathy, I love you', and (he) could not (say) it no matter how many times (he) tried.'

Alfonso (1966:517-8) characterized the type of *kedo*-clauses we have seen in (2) and (3) as 'prefatory statements'. *Kedo*-clauses in these cases in fact function as a prologue to set the stage for the main portion of the narrative.

Non-contrastive *kedo*-clauses in narratives are sometimes used to make a parenthetical remark on an event being reported. These parenthetical remarks are outside the main sequence of the narrative and are placed in a time and place different from those in the narrative, usually the time and place of speech, or the 'here' and 'now'. This type of *kedo*-clause is often inserted in the middle of an on-going clause, as can be seen in Examples (4) and (5). In (4) and (5), the parenthetical *kedo*-clauses are indicated by square brackets:

(4)   maa ima hayarino   ..enkyori   renai   toyuuno o
        well now commonly.done long.distance relationship QUOT   ACC

        nannenkanka,
        for.some.years

        [..maa ..enkyori   to   iimashi temo,
          well long.distance QUOT call   although

        kanarino enkyori   desu **keredomo**],
        extreme long.distance be

        nasatteta   wake desu keredomo,[4]
        were.engaging.in PRT be

        'Well, they were maintaining a long-distance — it was truly 'long-distance' in their case — relationship.'

_____

[4] This *keredomo* is performing a similar function as in (2); based on the background situation described here, the narrative goes on reporting what happened during that period.

(5)   ano,
well

aru-,
one

[koko ni,
here LOC

konoba ni   wa   chotto= kyoo wa   shussekishite nai n
this.place LOC TOP well   today TOP attend   NEG NOM-IZER

      desu **kedo**],
      be

aru jyosee no,
one lady   GEN

maa warewareno ..dooki   no onnanoko ni   desu ne,
well   our   same.class GEN girl   DAT be   PRT

e=,
well

'*Kathy, I love you*',

tte   iu serifu ga   attandesu kedo,
QUOT say line   NOM existed

'Well, (he) had a line that said 'Kathy, I love you' to one — one
who is not attending this reception — girl who was in our class ...'

In (4), the speaker is explaining that the bride and the groom kept
their relationship going while they were separated between Japan and the
United States. After he says *enkyori* 'long distance', before finishing the
clause, the speaker comments on the appropriateness of the expression. In
(5), the speaker starts talking about a woman who was their classmate. But
before even completing the noun phrase, he inserts the *kedo*-clause in order
to provide information about the woman which is not directly relevant to the
event he is about to report. In these cases, the *kedo*-clauses are used to
make parenthetical remarks which themselves are not part of the main
sequence of the reported events.

      In his 1979 article, Hopper made a distinction between parts of
narratives that he called FOREGROUND and BACKGROUND. While
FOREGROUND includes the parts of the narrative which correspond to the
actual story line, BACKGROUND includes the parts which 'support, amplify,
or COMMENT ON the narration' (215) consisting of 'supportive material
which does not itself narrate the main events.' (213) The non-contrastive
kedo-clauses we have seen in our narrative data can be characterized as part

of the background portion of the narrative in that they convey information which is not directly incorporated into the sequence of main events.

The backgrounding function of the *kedo*-clauses in narratives can also be reflected in the grammatical characteristics of the clauses. Hopper (1979) observed various linguistic properties associated with backgrounding clauses, including imperfective aspect in the verbs used in the clauses. In their investigation of 'transitivity' in discourse, Hopper and Thompson (1980) found that backgrounded clauses tend to be low in transitivity, and imperfective aspect is one of their low-transitivity features. The *kedo*-clauses of backgrounding function in our data strikingly confirm these correlations: the verbs in the backgrounding *kedo*-clauses in our data are either stative verbs, as in (3) and (4), or take the durative *-te iru* form, as in (2) and (5), and they are all intransitive.

Thus, the non-contrastive *kedo*-clauses in our narrative data serve to provide background information for the main line of the narrative, and the particle *kedo* in these cases functions as an indicator of backgrounding.

3. *Kedo* in Conversation

Now we turn to the non-contrastive use of *kedo* in conversation. Our conversational data consist of 6 segments of conversations, ranging from 3 to 9 minutes in length. Each conversation is produced by 2 to 3 speakers in their 20s who are good friends. In these conversations, in 10 out of 40 cases, *kedo* does not express any contrastive relationship. In these cases, however, the non-contrastive *kedo* is used quite differently from its use in narratives. The most prominent tendency found in the conversational data is that *kedo* often appears at the end of a turn without any identifiable 'main' clause.

In many of these cases, *kedo* is used after an utterance which presents the speaker's knowledge or opinion. For example, in the stretch of conversation where (6) occurs, the speakers are gossiping about a student who had been recruited by their department but has turned down the offer. After one of the speakers says, 'Wasn't she from UCSD?', speaker Y responds with the following utterance:

(6) Y: *San Diego State* tte　　uwasa o　　kiita **kedo**.
　　　　　　　　　QUOT　rumor ACC　heard
　　　'I heard (she) is from San Diego State (University).'

Adding *kedo* at the end of the utterance has the effect of making the tone of the assertion more attenuated. In this way, speaker Y is able to avoid direct confrontation with the other speaker, who seems to have a different opinion.

This use of *kedo* is also found in contexts where no possible conflict of opinion is present:

(7) T: tabemono niyoru   sa   tteno mo ookii toshite,
       diet   according.to difference QUOT too large granted

jinshu sa   mo aru kamoshirenai **kedo**.
racial difference too exist maybe

'Granted that difference in diet is a significant factor, I presume racial difference is also a factor.'

In (7), speaker T states his opinion about possible reasons why stomach cancer is more common among Japanese while cancer of the large intestine is more common among Americans. T is a physician specialized in cancer treatment, and there is no other speaker who T could be in conflict with. T adds *kedo* to soften the assertive tone of the utterance and avoid being imposing or sounding like a 'know-it-all'.

In these cases, *kedo* seems to function like other final particles in Japanese in that it reflects the speaker's interpersonal concerns (cf. Maynard 1989). In particular, it serves to mitigate the force of illocutionary acts in order to maintain harmony among speakers.

4.   From Contrastive to Non-contrastive Functions

In the previous sections, we have seen different types of non-contrastive uses of *kedo* in narrative and conversational data. The next question would be: is there any relationship between these non-contrastive functions of *kedo* and its 'basic' contrastive function? We would like to argue that these non-contrastive functions of *kedo* have developed from its use as a contrastive conjunctive particle through the process of GRAMMATICIZATION (cf. Heine et al. 1991; Hopper and Traugott 1993).

4. 1   Unidirectionality in GRAMMATICIZATION

GRAMMATICIZATION is a dynamic process by which a lexical item assumes a grammatical function or a grammatical item assumes a more grammatical function (cf. Heine et al. 1991; Hopper and Traugott 1993). Although grammaticization has typically been discussed as a diachronic process, it has been claimed in recent years that the notion of grammaticization can also be applied to synchronic grammatical analyses (e.g. Lehmann 1985; Traugott 1986; Thompson and Mulac 1991). Based on observations of many instances of grammaticization in typologically diverse languages, linguists have been able to identify a set of universal principles underlying the process. Based on these principles, multiple functions of a certain linguistic form at a given time can be arranged into a hyothesized order of development.

One of the basic principles of grammaticization is the unidirectionality of the process. As summarized in (8) below, the changes which occur during the grammaticization process tend to proceed in only one direction within various aspects of grammar. For example, the meaning of grammaticizing material tends to change from concrete and specific to more abstract and general, but not vice versa (a process often referred to as 'semantic bleaching' or 'generalization'). This semantic reduction tends to correlate with phonological reduction; the formal or phonological substance of grammaticizing material will be reduced during the process of grammaticization (Bybee et al. 1994). At the same time, material which was used only in a certain grammatical context comes to appear in a wider set of contexts (Bybee et al. 1994). While the semantic content of grammaticizing material may be reduced, its pragmatic meaning tends to increase, in that material with largely propositional content gains textual (cohesion-making) and/or expressive (modal, and other pragmatic) meanings ('pragmatic strengthening' or 'subjectification') (Traugott 1982, 1986, 1989).

(8)   **Unidirectionality in grammaticization**

     (a) semantic bleaching: concrete > abstract
     (b) phonological reduction: long > short
     (c) range of syntactic applicability: narrow > wider
     (d) pragmatic strengthening:
          propositional > textual > expressive

When considering the different functions of *kedo* in terms of these parameters, we are able to project possible grammaticization pathways in the development of the particle.

4. 2   Grammaticization paths in the development of the non-contrastive functions of *kedo*

The BACKGROUND function of *kedo* we have seen in our narrative data can be considered to represent the earlier stage of grammaticization as the concessive particle moves away from its original function. As a concessive conjunctive particle, *kedo* expresses a contrastive relation between two propositions by setting up a ground or a reference point for contrast with the clause to which it attaches. We hypothesize that, over time, this specific contrastive meaning of *kedo* has become bleached, and the use of *kedo* is extended to the general indexing of a discourse reference point or background information. In other words, the function of *kedo* shifts from indicating a relation between propositions to serving as a device for textual, discourse organization.

The SOFTENING function of *kedo* that we have seen in our conversational data can be hypothesized to represent a later stage of grammaticization. In her description of the softening function of *kedo*, Maynard (1990) explains that this meaning comes from a 'feeling of incompleteness' caused by the 'deleted' main clause. In examples like (6) and (7), however, there seems to be no 'main' clause or proposition left implied or suggested. Instead, the clauses followed by *kedo* themselves express the speaker's main assertion. It is therefore more appropriate to consider these clauses to be grammatically and pragmatically independent, and *kedo* in this function is used as a final particle rather than a conjunctive particle.

Our alternative to Maynard's analysis is the proposal that the softening meaning comes from the function of *kedo* as an indicator of a reference point or background information. When attached to independent clauses, the particle conveys a sense that the clause expresses background or peripheral information. It is this 'backgrounded' sense which gives a softening tone to the assertion. Thus, *kedo* in this function has developed an expressive meaning: by using this particle, the speaker can manipulate the way the assertion is delivered. As a final particle, *kedo* has a wider grammatical distribution in that it no longer has to connect two clauses but can potentially attach to any independent clause.

The hypothesized grammaticization pathway of the development of the non-contrastive functions of *kedo* is summarized in (9).

(9)   **Grammaticization path in the development of the functions of *kedo***

CONCESSIVE > BACKGROUND > SOFTENING

Semantics: contrastive --------------------------> non-contrastive
Syntax: conjunctive particle ----------------> final particle
Pragmatics: propositional ------> textual ------> expressive[5]

The parameters of 'semantic bleaching', 'range of syntactic applicability', and 'pragmatic strenghening' all suggest the order of concessive > background > softening functions of *kedo*. It should be noted, however, that (9) does not mean that the softening function necessarily arises through the backgrounding function of the particle. It only indicates that the former function shows a greater degree of grammaticization and has possibly developed later in the course of time than the latter has.

5.   **Discourse Genre and Motivation for Grammaticization**

As described in the previous sections, most of the non-contrastive uses of *kedo* in our narrative data show the backgrounding function, while most of the non-contrastive uses in our conversational data show the softening function. This skewing of the distribution of the functions does not seem to be accidental: it seems to reflect the difference in motivations

---

[5] The parameter of phonological reduction could be included as evidence for this grammaticization pathway. According to Doi (1969), shortened forms of *keredomo*, first *keredo* and then *kedo,* started to be used later in the modern period. While in our data the softening function tends to be executed by the shortest form *kedo*, the association between the forms and the different functions of the particle needs to be examined with more extensive data.

for grammaticization present in each genre. Different genres have different discourse dynamics, such as the way discourse is planned and laid out, the way information is arranged, and the way participants interact. We would like to argue that it is this difference in discourse dynamics that gives rise to the different functions of *kedo*. And the distribution of the different functions of *kedo* is very well motivated by the discourse dynamics typical in each genre.

In narratives, the main discourse goal is story-telling. The purpose of the speeches at the wedding reception in our narrative data, for example, is to tell anecdotes about the bride and groom. In narratives, the speaker is required to build a structured, extended discourse. Such a communicative goal calls for and motivates the development of text structuring devices, such as one that facilitates the systematic differentiation of background information from the main events of the plot.

In conversation, on the other hand, what is important is interactional considerations. When conversing with other speakers, Japanese speakers try to minimize potential threats to the interactive ideal of harmony, such as conflict with or offense against others. In this genre, therefore, there is motivation for grammaticizing a device to mitigate or soften the force of illocutionary acts.

We are not arguing, of course, that the backgrounding function of *kedo* is exclusive to narratives nor the softening function to conversation. In fact, in our narrative data, there are a few cases in which *kedo* is used to soften the assertion when the speaker states his/her own intention or desire. Although our conversational data are highly interactive, there are a few occasions on which the speaker produces a small narrative and *kedo* shows the backgrounding function. It is still true, however, that the different uses of *kedo* arise in response to the different communicative needs. The different distribution of the functions of *kedo* across the genres is a reflection of the communicative needs which are typically present in each genre.

6. Conclusions

In this paper, we have investigated two non-contrastive functions of the Japanese particle *kedo*, i.e. BACKGROUNDING and SOFTENING, by examining its occurence in two different discourse genres, narrative and conversation. Based on the principles established in the theory of grammaticization, the backgrounding and softening functions are placed along possible pathways for the development of *kedo* originating from its function as a contrastive conjunctive particle. The distribution of the different functions of *kedo* in narratives and conversation is associated with the different discourse dynamics of each genre, which we argue serve as the motivation for grammaticization of the different functions of *kedo*.

References

Alfonso, Anthony. 1966. Japanese language patterns: a structural approach, volume 1. Tokyo: Sophia University L.L. Center for Applied Linguistics.

Bybee, Joan, Revere Perkins, and William Pagliuca. 1994. The evolution of grammar: tense, aspect, and modality in the languages of the world. Chicago: University of Chicago Press.

Chafe, Wallace. 1987. Cognitive constraints on information flow. Coherence and grounding in discourse, ed. by Russell S. Tomlin, 21-51. Amsterdam: John Benjamins.

_____. 1994. Discourse, consciousness, and time. Chicago: University of Chicago Press.

Doi, Akira. 1969. *Keredomo - setsuzoku joshi <gendaigo>*. [*Keredomo -* conjunctive particle <modern Japanese>.] *Kotengo, gendaigo, joshi jodooshi syoosetsu* [Detailed analyses of particles and auxiliaries in classical and modern Japanese], ed. by Akira Matsumura, 415-420. Tokyo: Gakutoosha.

Du Bois, John, Stephan Schuetze-Coburn, Danae Paolino, and Susanna Cumming. 1993. Outline of discourse transcription. Talking data: transcription and coding methods of language research, eds. by Jane A. Edwards and Martin D. Lampert, 45-89. Hillsdale, NJ: Lawrence Erlbaum.

Heine, Bernd, Ulrike Claudi, and Friederike Hünnemeyer. 1991. Grammaticalization: a conceptual framework. Chicago: University of Chicago Press.

Hopper, Paul J. 1979. Aspect and foregrouding in discourse. Discourse and syntax, ed. by T. Givón, 213-241. New York: Academic Press.

Hopper, Paul J. and Sandra A. Thompson. 1980. Transitivity in grammar and discourse. Language 56(2): 251-299.

Hopper, Paul J. and Elizabeth Closs Traugott. 1993. Grammaticalization. London: Cambridge University Press.

Lehmann, Christian. 1985. Grammaticalization: synchronic variation and diachronic change. Lingua e Stile 20(3): 303-318.

Martin, Samuel E. 1975. A reference grammar of Japanese. New Haven and London: Yale University Press.

Makino, Seiichi, and Michiko Tsutsui. 1986. A dictionary of basic Japanese grammar. Tokyo: Japan Times.

Maynard, Senko K. 1989. Japanese conversation: self-contextualization through structure and interactional management. Norwood, NJ: Ablex Publishing Corporation.

_____. 1990. An introduction to Japanese grammar and communication strategies. Tokyo: Japan Times.

Thompson, Sandra A. and Anthony Mulac. 1991. A quantitative perspective on the grammaticization of epistemic parentheticals in English. Approaches to grammaticalization, volume II, eds. by

Elizabeth Closs Traugott and Bernd Heine, 313-329. Amsterdam: John Benjamins.

Traugott , Elizabeth Closs. 1982. From propositional to textual and expressive meanings: Some semantic-pragmatic aspects of grammaticalization. Perspectives in historical linguistics, eds. by Winfried P. Lehmann and Yakov Malkiel, 245-271. Amsterdam: John Benjamins.

_____. 1986. From polysemy to internal semantic reconstruction. BLS 12: 539-550.

_____. 1989. On the rise of epistemic meanings in English: an example of subjectification in semantic change. Language 65(1): 31-55.

How 'Seeing' Approaches 'Knowing' in Korean, Japanese, and English: An Analysis of *pota, miru, and see**

YONG-YAE PARK & SUSAN STRAUSS
University of California, Los Angeles

1. Introduction

This study represents the initial stages of our research on the semantic scope of the verbs related to visual perception in Korean, Japanese, and English. Our departure point in the study primarily included Korean *pota*, Japanese *miru*, and English *look, see*, and *watch* We will attempt to determine to what extent Japanese *miru* can be a counterpart of Korean *pota* and how each lexical verb in Japanese and Korean patterns against the three seemingly similar verbs of visual perception in English. By using a variety of spontaneous spoken data, we will also attempt to demonstrate how the concept of seeing approaches the concept of knowing by illustrating some of the most striking similarities and differences between these five verbs as they occur as lexical verbs in the three languages. We will conclude by comparing and contrasting the use of these verbs in auxiliary constructions, i.e. *-te miru* in Japanese and *-a/e pota* in Korean. In addition to some surface similarities in the structure and function of these auxiliary constructions, we have discovered some significant differences. We will maintain that these crucial differences are due primarily to the semantic scope of each verb as a lexical verb, or more specifically, how closely the notion of 'seeing' actually approaches the notion of 'knowing'.

---

* We are grateful to Prof. Noriko Akatsuka and Prof. Roger Andersen for their suggestions, comments, and encouragement on this paper.

2. The Data

The data we used are all from spontaneous spoken speech including both narratives and conversations; the data types and sources have been summarized in Figure 1.:

A) Pear Narratives
English 11 Pear Story narratives
Japanese 11 Pear Story narratives
Korean 11 Pear Story narratives

B) Personal Narratives and Conversation

    i. Personal Narratives

    a. English:
        1) 6 near-death narratives collected by Elinor Ochs, et al. (1976-1977)
        2) 14 "authority-encounter" narratives collected by Anna Gutherie
    b. Japanese: 12 near-death narratives from Iwasaki (1988)
    c. Korean:
        1) 7 memorable trips/ near-death experience narratives collected by Y. Park (1992)
        2) 1 Grandpa narrative collected by H.S. Lee (1987)

    ii. Conversation

    a. Japanese: 12 phone conversations (Szatrowski, 1991)
    b. Korean:
        1) 12 phone conversations (Y. Park, 1994)
        2) one face-to-face conversation (Y. Park, 1993)
        3) 2 phone conversations (H.S. Lee, 1987)

Figure.1

For the English and Japanese Pear narratives, we used the original narratives collected by Chafe et al. (1980); and for Korean we used a combination of data more recently collected by Kyu hyun Kim (7 narratives) in addition to the two collected by H.S. Lee (1987).

From this database, we isolated a total of 541 tokens of verbs of visual perception across the three languages and coded them according to a variety of criteria using the Paradox database management system.

3. Analysis
3.1. Pear Story Narratives

The first data type we would like to discuss is the pear narratives. The story is about a boy who comes by on a bike and steals a basket filled with pears from a farmer who was picking pears up in a tree. Because the farmer was so involved in his work, he wasn't paying attention and the boy got away with an entire basket. While he was riding away on his bicycle, the boy passed a girl coming from the other direction. As the boy turned to look at the girl, his hat flew off. His bike then hit a rock that was in the middle of the road and he fell. Meanwhile, three other young boys witnessed this sequence of events and went over to help the boy. In return for their help, he hands a pear to each. At the end of the film, the man comes down from the tree and sees that a basket of pears is missing. At that moment, the three boys pass by, eating pears and the farmer wonders whether those pears are his.

We found the pear film narratives especially useful for this study because the task involves two different layers of visual perception, that is, the visual perception of the narrators who recount the events of the film and the visual perception by the characters in the film. Additionally, as a result of this research focus, we have begun to uncover not only lexical differences in how speakers of these languages describe what they see, but perhaps even more importantly, what grammatical means speakers of Korean, Japanese, and English employ to talk about objects, events, and actions coming into view.

As shown in Table 1, the range of verbs of seeing used in each language seems to vary substantially. Note that English (Table 1.3) and Japanese (Table 1.2) demonstrate a much wider variety in choice of verbs, in contrast with Korean (Table 1.1), which uses *pota* or a variation of it almost exclusively. As noted, *pota* is used as a lexical verb to mean 'see', 'look', and 'notice,' displaying a frequency of 67.9%. With the exception of the last four verbs on the list, the remainder of the verbs of seeing in Korean are all directly derived from *pota*.

In contrast with Korean *pota*, Japanese *miru*, is used to express the actions of seeing and looking only. As shown in Table 1.2, *miru* clearly does not encode the cognitive notions of 'realize' and 'notice', which instead are conveyed through expressions such as *ki ga tsuku* and *kizuku.* Visual perception involving a directional action similar to Korean *twuitolapota* and *tolatapota*, meaning to turn around, is expressed in Japanese through verbs such as *muku, furimuku,* and *yosomi suru.*

Table 1. Pear Data: Verbs of Visual Perception
(# of Tokens: percentage (raw frequency))

Table 1.1 Korean

Token	Gloss	# of Tokens
pota	**see, look, notice**	**67.8 (57)**
chietapota	**look up**	**8.3 (7)**
tola(ta) pota	**turn around**	**4.7 (4)**
twuitolapota	**look back**	**1.2 (1)**
poita	be visible	1.2 (1)
-unka pota	look like	3.6 (3)
-ale pota	Conn.+ see	2.4 (2)
-ko pota	Conn.+ see	1.2 (1)
palkyenhata	discover	2.4 (2)
cengshiniphallita	be distracted	1.2 (1)
shinkyengssuta	pay attention	1.2 (1)
moluta	not notice (not know)	3.6 (3)
alta	notice (know)	1.2 (1)
Total		100 (N=84)

Table 1.2 Japanese

Token	Gloss	# of Tokens
miru	see, look	29.2 (26)
ki ga tsuku	notice	14.6 (13)
kizuku	notice	3.5 (3)
miageru	look up	1.1 (1)
mieru	be visible	2.2 (2)
mikakeru	be found	2.2 (2)
miokuru	gaze after	1.1 (1)
misugosu	overlook	1.1 (1)
mita kanji	impression	1.1 (1)
mitai	(look) like	16.9 (15)
mitoreru	distracted	7.9 (7)
mitsukeru	find	4.5 (4)
-ku mieru	look+adj.	1.1 (1)
ki o torareru	be distracted	2.2 (2)
me no mae o	in front of one's eyes	1.1 (1)
furimu ku	look back	1.1 (1)
muku	turn one's head	3.5 (3)
yosomi suru	look away	1.1 (1)
shiru	know, be aware	2.2 (2)
wakaru	know, notice	2.2 (2)
Total		100 (N=89)

Table 1.3 English

Token	# of Tokens	
see[1]	**25.7 (27)**	
look	**23.8 (25)**	**66.6%**
notice	**17.1 (18)**	
watch	3.8 (4)	
catch attention	1.9 (2)	
come across	1.9 (2)	
discover	1 (1)	
find	1.9 (2)	
know	1.9 (2)	
let's see	4.7 (5)	
look like	3.8 (4)	
pay attention	1.9 (2)	
realize	2.9 (3)	
run across	1 (1)	
show	1 (1)	
take a look	1 (1)	
turn	4.7 (5)	
Total	100 (N=105)	

The distribution of the verbs of visual perception in English shows a clustering of the greatest percentage for *see, look,* and *notice,* comprising a total of 66.6%.   *Watch,* which could also be considered a counterpart of both *miru* and *pota,* was used only four times throughout the 11 narratives, which we found somewhat surprising.

These pear narrative data provide us with convincing initial evidence that *pota* and *miru* pattern quite differently from each other, in that *pota* seems to express a wider range of meaning including a more complex type of cognitive processing than *miru.*

---

[1] Other tokens such as *you look* (2); *you see* (28); *you watch* (2) with indefinite 'you' as in: 'there's a man at the top of the ladder and *you see* him plucking a pear from the tree' appeared in the data. However, since this use of perception verbs is not found either in Japanese or in Korean, we have not included it in this table for the purpose of the current discussion.

3.2. Semantic Schema for *miru* and *pota*

To account for these apparent differences between *pota* and *miru*, we would like to suggest the following schema. We base this schema on a variation of Tobin's (1993) framework for *look* and *see*. Tobin basically proposes a system whereby *look* would be the unmarked form to express PROCESS OR RESULT connected with visual perception, whereas *see* is the marked form only for RESULT. Our schema for *pota* and *miru* is shown in Figure 2.

Semantic substance	form	meaning
	miru	MEANS[2]
perception of object, state, event, or overall view		
	pota	MEANS/ END

MEANS: 'look at', 'see' (i.e., apprehend objects by sight), 'watch', 'check out a situation or surroundings'

END: 'notice', 'realize', 'know', 'recognize'

Figure 2

Activities of visual perception such as 'look at', 'see' (in the sense apprehend objects by sight), and 'watch', in the sense of generally checking out a situation or surroundings would be considered as expressions of MEANS rather than END, since such activities involve visual perception only without extending into more complex mental processing. In contrast, our categorization of END denotes more complex mental activities such as 'notice,' 'realize,' 'know,' and 'recognize' since the activity transcends beyond the sight of the perceived object. Bear in mind, however, that *pota* signifies both a MEANS as well as an END type of activity. This schema will become crucial in our endeavor to trace the path between seeing and knowing as it relates to both *miru* and *pota*.

---

[2] The terms, MEANS and END in our schema correspond to Tobin's notion of "process" and "result", respectively.

3.3. Semantic Scope for *miru* and *pota*

Table 2 provides a breakdown in finer detail of the types of objects, events, or states occurring as the complements of *miru*, *ki ga tsuku* ('realize'), *pota*[3] from Pear story and personal narratives.

Table 2 Types of Complements of 'See' (percentage)

		Japanese		Korean
		miru (N=26)	*ki ga tsuku* (N=13)	*pota* (N=57)
1. Simple Noun Object		27	0	38.2
2. Other	a. Event in progress	0	0	10.9
Object	b. Event complete	7.7	15.5	0
Types	c. State	11.5	7.7	21.8
	d. Direction	0	0	0
Object sub total		46.2	23.2	70.9
3. State		0	38.4	1.8
4. Overall		34.6	0	21.8
5. General awareness		11.5	38.4	1.8
6. Others		7.7	0	3.7
Total		100	100	100

Note in particular the overwhelmingly high frequency (71%) of *pota* occurring with object complements, in contrast with the (46%) of *miru* tokens for the same category. Examples of this type of object complementation in each language are shown in (4).

(4) coding category 1-- simple object
[Korean]
(4a)
pay -lul   hancham   po -ko iss -te   -ni
pear -OM   for:a:while   see -PROG -RETRO -DET
'after he (the bike boy) was looking at the pears for a while'   [Pear 9]

---

[3] Due to space constraints, we have reserved of our discussion of the English data for a future paper.

(4b)
ku acwu isangha -n nwuncholi -lotaka ku ai -tul -ul po -nta -kwu
like quite strange -ATTR corner:of :eye --INSTR **that child -PL -OM**
see -DECL -CONN
'With mystified eyes, he (the farmer) looks at the boys'　　　[Pear 11]

[Japanese]
(4c)
*sono kago no **nashi** o koo jitto **miru** wake ne, HOSHI, hoshikute*
that basket GEN **pear** OM like:this intently **see** PT PT want want -TE
'He (the bike boy) looks at the basket intently like this, wanting..'
[Pear 1]

(4d)
*sannin no sugata o ojisan ga chotto fushigisoo ni **mite**-re n de
owatta*
three people PT appearance OM old:man SM a:little strangely
look PROG PT end -PST
'The old guy was looking a little strangely at the 3 boys' back and then it
was over'　　　[Personal 4]

Interestingly, not only does *miru* display a much lower frequency of use
with concrete objects, it actually displays an even split with what we
have categorized as Overall (from category 4) and General Awareness
(category 5), the combination of which also totals 46%, thus underscoring
its use as a MEANS rather than as an END. The latter two types of
visual perception are exemplified in (5) and (6).

(5)　　　coding category 4. -- Overall
*Kodomo ga jitensha ni notte arawarete, de **mite**,*
child　　　SM bicycle on ride-TE appear-TE and **look-TE**
'and a child riding a bike appears and looks [around]'　[pear 8]

(6)　　　coding category 5. -- General Awareness
*Nanka na **mite** nakatta shi ne ano- ojisan mitai na hito ga*
SOF　　　**watch-TE** not-PST and P, HDG old-man look like SM
'a person who looked like an older guy wasn't watching and...'
　　　　[Pear 7]

Thus far we have seen how *pota* tends to occur most frequently
with a concrete direct object, hence indicating a more focused type of

vision, in sharp contrast with the types of object complements that follow *miru*.

In addition to these more simple differences in the use of *pota* and *miru* as they occur with different types of object complementation on the sentence level, we would also like to point out some significant differences in how speakers of Japanese and Korean express visual perception on the level of the event.   Perhaps the most striking episode where these differences become salient is the one in which the boy hits the rock while riding away on his bicycle.   In the Korean data, four of the eleven speakers explicitly mention the fact that the boy did not see the rock in the middle of the road.   These four utterances have been reproduced in (7):

(7)

• *aphey issnun khetalan tolmayngilul poci mos hayse phihacilul*
  front -LOC exist -ATTR huge rock -OM see NEG -PRECED avoid
  'He didn't see the rock in front and couldn't avoid [it]'   [Pear 1]

• *aphey issnun tolul mos poakaciko nemeciesse*
  front -LOC exist -ATTR rock -OM NEG see -PRECED fall -PST -
  IE
  'He didn't see the rock and fell down'   [Pear 2]

• *aphey issnun tolul poci moshako nemeciesse*
  front -LOC exist -ATTR rock -OM see NEG(POT) -CONN fall -
  PST -IE
  'He didn't see the rock and fell down'   [Pear 4]

• *aphey toli issnun kesul poci moshako ku toley pwutichiesse*
  front -LOC rock -SJ exist -ATTR thing -OM see -NEG(POT) -
  CONN that rock -LOC hit -PRECED
  'He didn't see the rock in front and hit it'   [Pear 6]

In addition to these four tokens of *pota*, we had one token of *moluta*, literally meaning 'not know', but used here in the sense of 'didn't see', as in (8).

(8)

*aphey tolul **molukosenun** cacenke-ka tulipatakaciko cacenke ka*
ssuleciesse   [Pear11]
front -LOC rock -ACC **not:know** -PRECED -TOP bike -SJ hit -
PRECED bike -SJ fall:down -PST -IE
'He didn't see the rock in front and the bike hit it and fell down'

In sharp contrast, from the data that we used for this study, not a single Japanese speaker used the word *miru* in connection with the direct sight of the rock. Rather, we noted a combination of strategies whereby narrators would indicate that the boy was looking away and hit the rock, as in (9),

(9)

*sorede **yosomi shitete**, ooki na ishi ni butskatte*   [Pear 1]
and so **side-look do-PRG-TE** big rock LOC hit-TE
'And so he was **looking to the side** and hit a big rock'

or would simply use the existential verb *aru* to indicate the existence of the rock, which was the case in five of the eleven narratives, as in (10).

(10)

*omake ni ookii ishi ga **atta** n de, soko ni jitensha ga butsukatte*
in addition big rock SM **exist-pst** PT and, there LOC bicycle SM hit-
TE
'On top of it all, **there was** a big rock and the bicycle hit it and...'
[Pear 4]

A similar pattern is also evidenced toward the end of the film when the man discovers that one basket of pears is missing. Note the use of *pota* in Korean in (11) in which the reading is clearly 'notice', since the ensuing activity involves the man counting the baskets of fruit to verify his suspicion.

(11)

1 *halabeci ka naylyeoase...hana ka epsecin kelul pokose*
  old:man SJ come:down CONN one SJ not become thing ACC
  see CONN

2 *ku halapeci ka ku kwuail pakwuni-lul seyssci* [Pear 1]
  that old:man SJ that fruit basket -ACC count -PST -COMM

'The old man comes down and sees (i.e. **notices**) one [basket] is gone. So, he counted the number of the baskets'

None of the Japanese counterparts to this episode employ the verb *miru* to express the man's noticing the missing basket. Instead, verbs such as *ki ga tsuku* or *kizuku*, both meaning 'to notice', are used, as in (12),

(12)
*hashigo kara orite kite ne, hitotsu ga nai to omotte, **kizuite ne***
ladder from go down-TE come-TE PT one SM not exist QT think-TE **notice-TE PT**
'He comes down from the ladder and thinks there's one missing, he **notices** and...' [Pear 7]

or, there is no use of any type of perception verb at all, as in (13):

(13)
otokonohito ga orite kite nashi ga nakute okashii na tte yuu
man SM go down-come-TE pear SM not exist-TE strange PT QT say
'The man comes down and since the pears are gone he says "hmm, that's strange"' [Pear 12]

Thus, we have seen in the pear data and specifically in these two particular episodes how the narrators' use of verbs of perception reveals differing semantic scopes for *pota* and *miru*, with the primary difference being that the meaning of *pota* stretches from concrete visual perception to more abstract notions (in accordance with Traugott 1985 and 1992) and embraces the notion of knowing and a deeper understanding of the issue at hand, while *miru* appears to remain more at the level of seeing as a MEANS or PROCESS rather than as an END.

   The same tendency involving both verbs is observed in the second type of data, namely the personal narrative and conversational data for Korean and Japanese. In fact, our hypothesis established with the pear data is confirmed with greater strength in this second type, especially since these data involve spontaneously occurring speech with a much broader variety of topics and situations. The results of our analysis for *pota* and *miru* as lexical verbs are shown in (14)[4]:

(14)

a) *pota* as a lexical verb (Total # of tokens: 40)	b) *miru* as a lexical verb (Total # of tokens: 19)
<u>meanings</u>	<u>meanings</u>
suffer a loss (idiom)	look at
take an exam (idiom)	witness
turn and look	catch a glimpse
catch sight of	look around
gaze	watch
watch	attend (as in a movie)
be aware of	distinguish kind
witness	check out
spot	
scrutinize	
read	
notice	
realize	
recognize	
evaluate	
await outcome	

The list of meanings under *miru* involves the same type of actual, concrete visual perception, thus confirming our assignment of meaning to *miru* as MEANS. In contrast, the meanings listed under *pota* show that *pota* extends from the domain of concrete perception into the domain of the abstract, thus again confirming our analysis of *pota* expressing both MEANS and END. Recall that END necessarily involves an incipient knowledge state as in verbs such as 'notice', 'realize', and 'evaluate'.

---

[4] Note that these lists are not intended to be exhaustive and that other meanings also appear in other contexts for each verb.

3.4. -a/e pota vs. -te miru

The auxiliary constructions of -a/e pota and -te miru are usually both introduced in reference grammars and language textbooks as meaning 'try doing something and see' or 'try to do something' (cf. Alfonso 1966, Lukoff 1982, Martin 1975, H.M. Sohn 1994). Keedong Lee (1993) provides the most comprehensive and insightful account of pota and -a/e pota that we have located so far.

Table 3 shows a summary of main verbs used with -a/e pota and -te miru from the personal narratives and conversation data.

Table 3. Summary of Main Verbs with -a/e pota and -te miru

a) -a/e pota auxiliary   b) -te miru auxiliary
(36 tokens total)   (20 tokens total)

Main Verb	Gloss	Main Verb	Gloss
kata	go	*iku*	go
mutta	ask	*kiku*	ask
cenhwa hata	to telephone	*denwa suru*	to telephone
sayngkak hata	think	*kangaeru*	think
hata	do	*suru*	do
twuicita	hunt everywhere	*sagasu*	look for
ipta	put on, wear	*kaette kuru*	come back
kitalita	wait	*hajimeru*	begin (*vt*)
mannata	meet	*miru*	see, look, watch
phiwuta	smoke		
kyekta/ cinayta	go through, experience		
tutta	hear about		
alta	know		

At first glance, these main verbs seem semantically parallel in Japanese and Korean as in [15]:

(15)
a) *mata atode denwa kakete miru wa*   [ps -- conversation]
'I'll call again later'

b) *keki cenhwahay posipsio*   [s1- conversation]
'please try calling over there'

However, closer examination reveals semantic distinctions between -*te miru* and -*ale pota* as in (16) and (16').

(16)
a) *juunigatsu **mite miruto** fuyu yasumini hairu made wa ne*
[ps -- conversation]
'looking at December's calendar, [I'll be having classes until 4:15] until winter break'

b) *yoosu o **mite mimasu** node*   [ps -- conversation]
'I'll check out the situation and let you know'

c) *jaa naka o chotto **mite miyoo** to yuunde sono kaidan o nobotte*
[pn8 - narrative]
 'I thought I would take a look around (the room), so I went up the stairs...'

Note that -*te miru* with *miru* as a lexical verb is possible in (16), whereas the Korean counterpart does not necessarily take the lexical verb *pota* with -*ale pota*, as demonstrated in (16').

(16')   ?poa pota (Korean counterpart)
a') *?sipiwelul*   **poa** *pomyen kyewul panghak hal ttuykkaci*
                pomyen
'looking at December's calendar, until winter break, ...'

b') *? sanghwangul*   **poa pokose**
                      pokose
'after I check out the situation'

c') *? pang ul han pen*   **poa po** *ayaci hakonun kyeytanul olakase*
                po ayaci
'I thought I would take a look at the room and went up the stairs'

Conversely, (17) represents an example where -*ale pota* can be combined with the verb *alta*, meaning to "know", whereas in Japanese, the -*te miru* auxiliary cannot be combined with either *shiru* or *wakaru*, both meaning 'to know'.

(17)   a) *emeni ka mos al -apotelakwu*   [pn1 - narrative]
        'My mom didn't recognize me'

b) *program ey kaipul hasiessna an hasiessna al -apolyeko*
[11-conversation]
'[I called] just to find out whether you joined the program or not'

In fact, this particular combination of main verb *alta* + *-ale pota*
represents a prime example of grammaticalization in that a single verb
alapota appears as an entry in the dictionary. Once again, (17')
demonstrates the grammatical incompatibility of the Japanese verb *shiru*
"know" with the *-te miru* auxiliary.

(17')   *shitte miru
a') *watashi ga wakaranakatta*   [cf. *wakatte minakatta*]
b') *AT&T ni haitte iru ka doo ka kiite miru tameni*
[cf. *shitte miru tame ni*]

We attribute the problem in (17') to not only the semantic
differences between *pota* and *miru*, but also to the semantic differences
between *alta* and *shiru*[5].

Thus far, we have observed that many parallels exist between *-ale
pota* and *-te miru* from the point of view of the types of main verbs with
which they co-occur. In many instances, the messages themselves are
parallel. In other cases, as we have seen, combinations of certain main
verbs are not at all compatible with the auxiliary construction in one
language, while they seem perfectly compatible in the other.

Now we will examine another facet of the *-ale pota* construction,
which reveals a significant distinction that has not been recognized to
date. Note how (18) and the Korean counterpart in (18') express the same
meaning.

(18)   itte miru
*yonkai gokai made **ittemitan** desuyone*   [pn8-narrative]
'I went upstairs up to the fourth or fifth floor'

(18')   ka pota
sa chung inka o chung kkaci ola ka poassnuntey
'I went upstairs up to the fourth or fifth floor'

However, as noted in example (19), *-ale pota* also denotes an
experiential meaning, whereas the *-te miru* counterpart in Japanese clearly
does not. In order to convey the same meaning, which is also similar to

---

[5] This distinction is the topic of another study.

Korean *un ceki issta*, Japanese would employ a construction such as *koto ga aru*, as noted to the right of each example.

(19)

tule pota   Japanese
(a) *ney Tulepoasseyo*   [pn-narrative]   cf. **kiita koto ga aru**
'Yes. I've heard of that place'

ka pota
(b) *Na keki ka poasse*   [pn-narrative]   cf. **itta koto ga aru**
'I've been there'
(c) *aniyo Checwuto an ka poasseyo*   cf. **itta koto ga nai**
'No. I haven't been to Cheju Island'   [pn-narrrative]

4. Conclusion

We propose that the examples presented in (16) through (19) can be accounted for on the basis of our MEANS / END framework such that *miru* expresses a MEANS or PROCESS of visual perception and falls short of reaching a state of knowledge; while *pota* expresses both MEANS as well as END, in the sense that its meaning extends into the domain of an incipient knowledge state. The schema shown in (20) encapsulates our semantic categorization established as a result of this study for *pota, miru,* and *see.*

(20)

Korean		Japanese		English
pota		-al-e pota*	*miru*		-te miru*	'see'
↓		↓		↓

ACTUAL PERCEPTION
↓   ↓   ↓

ABSTRACT
↓   ↓   ↓

realize/ | 'do x and see' | 'do x and see'

notice

figure out| 'try doing x'   ↓ | 'try doing x'   ↓

recognize

                         ↓   ↓
                         ————   ↓

↓

EXPERIENCE

(*al -a pota*: 'investigate'/   (**shitte miru* /

         'recognize)   **wakatte miru*)

know + see   *know + see   ↓

        ↓

                                           ↓

(e.g. 'I see what you mean')

                                           ↓

KNOW

    For further study, we plan to first increase our database for the Korean pear narratives since there are only 11 currently available to us (and as such, our database is admittedly small), and to then analyze a greater number of the existing Japanese and English narratives in comparison with the Korean. We also plan to analyze English 'see' and other related verbs in finer detail in order to more effectively compare and contrast them to the Japanese and Korean, especially with respect to the correlation between 'seeing' and existence, or *miru* and *aru*.

    We will be focusing our attention more closely on the grammaticalization of *pota* and *miru* into other forms such as auxiliaries and the dative marker *poko*, in the hopes that this type of comparative study will shed more light on the grammars of Japanese and Korean, since they appear to be so similar on the surface, yet, as we have tried to show here, function sometimes quite differently.

References

Alfonso, A. 1966. Japanese Language Patterns - A Structural Approach. Vol.1. Tokyo: Sophia University L. L. Center of Applied Linguistics.

Bybee, J., Perkins, R., and Pagliuca, W. 1994. The Evolution of Grammar: Tense, Aspect, and Modality in the Languages of the World. Chicago: University of Chicago Press.

Dretske, F. 1973. Seeing and Knowing. Chicago: University of Chicago Press.

Gruber, J. 1967. Look and see. Language. Vol. 43 (4) pp. 937-947.

Lee, H.S. 1987. Santa Barbara Papers in Linguistics. Vol. 1. Korean: Papers and Discourse Data (eds. H.S. Lee and S. Thompson).

Lee, K. 1993. Korean Grammar on Semantic-Pragmatic Principles. Seoul: Hankwuk Mwuhwasa.

Lukoff, F. 1982. Introductory Course in Korean. Seoul: Yonsei University Press.

Martin, S. 1975. A Reference Grammar of Japanese. New Haven: Yale University Press.

Martin, S. 1992. A Reference Grammar of Korean. Tokyo: Charles E. Tuttle Company.

Sohn, H.M. 1994. Korean. New York: Routledge

Sweetser, E. 1990. From Etymology to Pragmatics: Metaphorical and Cultural Aspects of Semantic Structure. Cambridge: Cambridge University Press.

Szatrowski, P. 1991. Nihongo no danwa no koozoo bunseki (Analysis of the Structure of Japanese Discourse). Ph.D. dissertation. Tsukuba University, Japan.

Traugott, E. 1982. "From propositional to textual and expressive meanings: Some semantic-pragmatic aspects of grammaticalization." In Lehamann & Makiel (Eds.) Perspectives in historical linguistics. Amsterdam: John Benjamins. pp. 245-271.

Traugott, E. 1989. "On the rise of epistemic meanings in English: An example of subjectification in semantic change." Language. Vol. 65:1 pp. 31 - 55.

Tobin, Yishai. 1993. Aspect in the English Verb. London & New York: Longman.

Abbreviation

ANT	Anterior Suffix
ATTR	Attributive
CIRCUM	Circumstantial
COMM	Committal
COND	Conditional
CONN	Connective
CORREL	Correlative
DCT:RE	Deductive Reasoning
DECL	Declarative
DM	Discourse Marker
HEARSAY	'Hearsay' Evidential
HONOR	Honorific
IE	Informal Ending
IND	Indicative
INTERR	Interrogative
JUDG	Judgmental Suffix
LOC	Locative
NECESS	Necessitative
NEG	Negative Particle
NOML	Nominalizer
OM	Objective Marker
PASS	Passive
POL	Polite Suffix
QUOT	Quotative
RETROS	Retrospective
SM	Subjective Marker
TOP	Topic
TRANS	Transferentive
PT	Particle

Discourse Motivations for Referential Choice in Korean Acquisition

PATRICIA M. CLANCY
University of California at Santa Barbara

Introduction

The phenomenon of referential choice has been approached in at least two fundamentally different ways in linguistics: from the perspective of formal syntactic theory and from the perspective of discourse analysis. Referential choice has been an especially important and controversial topic for language acquisition researchers, since young children tend to overuse elliptical reference. From the perspective of formal syntactic theory, Hyams' (1986) parameter-setting account, which proposed that all children have an initial default parameter-setting of [+ pro-drop], has been especially influential (see also Jaeggli and Hyams 1988, Hyams 1991). While a number of studies have proposed alternative explanations for children's subject ellipsis in English (e.g. Bloom 1990, O'Grady et al. 1989, Valian 1991), there has been comparatively little research from the perspective of discourse analysis on referential choice in early caregiver-child interaction.

In this paper I will analyze referential choice in Korean acquisition, drawing upon the substantial body of cross-linguistic, discourse-based research on reference and anaphora that has been accumulating during the past two decades. This research has identified a number of discourse factors that influence referential choice in adult and child speakers, including the importance of the referent, e.g. the main character in a narrative (e.g. Karmiloff-Smith 1981, Hickmann 1982, Bamberg 1987, Clancy 1992), the position of the referent in conversational sequences (Fox 1987), prior mention of the referent and recency of the mention (e.g. Chafe 1987, Givón 1983), and the speaker's affective stance toward the referent (Lee 1989). Studies of Japanese (e.g. Hinds 1978, 1983, Clancy 1980) and Korean (e.g. Kim 1989, Lee 1989) have demonstrated that adult speakers' choice of referential form is highly sensitive to discourse contexts and interactive goals. While previous discourse-based studies of the acquisition of reference have focused on the narratives of children above two years of age, in this paper I will consider the impact of discourse variables on referential choice in children's conversations with caregivers at an earlier stage.

Data and Method

The data for this study consist of longitudinal records from two Korean-speaking girls, Wenceng and Hyenswu, whose speech was recorded over the course of one year. The children's fathers were graduate students at Brown University, and their families were part of a small, close-knit Korean community. At the start of the study, Hyenswu was 1 year, 10 months old and Wenceng was 1 year, 8 months. The children were recorded at home in interaction with their mothers in one-hour sessions every two weeks, as they engaged in ordinary activities such as playing with toys, looking at storybooks, and having snacks. Research Assistants who were native speakers of Korean participated in the recording sessions; one of them transcribed each tape as soon as possible following the sessions. All transcriptions were then checked again by a different native speaker.

For this paper, 13 samples of conversation taken at approximately one-month intervals have been analyzed. Every utterance with an overt or recoverable verb was identified, and what would be considered the subject and direct object in adult language were included in the database.[1] Each of these referents was then coded for linguistic form,

---

[1]The arguments of embedded predicates were not included in the database. *Toyta* as a deontic modal or as the single-word negation *antway* 'no', and the backchannels *kulay* and *olci*, were not counted as having codable subjects. To increase the comparability of subject and object referents, the following types of direct objects were not included: verbal noun objects of *hata* 'do', object complements, and uses of *hata* in which an adverbial seemed to carry the reference to the action, e.g. where *ilehkey hata* 'do like this' means 'do this'. Both primary arguments of transitive predicates taking double nominative casemarking were included, counting the second argument among objects.

the most common of which were: 1) ellipsis, 2) pronouns, e.g. *na* 'I', *ne* 'you', *wuli* 'we', and the third person demonstratives *i-ke/yo-ke* 'this-thing' and *ku-ke* 'that-thing' and 3) lexical noun phrases. The overall distribution of referential choices was then calculated for each child.

To analyze the potential discourse motivations for the choice of nominal, pronominal and elliptical forms, the referents in the database were coded for the following discourse variables:

QUERY: The referent is being queried with a wh-form, or is a response to a wh-query.

CONTRAST: In the context (the speech situation or prior discourse), there is another referent bearing the same relation to the same predicate (e.g. two actors wish to perform the same action) or bearing a parallel relation to a similar type of predicate (e.g. a series of pictures are labeled one after another).

ABSENCE: The referent is absent, i.e. not present in the room with the speaker, or in a location unknown to the speaker, at the time of utterance.

PRIOR MENTION (based on Chafe's (1987) notion of ACTIVATION STATE, but limited solely to prior mention in the discourse):

GIVEN: The referent was mentioned in the prior main clause or its embeddings.

ACCESSIBLE: The referent was mentioned before, but not in the immediately preceding main clause or its embeddings; most are cases of switch reference, i.e. subjects having a different referent from that of the prior main clause subject.

NEW: The referent is being mentioned for the first time.

Certain types of referents were not codable for each of these variables;[2] many referents were codable for more than one. The distribution of

---

[2]Generic subjects (translatable as 'you' or 'one') were not coded for any of the variables; wh-words were not coded for absence or prior mention; subjects and object with abstract referents, e.g. *appa ilum* 'daddy's name', or which referred to actions or events, were not coded for absence. Subjects of imperatives were coded, and the transcriptions of all imperatives with overt subjects were re-checked by a native speaker to differentiate vocatives from subjects.

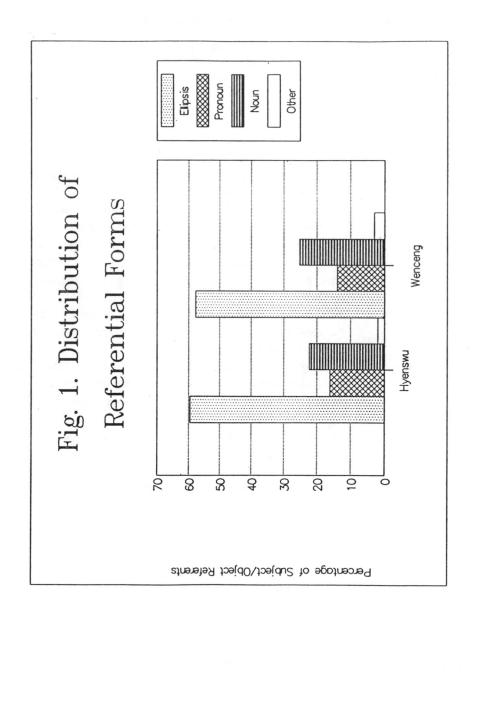

Fig. 1. Distribution of Referential Forms

referential forms was then analyzed with respect to each discourse variable.

Results

Fig. 1 shows the percentage of nominal, pronominal and elliptical referents in the database. Clearly, the most frequent form of reference for both children is ellipsis, which accounts for more than half of the referents. These results are consistent with Cho (1994) and Kim (to appear), who also report very high rates of ellipsis in Korean two-year-olds' speech. Noun phrases account for approximately one-quarter of the referential forms in the database, while pronouns comprise about 15%. Despite individual differences that will be discussed below, the overall distribution of referential forms for the two children is very similar.

What motivates the children's use of each referential form? A very important factor is whether the referent is being queried or is a response to a wh-question. The data indicate that both children know how to use overt pronouns or noun phrases to respond to wh-questions. Examples (1) and (2) are typical.

(1) Wenceng at 1;8. (Research Assistant K is looking at scribbling in a book.)

K: *i-ke-n   nwu-ka   kuli-ess-e?*
   this-thing-TOP who-NOM write-ANT-IE
      'Who wrote this?'

W: appa   ha-ess-e.
   daddy do-ANT-IE
      'Daddy did it.'

(2) Hyenswu at 2;4. (Hyenswu and K have a picture book, and are looking at a picture of people eating.)

K: *hyenswu achim-ey   mwue mek-ess-ni?*
   Hyenswu breakfast-at what eat-ANT-INTERR
      'What did you eat for breakfast?'

H: *pap mek-ess-e.*
   rice eat-ANT-IE
      'I ate rice.'

Fig. 2 displays the percentage of different forms that each child used for referents appearing in wh-questions/answers, as compared with referents appearing in other contexts. On the left side of Fig. 2 are given

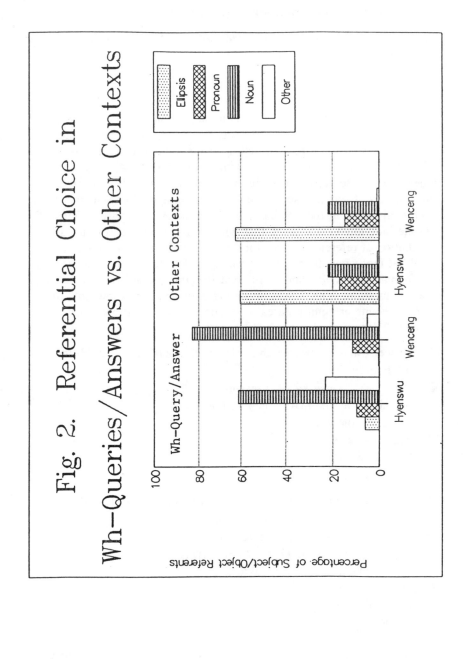

Fig. 2. Referential Choice in
Wh—Queries/Answers vs. Other Contexts

the distributions of referential forms used in producing and answering wh-questions in each child's speech; on the right side are the distributions for referents not involved in wh-questions or answers. It is clear from a comparison of the distributions on each side of Fig. 2 that both children use overt nominal reference much more frequently in answers to wh-questions than in other types of utterances. Overt reference is to be expected, of course, if the children understand that elliptical answers to wh-questions are infelicitous.[3] The other category of referential forms, which includes interrogative pronouns such as *mwue* 'what' is (by definition) more common in wh-questions; this is especially evident for Hyenswu, who frequently asks *mwue hay* 'What (are you) doing?' questions. In sum, the children are clearly able to provide nominal answers to wh-questions, and are also learning to query referents with wh-forms, primarily *mwue* 'what'.

Both children also know that overt mention is important for conveying contrast. When contrasting referents, they rely on both pronominal and nominal reference. In Example (3), Wenceng and her mother repeatedly use lexical mentions to contrast coca-cola with juice.

(3) Wenceng at 1;8. (Wenceng is watching Research Assistant T as he drinks a coke. Her mother (M) does not allow her to drink coke.)

W: *emma,   kholla mek-e.*
mommy cola   eat-IE
   'Mommy, I'll have a coke.'

M: *kholla   mek-ci   mal-ko,   ne-nun   cwusu   mek-e. ung?*
cola   eat-COMM   stop-CONN   you-TOP   juice   eat-IE   huh
   'You won't have a coke, you'll have juice. Right?'

W: *kholla.*
cola.
   'A coke.'

M: *kholla   mek-umyen emma   ippal   pelley   mek-nun-ta-ko*
cola   eat-if   mommy teeth bacteria eat- IMPFV-DECL -COMP
   'Didn't I say that if you drink coke, your teeth will decay?'

---

[3]The children did sometimes produce elliptical references where answers to wh-questions would have been expected. In most cases, however, they appeared to be ignoring the question altogether, e.g. reiterating their own prior utterance, rather than attempting to answer the question with ellipsis. Elliptical answers were coded only when it was clear that the child intended the elliptical referent as the answer to the question, e.g. when the ellipsis was accompanied by a gesture pointing at the referent.

kulay-ss-ci?   *aya ha-n-ta-ko*   *kulay-ss-ci?*

say-ANT-COMM   ouch do-IMPFV-DECL-COMP say-ANT-COMM

   'Didn't I say it would hurt?'

W: *cwusu mek-e.*

   juice eat-IE

   'I'll have juice.'

M: *ung.*   *ne, cwuswu   mek-e.*

   uh-huh you juice   eat-IE

   'Right. You drink juice.'

In Example (4), Hyenswu insists on being the one to perform the action. In the data, pronouns and nouns commonly appear when the child is contrasting 'I' and 'you' as potential performers of actions that the child wants to do herself, or that she wants the addressee to do for her.

(4) Hyenswu at 2;5. (Hyenswu and a boy named Forum are playing with lego at Hyenswu's house, when Forum takes a piece of lego.)

H: *nay kke.*

   my thing

   'It's mine.'

K: *Forum-to   com   kacko nol- key   hay.*

   Forum-ADD a.little with   play-COMP do:IE

   'Let Forum play with it a little too.'

H: *No. na ku-ke   ppay-llay.*

   no I   that-thing take.apart-VOL

   'No. I'll take that apart.'

Fig. 3 compares referential choices in contrastive contexts (on the left) vs. non-contrastive contexts (on the right). The differences in distribution indicate that contrast is also a powerful variable in eliciting nominal and pronominal reference. The percentage of pronominal reference is more than three times higher in contrastive contexts, and the percentage of nominal reference is about 15% higher. The rate of ellipsis, on the other hand, drops to about one-third of the percentage in non-contrastive contexts. Thus both children use overt mention as an important strategy for contrasting referents.

The conversations of young children with their caregivers are typically about the here-and-now. Fig. 4 presents the distributions of referential forms in the unusual context of talking about absent referents

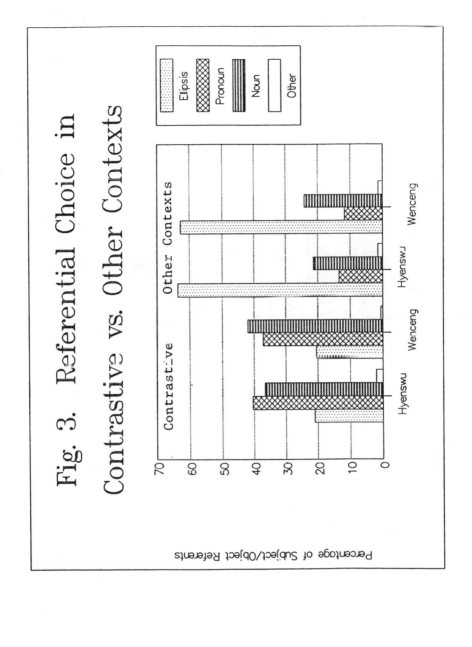

Fig. 3. Referential Choice in Contrastive vs. Other Contexts

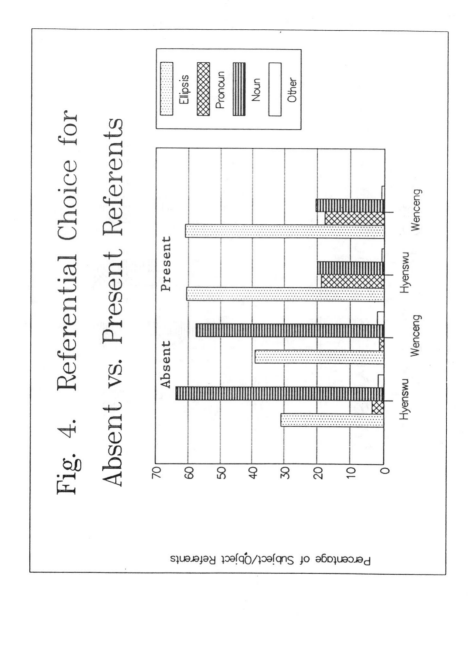

Fig. 4. Referential Choice for Absent vs. Present Referents

(left side) as compared with the typical situation of talking about present referents (right side). For both children, nominal reference is the most common choice for absent referents, while ellipsis is the most common choice for present referents. Pronouns are used for somewhat less than 20% of present referents, including all first and second person referents. Absent referents are almost never pronominal; virtually all third person pronouns in the data are deictics, such as *i-ke* 'this-thing' and *ku-ke* 'that-thing', used for present referents. Although absent referents that have already been introduced into discourse can be ellipted, there are cases in which a noun phrase is used again and again for an absent referent, as in Example (5).

(5) Wenceng at 2;3. (Wenceng and T have been playing with various toys. Myengcin, a friend of Wenceng's mother, is not present.)

W: *i-ke   myengcini-ka   cwu-ess-e,   myengcini.*
    this-thing Myengcin-NOM give-ANT-IE   Myengcin.
      'Myengcin gave me this.'

T: *myengcini-ka   cwu-ess-e?*
    Myengcin-NOM   give-ANT-IE
      'Myengcin gave you it?'

W: *ung.*
    uh-huh
      'Yes.'

T: *ung.*
    uh-huh
      'Right.'

W: *i-kes-to   myengcini-ka   cwu-ess-e.*
    this-thing-add Myengcin -NOM give-ANT-IE
      'Myengcin also gave me this.'

T: *kulay. i -kes -to cwu - ess-ci   myengcini-ka.*
    right this-thing-add give-ANT-COMM   Myengcin-NOM
      'Right. Myengcin gave you this too, didn't she.'

The final variable to be considered is prior mention. Fig. 5 shows Wenceng's distribution of referential forms in three discourse contexts: when the referent had been mentioned in the immediately prior clause (GIVEN), when it had been mentioned in a more distant clause (ACCESSIBLE), and when the referent is being mentioned for the first time in the conversation (NEW). As Fig. 5 shows, Wenceng clearly differentiates all three contexts: the percentage of nouns is highest for

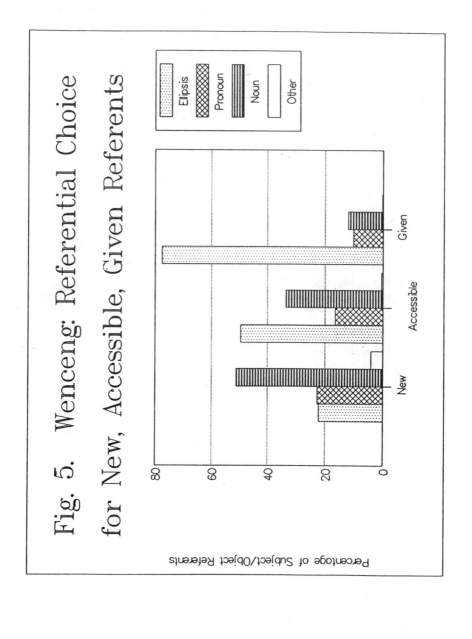

Fig. 5. Wenceng: Referential Choice
for New, Accessible, Given Referents

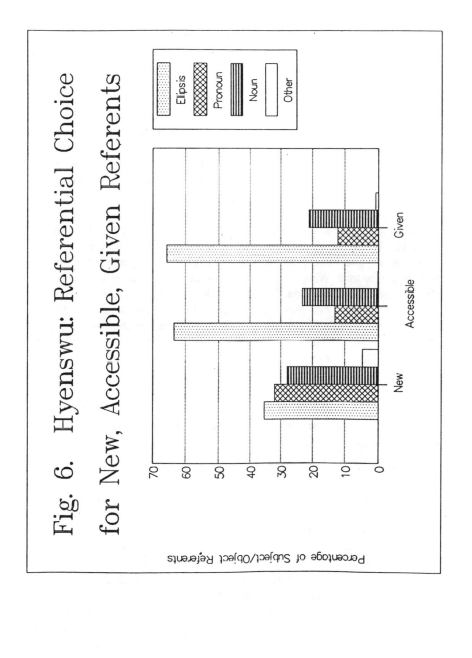

Fig. 6. Hyenswu: Referential Choice for New, Accessible, Given Referents

first mentions, decreases for accessible referents, and is the lowest for given referents mentioned in the immediately prior clause. Ellipsis presents the opposite pattern, with the highest percentage for just-mentioned given referents and the lowest for new mentions. Pronouns show a much weaker tendency to follow the pattern of nouns.

Fig. 6 presents the corresponding distributions of referential forms in Hyenswu's data. The differences between the two children are striking. Hyenswu does not differentiate between accessible and given referents, treating all previously mentioned referents with high frequencies of ellipsis and low rates of pronominal and nominal reference. She does differentiate first mentions from given and accessible referents, however. The percentage of ellipsis is the lowest for first mentions, while pronouns and nouns are more frequent in introducing new referents. Although Hyenswu clearly responds to the first mention context by reducing her use of ellipsis, she has a higher percentage of elliptical new referents than Wenceng. It is not necessarily inappropriate to use ellipsis for a first mention if the intended referent is clear from the nonverbal context, but Hyenswu is more likely than Wenceng to use elliptical first mentions that her interlocuters cannot understand.

Examples (6-9) illustrate the children's referential choices with respect to prior mention. In Example (6) Wenceng uses an overt pronoun, *i-ke* 'this-thing', for the first mention of a new referent.

(6) Wenceng at 1;10. (K urges Wenceng to look inside the baby-care set that comes with the new doll K has given her for Christmas.)
K: *acwumma-lang hanpen po-ca.*
    auntie-COM once   see-let's
      'Let's take a look.'
W: (pointing to the doll's shoes)
    i -ke -i mwue-kko?
    this-thing-NOM what-INTERR
      'What's this?'

From the beginning of the study, Wenceng can also use explicit reference for accessible referents that had already been introduced into discourse but had not been mentioned for a few clauses. In Example (7), the Research Assistant shows Wenceng a catalog, asks her what it is, and then starts pointing at pictures of specific items and eliciting their labels. After a few turns, Wenceng returns to focus on the catalog, which she calls *chayk* 'book', and comments on its size.

(7) Wenceng at 1;8. (Wenceng and K are looking at a catalog.)

K: *ku -ke - i   mwue ya   wenceng-a? i -ke - i   mwue ya?*

   that-thing-NOM what COP:IE wenceng-VOC this-thing-NOM what COP:IE

   'What's that, Wenceng? What's this?'

W: *chayk.*

   book

   'A book'.

(After K elicits a label for a picture in the catalog, she says:)

K: *i - ke - n   mwue ya?*

   this-thing -TOP what COP:IE

   'What is this?'

W: *nemu khe,   chayk-i.*

   too   big:IE book-NOM

   'The book is too big'.

Hyenswu is less sensitive than Wenceng to prior mention. In the early months of the study, for example, she often maintains nominal reference from the prior speaker's utterance, as in Example (8). She thus ends up overusing explicit nouns for given referents, which usually are ellipted.

(8) Hyenswu at 1;11. (T has taken off his glasses.)

M: *acci ipp   -e?*

   uncle pretty-IE

   'Does uncle look nice?'

H: *acci ipp -e.*

   uncle pretty -IE

   'Uncle looks nice.'

Hyenswu also has the opposite problem: a tendency to use ellipsis for first mentions of new information. The last line of Example (9) illustrates this: Hyenswu introduces her hairpin into the discourse with ellipsis, relying on gesture to indicate her intended referent.

(9) Hyenswu at 1;11. (Hyenswu and her mother have been talking about the clothes Hyenswu is wearing, which belong to her sister.)

H: (touching her clothes.)

yeki iss-ta.

here exist-DECL

'Here it is.'

M: *kulay. yeki iss-ta.*

right   here exist-DECL

'Yes. Here it is.'

H: (touching her hair pin.)

yeki iss-ta.

here exist-DECL

'Here it is.'

As the year progressed, Hyenswu began to develop more adult-like referential choices with respect to prior mention.

Table 1 summarizes the findings presented above, showing the relationship between referential forms and the four discourse variables: wh-query/answer, contrast, absence, and prior mention. For each variable, an X indicates the most common referential form(s) used in that discourse context. When a form was (one of) the most common choice(s) for just one child, that child's initial is given in parentheses.

	Query/Ans.	Contrast	Absent	Prior Mention		
				Given	Accessible	New
Ellipsis				X	X	(H)
Pronoun		X				(H)
Noun	X	X	X		(W)	X

Table 1. Summary of referential choice and discourse variables.

As Table 1 shows, noun phrases are the preferred form for answering wh-questions and for mentioning absent referents. When contrasting referents, pronouns and nouns are both common choices. For referents that are given by virtue of mention in the immediately preceding clause, ellipsis is the favorite choice. The children also use ellipsis for accessible referents mentioned before the preceding clause. Explicit nominal reference is used by both children for introducing new referents. Individual differences are apparent in the treatment of new and accessible referents: Wenceng, but not Hyenswu, often uses noun phrases for accessible referents, while Hyenswu often uses pronouns and ellipsis for first mentions of new referents. Thus each referential form has a different profile of usage with respect to the set of discourse variables.

Discussion and Conclusions

What are the implications of these results for our understanding of the acquisition of referential forms? First of all, the results clearly indicate that it would be an oversimplification to analyze referential choice in terms of a binary opposition between ellipsis vs. overt reference. Ellipsis, pronouns, and nouns have different distributions with respect to discourse variables, indicating that each option has different discourse functions. These functions presumably must be learned, even in the case of ellipsis, the most common referential form, and apparently are learned very early. The children strongly differentiate between ellipsis and nominal reference from the beginning of the study, before they are two years of age. They use ellipsis much more frequently in certain contexts, such as immediate prior mention, than in others, such as contrast. The differences between the two children, as well as their errors, e.g. Hyenswu's overuse of ellipsis for first mentions and underuse of ellipsis for given referents, provide further support for a process of learning. For each referential form, the children are acquiring a complex set of functionally motivated relationships between that form and specific discourse contexts.

Recent cross-linguistic research also emphasizes the role of learning in young children's acquisition of referential forms. Valian (1991), for example, has shown that English-speaking children, from the earliest stage of acquisition, use overt subjects more than twice as frequently as Italian children; she relates these differences to adult input as well as to performance factors. Based on her study of the acquisition of subjectless sentences in Hebrew, which are governed by a variety of discourse and grammatical factors, Berman (1990) concludes that children acquire appropriate use of ellipsis in developmental stages over a number of years. Wang et al. (1992), based on their analysis of null subjects and objects in Chinese and English acquisition, propose that pragmatic learning is necessary following parameter-setting, and that parameter re-setting may be a gradual, time-consuming process. To the extent that a gradual process of learning from input is necessary, the potential advantages to the child of having an innate pro-drop parameter are reduced. Even if Korean children, for example, were assumed to begin acquisition with an innately specified [+ pro-drop] parameter setting, they would still need to learn which discourse contexts are appropriate for ellipsis and which are not. A child equipped with the ability to learn referential forms and their discourse contexts from caregiver speech would seem to have little use for a two-value, innate pro-drop parameter. Thus the child's task in acquiring referential forms may not be substantially facilitated by postulating a parameter-setting account of early referential choice.

At a general theoretical level, the findings of this study raise important issues concerning the relationship between grammar and discourse. Analyses of reference from the perspective of formal syntactic theory have proposed that the principles governing certain referential forms fall within the domain of grammar and have a genetic basis, while the principles governing other referential forms fall within the domain of discourse and must be learned. Thus the pro-drop parameter equips children with innate, a priori expectations pertaining to ellipsis vs. overt reference, but leaves them to discover the differences between overt pronouns and noun phrases on the basis of experience. This implies a strict grammar/discourse dichotomy that is inconsistent with the functional unity of referential choice as a linguistic domain, as well as with the great variety of referential forms and discourse functions to be found across languages (cf. Givón 1983). A more unified approach to reference and its acquisition might start from a discourse analysis of the full set of available referential devices in a language, as in Berman (1990), and then explore the relationship between discourse function and referential form in the process of development. An adequate understanding of the discourse bases of referential choice in adult and child speech will require systematic empirical investigations of a variety of typologically different languages.

The findings of this study also have important implications for the acquisition of argument structure and casemarking in Korean. Since each referential form is used in specific discourse contexts, the Korean child will hear surface arguments of predicates only in those discourse contexts which motivate the use of overt pronouns and nouns. This means that the Korean child's exposure to argument structure is dependent upon discourse context (Clancy in press a). Furthermore, since only overt pronouns and nouns can receive casemarking, the child's exposure to casemarkers is also dependent upon discourse context (Clancy in press b). Thus Korean children will hear surface arguments of predicates, and therefore will hear casemarking, only in discourse contexts that foster overt reference, e.g. in answers to wh-questions, first mentions of a new referent, and contrasts between two referents. As a result, for the Korean child the acquisition of argument structure and of casemarking will be inextricably linked to the acquisition of the discourse motivations for referential choice. The intimate relationship between grammar and discourse in the experience of the language-learning child serves as a powerful motivation for abandoning the grammar/discourse dichotomy in favor of a more unified approach.

Abbreviations (from Lee 1991)

ADD - additive	IE - informal ending
ANT - anterior	IMPRFV - imperfective
COM - comitative	INTERR - interrogative
COMM - committal	NOM - nominative
COMP - complementizer	TOP - topic
CONN - connective	VOC - vocative
DECL - declarative	VOL - volitional

References

Bamberg, Michael. 1987. The acquisition of narratives: Learning to use language. Amsterdam: Mouton.

Berman, Ruth. 1990. On acquiring an (S)VO language: Subjectless sentences in children's Hebrew. Linguistics 28.1135-1166.

Bloom, Paul. 1990. Subjectless sentences in child language. LI 21.491-503.

Chafe, Wallace L. 1987. Cognitive constraints on information flow. Coherence and Grounding in Discourse, ed. by Russell S. Tomlin, 21-51. Amsterdam: Benjamins.

Cho, Sook Whan. 1994. The grammar of null arguments and mood categories in early child Korean. Theoretical issues in Korean linguistics, ed. by Young-Key Kim-Renaud. Stanford: CSLI Publications.

Clancy, Patricia M. 1980. Referential choice in English and Japanese narrative discourse. The pear stories: Cognitive, cultural, and linguistic aspects of narrative production, ed. by Wallace L. Chafe, 127-202. Norwood, NJ: Ablex.

Clancy, Patricia M. 1992. Referential strategies in the narratives of Japanese children. Discourse Processes 15.441-467.

Clancy, Patricia M. To appear a. Referential strategies and the co-construction of argument structure in Korean acquisition. Studies in Anaphora, ed. by Barbara Fox. Amsterdam: Benjamins.

Clancy, Patricia M. To appear b. Subject and object in Korean acquisition: Surface expression and casemarking. Harvard studies in Korean Linguistics VI.

Fox, Barbara. 1987. Discourse structure and anaphora: Written and conversational English. New York: Cambridge University Press.

Givón, Talmy. 1983. Topic continuity in discourse: A quantitative cross-linguistic study. Amsterdam: Benjamins.

Hickmann, Maya. 1982. The development of narrative skills. Doctoral dissertation, University of Chicago.

Hinds, John. 1978. Ellipsis in Japanese discourse. Alberta: Linguistic Research, Inc.

Hinds, John. 1983. Topic continuity in Japanese. Topic continuity in discourse: A quantitative cross-linguistic study, ed. by Talmy Givón, 43-93. Amsterdam: Benjamins.

Hyams, Nina. 1986. Language acquisition and the theory of parameters. Dordrecht: Reidel.

Hyams, Nina. 1991. A reanalysis of null subjects in child language. Theoretical issues in language acquisition, ed. by J. Weissenborn, H. Goodluck and T. Roeper. Hillsdale, NJ: Erlbaum.

Jaeggli, Osvaldo and Nina Hyams. 1988. Morphological uniformity and the setting of the null subject parameter. NELS 18.238-253.

Karmiloff-Smith, Annette. 1981. The grammatical marking of thematic structure in the development of language production. The child's construction of language, ed. by W. Deutsch, 121-147. New York: Academic.

Kim, Haeyeon. 1989. Nominal reference in discourse: Introducing and tracking referents in Korean spoken narratives. Harvard studies in Korean linguistics III, ed. by S. Kuno et al., 431-444. Cambridge, MA: Harvard University & Seoul: Hanshin.

Kim, Young-joo. To appear. The acquisition of Korean. The cross-linguistic study of language acquisition, vol. 4, ed. by Dan I. Slobin. Hillsdale, NJ: Erlbaum.

Lee, Hyo-Sang. 1991. Tense, aspect, and modality: A discourse-pragmatic analysis of verbal affixes in Korean from a typological perspective. Doctoral dissertation, UCLA.

Lee, Won-Pyo. 1989. Referential choice in Korean discourse: Cognitive and social perspective. Doctoral dissertation, University of Southern California.

O'Grady, William, Ann Peters, and Deborah Masterson. 1989. The transition from optional to required subjects. Journal of Child Language 16.513-529.

Valian, Virginia. 1991. Syntactic subjects in the early speech of American and Italian children. Cognition 40.21-81.

Wang, Qi, Diane Lillo-Martin, Catherine T. Best, and Andrea Levitt. 1992. Null subject versus null object: Some evidence from the acquisition of Chinese and English.

On the Function of the Japanese Particle *wa*: New Light on Two Distict Uses of the *te-wa* Construction

SETSUKO ARITA
Kyushu University, Fukuoka

0.   Introduction

This paper deals with the *te-wa* construction in Japanese which, I propose, consists of the *te*-inflectional form of a predicate and a particle *wa*. The construction has two meanings; one is a conditional reading which has a negative implication; the other is a nonconditional reading which implies that one type of event occurs repeatedly during a particular interval.

The purpose of this paper is to show that these two seemingly unrelated uses are derived compositionally from the function of *wa* and the nature of the *te*-clause. In other words, I would like to show that the Japanese particle *wa* in the *te-wa* construction can be treated in the same way as in the NP-*wa* construction in terms of its operating nature: 'domain setting for predication' which captures and generalizes a variety of uses of *wa*.

1.   Two Distinct Uses of the *te-wa* Construction

The *te-wa* construction has two distinct uses exemplified in (1) and (2).

(1) *Tomodachi-wo uragit-**te-wa** shinyo-sare-naku-naru*.
    friends-ACC   betray   trust-PASS-NEG-become
    '**If** you betray your friends, you will not be trusted. (So you should not betray your friends.)'
(2) *Tomodachi-wo uragit-**te-wa** sute-ta*.
    friends-ACC   betray   throw-off-PAST
    'He betrayed and threw off his friends (**again and again**).'

Example (1) has a conditional interpretation; on the other hand example (2) means the repetition of a series of   actions.   We will call the type (1)

661

'conditional *te-wa*', and the type (2) 'repetitive *te-wa*'.

Conditional *te-wa* has such an implication as represented in the brackets in example (1), which asserts that the action described in the subordinate clause should not happen. (We call it 'negative implication' from now on.) This implication has been often discussed in previous studies. It has been treated as the basic meaning of the *te-wa* form (or the *te-wa* construction) there. If its treatment is adequate, the repetitive use of *te-wa* should be regarded as an idiom or should be explained in terms of a semantic extension of the conditional use. The repetitive use should not be treated as an idiom because, as we will see in the next section, it is predictable from syntactic and semantic environments whether the construction carries repetitive meaning or not. The repetitive use should not be the semantic extension of the conditional one either, because it does not have such negative implication as the conditional use has. Therefore, the relationship between the two uses of *te-wa* construction cannot be captured straightforwardly by the extension of previous research.

The purpose of this paper is to solve two problems. The first is to consider why the construction has two seemingly unrelated uses, conditional and repetitive. The second is to consider how each of the uses is derived. To answer these questions contributes not only to the research of *te-wa* but also to that of the particle *wa*. This particle is dealt with as a topic marker in most of the previous research because it usually marks NP which expresses given information in most cases. However, this particle has a variety of uses which cannot be captured by static function such as 'topichood'. In this paper, I will propose a dynamic function of *wa* which can explain not only the case in which *wa* marks a NP (or 'NP-*wa* construction') but also the case in which *wa* marks a clause (or '*te-wa* construction'). In other words, I will show the adequacy of the dynamic function of *wa* by considering the *te-wa* construction.

2.   The Differences Between the Two Uses

In this section, we will describe the two uses of the *te-wa* construction. And we will conclude that they should be distinguished both syntactically and semantically: the conditional *te-wa* clause has tense and its semantic type is a proposition, whereas the repetitive *te-wa* clause does not have tense and its semantic type is an action.

2.1   Tensed vs. Nontensed

Conditional *te-wa* allows an overt subject in the subordinate clause distinct from the main clause subject.

(3) a. *Taro_i-wa [[pro_i zibun de   yara-naku-] te-wa] ki ga suma-nai.*
        Taro-TOP   by oneself do-NEG   satisfy-NEG
        'Taro does not satisfy himself unless he does it by himself.'
    b. *Taro-wa [[Jiro ga yara-naku-]te-wa]] ki ga suma nai.*
        'Taro does not satisfy himself unless Jiro does it.'

The *te-wa* clause of (3a) has a subject coreferential with the main clause subject, while that of (3b) has a distinct subject from the main clause subject. Both examples are grammatical.

On the other hand, as we can see from the examples (4a) and (4b), repetitive *te-wa* does not allow a subject distinct from the main clause subject.

(4) a. *Taro$_i$-wa [[PRO$_i$ hon-wo   toridashi-]te-wa]narabe- ta.*
    Taro-TOP   book-ACC take out   arrange-PAST
    'Taro took out and arranged a book again and again.'
   b. **Taro-wa [[Jiro ga hon wo toridashi-   ]te-wa] narabe ta.*
    'Taro took out a book and Jiro arranged it again and again.'

In (4b), the *te-wa* clause has an overt subject *Jiro,* so it is ungrammatical.

Whether or not the subordinate clause has an overt subject is crucial for classifying subordinate clauses in Japanese. Nonfinite clauses such as *mama, nagara* cannot have an overt subject exemplified in (5) and (6).

(5) a. *Taro$_i$_wa [[PRO$_i$ fuku-wo   ki-ta-]mama] oyoi-da.*
    Taro-TOP   clothes-ACC wear-ing   swim-PAST
    'Taro swam keeping his clothes on.'
   b. **Taro-wa Hanako ga fuku wo ki-ta mama oyoi-da.*
(6) a. *Taro$_i$-wa [[PRO$_i$ terebi-wo   mi-]nagara] yuushoku-wo tabe-ta.*
    Taro-TOP   television-ACC watch while   dinner-ACC eat-PAST
    'Taro ate dinner while watching television.'
   b. **Taro-wa Hanako ga terebi-wo mi-nagara yuushoku-wo tabe-ta.*

On the other hand, finite clauses such as *node* do not have such a restriction on their subject as in nonfinite clauses.

(7) a. *Watashi$_i$ wa [[sakuya   pro$_i$ nakiharashi-ta]   node]*
    I   TOP last night   cry-one's-eyes-out-PAST because
    hitomae ni   de-taku-   nak-atta.
    in the public eye be want to not PAST
    'I didn't want to be in the public eye because I cried my eyes out last night.'
   b. *Watashi wa [[sakuya otto-ga   nai-ta]   node]*
    I   TOP   last night husband-NOM   cry-PAST because
    hitomae ni   de-taku-   nak-atta.
    in the public eye be want to not-PAST
    'I didn't want to be in the public eye because my husband cried last night. '

From this point of view, we may naturally say that the conditional *tewa* clause has tense, while repetitive *tewa* clause does not have tense.

2.2   Proposition vs. Action

We will present three arguments which reveal the semantic distinction between the two uses.

First, in conditional *te-wa*, the scope of frequency adverbs does not extend over the *te-wa* clause.

(8) a. *[[[Tomodachi-wo uragit-]te]-wa] shinyo-sare-naku-naru*.

b. *[Nando-mo [[tomodachi wo uragit-]te]-wa] shinyo-sare-naku-naru*
'If you betray your friends **many times**, you will not be trusted.'

A frequency adverb *nandomo* 'many times' in (8) can modify only the *-te-wa* clause event and not the main clause event.

On the other hand, in repetitive use the frequency adverbs can take scope over the whole clause. As seen in (9b), *nandomo* modifies not only the first conjunct but also the second.

(9) a.*[[[Tomodachi-wo uragit-]-te]-wa] sute-ta.*

b. *[Nando-mo [Tomodachi wo uragit-te-wa sute-ta]]*
'He betrayed and threw off his friends **many times**.'

Secondly, while conditional *te-wa* allows stative predicates in the first conjunct, repetitive *te-wa* does not allow them in the first conjunct. Compare (10) with (11a).

(10) *[[[[Tomodachi-wo uragit-]tei-]te]-wa] shinyo-sare-naku-naru*.
'If you have betrayed your friends, you will not be trusted.'
(11) a **[[[[Tomodachi-wo uragit-]tei-]te]-wa] sute-ta.*
'He betrayed his friends again and again and threw them off.'

b. *[[[[Tomodachi-wo uragit-]-te]-wa] sute-] **tei**-ta.*
'He betrayed and threw off his friends (again and again).'

An aspect marker *tei*, which represents the continuation of an event,   can appear in the conditional *te-wa* clause but not in the repetitive *te-wa* clause.

Thirdly, conditional *te-wa* can be paraphrased by *no-de-wa*[1]*)*, whereas repetitive *te-wa* cannot be paraphrased by *no-de-wa*, as seen in (12) and (13).

(12) *[Tomodachi-wo uragit-ta]-**no-de-wa** shinyo-sare-naku-naru*.
'If you betray your friends, you will not be trusted.'
(13)**[Tomodachi-wo uragit-ta]-**no-de-wa** suteta.*

---

[1]*No-de-wa* can be analyzed as a compound consisting of *no*, the inflectional form of copula *de* and the particle *wa*. *No* is a complementizer in Japanese, whose function is generally regarded as nominalizing a proposition.

The three points examined above reveal that conditional *te-wa* clause represents a proposition; on the other hand repetitive *te-wa* clause does not represent a proposition but an action. This semantic distinction conforms to the syntactic one discussed in the previous subsection.

Table 1.

te-wa	Syntactic Property	Semantic Type
Conditional	Tensed	Proposition
Repetitive	Nontensed	Action

The next section will discuss these syntactic/semantic distinctions between the two uses of *te-wa* clause and show that they should be ascribed to a property of *te* as a connective.

3. Two Distinct Uses of *te* Clauses

I will overview the uses of *te* of Japanese. *Te* is an inflectional form of an aspectual marker which represents 'perfect'. Its basic function is regarded as connecting two predicates. It has a variety of syntactic functions i.e. a part of complex predicate[2]) which represents an aspectual concept, an adverb, and a connective which combines two sentences. The last one is relevant for the discussion here.

There are two uses of *te* as a connective: causal and sequential. Causal *te* is shown in example (14). The first conjunct is the 'cause' of the second conjunct. And sequential *te* is as in example (15). It means that one action occurs and another action follows it.

Causal:

(14) *Taro_i-wa [pro_i shigoto-wo   oe- te] hottoshi-ta.*
　　 Taro-TOP　　 work-ACC　 finish　feel-relieved-PAST
　　 'Taro felt relieved to finish the work.'

Sequential:

(15) *Taro_i-wa　 [PRO_i heya-ni　　 hait- te] booshi-wo nui-da.*
　　 Taro-TOP　　　　 room-OBL　enter　　cap-ACC　take-off-PAST
　　 'Taro entered the room and took off his cap.[3])'

2　　See McCawley and Momoi (1986).

[3]I will use the term 'sequential' to refer to the succession of two actions which form a single event. In the actual uses of *te*, there are some instances in which it is not clearly　determined whether it represents causal meaning or sequential meaning. We can find the examples which are interpreted as sequential but represent a relation between two events.

We will find exactly the same parallelism between causal *te* and sequential *te* as that between conditional *te-wa* and repetitive *te-wa*. As for the possibility of an overt subject in the first conjunct, causal *te* allows an overt subject in the *te* clause distinct from the main clause subject as seen in (16b). On the other hand, sequential *te* does not allow a distinct subject from the main clause subject as seen in (17b).

(16) a. *Taro*$_i$*-wa [[pro*$_i$ *shigoto-wo oe-]* **te]** *hottoshi-ta.*
   'Taro felt relieved to finish the work.'
  b. *Taro-wa* [[***Jiro-ga*** *shigoto-wo yari-oe-]**te**] *hottoshi-ta.*
   'Taro felt relieved since Jiro finished his work.'
(17) a. *Taro*$_i$*-wa [[* **PRO**$_i$ *heya-ni hait-]* **te]** *booshi-wo nui-da.*
   'Taro entered the room and took off his cap.'
  b. **Taro-wa [[***Jiro-ga*** *heya-ni hait-]* **te]** *booshi-wo nui-da.* [4]
   'Jiro entered the room and Taro took off his cap.'

As for the scope of frequency adverbs, in causal *te* the scope of frequency adverbs does not extend over the *te* clause. As seen in (18), *nandomo* modifies only the causal *-te* clause. On the other hand, in sequential *te* the frequency adverbs take scope over the whole clause. In the example (19), *nandomo* modifies not only the sequential clause but also the main clause.

(18) *Taro*$_i$*-wa* [***nandomo*** [[*pro*$_i$ *shippaishi-]***te***]] *tsuyoku-nat-ta.*
   'Taro became strong since he had failed many times.'
(19) *Taro*$_i$*-wa* ***nandomo***[[*PRO*$_i$ *koron-de*] *kega-wo shi-ta*]. [5]
   'Taro fell down and got hurt many times. '

As to the aspectual status of the first conjunct, judging from the difference of grammaticality between (20) and (21), we may say that the causal

---

te allows stative predicates in the first conjunct, while the sequential *te* does not allow stative predicates in the first conjunct.

(20) *Taro$_i$ wa [pro$_i$ nemut-**tei-te**] sensei-ni   shikar-are-ta.*
       Taro-TOP   sleep ASP   teacher-OBL   scold-PASS-PAST
       'Taro was scold since he was asleep.'

(21) a. **Taro$_i$ -wa [PRO$_i$ koron-   **dei-te**] kega-wo shi-ta.* [6]
             Taro TOP   fall-down-ASP   take-hurt-PAST

     b. *Taro$_i$ _wa [PRO$_i$ koron-**de**] kega-wo shi-**tei**-ta.*
          'Taro was injured when he fell down.'

Finally, as for the paraphrasability of *no-de*, the causal *te* can be paraphrased by *no-de*, but the sequential *te* cannot be so paraphrased. The function of *no* of *no-de* is regarded as an example of the nominalization of a proposition just as that of *no* of *no-de-wa*.

(22) a. *Taro$_i$-wa [pro$_i$ shigoto-wo oe- **te**] hottoshi-ta.*
          'Taro felt relieved to finish the work.'

     b. *Taro$_i$-wa [pro$_i$ shigoto-wo oe-ta-**no-de**] hottoshi-ta.*
          'Taro felt relieved because he finished the work.'

(23) a. *Taro$_i$-wa   [PRO$_i$ heya-ni   hait- te] booshi-wo nui-da.*
          'Taro entered the room and took off his cap.'

     b. *#Taro$_i$-wa [PRO$_i$ heya-ni   hait-ta-**no-de**] booshi-wo nui-da.* [7]
          'Since Taro entered the room, he took off his cap.' (causal reading)

We can summarize the above arguments as in table 2.
Table. 2

te	Syntactic Property	Semantic Type
causal	Tensed	Proposition
sequential	Nontensed	Action

Table 2 leads us to conclude that the distinctions between the two uses of *te-wa* discussed in the previous section are determined by the nature of *te*.

---

6 *Dei* is an allomorph of *tei*.

7 When this sentence is regarded as grammatical, it does not mean the succession of two actions but two independent events.

4. The Function of *wa*

In this section, we will consider the particle *wa* from a dynamic viewpoint applicable in the case of *te-wa*.

As seen in (24a) and (24b), the English sentence 'Taro came' has two options for translation in Japanese.

(24) a. *Taro-wa ki-ta.*
'Taro came. '
  b. *Taro-ga ki-ta.*
'Taro came. '

Wa and *ga* should be distinguished in that *wa*-marked NP but not *ga*-marked NP can be connected with 'an individual-level predicate'. (Carlson 1977) Compare the examples (25) with (26). An individual-level predicate *shinsetsuda* 'kind' can be connected with *Taro-wa* but not with *Taro-ga*.[8]

(25) *Taro-wa shinsetsu-da.*
'Taro is kind.'
(26) **Taro-ga shinsetsu da.*

So, we can say that *wa*-marked NP denotes an entity existing over stages while that *ga*-marked NP denotes an entity whose existence is restricted in a particular stage.

In predicational relation, the entity to be predicated has to be identified. In other words, the existence of the entity is presupposed in the predication. Suppose that both of *ga* and *wa* sentences express a certain predicational relation. Since *ga* sentences are restricted to a particular stage, the entity to be predicated can be identified by the stage. Whereas, *wa* sentences are not restricted to the particular stage but hold over stages. Then how is the entity identified?

We propose that in *wa* sentences the entity to be predicated is identified by a set of properties necessary for identifying the entity itself. Given that a NP denotes a set of properties of a certain entity, the particle *wa* serves to separate the properties of the entity into two parts: a set of properties necessary for identification and a set of predicates to be assigned to the entity.

---

[8]*Ga*-marked NP can be connected with an individual-level predicate in the case of its having an 'exhaustive listing' reading (Kuroda 1965, Kuno 1973) as the example below:

> *(Kono risuto no naka de wa) Taro-ga shinsetsu da.*
>   this list of in   TOP Taro   kind
> 'It is Taro who is kind in this list.'

This reading should be treated in the other way, since it should be dealt with as having a focus structure judging from its intonation pattern.

For example, a proper noun *Taro* denotes the following set of properties.

(27) ⟨Taro⟩   'Taro'
             24 years old
             male
             a student of Kyushu University
                    ......
             kind
             coward
             poor

                    ......
             having a girl friend

Wa divides the set of properties above into two parts: P={'Taro', '24 years old', 'male', a student of Kyushu University} and Q={'kind', 'coward', 'poor', 'having a girl friend'}. A *wa*-marked NP in example (28) should denote the set P and a predicate *shinsetsuda* 'kind' should be included in the set Q.

(28)   *Taro wa shinsetsuda.*
       'Taro is kind '

We propose that a set of properties for identification or the set P can be easily reinterpreted as a set of entities which have these properties. The process of reinterpretation has marvelous effect in the case where *wa* marks a common noun.

(29)   *Seijika wa kanemochida.*
       'A politician is rich.'

It is largely agreed that a *wa*-marked common noun such as *seijika wa* in (29) has a universal interpretation. So, the interpretation of (29) can be represented as in (29)'.

(29)' $\forall x \, (politician(x) \rightarrow rich(x))$

The universal reading can be accounted for by the process of the reinterpretation above. In (29), the set P which consists of a property 'be a politician' is reinterpreted as a set of politicians. As we will see below, this process plays a crucial role on the *te-wa* construction.

The function of *wa* of NP-*wa* construction argued above can be summarized below:

(30)   The function of *wa* is to separate the properties of the entity into two parts: a set of properties for identifying the entity itself and a set of predicates

to be assigned to the entity, where the set of properties can be reinterpreted as a set of entities which have the properties. [9]

5. The Derivation of the Two Distinct Uses of the *te-wa* Construction
5.1 Anchored/Unanchored

Now we move on to the main topic of this paper: how each of the two uses of the *te-wa* construction is derived. We propose that the analysis of NP-wa construction considered above can apply to the te-wa construction.

Note that a causal *te* clause have tense while a sequential *te* clause does not have tense as we discussed in the section 3. The former should denote an anchored event, whereas the latter should denote an action unanchored.

It is desirable to describe the term 'anchor' before moving on to the main task. Enç (1986) argues against analyzing natural language tenses as sentential operators on the grounds that only verbs are necessarily interpreted relative to the time provided by the tense. She claims that nouns and verbs must be provided with temporal arguments and that the temporal arguments of the verb is the time provided by the tense in the sentence assuming a referential theory of tense where a tense simply denotes a time. We define the term 'anchor' as assigning a certain index of time and location to a temporal argument of the verb within Enç's framework. A tensed clause should have a temporal argument assigned a particular index of time and location, whereas a nontensed clause should not have one. The nontensed clause should be interpreted relative to the main clause.

A sequential *te* clause does not have a tense independent of the main clause tense.

---

[9]The function of *wa* we are proposing here should be differentiated from such an function as marking given information or topicalizing. The next example demonstrates that clearly.

    A: *Kinoo   Taro-ni   at-ta   yo.*
      'I saw Taro yesterday.'
    B: *Taro-tte/*wa dare?*
      'Who is Taro?'
    A: *Tenisubu-no   fukusho   da yo.*
      'He is a subcaptain of the tennis club.'

Tte is also one of the topic markers in Japanese. A *tte*-marked NP *Taro-tte* can be treated as given to the extent that it refers to the entity previously introduced in the dialogue. However, the NP cannot be marked by *wa*. This contrast between *tte* and *wa* shows that the 'identifiability' is crucial for the selection of *tte/wa*. In the example above, the speaker B does not identify who Taro is, so (s)he cannot use *wa*. In other words, only *wa*-marked NPs but not *tte*-marked NPs can denote a set of properties for identification. (See Takubo 1989, Arita and Takubo 1995)

(31) a. *Kinoo   Taro$_j$ wa   [PRO$_j$ tegami$_i$-wo kai-te] ϕ_i yabut-ta.*
        yesterday   Taro TOP   letter-ACC write   tear-PAST
        'Taro wrote and tore letters yesterday.'

   b. *Kyoo Taro$_j$ wa [PRO$_j$ tegami$_i$-wo kai-te] ϕ_i yabur-u.*
        today TaroTOP   letter-ACC write   tear-PRES
        'Taro writes and tears letters today.'

   c. **Taro$_i$ wa   [kinoo   PRO$_j$ tegami$_i$-wo kai-te] kyoo ϕ_i yabur-u.*
        Taro TOP   yesterday   letter-ACC write today   tear-PRES
        'Taro wrote letters yesterday and he tears them today.'

It is assigned the same time/location index as the main clause. On the other hand, a causal *te* clause have tense different from the main clause tense.

(32) a. *Taro$_i$ wa [pro$_i$ shigoto-wo oe-te] hottoshi-ta.*
        'Taro felt relieved to finish the work.'

   b. *Taro$_i$ wa [kinoo pro$_i$ shigoto-wo oe-te] kyoo-wa hottoshi-teir-u.*
        'Taro feels relieved today because he finished the work yesterday.'

As we will see in the next two sub-sections, this syntactic difference between the two uses of *te* become more conspicuous in the *te-wa* construction.

5.2   Repetitive Use of *te-wa*

In this sub-section, we will show that the repetitive use of *te-wa* is derived compositionally from the function of *wa* and the syntactic/semantic properties of the **sequential** *te* clause.

Given the function of *wa* described in (30), when the particle *wa* marks sequential *te* clause, it should serve to separate a set of properties of an action denoted by the sequential *te* clause into two parts: a set of properties for identifying the action itself (set P) and a set of predicates to be assigned to the action (set Q). The set P consists of a property 'followed by another action'. We propose that the set can be reinterpreted as a set of actions which has the property. Thus **the set of actions** should be the domain of predication.

Since the actions have not been anchored, they need to be anchored as well as to be predicated. As a result, each member of the set has to be assigned an index of time and location from a corresponding event following it described in its main clause. Then the relationship between the two sets is reanalyzed as an accumulation of actions. In other words, instances of association between each member of P and its corresponding member of Q are foregrounded. This process produces the repetitive interpretation. [10]

---

10 I was questioned by a member of the audience in the 6th J/K Conference with regard to where the plurality of the main clause is induced. I can answer the question in part at present. Let me stress that the plurality concerned here is merely 'implication' induced from the concept 'set', where it is ordinarily agreed

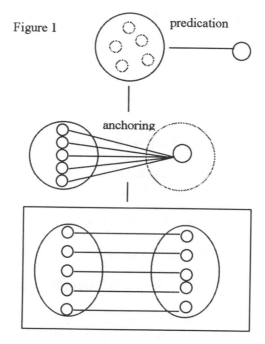

Figure 1

predication

anchoring

5.3 Conditional Use of *te-wa*

In this sub-section we shall discuss the process how the conditional use is induced. As for the negative implication carried by this use, we will take up in the next section.

The conditional use of the *te-wa* can be derived from the function of *wa* and the nature of **causal** *te*. Causal *te* clauses denote an anchored event. Since an anchored event denoted by causal *te*, by definition, has a temporal argument assigned a index of time and location, it does not need to be assigned by its main clause, resultant event, unlike in the case of sequential *te*.

When *wa* marks causal *te* clause, *wa* serves to separate a set of properties of the event into two parts: a set of properties for identifying the event itself (set P) and a set of predicates to be assigned (set Q). The set P, which consists of properties such as 'causing another event as a resultant' and 'having an index of time/location', is reinterpreted as a set of anchored events which cause the resultant event. Thus **the set of anchored events** should be the **domain** of predication.

These anchored events can be interpreted as the event holding over the particular time/location. In other words, they can be easily shifted into the general event.

---

that more than two elements are included. The main clause of a *te-wa* construction representing the property which is assigned to each member of the set denoted by the *te-wa* clause in our analysis should be reanalyzed as plural on the whole.

In the process of predication, the general event is assigned its resultant event, which should be also a general event. These two general events which are in the causal chain produce a general causality. Conditional sentences, generally agreed, represent general causal relation between two propositions, which shares the generality with the *te-wa* sentences discussed here.

Figure 2

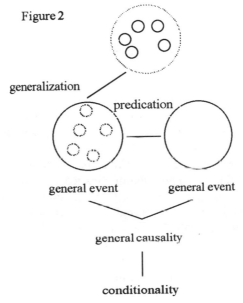

generalization

predication

general event   general event

general causality

conditionality

6.   Negative implication in Conditional *te-wa*

This section concentrates on the negative implication in the conditional use of *te-wa*. This implication can be also captured by the procedures discussed above.

Observing the interpretations of the conditional *te-wa*, we will see the following two types of implication: one is the type as in (33), where the speaker expresses indirectly his intent to avoid the subordinate clause event happening by describing an undesirable result in the main clause.   The other is the type as in (34) and (35),   where the speaker expresses that the main clause event occurs naturally as the result of the subordinate clause without any relevance to his intent.   So, strictly speaking, only the former type should be called 'negative implication'.

(33)   *Taro-ga   it-te-wa minna-ga meiwakusur-u.*
        Taro-NOM go   all-NOM be-annoyed-PRES
        'If Taro goes, all other members will be annoyed.'
(34)   A: *Onegaidesukara, sono hon-wo kashi-te-kudasai.*
              'I ask you as a favor to lend me the book.'
        B: *Anata-ni tanom-are-te-wa kotowar-e-nai.*
              from you ask-PASS   refuse-PASS-NEG
              'I cannot refuse at your request.'

(35) A: *Kinoo Hanako-to arui-teir-u toki, saifu-wo sur-are-teshimatta.*
'Yesterday I had my purse stolen when I was walking with Hanako.'

B: *Saifu-wo   sur-are-te-wa tanoshim-e-nakat-ta-daroo-ne.*
purse-ACC **steal-PASS**   enjoy-POT-NEG-PAST-MOD-MOD
'Since you had your purse stolen, you could not enjoy yourself, I guess. '

The negative or undesirable event described in the main clause of example (33) ought to be also both natural and inevitable as a result of its causal event described in its subordinate clause. We might say that the inevitable causal relation between two events strengthens an illocutional force of the sentence: warning. Therefore, what is crucial for the conditional *te-wa* construction is 'inevitability', which is naturally induced from the procedures proposed in the previous section.

Thus, we have to explain why some conditional *te-wa* sentences have 'negative' implication and how the implication is derived from the procedures in the previous section. For the first question, I propose, whether the subordinate clause event is realized or not is crucial. More specifically, whenever the *te-wa* clause denotes an event which does not happen yet, the sentence implies 'negativity'. Observing examples (34) and (35), we can find that our observation is adequate. It is natural that only a future event but not a past event be prevented from happening.

As for the second question, it is crucial for the derivation of the implication that a future event has two possible cases: realized in the future and not realized. So, in the process of predication, a predicate should be assigned to both of the two sets: a set of events realized in the future and a set of events not realized. In other words, the predicate should be a result of the subordinate event as well as it should be an event prevented from happening by the speaker or the hearers. In the case, the predicate is nothing but an undesirable resultant event.

It is worth while noting some constraints of the main clause regarding modality. Such subjective expressions as request and order never occur in the main clause.

(36) a. *Taro-ga it-ta-ra ki-wo tsukero.*[11]
'If Taro goes, be careful of him'.
b. **Taro-ga it-te-wa ki-wo tsukero.*
'If Taro goes, be careful of him'.
(37) a. *Taro-ni at-ta-ra yoroshiku-to tsutaete.*
'If you meet Taro, please say hello to him.'
b. **Taro-ni at-te-wa yoroshiku-to tsutaete.*

---

[11]*Ra* is one of the ordinary conditional markers in Japanese.

'If you meet Taro, please say hello to him.'

Request and order have an illocutional force which urges the occurrence of an event in the future. They can be regarded as a cause of the event. The sentences as in (36) and (37) should express **cause-cause** relation but not cause-effect one. (Murao (p.c.)) The *te-wa* form cannot occur in this situation because it is used as expressing cause-effect relation.

7. Concluding Remarks
In this paper, I have proposed a domain setting function of *wa*. This function is essential to the analysis of *wa* marked NP as discussed in Takubo 1989, 1990, Arita 1992, and Arita and Takubo 1995. The importance of this function does not appear to be clear in the analysis of *wa*-marked NP. However, it is indispensable for the analysis of *wa* because as we have seen in this paper, it is necessary for explaining the two uses of a *wa*-marked *te* clause, or two uses of the *te-wa* construction.

Acknowledgements:
    I am grateful to Toshiaki Inada, Yukinori Takubo, Haruhiko Murao, and many others for their invaluable comments and support.

References:

Akatsuka, Noriko and Sung-Ock S. Sohn. 1994. Negative conditionality: The Case of Japanese *-tewa* and Korean *-taka*. *Japanese Korean Linguistics* Vol. 4, ed. by Akatsuka, Noriko. Stanford: CSLI. 203-219.
Arita, Setsuko. 1992. Nihongo-no jooken-to shudai-no yuuwa-ni tsuite: danwa-ni okeru Setting kinoo (On Syncretism between Conditional Form and Topic Form in Japanese). *Proceedings of 14th Annual Meeting of the Kansai Linguistic Society.* 110-119.
Arita, Setsuko. 1993. *TE-WA* bun-no koozoo-to imi-ni tsuite (On Syntactic and Semantic Structures of *TE-WA* Construction). ms.
Arita, Setsuko. 1994. Bun-no imikaishaku-ni okeru gooseisei: *TE-WA* bun-no imikaishakuk-ni tsuite (On Compositionality in Interpretation: On Interpretation of *TE-WA* Construction). ms.
Arita, Setsuko and Takubo, Yukinori. 1995. Nihongo-no teidaikeishiki-no kinoo-ni tsuite (On the Discourse Managing Functions of the Japanese Topic Markers). *Human Science vol. 1.* Fukuoka: Kyushu University. 43-63.
Arita, Setsuko. to appear. WA no domain settei kinoo to *TE-WA* bun no futatsuno kaishaku. (On Domain Setting Function of a Japanese Particle *wa* and Two Distinct Interpretations of the *TE-WA* Construction. *Koizumi Tamotsu Sensei Koki Kinen Ronbunshu.* Tokyo: Daigakushorin. 21-34.

Carlson, Gregory N. 1977. *Reference to Kinds in English*. Ph. D. Dissertation, University of Massachusetts, Amherst. Published 1980 by Garland Press, New York.

Clark, Hubert. 1992. *Arenas of Language Uses*. Stanford: CSLI.

Enç, Mürvet. 1986. Towards a Referential Analysis of Temporal Expressions. *Linguistics and Philosophy* 9. 405-426.

Fauconnier, Gilles. 1985. *Mental Spaces*. Cambridge, Mass.: MIT Press.

Hasunuma, Akiko. 1987. Jookenbun ni okeru nichijooteki suiron (Everyday reasoning in conditional sentences). *Kokugogaku* vol. 150. 1-14.

Kuno, Susumu. 1973. *The Structure of the Japanese Language*. Mass.: MIT Press.

Kuroda, Shige-Yuki. 1965. *Generative Grammatical Studies in the Japanese Language*, Doctoral Dissertation, MIT, reprinted, New York: Garland Press. 1979.

Kuroda, Shige-Yuki. 1972. The Categorical and the Thetic Judgment. *Foundations of Language 9*. 153-185.

Kuroda, Shige-Yuki. 1992. Judgment Forms and Sentence Forms. *Japanese Syntax and Semantics*. Dordrecht: Kluwer Academic Publishers. 13-77.

McCawley, James D. and Momoi, Katsuhiko. 1986. The constituent structure of -te complements. *Papers in Japanese Linguistics* 11. 1-60

Miyagawa, Shigeru. 1987. Wa and WH phrase. *Perspective on Topicalization: The case of Japanese 'Wa'* , eds. By J. Hinds, S. K. Maynard and S. Iwasaki. Amsterdam: John Benjamins. 185-217.

Nishiyama, Yuji. 1990. 'Kakiryori-wa Hiroshima-ga honba-da' koobun-ni tsuite: hoowa meishiku-to hihoowa meishiku (Remarks on the "Kakiryoori wa Hiroshima ga Homba da" Construction: Saturated vs. Unsaturated Noun Phrases). *Reports of The Keio Institute of Cultural and Linguistic Studies* No. 22. 169-188.

Onoe, Keisuke. 1981. 'WA'-no Kakarijoshisei-to Hyogenteki-kinoo. *Kokugo-to Kokubungaku 58-5*. 102-118.

Sakahara, Shigeru. 1990. Yakuwari, ga/wa, Unagi-bun (Roles, the Particles ga/wa, 'eel' Sentences). *Advances in Japanese Cognitive Science,* Vol. 3. Tokyo: Koodansha. 29-66.

Takubo, Yukinori. 1989. Meishiku-no modariti (Modality of Noun Phrase) . *Modality in Japanese*, eds. by Nitta, Yoshio and Masuoka, Takashi. Tokyo: Kuroshio Publisher. 211-233.

Takubo, Yukinori. 1990. Taiwa-ni okeru kikite ryooiki-no yakuwari-ni tsuite: Sanninshoo daimeishi no shiyoo kisoku-kara mita nichi-chuu-ei kakugo-no taiwa koozoo-no hikaku (On the Role of Hearer's Territory of Information: A Contrastive Study of Dialogic Structure in Japanese, Chinese, and English as Manifested in the Third Person Pronoun System. *Advances in Japanese Cognitive Science,* Vol. 3. Tokyo: Koodansha. 67-84.

A Cognitive Account of the Korean Morpheme -*se*: A Marker of Inclusiveness*

SUSAN STRAUSS
University of California, Los Angeles

1. Introduction

This paper will attempt to shed new light on one aspect of Korean grammar by focusing on a single unit, -*se*, as it functions in Modern Korean. This component is generally not recognized by linguists as being meaningful in and of itself, and in this respect it is hoped that the current analysis will ultimately serve as a window to certain patterns of form and function in Korean which would otherwise remain virtually ignored and unnoticed. This paper is intended as a novel but tentative approach to the analysis of Korean grammar in the hope that it may begin to be re-analyzed as a more independent linguistic system, vastly rich in its own grammatical phenomena, and will suggest that Korean grammar has been viewed perhaps too strongly through the lenses of Western linguistic tradition.

2. The problem: is -*se* meaningful?
2.1   Traditional views

Modern Korean possesses a number of contrastive morpheme pairs in which the second member differs from the first, just by virtue of the existence of an additional final syllable -*se*, as in (1) a) and b):

* I would like to thank Professors Noriko Akatsuka, Robert Kirsner, Sung-Ock Sohn, and Misato Tokunaga for their encouragement and comments on an earlier version of this paper. I am deeply grateful to Ms. Yong-Yae Park for her assistance with the Korean examples and for her invaluable insights and support and encouragement throughout every facet of this study, from the initial abstract stage through the current version. Thanks also go to Dr. Shoichi Aoki (Inter-University Center) for his patient listening and thoughtful comments.

(1)

(a)	(-∅-)	(b)	(with -se)
ey	'to' (inanimate)	*eys e*	'from' (inanimate)
eykey	'to' (animate)	*eykeys e*	'from' (animate)
hanthey	'to' (animate)	*hantheys e*	'from' (animate)
kkey	'to' (hon. dative marker)	*kkeys e*	hon. subject marker
myen	'if', 'when'	*myens e*	'while', 'although
kulemyen	'then', 'if that's the case.	*kulemyens e*	'while doing so'
(u)lo	'direction toward'	*(u)los e*	'as', 'in the capacity of'

What is interesting in this regard, however, is that virtually all reference grammars and textbooks, and the majority of traditional accounts of the Korean language (cf. Lee 1993, Lukoff 1982, H.M. Sohn 1986, H.M. Sohn 1994, inter alia) treat these contrastive pairs as single morpheme oppositions, such that *ey*, for example simply means 'to', expressing a GOAL and *eyse* means 'from', expressing a SOURCE. There seems to be no explicit mention in these accounts of the semantic contrast between the honorific dative marker *kkey* and its corresponding subject marker *kkeyse*. Similarly, there seems to be no correlation drawn between the conditional marker *myen*, generally meaning 'if' 'or 'when', and the adverbial *myense*, meaning 'while' or 'although'; nor the directional marker *(u)lo* 'toward' and the adverbial meaning 'as' or 'in the capacity of', which could be viewed as a compound adverbial *(u)lose* comprised of the same directional marker *(u)lo* plus the morpheme -*se*. In short, these traditional accounts clearly do not seem to consider -*se* as a meaningful morpheme. Furthermore, all native speakers, (both linguistically trained and not), informally surveyed throughout the various initial stages of this research, unanimously considered the -*se* marked counterparts as independent semantic chunks, and not as compounds divisible into the types of base components as noted above plus -*se*. Simply put, the unanimous response among my native speaker informants was that -*se* alone means nothing.

2.2 Some early views of -*se* [1]

While the vast majority of traditional grammars and native speaker surveys do not seem to recognize -*se* as an independent semantic element, a few linguistic accounts of this unit do exist which contain observations that it does carry some type of meaning. Kim (1984) provides an overview of the four previous accounts known to date in the following encapsulated way: Ko (1968) indicates that -*se* functions as a subject marker; Swung-Nyong Lee (1976) traces -*se* to one of the 15th Century existential verbs *sita*; Song (1979) states that -*se* has the meaning of existence; and Keedong Lee,

---

[1]   I am grateful to Prof. Sung-Ock Sohn for providing me with these articles.

(1981) demonstrates that -se is a single morpheme, although its exact underlying meaning and overall grammatical functions are not explicated in detail by Kim. Kim then provides his own commentary with respect to the previous literature, rejecting Ko's account of -se as a subject marker, calling it instead a supplementary particle and in accordance with Lee and Song also maintains that its core meaning has something to do with existence. However, these five accounts including Kim's focus mainly on a limited number of grammatical constructions in which -se occurs (e.g., as a subject marker and with locatives) rather than treating its full range of possible occurrences in the grammar, and other than perhaps suggesting an underlying meaning of 'existence' for this morpheme, no unified analysis has been provided thus far which could also systematically account for a fuller range of its usage throughout the grammar of Korean. Moreover, these five earlier accounts of what promises to be a fascinating and powerful linguistic element do not appear to be very well known to Korean linguists at all, at least in the U.S., and thus remain all the more beyond the reach and recognition of general linguists as well.

The goal of this paper is to continue the ideas proposed by Ko, S-N. Lee, Song K. Lee, and Kim, that -se indeed carries meaning, and to attempt a preliminary hypothesis which would account for its meaning in a broader and more unified way. I will suggest that one of the primary meanings conveyed by -se is that of INCLUSIVENESS[2]. By assigning the meaning of INCLUSIVENESS to this morpheme, I will attempt to illustrate its power as a linguistic device which serves to link entities at the concrete and spatial level as well as at the clausal level: In the case of the former, -se will be explained as a device which links a particular entity to a particular location; in the case of the latter, it will be shown to temporally link clauses together on the basis of simultaneity, cause-effect, or sequentiality. In the process of explicating its use in these ways, I will also demonstrate that one of the crucial functions of -se is to transform the realm of IRREALIS into the realm of REALIS.

3. Is ey vs. eyse simply goal vs. source?

From the list in (1) I have separated out three contrastive morpheme pairs which express GOAL/SOURCE relationships in Korean, shown in (2):

---

[2] This feature of 'inclusiveness' appears to be related to Chesterman's (1991) discussion of definiteness. The potential relationship between -se and the overall concept of definiteness is currently being investigated more deeply by the author.

(2) postpositionals expressing 'goal' and 'source' relationships

ey	(to [place])	vs.	*eys e*[3]	(from [place])
eykey	(to [animate])	vs.	*eykeys e*	(from [animate])
hanthey	(to [animate])	vs.	*hantheys e*	(from [animate])

As should be clear by the approximate English counterparts provided in parenthesis, the elements in the left column all express directionality towards some place, being, or entity (goal), and those in the right column, directionality from a place, being, or entity (source), as illustrated in the full sentence examples in (3), (4), and (5):

(3) [adapted from Park (1968:69)]
 a) *Hakkyo -ey kapnita*
 School-**ey** go-FML
 '[I] go to school'   [goal]

 b) *Ce nun Seoul -eyse opnita*
 I   TM   Seoul-**eyse** come-FML
 'I'm coming from Seoul'   [source]

(4) [adapted from Park (1968:345)]
 a) *I chayk -ul Kim sensayng eykey tulisipsiyo*
 This book-OM Kim teacher   **eykey**   give-hon-IMP
 'Please give this book to Mr. Kim'   [goal]

 b) *Pak sensayng ekeyse ku mal ul tutko, nollassupnita*
 Park teacher **eykeyse**   that word OM   hear-GER   surprise-pst-FML
 'I was surprised to hear that from Ms. Park'   [source]
 (lit. 'I heard that word from Ms. Park and was surprised.)

(5) [adapted from Lukoff (1982:424)]
 a) *Nwukwu hanthey phyenci lul ssuni?*
 Who   **hanthey**   letter   OM   write-INTER
 'Who are you writing a letter to?'   [goal]

In Quechua, the dative marker <u>man</u> and the source or ablative marker <u>manta</u> could possibly be manifesting a similar phenomenon, although native speakers consider <u>manta</u> to be a single meaningful chunk and not a composite of the dative marker (man) plus the accusative markder (ta). This is simply an observation at this point and requires further investigation and analysis.

b) *Nwukwu hantheyse   phyenci   ka   oassta?*
    Who **hantheyse** letter   SM   come-PST-PLN
    'Who is the letter from?'   [source]

Based on these example sentence pairs, it becomes clear that a great number of grammatical and linguistic accounts of these postpositions (e.g., Lee 1993, Lukoff 1982, H.M. Sohn 1986 and 1994, Park 1968) seem to maintain a strict distinction, either implicitly or explicitly, between the seemingly antonymous meanings of goal and source for each form.

One such explicit characterization of the goal-source opposition for *ey* and *eyse* is H.M. Sohn (1986). While considering *ey* as the polar semantic opposite of *eyse*, Sohn's analysis departs from the traditional view which attributes this marker with two distinct meanings, i.e., locative *ey* and goal *ey*. Instead, Sohn posits a single underlying meaning of 'goal,' hence his unitary interpretation for *ey*, basing his analysis on semantic evidence from Korean 'motional' and existential verbs and on the patterning of the locative/goal marker *ni* in Japanese: In essence, the traditional bisection between location and goal for Korean *ey* is in a sense superfluous since the concept of what it expresses in combination with a range of motional and existential verbs is simply 'a scale of various degrees of goal meaning' (p.246). This is illustrated in (6), (7), and (8), originally appearing as (5) a), c), and d), respectively (p. 245):

(6) *hakkyo-EY   kanta*
     school-to   go-PLN
     '(He) is going to school'

(7) *hakkyo-EY   namnunta*
     school-at   remain-PLN
     '(He) is remaining at school'

(8) *cip-EY   issta*
     house-at   exist-PLN
     '(He) is at home'

Similarly, the same justification holds for Sohn's rejection of the traditional bisection of *eyse* into separate locative and source markers. Here again, this distinction is equally superfluous since underlyingly 'the *eyse* locative serves, in our conceptualization, as the place or source from which the activity state of a theme's referent starts or rises' (pp. 249-250). The varying degrees of source meaning are illustrated in (9), (10), and (11) below, originally appearing as (9) a), c), and d) respectively (p. 249):

(9) *hakkyo-EYSE onta*
     school-from come-PLN
     '(He) is coming from school'

    (10)   *hakkyo-EYSE nonta*
            school-at   play-PLN
            '(He) is playing at school'

    (11)   *hakkyo-EYSE issta*
            school-at   exist-PLN
            '(It) takes place at school'

Thus, while H.M Sohn does propose an insightfully sound analysis of these two locative expressions and provides convincing evidence in favor of a neater and more simplified account with respect to how we as human beings conceptualize and express relations between entities in a spatio-temporal domain, it would appear that the analysis of these two morphemes should by no means end at this point.

I would like to propose an even simpler analysis and as such a more unified view of these expressions--an analysis in which *ey* and *eyse* are not just dichotomous manifestations of two polar opposite concepts. Rather this new analysis is one which first recognizes -*se* as a morpheme signaling INCLUSIVENESS whose function is basically that of a definiteness marker. From there, it is expected that the analysis will be able to account for not only the distinctions between *ey* and *eyse* but the other grammatical patterns in which -*se* appears as well.

4.   From IRREALIS to REALIS--The definiteness continuum

4.1 INCLUSIVENESS--LINKING TRAJECTORS WITH LOCATIVES
4.1.1   'goal' vs. 'source' relations

As we have seen from the above examples, it is entirely possible for -*se* to attach itself to a number of other morphemes thereby effecting a relational shift between at least the notions of goal and source. As H.M. Sohn keenly observes, there does indeed appear to be a kind of scale of 'varying degrees of meaning' for both goal and source. However, in contrast with Sohn, rather than two separate scales, i.e., one for goal and one for source, I would propose that there is only one scale along which a kind of definiteness continuum would run. The basal, minimal, or least definite element on the scale is the goal element; the maximal or most definite element is the source element. This definiteness continuum is represented below in (12).

(12)

GOAL	location w/stative verb	location w/active verb	**SOURCE**
ey	*ey*	*eyse*	*eyse*
eykey	---	---	*eykeyse*
hanthey	---	---	*hantheyse*

LOW DEFINITENESS > > > > HIGH DEFINITENESS

As noted, for the case of -*se* occurring with the postpositionals *ey, eykey, and hanthey*, the definiteness continuum would be grounded in a spatio-temporal framework whereby notions such as goal or dative would represent the lowest degree of definiteness, and the notion of source, the greatest. Regarding the intermediary elements, i.e., *ey* vs. *eyse* with stative verbs or actions verbs, the choice of the appropriate locative marker would fall in between the two extremes, depending upon the type of verb with which it occurs. This is, to a certain extent, similar to Sohn's examples as shown in (6) - (11)[4].

Given that a goal or dative element is, by its very definition an as yet unachieved location or entity, one could readily consider this element as belonging to the domain of IRREALIS, in the sense that the referent in question is, by virtue of it being a goal, an unrealized entity. Conversely, the quintessential nature of the concept of source indicates that the action originates from some specified area, and as such, would be considered not only HIGHLY DEFINITE, but within the domain of REALIS as well. Thus, it will be shown just how -*se*, as an indicator of inclusiveness can transform the realm of irrealis into the realm of realis. Note example (13):

(13) a) GOAL [low spatio-temporal definiteness] / IRREALIS

hankwuk-**ey**   ka -yo
Korea -**LOC** go -POL
'I'll go **to** Korea'
[entities: 'I' : 'Korea' = NOT LINKED]

b) SOURCE [high spatio-temporal definiteness] / REALIS

chinkwu -ka   hankwuk-**eyse**   o   -ayo
friend   -SUB Korea-**ey + SE** come -POL
(My) friend is coming **from** Korea'
[entities   '(My) friend' : 'Korea' = LINKED]

---

4   The alternation of *ey/eyse* (and Japanese *ni/de*) with various verbs is a topic which is currently being investingated by the author on the basis of this defniteness framework and will be explicated in detail in a future study.

With -*se* carrying the meaning of INCLUSIVENESS we can see how it functions in the above examples which illustrate the so called 'goal' vs. 'source' opposition. In (13) a), denoting goal, and hence an irrealis state, the entity or trajector in question, i.e., 'I', is not 'linked' to 'Korea', while in (13) b) the underlying semantic link is clear by virtue of 'Korea's' status of source, i.e., the trajector '(My) friend' can be considered to have been linked to the source element 'Korea.' The identical operation of inclusiveness and hence degree of definiteness affecting the concept of GOAL / IRREALIS on the one hand and SOURCE / REALIS on the other can be seen below in (14) and (15) with the dative makers *eykey* and *hanthey*, respectively:

(14)   *eykey / eykeyse*
   a)   *I   chayk -ul Kim   sensayng -**eykey** tuli -si -psiyo*
      'Please give this book t o Mr. Kim'   **GOAL**
                                       LOW DEFINITENESS / IRREALIS
                    [entities: 'book' : 'Mr. Kim' = NOT LINKED]

   b)   *Pak sensayng -**ekeyse** ku mal -ul tut -ko, noll -ass -upnita*
      'I was surprised to hear that **from** Ms. Park   **SOURCE**
                                    HIGH DEFINITENESS / REALIS
                    [entities: 'that word' : 'Ms. Park' = LINKED]

(15)   *hanthey / hantheyse*
   a)   *Nwukwu -**hanthey** phyenci -lul ssu -ni?*
      'Who are you writing a letter t o?'   **GOAL**
                                        LOW DEFINITENESS / IRREALIS
                    [entities: 'letter ': 'who' = NOT LINKED]

   b)   *Nwukwu -**hantheyse** phyenci -ka o -ass -ni?*
      'Who is the letter **from**?'   **SOURCE**
                                    HIGH DEFINITENESS / REALIS
                    [entities: 'letter': 'who' = LINKED]

Thus, it should be clear from these examples that the relationship between the trajector element and the source element are semantically linked when -*se* is present and not linked when it is absent. These few examples alone indicate just to what degree -*se* can be considered to carry significant meaning--strong preliminary evidence with respect to the semantic power of -*se*.

4.1.2   Moving toward a state or condition vs. being in a state or condition: The case of *(u)lo* vs. *(u)lose*

Perhaps one of the least obvious yet most striking contrastive pairs which demonstrates the phenomenon of -*se* attributing definiteness to a particular entity or grammatical construction is the *(u)lo* / *(u)lose* contrast. Generally speaking *(u)lo* is used with motion verbs to express some type of directionality as in (16).

(16)　*Wuli nun　　Seoul l o kal keyeyo*
　　　 We　　TM　　Seoul to　go-FUT
　　　 'We'll go t o Seoul'

　　　　　　　　　　　　　(u)lo -- **'into/direction toward'**
　　　　　　　　　　　　　LOW DEFINITENESS / IRREALIS
　　　　　　　　　　　　　[entities: 'We ': 'Seoul' = NOT LINKED]

It can also be used with verbs such as *pyenhata* 'to change', *mantulta* 'to make', and *khiwuta* 'to raise', all of which still indicate a type of direction and at the same time, a process as in (17).

(17)*Wuli -nun　i ai　　　　lul　　hwulywungha　-n sensayngnim-u l o*
　　　 We-TM　　this child-　　OM　　great-　　　　RC teacher　　　**into**
　　　mantu/ khiwu -l ke i -eyo
　　　 make/raise-FUT-POL
　　　 'We will raise him **to be** (become) a great teacher

　　　　　　　　　　　　　(u)lo -- **'into/direction toward'**
　　　　　　　　　　　　　LOW DEFINITENESS / IRREALIS
　　　　　　　　　　　　　[entities: 'him' ; 'teacher' = NOT LINKED]

Note that in both (16) and (17) *(u)lo* functions to express some type of goal relationship (or a low definite entity and an IRREALIS domain), whether it is a physical location as in (16) or a state or condition, as in (17). What is particularly striking is that the addition of -*se* here as in (18), moves the entity which *(u)lo* designates from the realm of IRREALIS into the realm of REALIS, and in so doing, links the entities together, i.e., 'you' and 'teacher' are linked by -*se*.

(18)
　　sensayngnim-ulose　　　　　kulehkey　　　hamyen an twayyo
　　 teacher　　-**in the capacity of** in that way　　do-shouldn't
　　 '**As a** teacher, you shouldn't do such things'

　　　　　　　　　　　　　(u)lose --**'in the capacity of'**
　　　　　　　　　　　　　HIGH DEFINITENESS/REALIS
　　　　　　　　　　　　　[entities: 'you' : 'teacher = LINKED]

Thus far we have seen in a number of different constructions how -*se* functions as a marker of inclusiveness by linking entities at the concrete and spatial level, and as a result serves to move an entity from the domain of IRREALIS into the domain of REALIS. The next section will demonstrate a similar function of *-se,* and how it operates at the level of the clause.

4.2 INCLUSIVENESS--LINKING CLAUSES

As noted, the use and function of *-se* is not limited to a linking of entities in the domain of space or at the level of the concrete. As will be demonstrated in this section, *-se* functions in a strikingly parallel manner at the level of the clause as well. As a clause connector, we will examine first one additional contrastive pair consisting of a non-*se* marked element and its *-se* marked counterpart (*myen* vs. *myense*) and will then briefly look at the construction *-a/e se* (i.e., occurring alone with the *-a/e* form of a verb) as a clause connector.

4.2.1   Conditional vs. concession and simultaneity: The case of *myen*   and *myense*

The Korean conditional marker *myen* and the marker of concession or simultaneity *myense* represent a similar contrast between one grammatical form and its variant which seem to differ solely by the addition of the final syllable-*se.* These two forms are shown in (19) for reference.

(19)   a)   *myen*   CONDITIONAL
      b)   *myense*   CONCESSION / SIMULTANEITY

Myen   is the prototypical conditional marker in Korean, meaning 'if' or 'when' and its function is illustrated in (20), adapted from K. Lee (1994:484):

(20)   *nwun   i   omyen   pakkey   nakaca.*
      snow   SM   come-**if**   outside-to   go-PROP
      'If it snows, let's go out"

The second form, *myense*   seems to demonstrate certain similarities to English 'while'. Like its English counterpart, it conjoins clauses to express the simultaneity of two actions as illustrated below in (21), adapted from Lee (p. 492):

(21)   *na   nun   kwacalul   mekumyense phyencilul ssessta.*
      I TM   cookies-OM   eat-**while** letter-OM write-PST-PLN
      'I wrote a letter while eating cookies'

Also like English 'while', *myense* can take on a type of concessive speaker stance, conveying a feeling of dissatisfaction and carrying a tone similar to one which might accompany the expression 'even though' as in (22), adapted from Lee (p. 495):

(22)

kunun	*yenphilul*	*ssuci*	*anhumyense*	*an pillye cwunta.*
he-TP	pencil-OM	use-NOM	not-**while**	not-lend give-PLN

'he does not lend me his pencil even though he is not using it'

It is in the analysis of these two clause connectors that the distinction between the domains of IRREALIS and REALIS and the phenomenon of the definiteness continuum become the most salient, although here, the issue of definiteness does not apply to spatial relations as we saw clearly in the case of the postpositionals. Rather than linking entities in the spatial domain, the concepts of definiteness and REALIS affect the relationship between the two clauses. The definiteness scale for these connectors is shown in (23):

(23)

CONDITIONAL 'if'   TEMPORAL 'when'   SIMULTANEOUS 'while'
   myen   *myen*   *myense*
LEAST DEFINITE > > > > > > >MOST DEFINITE

The range in degree of definiteness as it applies to the uses of *myen* and *myense* is illustrated in examples (24) a), b), and c). (24) a) has been adapted from Lee (p. 489) and b) and c) were constructed by the author:

(24) a)

kunun te ilccik wasstelam y e n ku sensayngnimul mannasul kesita
he-TM   more early come-PST **i f** that teacher-OM meet-pst would probably
'If he had come earlier, he [that person] could have met the teacher'

myen -- 'if'
LEAST DEFINITE / IRREALIS

(24) b) *i chayk -ul ilkum y e n, te cal alkeytway l keeyo*
This book-OM read-**if/when** more well understand -will probably
'**If/when** you read this book, you'll understand better.'

myen -- 'if/when'
MORE DEFINITE/MORE REALIS

(24) c) *na nun pothong i chayk -ul ilkumyense, papul meknunta*
I OM usually   this book-OM read-**while**   rice-OM eat-PLN
'I usually eat **while** reading this book'

myense -- 'while'
MOST DEFINITE/REALIS

Since the semantics of *myen* actually span a wide range from extreme IRREALIS to some degree of REALIS by virtue of its meaning range from 'if' to 'when', the sample sentence in (24)a from Lee was expressly chosen because it represents a counter-factual conditional--the type of conditional representing the absolute lowest degree of REALIS. Note that the relationship between the two clauses in (24)a is one of extreme disjunction, in the sense that, both logically and pragmatically, a wide variety of possible consequent clauses could follow the conditional clause. If one overheard just the antecedent clause from (24)a, it would be difficult to predict what would follow in the consequent clause. As we progress toward a higher degree of definiteness, hence REALIS, as in (24)b which expresses the future temporal relation of 'when', there appears to be a substantially tighter logical and pragmatic relationship between the two clauses, in the sense that one would expect a particular outcome to result in the consequent clause. The range of possible or predictable outcomes is much smaller than the range of possible consequent clauses in (24)a. Going further up the REALIS continuum, we see in (24)c that the two actions expressed through the *myense* clause are simultaneous, and as such the two clauses are temporally linked in an exceptionally strong way by *-se*. In fact, if the two actions linked by a *myense* clause do not occur at the same time, the sentence would be ungrammatical. This simultaneity constraint for *myense* becomes strikingly obvious in (25), also adapted from Lee (p. 483).

(25)
? kunun hamonikalul pwulmyense, nolaylul pwullessta
he-TP harmonika-OM blow-while song-OM sing-PST-PLN
'He was playing the harmonica and sang songs'

As noted by Lee, what renders the above utterance ungrammatical or at best questionable is the fact that it is physiologically impossible for one normal human being to accomplish both tasks at the same time. In addition to providing a neat illustration of the simultaneity constraint surrounding *myense*, this example also demonstrates how an extreme degree of definiteness can be achieved by the combination of the conditional/temporal *myen* plus the marker of inclusiveness *-se*, although Lee does not seem to draw any explicit parallel between the conditional/temporal and IRREALIS marker *myen* and the REALIS marker *myense*, nor does he suggest that the latter may have derived from the former.[5]

---

5   A similar sort of alternation occurs between the domains of IRREALIS and REALIS in terms of hypotheticality and simultaneity in the following contrastive pair: *kulemyen* 'if that's the case' vs. *kulemyense* 'while doing something'.

4.2.2 The verbal connective -*a/e se*

-*A/e se* is one construction typically used to combine clauses in Korean to express cause and effect relationships, reasons, and sequentiality. A number of syntactic and semantic constraints surround the appropriate use of this connective, and it will be demonstrated here that the semantic function of -*se* is identically parallel to that in the other instances already examined and as such can account for these constraints In essence, all of the examples that follow in this section will illustrate just to what degree the morpheme -*se* as an inclusiveness marker functions to link the elements in the two clauses, whether the relationship involved is a causal or sequential one. Example (26), invented by the author, illustrates the function of -*a/e se* in expressing cause/effect or reasons:

(26) *cinan cwu nun mom i aphes e, il hale   kaci anhasseyo*
        last week TM body-SM sick-**e s e** work do-PURP go-NOM not-PST-POL
        'I was sick last week, so I didn't go to work'

In (26), there is a contingent relationship between the speaker's being ill and his not going to work last week. Similarly, as pointed out by S. Sohn (1994:352), -*ese* requires that there be a consecutive relationship, i.e., that 'the situation being described follows on some previously mentioned situation,' as in (27), adapted from Sohn:

(27) *Minca-nun nemwu aph-ase keylsekhayssta*
        'Minca was so sick that she was absent (from school)'

The strength of -*se* as an inclusion marker becomes even more salient when contrasted with another clause connector *ko*. Examples (28) and (29) below (both are invented examples) illustrate such an opposition:

(28) *tosekoan   ey   kas e   kongpwu haysseyo*
        library   to   go-**s e**   study   do-PST-POL
        'I went to the library and (I) studied (there)'

(29) *tosekoan   ey   kako   kongpwu hesseyo*
        library   to   go-**k o**   study   do-PST-POL
        'I went to the library and then studied (either somewhere else or at the library but at some other time'

Note that in (28), 'the library' is at the same time the goal of the motion of the verb 'go' as well as the location of where the studying took place, and it is through the use of -*se* that this cohesive interrelationship or linking of activities ('go', 'study'), trajector ('I'), and goal/location ('to the library'/ 'there', i.e., 'at the library') is achieved[6].

In contrast, in (29), the elements of activities, trajector, and goal/location are not at all connected. In fact, it is the connective -*ko* , or more precisely the absence of -*se*,[7] which indicates that the location of the studying is either somewhere other than the library, or that the two actions were at least not sequential. Lee (1994) also substantially supplements the analysis of the temporal/causal sequence constraint for -*se* and provides a deep and insightful analysis of this construction through a set of well-thought out examples with -*ese* as well as with a number of contrasting connectives such as -*ko*. What has not been previously pointed out, however, is the absolute strength of -*se* to link entities and clauses, a finding which emerges transparently when the presence of -*se* is analyzed in contrast with parallel situations in which it is absent.

4.3 INCLUSIVENESS--LINKING SUBJECTS

The final area that this study will address involves the usage of -*se* with subject markers[8]. Examples (30) - (32) adapted from Kim (1984) poignantly and pellucidly illustrate the power of -*se* as a marker of inclusiveness. Note that the Korean versions of the three sentences are identical, with the exception that (30) includes subject marker *i* + -*se*, (31) includes only the subject marker *i*, and (32) includes the double subject marking *i* + *ka*:

---

[6]   What is intrestesting here is that example (28) would translate into French as noted in (28'):

28')   *tosekoan -ey   ka -s e   kongpwu   hay -ss -eyo*
         library   to   go-s e   study   do-PST -IE
         'I went to the library and (I) studied (there)'
         [French: je suis allé à la bibliotheque et j'**y** ai étudié.]

In the French example, the pronoun 'y ' ('there') would be obligatory in order to express the locative relationship between the two actions, which points to some interesting implications vis à vis Korean -*se*. This is currently under investigation by the author.

[7]   As pointed out by K. Lee and S.-O Sohn (both pc) the combination of both verbal connectives *ko* + *se* is also possible. Examples from actual discourse are currently being sought and this issue will be addressed in detail in a future paper.

[8]   Because of space limitations, the actual usage of -*se* with and as a subject marker (e.g., *kkey* vs. *kkeyse*) is broader than what will be addressed in this section, however the basic claim with respect to the underlying semantics and operations of this morpheme is expected to be applicable to the entire range of its usage.

(30)
chwulyenca   seys -i -s e   nolay   han kok -ul   pwull -ess -ta
performer   three -SM -s e   song   one CL -OM   sing -PST -DECL
'Three singers sang a song'   [i.e., all three sang together]

(31)
chwulyenca seys -i   nolay   han kok -ul   pwull -ess -ta
performer   three-SM- song   one CL -OM   sing -PST -DECL
'Three singers sang a song'
[ambiguous -- as to whether they sang simultaneously or separately]

(32)
chwulyenca seys -i -ka   nolay   han kok -ul   pwull -ess -ta
performer   three -SM-SM   song   one CL -OM   sing -PST-DECL
'Three singers sang a song'
[ambiguous -- as to whether they sang simultaneously or separately]

As indicated, (31) and (32) it is unclear as to whether the three singers all sang together or separately. (30), on the other hand, is not at all ambiguous. The only possible interpretation here is that all three sang at the same time, and this is due, not surprisingly, to the mere existence of -*se*.

5.   Conclusion

While this analysis is still tentative and represents just one preliminary phase of an on-going study[9], I have tried to demonstrate that -*se* is indeed a morpheme in Korean and that its function as an inclusiveness marker is manifested uniformly and consistently throughout all instances of its occurrences in the language. Those areas which have been explicitly dealt with in this study have been summarized below in (33):

---

[9]   A larger scale study which also includes the analysis of Japanese *e, ni, de* and -*nagara* within this framework is also currently under way.

(33)   *-se* conveying the meaning of INCLUSIVENESS

Form:	entities linked	semantic effect
eyse	trajector + location	ACTION SOURCE/LOCATION
eykeys e	trajector + location	ACTION SOURCE/LOCATION
hanteys e	trajector + location	ACTION SOURCE/LOCATION
(u)los e	subject + process endpoint	IN THE CAPACITY OF
myens e	activity + activity	SIMULTANEITY
-a/e s e	action + action	SEQUENTIALITY or CAUSE/EFFECT
SM-s e	subject + subject	SIMULTANEITY

-Se appears to demonstrate a striking systematicity in all of its occurrences throughout the grammar of Korean and it is only by isolating this type of systematicity that we may begin to be able to account for its grammatical, syntactic, and semantic constraints in a unified and consistent manner.

I hope to have shown that not only is this element meaningful, but that its meaning is quite powerful, demonstrating strong potential relationships to other areas of semantics and grammar such as definiteness and the domains of REALIS and IRREALIS. As such, it is also hoped that Korean grammar will begin to be re-analyzed as an important tool which can shed new light on these linguistic phenomena.

References

Chafe, W. 1980. (1976) Givenness, Contrastivesness, definiteness, subjects, topics, and point of view. In C. Li (Ed.) *Subject and Topic*. New York. Academic Press.

Langacker, R. 1987. *Foundations of Cognitive Grammar*. Stanford. Stanford University Press.

Langacker, R. 1990. *Concept, Image, and Symbol The Cognitive Basis of Grammar*. Berlin: Mouton de Gruyter.

Kim, I. 1984. *Towum thossi '-se'ey tayhan yenkwu*. [A study on supplementary particle "-se"] in *Kuwke Kwukmwunhak* [Korean Linguistics]. Vol. 22. pp. 439-453.

Ko, Y. 1968. Cwukyek cosaui han conglywuey tayhaye [On a Subject particle]. Hyuntay Kwuke mwunpep [Modern Korean Grammar].

Lee., K. 1993. *Korean Grammar on Semantic-Pragmatic Principles.* Seoul: Hankwuk Mwuhwasa.

Lukoff, F. 1982. *Introductory Course in Korean.* Seoul: Yonsei University Press.

Prince, E. 1979. On the given/new distinction. In W. Hanks, C Hofbauer, and P. Clyne (Eds.) *Papers from the Fifteenth Regional Meeting of the Chicago Linguistic Society.* Department of Linguistics. University of Chicago. pp. 267-278..

Prince, E. 1980. Toward a Taxonomy of Given-New Information.

Sohn, H.M. 1986. Goal and Source in Korean Locatives with Reference to Japanese, in *Linguistc Expeditions. Seoul: Hanshin.*

Sohn, H.M. 1994. *Korean.* New York. Routledge.

Sung, K. 1979. *Kwuke cosaui yenkwu* [A study on Korean particles]. Seoul: Hyengselchwulphansa.

The Discourse Function of the *-myen* Clause in Korean*

CHANG-BONG LEE

University of Pennsylvania

1. Introduction

The *-myen* clause in Korean as exemplified in (1) below was once believed to function only as a conditional clause in the previous literature as in Bak(1987). [1]

(1)   Chelswu-ka   o-*myen*,   ce-to   ka-keyss-eyo.
        Chelswu-NOM come-*if*   I-too   go-will-DEC
        'If Chelswu comes, I will go, too.

----

* I want to thank Noriko Akatsuka, Young-Joo Kim and Kee-Dong Lee for their valuable comments. Special thanks go to Ellen Prince for leading me to investigate this topic based on the corpus data in natural discourse.
1. Throughout this paper the following abbreviations will be used in the gloss.

NOM-nominative	ACC-accusative	COMP-complementizer
DEC-declarative	EXCL -exlamatory	HON-honorific
MOD-modifying ending	PAST-past	Q-question marker
TOP-topic		

This paper challenges Bak(1987)'s claim and argues that the -*myen* clause functions not only as a prototypical conditional clause but it is also used to evoke various kinds of non-conditional readings. Evidence of data is presented from a chosen collection of corpus data in natural discourse. In doing so, we discuss a wide range of discourse functions of the -*myen* clauses by characterizing their acceptable domains in discourse context.

The paper proceeds as follows. In section 2, for the theoretical background for subsequent discussion, we review Akatsuka(1985)'s characterization of the conceptual domain of conditionals in general. In section 3, we discuss the discourse functions of the -*myen* clauses as reflected in the corpus data in natural discourse. We characterize their acceptable domains into two types. One is the type where their functions are characterized by identifying what kinds of speaker attitude are expressed over p in the 'p-*myen, q*' structure. The other is the type where their functions are understood by noting what p does functionally with respect to q. We observe, in both types of context, that the -*myen* clauses can sometimes evoke non-conditional readings as well as conditional ones, contra Bak(1987)'s prediction. We further observe that the non-conditional readings they evoke are highly constrained. I argue that the nature of this constraint is explained by considering the irrealis feature that the morpheme -*myen* carries inherently. In section 4, the main arguments are summarized with concluding remarks.

2. The Domain of Conditionals

The conceptual domain of conditionals; that is, the context that is acceptably subject to conditionality has been characterized by resorting to various kinds of terminology in the traditional literature; e.g., IRREALIS, HYPOTHETICAL, or POSSIBLE WORLD. However, the most recent and succinct account on this issue is found in Akatsuka(1985).

Akatsuka argued that the conceptual domains REALIS and IREALIS form an epistemic scale and explains the domain of conditionality. Akatsuka(1985:636) arrived at the following scale of realis and irrealis continuum representing the speaker's subjective evaluation of the reality of a given situation as in (2).

(2)   **REALIS**   **IRREALIS**

----

know   *get to know*   *not know*   *know*

(exist x)   *(exist x)*   *(exist x)*   *not (exist x)*

                newly-learned uncertainty   counter-
                information   factual

The UNCERTAINTY and COUNTERFACTUAL attitudes were already captured by such terms like HYPOTHETICAL, UNREAL, or COUNTERFACTUAL in the traditional literature. Akatsuka's new contribution is the addition of NEWLY-LEARNED INFORMATION in the irrealis domain. She observed that the antecedent of a conditional can express information which the speaker has just received from his interlocuter. [2]

Let us consider one of her examples.

(3)   A: Ken says he lived in Japan when he was a kid.
        B: Gee, if he lived in Japan when he was a kid, why
               doesn't he have an accent?
                                            Akatsuka(1985:628)

Akatsuka observed that the antecedent of a conditional sentence in (3) expresses NEW INFORMATION that has just entered the consciousness of the speaker at the discourse site. She argued that the reason this kind of new information is acceptable to be conditionalized is that it takes time for the speaker to accept this kind of newly-learned information in his/her state of knowledge and until then this information is still in the irrealis domain.

----

2. Akatsuka(1986:339) proposed to call this newly-learned information as contextually given *p* in the sense that the content of the antecedent has just been given to the speaker at the discourse site. What is interesting is that Korean marks this type of conditional construction by reserving a particular conditional marker (-*tamyen*) for this function. Refer to Lee(1995) for relevant examples and discussions. This observation strongly supports Akatsuka's motivation to identify this type of speaker attitude as one of speaker attitudes comprising the domain of conditionals. However, I do not agree with Akatsuka on the hypotheticality expressed in the conditional antecedent in this context. She viewed this kind of speaker attitude as being in the highly probable realm of irrealis domain. However, I argue in Lee(1995) that the speaker takes either a neutral attitude or a highly hypothetical attitude over the probability (truth) of the content of the antecedent in this type of conditional.

In the similar vein, Akatsuka also observed that the antecedent in a conditional sentence can express the speaker's attitude of SURPRISE or SUDDEN REALIZATION that something totally unexpected has happened. Consider her example in (4).

(4)   (Visiting his friend in the hospital, the speaker says to himself:)

J.   Konna ni   yorokonde   kureru no   *nara*,   motto
        this way in   happy   give that   *if*   more
        hayaku   kite   ager-eba   yokatta
        early   coming   give-if   good-was

E.   If he's so happy to see me, I should have come earlier.

                                            Akatsuka(1985:630)

Akatsuka observed that what the speaker connotes in using this type of conditional in '*If* S1, S2' structure is not 'I know S1' but rather 'I didn't know S1 until now!'. (4) shows that what the speaker realizes unexpectedly is subject to be marked by the conditional antecedent and the speaker's attitude of surprise is expressed by it.

Summarizing Akatsuka(1985)'s account of conditionals, conditionals are identified by the speaker's subjective attitude over the reality of a given situation in the epistemic scale of realis and irrealis continuum; that is, only the following range of speaker attitudes in the irrealis domain are acceptable to be conditionalized as in (5).

(5)   SURPRISE/SUDDEN REALIZATION
                'I didn't know this until this moment!'/
                'I just realize this.'
        UNCERTAINTY   'I don't know if this is the case.'
        NEGATIVE CONVICTION 'I know that this is not the case.'

What is excluded is the POSITIVE CONVICTION in the realis domain; that is, 'I know that this is the case'. This account explains why the speaker's direct (patent) knowledge is not allowed to be conditionalized as in (6).

(6)a.   Son: (looking out of the window):
                It's raining, Mommy.
        Mother: If it's raining (as you say), let's not go to the park.
    b. Son: (Looking out of the window and noticing the rain):
                *If/Since it is raining , let's not go to the park.

                                            Akatsuka(1986:341)

Akatsuka(1986:341) observed that the son, the direct experiencer of the given situation, cannot conditionalize it as in (6b). However, the same propositional content of the given situation is subject to conditionality by the mother in (6a) because she is not the direct experiencer; that is, the content of the IF-clause belongs to the irralis world for her. The discussion here confirms Akatsuka's position that what is crucial in defining the domain of conditionals is the understanding of what is registering in the speaker's consciousness at the time of utterance.

3. The Discourse Function of the -*myen* Clause and its Acceptable Domain

In this section, we discuss the discourse functions of the -*myen* clauses by noting two types of their acceptable context. One is the type which is characterized by identifying what kind of speaker attitude is expressed over p in the 'p-*myen*, q' structure. The other is the type where its context is best understood by noting what p does functionally with respect to q.

3.1. Speaker Attitudes in the -*myen* Clauses

3.1.1. Conditional Speaker Attitudes

1) SURPRISE/SUDDEN REALIZATION
Akatsuka(1985) paraphrased the speaker attitude of surprise/sudden realization by 'I didn't know this until this moment' or 'I just realize this'. Now consider (7).

(7)   (A and B opens the refrigerator door and finds that there are some beer stored inside:)

a. A: nayngcangko-ey   maykcwu-ka   iss-*umyen*,
        refrigerator-in   beer-NOM   exist-*if*,
        hancan   ha-yeya-ci.
        a cup   drink-have to-DEC
        'If there are some beer in the refrigerator, we have to drink some.'

b. B: mwulonici.
        absolutely
        'Absolutely!'

Notice in (7) that what the speaker intends to say by uttering this -*myen* clause is something like 'I just realize that there are some beer in the refrigerator. I am so happy to find some, so we surely should enjoy drinking some.' Thus, the speaker A expresses sudden realization attitude by uttering a -*myen* clause in (7a).

Bak(1987) discussed the following example to argue that even the realis situation can be exceptionally conditionalized in Korean. Consider his example in (8).

(8)   (to an old man who is standing in the middle of a street:)
        keki   sekyeysi-*myen*   wihemha-pnita
        there   stand-*if*   dangerous-DEC
        'If you stand there, it is dangerous.'   Bak(1987:168)

Bak argued that in (8) the content of the -*myen* clause is what the speaker directly perceives with his/her own eyes and this belongs to the realis domain. Then, he counted this example as one piece of supporting evidence for his argument that even the realis situation can be exceptionally conditionalized in Korean, contra Akatuska(1985)'s prediction. However, notice here that Bak misinterpreted the data in (8) above. In (8a), what the speaker connotes by uttering the -*myen* clause is 'I just realize that you are standing in the middle of a street and want to warn you that such situation is dangerous.'. The speaker's attitude here belongs to the sudden realization attitude that is acceptable to be conditionalized in the irrealis domain; that is, the situation described in this -*myen* clause is in the irrealis domain. This shows that unlike Bak's argument, (8) cannot be interpreted to show that even the realis situation can be exceptionally conditionalized in Korean.

2) UNCERTAINTY
Akatsuka(1985) paraphrased the speaker attitude of uncertainty by 'I don't know if this is the case'. Consider (9).

(9)   (A and B are inside a car on their way to A's place. A is not sure whether there are some beer stored in the refrigerator:)
a. A: nayngcangko-ey   maykcwu-ka   iss-*umyen*,
        refrigerator-in   beer-NOM   exist-*if*,
        hancan   ha-yeya-ci.
        a cup   drink-have to-DEC
        'If there are some beer in the refrigerator, we have to drink some.'

b. B: mwulonici.
       absolutely
       'Absolutely!'

Notice in (9) that the propositional content of each sentence is exactly the same as in (7). The only difference is a contextual difference. We can notice that the speaker attitude in uttering a *-myen* clause in (9a) differs from that in (7a). What s/he intends to say in this situation is something like 'I am not sure whether there are some beer in the refrigerator, when we arrive at my place. However, if there are some, we shoud enjoy drinking some.'. Thus, in this situation, s/he expresses the attitude of uncertainty 'I don't know if this is the case'.

By comparing (9) with (7) earlier, notice that a propositionally identical *-myen* clause is read in two different ways depending on the attitude the speaker takes toward its content at the time of utterance. This observation clearly suggests that what decides the type of reading in the use of a *-myen* clause is the speaker's subjective attitude toward its content at the time of utterance.

3) COUNTERFACTUAL
According to Akatsuka(1985), the counterfactual attitude expresses the speaker's negative conviction 'I know that this is not the case'. Akatsuka(1985:627) discussed the following example from Japanese as in (10).

(10)   Kono ko ga   otoko dat-*tara*, ii   noni   naa!
        this child-SUBJ   male   be-*if* good   though EXCL
        'If this child is a boy, I'll be so happy!'
        'If this child were a boy, I'd be so happy!'

Akatsuka observed that (10) is ambiguous. If a pregnant woman utters (10) before the delivery (assuming the normal circumstances where she does not know the sex of her baby), then (10) expresses her hope of having a son. However, if (10) is uttered after the delivery, it automatically becomes a counterfactual conditional.

The Korean equivalent of (10) is expressed by using a *-myen* clause as in (11) and the same ambiguity is observed.

(11)   i   ai-ka   atul-i-*myen*   coh-ulyenman
        this   child-NOM   son-be-*if*   good-EXCL
        'If this child is a son, I'll be so happy!'
        'If this child were a son, I'd be so happy!'

Akatsuka(1985:627) pointed out further that many East Asian languages- e.g. Japanese, Chinese, Korean, Mongolian, Semai, and Thai- make no grammatical distinction between subjunctive and indicative moods. However, this generalization seems to be too strong. [3]

I find that this generalization does not hold true at least in Korean. I find that a conditional sentence cannot be interpreted as a counterfactual without back-shifting when the verb in the antecedent is other than the copula 'be'. [4] Notice that unlike (11), (12) cannot be interpreted as a counterfactual; that is, it expresses only the speaker's hope of passing the upcoming exam.

(12)   ipen   sihem-ey   hapkyekha-*myen*   coh-ulyenman.
         this   exam-in   pass-*if*   good-EXCL
         'If (I) pass this exam, I will be happy.'
         '#If I passed this exam, I would be happy.'

When the speaker desires to express a counterfactual attitude after taking the exam, s/he must add the past infix -*ess* inside the verbal morphology of the -*myen* clause as in (13).

(13)   ipen   sihem-ey hapkyekha-ess-*umyen*   coh-ulyenman.
                               -PAST-*if*
         'If I passed this exam, I would be happy.'

---

3. Akatsuka pointed out (personal communication at the conference site) that she didn't intend to make a strong postion as I interpret it here in this paper. She mentioned that by bringing this kind of example she meant to show that East Asian languages like Korean and Japanese do not mark the difference between subjunctive and indicative moods as strongly and consistently as observed in other languages (e.g. English).

4. Regarding this example, Young-Joo Kim made a very interesting observation, saying that those verbs that need the help of back-shifting to express counterfactuality seem to be restricted to ACTION VERBS, whereas STATE VERBS do not employ back-shifting and therefore evoke ambiguous readings. This dichotomy of 'state verbs vs. action verbs' seems to be quite relevant in figuring out why some verbs are formally marked to express counterfactuality but others aren't. I leave this question to a further study.

This data clearly shows that, contra Akatsuka's generalization, Korean indeed makes a grammatical distinction between subjunctive and indicative moods. The availability of expressing the counterfactual attitude over the past event by the use of a morphologically pluperfect form as in (14) again supports the claim that Korean formally marks the distinction between subjunctive and indicative moods.

(14)   cinan sihem-ey   hapkyekha-yess-ess-*umyen*
         last exam-in   pass-PAST-PAST-*if,*
         coh-ass-ulyenman.
         good-PAST-EXCL
         'If I had passed the last exam, I would have been happy.'

3.1. 2. A Non-Conditional Speaker Attitude: -*myen* as a 'even though p' marker

In some occurrences of the -*myen* clauses, we find that they are best translatable by the 'even though' clause in English. Consider (15).

(15)   (to her own older sister:)
         ney-ka   enni-*myen*   ceyil-i-ya?
         you-NOM   elder sister-*if*   best-be-Q
         'If you are my elder sister, can you do anything?'
                                             Bak(1987:168)

The speaker uttering the above sentence patently knows the content of the antecedent clause. (15) can be felicitously uttered by a younger sister to her elder sister in the appropriate context; for instance, when she is upset about her sister's arrogant/bossy attitude.

    Bak(1987:168) interpreted this data as showing that even the realis situation can be exceptionally conditionalized in Korean. However, Bak's argument is again misleading. His argument is based on his assumption that every occurrence of the -*myen* clause should be counted as a conditional clause and under this assumption he must view this example as a conditional construction.

    However, I argue that (15) cannot be an instance of a conditional. In the situation where the speaker obviously knows the content of the -*myen* clause in the realis domain, the utterance of the -*myen* clause in this context does not evoke the IF-conditional reading but rather it creates a 'even though p' reading. Notice, in (15), that the younger sister who is talking with her older sister won't take the hearer's being her sister to be a hypothetical possibility unless she is insane or joking for sarcastic purposes, since the relationship of sisterhood is innately given. In this situation, the only available reading of the -*myen* clause is a 'even though *p*' reading. In other words, the speaker's attitude in uttering this -*myen* clause in (15) does not belong to the range of speaker attitudes which are acceptable to be conditionalized as defined in Akatsuka(1985). This leads us to view (15) as not constituting the data of conditionals in Korean. Having proved that (15) is not an instance of conditional, the fact that the -*myen* clause can mark the realis situation in this example should not lead to the conclusion that even the realis situation can be a conditional target in Korean.

Here the question arises as to whether -*myen* can function as a 'even though *p*' marker in every context where the use of a 'even though' clause is felicitous. To answer this question, let us consider a pair of constructed examples in (16) and (17).

(16)　　(the speaker is the secretary of the executive director of a
　　　　company; after she gets criticized harshly by her boss
　　　　she slams down the document on the table upon his leaving:)
　　　　ci-ka　　　　sangkwan-i-*myen*　　ta-ya?
　　　　he-NOM　　　boss-be-*even though*　everything-Q
　　　　terew-ese　　mos haymek-keyss-kwuman
　　　　dirty-because　can't work-DEC
　　　　'Even though he is my boss, does that mean he can do anything?
　　　　I can't work like this. '

(17)　　(the speaker B says to her friend A that she really likes her
　　　　boss because he treats her like his close friend:)
a. A:　ce pwun-hako　　　ilhaki-ka　　　　　ette-ni
　　　　him-with　　　　　working-NOM　　　how-Q
　　　　'How is it to work for him?'
b. B:　cengmal　　　cohun　pwun-i-ya
　　　　really　　　　nice　guy-be-DEC
　　　　'(He) is a really nice guy.'
　　　　ku pwun-i　　sangkwan-i-(#*myen*)
　　　　　　　　　　　　　　　　-i-*ciman*
　　　　that guy-NOM boss-be-(#*if*) *even though*
　　　　chinkwu-cherem　　　casangha-si-e.
　　　　friend-like　　　　　kind-HON-DEC
　　　　'Even though he is my boss, he is kind (to me) like a friend.'

In (16), the speaker feels that being somebody's boss does not mean that s/he can criticize that person too harshly. The speaker's attitude by uttering the -*myen* clause in this context is something like 'I know that p is a given fact. However, I strongly disagree with the kind of attitude you have over the reality of p.'. This attitude is sharply contrasted with the one observed in (17). The speaker's attitude over p in this context is far different from that in (16); that is, something like 'unlike the common expectation by the reality of p'. We find in (17) that -*myen* cannot be used to evoke a 'even though p' reading to replace the function of the prototypical 'even though' clause marker -*ciman*, which is perfect in this context.

What this observation suggests is that -*myen* cannot be used to mark every context of the 'even though' clause. Instead, we find that -*myen* is licensed to mark such context only when the speaker carries a specific kind of attitude over p in the 'p-*myen*, q' structure; that is, the attitude of disagreeing with someone over his/her attitude over the reality of p. I propose to identify this type of attitude as $Disagree_{realis}$ based on the sense that the speaker expresses his/her attitude of disagree concerning a given fact in the realis domain. [5]

Here the question arises as to why this use of -*myen* requires the speaker to carry such specific kind of attitude. I propose to seek the answer for this question by assuming that -*myen* carries the inherent semantic feature as the irrealis marker. Interpreting the $Disagree_{realis}$ attitude from the angle of the epistemic scale of realis and irrealis continuum, this attitude must belong to the realis domain objectively but it can be viewed by the speaker as residing in the irrealis domain temporarily at the time of utterance. The speaker carries such attitude like 'I know that p is in the realis domain objectively as a given fact. However, I don't feel like accepting it as a given fact at this moment. I want to consider it to be in the irrealis world for me at this moment.'. I hypothesize that this irrealis flavor comes from the irrealis feature which the morpheme -*myen* carries inherently. This hypothesis explains why the use of -*myen* as a 'even though' clause marker is highly restricted to express only this kind of speaker attitude having the irrealis flavor.

---

5. The further restriction represented by the subscript expression (realis) is motivated to distinguish this use of -*myen* from the use of another form of conditional marker -*tamyen* which is used to express the speaker's disagree attitude against someone's belief or opinion in the irrealis domain. Refer to Lee(1995) for relevant discussion.

3.2. The Function of the -*myen* Clause with respect to its Consequent

3.2.1. 'SCENE-SETTING' Function

The functions of the -*myen* clauses that we are going to observe in the following two sections are understood by their ability to provide a temporal or spatial background for the main clause. In this regard, this function of the -*myen* clause is best understood as the 'scene-setting' expression which was originally discussed by Kuno(1971). We observe that the use of the -*myen* clause for this function is significantly constrained and the nature of this constraint is also explained by considering the inherent irrealis feature of -*myen*.

1) TEMPORAL SETTING
Bak(1987:167) brought up the following data in (18) as another piece of evidence to argue that even the realis situation can be subject to conditionality exceptionally in Korean, contra Akatsuka(1985)'s prediction.

(18) a. pom-i   o-*myen*, isa-lul   ha-l   yeyceng-i-ta
         spring-NOM   come-*if* moving-ACC do-MOD plan-be-DEC
         'If spring comes, I am going to move.'
     b. yel si-ka   toy-*myen*   cong-i   wullin-ta.
         10 o'clock-NOM become-*if*   bell-NOM   ring-DEC
         'If it gets to be 10 o'clock, the bell rings.'   Bak(1987:167)

Bak(1987:168) argued that the antecedents in (18) above represent what he called GIVEN events that must occur in the course of time due to the nature of things. He viewed this given situation to be in the realis domain and argued that the fact that -*myen* is appropriate in this context shows that even the realis situation can be a conditional target exceptionally in Korean.

However, Bak's argument is again misleading. Notice in (18) that the most appropriate interpretation of each example should be temporal, but not conditional. For instance, in (18a), the fact that spring comes is so natural that nobody will assume it as a possible condition; that is, the speaker doesn't mean, by uttering this -*myen* clause, that under the condition (possibility) that spring comes, s/he will move, but rather it is interpreted as meaning that when (after) spring arrives, s/he will move. Thus, the speaker attitude in this context is not characterized by one of those speaker attitudes evoking conditional readings as defined in Akatsuka(1985). This discussion leads us to view these -*myen* clauses in (18) as temporals rather than as conditionals.

It is observed that those phrases consisting of a noun denoting a period of time or a point of time plus the verb like *toyta* ('to become') or *ota* ('to come') realized by -*myen* in the antecedent typically evoke a temporal reading as in (19). [6]

(19)   nuc kaul-i   toy-*myen*,   cwupwu-nun
        late fall-NOM   become-*when* housewife-TOP
        weltongcwunpi-lul seysimhakey kyeyhoykha-yeya ha-nta.
        winter preparation-ACC carefully plan-have to-DEC
        'When it becomes late fall, the housewife has to make a
        careful plan to prepare for the upcoming winter.'

Then, does this mean that -*myen* can function as a separate temporal marker? If we think of -*myen* as a separate temporal marker, it is expected to be interchangeable with a prototypical temporal marker -*ttay*. However, it turns out that -*myen* is not always interchangeable with -*ttay* . Consider (20).

(20) a. Chelswu-ka   cip-ey   tochakha-yess-*umyen*,
      Chelswu-NOM   home-at   arrive-PAST-*if* (#*when*)
      cenhwaha-lkeya.
      call-will-DEC
      'If (#when) Chelswu arrived at home, (he) will call.'
    b. Chelswu-ka   cip-ey tochakha-yess-*ulttay*(#*umyen*),
      Chelswu-NOM home-at arrive-PAST- *when* (#*if*),
      cenhwaha-yess-ta
      call-PAST-DEC
      'When Chelswu arrived at home, (he) called (me).

Notice in (20b) that the -*myen* clause cannot replace the function of the -*ttay* clause to describe the simultaneous temporal relation between two past events. The use of the -*myen* clause with the past tense form of the verb creates only the conditional reading as in (20a). If we take the position that Korean has -*myen* as a separate temporal marker in the lexicon, we have no answer to explain why (20b) with -*myen* should be bad. This discussion proves that the temporal reading in the use of a

––––––––––––
6. This examples is from Lim, Chong-Chul (1993:48) *Socwunghan phyenci, Cakun kaluchim* (Precious Letters, Little Teaching), Tongpanin Pub. Co, Seoul, Korea

-myen clause does not result from *-myen* being a separate temporal marker but rather it is a side-effect reading of the *-myen* clause as a whole in the appropriate context.

Then, the important questions to answer will be what are the acceptable contexts where the *-myen* clauses can appropriately evoke temporal readings and how to characterize them. We should notice first that in those examples where the *-myen* clauses are interpreted as temporals as in (18) and (19), they describe the obviously expected future events. On the contrary, notice that the *-myen* clause cannot evoke a temporal reading when it refers to the past event as in (20a). This contrast predicts then that the *-myen* clause will evoke a temporal reading only when it marks the obviously expected future event from the speaker's point of view. Since any future event belongs to the irrealis domain no matter how obvious it is from the speaker's point of view, this seems to suggest that the constraint in the temporal use of *-myen* results from the inherent irrealis feature of *-myen* .

However, the following data shows that the story is not that simple. Consider (21). [7]

(21) (the speaker/writer talks about the memories of his/her childhood:)

a. nwukwuna kulehtusi   ce-to elin sicel-uy   chwuek-i
     everybody as it is the case I-too childhood-of memories-NOM
     kakkumssik   tteolu-pnita
     occasionally   arise-DEC
     'As is the case for everybody, I occasionally think of the memories of my childhood.'

b. yerumbanghak-i-*myen*   sikol oykacip-ey ka-se
     summer vacation-be-*when*   rural relatives-to go-and
     tongney sinayska-eyse   mwulcangkwu chi-ko
     village brook-in   water splashing do-and
     nolkon ha-yess-ciyo
     play around-PAST-DEC
     'During summer vacations, I used to visit my relatives in the rural area and play around doing water splashing in the brook of the village.'   (from 'memo' section in KIDS)

----

7. This example is taken while running the KIDS program, which is a world-wide e-mail communication network for Korean-speaking people. I thank Jin-Young Choi for providing the program instructions.

Notice in (21b) that the -*myen* clause can evoke a temporal reading even when it describes the past event. In the context of (21), the speaker is apparently describing the past event.

However, when -*myen* refers to the past time, it is found to be much more restricted than when it refers to the future time. First, notice in (22), -*myen* cannot be used to refer to a past point of time by replacing a prototypical temporal postpositional marker -*ey* (=at, in).

(22) ecey ohwu   twu-si-ey (#i-*myen*)
      yesterday afternoon   2 o'clock-at (#be-*if*)
      sensayngnim-ul   manna-ss-eyo
      teacher-ACC   meet-PAST-DEC
      'I met (my) teacher at 2 yesterday afternoon.'

Notice, by going back to the example in (18b), that -*myen* can refer to a point of time (10 o'clock) in the future. Thus, when -*myen* refers to the past time, it seems to be restricted to refer to only a period of time expression like *yerumbanghak* (summer vacation) as in (21).

However, it turns out that this is not the only restriction. Consider (23).

(23) caknyen yerumbanghak- ey (#i-*myen*)
      last summer vacation during(#bc *if*)
      oykacip-ey   ka-kon hay-ss-ciyo
      relatives-to   used to go-PAST-DEC
      'During last summer vacation, I used to go to my relatives.'

Notice in (23) that the use of -*myen* is infelicitous when it refers to such time expression 'last summer vacation'. This is contrasted with (21). The only difference in two contexts is the SPECIFICITY of the time expression that -*myen* refers to. In (21) -*myen* does not necessarily refer to any specific period of time in the past. In other words, the reference of time expression in this context is non-specific in the sense that the speaker does not have any particular period of time in his/her mind at the time of utterance. However, in (23), the time expression 'last summer vacation' describes a specific period of time; that is, the speaker has a particular period of time in his/her mind at the time of utterance. This contrastive fact suggests that -*myen* is only allowed to refer to the non-specific period of time expression when it refers to the past time.[8]

Summarizing the observations so far, the temporal use of -*myen* is much more restricted when it refers to the past time than when it refers to the future time. It is allowed to refer only to the non-specific period of time expression in the past, whereas the only restriction in the future time reference is that the -*myen* clause should describe an obvious future event from the speaker's point of view.

Then, the question arises as to what explains the nature of this constraint in the temporal use of -*myen*. I again propose to argue that this constraint is explained by the inherent irrealis feature of -*myen*. The fact that -*myen* is used to refer to the future time is not surprising when we consider that any future event is in the irrealis domain no matter how obvious it is. Then, what about the constrained use of -*myen* in referring to the past? We observed that it is restricted to refer only to the non-specific period of time expression. I note that when something is non-specific, it is somehow connected to the attitude of uncertainty because the speaker has no particular set of time reference but rather a random set of time reference is evoked. The attitude of uncertainty certainly carries the irrealis feature. This reasoning shows that the temporal use of -*myen* is restricted to expressing only those speaker attitudes having the irrealis feature.

2) SPATIAL SETTING

We observe in this section that -*myen* is also used to make a spatial setting for the main clause. Consider the following examples in (24). [9]

---

8. Here some may note a contextual factor by saying that what explains the fact that the specific time expression is disallowed in (23) is not the presence of -*myen* but it is because (23) describes the habitual past but not the simple past event. However, there seems to be nothing inherently odd about the semantic combination of describing the habitual past over a specific period of time in the past. If the requirement for the non-specific period of time expression comes from this contextual factor, (23) should be predicted to be bad, when -*myen* is replaced by the prototypical temporal postpositional particle -*ey* . However, the resultant sentence is fine. This proves that what is responsible for the restriction in (23) is the presence of -*myen*.
9. I thank Seo-Young Chae who provided me with a tape that recorded interviews with two native speakers of Korean in Seoul.

(24)a. yessnal-ey   Ulciro saka-ey   ka-*myen*
      long time ago   Ulciro 4th St.-to   go-*if*
      OB Cabin-ilako kyenghyangsik-cip-i hana iss-ess-ci
      OB Cabin-called restaurant-NOM   one exist-PAST-DEC
      'Long time ago, at Ulciro and 4th St., there was one western
      style restaurant called OB Cabin.'

    b. Koryongtong   ka-*myen*,   kutangsi   naysi-na
      Koryongtong   go-*if*   at that time   eunuch-or
      kwungnyetul-i   manhi sal-ass-ko
      maids of honor-NOM   many live-PAST-and
      Ankwuktong-ey ka-*myen* pwuca-ka   manh-ass-e
      Ankwuktong-to go-*if*   rich people-NOM many-PAST-DEC
      'In Koryongtomg, at that time, there lived many eunuches and
      maids of honor, and in Ankwuktong there were many rich
      people.'
      (from the taped-conversation recorded by Seo-Young Chae)

In both examples of (24) above, the speaker describes a state of the past by giving a spatial setting with a -*myen* clause. Notice that there is a specific pattern to introduce a spatial setting with -*myen* ; that is, -*myen* is attached after the verb stem *ka* ('to go') preceded by the string 'location expression-*ey* (to)' evoking such underlying meaning 'if somebody goes to such and such place'. One of the notable structural features in this pattern is that the subject of *kata* ('to go') is not specified. In such dialogue context as in (24), this unspecified subject is usually understood as the addressee evoking such underlying meaning 'if you go to such and such place'.

Notice in (24) that the English translations of the -*myen* clauses are captured by the locative prepositions. This might lead us to view the -*myen* clauses in (24) as not constituting the data of conditionals. However, we should note the underlying meaning of the -*myen* clauses in this context. The pattern 'location expression-ey ka-myen' evokes such underlying meaning 'if you go to such place' which expresses the irrealis attitude by the speaker. Since we define conditionals conceptually by noting the underlying speaker attitude over p in the 'p-*myen*, q' structure, this leads us to view those -*myen* clauses in (24) as examples of conditionals of which the surface translations are captured by simple locative prepositions. In other words, the -*myen* clauses in (24) are conditionals in terms of conceptual identification, but they function as locative phrases in surface.

3.2.2. GENERIC CONDITIONALS

Reilly(1986:313) identified the following type of conditional in (25) as GENERIC CONDITIONAL and observed that it is typically used to describe a rule or to predict a law-like consequence between two events.

(25)   a.   (pouring water on cement:)
                If you put water on it, it sparkles.
       b.   If Jamie drinks cranberry juice, he gets a rash.

Reilly(1986:313)

Consider one such type of *-myen* clause in (26).

(26)   i   tanchwu-lul   nwulu-*myen,*
       this   button-ACC   push-*if*
       cenki-ka   tuleo-pnita
       electricity-NOM   get turned on-DEC
       'If you push this button, the electricity gets turned on.'

(26) describes a co-occurrence relation between the pushing of a button and the resultant power-on of an electrical appliance. In this kind of context, the *-myen* clause is simply a part of stating this co-occurrence relation as a condition for a rule-like consequence. Thus, its function is characterized not by the speaker's subjective attitude over the probability (truth) of *p* in the '*p-myen, q*' structure but rather what it does functionally with respect to *q*.

       Let us note another example of this type in the corpus data as in (27).

(27)   sam nyen   mwupyengha-*myen*   pwuca-ka toynta-nun
       three years   not get ill-*if*   get rich-MOD
       yess mal-i   iss-ta
       old saying-NOM   be-DEC
       'There is an old saying that if you don't get ill for three years, you become rich.'

[from Lim, Chong-Chul (1993:28)]

Notice above that the speaker cites an old saying inherited from the ancestors in the Korean history. This saying states a law-like lesson in a conditional form and the *-myen* clause functions as an antecedent clause to be a part of such a law-like statement.

3.2.3 SPEECH ACT CONDITIONALS
One of the most frequently observed types of conditionals I encountered in reviewing the corpus data of -*myen* clauses is of the following type as in (28).

(28)
hakkyo	tani-l-ttay	manna-n kes-to,
school	go-MOD-when	meeting-too,
ettehkhey	po-*myen*,	
differently	see-*if*	
pan-un	cwungmay	pan-un	yenay-lako
half-TOP	introduction	half-TOP	affair-COMP

pol-swu iss-nuntey.
see-can-DEC

'We met while I was attending school; if viewed in a different angle, it was possible half by family introduction and half by love affair.'
(from the taped conversation recorded by Seo-Young Chae)

The function of the -*myen* clause here is not naturally characterized by one of those attitudes that Akatsuka(1985) claimed comprise the domain of conditionals. In this context, by uttering this -*myen* clause, the speaker expresses neither the sudden realization attitude nor the counterfactual attitude. It is also hard to view the speaker attitude over this -*myen* clause as expressing the uncertainty attitude 'I don't know p'. In uttering this -*myen* clause, the speaker does not mean to say 'I am not sure whether I can view it differently.' but rather what the -*myen* clause does is providing a parenthetical felicity condition for the utterance of the main clause. Thus, this type of -*myen* clause is more readily characterized by noting what p functionally does with respect to q in the 'p-*myen*, q structure.

This type of conditional clause was identified as SPEECH ACT CONDITIONALS as in Van der Auwera(1986) or as RELEVANCE CONDITIONALS as in Iatridou(1990). This type of conditional is characterized by the fact that the antecedent contains a (relevance) condition for the speech act expressed in the consequent; that is, the conditional antecedent of this type does not specify the condition for the truth of q in the 'p-*myen*, q' structure but rather specify the circumstances in which the consequent is relevant.

4. Conclusion

This paper discussed the discourse functions of the -*myen* clauses in Korean. To do so, we noted two types of contexts where the -*myen* clauses are used. The first was the type where their functions are characterized by identifying what kinds of speaker attitude are expressed over p in the '*p-myen, q*' structure. The second was the type where their functions are understood by noting what p does functionally with respect to q. We observed, in both types of contexts, that the -*myen* clauses can evoke non-conditional readings as well as conditional ones, contra Bak(1987)'s prediction. We also observed that the non-conditional readings of the -*myen* clauses are highly constrained. I argued that the nature of this constraint is explained by considering the irrealis feature that the morpheme -*myen* carries inherently.

I believe that data gathering and argument building feed on each other in a linguistic research. In further studies, I expect to find more data of the -*myen* clauses that may influence to revise the current arguments. I also expect that a new perspective can be adopted in buiding an argument to guide me to pay attention to the data that I might have ignored before.

References

Akatsuka, N. 1985. Conditionals and the Epistemic Scale.
    Language. 61:3.
Akatsuka, N. 1986. Conditionals are Discourse-bound. On Conditionals.
    Traugott, E. et al.
Van der Auwera, J. 1986. Conditionals and Speech Acts.
    On Conditionals. Traugott, E. et al.
Bak, Sung-Yun. 1987. Conditionals in Korean. Harvard Studies in
    Korean Linguistics II. Ed. S. Kuno et al. Seoul: Hanshin
Iatridou, S. 1990. Topics in Conditionals. Ph.D dissertation. MIT.
Kuno, S. 1971. The Position of Locatives in Existential Sentences.
    Linguistic Inquiry. 2:3.
Lee, Chang-Bong. 1995. A Pragmatic Study of Korean Conditionals.
    Ph. D dissertation (in progress). University of Pennsylvania.
Lyons, J. 1977. Semantics . vol 2. London: Cambridge University Press.
Reilly, J. 1986. The Acquisition of Temporals and Conditionals.
    On Conditionals. Traugott, E. et al.
Traugott, E.et al.1986.On Conditionals. London: Cambridge Univ. Press.

Index

Other titles of interest
Studies in Japanese Linguistics
A series copublished with
Kurosio Publishers

Theory of Projection in Syntax
Naoki Fukui

Proposing a theory of phrase structure in which structures are built by a simple adjunction operation, and specifiers are solely characterized by agreement, this work proposes what came to be known as the "relativized X'-theory." This theory, which draws a fundamental distinction between lexical and functional categories, is the most widely discussed alternative to the so-called standard X'-theory, and plays an important role in current research not only in syntax proper but also in language acquisition and language typology.
160 p. ISBN: 1-881526-35-6 (cloth); ISBN: 1-881526-34-8 (paper)

The Syntax of 'Subjects'
Koichi Tateishi

Many linguists argue that there is no formal syntactic position for the subject of Japanese. Tateishi does deeper research on the surface syntax of the subject, and looks in particular at the syntax of the subject and phenomena that have been treated as S-adjunctions. This work ultimately demonstrates that Japanese is in a sense more configurational than the so-called configurational languages.
232 p. ISBN: 1-881526-46-1 (cloth); ISBN: 1-881526-45-3 (paper)

A Study of Japanese Clause Linkage in Japanese
The Connective TE in Japanese
Yoko Hasegawa

Employing a hybrid theoretical framework of Role and Reference Grammar and Construction Grammar, this volume investigates the syntactic, semantic, and pragmatic properties of the diverse families of Japanese constructions in which the verbal suffix TE (approximately English 'and') is a linking device. The TE suffix is the most frequent and versatile connective in Japanese, able to link all three types of verbal constituents. Because the semantic relations obtainable between the conjuncts are heterogeneous, the prevailing view is that TE-linkage is a mere syntactic device with no semantic content; and the interpreter must infer intended semantic relations based on extralinguistic knowledge. However, closer examination reveals clear correlations between its syntax and semantics that have been obscured in previous studies which did not investigate TE-constructions as pairings of form and meaning. Detailed analysis of TE-linkage is of special significance to linguistic theory because it inevitably involves the search for an adequate descriptive framework for representing connectives.
254 p. ISBN: 1-57586-027-9 (cloth) ; ISBN:1-57586-026-0 (paper)

Complex Predicates in Japanese
A Syntactic and Semantic Study of the Notion 'Word'
Yo Matsumoto

In this thoroughly revised version of his 1992 Stanford dissertation, Yo Matsumoto presents an extensive discussion of Japanese complex predicates. A broad range of constructions and predicates are discussed, including predicative complement constructions, light verbs, causative predicates, desiderative predicates, syntactic and lexical compound verbs, and complex motion predicates. A number of new interesting facts are uncovered, and a detailed syntactic and semantic analyses are presented. On the basis of the analyses, Matsumoto argues that the notion 'word' must be relativized to at least three different sense: morphological, grammatical (functional), and semantic; and that this observation can be insightfully captured in the theory of Lexical-Functional Grammar. Previous proposals for each type of predicate that involve such mechanisms as argument transfer, incorporation, restructuring, etc. are thoroughly reviewed. Concrete proposals on the constraints on semantic wordhood are also made (an issue rarely discussed in the literature), drawing insights from cognitive linguistics.

345 p. ISBN: 1-57586-060-0 (paper); 1-57586-061-9 (cloth)

Other CSLI Publications Titles

Theoretical Issues in Korean Linguistics
Edited by Young-Key Kim-Renaud

This volume contains a selection of papers presented at the Eigth International Conference on Korean Linguistics. Areas represented include theoretical phonology and syntax, semantics, historical linguistics, discourse/pragmatics, and first language acquisition. The contributors include Sang-Cheol Ahn, Young-mee Yu Cho, Sharon Inkelas, Eunjoo Han, Gregory K. Iverson, Hyang-Sook Sohn, Sun-Ah Jun, Hyunsoon Kim, Yongsung Lee, Mira Oh, Jeong-Woon Park, Sung-Ho Ahn, Jung-Tag Lee, Sung-Yun Bak, Dong-In Cho, Jai-Hyoung Cho, Hyon Sook Choe, Yookyung Kim, Chungmin Lee, Myung-Kwan Park, Barbara Unterbeck, Jae-Hak Yoon, Ik-San Eom, Pung-hyun Nam, John Whitman, Sook Wh Cho, Alan Hyun-Oak Kim, Hyon-Sook Shin, Haeyeon Kim, Hyo Sang Lee.

555 p. ISBN: 1-881526-51-8 (paper); 1-881526-52-6 (cloth)

Context and Binding in Japanese
Masayo Iida

In this book, Masayo Iida investigates the proper treatment of *zibun*-binding, reviewing the status of the syntactic subjecthood condition. She proposes a conjunctive theory of *zibun*-binding in which both a syntactic condition and a nonsyntactic condition apply to every instance of *zibun*-binding. This approach is contrasted with a disjunctive approach adopted in many theories of *zibun*-binding, which views the subjecthood condition as a fundamental licensing condition, supplemented by semantic or discourse binding condition to account for nonsubject binding, when the syntactic condition would be violated.

Observing the fact that *zibun*-binding is affected by or interacts with various kinds of discourse information, and that the syntactic subjecthood condition does not impose its constraint independently, contrary to expectation, Iida claims that *zibun*-binding should be captured by a conjunctive theory, where the syntactic constraint minimally refers to a coargument relation between *zibun* and its antecendent, but not to subjecthood, while the discourse constraint licenses any actual interpretation. The relevant discourse factor of *zibun*-binding is identified, inspired by previously proposed factors, which are all related and often presented under the general term "point of view". The discourse notion of *deictic perspective*, the same notion that is relevant for the interpretation of deixis, is proposed. Discourse factors such as "empathy", "logophoricity", "awareness" are reviewed in detail and compared with the notion of *deictic perspective.*

The interpretation of so-called 'zero-pronouns' is also discussed. Like *zibun*-binding, zero pronoun binding is affected by a discourse factor, in this case *attentional focus*. The conjunctive approach in which a syntactic condition is minimally stated is also shown to be adequate in accounting for the interaction of syntax and discourse in zero pronoun binding.

The approach of this book is supported by the uncontroversial assumption that the syntactic binding ought to be available whenever the syntactic condition is met. Iida concludes that it is more plausible to think of grammar as providing some definite constraints, and what discourse factors do is to apply disjunctively or conjunctively with respect to those constraints. Violation of any constraint, syntactic or discourse-based, will lead to unacceptability which cannot be "repaired" by another component.

374 p. ISBN: 1-881526-74-7 (paper); ISBN: 1-881526-75-5 (cloth)

For a complete list of our titles, please visit our World-Wide Web site at:
http://csli-www.stanford.edu/publications/